FOR WANT OF
THE GOLDEN CITY

FOR WANT OF
THE GOLDEN CITY

SACHEVERELL SITWELL

THAMES AND HUDSON
LONDON

ISBN 0 500 01096 X

to
Georgia
with all my love
& loving
thanks

Contents

A Note of Explanation

BOOK ONE

The book opens with *Death of a Flie* which is even spelt that way in order to put particular emphasis upon this very small creature in our lives. It is the point of this opening chapter to show how important the moment of death must be to even the humblest being that has ever been alive. After this comes *Credo*, of which the first sentence: 'How marvellous to be living!' should carry or express the meaning. '*I'll build you a stairway to Paradise*' starts cynically on a school fire-escape to end in a nightmare on the flying buttresses of Bois-le-Duc, or 's Hertogenbosch, among the cripples and beggars of Hieronymus Bosch who was born there. In *Trampoline* this theme dear to the painter just named, to Pieter Bruegel, Rembrandt, Brouwer, Salvator, Magnasco, too, to no more than mention in his own sphere the poet Villon, is brought nearer home to haunt the streets of London. And these episodes conclude with the *Postscript* to a book which has already appeared, but on a theme that is equally contingent and appropriate to the work in hand. With this in mind it will not, I hope, be regretted by the reader.

Book Two is now introduced by the first of the *Entr'actes*, which is on the ice or skating scenes of Hendrik Avercamp, and not only because I had always promised myself I would write this. But his paintings in spite of their being crowded with figures afford the perfect illustration of the small and isolated communities of the past. More so indeed than the interior intimacy of Vermeer, or the kitchen backyards of de Hooghe, where the isolation is only momentary and the amber'd calm but waiting for irruption from some outside person. With Hendrik Avercamp it is the true solitude of some small village in ice and snow upon an inland sea, and the absolute antithesis to the sprawling overcrowding of today.

BOOK TWO

'*Photographies des temps passés*' is the expression of a desire for exact and precise information about the recent past. Of the sort, even, that could be given by a complete photographic documentation, in default of which persons of such recent history as Wilde or Beardsley, let alone Chopin or Mozart, remain shadowy and indistinct. Of the two first mentioned, we could have obtained more information by simply questioning those who knew them, but such opportunities are nearly always lost. Aubrey Beardsley, who died aged twenty-five, is perhaps the extreme example of young genius that might have come within the scope of one's own acquaintance; while the link of their both dying from consumption, though Chopin died fourteen years older, only makes more pitiful the little we know about him too.

Siesta Thoughts is a chapter of autobiography in terms of books written over a particular span of years. But it deals especially with books treating of certain subjects that I have tried to make my own. Thus, what I may, myself, consider to be the best things I have written are not even mentioned here. Those are the sequence of six books that include *Dance of the Quick and the Dead, Sacred and Profane Love, Splendours and Miseries,* and *Cupid and the Jacaranda.* They were published in the years between 1936 and 1952, are all out of print, and quite unknown to the present generation. But in this instant, and at this present, it is the genesis of the first popular book dealing with architecture and decoration in England during the seventeenth and eighteenth centuries that is under discussion. And in sequel to this there is the book I wrote upon *The Netherlands* wherein I may lay claim, I think, to certain discoveries, the old family houses by Daniel Marot at The Hague, the marvellous old synagogue of the Portuguese Jews at Amsterdam and the discovery, for it really was the discovery of Friesland; the golden-casqued Frisian women, the extraordinary costumes, the town-halls with their burgomaster's rooms painted with chinoiseries, and so forth. It was at least a picture of Holland that had not appeared before.

There followed close upon this the book that I wrote on *Spain* in the not altogether vain hope, I have to admit, of vying with Ford and Borrow, but there was at least a good deal to be added to their view of Spain. George Borrow makes the one prophetic remark as to *The Burial of Count Orgaz* but, that apart, neither author has 'truck' or contact with El Greco. Also, their interest ends, even if it extends to the Escorial; and the gaiety and brilliance of the later architecture quite eludes them, just as it might be said that no work on Spain is complete that does not mention its protean master and genius of our day.

The second and ensuing part of this chapter deals with another subject of personal predilection, of which I was the first person to write an appraisal in our language. For I published a work on German Baroque as long ago as 1927, and the next books to appear in English on this subject came out thirty years later in, respectively, 1958 and 1959. It was in praise of the brothers Asam and brothers Zimmermann, of J. B. Neumann, architect of the palace of Würzburg and the church of Vierzehnheiligen; of J. M. Fischer, creator of the magical abbeys of Ottobeuren and Zwiefalten; of J. G. Fischer, not to be confused with the foregoing, and putative architect of Maria Steinbach; of Count Cuvilliés, Court-dwarf and genius of the Residenz Theatre at Munich and of the Amalienburg; and of the bucolic-sounding, but anything but bovine in the results, Peter II Thumb, architect of the church of Birnau on the shores of Lake Constance. These men; and their attendant craftsmen, carvers of pulpits, stalls and organ-cases, fresco-painters, sculptors, stuccoists. They are difficult names, but no more so than the characters in any Russian novel. The church of Die Wies, the pavilion of the Amalienburg, the glittering grotto-cavern of Zwiefalten, are probably their masterpieces. It will be admitted, I think, that their works are something added to the pleasures and graver gaieties of life. That they may be the last light-hearted and confident works of art ever to be created, in no way lessens their appeal.

Tierra Caliente is a celebration of another sort. A very early interest of mine lay in Mexico, of which I wrote thirty years before I set foot there, making it the scene for the last chapter of my first prose book, *Southern Baroque Art*, which came out in February 1924. I am almost inclined to say that it preceded the quasi-Mexican, and probably Southern Californian or New Mexican background for my favourite 'Westerns'. But, certainly, with its clear mountains, *haciendas*, half-ruined churches, and Zapata-like personalia, it is the ultimate in picturesqueness. *Tierra Caliente* celebrates, therefore, the arrival by sea at Acapulco; and then launches into a perhaps rhapsodic description of the semi-tropical fruits and flowers, and cactuses. But it was a long time before I reached Mexico, and I enjoyed it when I got there; this last occasion being in fact the third time that I went to Mexico. There follows a more depressed view of the contrasting worlds, and of the future generally.

ENTR'ACTE: *On the San Sebastián of Palencia Cathedral*

Probably the strongest and most violent impression still to be derived from any picture is still that produced from one of several paintings by El Greco. Not Jackson Pollock on any account, but not Picasso, not even Cézanne, can approach him. His *Burial of Count Orgaz*, his *Martyrdom of St Maurice and the Theban Legion*, his *View of Toledo in a Storm* are astonishing masterpieces of this kind. But there are other paintings by him which are no less awe-inspiring and extraordinary. It has been my good fortune to know two of these three paintings since I first went to Spain in 1919; and perhaps his strangest and most extreme painting of all, *The Opening of the Fifth Seal*, I saw as long ago as 1926 when it was in the collection of the painter Zuloaga in his villa at Zumaya, on the Basque coast. I have become, therefore, I like to think, tolerably familiar with his distortions, mediumistic flashes of light, 'materialized' flowers, and other séance effects. It is not completely, or altogether surprising in view of this, that I seem to have convinced myself that I saw a painting of San Sebastián by El Greco in the sacristy of Palencia Cathedral in the somewhat dramatic, if actual circumstances described in these pages. But I did not see this painting. For it was not there. It has in fact only recently emerged from a private collection and been added to the new acquisitions in the Prado.* How this confusion can have arisen I am unable to

* This painting of St Sebastian by El Greco is illustrated on p. 350 of *Apollo*, for May 1970. An article by Victor Nieto Alcalde describes it as 'a particularly exciting acquisition to the Prado, which has been dated by various authorities between 1604 and 1614'; and adds that 'a fragment depicting some legs which could belong to the picture was found in 1962'. The painting had been in the collection of a Spanish marquis.

explain, but my wife also has a clear recollection of the incident as I have described it, and recognized the painting at once from the photograph. There is indeed another St Sebastian by El Greco, but of decidedly uninteresting character. Certainly, somehow I knew, or had seen photographs of the painting I describe. And in spite of its not being there, and it being some sort of over-enthusiastic hallucination on my part, the picture at least exists apart from its imaginary setting and so I have thought my *Entr'acte* worthwhile retaining.

BOOK THREE

Globe-Trotting signifies the prelude to a period of intensive travelling, with its title given a literal interpretation from the two men on a world tour, rolling the globe before them in which they lived and slept. The thought of their experiences and occupational difficulties leads naturally enough to the theme of Hannibal crossing the Alps. There follow relevant facts touching the Hospice of St Bernard, to conclude with the goitres and cretins of Aosta.

V.I.P. Lounge. Much more than any railway station the symbol for departure, since it leads almost inevitably to foreign lands. Other travellers come in; the husband and wife of every advertisement; and the phantom of St Sepulchre's, an 'eccentric' seen and studied from the life. The *zakuska* hour, and *hors d'oeuvres* are handed round. Air-hostesses compared to the *Fates* or *Parcae*, which leads on to a nocturnal experience in St Martin's-in-the-Fields. Possible V.I.P.'s of the past considered in ratio of their real importance, when Ramses II would have equal precedence with Rembrandt's *Rat-Killer*. Impending departure, and a slight misunderstanding.

Tropicalia which could be taken, too, as the alternate or Eastern hemisphere in comparison to that of *Tierra Caliente* which is in praise of semi-tropical lands like Mexico or Guatemala. But, as well, it is the assertion of a wish to extend my own boundaries beyond Spain and Italy and the Mediterranean; in pursuance of which I went to Brazil, Peru, Bolivia and Ecuador, and in the other direction to Persia, India, Ceylon, Nepal, Thailand, and most rewarding and interesting of all, Japan. But the method in *Tropicalia* is to be thinking of such experiences in retrospect while walking through a Victorian shrubbery at my home. Thus, accounts of it in spring, summer and winter are interwoven with first intimations of the Orient during childhood in Venice, and later, with the first vision of tropical flowering trees at Madeira. There is the sensation of arriving from Brazil in the middle of the night in Senegal, which experience of Africa and its unending strangeness is summarized in the microcephaloid of Dakar.

From now on to the end of this chapter it is India and Further India. The object of all this journeying having been in order to see the temples and works of art, out of which number Angkor Wat and the dance-temple of the Kailasa of Ellora stand out as supreme. But, also, a secondary object was the tropical flowers and flowering trees of which I was at great pains to discover the essence, so to speak, if that could be expressed in writing. I think the possibilities of tropical gardening would dawn upon anyone who has had the good fortune to visit the, now, more than century-old botanical garden at Peradeniya, near Kandy in Ceylon. Here, one sees the Amherstia nobilis, cassia or 'golden shower', ipomaeas, bauhinias, bignonias, to perfection, with more exotic curiosities such as the flowering cannonball tree. Of such will be the gardens of the future, a future that has begun already in the Caribbean, in Queensland, and elsewhere, the possibility being lost and gone in most of Africa and the East Indies. Further than this, I have tried to bring them into poetry by writing groups of poems on tropical flowers, and in particular the frangipani, but on many others, also. And the chapter ends with mention of the Indian temples of Khajuraho and the 'Black Pagoda' and their sculptures, which are, also, the theme of long, and as yet unpublished poems; as, too, 'the golden swing in the sky' or swinging festival of the Brahmins, which takes place at the temple of Wat Prajohit at Bangkok.

ENTR'ACTE: *A frieze of pigs' heads*

An account of a butcher's window in a local town just before Christmas forms a prelude to subjects of another nature altogether. The severed pigs' heads recall the helpless and harmless Louis XVI, but, also, the busts of Roman Emperors and the uniquely horrible Twelve Caesars.

BOOK FOUR

Matterig. Why this account of a dreadful and maniacal suicide which took place more than a hundred years ago? Because, indeed, it is so mysterious and frightening to read of, and so haunts the mind. And yet is no more awful than the fly's death-struggles in my opening pages. But despite this, Matterig, whoever he may have been, grows in stature and becomes something of an archetypal figure like, I have said, the Flying Dutchman or the Wandering Jew. I would be surprised if the experts on forensic medicine could produce from their records anything more extraordinary than this true story. But I will not altogether deny that its inclusion just at this point, less than half-way through the book, may be in part, perhaps a ruse to hold the reader's attention and induce him to read on. To which end I have tried all I know to bring the dead Matterig alive for these few moments.

'*Actor found dead in an empty flat*'. Another curious and most absorbing mystery, symbolic of much that has happened since. To myself, remembering the year 1910, it is most redolent of the time. The mere title, as it may have been shouted out by newspaper boys and read upon the placards, is dramatic enough. And like all good mysteries it has stayed insoluble.

Paraphrase on the dead actor. This is treated in the manner of a Liszt paraphrase upon an opera, with some attempt at the effects to be expected in his *Réminiscences des Huguenots*, or the *Grande Fantaisie sur Norma*. It is perhaps inevitable in view of my birthplace that it should begin with memories of the pierrots on the sands. There follow remarks on Little Tich and other music-hall comedians of my youth, by which time, I would hope, we are well inside the theatre.

The paraphrase continues with an incursion into the Kabuki theatre of Japan. For good reason, because they had dynasties of great actors there; and much more so, I think, than there ever were in China. The proof of this lies in the prints of actors by a whole group of woodcut masters; among them one astonishing genius, Sharaku, whom I have only abstained from writing about because I have written of him before, and have had to content myself this time by attempting to invoke the actor prints by Toyokuni. These are melodramatic beyond credibility; and in defiance of the anachronism, or 'mistake in time', one would wish Toyokuni to have been shown the posters of the Moulin Rouge by Toulouse-Lautrec. Both artists were noctambulists and lovers of the false daylight of the stage. From this we arrive by easy involvement to murder in the theatre, of which there have been notable and dramatic instances, and from that to the death of an old derelict actress in her caravan on the common at my old home. Thence, to the theatre of the golden caryatids, which are as a theatre should rightly be, and to the lowering of the curtain upon the scene.

ENTR'ACTE: *A breath from the Jasmine Kingdom*

This is to signify a return from murder and melodrama to gentler things, of which the Jasmine Kingdom is symbolic, and it brings us to a field of flowering yellow Crown Imperials looking down upon the blue domes of Isfahan.

BOOK FIVE

Flight of the Dragonfly signifies just what it says, the darting, hovering of an intelligence over subjects and themes of interest. The brilliant and marvellous ornaments of the birds of paradise; by whom devised and ordered, and for whose pleasure? To what end? And preliminary to that, the scents of roses. A quickening or speeding up of evolution as practised by the hybridists. There must have been a time when no winged creatures were in the air and, as obviously, a day when the first bird made its unaided flight from bough to bough. Were the birds of paradise extant, and just as they are now, in the days of the first Pharaoh? Or have they developed within historic time? How much of what has been painted, or composed, or built, or written in this century will be remembered in another hundred years from now?

The Workroom is an excursion out of ourselves and into the common pool, or workroom, or studio of ideas. There follows a momentary refuge from public entertainment, via the mass media, to the early morning of the world, of the world which is among primitive monuments and giant goddesses, watching the *lampuki* or dolphins scudding through the waves. The giant women of Picasso's curtain restore or put back the canon of painting and make that possible again. How is it that some primitive races had the gift for drawing? But something has gone wrong, and no one knows how to put it right and get it started again. Equality of opportunity is the sure path to destruction from inanition; rapidity of communication becomes in itself its own worst enemy; too good taste is enemy to creation. Of such are the arguments in this chapter, and it continues with a discussion of the 'staying' or lasting powers of music.

ENTR'ACTE: *Le Grand Gilles*

The Second Empire of Napoleon III as one great and glittering sham or fiction. Impersonation of character as a primitive form of magic, and the consequent horror of priests acting as gods in primitive races. In which context the heroes and villains of all-in wrestling have their part to play. Buster Keaton as dumb comedian foreshadowed in Le Grand Gilles of Watteau.

BOOK SIX

'*Say, what is love?*' Love has many meanings, in most of which it has no say at all. The contradictions thicken and crowd in upon themselves. Inanity and entire lack of talent in pop music. What is the I.Q. level among the readers and public for James Bond books and films? The parade of rockets through Red Square in Moscow is contrasted with the festival of the Dionysia in Alexandria of the Ptolemies during the carefree pre-Christian days. State of living in Whitechapel and the London slums, generally, in Jack the Ripper's time. The 'Floating World' of Panton Street and the Haymarket. The great cities of the Pax Romana were to be preferred to the cities of our industrial age. 'Hippy'-pattern austerities of the Egyptian and other hermits of the Eastern Church. Malraux's 'révolution à base d'érotisme'. The beggars are really and truly 'coming to town'. There is a law for the eagle and another for the sea-anemone; and so everyone to his, or their bed-sitter while there is still time.

ENTR'ACTE: *À la Japonaise*

This is at its start the sequel to the ice-scenes of Hendrik Avercamp. It contrasts the rain and mist and snow-scenes of Hiroshige which lead on, as diversion, to a few pages about the many wonders of Kyoto.

BOOK SEVEN

I came sad home': Disintegration of places, persons, things. Disillusionment of a lifetime of affection. Refuge taken in Rome. Versailles collapses like a house of cards. Its garden statues contrasted with those of Giovanni da Bologna. Fall to music of the faun-caryatids and pagan world of Caprarola.

Irresponsibility of Italian painting. Opera season as the true *métier* of their later painters. Mosques compared to churches, to the detriment as buildings of the big churches in Florence and Venice.

Deterioration of his own characters in Tolstoy's *War and Peace*. Depression of his Epilogues. Holocausts and hecatombs. The Anabaptists in Münster. Death of their leader Knipperdollinck, and end of Catinat and Ravanal, two leaders of the Camisards.

'For want of the Golden City'. The simple words of a children's song express a longing we all feel, and have perhaps enjoyed now and again for a few hours. But a ghost is invoked by a chance remark, and the friend in question appears in the doorway. And gradually the restaurant fills with *habitués*. Another long-dead friend is recalled. I am reminded of my first escape from home to *The Complete Angler* at Marlow, and evenings in London at the *Eiffel Tower*. First experiences of the Ballets Russes; and to memories of barrel-organ music the scene fades out.

There could be no deeper contrast to the memories of dead persons than sitting lazily in the sun, or lying warmly in bed. Which recalls an eerie and transcendental experience of owls hooting in the moonlight. Impossible, after what has gone before, not to think on and on about the problems of death and burial. The dead are dead, and that is the end of it. But there was virgin soil till not long ago, and how wonderful to have settled on it! There is, also, a longing for knowledge as a spur to living, but the miasma descends of the huge cities. What a contrast to New York was Vermeer's *View of Delft*; or even the Haarlem of Frans Hals! And again, the huge and diverse area of the Arcadia of rich peasants, stretching from villages in the Black Forest all through the Balkans to the white houses and chapels of the Cyclades. The hotchpotch, or charivari of different races. That there was as rich and varied a life as this in England is proved in the buildings in our villages and small towns, to end, even, or be revived in the red brick cottages and mullioned windows of Bedford Park.

From the movements of the celestial bodies, we infer the ordered activities of the world of ants. But they live in cities, and human beings are wearying of living in huge cities. Probably the last one worth living in was Paris during the Second Empire. Women's dresses of that day down to the time of Helleu and of Boldini. Destruction of the human environment while human intelligence is on the increase. But the beautiful solitude is going, and with it any hope of the 'Golden City'.

Persona perturbata. It will be obvious to the reader that the author has had difficulties which thwarted and impeded him, spread out over most of the two years that the greater part of this present work has taken in the writing. A simple restorative and antidote has been in reading Trollope, the common sense and humour of whose novels is enough to restore any unequal balance in one's nervous system. The cure amounts to a nightly sojourn of half-an-hour or more in another world free of the cares and worries of a would-be poet and aesthetician. And from this point the work in hand becomes for a few pages, more or less, a chapter of personalia. In the which a family picture which has been distorted takes on its truer colours.

ENTR'ACTE: *On Luca della Robbia*

The genesis and reason for the pages that follow have been recounted, and the *Entr'acte* opens with a picture of the Florentine spring, or *primavera*. This is followed by the later Florence of the Medici Grand Dukes. And now for Luca della Robbia and his *stemma* of King René of Anjou, in the Victoria and Albert Museum in London. His majolica roundels of fruit, flowers, and vegetables are examined. His ceramic cupola to the Cappella Pazzi which, the tiled domes of Isfahan and Samarkand apart, is one of the triumphs of architecture in colour. And the variety in his figures of Madonnas, their physical beauty, and the different poses of the child Jesus. The Tabernacle at Peretola, outside Florence, and the works by the family in the three churches of St Francis's convent of *La Verna* conjectured, if not seen.

BOOK EIGHT

Concorde and Concordia. Content and peace of mind are recovered on visiting again the old town of Bamberg after half, or more than half a lifetime. Bamberg being one of those old Imperial cities like Ratisbon (Regensburg) which bespeak the Holy Roman Empire and not the Teutonic Germany of Nuremberg and Rothenburg-ob-der-Tauber, and are on the level of interest of old towns in Italy or Spain. The Concordia, a lovely old house beside the river, seems to epitomize this past. And what a delight it is to think of the Councillor, Hofrat Böttinger, who built it in about the time of our Queen Anne, and to discover that Bamberg has close associations with E. T. A. Hoffman, who with his *Tales* for theme is as near to opera and ballet as Pushkin to the opera of his native Russia. But more exciting still to remember that Doctor Faustus was a guest of the Prince-Bishop and must have looked down on the city from that Kremlin-Hradschin of a palace-fortress above the river. The Concordia in its architecture as symbol of a balanced mind and controlled population. The balance of nature exemplified by the rows of dead children on old tombs. Youthful intimations of the cruel world in Cruickshank's drawings for *Oliver Twist*. Could the right priorities assert themselves again?

ENTR'ACTE: *Triptych*

One occasion suggests another, and my nerve having failed me in securing an interview with Dr Faustus during our stay in Bamberg, I 'opt' instead for the Ugly Duchess, and we set forth for her castle in the Tyrol, transferring it *en route* to Transylvania for the whiff of Count Dracula in the mountain air. The castle of Princess Tamara in the Caucasus also comes to mind, and strains of the *lezghinka* are ringing in our ears. And with little more ado we are in her horrific presence. It impels a recourse to dictionaries and natural history books, but first she is described as from the picture of her by Quentin Matsys, familiar to us all from Tenniel's drawings of the Ugly Duchess in *Alice in Wonderland*. A comparison is invoked between her and the man-eating plants, or *nepenthes*. And then comes the true history of Margaret 'Maultasche', or 'pocket-mouthed', Duchess of the Tyrol; and it would seem she was the aunt, or great-aunt, of Anne of Bohemia, Queen of King Richard II. What is there in a name? And it is irresistible to retail the names of the Swiss physician and alchemist Paracelsus.

'*A froggy would a-wooing go*'. We are driven to a palace to present our credentials, if any, and this evokes Cinderella's glass coach the like of which, improbably, was not so rare a sight in Mayfair only a generation ago. Was the texture of the coachman's spun-glass wig like that of a solidified foam-bath? But now there comes a fanfare of trumpets and a Virgin Queen is borne past in a litter or palanquin. It is the moment of her hypothetical love affair with her 'Frog Prince'. She has just sent him a basket of apricots for a present which inspires thoughts of poetry. And from poetry to lute music and a beautiful madrigal of Roberto Greene. Swinburne's metaphor for the sound of lute music.

Sketch for a portrait of the princess of the aphidae. Her suitability to have been a nun of the convent of Las Huelgas. The sandalwood boxes on her dressing-table.

BOOK NINE

The Green Boy and Girl. This is a return to the mystery of living, and I have taken for this purpose the Green Boy and Girl out of an old legend or folk-tale. They come up in mystery into the world, and are in symbol for what is instinct in the arts and is not born of learning and acquired knowledge. There is mention of them in my *Journey to the Ends of Time*, where there was promise of them which has not been fulfilled. They come up in the harvest field on a morning of hallucination at no certain date or time. They are caught and taken to a cottage, and little or nothing more is heard of them.

Born Again. Their birth is then parodied or burlesqued as if it were to happen now, but with ludicrous consequences for the modern age is not suited to miracles. They come up again in the harvest while jet planes are flying overhead from the USA airfields in East Anglia, and at once begin eating deadly nightshade. An uneasy future is foretold for the Green Boy, and they appear on earth at the poltergeist age which is the age of puberty. A world of promise is open to them but they will not fulfil it. But there are eye-witnesses' accounts of their re-appearance; a Gypsy woman and a postman turned amateur scientist give their stories. Foster parents are found for the Green Children, and the Green Girl would like to go to work in an aluminium factory. Meanwhile the Green Boy goes on holiday to a temperance hotel on the coast of Eire. The Celtic nonsense begins at once, and we are told the story of the mermaid and the fisherman's son. By the time this is finished the stop press is that 'Wendy', as the Green Girl likes to be known, has run away from home. Her foster-mother keeps her bedroom ready for her, but no more is heard of her. And the Green Boy dies, and medical opinion is that he would not have made a success of his life.

Morning Glory. This is again in sort a Messianic exercise. The circus troupe arrive on a never-to-be-forgotten day and the big tent is put up. Extraordinary and wonderful human beings emerge out of the motor-trailers on that transcendental evening. We are admitted into the dressing-room of the old clown who now transcends his stature and has the countenance of God. We are now outside the world of the Christians and at Polannaruwa in Ceylon, a very holy place of the Buddhists, and a place attuned to spiritual messages and emanations as conveyed in particular by a beautiful yellow-flowering tree. This seemed indigenous and endemic to this holy place, but emerges after long inquiry as of origin from Maryland, USA.

Vaudeville of the Living and the Dead. So we return to the circus tent for a repetition, if possible, of the first night of Offenbach's *La Vie Parisienne.* Constellation of Capricorn over gas-lit Paris and 'name-dropping' of the *hetairae* of the Second Empire. The extremes of fashion shown in colour by Compte Calix and in sepia drawings by Constantin Guys. The exaggerated fashions of the time demanded an artist of the calibre of Utamaro to depict their chignons and huge crinolines. Choice of subjects for Utamaro or for Kiyonaga. Music of *le grand écart.* Shakespeare on hounds 'with ears that sweep away the morning dew'. Paintings of angel-musketeers from Andean churches in Bolivia and Peru. Pharaonic mummies in contrast to the skull and crossbones of the German *Totentanz.*

Jewelled Skeletons. We are alone and left to our own devices. Is it all accident, or intention? If it was even an intention; or just a movement, once started, that goes on moving? Could it be the dawning of the Dark Ages for the second time? More serious research done in stone-age temples and stone circles than in twenty centuries of church going. Jewelled skeletons of saints in Spanish Court dress as a theme for Baudelaire, and his initiation in the Jesuit church of St Loup at Namur. Pitiful fewness of his own personal belongings. Probable Papal ban on exhibition of the bedecked skeletons.

ENTR'ACTE: *'Grand Pas de Deux' from Tchaikowsky's 'Casse Noisette'*

Towards the end of masques or ballets there is, traditionally, a set number or *pas de deux.* This tradition is upheld faithfully by both Delibes and Tchaikowsky. In *Coppélia* it takes the form of a solo for Frantz with music suggestive of soaring, ascending leaps for the male dancer followed by the clipped and slangy run-out of his dance marvellously evocative of its day and hour as of running out of the theatre through the summer traffic in order to get something to eat in the traditional haste of the dancer. No longer are we 'in a square in a small town on the borders of Galicia', as reads the stage direction. It is *'le plein Paris'* of 1869 or 1870. But the solo for Swanilda is in Spanish overtones; a set piece from the dancing schools of Córdoba or Seville in convention of the high comb, the mantilla and castanets.

Our *Entr'acte* which now follows is modelled upon music of a more serious nature, deeper indeed and more tragic than its rôle demands. It is the *Grand Pas de Deux* towards the end of Tchaikowsky's *Casse Noisette.* This must be the supreme masterpiece of its genre of music, in its warning that a most ethereal and extraordinary pair of human beings are about to come on from the wings. For it is as immediate as that. The music for their appearance is inimitable in the sweeping and gliding of the strings to suggest their entrance, which when it comes and we can see them, is in *diminuendo* to that music for in fact they walk on with little quick steps into the middle of the stage. And all the time it is accompanied by long-drawn sighing and lamenting of the wind instruments and brass, building up in tragic intensity, to a fever pitch of excitement which is more than just the composer's skill and his pleasure in the instrumentation. It is of the dilemma in his mind and soul, as clearly expressed here as in the 'Letter Song' in *Eugène Onegin*, but in less earthly terms, and as of immortal spirits. And in slackening that rage and intensity for a moment to allow of the intricacies of the dance, but resuming it again in full force to the despairing end.

BOOK TEN

À la Mexicaine. The despoiling of the world is touched upon, as, also, the system by which one section of the community can make life unendurable for another. But there would seem to be one country, at least, where the gadgets of 'civiliza-tion' still hold magic for the pawns who work them. For how much longer till they are disillusioned? It cannot lie far ahead in time, but meanwhile it is their honeymoon with the machines. Morning drive into the valley of the sugar-mills through the Mexico of 'le douanier' Rousseau. Even the beehives beside the road sell radio-active honey. Departure for lands of the flamboyant in all the excite-ment of seeing places I have thought and written of since 1920. Arrival at Queré-taro, and inquiry for the convent-churches of Santa Clara and Santa Rosa di Viterbo. Walking to them through the town and finding Santa Clara had shut its doors a few minutes before, at midday. Thence to Santa Rosa only to find that shut, too. Disappointment of long years of a working life till the truth comes that it is best not to have seen them and to leave these stones, at least, unturned. Their exteriors fulfilled, and the rest still left to the imagination. Celaya, that other town gone by, with just its domes and towers upon the skyline.

But the balance is redressed by providence in announcing the Strawberry Feast at Irapuato with bull fights in the evening as though in tardy recognition of a group of poems from a lifetime of prose and poetry. The revelation, too, of Guanajuato as compensation for the disappointment, with its three or four façades to churches of true Mexican-Indian intricacy and controlled abandon, the fretted pilasters looking as though they could spin round and revolve of them-selves, soundless, noiseless, in their perfect finish. The church of La Valenciana entered and attained at last. Roll-call of the golden altars of Mexico. Return to Irapuato of the 'strawberry feast', and provincial boredom of Morelia. Thence, over a desert road to San Miguel de Allende revealing itself out of nowhere down a steep hillside. Full moon seen as never before in that clear evening air. Drive to the intangible lake of Patzcuaro. Incredible that there should have been a Spanish bishop, near by at Quiroga, sent out by the Emperor Charles v nearly four hundred and fifty years ago. Reminder of the hovel-home of Pizarro, conqueror of Peru, at Trujillo in distant Estremadura.

One Town: One Voice. Museum director or prison governor away on holiday as responsible for state of world affairs. What is it all about, and why? The true discoverers, and the meeting of Cortés and Moctezuma. Bus or air tours every-where with no respite.

The ideal of Aristotle for the capitals of the Greek states. William Blake in

'The House of the Interpreter'. The voice of the fish-wife over a whole town. Agrigento, the ancient Acragas. The siting of their temples. Offering to a corn goddess. The Korai and the athletes. Voices of the long-crowers in the dawn. Peepshow in a railway station. Weather control. Demerits of a classical education. The spectacle of London in the nineteenth century. Low tide upon the sands. Futile visit to the painter Modigliani. Death of a fly recalled, and final fanfare.

ENTR'ACTE: *Pourriture Noble*

What is *pourriture noble*? Its picaresque connection. The demon of Matthias Grünewald. *Butch Cassidy and the Sundance Kid*. Swashbuckler plates of Montelupo. Fiasco of le baron Gros. The darkened fingernail of Cruickshank. The golden period of our language and the gift of tongues. Prize ring at Lillingston Lovell, as pendant to which, Borrow's account of Thurtell at the tent door of Jasper Petulengro. The tradition of violence from the vagrants in the reign of Henry VIII. First memory for the highwayman James Dalton. Puget's *'mélancolique empereur des forçats'*, and Puget in his dockyard workshop. Bronze group of *I Quattro Mori*. Report from the town clerk of Macclesfield. Return to Nova Scotia Gardens. Mayhew's supper to inmates of the twopenny lodging-house. The spectre in lace-sided bootees. Gustave Doré's drawings of the London slums. Cruickshank's *Early Morning*. The hansom cab and top hat. Eulogy of St Martin's-in-the-Fields. The Chicago of Al Capone. And for contrast the 'Redskins' of George Catlin. Hung in chains on Hounslow Common. Footnote after Thomas Rowlandson.

BOOK ELEVEN

Personalia. The time has come to reveal a few of the personal idiosyncrasies of the author. His writing room with an early version of *The Triumph of Death* by Bruegel, and the view out of his window. Bird life on the green lawn outside. Choice of prints and drawings for the room itself. The frontiers of Ruskin's knowledge. Alternatives to the habit of 'counting the sheep'. Farewell to the Val di Pesa. Two focal experiences; the first view of Naples, and a late look at Japan. Vision of St Petersburg. Places and things unseen, or left till last. The mirage of Plougastel and of Tønder in Denmark.

Prospect of Venice. Why are there no statues in the water? Finding of Magnasco. His banditti paintings. Tiled stoves and pretty ceilings of the north. Pictures by Fuseli. Portrait drawings by Ingres. Oncocyclus and paradoxa irises. White cubist houses of the Cyclades.

Red Raku Tea Bowl. Moonlight Revelry at the Dozo Sagami. Moonlit landscape by Utamaro. Flower festival at the Yoshiwara in comparison with Piccadilly Circus. Boat show at Earls Court. The painter and sword specialist, Hon-ami Koetsu. His sand pictures and pictures on the sands. The Red Raku Tea Bowl. Moonface, or atomic cloud?

The Garnering of the Cornstooks. Harvest sounds on the August evening. The flow of numbers compared to the counting mania and funeral obsessions of Anton Bruckner. In limbo with *The Tyro* and *The Enemy*, self-named. The uneasy fame of Eliot. A dictionary of poets? Poems by Mallarmé and by Góngora. Torquato Tasso. Herne the Hunter on a foggy afternoon in November. Glass anthills of New York. Brett's *The Stone Breaker* and his *Vale of Aosta*. Andy Warhol and Jan van der Heyden. Ingres and the daguerreotype. Vendemmia and treading of the grapes.

CODA: '*I return you now to the studio*'

Note. It is perhaps necessary to point out that the different chapters and episodes in this book were not written in chronological order, one after another. A few of them, or parts of them, date from as long as seven or eight years ago. But the bulk of them, to the extent of more than three-quarters of the whole, are the work of the last couple of years. It is hoped that this footnote will elucidate any apparent discrepancies in their timing.

This work would never have attained its present form without the help and encouragement of Michael Raeburn, who has spent many hours revising it and ridding it of repetitions and redundancies thus making it, or so we hope, a little easier to enjoy and read.

21 October 197

BOOK
ONE

Death of a Flie

I witness the death of a fly on the table beside my bed, on an October night when nearly all the race of flies are dead.

It had been buzzing, as flies do when they are on their backs, and was propelling itself in little short jerks or bouts between the books beside my bed. I hate flies, and wanted to go on reading, but the intermittent whirring and buzzing as of some costive and halting engine made this impossible.

And now a particularly loud, an ominous hornet-like noise, as of a spring released in perpetual motion, venomous and drilling; altering key to a piercing, screaming, whirring – and the living animal in a paroxysm or despairing frenzy scuttles round like a blind thing beside my bed, spinning round and round – then moving straight as though travelling on a beam for a few inches, collapsing, and as suddenly, stilled.

It must be dead. I touch it with a pencil. Nothing. No reaction. And now a little harder push, and it is off again. But this time staying in place, as when an aeroplane having turned into the runway, tries its engine, and its whole fabric shakes, and trembles, tied down, lashed, as it were, to the cement scaffold. The noise rises shrilly to an unbearable intensity, continues in that for a second or two, and stops dead. Ceases.

All this time I have not looked closely at the creature, having a loathing for six-legged insects. But it is a live animal, not a piece of machinery; just now in some kind of trauma of exhaustion, but lying dormant and gathering strength. And now, horribly, it waves its front pair of legs, even rubs them together with a soft scraping sound that some auditory device could record and play back to us, much magnified.

The creature, or housefly beside me has a chocolaty carapace marked off in segments as to its underneath or belly, like a Mills bomb, as though for dismantling or explosion; and now I remember that flies turn this colour during the winter from weakness and want of food. By the time the few survivors crawl from the cracks and crevices where they have hidden into the first spring sunlight upon the windowpane, their bodies are grey-green, and they are thin as ghosts. Always, nearly always, they are mistaken and die that night of cold.

This one has tried to hide itself among my books, where it would be dislodged sooner or later by the duster. In the meantime the flat table-top is its parade or exhibition ground. And once again it is 'travelling blind', buzzing and knocking itself against the edges of my books.

Next, it puts on a held, high tension crisis of a wiry humming that lifts or drops a semitone but it is as that lift from the empyrean into the stratosphere, out of some element into another, and it is a dimension of noise in which it is impossible to sleep. And now gone. Stopped. Without even the broken stalk of sound behind it.

It is the moment to open a book and go on reading, if the housefly will allow of it. But the 'father or mother of all bluebottles' at once enters an objection. It starts an invisible, subfusc whirring, as of but one side of wings from some dark corner.

And it continues so that I must look for it, upsetting a book, which, I think momentarily, may have killed it. But it sails into sight again, serene and round like one of the moons of Saturn along the tundra or pampas of my bedtable, not in fact airborne, but coasting as on a cushion of air along that table-land. The pallor of electric light accentuates the lunar whiteness. And slowly it crosses the meridian and dips into darkness where the table has a rim. It has taken an instant, a day and night, a lunar year.

For the moment it is out of my mind.

Instead, and like a stale newsflash from the days before they were invented, I have the whiff of a tramps' bonfire in my nostrils. The whirring has taken me back to the summer term beyond the streams and the pollard willows. It was beyond those that the early bird-man had his aeroplane. He was a hawk-nosed American, and it never left the ground.

This early airman, we were told he was American, kept his machine beyond the butts and the water meadows on the way to Slough. In those days there were tramps' fires on the outskirts of every town, with that acrid smell as if they were burning their old boots. It was 1913 or '14, the summer of Léon Bakst and of Nijinsky even to a sixteen-year-old schoolboy, not long after Blériot had flown the Channel, not long before the First World War began.*

Several times on Thursday or Saturday afternoons that summer term I had watched him trundling it from its shed, the word 'hangar' was not yet invented. Probably he came down from London every day after finishing some other work. Because of his hawk-nose I imagined that he must have Red Indian blood. I often wonder who he was, and whether he is still alive. But it is not likely after two world wars and over such a chasm or abyss in time.

So here we were, myself and my two school friends, both of them destined to be killed in a few months' time before they were nineteen, having pushed to the far edge of our world of school, looking from the willow trees to the flying machine that could not leave the ground. It is all gone now. My two friends have been dead for fifty years. I would not be able now to find the stream or the pollard willows. Long ago it was all built over as part of a factory, or huge housing scheme.

* The first aeroplane I saw was from the train window going to Bournemouth in April 1910 or 1911. It was over Brooklands.

And on the way back I would smell the smoke of the tramps' fire once more, thinking too, of the round-faced Romīs, a ragged man and two young girls in long skirts with round, round faces whom I had seen upon a winter evening leading a bear by the school library as it was getting dark. The man had a thick stick in one hand and was leading the bear, a yellow bear upon a chain. I remember the cheap look of its fur, and wondering whether they huddled against it for warmth at night. There was only a little moment to ask them who they were, and one of the young girls answered 'Bohémiens' to the young boy in top hat and tailcoat who was myself, and certainly no less far-fetched and peculiar in her eyes.

I still hear the buzzing and revving of the early aeroplane engine.

But I remember the dying fly and look for it, and cannot see it. If it were alive it would have crawled out into the light. With the whole of its body spinning, spinning, it would have come across the calm to the lamp, longing, of instinct, to buzz inside the lampshade. But not a sound.

It can no longer use its wings to fly. In fact, it turned over onto its back from buzzing its wings too furiously, and overbalanced just as if its motor or engine were too strong for it. Far from being lifted and airborne, it was capsized. I suppose a speedboat with too powerful a motor might turn turtle, or just go round and round in mad circles like the rings upon a pond.

This is what the moribund fly was doing until a moment or two ago. Travelling round on its back with all six legs in the air. Trying to right itself and get its feet upon the ground again. It has lost all direction as though its eyesight is gone; those multiple eyes that are like facets, like the reflectors in a lighthouse, or the florets of a hydrangea head. Moving at high speed like a water-beetle; a few of which creatures together on a pond seem to be moving to order in obedience to some remote control. As part, even, of an overall design; no less, or more mysterious than the celestial bodies out in space.

At this point I must have dropped off to sleep. It was one of those spells of a couple of hours or so which refresh but seem over in a few minutes, and one wakes up as if from a century of sleep with the feeling that one needs no more of it and is rested. But the greater depths of that ocean are there in front of you. You can even feel them on its surface, as though there is a hollow sound where the lead goes down into the deep.

I wake up once more, and fancy I can hear it buzzing but cannot be bothered, and turn over on my other side.

At five o'clock it is still entirely dark. There is not a hint of day. It is the true main, or island-less profundity of night time, with all alternative forgotten, and only creatures of the night awake and abroad; but it is a darkness which is anything but death.

I turn on the light once more to know what time it is, and this is what I see.

It is sitting nearer to me on the table. No more than a foot away. Sitting there. No longer struggling on its back.

Somehow, somewhere, it has got onto its legs again. But the insect is too weak to stand and is sitting down.

Sitting in the semi-human posture some animals, lions and dogs, can assume, with its forefeet to the ground. The front pair of its six legs, that is to say. Sitting in fact with its haunches on the ground. Its four hind-haunches.

We are in the world or bestiary of eight-wheel lorries. Eight wheels to a side, sixteen in all, as on the Brazilian iron-ore road from Ouro Preto to Belo Horizonte through the red-rust, red-dust nightfall with our one-eyed driver, and on arrival the huge town, unheard of, with high buildings, was one quarter slant-eyed Nipponese. And in momentary vision, like another newsflash, are the lorries delivering new cars from Coventry. So do the young progeny of toads, toads of the year, ride their parents' backs and stifle them, in parody on the bottle-neck and traffic problem.

And for some moments I thought 'Mosca', the housefly, was just sitting there.

Sitting there because it had nothing better to do, and in a way of sleeping. And because it is too weak to stand.

But not at all. It has another purpose.

It is trying to lick a sugar-coated pill which is on the table beside me. A pill that fell out of the pill-box, or which I have forgotten to swallow. It clasps the white ovoid with its front legs and is trying to lick the sugar with its knobbed proboscis of a tongue.

The pill is as high, or higher than its head. As to the Augaean or Rabelaisian propensities of that pill we are silent for this is no Gargantua or Pantagruel. Or it might have no effect at all. Who knows?

But the fly has eaten nothing for many weeks. What in fact do they live on? I am no entomologist, but it must be evident that there has been nothing for it to eat since it flew into the room, perhaps one day in August or September. How much is known, or has been written about the life cycle of this race of insects? Of whom another, as I write this, has just arrived upon the window-pane but is, as quickly, gone again. Can they live on air? They must have the ability to exist for weeks on end, in rare instances all through the winter into spring, on no food at all.

So this fly has found for itself the sugar-equivalent of a gold mine. Towering above its head, more than life-size, and white as chalk or salt.

And I have at the back of my mind the white pyramids of the *salinas* or salt marshes, 'glistening like the white ghosts of the tents where our redjackets were quartered in the wars of Wellington'. This, from Cádiz on the road to San Fernando, passing the Isla de León 'where chameleons abound', and the red cattle of Geryon were pastured which were stolen by Hercules. How red were they? And had they the white eyelashes of the bulls that roam beneath the centenarian pear trees? More than a hundred varieties of perry pears, ragged or full of shape in blossom, on the red lands where those herds graze and perry wine was pressed?*

The insect beside me looks at this moment like a cosmonaut just landed from his capsule and struggling with elements and forces he does not understand. Is he emerging from the egg, or trying to get back into it?

* In the counties of Gloucester, Worcester, Hereford, and part of Monmouth. A hundred varieties found, and perhaps another twenty more to find.

It seems improbable this is his first meeting with it. Has he been tied up inside it as if to practise weightlessness? Or simulate the right, or wrong conditions? And stayed inside a day, a whole week, a long winter for a fly?

There is a languid air about its gestures with its forearms. Which does not come only from the waving of their three joints where we are used to two. But, then, we have our hands at the end of them, with our four fingers and a thumb. In place of their padded feet, with suction disks and all the armature of the lamprey, which fastens by suction on another fish body and sips its juices. Limbs, though, that are awkward to move and not co-ordinated.

Not so, though, when it releases hold and springs into the air, and is master of its element. Where it can land on you and take off again several times in a minute, its plan being to annoy and tease for it is both curious and inquisitive. But no longer. This fly, indeed, is on the threshold of another world.

It has effected a lunar landing. And what to do next? It is merely a probe and not a real invasion. And now it is absolutely alone on the table beside my bed. Alone, with no worldly possessions, of this world, or of any other. What does it make of the switching on and off of the electric light, which is one of the hazards of the race of flies? It is a new risk, but I do not remember the world without it, and my span of life would probably cover two thousand years of flies' lives. To land on an electric light bulb is to them only less dangerous than a lunar landing, dependant on a human whim which is as arbitrary as a change of weather! To join the throng of insect peripatetics padding round with blistered and scorched feet is worse than a lifetime in the Australian desert, the span of a human generation being equivalent to those few hours of evening when the light is on! Hot electric bulbs are dangerous to flies, but so are wars to human beings. Yet, as techniques improve, wars get worse, not better, it should be obvious.

But another whirring and buzzing that is nearly a note of agony.

In fights between insects there are no cries of pain.

The six- and eight-legged creatures are all masked. They wear masks or visors. They show no emotion.

The praying mantis is expressionless. As though of green painted wood while she devours her lover. Cruel, with helmet head and toothed arms like saws, but not voluptuous.

Not so the octopus who capers before his meal, who hurries to it, hand over hand, out of his cavern. But the octopus is a solitary and a recluse; he does not hunt in packs or nations. He sprays with ink, and not with napalm. His natural juices make sepia, and not jellied petrol.

To be eaten by an ogre lingering over his meal; or, like Servetus, burned at the stake in Geneva with a crown of thorns steeped in phosphorus put upon your head, for having opposed infant baptism, denied original sin, opposed the doctrines of the Trinity, and confounded the Creator with his creatures?*

After the names of persons burned by the Inquisition, or Holy Office, is

---

* Michael Servetus, a Spanish physician (b. Tudela 1509) who had written against the Trinity (*De Trinitatis Erroribus*), and who was 'only a visitor to Geneva', was arrested by order of Calvin, condemned by the Great Council, and burnt 27 October 1553.

written the laconic phrase, 'convictus et combustus'. How many hundreds and thousands burned at the stake, and never a finger raised to help them! Surely, if there be a god? But he will not help in this world!

Criminals broken on the wheel were in no better plight. In his travels through France, Tobias Smollett has an account of seeing a young robber broken on the wheel, at Dijon in 1754, as night fell in that year of the Louis Quinze snuff-box. While the scaffold was building, an old woman lit the fire, and helped generally. She was both the executioner's mother and his assistant, a wonderful instance of French thriftiness! Smollett tells of the dreadful hammer blows; two to each forearm and to the upper arm; two to each shin-bone and then to each upper leg between the knee and hip, and then the 'coup de grâce' delivered on the chest above the heart. All that time the old woman was helping and watching, and holding for her son. Could a stranger deathbed be imagined! To die in lingering agony, with the old crone at your side, and her son slowly killing you, to whom she had given birth in pain and agony! And when it was over, the old woman and her son, collecting the instruments of their trade came down from the stage into the thinning crowd, and walked off into the darkness.

It was Henry Fielding, the other inventor of the modern novel, who was taken to Lisbon to die, and describes how the crowds at the London docks laughed at his infirmity as he was carried aboard. Fielding, who was a Bow Street magistrate and a human one, knew so much of the slum dwellers of London.

But where is the fly? Where is it? For there is not a sound. It cannot have gone far. For of course this one, though it has wings, is flightless. It cannot leave the ground. It is like a sheep lying on its back in the middle of a field; and I am countryman enough to know that all you need do is to take it by its wool, or by a pair of legs, and turn it round. It will scamper away, white-faced, and sillier than ever, but it would have been dead in a few hours.

This flat disk of a fly on its back with its aureole of legs, three joints to each of these, waving about like a clown's fringe of hair, is as intangible in the darkness as a flying saucer and would not even show upon the radar screen. Will it reverse direction and fly off, climbing almost perpendicularly at terrific speed? But always soundless. Remember, they make no sound.

There is quiet for a few moments as though its gyro-mind is disconcerted for it has the brain cells of a spinning-top. But in the darkness it tries to spring a mine. It whirrs again as if within an inch of me, or on my pillow. I listen, and do not like to feel for it because of the horror of touch. It may have crawled even underneath my pillow.

It is invertebrate, which means it has no vertebral column, 'is destitute of a backbone'. Has it a heart or lungs? I am not sure. Certainly it eats and defecates. And procreates and fornicates. And can see, but, I think, not hear. Or, if it has hearing, it is tuned in to another dimension of sound. Not that its buzzing is not intended as a warning? But if it can hear its buzzing can it hear a human voice? Or the ringing of the telephone? Or the far off, far up whirring round half-past five in the morning which is a jet-plane flying in from America at no-man's hour and nearing London.

What does it know? And what does it not know? All it possesses in any case is instinct, and not knowledge. It must be aware that it is dying. Any creature that has the instinct to get out of the way, or hide itself, must know it is in danger. And danger means death. So there is another state from living which is death. And it does not want to die.

If there were true inheritance of instinct it would be wiser than to fly straight into a light. How is it they know how to fly out of the way if you lift your hand, which is something they have learnt, and yet the madness takes them once the light is on? The sugar-coated pill must be a godsend hunched there under the lamp in their world where every electric bulb in its working hours is another solar system.

In fact the housefly sampling the sugar-coating is copying the basic instructions to the cosmonaut which are to take specimens of rocks and soil just as though arrived at a new Rand of precious minerals. Gold and diamonds, coal and oil, may be there for the asking, and all sorts of other more personal data of action and reaction are to be filled in on the appropriate forms. After which it is time to sit down and think; and indeed it could be that there is nothing else to do for all eternity.

Is earth in fact visible from there? It should occupy a much bigger space in the sky, and perhaps they get the dimmed outline of the Atlantic Ocean and of both Americas. Which should heave slowly out of, or into vision during a sleepless night? Is there that cold lunar pallor? Because it is dead. It is a dead place. There is no doubt of that. But this should be another colour. Not green which is the livery of nature. But, here, are too many areas of ice and water; too many mountains, Alps and Himalayas, and too much sound. Those could be little more than markings on the terrestrial physiognomy. It must be a curious sensation on a starlit night to look from an extinct world of rocks and sand to one of living beings.

The dead world to which this insect on my table is going in a few minutes is not bleaker or more purposeless. At least it has no landscape. No landscape, and no light whatever. It is a question of darkness or illumination. There is no lit globe, no simulation of a solar system. And as it is nothing, once there, there are no regrets. As you have no existence, you can be neither glad nor sorry. You have lost your right to live. Perhaps once there was something living on the lunar satellite, but it perished in the cataclysm in which it was created, and by which it gained dead independence. It was stillborn because of some disaster that befell the parent. It broke away. It cannot have approached and been rejected. Therefore, in a sense there is a dead being trailing after us; and I do not think that in the mythology of any race whatever the satellite has been thought of as anything but feminine. The sun-god is always male; and the moon is female, and past child-bearing.

In the meantime the sugar-coated pill has shifted a little on its axis. It has slanted and the rim of the ovoid rests upon one of the fly's feet, which is quickly put right by the pencil which is always by my bed. It has not hurt the insect at all, which soon withdraws its leg. What more indeed can one do for a fly except free it from a spider's web? Close up against the sugar-pill, the mass of it must look like the moon seen from near to, perhaps only a few hundred miles away, as the astronaut is hurtling towards it. The white light of it, the bland openness of its countenance, must be nearly blinding. Not its own light, but a reflected light like that thrown on the sugar-pill by the reading lamp, while hurrying towards it at so many thousands of miles an hour. And the perfect ovoid of its shape rouses speculation as to whether it may not go up perpendicularly into the air, swerve away, or behave, in short, like the UFO's of the evening papers.

But now things are happening. There's a movement on the part of the fly.

I watch it in horror topple over on its back, buzz its wings – which is something we cannot do, who can only get above the clouds in a machine worked by a motor – and twice get up again. I cannot kill it, though I should, but have to watch its death struggles.

This time it has toppled over. Not been thrown over; but, as before, overturned by the extreme force in the buzzing of its wings. So did the gyroscope tops of childhood turn turtle and spin round upon their backs. And for a moment it hurt to touch them until the force ran out of them and they fell. With a little movement in reverse right at the end and as though to settle down comfortably, ready to be spun again.

But to my horror by one pair of legs after another it gets up again. First sitting up, in the lion or dog attitude, collapsing again, then, by a huge effort hauling itself onto its front pair of legs; after which like the treads of a tank moving over difficult country, and rotating hopelessly before they get a grip, the fly flutters its four back legs which are too flimsy to hold their ground, while it trails its hindquarters as though for egg-laying in autumn on the windowpane. A squirting of ectoplasm from some faecal tube or syringe, gelatinous, not soft and rubbery like new laid turtles' eggs; nor do their young, of instinct, make in a straight line for the cleansing, salt oceans. But these cluster upon the ceiling, and the airs can hum with the whirring of so many embryo wings.

It rights itself, gives a shake as though in reassurance which, magnified, would make a curious sound, and shrinks forward, caterpillar-like, its own body length. No more than that. Then, quite still, as if thinking. What to do next is its own decision. There is nothing implicit one way or the other. It has power of choice, as much so as the horse in a field.

Instead of which, it topples and falls down once more. Turns over, as if fated, and waggles its six legs. Rotates on its back, but not a full circle. And now it is evident to me that I should put it out of its agony and kill it.

But I cannot kill it. I have to watch its death struggles which are prolonged and fearful.

Quite still for a moment. And then, as if to the bite of the tarantula, it is convulsed, kicks out in all directions and contrives to move an inch or two. Were there an edge to my bedside table it would hurl itself over, but we know they are too light to hurt themselves and have always a safe landing.

But there is a rail, and it rebounds from that for another figure in its dance of death.

Tacking under steady sail at a diagonal right across the table to the other side. Scuttling, as though nothing was wrong with it, and making port with no visible effort at all. Lying off shore at anchor under the breakwater of a pile of books.

Revictualling. Taking water on board. Trying out its turbine engine for it sails just as well backward as forward. Raising and dropping anchor playfully. For that is what it is doing, I imagine, making a few lazy movements, then lying still. Taking it easy, and grateful for 'the breather', as in a bout of 'all-in' wrestling when one of the heavyweights will sham dead and let himself almost be counted out in order to recover strength and down his opponent when he stands up again.

A shudder of all six legs, and after that perfectly still. Not a movement.

And now careering away with the bit between its teeth in a last fine frenzy, given maniacal strength and gaiety. With the strength of ten flies it emulates tank manoeuvring, moving bumpily at outrageous pace, still on its back, but buzzing its wings and agitating both sets of legs. It remembers being free of the air and long days upon the wing.

But it is no nearer flying than the early bird-man in his shed near Slough. How often he must have been angered by the ease of the sparrow with its one hop and in the air; or when brushing a fly from his hand or forehead! And, once more, I wonder who he was, and what has become of him? I get the smell of the world that lost itself in the First World War. And the stab of nostalgia from that bonfire smoke brings me to all manner of strange places, the Moldavian horsefair and the caves of Guadix. But I force myself away from them and back to the Salisbury Plain and the Naumachia beside my bed.

In time to see the insect right itself and with a fearful convulsion of limbs and body stagger to its feet. This is its death agony which is horrifying to watch. And with human beings? This is when we read: 'At about two o'clock the next night, he rose up in delirium from his bed, uttering the most appalling cries, and possessed of such strength that he knocked down his servant who tried to calm him.' But he lived through the day and did not die till ten o'clock that night.

Or, 'soon after five o'clock', in the early morning of course, 'there came a flash of lightning accompanied by a peal of thunder. . . . He opened his eyes, lifted his right hand and looked up for several seconds with his fist clenched and a very serious, threatening expression', and let his hand sink to the bed, and was dead in a few moments. This was the deaf man of genius; and the peal of thunder may have been the only noise – and the first music – he had heard for years. But it was more likely the flash of lightning that awakened him to die.

I have written down the first two deathbeds that came to hand. The dying men are Beethoven and Franz Liszt, in reverse order.

But the dying insect goes down like a horse in the knacker's yard. On its haunches, one moment, and then slumps down dead, legs in the air like a babe in its cradle, or a dead bull. Waiting for the mule team to drag it by the horns round the ring in triumph, and out from the arena into. . . . ? While the dead fly in fact goes on an envelope or an old letter into the wastepaper basket, and down the lavatory.

Credo

How marvellous to be living!

You can touch dead stone or metal with your hand and almost feel pity for them, except that the hot sun of the morning is in them, too, even in the white metal handrails of the omnibus soiled by so many tens of thousands of fingers, white and black, but rubbed with a rag by a 'polisher' in the cold dead hours of night.

Men from Post Office Telephones are in and out of the kiosks, unscrewing and disinfecting the mouthpiece. Bill-posters are at work on the Tube platforms.

A morning of spring when women are beautiful as flowers, as though they are lovely animals, awoken and come out into the sun.

A dog trots on the pavement, lively as the morning, carrying a shopping basket in its teeth.

Here are three pennies (it is two new pence now!). Go into the telephone box and ring up anyone you please.

Wrong number; or number engaged, an intermittent, high pitched buzzing note. Will you wait until the operator calls you? Or try again. Dial the number code of the exchange; and wait for the 'pip-pip' signal or the operator's answer.

Perhaps it is not so simple as that. In which case dial 999 for the police, or in case of fire, or for the ambulance services.

Did you not get the dialling tone? Then, dial 100. Or, if you wish to make a trunk call to a particular person, you will probably find it advantageous to book a 'personal call' to the person required. Your name will not be given to the called number if you ask for it to be withheld.

No reply. It means that everyone is away. Or the line is out of order and the operator will check for you.

Everything in the world, but not the thing you want.

Up in that aeroplane, from where the blue empyrean over the chain-store turns to awful, unfathomable black-purple, looking down – or is it up or down, or neither? – the individual soul is no more than the one hundred and ninety thousand numbered souls of Hiroshima.

The ant-heap pullulates; and is in an instant stilled.

Looking out of the window where I sit, writing, this February morning, dead leaves are blowing to and fro over the snow, still and inert for long moments together with no life in them, and of a sudden, whirled hither and thither, or, surprisingly, taken up and capering furiously in a mad, vertiginous gallop, which is ridiculous and as though an old lady, or anyone's grandmother or great aunt, was run down a steep hill by invisible agents holding her by each arm, and you know she will fall at the bottom and break both legs, and other bones as well.

In music, as in life, this is the *Galop Infernale*, the *Course à l'Abîme*, or *Ride to the Abyss*.

Was it Nero, or Commodus, who 'did not hesitate to expose decent house-wives and old charwomen' to the fury of the wild beasts in the arena? What else are the blindfold nags ridden by the picadors in the bull-ring, except that Spanish 'chivalry' will not permit of an old mare being sent to the bulls, and so they are always decrepit, worn-out horses?

It is said that mushrooms are full grown in three or four hours so that one could fall asleep in a field, lying within a fairy ring where it makes a dark circle on the grass, and awaken in a Kitaigorod, a Kremlin or Tartar encampment of domes and phalluses. There is a very good restaurant under the Governor's house where an excellent dinner may be obtained. Near-by is the famous suburb called Kunavin, dedicated to pleasure, with open air pantomimes, Gypsy singers and bands, and a theatre where there is generally a good ballet. The river looks like a broad blue riband stretched over the country from one extremity of the country to the other, and coming up from below the terrace you hear the noise and excitement of the Great Fair.

The wind in the dead leaves was but a catspaw and a scherzo. A device in order to effect a touch of magic. The transference of magical impulse is as easy as that. It is as quick as moving in a sentence from the mushroom field to the fair of Nijni-Novgorod.

What would it be if animals ceased to increase, but machines of a sudden began to procreate?

If the tractor-combine shrouded for the night was found at early morning with an infant harvester in the dew beside her? If we could assist, not at leviathan-amours in the deep, but at the loves of the steam-rollers? If the sewing-machine gave birth in the back bedroom of the seamstress, and there were children of the typewriter and the telephone?

For it is as simple as that.

Unless we are willing to believe in a little thing that cannot be explained, then all explanations become meaningless. And there may well be things which have no meaning. Their purpose has been diverted, or they have lost their meaning. There could be celestial bodies as pointless in their behaviour, as obsolete, and as far removed from the mathematical utilities, as the sentry posted at one of the Russian palaces in the time of Catherine the Great to mount guard over a rose-bed, who was relieved night and day for more than a hundred years after the Empress was dead and the garden had been swept away. Truth is proved more by its contradictions than its agreements. That there should be black swans only makes a snow-white swan the more beautiful in imagery.

But we are, and remain, what we were born, with little alteration or improve-ment.

The foreigner in a kilt is not more absurd than the Englishman pretending to be anything else than what he is. We cannot turn ourselves into Balinese rajahs any more than into Red Indian 'braves'. And an Englishman in the world of nine-year-old bayadères in golden diadems with frangipani blossoms in their hair is incongruous as the black face and bright blue suit on a wet afternoon in Totten-ham Court Road.

It is not enough to wear a knitted cap upon the bay of Hammamet in order to become an Arab; nor could I pretend to be a miner in my native Derbyshire.

Born in the north of England, and born a younger son, I do not like to think what my life would have been had I not caught the germ of poetry from my brother and sister for it is contagious, and known I had a lode or vein to work in order to transcend my own reality. It is only in virtue of it that I have got outside or surpassed my physical self, which was intended, obviously, for pursuits in which I have never engaged because I have no liking for them. Those have been the identical circumstances of how many other writers and poets of all ages in every land from China to Peru, and it is the background for what has stupidly been called the 'mandarin', as opposed to the worker or proletarian writer or artist, as though either implied a greater, or lesser degree of pain and difficulty in attaining the ideal.

There are beauties which are imponderable; or human beings of their skill could match the roses in a maiden cheek; the rose being of another order of beauty from the night-hyacinth, or of a different temperament, as a lily to a rose.

Tear a rose-petal, or dig your nails into the lily; and in texture they are little more than paper, but paper that does not make a sound when crumpled. They will rub between the fingers till nothing is left of them; until the petal with dark marks in it from the finger nails is but a pulp, and a ghost of dew still haunted by the scent.

The lily flesh bruises; and we can effect in a moment what the hand of time does to the maiden.

Ah! while we are young we do not think of that, or only witness it by proxy in a third person, without emotion.

A railway runs along the whole Mediterranean shore of Spain, from north of Barcelona as far down as Málaga or Almería. Why? For the same reason that every house in Spain, even the cave of the troglodyte and the hut of the Gitano behind the blue cactus hedge, has its number painted on it.

There is a story of how guests staying at Glamis Castle went into each room in the house and tied a handkerchief to every window in order to discover the ghost room wherein the legendary 'monster' had been imprisoned.

Would it not be as sensible to stencil a number on every orange in the orange grove? But you cannot number the orange blossom; nor is there dimension or measurement to its divine breath.

How many centibels of sound are there in the song of the nightingale? Or can the darkness of the velvet night be measured?

To number every house in the country is to look for something which you will never find. Till the numbers are, themselves, obsolete, or no one travels on the railway line.

'I'll build you a stairway to Paradise'

But all things in their proportion and before there is time to think I am back on the playground at St Hubert's on the morning they tried the new fire-escape. Crossman, a loathsome child from Lancashire, stands near me. Worse still, he sleeps in the next bed to me in the dormitory and is awake early on those interminable and tormented Sunday mornings in the summer term. For many years – but not now – I hated fine weather because it meant 'nets', which portended cricket-balls bowled or thrown at one by Wallace, the sadistic classics master. At least the fire-escape meant an hour 'off' from Greek grammar in the Inquisition setting he had devised for it.

Another child-beast, Crompton, who says all flowers 'stink' – what his home must be like! – is kicking a football with idiot vacuity only a yard away. So it is the winter term (Michaelmas) – why 'Michaelmas'? – which is the longest and darkest in the year. Ah! well! most of them are dead by now; the masters, surely, and after two world wars, more than half the boys. And St Hubert's is gone with all its totem-shields of athletic 'wins' hung up like so many scalps, its initiation rituals, and to paraphrase the 'brothel paraphernalia' reported in the papers as removed after a police raid, we could say its team-spirit relics, and pseudo-Red Indian insignia and nonsense.

But in the same instant, before we can breathe we are back there. The long corridor of sacking, now hanging limply, is lowered from the window of 'B' dormitory, high in St Hubert's, where the little brute Nesfield is tyrant. Who was it that he made stand with his head up the chimney all night long? His horrid little face looks down at me from the other window. And now someone's coming down the chute, slowly, slowly, as an example of course to others, holding to the rope inside. And in a voice of mounting excitement as, nowadays, the commentator at a race-meeting, rising to a screech, 'It's Mr Hankey; no, no, it's Galbraith. I'm sorry Mr Galbraith' – in Holy Orders, but just why is that? – and with a yell, 'It's Mrs Williams!' (the headmaster's sister). And now we all go up in turn, half a dozen at a time, and one after another climb onto the windowstill, put our feet into the sack, and are given the push, 'launched into eternity', as it were, by Hewitt the 'odd man' and general factotum of the school, who was kind and whom I liked, but who came round in the mornings at seven o'clock sharp, to pour cold water into the tin-bath which was under every bed. How I loathed it all, and hated my red school-cap and loathed even my locker No. 54 in the changing-room, and missed my mother and my brother! And it was endless. I had to endure four years of it, and am only surprised it is not still going on now.

We are not only coming down the chute, but climbing up the rope again.

Hewitt teaches us to climb ropes in the 'gym' among the parallel bars and the rest of the paraphernalia. It is a condition of endless climbing up and down like that in drawings I have seen of Indians fetching water up and down ladders in a cenote in Yucatán; and again in double meaning, for except for the necessity of having water, it is as useless as the ants following each other round the rim of a bowl for hours on end.

And now it is cold and hot at the same time as with a touch of fever; and I am astride a flying buttress in a pea-soup fog. Not 'a' flying buttress, but 'the' flying buttress, which one must keep one's eye on as on a high wire or tightrope all the time, and not look down. If you look below you are lost and gone. And if someone or something comes crawling along it towards you? What, then? And not 'then' but now. You cannot step over it, or go backward. It stretches up and up, and you cannot see the end of it. And it is not round like a rope. It has a sharp edge of stone, like a stone rail. And there are the obstacles. At moments there is quite a depth of stone, greenish stone, beneath me; and then it narrows and other shafts of stone join into it on both sides, and I must lift my feet over them, carefully, one at a time. And the next moment there is that frightening thinness of support under me where the stone narrows again and is no more than a few inches thick. Soon, a few feet ahead of me it ends altogether and joins up into a blank wall. One is at the same moment out in the cold high up in open air, and could as well be deep in a coal-mine thanks to the pea-soup fog. But it all changes. It all passes. In a moment it has gone as completely as those unhappy school days.

What we see now is a fat man in a furry hat enthroned on a sort of four-legg'd stool, but he has only stumps for legs, holds a stick in walking-stick position a little behind him in his left hand, while in his other hand he brandishes a longer stick, handle-upward, like a croquet-mallet. He is one of the static, the immovable ones, who has to be carried out and lifted home at evening, and must be some kind of Roi d'Yvetot, or beggar-king. Waddling away from him with his back to us, another fat figure in a like furry hat, guitar on back, almost round of circumference – there are fat as well as thin ones! – pegging away from us upon his pair of stumps. Their ladies, whether queens or beggar-women, wear the high head-dresses of cambric and lace of the Pays de Caux.

Then, in a kind of pointless frenzy, reeling from side to side and half-staggering sideways and backwards, a victim of chorea, but of course this is before the disease has been given its collector's name. And a pair of cripples, both on crutches, hurrying, hurrying, and they have got their two pairs of legs crossed and entangled. There is a beggar, also on crutches, trailing a deformed leg like a thin, bent stalk behind him. And a 'hopper', guitar or mandoline on his back, hopping and jumping on his one leg and a stick; and two of the quick-moving sort, they can go nearly as fast as skaters so long as they are on level ground, their feet on bits of board which they have learned not to knock against each other, while they dart forward by means of what looks like a flat-iron on four points which they hold in either hand.

They are but a few of the beggars who are as many as the rooks at this moment building their nests in the high elms on a windy day. There is no background at

all. It is as flat as a sheet of paper. And a sheet of paper it is; what else, indeed?*
So much for the beggars who are inevitable as the flies of summer. But who do
not die so easily; nor do they procreate, yet are here and there in hundreds. Or,
as about to be encountered, one at a time.

* A sheet of drawings of beggars and cripples by Hieronymus Bosch, at the Albertina in
  Vienna.

Trampoline

I am thinking of 'the Captain'.

I used to pass him so often in the street when we came to London during the summers between the two world wars. When it was nearly always so hot every night that one had only a sheet on the bed and no blanket, which never happens now.

I did not see him anywhere but along Piccadilly, always on the south side, and down as far as Leicester Square. I have seen him, twice at least, sitting on one of the blank windowsills of the arcade underneath the Ritz, outside Fortnum and Mason's; outside Prince's and in the forecourt of St James, Piccadilly. Also, in Coventry Street, outside the Criterion, and in the garden in Leicester Square.

In all, over the years I may have seen him a couple of dozen times. After a while I began to nod to him, or murmur 'Good Morning'. And so he got to know me by sight.

One day not long before the war there he was on a bench opposite the Green Park. And I knew this was the moment and sat down by his side.

More than ever like a ventriloquist's dummy, and shedding for a foot or two round him what I would call 'the all-night smell'.

Wearing two overcoats which were in a state of coalescence. Beside him on the bench were three or four parcels wrapped in old newspaper and tied with string.

I could say he was more like a waxwork of himself than his own person, I suppose from exposure to winter nights and from never washing.

He wore a cap which looked as though it had descended to him from ten generations of coalheavers. The sort with sacking over their heads, and in the past, a gold ear-ring.

His boots were like clowns' boots at the circus. Like the boots of the Augustes, a dying breed, who roll up the carpets and get in the way of the stage hands before the teams of horses and the equestriennes come on.

And in fact my friend's face, red from roughness and from outdoor days and nights, was much like a clown's face. Like the clown's make-up which the secretary and founder of the Clowns' Club, a retired chemist living in South London, designs for them and paints their faces upon egg-shells; and I have thought them beautiful and nostalgic objects, intrinsically valueless, but worthy of a place beside fine Louis Quinze snuff-boxes though derived, as they are, from Hoxton by courtesy of the clowns' church in Clerkenwell.

It is long ago now. What did he tell me? It is of little interest what I said to him.

He told me the police called him 'the Captain'. That he often slept in the park, and the police knew him and did not disturb him. But on winter nights – and this, helpfully, as if giving me a useful tip – he would stand on the glass tiles in the pavement outside the Palace Theatre in Shaftesbury Avenue, in order to get warm. The heat came up, I fancy, from a lounge or bar beneath.

Then, I asked him where he came from. And this was interesting. He told me and I did not believe it at first, that he had been clerk to the magistrates in one of the towns round Sheffield. I think it was Darnell, which interested me because my childhood home was not far from Sheffield. Certainly he knew the country round there, including Eckington which was our village.

How long had he been 'living rough'? He said for twenty years, which brings us back to the great days. And what made him take to the life? I did not like to ask him.

For I now felt more certain than ever that there had been a big gap in his life. That something had happened to him which altered everything. After which he was not the same person again. Perhaps he had been put away. It could not have been for murder. At that time he would have been hanged.

Attacks on children? I wondered. Holding a bag of sweets, and looking both ways at once. And afterwards sorry for what he had done; and pleading guilty to spare them giving evidence. Or perhaps not? And only waiting for the next chance.

But he was past it. Yet I fancied that like a clown he could still run pretty fast in his overcoat and baggy trousers. Carrying his parcels?

Or was it merely a book affair? Cooking the books, in fact, and doing everything but eating them. Fraudulent conversion; and the solicitor's clerk 'attributed his ruin' to horse racing. Minor peculation that had gone on for years and years.

Or housebreaking? 'Entering with intent', which has the sound of breaking glass? Wearing gloves, a stocking-mask, and carpet slippers?

I could only see him sleeping in barns and empty buildings. In the grimy purlieus of Sheffield, but there is unspoilt country only a mile or two from the city as though to put on view what man has done to it? In kilns? Yes, sleeping in the brick kilns, where the track is of coal dust, and there is dirt on the dock-leaf near the bed of nettles. Pink willowherb waves on the slag-heap; the steep cornfields are flaxen as the hair of children you meet blackberrying, and there is always somewhere in the distance a panting engine, a ghost of iron and steam.

Listen for it! And you hear it, as I said you would. The 'penny-engine', panting through Foxton Wood on the way to Hornthorpe colliery through the dark glades, saturnine with blackberries and wild garlic.

But maybe there was no trouble at all and it was only that he was eccentric. He altered, and grew rather odd, and seemed to resent spending money on his lodging. And would never sit down for a meal, but buy something, and then eat it, standing. Like a dog, afraid that someone might come up and take it from him. Or just that he did not appreciate his fellow creatures, and soon became peculiar as to his clothing?

He wore the same pair of overcoats for years, and you felt they would stand up on their own without him. Imagine a tortoise out of its shell, or the shell without the tortoise, and you will get my meaning. His overcoats and his boots had become not only his clothing but his carapace or armature. I suppose he only took his trousers down once a day, if that, in one of the 'gents' in the Borough of Westminster, and no pennies to spare for a wash and brush up. When I think of it, I see the lifting and lowering of the Tower Bridge, and the river Thames widening below that into the Pool of London.

What, then, was in those parcels? And did he ever undo the knots just for the fun of wrapping and tying up again? Whatever was inside the parcels would be useless and inappropriate, that is certain. It may well be that he was carrying round pyjamas, a dressing-gown, or even a salver and silver knives and forks. Or had, as a sign of respectability, absconded with the charge-book from the magistrates' desk.

I found there was something missing even in a simple conversation with him. Some string or line of communication had broken. Had sagged, or become disconnected. One, or more, of the mental points of contact had been removed. His voice was slurred, but educated, and the slowing down or the distortion were between his brain and his speech. Not, I am sure, from drink but in consequence of some accident or brain injury.

During those few moments I knew him, he seemed to have no relations in the world. To have occurred up there, somewhere near Sheffield, without parents. Like a natural phenomenon, a rise or fall in the ground, or the view out of the court house window onto the slag-heap and some ash trees. He must have gone to school and have had childhood memories. More likely a grammar, not a villag school, and may have known some words of Latin.

But now he had said enough and was no longer talkative. Had dropped three-quarters of his words for he did not need them. Who was there to talk to? A word or two with the police was enough to keep on good terms with them.

I never saw him begging, and am led to think he must have had some small sum he drew weekly from one of the banks between Piccadilly and the Strand, a bank where he must have been well known and addressed as 'Mr' by the bank clerk. There was no National Assistance then, it was before the welfare state; and as he did not beg and slept out it is reasonable to think he lived on an allowance or small income. My old friend (when I was young) W. H. Davies, 'tramp poet', and Brodribb cousin to Sir Henry Irving, was left a legacy of thirty-six pounds a year by an aunt, slept out on that, and went to prison for the winter. I see his fine dark features, so much in the cast of his actor-cousin, as I write this, and hear his voice calling me 'Sush' in his very special accent.

Indeed 'the Captain' was a man of property, free as air, moving or treading the hub of Empire which is the statue of Eros in Piccadilly Circus, given the liberty of that area between Piccadilly and Leicester Square, at a time when the King-Emperor still ruled India, 'untouchables' and all. Toronto, Ottawa, Jo'burg, Bombay, Calcutta, Sydney, Melbourne, and the rest of them, were our Alexandria, our Ephesus, our Antioch; and Glasgow, Sauchiehall Street, Gorbals and all, was the second biggest city of Empire. To have been a vagrant in Rome of the Caesars was still something of an experience. There were porticos to sleep under, and the nocturnal conversation was more worldly wise than the grunts and monosyllables in our nights of fog and rain.

A rather special area with minimal night population, though indeed it is difficult to know why the Embankment has become a synonym for sleeping out. A cold and draughty stretch of river above and below Cleopatra's Needle (which has looked down upon warmer climes), with ramparts of black, granitic stone and cold damp exhalations from the water. I think, myself, from midnight observation upon more than one occasion out of the moonlight into those pools of dark, that it would be better to be a beggar under the walls of Fez. The dusty environment being more human, however cruel and bloodstained.

And so back to w.1. There is a chemist or two open all night long. There are the police on the beat and at headquarters. There are the drudges of the telephone exchange; and almost the only other night apparition is, or was, the tramp-philosopher who haunts that narrow passage or alley-way between Jermyn Street and Piccadilly, and who was to be seen for many years – I have not noticed him lately – next to the telephone booth. A rather tall old man, in tramp's boots and overcoats, grey bearded, with the inevitable pile of parcels at his feet.

All his character was in his hat, which I can only describe as the hat of a Roumanian Ciganje. Anyone who has seen the photograph of a Roumanian Gypsy will know just what I mean. That is what it looks like now, but it had a different beginning. A velour or stetson of respectable origin come down in the world but, as certainly, come up again. Transformed, given by magical means a wider, more bohemian brim, with its 'crown' blown up, stretched to its height, the crease and division of convention and respectability lost and gone for ever; and in its stead this high, ascending balloon-crown of Parthian shape, dusted with desert and dust of ages above the beard and cunning eyes. Seen, on occasion, smoking a pipe, having been at some time a pupil of the Cynic philosopher who was banished for coining false money. Who retired into a barrel 'which served him as a house and place of repose', 'gave way to the most vicious indulgencies, and whose unbounded wantonness', I quote from the *Classical Dictionary*, 'caused some to observe that the bottom of his tub would not bear too close an examination'. Only once did I see this Diogenes and my tramp acquaintance cross each other's paths; and then 'the Captain' shuffled by the telephone booth, the pair of overcoats or garments which distinguished this all-weather Cynic, philosopher's hat, beard, pipe, newspaper parcels and all, and never once looked back at him.

Thinking all of which over you may conclude, as I do, that the typical ghost or phantom of this stretch of London pavement, together with 'Burlington Bertie' or the 'Bond Street Beau' of Concanen, is some such character as 'the Captain', or this other whom we are about to encounter.

Of whom the early warning is his shouting which causes us to turn round. And we see a man walking along with determined stride, swinging his arms. His loud shouts come nearer and nearer, and several persons turn round to look at him. He shouts incoherently, making no sense at all. Any more than the stone-deaf man of my childhood whom we used to meet walking on the sands at low tide, who asked if he might go into one of the churches, I think it was Christchurch where I was christened and only a few paces from where I was born, and shout as loud as he could in order to hear the sound of his own voice. He heard not a word. And this street-shouter is no more intelligible.

Just when he has caused a little sensation and people are stopping to look at him all along the street, he crosses over with the traffic-lights against him in front of a double line of moving motor-buses, and continues his shouting along the pavement opposite. No one is chasing him. Yet he likes to believe in it, and it is not his delusion but his double life of fact and fancy. There is one at least of these shouters in every town of any size. You could mistake him in the first moment for one of the prophets of imminent doom, calling for repentance, and probably hoping his appeal is falling on deaf ears. But religion has no part in it. Neither has sex.

The true eccentric of the streets is very near in effect, and in details of appearance and behaviour to the highly studied 'eccentrics' of the old music-hall. The unfrocked clergyman's long coat which had come down towards the gutter, the clerical, if bibulous manner, 'billycock' hat and cane, which were George Robey's additions and embellishments to the truth, were no more unlikely and outrageous than these natural eccentrics of the pavement and street corner. Where, indeed, could you hope to meet those black eyebrows and that red nose? In what Elysium of the engraved plate-glass window, near to the polished brass rail and the aspidistra? To what talk of fallen actor talent and late night, return home escapade? A person of some learning and small independent income, enough to pay for half his drinks and cadge the rest. Flush at the beginning of the week and quite out at the end.

And the whole repertory of the music-hall eccentrics offers its far-fetched and strange inventions. The staccato Bren gun-fire delivery of a song which was the special trick of certain comedians; an abruptness that in the real life of the comedians grew upon them and took possession of their persons, to end – in exaggeration upon the phrase 'living their parts' – in several instances of suicide. It would be of no use to recall dead comedians of talent or genius by a mere list of names.

But Little Tich was no more of an exaggeration or distortion of a human being than the red-haired, red-bearded dwarf who works as motor-mechanic in a near-by market town, in the next county. The little satyr is as clear in outline as a Dürer drawing, and of a jovial, intense savagery; to be seen mounting his motor-bike, jumping into the saddle with his short, springy legs, and roaring off with all the noise he can make. With a shout or two in a deep-gruff voice, no mannikin he, but satyrous, and the red-bearded troll or Hafner of South Bar and the red houses down by the iron bridge over the canal. But he is not the only dwarf in the place. There are at least four others; two mannikins, one of them an old friend, 'Ida'; and a 'big-head' (hydrocephaloid) man and big-head woman. This, I think, by way of proving it is an old town.

And here I am, still sitting on the bench opposite the Green Park, listening to 'the Captain'. Think of the West End, then, of 'the Captain's' beat, from Apsley House to Leicester Square, and compare it in your mind with the Rue de la Paix, Fifth Avenue, the Grand Canal, Nevski Prospekt, and so on! The Rue de la Paix and its jeweller's showcases ... Fifth Avenue, and the massed skyscrapers on and between that and Madison, in the semi-Semitic Babylon of the modern world; the slap-slop of waters upon the weedy green waterstairs of Venice, and the midnight, moth-gondola in the hissing spitting downpour and drum-boom of the thunder; the Muski of Cairo, dusty and long, but not far from the balconies and melon-domes of the Mamelukes; the Nevski Prospekt and its smooth snow-sledges, a military band in the distance, for what hidden meaning that may have had for him, in the scherzi of Tchaikowsky's symphonies, and always, nearer at hand, some drunken singing; down to the traffic-less Platería of my favourite Murcia of the china domes beyond the casaurina trees; and to the Sierpes of Seville, now without character, but as I remember it, or tell myself I do, with the *majos* of Andalusia standing at one corner, striped blanket on shoulder, stalwarts of the *afición* or 'fancy', long, whittled stick in one hand, and past the plate-glass club-windows to the bullfight posters at the other, or cathedral end.

All the character gone now, except perhaps for Fifth Avenue, in prototype, and for the Ginza of Japan. And how would 'the Captain' have fared on any or all of these famous thoroughfares? Of a certainty he could have been stared at on them all, if least perhaps on the Nevski Prospekt where every phantom of drunkenness must have wandered, must even have fallen, from time to time. And it is for a drunkard that 'the Captain' would have been miscast and mistaken in most of these cities.

But not along the Ginza in Tokyo. There it would be different. And it was on the Ginza that I had a curious experience. Twice on one day in this city of eight million inhabitants, in 1958, I saw the same beggar in different parts of the town. That morning I saw him watching Sumô (Japanese wrestling) on the television screen in a shop window. He saw my reflection in the shop window and turned to look at me. He had a thin black beard, which makes it more probable he was Korean, and not Japanese, while his rags and professional thinness made me wonder if he was a wandering priest from the forest cells of Koyasan. The chances were eight million to one against my seeing him again in another part of the city on the same day.

But that afternoon I saw him again on a far part of the Ginza. Our eyes met, and it was obvious he remembered me. The last I saw of him was the back of his head as he walked away with his bare elbows showing through his ragged sleeves. And it was in this manner that I saw 'the perpetual and ghostly jay-walker of the Ginza of Tokyo, too quick to get run over in the traffic, but too slow to be caught up into life'. Perhaps he recognized another in the same category, however diff-- erent, when he passed him in the street.

Whereon, upon the Ginza that is to say, I have no doubt at all that 'the Captain' would have been taken for an actor from the Kabuki theatre. Sitting, in order to bring it nearer into focus and make it more real, on the sidewalk outside the Mitsukoshi Department Store, which is one of the four big stores (the others, for the sake of their names, are Takashimaya, Shirokiya, and Matsuya) just at the moment when stalls selling all kinds of things are being set up for the evening promenaders. A beggar in a play, in fact, and not the real thing.

Any more than a member of one of the great dynasties of Japanese actors in Piccadilly, sitting, for as long as the police allowed of it, let us say outside Hatchard's, at the door of Swaine, Brigg and Adeney, the walking-stick and umbrella makers. Sitting on his mattress, or a roll of bedding, with his legs tucked beneath him, a fan in one hand. Wearing a kimono, of which the pattern, so wide apart as to come twice only down all his arm, is of three black triangles arranged so as to have a white triangle enclosed in them, which is his actor's family crest. It appears twice again round his waist, and once more on the collar of his kimono.

But it is his face, that is to say his make-up, which is interesting. Black lips, black lines to his eyelids, and a positive clown's dark eyebrows with bald head, all bald except for a tiny tuft of hair. He turns his head slightly in order to look at us, and we have a clown of the old English pantomime before us. Round, blanched face, shaved occiput, every detail perfect except for the red nose. More immaculate than the clown, not carrying a sheep's heart or a string of sausages as in the old spangled prints, 'penny plain, tuppence coloured'. And not wearing the baggy pantaloons, the *bragou bas* of the Breton peasant come down in time from the gallants and courtiers of Queen Elizabeth's reign. It is an even more surprising addition to the *dramatis personae* of all poetry than in the person of Willett, who altered the clown's original costume in several respects, grew a forked beard, and announced himself on the theatre bills as being in theatrical attendance upon Queen Victoria though in the prints he looks more like her wizard or astrologer. No less of a departure from tradition is this pierrot-like apparition sitting, or, rather, squatting motionless, who will rise to his feet, gird himself with a pair of swords, and turn into a ferocious, head-lopping warrior or samurai.

Then, back to the Ginza of Tokyo where 'the Captain' is sitting, huddled, and looking strange. And in the flicker of the same eyelid back to the bench in Piccadilly, opposite the railings of the Green Park. Where he has been all the time – but no longer, now, the bench is gone – and it is just that I cannot pass the place on the top of a bus, in a taxi, or on foot, and not think of him, and wonder what became of him. I have not seen him since soon after the war began. Since the summer of 1940, let us say. I think something must have happened about then. There was the 'blitz', that second autumn of the war, and he may have left London, and I daresay that killed him. I think there were few persons, if any, sleeping out in London in the 'blitz'. Certainly he would not have liked to be 'evacuated'. I suspect, as can happen, and as many soldiers of the two wars will bear witness, that after sleeping out for so long he caught pneumonia, as soon as he was forced to sleep indoors. In fact, this is the corollary to its own direct opposite; and we would most of us be down at once with pneumonia if driven out into the woods or fields. I think he was killed off by the war in this back-handed manner.

'The Captain' was someone of a little education. What would be his comment if shown the persons, the tens of thousands of persons, sleeping out in the streets of Calcutta and Bombay? Eighteen miles from the airport, through the forests of palm trees into Bombay, and for the last ten or a dozen of those miles, sleepers in their hundreds on the pavement or on the humid earth, with their white cotton garments pulled up to hide their faces and eyes. In Calcutta from all accounts it is much worse. Tens of thousands who have no home at all, who sleep in the street and have never in their lives had a roof over their heads. It is one of the more extraordinary sensations of the modern world to encounter this spectral night population for whom there is in fact no hope at all. Bombay and Calcutta are in fact horizontal Gorbals for Indians, with bedding unneeded and no roof required. And the others? The Indian, the shadow Indian or *mestizo* inhabitants of the *barrieras* outside Lima, in Peru.

But talk ran out. And getting up from the bench beside 'the Captain', I said 'Good Morning' which was in fact a long 'Good Bye'. I thought I would be seeing him again soon, and looked forward to continuing our conversation. So I put half-a-crown into his hand, and he said to me, 'If you can spare it, brother!' It would buy at least three times, then, what it would buy today. And I never set eyes on him again.

Postscript: a backward look at Gargoyles and Chimaeras

It must have come within the experience of many writers, only to discover the answer to something they wanted to know long after their book has been published. As we grow older it could be this curiosity, as much as anything else, that keeps us alive. For there are questions to which every human being would wish to know the answer, and be told the truth before he dies. But there can be other, if lesser ones, that are no less obsessive. As could be; what has happened to so and so, not seen for many years, and with whom there is no apparent means of getting into touch again? Lost, in fact; but who could be still alive. Someone, perhaps, who could tell us something we desperately want to know. It might be no more than one little item of fact that could fit so much else into its place. Or, again, that could alter the entire scheme of things and bring down the whole existing fabric. Or complete and fill out something already thought of, or attempted and begun.

Of which a conspicuous instance lies immediately to hand. For in a book published in this present year (1969) on *Gothic Europe*, I wrote of my regret at not having been able to compile a demonology of gargoyles, as had been my intention, continuing that 'for many years I had been hoping to find a work on gargoyles, similar in scope and in patient labour, to the mid-Victorian *Spires and Towers of England*, in three volumes (1853–5) by Charles Wickes' . . . making a total of some hundred and thirty separate drawings and as many, or more visits, of course, to the towns or villages concerned. The book on gargoyles could be in any language; and I have felt sure there must be someone going round the gargoyle countries – which are France, England, Germany, and the Low Countries – patiently with camp stool and field glasses, rain or fine, to make the drawings. But I have failed to find him. What a compilation it could have been! And what an anthology or dictionary of oddities, from which of a certainty some secrets would have emerged by now.

That there were such characters afoot, and willing to devote the leisure hours of a lifetime to such projects, is certain enough. As, for proof, the double page of ten drawings, containing a dozen rose windows in Italy, Germany, France, and England, reproduced in my work in question, and drawn by Rev. Thomas Kench, an early nineteenth-century amateur of rose windows. It was this cleric who wrote of a window in the south transept of Lincoln that it reminded him of two dead leaves lying side by side, a remark, or simile, that endeared him to me. I have no further information of him than from his drawings, but can form a mental picture of him at Cremona, Reims, Oppenheim, or Orvieto, sketch book in hand. It was his hobby, and it was ground work, in the sense that it could be done from floor or pavement level, and did not take him aloft into gallery or clerestory.

Many a drearier holiday task can be imagined than that of travelling about collecting and comparing rose windows. Not so long ago, there were such amateurs in plenty, who spent their time in writing down the Latin inscriptions upon wall tablets and tomb stones. But that was in the age of Latinity; though I have even met in the Baptistery at Pisa an American lady and her daughter who told me that their hobby was going round such buildings collecting echoes *and* inscriptions!

I had thought it certain there would be a book on gargoyles, or, at the least, an illustrated paper in the pages of some learned journal. There are works after all dealing with so many other kinds of ecclesiastical minutiae; with church bells in the melodious interest and composed in the private vocabulary of the campanologist, not to omit what may have been written in Dutch or Flemish on the carillon music and church tower virtuosi of the Low Countries. No more modern work has ever equalled in effectiveness of illustration the original and best book on ornamental brasses, now more than a hundred years old. There are books innumerable on stained glass windows; learned articles with illustrations on the flushwork of East Anglia; volumes devoted to choir stalls, and in greater detail to misericords, the latter often with pornographic interest – and the most Rabelaisian in Europe, of a truth, are at Plasencia in Spain, by a German woodcarver Rodrigo Alemán, so called, a magician by repute, and at the least, a remote disciple of Doctor Faustus in that far off Estremaduran town. There are works in plenty on church monuments of all periods; on rood screens and roof bosses, the latter being more than a little curious of intention in that they are all but invisible in detail from the floor, can barely be seen through a pair of glasses, are on occasion set at such an angle that, once *in situ*, their subjects can never be visible again by human eye until taken down for cleaning and repainting; and beside their repertory of flower and leaf and petal taken from the local flora, possess their own macabre footnote or sub-chapter, as in the pair of roof-bosses in Salisbury Cathedral depicting the fearful end of Edward II, spoiler of Piers Gaveston, at Berkeley Castle.

Finally – for there must be an end to all this – there are works on heraldic hatchments, on sword rests, on encaustic tiles, and on the open timber roofs of East Anglia, the latter, again, a difficult subject because of the technical problem of how to get these wooden ceilings which resemble the inverted interior of a ship's hull on to paper. It is to be noted that no one has attempted a work on fan vaults illustrated with drawings. Here, the camera can accomplish in a matter of seconds a project every bit as painstaking and laborious as would be, as indeed, has been, a set of measured drawings of the stalactite and honeycomb ceilings of the Alhambra of Granada. But those fantasies and arabesques are, at least, nearer to eye-level. It is the perpendicular height, even more than the intricacy of the fan vaulting that makes it a labour and a pain to reproduce in drawing. Why bother, when it can all be done by photography? And indeed it is questionable whether such books of measured drawings will ever be made again. They were the symptoms, and the ill or malaise of their age, so long, that is to say, as we are willing to think of unnecessary pain and labour as a waste of time. Be that as it may be, no one appears to have devoted some years of his life to this task, simplified a little, as is the case, by its being locally peculiar to this island, for fan vaulting, proper, is only found in England.

There is not even a work confined to flying buttresses, a theme with engineering and quasi-acrobatic appeal of its own, and forming a chapter in what could be termed the aerial Gothic of height and slenderness for its own sake, as with the choir at Beauvais. But, in fact, one must go to France to see flying buttresses and need move no further than the exterior of Notre Dame. Someone surely must have been excited by the nicety in mathematical calculation, been thrilled by the thrust and yet attenuation of these tie-ropes in stone, and by their extraordinary problems in visual perspective. But there is no answer, and no such work has come to hand.

But, also, gargoyles and chimaeras pertain to this aerial Gothic. It is their especial province, indeed their perilous and airy kingdom shared out among their kind. In which indeed there are distinctions, as of rank or purpose as to whether they are of utility as rain spouts, or have been set up there not so much for ornament as to hold the attention from below, and clown-like, are less funny than they are frightening of effect. The amateur of gargoyles and chimaeras would have unnerving experiences, and not only those of looking down from sheer walls of stone. One would have to grow inured to this curious population of the parapets and ledges, and no longer be altogether surprised to find them a little changed of attitude or expression, having climbed and groped the way back to them in order to complete a drawing.

For it was not the innate sense of beauty in the mediaeval stone carver that inspired these figures. Nor was it purely and simply their sense of fun. They were out to frighten and haunt the imagination, and the sinister side of their minds seized the opportunity and was in the ascendant. It is possible, too, that they were allowed a freer hand along the parapets and roof-line, and had not to submit their carvings in detail to be passed in judgment by authority. The mediaeval sense of humour in any case was of the sort that laughs at sudden falls and infirmities, and we would find few of their jokes to be funny. The lame and the crippled, and even lepers, were half figures of fun to a population all of whom in large cities down to the youngest children, will have witnessed such horrors as public torturing and burning alive. The whimsical in them was allied to the horrible and they had little pity to spare for the old and ill. They had the excuse, too, of frightening for its own sake in reminder of the world to come. It was even their profession to spread alarm and terror and they were lax in their duty if they failed to do this.

For the draughtsman and amateur of such carvings there would be days spent aloft along the parapets and galleries. Steep turret stairs to climb, and to come down again in the semi-darkness of perhaps a late winter afternoon. A sudden shower to shelter from under a canopy of cold, rain-sodden stone. A sudden and strange illumination as if to draw attention to some detail not observed before.

Or as though it had some deeper meaning. A rest period with something to eat and drink while the jackdaws flew in and out of the stone openings just overhead. Or, even, in spring time with the twigs and straw from their nest strewn and fallen at your feet. A scramble on hands and knees to reach some point of vantage, and then the appalling drop below. An inaccessible Alp of stone offering a sheer rock face to climb. On occasion a sexton or sacristan, even odder of habit and appearance than his stone charges and who, uninvited, would climb to the roof and talk for some uncertain reason. A gargoyle, of necessity, because of the angle at which it leans out would be easier to draw from below, as with the long-necked gargoyles of the Sainte Chapelle of which the purpose was, as surely, to pour water on the spectator looking up at them as, simply, to dispose of the rainwater from the roof by channelling it away. But there were gargoyles, higher in the hierarchy, for a clear view of whom it was necessary to climb at peril, as it were, into the stone rigging.

Chimaeras, by contrary, for whom we now give the classical prescription or formula that they should have 'the front of the body that of a lion, the middle of a goat, and the hinder parts that of a dragon', were firmer of habitat. That is to say, they did not project their bodies from the stone shell of the church but, at the most, leaned with their elbows on the balcony, though at times like wire-walkers they are to be seen straddling the roof lines. There should be an instance of a chimaera atop a church spire where the weathercock should be. But it could be said that, in general, they are equivalent to the ship's crew manning the stone vessel of the building. Not too many of them at a time for, as aboard the huge oil-tankers that are half-a-mile long, the giant stone building in all its intricacy can be run or managed by a mere handful of chimaeras. Despite this, I have been left with a longing to see a full display of them, not hiding themselves in unlikely places, but drawn up along some parapet or balcony as on parade. Which is likely to have happened, I concluded, in but one or two places in France, and not elsewhere. At Notre Dame, certainly, where the old set of chimaeras was removed and destroyed before 1730 as being 'too barbarous and ugly' – but how one would wish to have seen them! – and the new set sketched by Viollet-le-Duc in his atelier in a matter of hours, and carved by the sculptor Dechaume and his assistants, was carried up and put in place in the 1850s.* The other possibility may have been Reims Cathedral before its destruction in the 1914 war. This from personal conjecture only, but we shall see whether mere guesswork is not some-times the correct and true guide.

For just when all hope had been abandoned of finding a nineteenth-century work on this subject illustrated with original drawings, a book with old if not early photographs of gargoyles and chimaeras came into my hands. I had never seen or heard of it before, and it may be imagined with what eagerness I fell upon it. How it can have eluded for me so long I cannot think, and am almost persuaded to believe it was reserved for me till now for some especial purpose. The terrain covered by the book is France alone but, even so, what a vast subject if only

---

*   The new set of chimaeras appear in Méryon's etching of *Le Petit Pont* where they appear, it is true, as taken for granted and not a new addition to Notre Dame.

with camera and not pencil, and in the land pre-eminently of gargoyle and chimaeras. It appeared as far back as 1930, or, indeed, forty years ago, and its author, Lester Burbank Bridaham, has no other work than this to his credit in the book catalogue of the British Museum Reading Room.* He is, then, the authority on his subject though his text of a handful of pages is disappointingly brief, and with this further stimulus I open the book in a fever of excitement for what I may find there waiting for me.

The introduction is by that ancient architectural authority Ralph Adams Cram who has little or no fresh light to throw upon his subject. But neither is the author's text particularly illuminating, though intriguing; and curious theories are advanced, if tentatively, and with little serious argument behind them. As to the origin of the chimaeras which indeed is somewhat of a mystery, 'Mrs Jameson believes their origin lay in the prehistoric diluvian remains of monsters dug up in the Middle Ages', which could on occasion have happened in a clay bed or river bank, but must have been of very rare occurrence; while the Abbé Auber 'considered them as representations of devils conquered by the Church and made her slaves to perform her menial tasks'. This is certainly a picturesque derivation for the stone crew of Notre Dame or Reims and one is loath to dismiss or disbelieve it altogether.

Then, the author in but a paragraph or two goes on to discuss their obvious connection with the dragons and other monsters which played so important a part in the religious festivals and processions of the Middle Ages. Nowhere more so than in France and Flanders, if with even more curious descendance or aftermath in Spain. But France is principal theme in hand, and attention is drawn to the *papoires* of Amiens, the creatures of wood and wickerwork carried in the Fieste de Saint Romain of Rouen, and of course the famous Tarasque of Tarascon. There are others at Reims, Beauvais, Sens and Metz; but their numbers are further swelled with mention of the Grande Goule at Poitiers, the Graouilly of Metz, La Chair Salée of Troyes; the Saint Georges of Mons and Le Dragon of Louvain, these two latter among the French-speaking Walloons; and Le Dou Dou of Saint Merlaine at Morlaix in Brittany, where now, alas! the local inhabitants no longer wear their penthouse brimmed hats, their loose trunk hose or *bragou bas*, their shaggy locks hanging like manes down their backs, all of which were thoroughly characteristic of 'la Bretagne Bretonnante', as it was not long ago. It is but a step from the 'monsters' of these processions, for the most part 'animated' by men walking inside them, to the *gigantes y cabeçudos*, the giants and 'big-heads' of Toledo, Burgos, and a dozen or more other towns in Spain.

It must, in parenthesis, be due to the Spanish influence persisting for so long in Flanders that so many religious ceremonies and processions have survived of an intensity and fantasy even surpassing those in Spain. The hooded penitents, 'en cagoules', carrying wooden crosses through the streets of Furnes on the last Sunday in July; the Sortie des Géants at Courtrai; la Ducasse at Ath, with a défilé de Géants, twelve to fourteen feet tall, Goliath and Madame Goliath, the

* *Gargoyles, Chimaeras, etc.*, by Lester Burbank Bridaham, New York 1930. This work has just (November 1969) been republished by the Da Capo Press in New York.

hero Bayard, Madame Victoire, and others, these are confusing and mysterious in origin; the dancing procession at Echternach in Luxemburg; or that at Binche with the dancers moving in slow, syncopated motion through the streets, wearing hats with huge ostrich feathers and ending in a battle, not of flowers but oranges; a fête long thought to have its origin in a celebration under Charles v of Pizarro's conquest of Peru, when the notables of Ath dressed themselves as Incas; or, in *diminuendo*, the *jet des craquelins* at Grammont, which from the sound of it nearly suggests a proto-Spanish ceremony held till not long ago in Mexico City, where 'on Good Friday', a peculiar apparatus housed in the tower of the cathedral made a loud cracking noise, which was supposed to represent the breaking of the bones of the thieves on the cross, but, in fact, at Grammont it was no more than a throwing of biscuits from a hill above the town, or from the balcony of the town hall into the crowd. How interesting it would be at some international festival of folklore to assemble these giants and carnival figures from all over Catholic Europe! It was in Spain, typically enough, that some years ago a start was made with this; as witness the photographs I published some years ago of the *Concentración de Gigantes y Cabezudos*, held first at Valls, and then in the bull-ring at Tarragona, attended by twenty-two *gigantes* and 'big-heads' or *cabezudos* from all over Catalonia. From Catalonia only, but their number could be increased many times if invited from all over Spain.

But now, with no further delay, to the gargoyles for whom such processional figures and grotesques are but the overture or prelude. At Saint Germain l'Auxerrois in Paris, but a few steps from the Louvre, are the pair of gargoyles of a 'fool', in the Shakespearean sense, standing on an old man's shoulder; and its pair or companion of a man being vomited from a dragon's mouth. Such 'telescoping' of figures when space permitted of it was a theme that endeared itself to the mediaeval mind, and 'tandem' subjects were particularly adapted to the projecting purposes of a gargoyle to carry out the rainwater well away from the wall of the building; as, again, in another instance, that of a monk in the jaws of a monster. Exaggeratedly long necks were a favourite device with these stone carvers; and it may be accounted an oddity that there is no record of a giraffe-necked gargoyle, something that would have been historically possible with stories of camelopards and the like, and would not have been an anachronism. Fabulous, not real monsters are of the repertory.

Of whom are the figures derived from woodcut illustrations to Leo Africanus and other early travellers, wholly fanciful creatures with florescent vegetable forms where should be their breasts; or double-headed beasts or men, the latter being natural freaks of immense rarity. But was there not the two-headed nightingale of late Victorian times that sang drawing-room ballads and duets; and the Patagonian two-headed giant not far short of seven feet high which was presented to King Charles II and of which the mummified body was preserved till a very few years ago on the iron pier (1,100 feet long) at Weston-super-Mare?* But mediaeval fantasy ran more to pairs of bodies joined at the waist, or three-legg'd men. There were, also, wild men, green men, and wydwoses in variety, hauntings

* From recent information this curiosity is still there.

maybe from Blue Man's Bower, a prehistoric earthwork near to my old home, of imagery perhaps inspired from vagrants and charcoal burners, but in any case figures of satyrous propensity and intended to be a little frightening.

Bat-ears and staring eyes are of facile imagery for the gargoyle carver, and of course it should be possible to identify certain masters who being sculptors of a minor order are not likely to have moved far from their own homes. Thus, at Le Mans, having studied the gargoyles at the cathedral it could be rewarding to recognize the same hand at Notre Dame la Couture, a smaller church in the town; at Troyes as well as the Cathedral of St Pierre there is, also, St Urbain; at Chartres there is, too, the church of St Pierre; and at Reims there is the abbey church of St Rémi. All these are town churches but there are the surrounding villages, as well, and churches up to perhaps fifty miles, or two or three days' journey away.

It is not to be thought that all gargoyles are mischievous of intent and delight to pour down water on the inquisitive and curious. At Notre Dame de Paris there are gargoyles that even empty the rainwater into channels in the flying buttresses in the complicated geometry of that exterior, though maybe there was a particular reason for this, an opportunity for the water to emerge again from lower down and drench the, by now, reassured spectator and not let the victim forget his visit to the gargoyle- and chimaera-infested cathedral on the island in the river, in midst of the green Île de France. There must be many a recognizable hand among the monstrosities, a predilection for satires upon monks for instance, or, as said above, of 'telescoped' animals, a snake swallowing a frog, or, for easier accommodation, Jonah and the whale. An entire bestiary is not uncommon; of animals above each other at times, as, in fact, two tiers or storeys of animals, the one throwing water out farther than the other, and a tendency to portray them all as screaming or bellowing with open mouth, as was, indeed, the necessity and trade secret of the profession. A face with a shut mouth is a near impossibility for a gargoyle. As, also, to twist the head on one side was a device learned quickly by the gargoyle carver.

Even so, the ingenuity displayed is formidable, more particularly in the matter of birds' heads, dragon shapes, and the multitude of minor forms or lesser demons. It is at St Ouen at Rouen that there is perhaps the widest choice in grinning faces, bat-ears, and staring eyes; while one especial gargoyle master was certainly at work outside the very late Flamboyant church at Louviers, long necks his speciality. For the demonologist at work on the sub-species where they approach and verge upon the cheiropterophile or bat-lover there is opportunity unlimited in the part of Normandy between Rouen and the peninsula of the Cotentin; while the lesser and more rustic breeds of demons abound farther to the west in Brittany where probably the mere fact of a different spoken language brought them into another mythology, and having sprung from other legends made them subject to other, and older forms of inspiration. The total of gargoyles in those two parts of France alone, Normandy and Brittany, with addition of the Île de France, the cradle of Gothic where the greatest flights of imagination are to be expected, must run into a population of many hundreds or even thousands.

But the chimaeras are a rarer breed, even with their sub-species which yet could be awarded varietal names and be classed as clones or cultivars deriving from ascertained and set types, when properly studied. There being for instance chimerical birds, a contradiction in themselves for chimaeras should be, as stated, part-lion, part-goat, and partly dragon. And again, there are lion-faced men, probably ... it is horrible to think, deriving from the lion-faced, thus named, stage of leprosy, there being, then, hardly even a small town without its lepers. At Poitiers there is a chimaera in lead upon a church tower, but principally of dragon conformation, darting its serpent tongue and with long dragon-scaled tail, and it would appear from the photograph, a pair of wings; very different of attention and appeal from the gilded chantecleer of the ordinary church spire. At Rheims there is a centaur, bow-in-hand, shooting down a row of smaller figures standing before him on the roof line. If, that is to say, the centaur is still there, for particular destruction was wrought among the chimaeras of Reims during the First World War.

This is what the dictionaries have to say on the subject of chimaeras: 'a wild fancy'; 'an incongruous and impossible conception of the fancy'; 'a symbol of any impossible monstrosity'; with adjective 'chimaeral' meaning 'purely imaginary'. In Nuttall's Dictionary, under the heading Chimaera Monstruosa, there is is even a fish called the King-of-the-herrings or rabbit-fish, 'a curious fish about four feet long, with a spiny knob on the head and a long finless, filamentary tail'. But Dr Lempriere, infallible as ever, adds the matter-of-fact information that it generally lived in Lycia, and was overcome by Bellerophon mounted on his horse Pegasus. He gives the classical prescription that it was part-lion, part-goat, part-dragon, and continually vomited flames, 'which fabulous tradition was explained by there being a burning mountain in Lycia whose top was the resort of lions; the middle, which was fruitful, was covered with goats; and at the bottom the marshy ground abounded with serpents'. The vomiting of flames was difficult to achieve with the stone chimaeras of the Middle Ages but there is an extraordinary photograph in the book under discussion, if indeed it is not the most interesting of all the illustrations. This must have been taken shortly after, or even during the First World War.* It shows a row of chimaeras' heads, and of gargoyles, as well, lying on the ground inside a shed; and the curious point is that the melting lead from the roof of the cathedral has in nearly every instance choked their mouths. The lead must have come running down like molten lava from above, and it drips from their mouths in a way only comparable to the blood pouring from the severed neck in Cellini's bronze figure of Perseus with the head of the Medusa (in the Loggia dei Lanzi in Florence). In this manner, and only after months of insensate bombardment, did the chimaeras of Reims breathe forth flame, but it was in fact molten lead which had the look of congealing blood.

So indeed the chimaera, under licence, took on any form of 'wild fantasy' or 'improbable monstrosity'. For instance there is, or was, at Reims, a figure of a

---

* During the 1914–18 war Reims suffered bombardment with varying degrees of intensity during forty-nine months, at the end of which time, the cathedral apart, twelve of its fourteen thousand dwellings were entirely destroyed, and the city was in fact a heap of ruins.

chimerical elephant, very small and squat in size, with a trunk as broad as its body, and not tapering, but of the same width down to the ground, an elephant with none of the other attributes of the chimaera, but a dwarf elephant none the less, that could only have been of the Melitan race which survived in Malta out of prehistoric times till late enough to become the household pet of Roman ladies. The 'purely imaginary' creature of the Middle Ages was more often compound of horse, tiger and eagle than of lion, goat and dragon. There is, too, a unicorn in lead at Poitiers, companion to the chimaera in lead upon a tower or steeple, but the pair of them though defined in shape are indeterminate and interchangeable. There were no field glasses in those days and hardly spectacles except for book-worms. Something or other was caught, or had twined itself round the church steeple, as though come out of a black cloud of rain, or just been found there in the morning. Of such were the lead chimaera and the unicorn of lead hoisted with such infinity of trouble upon the tower of Poitiers.

It is of course expecting to find something different that one would go as far as St Pol de Léon in the district of Finistère, of a comparable bucolic remoteness, unless you live there and it is the centre of your life, to Louth in the wolds of Lincolnshire which, also, is famous for its spire, of a flashing white limestone three hundred feet high. But at St Pol de Léon there are two towers, of the cathedral and of the Kreizker, another church, the latter nearly the height of Louth, both Breton towers being built of dark, greenish granite.* Before the terrible provincial quiet sizes down upon you, while there is still light, there are carved curiosities to look for in the form of gargoyles and chimerical animals, but of a mythology tainted by Breton legend and by the stone sculptures on the Calvaries, whereon the peasant *cornemuse* (bagpipe) often accompanies the entry of Christ into Jerusalem. How remote it must once have been! As much so as Spanish Galicia, or the south-western extremity of Wales; but it has no Santiago de Compostela to make with its arcaded streets and its fronts of churches a welcome of civilized architecture. There are only the spires of green granite, the near-contortionist sculptures of chimerical interest, and for the few that are left of them, the starched and lace steeples of the Breton women's head-dresses.

It is the Département de Finistère, one of the two Finisterras, and of the three Land's Ends of the Celts, all three of them granitic and one must stay here for the rest of one's life among the lobster-pots and market gardens, or be off at latest by the first light of morning, bound for the grander dramas of the Middle Ages. But the farther we go on this hypothetical journey the quicker our spirits rise. Beyond Rennes, probably the most depressing and widow-haunted of all provincial towns in France, we come to Anjou and then Touraine, the landscape is beautiful, there are vineyards and the, mostly hideous, French châteaux of the Loire. But it is not long before Gallic genius in the Gothic is at work, and play. It is in full spate when we get to five-portalled Bourges. But we are in search of

* 'A greenstone, peculiar to Brittany . . . believed to be a hornblende rock, with a mixture of oxide of iron, in particles partly disseminated . . . Its peculiarly bright green colour gives to a portal carved out of it the appearance of being cast in bronze.' Murray's Hand-book, 1864. But it is at its most depressing on a rainy day.

chimaeras and not stained-glass windows. For which reason even the sight and prospect of the twin towers of Chartres across the monotonous ploughland of La Beauce is no help.

This hypothetical transit finishes indeed in hypothesis and little more than that. At Reims where, rightly, it should have begun and ended. For there are but the two palladiums of the chimaera; one imaginary, or by proxy, and the other all but gone and vanished. Notre Dame de Paris having its parapets and balconies haunted in supposition, or by substitution, while Reims was the domus palatine or capitoline of the chimaera. What Viollet-le-Duc sketched in a few hours, on a morning or evening or two, upon his writing pad or blotting paper as quickly and easily as though they were 'floats' or figures for the carnival or battle of flowers, were carried up the turret stair and cemented upon the balustrading with little or no attention paid to them. Why does no Gothicist of the 1850s, or English clergyman on holiday in Paris, comment upon this sudden and new population of the towers? The scaffolding must have been removed in a matter of weeks when a very different vision will have been revealed to the spectator craning his neck to look up at them from below. No wonder that Méryon in his 'madness' put imaginary flying creatures in the clouds over Paris! For it can have been no more, or less extraordinary than that. To find the rooks and jackdaws back in their deserted nests where they had been for perhaps five centuries until but a hundred years before. Then, thrown down and carted away as being 'too barbarous and ugly', and not even a painting or a drawing made of them.

But it is always possible that the chimaeras of Viollet-le-Duc, however hastily sketched, were an improvement on what had stood there before. After all, the Queen's Beasts at St George's Chapel are quaint and delightful yet there has never been pretence that they are works of art. And the chimaeras of Notre Dame are less an ornament than a commentary. They are the witnesses who sniff the wind and smell pestilence and burning, and hear the tocsin. It is more than likely that some bits of them were left, or that there was some tradition of them. Were they, indeed, 'representations of devils conquered by the Church and made her slaves to perform her menial tasks'? In which case it was not to be expected of them that they should be agreeable of expression, any more than the forced crews aboard the galleys. They were up at their stations, rain or fine, in spite of themselves and hating what they looked down on from their points of vantage. Spectators sitting up there 'in the gods', and only enjoying themselves when things went badly and there was disaster and trouble for the human race below. Yet with some purpose or duty to perform, as scarecrows, or merely to frighten. With their lives spared and allowed to remain there on those terms, time-blackened brothers of the hangmen and the public executioner. Who, if they could, would flap down from their roosts and give help to heat the hot irons and pincers, and throw on the faggots. Outcasts and untouchables, being chimerical creatures of unholy union. Thus, the lion-faced men, those with beaks and claws; and others as though haggard from centuries of night watching.

But it is apparent that the grand collection of them was at Reims, the coronation church of the Kings of France, so that they were in some sense guardians of the 'sacre'. In one photograph they appear in extended line along a balustrade. Two or three of them may be the heads we have seen lying on the ground, with the molten lead pouring from their mouths like the congealing blood from the neck of the Medusa. They are not recognizable in the photograph. The exceptional array of them will have been because Reims was, so to speak, the flagship of the whole fleet. In point of sanctity it was the French cathedral of cathedrals. And among all the gargoyles and sculptured figures there was deck space enough for the captive crew.

Is the centaur still up there straddling a roof-line with all four hooves, aiming his arrow at the 'powder monkeys', for such they could be; far indeed from the plain of Thessaly and from Hippodamia of the amber waist? And were there more centaurs stabled upon the leads? But centaurs, being chimerical animals, ranked as minor devils. They could only, like the 'capos' of the concentration camps, being a little privileged, keep order among the other slaves. Of whom it is difficult in the forty-year-old photographs to make out the physiognomy, it being impossible in most cases to get near to them. They have been placed up there as a flag is planted on a mountain top, and it is not so easy to bring it down again. There is no scaffolding, and it is too dangerous on a ladder. But, also, it is perilous to climb into the stone rigging. It could be treacherous as any glacier or moraine.

The diabolism of the gargoyles and chimaeras was their equivalent to our crime reportage and to the folk hero-villains of our murder lists. Such and such was a face you would not like to see looking at a child on one of the roads to Cannock Chase. But for ever free to wander on the lead roof; or lean looking down at you from where you are used to him; and yet, in a sense, with all his companions for ever in the pillory. Not so much an introduction to, as an overture from the forces of evil. For there is another side to it. If you join them up there on the roofs and in the stone yards, it is some sort of life, not death. In scenes of the Last Judgment the demons are always enjoying themselves hugely. Or are they killed, themselves, later, as with the squads of renegades at the incinerators? In the *Totentanz* the skeletons are tasting all the carnal pleasures. There have to be partners in the Dance of Death.

One must not attach too much importance to the minor players. But, certainly, they catch and hold the eyes. Had one seen Reims in its glory – and are we to think that its triple portals and some five or six hundred statues were once painted and gilded, as at Chartres? – would one not have taken away with one a mental picture of the most beautiful of the statues but, also, some memory of the 'horror-comics'? The child remembers the harlequinade which comes at the end of the pantomime. This was the last opportunity to watch the full company of the chimaeras. One must remember they were not intended to be human beings but mythical animals of human attributes. And the sculptor's sense of evil was at play among this population who stay up there above the long line of paladins and Kings of France. Inhabitants only of the lower clouds that may touch the towers and turn to snow or rain. Of no involvement with golden sunbursts or rainbows, and other optimisms of the rising and the setting sun. But lurking in corners and hiding in the shadows. Messengers, all the same, not of death in life, but life in death; the mediaeval mind with all its fussiness of detail being unable to accept that there could be nothingness and annihilation. Even the emptiness for their satisfaction must be inhabited. Of whom, if there be survival of the soul, there follow later two instances, perhaps still wandering and not yet at rest. Who can on occasion, at thought of them, cause us to turn round and conjecture if we are alone. For a sort of pitiful companionship in their loneliness. And there are the myriads of others. But only the one or two sentinels upon the towers and parapets of death. Suicide and murders, both and for whatever reason, being chimerical and not natural forms of death. And the book of chimaeras and gargoyles is carried back to its dusty shelf again, and no more is said.

ENTR'ACTE
Hendrik Avercamp

It is no more than two or three years ago that a big and important painting by Hendrik Avercamp (1585–1630), indeed the largest known canvas from his hand – appeared for sale in a picture gallery in St James's, and at an opportune moment for myself. For I had had the intention for a long time, as expressed on an earlier page, to set forth for the snow scenes of Bruegel and of Avercamp pairing them with those from the other side of the world by Hiroshige; and sight of the painting in question confirmed and gave further strength to my resolution. For long enough now it has been but a matter of waiting for the right time; and what better moment than this of having finished writing of the Jasmine Kingdom, and as to the further pleasures of imagination almost bathed myself in tropical flowers and tropical flowering trees! Decidedly, although these passages will come later in the finished work, the time has come to take the first step into this world of winter scenes.

But there arises the immediate problem of whether to walk right into the picture from the foreground, or to come into it out of the empty distance for the particular wonder of this painting is just precisely the vanishing point. There is no other picture known to me in which the centre, or, to be accurate, a little left of centre in the painting is endless distance, indeed nothing but distance and emptiness. And lying not very far away at that. Let us think a quarter of a mile at most. There may be plenty of canvases by the Dutch little masters where the distance is all sky and clouds. Or the mists of evening. But not, as here, the pall of snow even if snow is not falling. And it would not be true to make trite use of the term 'low visibility', because the emptiness has substance as though it were a wall of snowflakes.

Stand still for a moment or two and listen, and you will catch the sound of church bells, but coming from a long way away. They even play a tune on the carillon at every quarter; but no more than a few bars of it; and the whole tune at the hour. Tunes which are either hymns or popular songs, but in either case with a sturdy and defiant air, for the Dutch are still fighting for their lives against the Spaniards. There are villages here you cannot get to all through the summer because of shoals and sandbanks. That is why you cannot row or sail to them but have to come the long way round. But you can walk to them in an hour or two across the ice. You make straight for the bells and indeed walk towards them. Or to where you think they must be; though they can be deceptive, too, for the snow play tricks and can both exaggerate and diminish distance.

It is the Inland Sea of Holland, and what a difference from that other! But with just as much of interest if we but use our eyes. These are not islands; Walcheren, Schouwen, Tholen, Overflakkee, and the others which are flat alluvial meadows steeping themselves in, and indeed flush with the North Sea. It is not Zeeland, the sea-province in the delta of the Rhine and Scheldt, rich farmlands where life may have been more fanciful still due to the preternatural dullness. If this is anywhere at all, which is far from easy to determine, it must be in the neighbourhood of Kampen, where Avercamp lived and died. But there is no reason to attach a particular locality to it; the painter probably took sketches of buildings, collected a stock of them, and made use of them when and where necessary.

And we decide to walk right into the painting as though paying a call from a village three or four miles away. Our shapes looming up, growing bigger, now arrived. A crowd of persons, men, women and children all looking in our direction into the snow. As if, indeed, which is the truth, we have come to them out of another world. Let us not forget the community of four hundred Esquimaux in the far north of Greenland who, when they were found, which was only late in the last century, believed they were the only race of human beings in the world. That was Thule, so called for good reason; but now become a USA air base of great importance, noisy enough, we would think, to shatter the Aurora Borealis and put to flight the Northern Lights.

But here are some fifty or sixty persons, all wearing the most extraordinary clothes. But it is always so in paintings by Hendrik Avercamp. They are 'got up' for an ice carnival. And it is their extreme isolation that is responsible. They are rich and prosperous and there is really nothing else for them to do. The horses are stabled. The cows are in their byres. Summer is the busy time. They take their holiday in winter when there is a hard frost and the ice will carry. The ice enlarges their world, and they meet friends and even strangers from other villages. This is too laborious in summer. And they have no time for it.

But did they in fact have white Christmases every year? The mystique of a 'white Christmas', largely the creation of Charles Dickens, was investigated by a niggling statistician, presumed lover or perhaps hater of the Christmas card, who was able to establish that there were no more than two or three 'white Christmases' during the whole of Dickens' lifetime. There is some evidence though that winters were colder during the reigns of James I and Charles I, which approximate roughly to the working life of Hendrik Avercamp. That being so, he may have seen not the inlets only but the whole of the Zuyder Zee frozen solid, an infrequent phenomenon made permanent in his imagination and for the purposes of his painting. It is tempting to remember that Kampen where he worked is only a little way inland, and was port of embarkation for Urk, the island little more than a mile in length lying right out in the middle of the inland sea, and having till a few years ago a community of fisherfolk no less curious in custom and habit than those of Volendam or Marken. Indeed, Urk lay out there some dozen miles into Avercamp's snow scenes, within reciprocal sound of the guiding church bells for which you would have to listen most carefully over the distance. Let there be no mistake about it! Twelve miles was for them four hours' walk away over the frozen sea.

We are making that crossing ourselves, and just emerging from the lilliputian infinity at first landfall which is a ship's hull careened over and lying on its side. The first persons we see are near to it, almost lost in the mist and snow with, a little unexpectedly, a horse quietly feeding near by. And now into the ice Kermesse, of which there are more brilliant examples, with the participants more fantastically prinked out with ribboned shoes and starched ruffs and feathers. But those we see are curious enough to find in this little place of a few hundred inhabitants, at most, on a frozen inlet of the inland sea.

Two or three persons are busily skating by themselves; one couple, he in Jacobean hat and Dutchman's baggy breeches, are figure-skating as if on an ice rink. Two more men in baggy breeches facing each other are just standing still and talking. More characters, younger men this time, are playing ice-hockey or a primitive form of it, for it does not take long to discover that a ball will roll further on ice than on the grass.

The scene closes in on both sides with buildings. But, in a sense, it is one-sided because all the set scene is to the spectator's right-hand side. A very tall old barn, half-brick, half-timber, with thatched roof thick with snow. But the inevitable barrel for rain water and long-handled broom, sign manual of the Dutch housewife, make one think this dilapidation must be inhabited. There is a flurry of old planks and fencing in the foreground which the painter must have enjoyed accumulating, at foot of the first of a pair of wintry trees, entirely leafless, but, noticeably, with no snow upon their boughs. They are gaunt, contorted tree stems with twisting branches as though, themselves, suffering the intense cold.

Now it strikes one that for Avercamp the inhabitants are almost poorly dressed, which gives verisimilitude and makes one think this largest of his pictures could be not an invention, but a real scene. Is that the reason for its unusual size? There are one or two persons pushing small cradle-like sledges which remind one of the shopping baskets on wheels propelled by elderly, mostly eccentric characters in suburban parts of London. The very vacuity of the painting makes it ring true as a real-life scene. No popinjays in the picture; and generally these are as frequent of occurrence in Avercamp as in Carpaccio; but with the latter painter one feels they are popinjays with more to talk about, and who in the Italian fashion would sing in the streets on their way home at night.

Only a quartet of well-dressed persons, but with little of his usual fantasy about their clothes; except for a man with his back turned to us like nearly all the other figures, and who has a huge fur hat with a wide brim, but shaped like a soldier's bearskin. And there are two or three of the ladies in long black mantles carried over their heads who appear in nearly all his paintings. These black cloaks which descend nearly to their feet seem to depend from the back of the head-dress which is a kind of widow's coif. There are always women dressed like this in all crowd scenes, whether Dutch or Flemish. There must be some dozens of them, thus portrayed, in the galleries of Brussels and Antwerp, let alone of Amsterdam and of The Hague. Why this communal dress? Who, and what are they? They look like inmates of a béguinage. From some quiet, swan-haunted backwater within sound of the carillon. In which case they would be Catholic ladies, which is not improbable even on the inland sea, the fisherfolk of Volendam having always been Catholic. But it remains as one of the little unexplained mysteries of Dutch painting; akin to that other which is why the filled wine glasses in their still-life paintings seem always to contain vin rosé? It cannot be just that the pigment has faded; and must only mean that their red wine was of this colour for one is unwilling to believe the Dutchmen added water to their wine. The white wine in their glasses is always the colour of Rhine wine; but their red wine is demonstrably, even blatantly pink.

And the dusk falls, and now all turn and begin to walk back to their houses, while the sun for a few moments shows its robin-redbreast in the wintry trees. And only one of the problems confronting us is that not one of the inhabitants will understand one word we say. The term 'double Dutch' takes on its full meaning. Yet there are villages round this inland sea, for we would hardly call them towns, for which mariners have set forth for the most distant parts of the world. By this time, or within a few years of it, the Hollanders will have possessed themselves of Amboyna and the Moluccas (how many persons of education could point to these with confidence upon a map!). They will have taken hold of Ceylon and of Formosa; established themselves at The Cape of Good Hope and in Java; their seamen will have seen, at least, the contours of Australia, of Tasmania and of New Zealand; and pushed through the Arctic ice to Nova Zembla. They have built the New Amsterdam upon Manhattan Island, and founded a colony at Recife or Pernambuco in Brazil; while their East Indian Company, founded in 1602, traded between the west coast of Africa and the east coast of North America, and was master of all commerce between The Cape and the Straits of Magellan.

Yet it is an entire vacuum upon this inland water. No one spoke a word of any language but their own; and even this in most individual dialect and pronunciation, did we but understand it. Intrepid and marvellous mariners they may have been, but as soon impute universal knowledge to the most highly trained technicians in human history who, at the time of writing, have just left their footmarks on the moon. Those have no power of healing, cannot perform miracles, or raise the dead. They are, almost certainly, completely and entirely uninterested in the human arts. If, as seems likely, they may be religious-minded, are they more simple, or more sensible, than we would give them credit for being? When they came down out of the heavens, and the world was given word of the first sighting of their fireball in that half-light of dawn, it was a return to earth no magician or human deity had achieved before so many witnesses. Yet the race who sent them up and brought them down are no better than the rest of us, and even lack the restraints and the wisdom of other peoples. Certainly their cities are little credit to them, and a multiplicity of gadgets can never usurp the place of even minor works of art. Radio pictures in colour bounced off a satellite in space make no substitute for great paintings, any more than top prices in the auction room make a true barometer of the value of any work of art.

Why are nearly all the figures in Avercamp's paintings shown with their backs turned, looking away from us into the waste of snows? Is it because of his affliction? For he was dumb. He was the 'deaf-mute' of Kampen; born, it is true, in Amsterdam, but living for most of his life in the dull, uninspiring little town of Kampen, near the not more interesting or lively Zwolle. They cannot all have their backs turned, as in a fashion plate, just in order to display their clothes. There must be some deeper reason for it; and it must be in unconscious demonstration of how he was cut off from the world. His infirmity, or, rather, his deficiency kept him apart and left him friendless, and we are to suppose, the object of curiosity and pity. Was his talent considered to be a weak talent in someone who was not quite normal? In the same way that, in *diminuendo*, blind persons are taught to do basket-work, and it is thought remarkable how good they become at it?

Yet the painter of this huge canvas was no little master. But, once again, none of his figures is paying attention to the painter. They are not too busy to stand talking on the ice, but not one of them is looking in his direction. They ignore and are oblivious of him. It is clearly a holiday of sorts, and all are out to enjoy themselves, but are not thinking of him. One could get the impression that he is left to get on with his painting in solitude; that they are used to seeing him at work, with nothing much to show as the result of it. He has been painting away, year after year, and no one else is interested.

Ice scenes were Avercamp's speciality in a land where there was a fever for painting and the profession had become specialized down to its smallest minutiae. Moonlight scenes by Aert van der Neer (1603–77) 'usually showing the canals round Amsterdam, where he lived'; Hendrik Vroom, the painter of ships lifting themselves like wooden castles or being hurled in and out of the waves; the two Van de Veldes, father and son, painters of sea-fights; Emmanual de Witte for the interiors of churches, and that much greater painter, Pieter Saenredam; candle-light scenes by Godfried Schalcken; poultry and peacocks by Hondecoeter; Willem Kelf for still-lifes of copper and glass vessels with objects reflected on their polished surfaces, 'and often a watch in front of the group'; the legion of flower painters; down to Balthasar Denner who painted the portrait of his wife and himself, 'in the manner of Rembrandt', which, *pace* Fuseli in his *Dictionary of Painters* (1810) is so minutely finished that (if writers may be credited) 'even the pores of the skin are visible'; and down to the painters of insects and butterflies like van Schrieck and to Jan Christiaan Sepp.

So Avercamp made ice-skating scenes his speciality, much as, in the great restaurants, there will be an under-chef in charge of the cold dishes, and perhaps even a specialist at ices in the friandises and patisserie department. There is even obvious advantage in this for if you are not an adept at most branches of the art, at least your ice scenes; copper pots and pans polished until they reflect like mirrors; or vases of tulips, roses and crown imperials, with dewdrops added, and perhaps a crawling insect, become your signature and are at once identifiable. It is better to do one thing all the time, however humble, than dissipate your talents. That is, if you are not certain of yourself. And if you are, then, surely, you will have failures and disappointments.

Of which not the least, in the case of Avercamp, could one but know that future, would be to have a picture sold three hundred and more years after one's death, as happened a year or two ago, at what even in the diminished value of money is certainly several times his entire life's earnings.* Posthumous fame is cold comfort to the recipient; and not a few, could they be consulted, might spurn this form of charity. It could be more irritating, by far, than having no success at all while living.

His painting referred to in the footnote is unusually full of figures. But all, or nearly all of them, as ever, with their backs turned, walking or skating away from us. And they are more gaily dressed, with their reflections showing on the ice they stand on. Skating, in fact, with their shadow images attached upside down to their feet, and jointly gliding across the ice. There are even a number of small boats stuck in the ice, and showing that the scene is a river running through the village, not a canal, nor a frozen inlet as in the former painting. A number of the ladies in long black mantles have come out from their houses, and their familiar silhouettes, five or six of them, 'in line ahead', show in the foreground. Buildings from his stock of sketches make the side wings of the picture, but not enough of them and with not the individuality to make it recognizable. It is a Dutch village, that is all; and in fact, this allowed, it could be nowhere else, and in no other country. But, also, the baggy breeches, and something about the stolid attitude of the standing figures, the skaters apart, proclaim that it is in Holland. This could not be a painting of a village in England by a Dutchman; it has all the cautious slowing down, or halt of time which is the national signature upon their paintings.

There is a curious problem concerning the drawings by Hendrik Avercamp, of which the largest number (more than one hundred of them) is preserved in the Royal Collection of Windsor Castle. It is that the contemporary costumes apart they could be the work of the brothers Maris, or other Dutch painters of the nineteenth-century school. To stretch the analogy perhaps a little far, they could even be sketches by Randolph Caldecott taken on a hypothetical journey to Holland, not in the eighteen-eighties, but early in the seventeenth century. Or, in other words, Avercamp's drawings surprise by their nineteenth-century handling, but are a disappointment compared to his paintings.

As remarked on an earlier page it is the Inland Sea of Holland, but with what a difference from that other! But, again, with just as much of interest if we but use our eyes. And to what else can it be compared? Having been lucky enough to see that other Inland Sea of Japan, I can only think of Lake Atitlán in Guatemala, with the twelve villages on or near its shores in each of which the Indians wear a different costume, and indeed three different Indian languages are spoken. It may be the most beautiful lake in either hemisphere, and I would write further of the

* A winter scene by Hendrik Avercamp was sold in Paris in 1967 for more than £30,000.

dazzling *huipiles* of Santiago Atitlán and of Solola, of the hibiscus, the allemandas, and the tropical flowering trees. But it is necessary to no more than mention those for contrast and condiment to the skating scenes of Avercamp and the more sedate wonders, now vanished, of the Zuyder Zee.

BOOK
TWO

'Photographies des temps passés'

An exceptional degree of interest attaches to the very slightest detail or scrap of information concerning Rimbaud who was the poetic phenomenon of the nineteenth century, if not of all time. For an example, when my wife and I, having not long been married, were staying in Rome in the winter of 1926–7 at the Hotel Majestic in the Via Veneto, every day after luncheon and dinner we would see an old man lying on a sofa in the middle of the large drawing-room of the hotel, lying on the sofa and looking up and laughing at the ceiling. It had an oval panel painted, as only Italians could render such themes, with Rome being crowned by Liberty, Fame, and several more female abstractions in the full absurdity and ugliness of the Victor Emmanuel II Monument in Rome. It was only later, as we were leaving for home, that we were told that this old gentleman who was staying alone in the hotel was the painter Forain who had known Rimbaud more than fifty years before, just after the Commune, when Rimbaud in the full tide of his talent at eighteen or nineteen years old was about to throw away his genius and go into obscurity. Another, and how different personality, staying in the hotel was the Princess Stéphanie, daughter of Leopold II (of the Congo), and widow of the Crown Prince Rudolph, the self-accomplice and victim of Mayerling. Often I used to pass her and her husband Prince Lónyay on the stair, and used to fancy she looked at me as though she would have liked to speak to me, and indeed there could, then and now, be no more interested audience to this unwilling participant in the Hamlet and Ophelia drama of the Crown Prince and the seventeen-year-old Baroness Vetsera.

The other link with Rimbaud, tenuous but irresistible in its pull or drag upon my memories of childhood, is the recent discovery by a scholar and research specialist that Rimbaud must have visited Scarborough with Verlaine, presumably during the unlikely time while the latter was acting as tutor or schoolmaster in Lincolnshire, and that there are notes or letters in their handwriting on the back of an advertisement for the Yorkshire Agricultural show, which show was almost certainly opened by my grandfather, in August 1872. Furthermore, it is thought that the hotel in the prose poem *Promenade*, in *Les Illuminations*, was inspired by the Grand Hotel at Scarborough, a new and sensational building only completed four years before this in 1867 – and the second largest hotel of its kind to be built in Europe after the Grand Hotel on the Boulevard des Capucines in

Paris. It may have seemed to the two poets as a symbol and paradigm of luxury with its gas-light and palm court with orchestra, dining-room looking out over the bay, and grand stair. No less was it a landmark in my childhood, being as prominent in any memory of Scarborough as is Vesuvius in any view of the town and bay of Naples; and indeed it is wonderful and extraordinary to think that Rimbaud, so unexpectedly, should have had this same image fixed on his retina and changed to poetry.

But, really, the present interest as with other lost or uncompleted works of genius is with Rimbaud's expressed intention to write a work called *Photographies des temps passés*, inspired maybe with somewhat of Salvador Dalí's contrariness when he says his ideal is to paint like the camera, or like Meissonier, expressing only a wish to have the past brought before one's eyes as it can so easily be done in our time, and as all of the past is entirely lost and gone from us until the earliest invention of photography not much more than a hundred years ago. Not even that with the invention of the camera the re-living of the past became much easier. À propos what I have written elsewhere about the nostalgia of seeing one of one's own old suits of clothes, let us but think of the photographs of Wilde before his crash came in 1895, 'camera studies' one or two of which must be familiar to every person who is likely to read these pages. They were most hauntingly dated even in 1925, the date of which I was writing, by the turn-up collar, huge tie-knot, stiff and affected pose, hair waved, and parted in the middle, and so on. This, of a person – and a personality – of whom on a wet day when I could make no progress with my own writing, I wrote down the names of between seventy and eighty persons I knew or had met, who had at least met or known him.

But of all such persons I knew – Robert Ross, More Adey, Max Beerbohm, Mrs Leverson, Reggie Turner, were all friends of his – it never occurred to me, probably out of shyness, to ask any real questions about his appearance, his manner, or the clothes he wore. The gulf of time separating them from their friend in 1918, or thereabouts, which is the time I am speaking of, was less than twenty years, but is now (1969) more than fifty years ago. So does the present run back at compound interest into the past, where it stays fixed and immovable. For it is in fact dead.

A living impression of that time, all time past being in reality equidistant and all alike dead and gone from us, was to be had, while there were living survivors, in mannerisms of speech. In the phrase, 'May I present to you', instead of 'Have you met?' or, 'Do you know?'. In certain formalities and inflections of speech, of which an instance, I think, is the letter written by Wilde to introduce Beardsley to the actress Mrs Patrick Campbell. This was in February 1894, during the run of Pinero's play *The Second Mrs Tanqueray* at the St James's Theatre. His letter goes as follows:

Box F. St James Theatre.

Dear Mrs. Campbell, Mr. Aubrey Beardsley, a very brilliant and wonderful young artist, and like all artists a great admirer of the wonder and charm of your art, says that he must once have the honour of being presented to you, if you will allow of it. So, with your gracious sanction, I will come round after Act III with him, and you would gratify and honour him much if you would let him bow his compliments to you. He has just illustrated my play of *Salomé* for me, and has a copy of the *édition de luxe* which he wishes to lay at your feet. His drawings are quite wonderful.

very sincerely yours,
Oscar Wilde

This seems to me the perfect letter with which to introduce a young genius. And what more absolute instance of that than the young Beardsley; then, not quite twenty-two years old (his birthday was in the next month)? These few words, which it occupies quite a moment in time to copy out, must have been scribbled in Box F during an interval, on a sheet of paper borrowed from the programme seller or the box office, and sent round backstage to Mrs Patrick Campbell. In this theatre where already 'Mr Wilde' was well known; where he was to produce *The Importance of being Earnest* in the following and fatal year of 1895; and where, we may surmise, he was already the subject of scandalous stories and anecdotes.

But the wording of the letter has the elegance one would expect from a D'Orsay or Beau Brummell had their literary style been equal to their taste in dress. It could not be improved upon in this respect. Beardsley was an artist whose short life – he died at twenty-five – was entirely conditioned by his dread disease which indubitably 'forced' his genius, and little as poor Beardsley enjoyed of it one would like to think that a like climate of not altogether fictional good manners and appreciation surrounded the greater and less morbid genius in the person of Mozart. He was, though, we may be certain, less of a phenomenon in his person; still less so in his character and personality. And in fact Mozart on examination of his list of works at nearly twenty-two years old by the end of 1777, his renown as a child-prodigy apart, had produced no great masterpieces. Works, typical of that and the year following, were his flute and harp concerto composed for a French Duke and his daughter. *Il Seraglio*, perhaps the earliest of his true master-pieces, was not written until 1782 when Mozart was twenty-six years old; while the dozen or more of his piano concertos which date from 1784 to 1786, and with the *Nozze di Figaro* of 1786 are the finest fruits of his genius, date from the years when Mozart was aged twenty-eight to thirty. That was the time when his astonishing talent deserved letters couched in these terms – and did not get them. Beardsley, due to illness, had the precocity which one might think would bring him recognition; instead of which, notoriety was his only gain, and on the authority of persons who knew him, he never got more than ten pounds for a drawing.

To follow his short career a little further, in May 1898 Beardsley made his second visit to Paris, 'where his personal elegance and fashionableness made a vast impression, but angered M. Whistler'. (I am ignorant of the source of this

---

* Mozart did, it is true, compose five of his violin concertos, K207, K211, K216, K218, K219, in 1775 when he was aged nineteen. How fresh and beautiful they are! But not faultless or of significance as works of art, being the more delightful for that very reason.

information.)* It is poorly expressed because Beardsley in person can never have been 'fashionable' in that sense. He had neither the means, the capability, nor the ambition. On the authority of Robert Ross who knew him well, Beardsley who had been working up to a few months before this time as a clerk with the Guardian Life Insurance – and was already at seventeen years old 'badly ill, with severe haemorrhages' – had a strongly marked Cockney accent. Ross told him he must get rid of his accent, and within six months, so Robert Ross told the writer, not a trace of it was left, and he had become an authority on eighteenth- and nineteenth-century French art and literature. Such was the young Beardsley, a youthful genius if ever there was one. Within a year of this visit to Paris he was to make the ten drawings and the cover design for Wilde's *Salomé* for which he got fifty guineas. He was not yet twenty-two years old, and less than four years later he was dead.

We would stay a little longer in momentary company, if ever there was the chance, with this individual of so fantastic and personal a talent, so much tied to and expressive of his short span of but six or seven years in time, and who could have appeared at no other moment in history than in the last decade of the nineteenth or English century with the Britons at their control-stations, with their sham-Gothic churches, their clubs, and their statues of the widowed Queen-Empress all over the world, at Gibraltar, Malta, Calcutta, Rangoon, Bombay, Singapore, Hong Kong, Sydney, Melbourne, Wellington, Vancouver, Toronto, Montreal, and so back home. Beardsley was a key to his day, but contrariwise or widdikins, a proving of the facts by contradiction, as indeed was only to be expected after the hypocrisies of Church and State. Not after, but during the appalling slums that were our legacy from the industrial age, even with their horrors dramatized by Marx and Engels on behalf of tens of thousands who would have preferred the drabness of the back streets, where at least there was company in their misery, to the dullness and the stultifications of the upper and middle classes by the rigours and inanities of our private and public school system.

So we go back a year or two in time to July 1891 when, not quite nineteen years old, with his sister Mabel, Beardsley called to see Burne-Jones in his house in Fulham thinking the studio was open on that afternoon to the public. Beardsley was mistaken in this, but Burne-Jones was shown the young artist's drawings and admired them, and he and his sister were then given tea in the garden with the other guests, who included Wilde and Mrs Wilde and their two sons. I have been told by someone, who had the experience, of what it meant in the early nineties to be taken to see Burne-Jones in his studio. It was almost equivalent to being admitted into Botticelli's presence so deep was the evanescent glamour and prestige of successive exhibitions at the Grosvenor Galleries. My informant told me that he felt like taking off his shoes and leaving them in the front hall, and that he dared not speak. We have said that Burne-Jones admired the drawings of the young genius, but what was not Beardsley to make of the Burne-Jones

* Quoted, with reluctance, from *Black and White; a portrait of Aubrey Beardsley*, by Brigid Brophy, London 1968, pp. 86, 87; as, also, a few words from a sentence below.

mannerisms by way of return! In two sepia drawings – one for *The Achieving of the Sangreal*, from *Le Morte d'Arthur*, and the other for *Siegfried, Act II* – in particular, which are transcendental performances for a draughtsman of his youth and inexperience, Beardsley contrived to inject a marvellous strain of equivocal and morbid sensuality into the Burne-Jones canon of languid and androgynous effeteness, and to make of it something unique in the history of drawing.

In both drawings in question the figures stand on a kind of ice or cliff edge a few inches high above dark and mysterious waters; and echoes of Filippino Lippi, of Pollaiuolo, even of the little known Alesso Baldovinetti, linger among the haystacks and poplars and the flooded fields over the, surely, black and green, absinthe-tinted nenuphars or nelumbiums of the foreground. As to the fruit of the plants shown in two of the drawings, are they not consciously intended for 'apples of Sodom'? Neither nymphaea, nor passion-flower, has fruit like this. As drawings they are marvellous in execution, and more morbidly interesting than any achieved fantasies of a youth not yet twenty years old.

The drawing for *Siegfried, Act II*, was given by Beardsley to Burne-Jones, whether on the occasion of this visit or of another is unknown; and on the death of the latter artist in 1898 was given back by Lady Burne-Jones to Beardsley's mother. It must have been drawn in fact with Burne-Jones especially in mind, and is not less than an extraordinary and transcendental *tour de force*, being equivalent to the injection of something superlatively sinister and even venomous into the placidly androgynous personalia of Burne-Jones's tapestries and paintings. The abnormal growth of the plants in question, a half-dozen of them in *The Achieving of the Sangreal*, and half that number of them for *Siegfried, Act II*, proffering themselves forward on their long and sinuous stems right into and across the Kelmscott-like landscape of flooded fields, is like the planting of a germ and the spreading of a disease. It could be true that tuberculosis as, too, other and more venal illnesses are the hot house and forcing place of talent, and that the implantation of such a germ into the body and bloodstream of a poet, a painter, or a musician of ordinary talents might achieve a miracle and make an exceptional artist of him.

And we come to the moment when Wilde and his ill-fated family, and Aubrey and Mabel Beardsley, rise from their chairs on the lawn to take their leave of the Burne-Joneses and walk back through the house and studio and down the steps into the waiting carriage. For Wilde has offered to drive the Beardsleys back to Chelsea, and knowing him as we do we may be certain it was no ordinary 'growler' or four-wheeler, but that he had ordered a cab and kept it waiting all that time. What would Wilde be wearing? Probably a frock coat and top hat because he was calling or paying a visit on the most famous living English artist. We see him, therefore, as in Frith's painting of the opening day of the Royal Academy in 1884, where he is to be seen with Mr Gladstone, Mrs Langtry, Sir Henry Irving, and other celebrities of the day, and a good deal taller than any other person in the room. We may be sure, too, that he had a characteristic stance and way of walking, while it could be said that we decidedly hear his voice in Max Beerbohm's drawings. And beside him goes the bony, angular figure of Beardsley who was to be so very much the greater artist of the two, and indeed the only true genius of the nineties. He will have been wearing a clerk's 'Sunday best', being short of pocket-money and not yet nineteen years old. In three years' time (July 1894), when he attended the unveiling of a bust to Keats, a fellow-victim of tuberculosis, in Hampstead Church, he was wearing the conventional grey trousers, black frock-coat, and carrying his grey top hat. It is so dressed that we see him, thin and cadaverous, in the portrait that Sickert did from memory (now in the Tate Gallery), on this occasion that Beardsley, already doomed, must have felt to be full of foreboding for himself.

And Wilde? On this occasion in Box F; and a year later in the stage box of St James's Theatre for the first performance of his play *The Importance of being Earnest*, 14 February 1895, only three months before disaster overtook him at his trial in the Central Criminal Court at the Old Bailey. We hear the poor creature's voice which surely must have so much irritated those who disapproved of him, and his many enemies. We hear his voice and way of speaking, and entering into his memory by way of the evidence at his trial can go through the list or catalogue of his terrible, his irredeemably awful 'young friends', one of them in particular, probably the worst of them all, who went to Paris with him in 1892. Mr Avery: 'How old are you?' 'I am twenty years old.'

'What is your business?' 'I have been a billiard marker. I have also been a bookmaker's clerk and a comedian. . . . I have a professional name. I have sometimes called myself Denny . . .'

Cross-examined by Mr Grain – 'Did you go to Scarborough about a year ago?' – 'Yes'. 'What was your business there?' 'I was engaged professionally. I sang at the Aquarium.'

. . . 'How much did you receive a week?' – '£4.10s.'

(Counsel wrote a name on a piece of paper, which was handed up to the witness.)

'Did you know that gentleman?' – 'No. I heard his name mentioned in Scarborough.'

'Did you ever speak to him?' – 'No. I heard other young men speak of him. He had a big yacht lying out in the bay.'

'Now, I put it to you, did not you and Burton obtain money from that nobleman to the amount of nearly £500?' – 'No.' etc, etc.

Whatever can his songs have been? And in what conceivable context can he have described himself as a 'comedian'? It has of course a particular and personal interest to the writer because of the mention of Scarborough. How well I remember the dingy, rusty underground Pompeii of the Aquarium, down near the Foreshore, in disuse in my time but entry to it was possible! And now I hear there is talk of 'restoring' it as a monument of 'Victoriana' during the golden age of this most northern of spas and European watering-places. I would be interested, too, it would be idle to deny, in the identity of the foreign nobleman whose 'big yacht was lying out in the bay'. There may be someone still living who could give the clue to this.

The terrible individual concerned in this dialogue, who had gone to Paris with Wilde 'in the Club train' in 1892, when living in Osnaburgh Street where Wilde visited him, 'had smallpox and was removed to the hospital ship'. Before he went he asked someone to write to Mr Wilde requesting him 'to come and see me, and he did so. I was removed to the hospital ship the next day.' It would have been a happier fate, as my sister remarked to me on reading his trial, had poor Wilde caught smallpox from this invidious friendship and died in the result. But it is exactly these friends of whom Wilde wrote in *De Profundis*: 'People thought it dreadful of me to have entertained to dinner the evil things of life, and to have found pleasure in their company. But they from the point of view through which I, as an artist in life, approached them, were delightfully suggestive and stimulating. It was like feasting with panthers. The danger was half the excitement. They were to me the brightest of gilded snakes. Their poison was part of their perfection.' So Wilde sought to exculpate himself in these matters by pleading that he approached them 'as an artist in life'.

But to continue with his friendship for the horrible Lord Alfred Douglas, and quote another sentence or two from his *De Profundis*: 'The Savoy dinners – the clear turtle soup, the luscious ortolans wrapped in their crinkled Sicilian vine-leaves, the heavy amber-coloured, indeed almost amber-scented champagne – Dagonet 1880, I think, was your favourite wine? – all have still to be paid for. The suppers at Willis's, the special *cuvée* of Perrier-Jouet reserved always for us, the wonderful *pâtés* procured directly from Strasburg, the marvellous *fine champagne* served always at the bottom of great bell-shaped glasses that its bouquet might be the better savoured by the true epicures of what was really exquisite in life – those cannot be left unpaid, as bad debts of a dishonest client.' And then, descending from grand luxe to bathos: 'Even the dainty sleeve-links – four heart-shaped moonstones of silver mist, girdled by alternate ruby and diamond for their setting – that I designed, and had made at Henry Lewis's as a special little present to you, to celebrate the success of my second comedy – these even – though I believe you sold them for a song a few months afterwards – have to be paid for. I cannot leave the jeweller out of pocket for the presents I gave you, no matter what you did with them. So, even if I get my discharge, you see I still have my debts to pay.' Despite the brilliance and wonder of his conversation and his good humour with never a sign of bitterness or self-pity in his last letters when he had come out from prison – was not Beardsley right when he said of Wilde and Douglas, of the pair of them, that 'they were really rather dreadful people'?

It is by one of the contradictions inherent in all human histories that Alexander Pope's *The Rape of the Lock*, another of those works of art to be classified as *arbiter elegantiarum* of its kind, and the poetic masterpiece of our own, if not of all, whatever, silver or Augustan ages there have ever been, should be the work as we might expect of a young man twenty-six years old when it was published not, a victim of tuberculosis in this instance, but a little hunchbacked dwarf only four feet six inches tall. The finish and elegance of the poem suggest a very different physique from that.

If we look for another instance of the transcendental in this context of extreme elegance and fastidiousness informed by genius there could be no more perfect example than the opening run or flourish of Chopin's *Twenty-four Preludes*, op. 28. I have tried to write in another place of the underlying, but most evident meaning in the 'Farewell Song' at the end of Mozart's *Il Seraglio*. In a miraculous way it has all the poignancy of a parting, but a stage parting. One is not to see the company of actors again, or hear the ravishment of the music again until next time, which could be tomorrow night, or never. But Mozart as a young man – indeed while writing this opera – has been in love with opera-singers, and knew what he was about. So it is not quite a parting for so far as he was concerned there was the certainty of meeting, but as though in another existence in a few hours' or even a few minutes' time.

Now, in the start to Chopin's *Preludes*, op. 28, a miracle of the same order of invention is achieved in the space of twelve to fourteen seconds which is all the time it takes to play, or to sing over to oneself in one's own head. And what does it suggest? Superficially, it could be the trying out of the piano's tone, or no more than a run to warm the fingers. Yet it is the lifting of the curtain, and an anticipation of what is to come. So that it is in a sense both the beginning and the end of all *Twenty-four Preludes*. It is this Romantic but reticent being, entire, within the confines of less than a quarter of a minute in time. I would say that it is the mood of Chopin in two, at least, of his *Études* which are among the wonders of his young genius, and unlike anything else there had been before in music. There is no shade in them of Field of the *Nocturnes*, or of the pieces by his female compatriot Szymanowska that I have heard. There is nothing in them of his loved Bellini. They are his genius at its purest, of an unequalled firing of the imagination; as of a wonderful series of happenings to look forward to, of meetings, of imagined love affairs. And it is both the pretence and the truth in works of art that we know they cannot happen or come to pass. The reality will be very different except in spirit. Yet, in truth, they have been and have happened for they are all there in the music. They have existence and permanence in that, and no other life than that is possible for them, and therefore they stay unspoilt and unsullied. But, too, they are the elegancies of a higher order of existence than ever happened.

They are the young Polish musician newly arrived in the French capital and giving music lessons, in certainly aristocratic circles to judge from his dedications,* which again is all in the music but transformed, and indeed transubstantiated. There can never have been such an elegance or chivalry of *milieu*, so that it is an enhancement or mystification of the ordinary which his genius has turned into poetry. There were ladies sitting in the Parisian salons of the eighteen-thirties whose grandmothers remembered the Court of Louis Quatorze, the *étiquette*, and the terraces and fountains and the clipped hedges, not, then, grown too tall. Now everything was different; but to Chopin, born in 1810, who could not remember the Napoleonic Wars or the '1812', it must have been a very strong

---

* It is not intended by way of criticism of Chopin in any way to point out that twenty-seven out of sixty-five of Chopin's opus numbers bear dedications to ladies of title; *cf.* the catalogue of works in Arthur Hedley's *Chopin*, London 1947, pp. 193–6. Radziwills, Potockis, and Czartoryskis are of frequent occurrence.

feeling to come from Warsaw to the French capital which was full at that time, and through most of the nineteenth century, with Polish exiles. The political refugee from Poland was as familiar a figure (forgive the comparison) as the English tourist or Italian organ-grinder. Alas! that he should continue and be perpetuated in our day while the other pair of types are gone and vanished!

The two *études* referred to a few lines back are op. 25 no. 10 and the second *nouvelle étude*, and they are something new both in poetry and music. They seem instinct with a nobility of decision to put things to right, while chosen for or granted the power to do so. In no political sense, or dreariness of speech-making and ballot-boxing. But on higher levels of physical health and rightness (again not in the political meaning) of ideas. Extraordinary emanations coming from this young Pole in his early twenties; two or three of the first set of twelve (op. 10) dating even from the time he was eighteen! Although it is always to be remembered that 'Chopin was one thing only – a musician working with musical materials for purely musical ends; his first concern was the solution of *musical*, not sentimental problems'.* Musical problems, yes! but their interpretation back again out of music into other meaning, if that is at all possible, suggests or reveals a very different world of both ideas and action.

It is enough to have been twice in a life to Łowicz, a town to which one went to see the peasants coming out of church in their striped dresses (in imitation of those of the Pope's Swiss Guard), some twenty miles from Zelazowa Nola the village where Chopin was born – and as many times to Warsaw to which Chopin was removed when a few months' old – to know that Poland is not Paris. The endless plain round Łowicz and on the way to Warsaw – if these are not present in Chopin's early music before he came to Paris, then there is nothing in an early environment and we are to believe that Chopin would have been no different in his music had he spent his childhood on the Bay of Naples, or been like Keats, a Cockney. Both the melancholy inherent from nationality and historical happening, and the sad landscape which led out of East Prussia in the one direction into Russia in the other, are present in his two piano concertos written when he was a boy of twenty; and how much more, one would imagine, in the *Fantasia on Polish Airs*, op. 13, and the *Krakowiak*, op. 14, both for piano and orchestra, which are of even earlier composition.† It must be the same setting and landscape for his early *mazurkas* (seventeen including some very youthful ones, written before he came to Paris) – while the forty more *mazurkas* he was still to compose must, and can only have been inspired by scenes and melodies he had carried in his mind from his native land. But the two *études* in question do not partake of this character, nor are they in the mood of the *valses* – written advisedly instead of waltzes – which beautiful as they may be are Parisian salon music elevated by his poetry and genius into works of art. Still less are they fiery and patriotic like his *polonaises*; nor yet are they 'musical material used for purely musical ends' like

* Arthur Hedley, op. cit., p. 143.

† An omission now repaired by the gramophone, and the best of them is surely the *Fantasia on Polish Airs*, op. 13, though one might be suspicious of some alien tinkering in the orchestration.

his 'Black Key' *étude*, no. 5 of op. 10, or *études* nos. 6, 8, and 9 which are studies in thirds, sixths, and octaves. But they are youthful, chivalrous and noble in intention with somewhat of the quality of a youthful masculine head as drawn by Leonardo or Michelangelo, conveying the same sensation of the world put to rights by youthful energy and genius, together with the underlying certainty that this has never happened and will never be. And yet in those few moments which amount to but a breath or two of time they are wearing, it could be said, the clothes of Schumann's Florestan and Eusebius with Chiarina and Estrella never far away, as though Schumann had in his turn borrowed them and used his lens on them from Chopin.

What a wonderful and eternally youthful world is left to us with this pair of *études* by Chopin and with the youthful violin and piano sonatas of Mozart, to which latter it is almost too sad and painful to listen because of their happy optimism and spreading of the wings of genius to such unrewarding ends! But it is only necessary to glance at the unfinished portrait of Mozart by the actor Josef Lange, who married Aloysia Weber and was his brother-in-law, to be certain in one's mind that worldly success would elude him.* And as for Rimbaud with whom these few pages of argument on the subject of youthful genius began, his uncouthness, savagery and bad manners would certainly have excepted him from any possibility of mundane wealth and ease, even if his pronounced political views would now in our time win him uncritical and facile entry. There could hardly be a greater contrast in genius than between Rimbaud and Mozart, their only point of contact or comparison being that both were equally unfortunate and doomed to worldly failure. But while the mere thought of the amount of work done by Mozart makes one feel ill, the boy-poet Rimbaud seems to have taken no trouble at all and just plainly been inspired. Perhaps his case is nearer to poltergeist phenomena than to any skill or knowledge in the acquired sense. The derivation in him of the imagery he uses is an entire mystery. How can he have attained to it; or got the knowledge? There is no explanation. It does not seem that he was particularly well read, but of course his is not a case of extended genius. It left him after a few months, or even weeks; that is to say, the *geist* or spirit that was inhabiting him just went away, as simply as that. What is unusual about Rimbaud is that he did not wish for its return.

How to explain this wind of inspiration! It could be as though a particular light fell on objects; a shaft of sunlight coming through a window and showing a portrait of an ancestor in an illumination never seen before. There is a ruby-red incandescence; a light of Bengal-fire in his sword-belt, never noticed up to this moment, and a red glow as of sunset in the sky behind him. On the far side of the fireplace in the drawing-room the young woman wearing a blue-green Van Dyck dress in the fashion of the time of George the Second now has her turn. The rouge on her cheeks shows up. We can see the dark brown 'spaniel' iris of her eyes, and

---

* In this portrait Mozart is looking down intently and, one would presume, sitting at the keyboard. Although by an amateur painter, it is beyond all value as a likeness of his features. The only good portrait of a musician in action is the picture of Gluck at the clavichord, both hands in the air. This is a pastel by Duplessis in the gallery at Vienna.

that her bodice and hooped skirt are of velvet. The sky behind her has a red glow in it, the low trees on the horizon seem to be bowed down in a sunset wind; and the focus slowly passes or slides over her, and is now but a patch of light upon a bare wall. In another moment the room is in semi-darkness. It is twilight, and the bat flits past the window.

Such is the transcendental within the walls of an ordinary room. But the sacred trance or ecstasy, which is an intoxication of the senses, can descend like a swarm of bees upon the blossoming apple trees.

I am thinking now of a painter who was inhabited for a year or two, or a few months only, by the genius of poetry, which bemused and possessed him, and then left him without warning. A visitation, again, as curious and beyond explanation as that of the poltergeist when that 'controls' a child, but which in his case was induced by reading poetry, or at the invitation of poetry; poetry being the drug or narcotic, but the effects of it wore off, or its potency could not be renewed, and the power left him.

He laboured all the rest of a long life to catch up with it again, but it eluded him; and only the titles he gave to his later paintings and etchings portray the ghost or echo he was seeking.* Long ago it had run into his arms and then escaped him, as transitory as the bright cloud behind the hill.

The pale fleeces move like a shadow over the meadow and we do not hear the bleating of the flock while the last sheep are folded. Magical, too, is his oaten moonlight with the owl calling out of the elm tree, could we but hear him. Samuel Palmer is not one of those masters that, once discovered, remain for all time in one's mind. But he had drunk of the fountain of the Ancients, in the House of the Interpreter, which was William Blake's slum lodging in Lambeth, and was bemused and intoxicated by the waters of that spring. He is, therefore, the purest clinical case of a person metamorphosed and inspired.

But there have been periods when this magic inhabited not only an individual person, but a whole town, or even a little country. Everyone has his or her own instance of this, according to taste, just as we can all remember hours of illumination when the bounds of ordinary life were transcended. There are exceptional times and places, just as there are individual persons who are exceptional, and those whom we all know in our minds to be lucky, or unlucky. They even continue in this course in spite of their own efforts as though their track is plotted for them and it is too late for them to change it.

How easy it is to understand that superstition of the Elizabethans that it was luckier to live in an unfinished, uncompleted house! Did not 'Bess of Hardwick' die on a day when snow prevented the builders from climbing into their scaffolding and so work was brought to a standstill! Are there not many authenticated cases of persons dying upon the day they have always dreaded? Or is it not better so than to be taken unawares? But it will come one day, and on a day of its own choosing. That you may think you have chosen the time and place is but to ask for your eyes to be blindfolded with your own handkerchief upon the fatal morning.

* *The Herdsmen's Cottage; The Sleeping Shepherd; Early Morning; Opening the Fold.*

But that is but the beating of the drum. Which could mean many things, and was the old way of announcing that a quack or charlatan had come into the town. I saw his descendant, only yesterday afternoon, selling cheap saucepans, near the corner of Cambridge Circus, if that is still what it is called. What soul or heart is there in thin metal surfaces that are japanned or tinned! One or two of the Tschoron and Demeter families (of Roumanian Gypsy coppersmiths or Calderarii) are in Tangiers and others are reported from Brazil. Do not expect to see any 'sights' but accidents along the arterial roads, either by day or under the neon lights! But, even now, one or two caravans are behind the hoardings, laundry is hung up to dry, and a piebald pony is hobbled on the grass verge. However, a certain number of persons of 'no fixed address' have taken to the road in order to avoid the 'Inland Revenue Boys'. And a few others live for the same reason on barges and houseboats on the canals. Do not imagine for one moment that they have escaped notice. The problem of such vagrant persons is constantly under review and comes up for discussion at regular intervals. An official spokesman states that it is only a question of completing certain reports. Names are known to the police and arrests are expected any day in the near future. Probably on Wednesday.

The curious point is that in spite – or is it because of? · · all this tabulation, there is a wave of crime. Murders are worse, and more far fetched, than ever before. Nothing is too fantastic. 'Jack the Ripper', or Gilles de Retz (much come down in the world), could be living in the next-door house where a suspiciously new-looking cement floor has been laid down in the garage. Did anybody living near-by notice a bonfire in the back garden, or curious smells from a smoking chimney, any time round the end of last November or the beginning of December? For it was about then that those two small children disappeared; last seen buying sweets at the tobacconist's in company with a young man, of about thirty years of age, no details known of his appearance, but he may have a slurred way of talking and carry the marks of recent scratches on his face and hands.

Next Sunday there is to be a visit from an American evangelist, and if he is correct nearly everyone will end in heaven. Despite its rapidly increasing population there is every hope that conditions there will not be widely different from those we are accustomed to down here. There could be even more relayed music, with all the song hits and popular old-time favourites; and no doubt sport will prove as big an attraction as ever. But, of course, no crime unless it comes to us by courtesy of the 'other side'.

New arrivals every day: familiar faces and old friends. Is it conceivable that it may be run rather on the lines of a comfortable, non-commercial guest house, with resident host and hostess who greet guests on arrival and do their best to make them feel at home? New arrivals are given a ticket with their name upon it to wear in their corsage or their buttonhole the first night at dinner. The hosts see to it that there is a gentleman sitting next to every lady at table; and after dinner while coffee is served conversation is general in the lounge, after which there is a tendency for guests to split into groups and join their friends. About once a fortnight there is a concert, generally upon a Saturday evening. A platform is put up; guests file back into the dining-room; and last week the resident host and hostess, Mr and Mrs Sarony is the name, gave a killing performance of 'Everything you can do, I can do better' (you remember), from *Annie get your gun*. They made all the movements and gestures. No one could believe they weren't singing, and all the time it was a gramophone record playing behind the curtain. It was most popular. When it was ended you could have tea and sandwiches; or the gentlemen could ask for minerals or beer. A quite delightful place for a holiday, with no snobbishness. Even if it rains there is always plenty to do, and people to talk to, and it is near the picture houses. Morning and evening services on Sundays in the dining-room; nearly always there is a clergyman or minister staying, and should there not be, Mr Sarony reads the prayers. They say Mr and Mrs Sarony formerly gave dancing lessons, and whenever there is a dance Mr Sarony always acts as steward. Mrs Sarony plays the piano. Unless someone else volunteers; in which case they dance a lot together, *The Boston* and *The Gay Gordons*; or something difficult like a reel or two. Soon after midnight it is all over and we go upstairs to bed.

When you come to think of it, falling asleep is like an easier and pleasanter form of dying. Except that, when you wake up again, you are still alive.

Siesta Thoughts

I

'Siesta – (se-esta) – n. a rest or sleep in the afternoon', so reads the dictionary. But in fact it is a word amounting almost to its own synonym for heat and sun. Which factors are not essential for a siesta is as effective with the snows of Canada outside, as I hope to prove later, when we advance from the world of Hendrik Avercamp to that of Bruegel, or of Hiroshige and Utamaro, the painters of deliberate winter scenes, and lose ourselves among their snows.

A word with its accompanying connotation of idleness which, also, is not entirely true. In siesta lands because of the heat the shops and offices are shut from two till half-past five or six o'clock or even eight. But they stay open working until ten or eleven at night. Siestas are not for the young. But for anyone over thirty years old a siesta is the hour of day for staying awake, thinking. Because it is free of the distortions of the night.

The heat I have found ever to be a marvellous catalyst. But with no more ado we will begin upon the points and pleasures, the illusions and disillusionments of the siesta. I have written before of the siesta hour in Seville, when, 'late in the afternoon, comes that extraordinary moment when from all over the town, in every direction, you hear the rattle and crackle of ten thousand castanets. The crowd is making for the Feria and the women are playing their castanets excitedly, and in anticipation, as they walk along.' Could there be anything more inspiring! It is of no use to compare this experience with that of watching the crowd arriving or departing at Wembley from the Cup Final. The two experiences are worlds apart.

It could be true that there is some little disappointment about Seville at other times than this. I have been there when there was nothing else to do but walk in and out of the Cathedral. When the Sierpes, that long narrow street of shops like the Mercería in Venice, and place of *paseo* for the warm Sevillan evenings, seemed little different, if at all, from the passages lined with bookshops and junk shops lying between Charing Cross Road and St Martin's Lane – except that there are no bookshops in the Sierpes. When one could not bear the sight of any more paintings by Zurbarán or by Murillo. When the famed Triana of the toreros and flamenco dancers had become a mean suburb of cement flats, approached over the Guadalquivir by an iron bridge that clanked noisily, day and night long. When it was raining in the Court of Orange Trees beside the Cathedral, and there must be fly-blown windows and magazines five or six years old in the dentist's parlour. But it can recover itself in a few moments and become again the city which was made the scene for four operas. If never quite as I remember it for the first time with the rose-beds in flower in February in the Plaza de San Fernando.

It is one of the cities in which to lie thinking whether by night or day, in a sense in which the boroughs of Marylebone or Kensington could not fill one's thoughts. And it can even, when one knows everything of Seville, produce a bonus for its admirers at a late moment in the form of the Capilla de San José. This is something owed positively to the Sierpes, and which would have to be imagined for it did not exist (the Capilla was badly damaged and has only been re-opened during the last year or two). It is a small chapel of about 1690–1700, by an architect Pedro Romero, who could have been a matador or bull-breeder by his name, with an interior of gilded woodwork which is no less than the perfect church setting for the fashion and *afición* of the Sierpes – as it was not long ago, with its *majos* in Andalusian dress which is that of Figaro in both operas, and with the infrequent young girls walking in pairs, in high combs and white mantillas, for whom the only simile is that they moved like laced fantail pigeons. The Capilla de San José, which by a lucky chance was withheld from me till last year although it lies at the corner of an alley off the Sierpes, as much as the Court of Orange Trees or the gardens of the Alcázar is the quintessence of Seville, and we are to imagine as in a vision the characters, just mentioned, pouring out from Mass onto the Sierpes.

It is important not to read but to let one's thoughts wander during the siesta. Reading is for night time; except for serious reading, the proper place for which is the Reading Room of the British Museum, or else the Bodleian, or the London Library. One must avoid all problems and difficulties of person. Things of which to think when one is sleepless belong to a different category of thought. They had best, therefore, be in series so that one can move from the first to the next with the hope of falling asleep in the middle. I find I can lie awake, and perhaps get to sleep in thinking of English cathedrals; beginning from Canterbury, and going round through Winchester and Wells (the most beautiful of all) to Salisbury; or moving up the east coast paragons, Ely, Lincoln, York, to culminate at Durham. Or trying, more exotically, to remember the oft-seen treasures of Burgos, Toledo, Santiago de Compostela; or, again, Seville.

Such, I say, are for sleeping, not for siesta. But regarding this latter subject there is so much to say and so many possibilities, realized or otherwise, that I know not where to start.

Let me begin by saying that on the fly-leaf of one of his publications of the late thirties, just before the war began, my old friend Harry Batsford printed a note to the effect that much as he would love to 'produce a work devoted to English architecture of the seventeenth and eighteenth centuries such a project was out of the question. No one would buy it. In the result it would be a dead loss. Sir Reginald Blomfield has essayed it with no great success.'

How difficult it is to credit that such was the situation less than thirty years ago! With some trepidation, therefore, I accepted Harry Batsford's invitation to embark upon this very subject which at least was familiar ground to me. The book was written at fair speed from my enthusiasm, and first published with great success in the spring of 1945, after a delay of more months than it had taken in the writing. It was indeed illustrated as only Batsford's books were illustrated, and published 'in the sixth year of World War Two', as it proudly proclaimed itself, at the now incredible price of 21s. net, which was a ridiculous sum to pay for a book with two hundred photographs and reproductions of engravings. I think it may be fairly said that *British Architects and Craftsmen* (*1600–1830*) broke the ice where books on this subject were concerned and that it made way for many subsequent publications on English art and decoration in general, and upon individual English architects in detail.

As a siesta theme or subject I sometimes try to think of buildings by the still under-estimated, or taken for granted universal architectural provider, Robert Adam; and try to remember individual rooms by him, or even pieces of furniture – with one of the finest of which, the chiffonier at Renishaw designed by Adam and made, it is said, by Chippendale – I have been familiar since childhood. Such is but a small detail in his vast output, the comprehensive listing of which would fill too long a footnote and obscure the page. Let us only think of his 'town houses', the three survivors among them being 20 Portman Square (now the Courtauld Institute), 'with its ceilings as complex and fine drawn as a spider's web upon a frosty morning'; Chandos House of 'the fluted pillars and neat neckings to them, and the ram's heads and garlands of the entablature'; or 20 St James's Square, built for the Welsh magnate, Sir Watkin Williams Wynn, with its pair of drawing-rooms, lately restored in bright colours from the original drawings, and in its day complete down to the sedan chair and the inkstand, the fire irons and the door knocker.

But there was, as well, Old Derby House in Grosvenor Square, long since destroyed, the most sumptuous of his London houses, '*clinquant* like all the harlequinades of Adam', but this is the old-maidish Horace Walpole's opinion. Other London houses now gone were Roxburghe House at the corner of Hanover Square, for which designs remain for a dining-room, two libraries and three drawing-rooms; and Cumberland House, Pall Mall, with one of Adam's 'Etruscan' rooms; while Northumberland House with a gallery more than a hundred feet long, and ceilings in Adam's 'harlequin' or parti-coloured manner, was pulled down to make way for the Thames Embankment. In respect of all of which it can be repeated once more that it was not only the Germans who set out to destroy the finest things in London.

But then, as well, we have to think of Lansdowne House and Kenwood, Osterley and Syon, which were, and miraculously still are, Adam's four great villas or houses in, or near London. When we add to this list Saltram and Shardeloes, Croome and Bowood, Kedleston and Harewood, Newby and Culzean, Headfort and Mellerstain, we see the true extent of Robert Adam's achievement. Beside which, there are hundreds of coloured drawings by him in the Soane Museum, in Lincoln's Inn Fields, from which with modern skill in reproduction it would be perfectly possible to achieve carpets, looking glasses, coloured stucco ceilings, furniture, silver, even whole rooms, and such extravagances as orangeries and unnecessary park bridges – drawings which remained on paper and were never realized. Besides this, there are drawings by him for works which were carried out – Luton Hoo, for instance, 'with a library of three or five rooms which, when the doors are open, make it appear one large room or gallery'; or Alnwick, 'with a grand staircase, singular but beautiful, expanding like a lady's fan' – but later demolished or destroyed. And in default of anything better, of which there is little hope, now or ever, the effects of such reconstruction at least would not be disagreeable.*

The next project to which I was invited by the omnivorous Mr Batsford – the war ended, in the summer of 1947 – was to write a book on Holland. Though not immediately appetizing, for my previous knowledge of The Netherlands was confined to a couple of two-day visits in the pouring rain, we spent two weeks in August seeing Holland in a very different light from that; finding for ourselves the old town houses along the Keizersgracht and Heerengracht, and the wonderful old synagogue of the Portuguese Jews; and after the August nightfall, when not delayed by Mr Batsford's passion for stray cats which led him through odd doorways and up still stranger stairs, we listened to the Gypsy bands which are no less unexpected a feature in the staid temperament of the Hollanders.† The old houses at The Hague by Daniel Marot, the Huguenot architect (1650–1714) – and one is tempted to add after his name the initials GP for general practitioner, since there is no detail to which he did not lay his hand, state coaches and iron-work, door furniture and watch cocks, not forgetting his tulip vases, veritable pagodas of Delft chinaware at Hampton Court – were all of them, I believe, first written about on this occasion.

But the true discovery, for I do think it amounted to that, was Friesland, the Dutch province with its own language of 'double Dutch' across the Zuyder Zee. Where else had the town hall of Sneek been even mentioned, with its *chinoiserie* room painted entirely in shades of green and gold? Or the Raadzaal or Court Room of the town hall at Dokkum with its beautiful paintings and grisaille panels! And the array of clay-pipes laid out ready on the table for the burgomaster's meeting! The Frieslanders, themselves, with their excessively fair hair seem a race apart and there is, or was, so much else peculiar to Friesland. The golden casques or *oorijzers* for instance of the Frisian women. The golden skull caps worn, also, by the Friesland noble ladies and to be seen at the opera at The Hague on a gala night as late as the end of the century, but now, I am afraid, no longer worn. Twenty years ago we saw no more than four or five of them. A friend who went to Friesland last summer saw not a single one. Yet when my book was published in 1948 I had a letter from a reader who had arrived to work as an engineer at, I think, Workum in Friesland in 1910 or 1912 and had been surprised to see what he took to be a group of firemen in their brass helmets in a garden just across the canal, and they were Frisian women busy with their washing. The costume, too, was strange and fantastic with the most extreme invention of all, the cartwheel hat or *deutsche muts* worn only in the little town of Makkum on the inland sea; while the inhabitants of Hindeloopen which was little more than a village, but a village

---

* It is curious that no coffee consortium or other body has ever thought to recreate Adam's British Coffee House in Cockspur Street, 'surely an adaptation of the Porta Aurea'. It is illustrated in his *Works*. Lansdowne House has of course been altered and truncated.

† There was a Gypsy cymbalom player, in particular, who performed the *lassán* or slow introduction before a *csárdás* in a manner recalling the remark of Casals that J. S. Bach must have had Hungarian blood, and that his *Chromatic Fantasy*, which has the character of a marvellous improvisation, should be played upon the cymbalom.

of mariners and sea-captains and their families, dressed themselves in Indian stuffs and chintzes, had painted furniture in the same style, and must have lived in a kind of innocent opium dream of distant lands and exotic countries.

This book, too, for some reason that I never discovered, but I think it was paper shortage, came out after nearly a year's delay, by which time I had embarked upon another subject. *The Netherlands*, I should add, was splendidly illustrated, if not quite with the lavishness of *British Architects and Craftsmen*, and came out at the now astounding price of 28s. net. My new and self-chosen theme was *Spain*, but it was not achieved, or rather started, without some difficulty. When I told Mr Batsford of my idea he immediately rang the bell in front of him on his desk, and when the lady assistant came up from the bookshop below he inquired how many persons had asked for a book on Spain during the previous twelve months. She answered 'four'; and I suggested we should print an edition of six copies, with one reserved for himself and one for the author.* From his office I went a little despairingly to see the editress of the leading fashion paper to say I was going to the Feria in Seville in a few days, and might I write an article for her? Her answer was that Spain was a back number and finished, and that no one would ever go to Spain again. She should have known better, and has been proved wrong.

I was soon able to bring round Mr Batsford to my point of view, by that time having already gone and come back from Spain. In fact during some weeks in the spring of 1947 and 1948 – and again in 1949 – I was enabled to make journeys in every direction from end to end of Spain. This was a wonderful and unique occasion, or, rather, series of occasions; and in the course of it I saw every cathedral in Spain excepting Burgo de Osma and La Seo de Urgel, and I think I can fairly say every town worth seeing excepting the twin Andalusian towns of Ubeda and Baeza with their late Gothic and Isabelline churches and palaces, and the green-tiled Mudéjar towers, more like minarets, of Teruel. I could wish, too, to have seen Albarracín, which lies twenty miles inland from Teruel with Moorish walls and towers and a stony stairway leading up to them.† The book which was the result of these journeys duly appeared in 1950 after, sadly, Mr Batsford was dead, and it has even, like *British Architects and Craftsmen*, sold well in paperback. It had been my ambition, and it has been my lifelong disappointment not to have been allowed to do this, to make the book on *Spain* twice as long as it is. The material is endless; inspiration came quickly, and I could so easily have

* I would like to add here, in the accumulated experience of more than half a century as a writer, that Harry Batsford came nearer to my ideal as a publisher than any of his rivals. That is to say, he did *almost*, if not quite believe in me, and appeared willing to print anything I wrote except poems.

† To which the perfectionist in me would add, on information, the 'magnificent carved brick' tower of 1756 of San Miguel, at Jerez de los Caballeros, between Badajoz and Seville; and at Caravaca, between Murcia and Cartagena, the church of Santa Cruz, 'in the Escorial style, but its fantastic portal of 1722 is rather Mexican in manner'. These two are for another time which probably will never be. But the interest of the brick tower of Jerez de los Caballeros lies in comparing it to the detached tower of Santo Domingo de la Calzada, the 'china towers' of Écija, or the towers of Santiago, all of which, *mutatis mutandis*, are among the lesser, but unforgettable sights of Spain.

achieved this. But a paper shortage intervened, or was made the excuse, and my half-attempt must remain but another of an author's disappointments.

The 'discoveries' in this book, and I lay no claim to being the first to find them, being a group of churches, or parts of churches, subsidiary to that perhaps most fantastic of all interiors, the *sacristía* of the Cartuja at Granada. They are the works of a forgotten architect, Francisco Hurtado Izquierdo (1669–1728), who is more easily accessible at another Cartuja, that of El Paular, in the pinewoods outside Segovia. There he is to be seen in fantastic vein and delirium of ornament: but money cannot have been so forthcoming and he is, comparatively, in simple mood at Priego, a little Andalusian town between Córdoba and Malaga, where he had not to rely on twisting Salomonic columns 'of a brilliant coral colour' and doors of scarlet and gold lacquer, but must depend on mere stucco ornament and brilliance of planning. It is the two-storeyed octagonal *sagrario* in the church of the Asuncíon which is the masterpiece of the style, and which raises it into the category of those masterworks of fantasy at the Wies church in Bavaria, or at Zwiefalten. And it could be added that Hurtado can be studied *in petto*, and on a diminutive scale in the *camarín* (1693–5) of the Iglesia de la Victoria, on the hills just outside Málaga where some little idea can be formed of his daring imagination and brilliant handling.* In short his is a name to be remembered in company with J. B. Neumann, J. M. Fischer, and the brothers Asam and brothers Zimmermann; those, too, unknown to fame not so long ago, but now familiar as artificers of delight and pleasure.

During the journeys in Spain I had intended to write a companion volume on Portugal. But the project was interrupted by illness and could not be resumed until 1953. The book appeared at last in the following year; and I would put forward, as siesta themes of the kind the mind delights on, my attempts to write as well as I could, at this and later opportunities, of such wonders of their kind as the Convent of Jesus at Aveiro, and the golden grottoes of São Francisco and of the convent of Santa Clara at Oporto. Some of these, and others, I had been able at least to touch upon in a book on *Spanish Baroque* published as long ago as 1931 when certainly such places as the 'sacred gardens' of Bom Jesus, the Santuario dos Remedios at Lamego, or a little gem of architecture such as the granite and white stucco Capela de Falperra, outside Braga, were as unknown, then, as the palace and vin rosé of Mateus, now of world-wide, even 'telly-wide' renown.

But its Elysian landscape apart, and it was acclaimed as such by the Roman legionaries who called the province of Minho the Elysian Fields, it is the huge and deserted nunneries and monasteries of Northern Portugal that are remarkable. To the extent even that they furnish and give character to the landscape as much as do the near-Mexican buildings as background to a good 'Western'.

---

* Information from Mrs Mary Fitton, *cf.* her book *Malaga, the Biography of a City*, London 1971, pp. 103, 104. It should be added that the octagonal *sagrario* at Priego de Córdoba is now attributed to F. X. Pedraxas, 'the last epigone of the school of Hurtado', born in 1736 after Hurtado's death, a singular and posthumous curiosity, or even minor wonder, of interior architecture.

Merely to mention Lorvão in its wooded valley, a Royal nunnery with the bodies of two princesses in silver coffins; Arouca with carved choir stalls for a company of eighty nuns; Pombeiro of the pelmets and golden woodwork; Santo Tirso of the double cloisters, and again extreme fantasy of golden carving; Tibães of the four cloisters, and church with golden pelmets and proscenium arch; near-by, São Frutuoso of the nuns, with gold woodwork, gold pelmets, and a *coro alto* with figures of cherubs holding chains of flowers; and for a conclusion, but there are several others that should be named, São Miguel de Refoios and Refoios de Lima, which pair have the gilt carving that is the Lusitanian equivalent to the stucco fantasies of Italy or of Bavaria. What are beautiful and unexpected in the old convents of Portugal, when we have grown used to the blue and white tile pictures or *azulejos*, are the marvellous wood carving, both gilded and in the natural mahogany or other hardwood, and the organ-cases. These latter form a subject to themselves, of unbelievable fantasy, it being not unusual to find an organ-case upheld by carved figures of mermen or satyrs, irrespective of propriety or purpose. The book on *Portugal* had of course to be printed in lesser number than the book on *Spain* and with fewer illustrations but, then, compared to that other it is decidedly a minor or provincial theme, notwithstanding the Manoelino style which added the Unfinished Chapels to Batalha and doorways with coralline motifs to the abbey of Alcobaça.

Having completed this companion volume to the book on *Spain*, and searching about in my mind for a Northern subject to form a pendant for *The Netherlands*, I thought it would be interesting to see what Denmark had to offer and went there with that intention in the summer of 1953. And here a delay imposed itself which is but another instance of the petty annoyances to which writers and, I think, all artists fall easy victims. An 'author' on the strength of a couple of novels, but I had never heard of him before or since and have now even forgotten his name, who must have known I was going to Denmark, went to the trouble of getting an article accepted in the leading Copenhagen newspaper, a much respected publication, to the effect that my brother and sister and myself were entirely finished as writers and that I was nearing my seventieth year. I was then fifteen years younger than that, was conscious that I was at my poor best as a writer, and so much resented this gratuitous unkindness and injustice that I put away the idea of writing a book on Denmark completely from my mind, and only came back to it after a couple of years, when I found I had enjoyed my experiences so much in retrospect that I could delay no longer. In the result the book was written in three weeks, between 13 July and 9 August 1955. Denmark is not an epic theme, but on a lesser level it has perhaps the most delightful country houses to be found anywhere out of England, only to mention Valdemar Slot and Wedellsborg, or Clausholm in Jutland which is the true castle of the *Sleeping Beauty*, with its stucco ceilings and memories of the 'conscience Queen'; down to other delights, the family portraits by Carl Gustav Pilo, unknown elsewhere; the lay-convents of Vallø and Gisselfeld with the portraits of the prioresses wearing the jewels and diamonds of their Order; the *cottage orné* of Liselund where I thought the dark-eyed Giselle should be waiting for a visit from the Prince of Courland and his daughter Bathilde, 'weary from hunting' as in the old ballet; and the heyducks of the Court of Copenhagen in their 'flower-pot' hats. Such may be bypaths, but they are far from unrewarding. And it may need no more than a notice put up on or near a bypath to turn it into a highway.

These, of course, are cool siesta subjects. As in a sense are those to do with eighteenth-century Austria, or Germany; or they are at any rate temperate, as opposed to semi-tropical or tropical. I wrote of them; and I think it was the first time they had been written of in the English language, in a book published as long ago as 1926. It was not even so long before then that they had begun to be appreciated in their lands of origin.

II

Perhaps the happiest way of willing oneself into siesta thoughts is in recalling the monasteries of Melk and St Florian and Wilhering which are the architectural wonders of the old Holy Roman Empire; the silly adage that it was 'neither Holy, Roman, nor an Empire', being quickly disproved in thinking how long it lasted, how important a part it was of the old Europe, and how easy it was to get oneself killed in fighting for or against it, over the centuries. The monasteries just mentioned are, at least, its monuments; as are the churches and palaces of Prague though imposed upon the Bohemians by an alien nation.

This is perhaps an idle moment to attempt to recall the impression left by Melk and St Florian, but it was certainly that of a lost entity which was the old Holy Roman Empire, no more and no less of an anachronism in its time than was, till so short a time ago, our Indian Empire. The buildings by Lutyens at New Delhi were built seemingly in the same confidence and security of tenure. And they were hardly finished before the transference of power.

Melk and St Florian at least fulfilled their expressed purpose for two centuries or more, and not for a mere twenty years, or less. Their churches apart, the monasteries were an initiation into the splendour of decorated libraries and Kaisersaals, architectural features apparently as indispensable to them as the dining halls to Oxford or Cambridge colleges. What a delight it was – I am thinking of early years between the two World Wars and before the coming of the Nazis – to arrive at some old abbey, Göttweig it could be, of the white stairway and the great urns at the turning of the stair; or Kremsmünster of the five colonnaded fish ponds for trout or carp – presumably – and if so far so good, why not indeed for crayfish? Or Seitenstetten with its unbelievably appropriate set of paintings of monastic subjects by Magnasco in the Abbot's Parlour, a feature one might have dreamed up for oneself in early days of enthusiasm for this rediscovered master.* Or the abbey of Altenburg, far away in the north of Austria and

---

* The painter and collector Italico Brass, whose studio in Venice I used to frequent at about this time next door to the church of the Madonna dell' Orto, with a vine-trellised garden where, he used to say, Titian entertained the Venetian courtesans to supper, had no fewer than fifty paintings by Magnasco in his collection. Most of these he had bought during twenty years before he knew the painter's name.

difficult to get at in those days, with the most splendid of all monastic libraries, wherein, could the ages but slide into each other and stay fixed in time, the monks surely should be reading gourmet menus and the fashion magazines. Even the Totentanz, painted in fresco on the walls and ceiling of the crypt below, makes death less of a disaster among the fountains, spouting dolphins and arabesques of a charnel-house become a set of garden grottoes.

If Austria personified itself in the apricot-espaliered Mirabell Garden at Salzburg; or the little town of Dürnstein on the Danube, where a mere evening stroll in the streets should be enough to convert an unfavourable predisposition into a sudden liking for obelisks and balconies and statues of saints disguised as garden statues, then it is only to be expected that the Bavarians should be more serious-minded even in their frivolity. It is the Teutons living within the boundaries of Germany who will carry an exquisite delicacy to excess. That is the only explanation for their extreme feats of virtuosity, not in architecture *per se* for it was only in interior planning and execution of detail that they excelled. The Danubian monasteries, in contrast, have the nearer influences of Italy upon them. Melk and St Florian are, so to speak, conceived externally, from outside in, as in Italian fashion which first thinks of the façade and then works within that for the interior planning. There is indeed no other fine exterior in Germany, whether of church or palace, after the Residenz at Würzburg; the palaces at Potsdam, marvellous as are their interiors, being pavilion-like structures no more serious of intention than the Amalienburg at Munich of which the destiny was pleasure. It is even difficult to detect a serious purpose behind the workings of their minds which on the evidence of their handiwork were possessed of an ebullient confidence. Their beliefs may have been infantine but full of wonder at being live beings in an improving, not a redundant and dead world.

I believe that no one even in disapproval of its exuberance could set foot within the abbey-church of Rottenbuch and not sense that it is a paean of pleasure at being alive. But it is not easy to see it as a church in the ordinary sense we are used to with pews and prayer books. It has the familiar trappings but with a great many others added; and the overall effect is that of the individual, even the group soul of a number of persons, singing, humming, even dancing. This is something there is not in the world in our time, but of which there is the evidence in other places; and perhaps only in our lifetime among the Balinese. But there were the two strains in these architects and craftsmen; the courtly and the peasant, and on occasion the two combined together. On the one hand J. B. Neumann, architect of the Residenz at Würzburg, was a military engineer of high qualifications; or Count Cuvilliés, page to the Elector in the beginning of his career because of his diminutive height, had shown talent and been sent to Paris to study under Boffrand; and as against this there were those others who were peasants, purely and simply. Or, an instance of the two strains in combination, the brothers Egid Quirin and Cosmas Damian Asam, who were rich peasant-farmers in origin, but had studied in Rome and drunk deep of the skill of Bernini and Borromini. This pair of brothers, like a great many other consummate artists, were considered old-fashioned in their time. They went on working in fact as they had learned when they were young, and between them they could design, build, and entirely decorate a building.* So, too, could the brothers Dominikus and Johann Baptist Zimmermann. While there were others who worked together rather as the *équipe* in a riding school, or, more still, on a French express train, where the menu in the restaurant car is signed by the *chef de brigade* who presents and presides over the meal. It was after this manner that huge affairs like the abbey-churches of Ottobeuren or Zwiefalten were produced, no one person, even be he a Bernini, being capable of such an area of fresco, statuary, and stucco.

There were architects, too, who were nothing else than that. Johann Michael Fischer for instance who built both the aforesaid Ottobeuren and Zwiefalten, and is given credit on his tombstone as being author of thirty-two churches and twenty-two monasteries which is surely beyond possibility of achievement except with this deduction made. He must have been consulted; he must have opposed, or given assent, but he was not responsible in minor details for more than possibly the designs for altars. It is this subordination or derogation of parts that was all-important to the achievement and about which much more should be known. But quite a few of the craftsmen were not highly literate and left little behind them beyond the works of their hands.

We must conceive of them, too, as speaking a wide variety of dialects; a craftsman from Vorarlberg will have had difficulty in making himself understood to a colleague from near-by Wessobrunn, or from villages on the lake of Constance; while we may be fairly certain that if they did not find it easy to converse with each other they will have found it more difficult still to read each other's handwriting. They worked in a world, we must realize, where they themselves and their like could cross indiscriminately from one small principality, or electorate, or bishopric, into another. Their range of activity being from St Peter in the Black Forest, where Peter II Thumb of bucolic appellation built the beautiful library,† – the whole of the Breisgau being curiously one of the hereditary dominions of the Habsburgs and a part of Austria, so that Austrian possessions until 1805 reached to the right bank of the Rhine – into the Swiss Cantons of yet more confusing history with the independent prince-bishoprics of Einsiedeln and St Gallen, both of which I would presume under pain of contradiction to have remained subject to the Holy Roman Empire until the time of Napoleon.

When it is remarked how very bucolic the names of these 'stuccoers and stuccoer-architects' – this awkward phrase in default of a better is borrowed from Dr Russell Hitchcock – we arrive at one of the minor mysteries of aesthetics. I am thinking of Johann Georg Fischer (not the same as Johann Michael Fischer

---

* The Asam brothers were in fact younger by a year or two than the brothers Zimmermann, but the works of the latter, e.g. the Wies church or Steinhausen, seem to belong to another generation, being in fact not late-Baroque but the high zenith of the Rococo. Neither of these paired talents are the worse or the better for this. Both, or, rather, all four of them, are supreme and invincible in their own way.

† Dr Henry Russell Hitchcock in his recent and learnedly entangling *Rococo Architecture in Southern Germany*, London 1968, p. viii, extends the range from a church by the same Peter II Thumb, 'west of the Rhine' at Ebermünster in Alsace, to 'one of J. G. Fischer's less important works across the present Italian border near Merano'.

of the more than fifty churches), Peter II Thumb, the three Schmuzers, as many Feichtmayrs, and Caspar Moosbrugger. It is a state of affairs not far removed from that of, say, villages in Persia or in India that were famous for centuries for carpet weaving, the facility for which remained in certain families. This would seem to have been precisely the case at Wessobrunn, where there was an ancient abbey, near Weilheim in the lake district of Southern Bavaria, and a group of stuccadors (the improved phrase *à l'Espagnole* being due to William Beckford) from at least as early as 1600. In fact, in a sub-alpine, or near sub-alpine landscape of fir-woods, lakes, green meadows, the dahlia, the autumn crocus, and the gentian. And how far is it across the mountains with the speed and rectitude that only a jet-aeroplane could take us, ignoring frontier posts and mountain passes, from Wessobrunn to Lugano in the Ticino? It cannot be much more than a hundred and fifty miles from this Bavarian village to Italian-speaking Switzerland, the other side of the Alps, where was another and more far-reaching trade and tradition of stuccador.* It was travelling stuccadors from the Ticino who made the plaster ceilings in the houses by Daniel Marot at The Hague; in the Danish Castles; in the Russian monasteries outside Moscow; and in old houses at Dublin before the Irish bred their own generations of craftsmen. In all humility, coming from a family of writers and poets, I do not find this ease of expression at all difficult to understand.

But the craft of stuccoist has to be associated as well with that of wood carving which is traditional in mountain regions. It is in essence the world of the cuckoo-clock, the châlet and the decorated *presepio* or Christmas crib. Are not the present-day Swiss the watch- and clock-makers of the world? And it is from just this world of precision-craftsmen that the brothers Zimmermann had their origin; in just the way, we could say, in which good musicians, painters, writers, are often the children of amateur or indifferent talents in the same profession. The brothers Dominikus and Johann Baptist Zimmermann, respectively, from stuccador turned architect, and from stuccador became frescoist, which on results seems to have come as easily to them as from cooking roasts to becoming specialist in sweets or ices. But the stuccoist has of course to be able to draw and prepare his designs.

Yet another minor mystery connected with this extraordinary blossoming of the arts in Southern Germany is that, just as in parallel instances in Tuscany or in Venice during their florescence, every detail had to be in accordance and obedience to most stringent instructions by the council of elders, or governing body, expressed in terms which left no latitude at all to the imagination. The craftsmen worked to a full, or overfull libretto, and it did not hinder them. What body in our day, we must ask, corporate, municipal, or private, would dare essay this with an abstract sculptor? But projects have to be judged by their results; and implicit belief in the mythology by which they had been surrounded since childhood, must have enjoyed, and had certainly never questioned, was productive of such paeans and dithyrambs of praise as the aforementioned Rottenbuch, which it is hard to believe was an older foundation altered and transformed by the Schmuzers within

---

* Franz Anton Bustelli, the modeller of Nymphenburg porcelain, was a native of Lugano. Borromini, also, came from the Ticino.

the existing mediaeval shell. The confidence and rationalized gaiety, admitting of no fears or misgivings but only intent on proving and revelling in its powers, are still more remarkable in the Wies church where at least Johann Baptist, one of the brothers Zimmermann, was of more sophisticated kind.* He had worked on the transcendent decoration of the Amalienburg and, we may think, long lost or transcended his rich peasant origin; these two, the Wies church and the blue and silver room of the Amalienburg, being in all certainty the most beautiful Rococo interiors in the world.

If Rottenbuch is by contrast Arcadian, in the sense of portraying a bucolic happiness and state of being which are nearly beyond comprehension to our troubled and tormented days, then, again, it is a therapeutic experience only to enter another work by the Zimmermanns, the oval pilgrimage church at Steinhausen. The mere ease and fluency in handling are enough to exacerbate some tastes, as compared to a world where all the arts are groping in different directions and there is nothing but experiment with no achieved result. Or we may take Peter II Thumb once more, this time at Birnau on the shore above Lake Constance, where the interior is predominantly white with pale rose and blue marbling in the balcony railing and the altars. Results of this order in eighteenth-century Germany are composite, we repeat, and it is the *équipe* or staff of assistants who should share the credit. As much so as with a finished print by Hokusai or Utamaro where the craftsman who cut the design on the blocks of cherry wood, others who printed it in colour, worked in with the artist, and it could be said, prompted and produced his personality; in just the way that the gag-makers and attendant wits help to effect the finished image of a film comedian like Bob Hope.

At Birnau, this other of the Rococo church-theatres with participant audience, the craftsman-in-chief was a member of the Feichtmayr family,† in whom amiable fantasy ran to the *Honigschlecker*, a statue of a cupid holding a beehive and licking his finger. It indeed expresses the spirit and intention of Birnau where, as I have written, 'the light-heartedness is continued into the painted ceiling, for standing in the right place on the floor you can look up into a piece of mirror in the hand of one of the angels and see yourself in heaven'. At the end of it all, for better or worse, this delightful interior is almost indistinguishable from that of the library – the white-statued library with winding gallery just as at Birnau by the same Peter

---

* Dominikus Zimmermann, the elder brother, appears to have been barely literate and to have had difficulty in preparing and measuring up his drawings. Not the least beautiful things to be seen in Southern Germany are the transformations of mediaeval churches, as at Rottenbuch, into large-scale oratories, or, even, they could be called sacred drawing-rooms or ball-rooms. Other examples that could be cited are Ochsenhausen, Schussenried, and Berg Andechs.

† Family of Feichtmayr (Faichtmair, Feichtmeier, Feichtmayer, Feuchtmair, Feuchtmayer) – what confusion! – of whom, according to Thieme-Becker, there were seventeen families documented in the parish of Wessobrunn. The *Honigschlecker*, at Birnau, is by Joseph Anton F. 1696–1770 – as you like it! – though the greatest artist in the family is considered to be Johann Michael II, 1709–72, on whom there is a monograph (1935) by E. Petri. There is also a monograph (1948) by Wilhelm Boeck on Joseph Anton F. I am indebted for this footnote to Mr Michael Raeburn.

II Thumb, with china-like figures standing on pedestals outside its balcony – this of St Peter's in the Black Forest, a monastic library which is not the less rewarding for being miles away from the part of Germany in which you look for such things, and which has therefore the added interest of remoteness.

There are fifteen or eighteen, or thereabouts, masterpieces of the Rococo in Bavaria and Franconia, named here in a footnote as the panacea they offer is not yet fully recognized and known.* Of course the names are confusing; but no more so, once attuned, than any others. In the aggregate they are a comfort and a reassurance in this wavering, or even quaking world of population explosions, and the threat of atomic bombs. They are an excuse for forgetting for a little and not asking questions for which we will never know the answers. On the evidence of their handiwork these architects and craftsmen were pleased and not sorry to be alive. It is such a little time ago in history and it can never come back again. A last message, therefore, but with contemporary if unconscious support of the greatest musicians there have ever been; in the greatest of whom the fundamental truths are expressed, or even proved arithmetically, but in mathematics clothed naturally and disguised as poetry. The architectural works just discussed, whether bucolic or Arcadian and the work of village masters, or more sophisticated and of access to Electoral and big-wigg'd Archiepiscopal presence, are, alike, non-faltering and self-confident. How much we must envy them! No longer obsessed with death and damnation, which are our self-same terrors only we are earthbound with no hope beyond the grave or plastic urn, they sing the praises of having been born into the living world. A world improved and tended by human skill which, it is true, is only possible with small numbers. That is the beauty and the tragedy of it; that it came before the swarming and the symbolic traffic jams. Now it is growing late and may not come again.

I would like to think I have done something, however little, towards the appreciation of these beautiful things. At the time I began to admire them they had not been studied for longer than a decade or so even in their lands of origin. Probably it was the opera of *Der Rosenkavalier*, joint production of von Hofmannsthal and Richard Strauss in 1911, that marked the real beginning of this new interest. But it is certain that hardly a single individual attending and applauding this opera in its pre-1914 War production in London would have known the names of the Asam brothers or the brothers Zimmermann. But, then, even to a sophisticated audience, not more than a handful, say, half-a-dozen at most, of Mozart's fifteen or so mature piano-concertos will have been known, in contrast to the huge audience now familiar with the whole lot of them, thanks to

* They are: Vierzehnheiligen and the Court Chapel of Würzburg by J. B. Neumann; Rohr and Weltenburg and the Asam Chapel (St Johann Nepomuk) in Munich, which are the most complete works by the brothers Asam; Osterhofen, Diesen, Rott-am-Inn, and the incomparable pair of abbeys, Ottobeuren and Zwiefalten, by J. M. Fischer; Wolfegg and Maria Steinbach by J. G. Fischer; Birnau, on Lake Constance, and the church and library of St Gallen in Switzerland by Peter II Thumb; and the library at Wiblingen, and the churches of Die Wies, Steinhausen and Günzburg by Johann Baptist and Dominikus Zimmermann. It is out of question to enumerate here the craftsmen who contributed to the achieved results.

the gramophone and radio, and awake therefore to some of the same delights that await them in this architecture.

NOTE

The lesser and more out-of-the-way examples of this art are not yet appreciated even in their land of origin, and are seldom to be seen in illustration; except perhaps for the Fisherman's Pulpit at Traunkirchen, on the lakeside near Gmunden, in Lower Austria. The two fishermen with their oars at bow and stern, the stalactitic pulpit-base, and dripping, golden fishing nets are beautiful indeed, in their bucolic sophistication. Much less known is the ship-pulpit at Irsee, near Kaufbeuren, where sermons were preached from a ship's bow with cupids on a rope ladder, raising the mainsail and busy in the rigging. Other ship-pulpits are reported from Altenerding and Niederling, a pair of villages not far from Munich. There is a pulpit amounting to a major sensation at Amorbach in Franconia, a wooden affair, half-balcony, half-state coach, with glittering canopy and long approaching stair, by J. W. von der Auwera, a sculptor born in Würzburg, and Beardsley-like of fantasy. Other notable pulpits are to be seen at Diessen, by J. B. Straub, the sculptor of many superb altars; with the twin pulpits at Maria Steinbach, near Memmingen; and at Mödingen, near Dillingen. Most notable of all are the pulpit at Ottobeuren which appears, literally, to be floating on the clouds; the pulpit at Vierzehnheiligen where the sounding-board is replaced by seven clusters of rays representing the seven gifts of the Holy Ghost; and the pulpit by Dominikus Zimmermann at Die Wies which interprets the theme of the Pentecostal Storm accompanying the Holy Spirit.

Much fantasy was expended upon organ-cases as well as pulpits; there are splendidly decorative examples, not so miniature temples of music in themselves, at Melk and St Florian and at Herzogenburg in Austria; and, as well, at Ottobeuren and Neresheim and Weingarten in Germany. Those in the grander churches are to be expected; but, also, there is the uniquely beautiful organ at Roggenburg, a small village not far from Günzburg; and a most fanciful organ-case, all stairs and balconies and cupids playing instruments, at the monastery church of Ochsenhausen, near Memmingen. These, lesser, pulpits, organ-cases, and so forth, are equivalent to the minor mediaeval wonders to be found in village churches all over England, cf. Orgel in Alter Welt: Organs of the World, by Walther Haache in Die Blauen Bücher series, 1965, in which the splendid, artillery-salvoing Spanish organs with horizontal organ-pipes pointing their broadsides laterally, instead of upwards, are well illustrated and also a surprising number of fine organ-cases in Poland and Silesia but, curiously, only one from Portugal, ignoring perhaps the most glorious specimens in all Europe, from the pair of huge organs upheld by tritons, dolphins and mermen in the Cathedral at Braga, in Northern Portugal, to others at Amarante, at N.S. do Porto de Ave, at Arouca, and the pair of portable organs in the Convent of Jesus at Aveiro.

Tierra Caliente

I

I have lived to see an appreciation of interest in widely different fields of knowledge that is extraordinary and beyond precedent. It is indeed astonishing to me to realize that when I wrote of Taxco in 1922, choosing that place for finale of the chapter on Mexico in *Southern Baroque Art*, my first prose work, the little town was still three days' ride from Mexico City over the stormy mountains of the state of Guerrero. For now with its lovely church, *chef d'oeuvre* of *le style Mexicain*, universally admired and the steep cobbled streets and silver shops swarming with visitors, Taxco is distant from Mexico City rather less than two hours on a motor-road. Little, if anything, had been written of the beauties of Mexico since Madame Calderon de la Barca's *Life in Mexico* (1861), even if inspiration could be found in the photographs in Sylvester Baxter's *Spanish Colonial Architecture* published in 1901.*

In Mexico, where the capital has trebled in population since I first remember it, the talk is now of a ten-thousand bedroom hotel in Acapulco, foretaste, it is only too probable, and for wider application, of worse things to come. And the shiploads coming down daily out of the clouds, with only a hornet's stinging note, but rising into a frightening stream of warning! And the dragon-fly disgorges through a vent or old wound in its belly, some of the passengers already wearing funny hats bought at the airport before embarkation. They are on holiday and have reached the 'fun-belt'. And now the next thing to do is to make friends with the barman. In half-an-hour the hotel is as though a flight of parrots had alighted in it. Would this be so, were they Latins or Slavs who had pullulated and filled the waste spaces of the New World? That is another question, and one which it is too soon to answer. Probably it is the mixture of races in the United States that has produced the parrot voices; that, plus the air and water.

But let us try to essay our arrival by sea at Acapulco.† My father, whose posthumous fame as an eccentric has obscured and distorted his true stature, said to me, prophetically, more than once, 'the last rich people in the world will have a wonderful time'. And he was right. They have had, and are still having it, if you know where to look for them.

So, then, the coast has been in view since early morning, and shortly we will be coming in to land. I was up on deck soon after seven o'clock, remembering the passage in Stephens' *Incidents of Travel in Central America, Chiapas and Yucatán* (1841), where he describes sailing along this coast and seeing nine smoking volcanoes at the same time. Or have I imagined this? Perhaps we passed them during the night for there is not a volcano in sight.

---

* D. H. Lawrence's *Mornings in Mexico* and *The Plumed Serpent* appeared, respectively, in 1927 and 1933.

† The first motor-car reached Acapulco as late as 1927, up to which time it took a week to get there from Mexico City.

It seems to get hotter every mile we move in nearer to shore. And now there is the rush and excitement of a two-weeks' voyage which took us through the Panama Canal coming to an end, for those of us at least who disembark here since the ship goes on half across the world to Sydney. It has been a long morning. A hurried luncheon is served, an hour earlier than usual, with the dining-room stewards, Goans and Britons alike, seemingly careless of whether they get a parting tip or not. Yet, last night, all were smiling and in good humour. Probably they disliked every passenger indiscriminately all the time from the start, and were merely pretending to be polite and obliging. Now, they only want to see the last of us. That has been it all along. Past the Canaries, first landfall since leaving England; to Fort Lauderdale and its performing dolphins; Bermuda and its pink houses and bougainvillea; and after a day and night, turn right into the Canal to Panama, where we landed, but could not reach the city because of the last day of Carnival and the huge crowds. I was sorry to miss the cathedral at Panama with its pearl shell windows, as, also, 'the cocktail of tropical fruits' at the Panama Hilton, and had to be content with the carnival floats and a single street of old houses with projecting balconies.

And now on deck again for a last hour while a magnificent bay slowly and gradually opens before us, the bay of the galleons and galeots, caravels or carabelos from Manila and China and the lacquered Indies. A bay as splendid as the Bay of Naples, the siren city and Parthenopaean shore, and only lacking one thing, a Vesuvius or a Fujiyama. Wanting in that, but entirely different, and growing more sensational at every moment as we come in nearer to shore by an island – or is it only a promontory? – that gets in the way and hides the view, but now sinks into the distance and we see the buildings. Which, viewed from here, consist only of houses and huge hotels; no streets and nothing of a port or harbour town. With a low white building on top of a cliff on the left hand, as we come in, that must be the night club where 'Indians' jump, lit torch in hand, from a hundred feet and more into the Pacific Ocean to entertain the diners.

And now other huge buildings which are more hotels at the far end of the town come into sight. Just as a diminutive tug appears and the pilot climbs aboard. The crew of the tug, more 'Indian' than Spanish, gazing sullenly up at us as though they resented our arrival. Next, gold-braided officials come up the rope-ladder from a motor-boat and we queue up to show our passports. And now we go ashore with our luggage in a pinnace through blinding heat, and it is the last we see of the ship's crew.

We have arrived. And are in the customs shed trying to pick out our suitcases and to persuade a young woman of mixed blood, who is like a too heavily 'made up' college girl, to pass our luggage, but she opens everything out of feminine curiosity, as the result of which one suitcase is left behind in the turmoil and I have to come back later, despairingly, but succeed in finding it. And into the furnace of heat outside, and off in a taxi to the hotel. Where we find a message to say that acquaintances for whom we have a letter, were waiting at the wrong pier, and will be coming round to fetch us in the middle of the afternoon.

And what a fruit market just next to the hotel! Every known and unknown fruit of the semi-tropics, and as it is impossible to remember them all I write down some names. From bananas, pineapples, lemons, oranges and limes, and every sort and variety of citrus fruit, to papayas, pomegranates, pitahayas, rose-apples, persimmons and caimitas or star-apples, mamayas, guavas, coconuts and mangoes. These, and as well, guanabanas, granadillas, zapotes, tamarinds and zapatillos, chirimoyas, aguacates and chicozapotes; not all of them we may be certain, as alluring or good of taste as their delicious-sounding names. Indeed, some few of the last of these, as you read of them, turn a little astringent, or too relaxing and deliquescent on the tongue.

The fish market and flower market, near by, are no less tropically abundant. The houses may be shabby and the streets dirty, but what sceptres or clustered heads of tuberoses! What rods or thyrsuses of lilies, only to think of lilies! We are in a country, we must remember, where the 'Indians' – but they are not Indians at all, and there is still no other name for them, they are, after all, the true Americans – sell gardenias that are lying in little crates of split bamboo at the wayside railway stations; gardenias in their macerated or softened ivory being the mere cowslips or buttercups of the *tierra caliente*. I say rods or thyrsi, even thyrsuses of lilies, but what would it be if the new age of the lily came true and the 'Indians' grew, not the ordinary lily, but the lily hybrids! It would be easy to write of this were they not named so stupidly, a fault that could be remedied by looking at any flower list of the seventeenth or eighteenth centuries and adapting and improving upon the old French, or Dutch, or English names for their carnations, auriculas, or tulips.

And what an intoxication there could be from the green or chartreuse-yellow of the skin or integument of the new lilies; their trumpets of rose-pink with frost of silver on the lily flesh; pendant, datura-like trumpets of canary-yellow with green throats, spotted black; others with glistening maroon deep in the flower-throat; the candelabra lilies with a dozen or more flowers on long stalks or pedicules; the striped in their newer forms with broad bands of gold and crimson on their petals; or the golden-rayed and crimson-spotted hill-lilies which are, and have been so since the sixteenth century, as can be seen on the embroidered robes of actors in Nōh plays in Japan, not less than living trees of lilies! The martagons, and the tigered and the leopard lilies! One could be made perfectly dazed and drunk with lilies!

To all of which there is the flowering accompaniment of the sub-tropics, flowering trees, some native, others imported; as the crimson or vermilion, tasselled and flanged petals of the flamboyant or Delonix Regia of Rajput India, as I see it in my mind because, although Caribbean of origin, 'there is hardly a tropical city or town park or formal garden without at least one specimen', but in my limited experience of the tropics and sub-tropics it seems particularly suited to the bare hills and marble forts of Rajputana; or, again, the scarlet and yellow cockscombs of Amherstia nobilis or Pride of Burma, by general consent, but not to personal agreement, the most lovely of all flowering trees.

I think there need be no hesitation in mentioning the Amherstia or other of these flowering trees more than once, as both in the Indies and in Central America, because they are now distributed far from their country of origin, have to that extent changed the look of their lands of adoption, and the natural flora is by now so muddled through foreign importation that these flowering trees have to be taken as found where in fact they are adding something which was not there in the first place. In fact, I think the flamboyant, known, too, as *arból de fuego* or fire tree, the *pata de león* or lion foot, the poinciana, and the *guacamaya* or golden mohur tree, to be altogether too vermilion or scarlet of effect, as of the scarlet uniforms of the Viceroy's Lancer Bodyguard showing against the pink sandstone domes and white marble inlay of Moghul India; while the long pendant racemes of the Amherstia with its sepals which are of the same red as the flower, even with its butterfly-winged and gold-tipped upper petals, too nearly resemble the fuchsias of the flower-pot and conservatory to be given the highest award for beauty. This said, having time and time again expressed admiration for the jacaranda which is of another order from the strident clarions and trumpet calls of the Amherstia and the flamboyant.

But there are the other flowering trees; the lagerstroemia, opening rose-pink in the dog-rose dawn, but darkening until by evening its cloak of roses has become purple as a bower of lilac; the yellow-flowering poui, giant of the tropics, which sometimes 'in virgin stands', grows, stem and crown together, for two hundred feet, 'its vast dome of foliage rising above the other flowering trees as a domed cathedral above the other buildings in a city', a tree of sulphur-yellow daffodils growing in clusters, but scentless; and the smaller pink poui or Tabebuia pentaphylla, only less sensational in flowering because it reaches to no more than seventy or eighty feet. There is the deep purple bauhinia or orchid tree, with its sub-variety which bears pure white orchids; the 'Rose of Venezuela', of composite inflorescence like a rhododendron; and another personal favourite, Spathodea campanulata or the African tulip tree, first sighted in the log-book of a trader out of Truro, Massachusetts, in 1723, who 'watched for the mouth of the bight between two sand bars, with a small hill to port growing trees with bright red flowers at their tops', which feature is characteristic of its growth. A tree with habitat between the Congo and Uganda, whence its local name of *bâton du sorcier* or *bwele ba bango*, for its timbers provide, alike, the wand of the witch doctor and the wooden war drums. Such are, or could be the gardens of the last rich men and women of the yachts and the executive aeroplanes. For it will not continue; or not further than the turn of this century.

Coming here by sea could be like setting foot on a new continent and arriving somewhere one has never been before. But, sadly, 'the beautiful people' are here already. And now tours are being laid on from twelve of the biggest American cities; and they in their turn will have to leave soon and look for somewhere else to go. We are taken to the new Acapulco Hilton with water-tank, as ever, on the roof, a functioning part of the modern building, as it might be, the bladder or urinary tract, which it is impossible to mask or conceal; elevator in a spinal column rising from top to bottom of the hotel and green-lit at night; cement ramps of identical rooms, all air-conditioned, with balconies; and it should be said, a row of shops on the ground floor which has more to offer than the usual international arts of the airport. But this is because the minor arts still flourish in Mexico, or were flowering until lately, as witness the shawls, or *sarapes* dyed with the cochineal beetle that still come in diminishing number from Oaxaca. But neither is it to be denied that the restaurant of the Hilton, on an artificial island with a serpentine swimming-pool around it, is remarkable and the herald of an age that has turned its back for ever on Italy as mother of the arts.

An age that has come via the Bauhaus and Mies van der Rohe, and the more sophisticated buildings of New York and Chicago, to rest on the Pacific and the Caribbean, not without innate, if unconscious influence of the native Mayan or other temples and their towering shapes recovered from the jungle, this being after all the 'classical' of the New World; and which with lessons learned from the Katsura Detached Palace, 'the most modern of all old buildings anywhere in the world' and the raked sand and rocks of Ryuanji and other Zen gardens of Kyoto, adds up to a civilization that is anything but Mediterranean by implication. But, rather, it tends to be of the Pacific seaboard, in extension to the Australian continent and embracing some of the Pacific Islands, with Japan or the Philippines for its far shore. Even 'Trader Vic' with his genial invention of a Polynesian cuisine that never had existence, with addition of dishes from Canton and Shanghai and repertoire of 'pirate' drinks of rum, makes a contribution to this new mythology. It is a plutocracy that can plan and afford to pay for these long journeys with its rich men richer than rich men have ever been before. Richer, but it could be, also, in greater danger. A vertical danger, in depth, and coming up on them from below.

And, besides, the pocket air-tour has arrived to spoil it all. Here, on the Pacific shore where the sunsets are unimaginable, the huge breakers roll in out of the distance; it is indeed the sharp edge or declivity of the West into the sea, and there is nothing but thousands of miles of ocean between ourselves and the never ending, if intermittent, illusion of the rising sun.

The problem is where to go from here, and the answer is farther up the coast. Of which till this present time there is still plenty and to spare, perhaps to the extent of a thousand miles or more. In the state of Nayarit, for instance, where the vegetation is richer than in the Antilles or Polynesia. But even now it is not easy to find written accounts, or meet anyone who has been there. I have found mention of 'rose-pink or flamingo-coloured villages'; and of an island on an inland lake with Korean-looking fishermen who have goatee beards, and Mongolian-looking women. Another writer tells of 'sky-blue churches with white lines or friezes, where the shadows are lilac-mauve'; and in another district, of 'rose or beige-coloured churches with violet-coloured domes'.

When I was in Mexico as lately as 1952 no one seemed to know anything for certain of the country – even round Puebla. Churches outside the town itself like San Francisco Acatepec with a tiled façade and tiles that spiral round its belfry and 'twist themselves into shiny blue columns like a field in summer sprigged with flowers',* was scarcely heard of. There was talk of a church with an interior

---

* Quoted from *Viceroyalties of the West*, by Roderick Cameron, London 1968; as also, the recipe from the nuns of Oaxaca on my page 108.

painted 'by the Indians' with flowers, probably at Tlacochahuaya, the mere appellation being a part of the fascination, but no one knew its name; or pronounced, or had ever heard of the other tiled village churches of Santa Maria Tonantzintla, or San Bernardino Tlaxcalalcingo. But back to the upper reaches of the coast where in the coffee-lanes you may pass 'cartloads of gardenias', where the women 'who are like Cantonese girls', wear 'huipils of cadmium red'; and in the hibiscus gardens the wings of the humming-birds make a soft murmur, and you may reach out and touch them with your hands.

But it is not all so soft and gentle as that. We are nearing the cactus lands, the limitless desert or wilderness of the cacti, 'where the *saguaros* stand upright like phantoms, their spectral arms stretched wide open, and tufts of hair in their armpits', as though effigies of elemental beings, not human, and studded with holes which are the nests of woodpeckers. Spectres that are fifty foot tall, full grown are five times as old as that, and formed of a cylindrical core of rods with vegetative power of blossoming, and with spine clusters in their flutings. Spectres with flower faces but no heads, their trunks rising like periscopes or organ-pipes in every direction, and all but ready to walk to each other. Or, as with an octopus, does a limb break off and cross the desert-bed to fertilize the female?

Arriving at a cactus that is like a mummy wrapped in a cocoon, neatly wound round, and flowering from its side in a cradle of its own felt; giants thirty and forty feet high, shining white in the sun; statues in long fleeces standing on the hills, or down the hot slopes of canyons, with shaggy crowns of their long white hair; not plants, but columns or statues to shepherd-caciques, and cotton-quilted kings? Cactuses that are as vegetable hills with wavy ridges dividing their ravines, and but few spikes; the body marked as though with sheep-tracks, or covered entirely in a tangle of long hair, with flowers emerging from their tufted crowns that could be old craters of volcanoes.

Flowers of another world, or not flowers at all; all, or nearly all of them from Mexico, from a different world of human beings with no communication, as separate as upon another star; artificially-deformed skulls and cross-eyes being their cynosure of human admiration. And yet the habitat of the humming-birds for which the Spanish 'picaflores' is the more lovely name; of the painted trogon in all its kinds; and the glorious quetzal bird trailing its green mantle.

To which the night cactus is only paragon, the blue cereus for a beginning, in flower on its ribbon-stem of electric blue, of same voltage as the electric flash of the blue lizards on the Faraglioni, facing south in the Tyrrhenian from Capri towards the Siren Isles; or the green cereus of greenish light as though from green grottoes in the sea upon that same goat-island; or another cereus of different habit for when it opens, and it can be watched opening by jerks and starts soon after sundown on a hot night, its rayed and pointed petals are as a rocket-burst at its greatest circumference before the rocket fades; the night-blooming cereus filling the night sky, every blossom of it, but only as a hood or protection for the night-scent, and for the protruding stamens of the cereus that come pouring from the throat of the flower, moon-pale, and like a rocket within a rocket. The moon-cerei being on thin stems, and climbing vine-like into the trees, the better to attract the moths their ghostly partners who come by night to fertilize them.

It would be difficult for anyone seeing them for the first time to forget the organ-cactus, simplicissimus of its kind, growing along the road between Acapulco and Cuernavaca. But this is a land in which alike to the trained and the untrained eye almost everything is extraordinary. And only now is notice, and as yet not too much notice, being taken of it. At the time I am thinking of, which is no more than twelve to fifteen years ago, there was entire conjecture and no precise knowledge as to what might be no more than a very few miles away, as with that interior of a church painted by the 'Indians' with bunches and festoons of flowers.

The only parallel situation to this in my own experience being at about the same time in Portugal where the 'port wine' families of English descent who had lived for generations round Oporto would talk, mystifyingly, of villages with strange-looking fishing boats up and down the Atlantic coast. The sardine boats of Nazaré with Phoenician-looking, goat-faced fishermen in their tartan shirts were, then, barely 'discovered'. As for the *esguichos* or the *moliceiros* of Aveiro, the first craft being like a sickle or a half-moon fishing boat, and the other swan-necked and used by the weed-gatherers and salt-collectors of the lagoons; or the fishing boats of Caparica that I saw, one day in the summer mist, riding like huge half-moons on the water, or drawn up tiered on the sands of the Setúbal peninsula opposite Lisbon, there was entire ignorance and no one even spoke of them. No one had heard of them, which happy time is now ended. But I have to add within this context that in the twenties people had all the sensations of 'discovering' for themselves villages in Wiltshire that appeared to be 'unknown' except to the vicar and the local squire – in other counties of England, as well, in Somerset and Dorset, and in the Cotswolds, but, as I remember, especially in Wiltshire. Perhaps it was the publication of *The Highways and Byways* series, from 1902 on no fewer than thirteen of them, with beautiful pencil drawings by F. L. Griggs, that started and sustained these innocent explorations.

11 VILLAS, VILLAS

Villas everywhere there is room for them, each with its own bathing-pool; implying a condition of euphoria and well-being that may have begun with gold-plated bath-taps and an ivory and gold telephone in the executive suite, and will end with a Renoir on the cocktail cabinet over the shelf of swizzle-sticks and the little flags. Renoirs, we all know, having become a form of currency that steadily increases in value, although he painted a total of twelve thousand pictures; and no wonder the crowds applaud now at public auctions, and the auctions have become 'pay-parties'. Wouldn't you applaud if you knew that something you could take down off your wall and send to auction any day you pleased was going up and up in value? It is you, the Renoir-owners, who are bidding and sending up the value of your own possessions all the time!

Most of these resorts are basically the same, but this is different and not just because of the 'Indians' coming round to sell orchids of the tropical forests from door to door. It is not only that a snow-capp'd volcano with a name like several explosions going off at the same moment hangs up there in the sky while you drink your breakfast coffee and eat fresh mangoes or papayas. That after all could be the enlargement of a coloured postcard, like the 'blown up' photograph on the end walls of offices and restaurants. There is more to it than the hedges of hibiscus and the flowering trees.

But these things have not made the slightest difference to those who live near by them. The notion that anyone at all, almost, is 'changed' by an object as beautiful as a jacaranda tree in full flower is too ridiculous to be taken seriously. For jacarandas, if you have not seen one before, are enough to take the breath away. They are blue trees, we know, and that they 'turn blue' in a night when they come into flower. But, in fact, blue does not describe them. The blossoms, which are the size of a snapdragon, are heliotrope, blue pastel, blue powder-blue; with the hush or gasp remembered of first seeing a blue flowering tree.

But, we say, they have not altered or made the slightest difference to those who live near by them. There are clouds overhead all day, and dawn and sunset, and they make no difference. It should after all be a sensation to arrive in a country where green parrots are flying about at liberty; where brilliant humming-birds are whirring and hovering at the red hibiscus, but we remain the same. Of course the parrots here are not as the green parrots I first saw at Agra, where they rose out of the branches in Kipling's phrase 'like a burst of green shrapnel'. That is another story. What do they mean to the Indians? They mean no more to them than the sparrows to ourselves; or the London pigeons. Does the West Indian porter at Paddington still marvel at the diesel engine that draws the train? More likely he hated it from the moment he first set eyes on it.

It is the same sensation here as everywhere else. The 'Indians' are starting to swarm. And one could say, the Americans, likewise, who arrive out of the sky a shipload at a time. What city in the modern world most resembles a parrot-house? And the answer is either New York or Chicago. There the polyglot has been melted down into an amalgam. And the resulting effect? Is it English, that is to say, Anglo-Saxon? Most certainly not. Or German? No. Or Italian? No. Perhaps having been Dutch for a considerable part of the seventeenth century, it still keeps some little aura of Holland. The grid-iron plan of New York, and even its old 'brownstone' houses are more Dutch than English. And the New Amsterdam, like the old, was a city of refugees where Dutch was not the only language. But the truer analogy is to Byzantium in its thousand years from Justinian until it was conquered by the Turks. Certainly it has nothing of the Byzantine tortuousness and slowness; but there is its geographical situation as the capital of the New World facing the Old World, and only comparable to Constantinople as the meeting place of East and West, of Europe and all Asia. That was Roman of intention, Hellenic by tongue; but much of Oriental Greek, of Armenian, even of Persian had crept in for it lies opposite and less than a few hundred yards from Asia. And, as inevitable as this, and unlikely as it may seem, New York has still something of the native 'Indian' about it, added to everything else of Central European, and of every other nation of East and West and of the dark, dark South.

The skyscraper is endemic to the scene with wigwam for direct ancestor at both New York and Chicago. Did never a medicine-man of the 'Indians' see the skyline of the one, or the glass towers of the latter city, in the smoke-cloud of his divination? One must be unwilling to believe there has been no prophecy. Are not towers of glass built in part for the noise they will make in tumbling? As motor-cars and railway-engines to collide with each other; and aeroplanes to fall down out of a clear sky? The dread is even part of the compelling ambition and the desire. One day, one night perhaps, their makers must hear the noise and enjoy the havoc. There are all the probabilities of upheaval from below. When drugs have sapped the vitality of how high a percentage of their youth? When there is burning hatred in the black ghettoes? When no one, male or female, can walk the streets at night in safety! And public parks are more dangerous than the forest or the jungle! All of which is true and factual here and now! The first stage, or launching of the capsule away from its parent body of old beliefs and conventions, having taken place already with objective nothing, or, in fact, the lunar emptiness from which to look back and see the home they've left behind them.

As soon as human beings are collected together in millions in their cities and can be destroyed a hundred thousand, or even a quarter of a million at a time, we know that their towns are not worth destroying. By the same token it was enough to read a year or two ago that the Chinese had set themselves a target of twelve million more Chinamen every year to know that numbers do not matter and only the individual is of any moment.

Numbers are nothing; or an aircraft-carrier would be a greater work of art than the Parthenon.

That is to think in terms of money, of what money can produce.

Yet extravagance pays big dividends, to the bankrupt's heirs. After Chartres Cathedral, Versailles which ruined the French monarchy is the greatest monument of France.

The arts move almost in inverse ratio to the increase in population. We have only to think of the Greek cities in contrast to the Roman Empire. No one who has seen a Greek temple will admire again a Roman circus or triumphal arch.

Once Italy, the most fertile soil for genius in the arts, was united, it produced not a single painter, writer, or musician of note. Germany, united in almost the same year into the German Empire, effected nothing.*

The most certain thing is that India with a population of more than four hundred millions, and China with nearly double that number of millions, will produce scarcely an individual of genius between them.

All the nations of Asia united will produce nothing.

Having stung and paralysed the coloured races over centuries, as in the wars of the insects, as in the eternal battle between the spider and the fly, they are beginning to revenge themselves upon us.

In North America all the black men who have the ability to do so leave the cotton swamps; they move up from the south to darken Pittsburgh and Chicago.

And the 'pale face' nations withdraw into themselves, draw in their claws.

* Verdi, Puccini, Toscanini, d'Annunzio, were all born before 1870, as was Richard Strauss.

Wanting all their fortune for themselves with none to spare for others. Bringing back their armies, the unwilling or half-willing legions; for to lay down your life for NATO is as uninspiring a trumpet-call to duty as would be the Thames Gas Board. Calling in the ships, leaving the airs unflown as they were before. Which return can only spread the disaffection, and they will infect each other until all have caught it. A virus that attacks again and nags and stabs its victims, and no stratum of the population is immune from it. Or immunity spells entire apathy and impotence. Which is the moment when the hordes of Tartary will move in and swarm across the small world of all that matters, and a few sealed railway trains will do the rest. It would only require a team of trained experts to organize this exodus; an exercise of the same technique that in miniature emptied the intelligentsia from the three Baltic mini-republics of Esthonia, Latvia, and Lithuania; as it could be, one day, East Anglia, New England, or California. A snake has been known to swallow and digest a deer, or other animal much bulkier and weighing heavier than itself. We must not think we cannot be devoured and eaten by a body smaller than ourselves; and when it comes to a body more than five times our size! Or there are fights between animals when both beasts are killed; and of the two alternatives we may ask ourselves which is the more probable!

The sanity lies in the smaller nations if they are permitted to live on. It all depends on the individual, and what the individual would want his life to be. There are the many who are contented with the football pool and the 'telly'. To whom crime reports are the salt and pepper, or the HP sauce upon the fish fingers, or the fish and chips. For, and on behalf of whom, these pages are not intended. But there are more and more tens of thousands of persons who will not be herded. Who know they only live once, and want to enjoy the wonder and beauty of the living world.

Which, all said and done, need cost no more than a paperback edition, or according to inclination, be of no more physical effort than the turning of a knob – and a knob on that same receiving instrument or mechanism that opens the flood gates to ignorance and vulgarity. An aerial on the roofs of nine houses out of ten, but it is the one in a hundred who is worth considering. It could be one house only in a red brick suburb, and perhaps one person in a family against the wishes of the others, who is not content with what is given him, and knows he has only to ask for more and he will get it. But it must not be made too easy. Some degree of opposition is needed, or there is no incentive.

There are degrees in appreciation for which the facilities are now more universal than they have ever been before. A choice from twelve thousand photographs taken over a period of fifteen years in a book on the great sculptor of our time, but not even a snapshot of Mozart or of Keats. That is the pity. There are those who have left their genius with us, but who are gone entirely in their persons.

There can come satiety from over-documentation. And of the greater fame of all, the less said the better, of which the eternal proof lies in the tomb at Stratford. Only a signature or two – the mere signing of his name and not always in the same spelling – and not a single surviving letter in his handwriting. And the little known of him is the seal or sanction on his immortality. In general, the less documenting the better and the more tempting and inviting. What mystery is strong enough to survive snapshots by the thousand, for in the end it is the mystery that lasts and not the explanation.

I have tried in my lifetime as a writer to widen my areas of appreciation. This is far from having been my only ambition, however limited its realization, but I have consistently over the years studied and written upon subjects which I hoped would be new to experience. It would be tedious to name them here, but I think this will not be denied to me if it is but the by-play of poetry, just as much as travel and the describing of actual scenes and places has been equivalent to a painter's reluctance, but his financial necessity, in having to paint portraits. And, also, primarily, it has been the means of getting to such places. It would have been impossible for instance for me to go to Japan without assistance. It is true to say that not one of the books I have written of this nature has been anything but a financial loss to me. And as to the months and years spent in writing poetry? But, equally, none of it was written to make financial gain. That was not the object.

And the theme at this moment is how in the possession of this acquired knowledge and sensibility there is a very real danger of losing it all; that, and everything else as well, from inability to help ourselves. Here I do not speak for myself; being no longer young, having worked hard since I started to write seriously in 1919, and having therefore little to lose and still less to gain. But it must be obvious by now that the much vaunted technological revolution has added to the noise and tension, without conferring benefit other than that the resulting and eventual unemployment will leave tens of thousands workless and without any idea of how to live and enjoy their leisure. Not that there could be the chance or even the desire that they should 'go artistic' in their millions. But, to take the tiny majority who might be interested, no one in his right senses would want to spend his life surrounded by reproductions of Impressionist and old master paintings, excluding from this the abstract painters whose works will surely perish with them, even in our lifetime.

Why should the days, still more the nights of a whole local population be made subject to air-travellers arriving a few minutes earlier in transit, or at their destination? There will have to be sumptuary laws imposed on noise and time.

Cannot order be put into the chaos so that it has signature and character and can be dated accurately in a hundred years from now? It is the disaster of socialism that it removes or makes impossible private patronage or enterprise and puts all decisions in the hands of councils or committees. There is increase in knowledge, but knowing is not making; any more than lecturing is creating. An art institute is indeed a contradiction in terms, for once it is institutionalized it is no longer functioning. This, again, is presuming that such academies and art-mortuaries will continue and not perish in the over-population and ensuing anarchy.

Concerning which one is powerless and can but continue to work as though nothing is happening. For the chaos may get duller and no more dangerous. Or, and it seems unlikely, the muddling fog may lift. But will it be any better when we can see where we have got to? In the meantime, and while waiting, let us enjoy ourselves if it be for the last time, in all the licence of tax-avoidance, as it were, and carefree as though young, with all the world to savour and enjoy.

Once again, though, it is the same trouble here as everywhere else. The 'Indians' have begun to swarm. One day it will be as bad here as the *barrieras*, the appalling slum outside Lima which I saw in the spring of 1960, and that must be worse still by now. So many thousands of miles from here, and about half-way down South America, a 'suburb' – but like no other suburb ever seen – of three or four hundred thousand *mestizos* and 'Indians' living in huts made of sticks and straw-lattice, with no water, no lighting, and no sanitation, and with only a piece of matting for roof because it has literally never rained here. With more 'Indians' coming down from the Altiplano, the 'high plain' of Peru, every year, to find work in the towns. And finding none, because there is none to find.

With, if only by coincidence, another suburb of like propensity, how far? – three, four, even five thousand miles over the Andes, across the forests of the Amazon and the Mato Grosso, on the Atlantic coast just outside Recife, in Brazil, the Pernambuco of old, which port is the nearest landfall to Europe and Africa from the whole of the South American continent. Only here it is not an Indian and *mestizo* but a Negro or mulatto population of two or three hundred thousand persons living on mud-flats outside the city, and deriving their food chiefly from crabs and other crustaceans found in those same mud-flats. Hundreds of the inhabitants, men and women alike, are daily to be seen picking out the shellfish from the mud, elbow-deep, with their hands; the crustaceans in their turn feeding upon the excreta and other waste products of the human population.

It is one of the most hideous of all life-cycles; which, yet, on closer thought, could be said to be very close to nature. Is it indeed worse than the life-history of almost any race of carnivores, not excluding that of the wolves and foxes? Or the hyenas who go with lolloping run after their prey, biting off pieces of their flanks or hindquarters as they run? What life cycle is pretty in contemplation but that of the trees and flowers? And not even all of these, from deadly nightshade to fly-eating orchid! Yet what person of energy would wish to be flower-like; or even inanimate as a centenarian oak? It is the case that such subjects are the less sordid when they are human in our own likeness, but at the furthest remove from that when the subject is no longer two or four-legg'd, but six-legg'd like most insects, or eight-legg'd like the spider. Thus, a lion licking and gnawing a lump of raw flesh is less horrifying than a praying mantis, even motionless, its saw-legg'd forearms ready in position; or than the spider scuttling up and down its web to seize and pinion a victim.

And yet! And yet!

Most unusual are the bowls with long sprays of white pikake of the heavenly jasmine smell, an Indian plant born for the necks and shoulders of the bayadères or temple dancers, but with another home for itself in Hawaii where it is a favourite flower for making leis. As, too, the hedycium or white ginger lily, another native Indian, with moon-white petals, moth-shaped; a pair of them being like the open wings of the moth, a third petal like its folded wings, and a filament in the centre which is like the moth's antennae. This comes in sprays cut from the plant's green spathes, and looks to be, and is indeed of water-habit. It, too, is scented to perfection, and carries all the potency of an unanswered question.

It is not possible for me to end this chapter without once more apostrophizing Mexico, the land which until more recently I travelled in Japan, has been the scene for so many of my siesta thoughts. I have indeed been thinking of it for nearly fifty years during which time it has emerged from part anarchy into near prosperity, with its huge variety of interest and beauty at last recognized. For the surpassing and fiery strangeness of which I feel I need do no more than to add yet another recipe to one, already published; but this time it is not the *Mole Poblana* of the nuns of Santa Rosa in Puebla, prepared by them in the blue-tiled kitchen of the convent. It is a recipe of the nuns of Oaxaca for a dish of chocolate; some of the ingredients for which were cinnamon, cloves, almonds, hazel-nuts, orange-blossom water, musk and vanilla. Once compounded, the mixture was coloured with achiote, an orange-yellow dye obtained from the Bixa orellana, or annatto tree. It is but another *chef d'oeuvre* of the Churrigueresque cuisine! But, then, Oaxaca is that much more sub-tropical than Puebla. And below Mexico lies Guatemala with its astonishing relics of the Mayan civilization; its carved stelae to astronomers and feathered caciques; its stepped pyramids still clothed in jungle; its nearly Tuscan glades of pinewoods, but with volcanoes in the distance, and orchids and iguanas never far away; its costumed 'Indians' and quetzal-haunted forests. It was an excitement but to be flying out from Guatemala over the Mexican province of Quintana Roo, with a stretch of well over two hundred miles below one marked with no name at all upon the map.

On the San Sebastián of Palencia Cathedral

What would Mussorgsky's projected 'Grand symphony with piano and harps' have been, could he only have controlled his alcoholism and got down to writing it! But, instead, he drank on, and died. Probably, even today, when no holds are barred, and there is anarchic permissiveness in all the arts, the brass instruments in *Boris Godunov* and in *Khovantchina* make their effect. Speaking for myself, I can never forget hearing *Khovantchina* at Drury Lane in 1913, at the age of fifteen. It was one of the musical sensations of a lifetime, and seemed to open the whole history of half a continent in a few blasts and mutterings of sound. Mussorgsky's was perhaps the most original genius in all music, even more than Berlioz and with more and wider achievement, although he died so young, at thirty-nine. No doubt, had he written his Grand Symphony before his powers were failing, it would have been unlike anything before or since in music. It goes therefore into the same category of lost masterpieces as Rimbaud's *Photographies des temps passés*, and perhaps we should be grateful that no fragments of either of the works in question have survived to disillusion and disappoint all expectation.

But if there be an original genius in any of the arts who always astonishes, that being self-evidently his purpose and intention, it is El Greco. A sensation directly comparable to that of hearing Mussorgsky's brass instruments for the first time was to be had from Greco's *St Maurice and the Theban Legion* when it hung in the Sala Capitular at the Escorial. If removed to the Prado, it has not the same effect, any more than *Khovantchina* would have had, if first heard not at Drury Lane but in the Albert Hall. But in March 1919, with the war just ended, and the snow lying thick outside the granite walls and upon the blue slate roofs of the Escorial, it was a sensation always to be remembered.

And hardly less so, *The Burial of Count Orgaz*, in the church of San Tomé at Toledo; extraordinary, then, and now, and always, as George Borrow saw it a century and a half ago when, indeed, it had been all but forgotten for two hundred years and more. And yet the clouds in the picture come too near the persons; they obtrude in an incredible and almost an annoying way, equivalent to some infallible doctrine one cannot stomach and that one's reason will not let one swallow. It is more than a little of a muddle low down there on the clouds, which are within arm's reach like the mists upon a mountain path. But the row of heads below that, all in starched ruffs, and the expressive gesticulating hands of the notables of Toledo are among the marvels of painting; while the construction and force of the picture are the sextet of main actors, not the audience of Spaniards, this sextet being the Franciscan monk and surpliced priest at either end, the arch-bishop and the handsome acolyte supporting the dead, mailed body of the Conde de Orgaz, with the most eloquent of all those pairs of hands showing above and below the acolyte's head against the Spaniards in their black clothes. These five, and the little kneeling, torch-holding page or boy servitor in the foreground, dressed like a small Spaniard, who has his knee directly touching upon a panel of embroidery on the acolyte's vestment which has the *Stoning of St Stephen* for subject, in itself a microcosm of El Greco's painting, and which would enlarge into no less tremendous a theme than *The Burial of Count Orgaz*. And yet, in spite of the marvels of its handling and the extraordinary quality of the painting, the upper portion of it congests and irritates. It is too much to believe in celestial bodies in such close proximity to human beings; to the chief male inhabitants of Toledo with their heads and the flames of their torches touching upon the saint and the martyr-bearing clouds.

At the time I am thinking of in Toledo, in that March of 1919, so soon after six months at Albuhera Barracks, Aldershot, in that extraordinary autumn and early winter of the incredible scenes upon the platforms of Waterloo Station and the pitiful, hopeless songs of 'Oh! What a Lovely War', it was possible to go into any church and not know what paintings by El Greco one might find. I am certain, in parenthesis, that more than one or two of those pictures have disappeared since then. But there was another painting in the town even more dramatic than *The Martyrdom of St Maurice and the Theban Legion* – that picture which astonishes as would do a miraculously hand-illuminated version, in large, of a Mannerist tapestry cartoon, but carried out in the spectrum of the Kingfisher or the humming-bird, and the more marvellous again because of the grey-yellow, granite Escorial, snowbound, as we saw it – a painting even more extreme and over the edge than *The Burial of Count Orgaz*. This was the *Baptism of Christ*, in the Hospital de San Juan Bautista or Hospital de Afuera, outside the walls of Toledo, and down below the town. It is the last picture that he painted and it was left unfinished at his death in 1614.

The moment of first seeing this painting is not to be forgotten. It is a tall narrow canvas on a side altar, not in a good light, but in an extraordinary gloom and darkness of its own. Again, the upper part which is the hierarchy of angels, is turgid and indigestible, in spite of the pair of them, decently clothed down to the ankle, of immense height – when 'grounded' they would be at least twelve feet tall – and with active and useful wings growing naturally with no nonsense about it from their shoulders. Here, again, it seems to be Greco's intention to prove his assertion and make his point by bringing his clouds and angels, and his mysterious mediumistic flashes of light down to earth, and indeed touching and impinging on the action. Once more, as in *The Burial of Count Orgaz*, the feet of one of them almost touch the outstretched hand of the angel below him, who stands firmly on the ground and appears to be shouting up to his friend or companion angel in the air above. He is next to the kneeling, naked figure of Christ; kneeling on one knee, with the other leg extended, but the whole of his naked anatomy is rendered with a flickering technique as if its substance was incandescent and compound of flame.

But it is the small, moronic head of Christ on his long, long body, and the foreshortening of his bent leg, that are inexplicable. He is in the canon of the giant races of the Nile and Congo, and could be all of seven feet six inches tall. But the small head and tiny occiput and the moronic expression are unmistakable. And the very same man appeared in Greco's more famous painting of the *Expolio* (Christ being stripped of his garments) which hangs in the Sacristy of Toledo Cathedral, though this was painted some thirty years earlier. He is near to, and almost touching the figure of Christ, looking indeed over his right shoulder with imbecile expression. And it is the fact that while there in Toledo, fifty years ago, we continually saw this same mad beggar who came up and accosted us, and whom we saw in at least four places in Toledo; outside the walls, near, in fact, to his portrait in the Hospital de Afuera; outside the west door of the cathedral; hanging round several times outside the late Gothic church of San Juan de los Reyes; and near the cafés of the Zocodover or main square of the town. I am not suggesting that it was physically the same person, but that it was a beggar exactly like him; and that over the centuries, and maybe even now, there have been vagrant and begging imbeciles in his likeness in Toledo. He is as much the typical inhabitant of this old Castilian city with its Judeo-Moorish and Berber overtones, and its undernote of Africa, as any of the hidalgos clustering round the dead Conde de Orgaz; and if you wish to see his like, look for him in the outskirts of any Moorish or North African town where the shacks and sheds of petrol tins begin. Why the painter chose him as his model is the mystery; but, most certainly, he is typical of Toledo, and in Greco's panoramic painting of the city spread out before one like a panorama surrounded by its green hills there is room and to spare for him in that warren of narrow alleys and old houses.

The same hand painted him that worked the incomparable portrait of the Grand Inquisitor Don Fernando Nino de Guevara, now hanging in the Metropolitan in New York. It is perhaps the most haunting and powerful of all Renaissance portraits, with the difference that it is specifically the portrait of a Spaniard by a pseudo-Iberian, or, at the least, Spaniard by adoption. What character there is in the Inquisitor's clenched left hand gripping the arm of his chair, with his other hand dropping languidly, aristocratically, and the two rings on each hand! The portrait by Velázquez of the Pamphili Pope Innocent x, in the Palazzo Doria in Rome, is of course most directly influenced by this portrait, but it has not the frightening impact of the Grand Inquisitor Don Fernando Nino de Guevara. The painting by Greco in the little convent church or Hospital de la Caridad, at Illescas, between Madrid and Toledo, of *San Ildefonso* sitting writing at his table, would seem to be of the same period and inspiration as the portrait of the Grand Inquisitor, and this, too, is astonishing in effect. Almost as much because of the box-like, velvet-covered table at which the saint is sitting, and which is as important as the saint himself, but redeemed and pulled back again into being a portrait by the rendering of his hand with spread-out fingers holding down the page; by the meticulous still-life painting of the objects on the saint's writing table; and by his other hand poised in air holding the quill, and looking towards the statue of the Virgin for inspiration. It is nothing less than a daily experience of sixteenth-century Spain, and an extraordinary conception to have him there sitting in front of one, more real than life, in fact with theatrical, nearly operatic prominence and emphasis as though in some scene or entr'acte from Verdi's *Don Carlos*. The rich impasto of the saint's robe, and of his velvet table-covering with its galleon gatherings, make of this a portrait of a person and not the mere painting of some saintly personage.

How lucky was this Cretan, but Venetian citizen, laden intellectually with the pictorial spoils of Venice and of Rome, to find for himself such a city as Toledo for his working centre! He would never have had such a career, or the opportunity for development of his personality, had he spent his best years in, perhaps Siena, or some lesser Italian city where the enmity of his fellow painters and Italians would, we may guess, have hampered him at every turn and impeded his fulfilment. At Toledo he was without rivals and removed to some large extent from argument and discussion. A person who could talk learnedly and with authority about Michelangelo and Tintoretto was in little danger of contradiction in late sixteenth-century Toledo. He arrived there when about thirty-five years old; was neglected by Philip II, art lover that he was, who collected the Italian masters, and at the same time had paintings by Hieronymus Bosch in his rooms at the Escorial; and during all his years in Toledo (1577–1614), he escaped the attentions of the Inquisition. These are a pair of omissions that it is difficult to account for, but he was left in peace in Toledo. And being no Spaniard he assimilated it without being born to it, and was able to paint the *View of Toledo in a Storm* (in the Metropolitan Museum, New York). It is a strange hallucinatory scene as though, itself, suddenly shown up in the blink of lightning, and about to 'go out' again while the thunder booms and rattles. The hills and trees and fields, though so recognizably Toledan, are seen by the unreal light of natural electricity which accounts, too, for the extraordinary hollows and flashing lights in the clouds. A monument of tension and suspense, or, in fact, perpetual thunder and lightning over Toledo.

El Greco is no different in mood on the occasions when he puts Toledo in the background of a painting. In his two pictures of *The Crucifixion*, for instance, again with mediumistic flashes of light in both paintings;* and in one of them with the Alcázar and the Cathedral, but again with black night, almost, above Toledo. A far more interesting painting is the little panel of *San José with the Child Jesus*, which I remember seeing in a small church in Toledo, but it is now in the Museo de San Vicente; an extraordinary affair because of the enormous height of San José, the angels brushing his head with their wings as though to prove the scene is gospel truth and incontrovertible, while the child Jesus is not like any other portrayal of him, being painted, it would seem, from an articulated

* In the art museum at Philadelphia, and at Cincinnati, USA.

doll or lay-figure of a child, but with the head painted in as a portrait. It is of weird effect. The view of Toledo behind their two figures, with the Puente de Alcántara to one side of them and the Alcázar to the other, is less stormy with fewer of the lights of trance or séance in the clouds. But it is a troubled sky higher up where this giant apparition stalks upon the hillside, some hundreds of feet tall against the clouds with the weird long-gowned little boy holding up his arm to San José for protection. It is a strange painting indeed, and Greco's usual inscription and signature in Greek letters on a paper lying on the hillside at the foot of the bridge of Alcántara that leads over the Tagus into the polyglot city, makes it odder and more peculiar still. This late painting by him shows how far Greco had moved from his Italian training. As to at least the lower portion of it, up to the head of San José against the traumatic lights and flashings in the sky, under the tumbling, winged apparitions come down with their olive wreaths, and their roses and lilies that are as flowers fraudulently materialized at a séance, it can truly be said that there is nothing even remotely resembling this picture in all Italy.

If his *View of Toledo* in the Casa del Greco in the city, with a youth holding the map of the town in the foreground, is indeed a pictorial plan more than a painting of the city, there is a marvellous rendering of it in all its strangeness, as Spanish as could be, and yet it might be Fez or Meknes, as background to Greco's painting of *Laocoon and his sons*. In the painting Toledo is the 'stand in' for Troy. But why are there four youths with the aged Laocoon when in the story he had but two sons? The painter was an educated man and something of a scholar. In the inventory of his effects at his death Greco had seventy-two books, including Homer, Demosthenes, Euripides, Lucian, and Aesop. In fact the subject was his excuse for painting the nude and he was as difficult about this as Cézanne. It would be interesting in fact to see the latter's three versions of *Les Baigneurs* hung in a room together with Greco's *Laocoon*. There is a conscious, and unconscious awkwardness about the naked figures in the *Laocoon*. It is different indeed from the ease with which Velázquez entered upon and achieved the 'Rokeby' Venus,* a painting of a naked woman who by inference was probably a Spanish dancer. There is no nervousness in the approach of Velázquez to his model.

But in the *Laocoon* the awkwardness makes the conception a little ridiculous, and the weird lights in the clouds over Troy introduce a hysterical note and only add to the affectation. Now in the *Baigneurs* of Cézanne it is not his technique, but his furious, desperate strivings for technique that make him a great painter. He triumphs in it but with clumsy hands; or he would not have wanted to paint three versions, to make three attempts at it. By his pains he achieves the transcendental. The 'bestial incompetence' of which Sickert accused him, here serves him well, and is the very weapon that he wields so competently. It is in virtue of it that he is himself. It has become not his defect but his quality. With the Cretan painter – although he could sometimes play at the naïf, probably with the memory of paintings in his native island as in his picture of *San José with the Child Jesus*,

* In the National Gallery, London.

which one would expect to find in some inaccessible village in the Cretan hills – there was no question of bungling or native awkwardness. He knew himself, and even vaunted himself, as the equal of Michelangelo. Therefore, in the *Laocoon*, it is his temperamental failing, or the unbalance in his nature. Of this there is further evidence if we examine the personalia in his paintings.

The Opening of the Fifth Seal is a wonderful and spiritual masterpiece compared to the too mannered and affected *Laocoon*. It is also probably the most extraordinary picture ever painted. For many years this picture hung, where I have seen it, in the villa of the painter Zuloaga at Zumaya on the Basque coast of Spain.* It would seem to be only part of, and not a complete painting. But although the kneeling figure of St John (?) on the left of it, with arms outstretched, and towering three or four times lifesize, is painted very obviously from a lay figure with articulated arms, dressed up for the occasion with the hem of his robe spread out around him, the effect of it is tremendous, and transcends any other painting. Not in beauty, but in force and drama, and as part of some convinced experience. It is the opening of the heavens, and what we see in the scripture are 'the souls of those who were slain for the love of God', but it is a more interesting experience than that, and of much deeper meaning. There is an unparalleled drama in the kneeling figure of the St John – in his outstretched arms and hands – and his enormous, uncouth clothed figure which in fact has hypnotic, or even idolatrous importance of the sort than can be induced by long staring and concentration on some perfectly still object. It is impossible to look at a living human being with this passivity for there are movements, if it is only that they are breathing. But if it is a doll or lay figure or puppet one could study it till one became hypnotized, and even a little frightened and in awe of it. This, in primitive form, is the juju or fetish of the West African tribes. And the next step is to invest it in one's mind with superstitious powers.

It is in this manner that the image becomes more powerful than the human being. Hence, the miracle-working statue; and, as well, the wax doll you stick pins in to bring misfortune to your enemies. There is a hypnotic fascination in marionettes or puppets; alike, in the now defunct Punch and Judy of the street corner, and in marionettes, as many persons would agree who have seen the puppet-drama or Bunraku of Osaka in Japan. The great dramatist Chikamatsu wrote his plays for the puppet-drama; the Kabuki players imitated the stilted movements of the puppets which were two-thirds lifesize, and had a chief-operator and a pair of assistants who could not only manipulate their limbs but roll their eyes and move their eyebrows. One has but to attend a performance of the Bunraku-za in Osaka, to grasp the potentialities of the puppet drama. Here, it seems to me, in this wildly impressive and dramatic painting of *The Opening of the Fifth Seal*, we have a lay figure with his arms stretched as high and wide as they will go; here, in Spain, the adopted land of the articulated statue and the carved and painted images to be carried in processions. Two of the other kneeling

* Now, all four pictures by El Greco, the *View of Toledo*, his portrait of *The Grand Inquisitor, Don Fernando Nino de Guevara, Laocoon and his sons*, and *The Opening of the Fifth Seal*, are in the Metropolitan in New York.

figures in the painting could be taken from the same lay figure, but unclothed, and nearly in identical attitude, its limbs being voluminously concealed and covered where it serves as model for St John.* He is the doll heightened ten-fold; and with this in mind the naked standing figures in the centre of the painting betray their identity and recall moments of passing by shop windows when the lay figures are standing or lying about naked before they have the clothes put on them and are lifted into position.

But what genius to proceed from this simple beginning to a spiritual experience of traumatic force and violence! There is nothing in painting more simple and more tremendous than this lay figure or giant puppet. It has even the true puppet's wooden vacuity of expression. The same mediumistic flashes of light in the sky as though at the moment just before some terrific manifestation, as in accounts of earthquakes when the birds and animals are violently disturbed and seem to know there is something coming. It is more than the Northern lights or summer lightning. And suddenly the huge kneeling figure is there, and whatever it is shows in the sky where he can see it, and it is coming down on us from above. The naked shop-dummies, it is true, gaze at one another and are not looking up into the heavens, but they have risen uncorrupted from their tombs and the 'white robes', not too literally represented by the painter, are descending on them out of the clouds. It is the revelation, more than the action subsidiary to it, that is the subject. That it is a supernatural happening is implicit in that huge kneeling figure with outstretched arms and hands and ventriloquist's dummy features.

There are other pictures in which El Greco has clearly taken inspiration from the carved figures of the 'pasos' or religious processions, notably the two different visions of Christ in the house of Simon the Pharisee,† which could almost be direct paintings of polychrome 'pasos' or passion groups by Zarcillo in the churches and the museum at Murcia. These are far from being the most successful of his paintings. But the strangest, and effectually most wonderful of all his pictures has not yet been mentioned. Its subject is more easily assimilated than The Opening of the Fifth Seal, so that it is less mysterious, but no less marvellous in conception and handling, and one of his very last paintings finished not long before his death.

This is a tall narrow canvas and hangs in the former church of San Vicente at Toledo. What a mercy, we may think, that it stays there and not in the Prado! Where it would be jaundiced by too close contact and competition from other paintings by the master. Its theme is the Assumption of the Virgin and this, so far as humanly possible, does still take place in the Museo de San Vicente among other pictures and works of art taken from the parish churches of Toledo. For the picture is of soaring, ascending effect. It is an Ascension, no doubt of that, and a projection upwards of enormous force. There is the thrust of the hugely

---

* On a table in one of the El Greco rooms at the Prado there is a small nude statue or mannikin said to be from his hand. It is, I think, a recent acquisition.

† Both paintings are in collections in the USA. The sculptor Francesco Zarcillo (1707–81), two centuries later in date than El Greco, was of Neapolitan origin, but spent his working life in Murcia. cf. Zarcillo's Last Supper (1733) in the Ermita de Jesús, 'with the disciples, two-thirds life-size, seated at a trestle table, on stools with cabriole legs'.

elongated angel on the right, who has just taken off from ground level with his bare feet still touching the 'materialized' roses and lilies. It is odd how Greco falls naturally into the jargon and séance paraphernalia of a later age! But this same angel just taking off into the strangely lit sky is but the first-stage rocket of the ascent. The thrust and energy come from him, and it is as though his body is some two hundred feet long, or longer, and already half-way between earth and sky. The foreshortening of the angel's body could only have come from someone who has had vivid traumatic experience of this scene, and indeed to that degree witnessed an ascension. You could almost hear the noise of his wings; the sabre-slice and flash of his left wing which has ended its stroke and come in close again, all pinions closed, and the spread feathers of the right wing, winnowing like a great fan of plumes.

There lies Toledo below, no doubt of that either, but just seen in its essentials, the thunderous hills and heights of the town, and only a ghost of the bridge of Alcántara. Above that the uncanny gleams and flashes in the clouds, and another soaring angel, like another up-surging and supporting rocket, cyclopaean in length, longer by far than any rocket paraded on May Day through the Red Square in Moscow, and with an instrument-playing angel alongside him, whose head reaches higher than the Madonna and who is therefore miles up, right into the sky. With still another angel, the other side of the Virgin, habituated to those heights and playing, a little incongruously, a full size double-bass or 'cello. Over all this a sort of penumbra as ceiling, with the dove of the Holy Ghost in the middle. The Virgin or main body of the rocket being positively enormous, as disproportionate as the carapace of Queen bee or hornet, many times longer than it could be in life, a thing of mystery, with her body above that, her chest and shoulders and her hands of normal size; and then the foreshortened, moronic or dummy features quite devoid of all but a sillily rapt expression.

Yet nothing can take away from this painting of *The Assumption*. It is a spiritual and psychical experience, even beginning at the roses and lilies of hallucinatory kind at foot of the picture. They could be real, or they could be paper flowers made by the nuns in a convent; but like the shower of rose petals at Lisieux their bodily existence must not be taken too literally. For a wonder there are no further and more improbable flowers high up near the 'cello-playing angel! Now one questions whether the Virgin herself and all three leading or principal angels in the picture were not painted from lay figures hung somehow in his painting room in the right positions. The initial or rocket-angel being most obviously the difficult one to place correctly, but in fact it would only need string or wires to hold him longitudinally along the studio with his head higher than his feet at that angle which from below looks as though he is climbing at terrific speed and soaring up into the sky. You would only have to stand beneath him and look up at him to imagine this. One by one, the three or four figures panto-miming this ascent into the upper airs could be painted in their trance-like hypnotic stillness and made to look as real as the figures in a dream. There is nothing insubstantial. You have the feeling you could touch their clothing which in fact would have been physically possible, or even to move their heads and open or shut their pairs of wings. Even give them a little push and leave them swinging from the ceiling. But, even so, what a rushing, roaring ascent into the skies! With fireballs, flashing lights in the clouds, all the abracadabra, alike of the séance and of the now familiar roaring departure of the lunar module on the way to the dead satellite; or for a permanence into the void with weakening messages coming through, and then an eternity of silence.

It is evident that Greco uses distortions of height when he wants to impress and frighten. There are so many instances of this, in *The Assumption* and in *San José with the Child Jesus*. But there is another extreme example in the convent church at Illescas where a painting of the *Madonna Caritatis* shows four or five Spanish hidalgos, half-length, praying and gesticulating with their hands under the cloak of a Madonna, full length and neither quite sitting or standing, but who would be two and a half times their height. With El Greco the rational vanished at once when dealing with the supernatural, and he followed his usual practice of bringing the two head-on together and touching. This on the whole in the past of painting has been allowed only in the case of Royal personages, and with ordinary people it is a little disconcerting. In this instance the Madonna is almost, literally, sitting on their heads, but it is true that she is of curious physical type perhaps in order to avoid any sense of impropriety, and in fact so small of head that in ordinary circumstances one would take her to be half-witted. It is interesting to speculate as to El Greco's degree of religious sophistication. In the paintings of his 'Venetian' period when still influenced by Tintoretto and Bassano, for instance in *The Cleansing of the Temple* (National Gallery, London), all is sanity except for the two beggar boys with their baskets, both showing the contortion of their features when looking upwards which was to become an obstinate habit and a hallmark in his pictures. It is equivalent to an insistence that this is how a human being looks from a certain angle however much they may flatter themselves that it is not so. Soon after his arrival in Spain he seems to have succumbed to the prevalent superstitions, or else it is that he 'painted down' to them. The impressively wonderful, and indeed hauntingly unforgettable *San José with the Child Jesus*, is a painting for an image-worshipping, an almost idolatrous audience or public. His *Gloria de Felipe II*, or *Philip II's dream of heaven and hell*, at the Escorial, his first and only partially successful attempt to gain the Royal patronage (*St Maurice and the Theban Legion* was his later failure) is exceedingly curious, but would have been hopeless as a large composition. It is as though the painter lost his nerve when confronted with some contact of patronage however remote with this great, if unlearned connoisseur of Italian painting. There he is, the King of Spain and Portugal, the Netherlands, ruler of Naples and Milan, titular King of England, the heir of America and the Indies, the only living human in the painting amid the hierarchy of the saints and martyrs, and of all heaven and hell. In fact, hell yawns a foot or two away from where he kneels upon an Oriental carpet, in the likeness of an open whale's mouth with a dripping fang or two, and all the damned are pressed together and are swallowed up into the monster's belly. There are too many persons in the painting; and bigotedly religious as the King may have been this picture did not recommend itself to him any more than had done the *St Maurice*, and this was the curtain to his patronage of El Greco.

His confrontation of the visible and invisible, or the material and the immaterial worlds, was habitual with the painter, as in his *St Maurice, The Burial of Count Orgaz*, and in nearly every painting mentioned. But whereas in pictures by other artists the heavenly hierarchy at least keep their distance and only descend from it with caution and discretion, with Greco they come into the greatest, and most intimate proximity, but he exaggerates their size; except where all concerned are immortal spirits as in the *Resurrection* (of the Prado) where the figures for that reason, the lack of competition, are all, approximately, ordinary lifesize.

It is probable that finding himself in Spain in the half-Arabic and even bilingual city of Toledo, very far in spirit from circles in Rome or Venice where much of the conversation would be of painting, he remembered his Cretan childhood and youth. It had been his home till he was twenty-five years old and came to Venice. Now, once more and for the rest of his life, he was in a mediaeval, semi-Oriental world, most unlike Renaissance Italy, and with this reversion to childhood must have come back memories of Byzantine chapels in Cretan villages. He most certainly knew about the Cretan school of icon-painting and traded upon and was proud of his Greek name.* It is more than probably a sophisticated simplicity that he was practising in his strangely distorted painting of *San José with the Child Jesus*, not uninfluenced by icons that he remembered in which the saints and anchorites were often of superhuman size. All traces of this have gone when he painted portraits. In these, his painting of *The Grand Inquisitor* apart, he often approximates to the Dutch masters in technique and handling, though it would be an improbable Hollander at work on the typical Spaniards in their black doublets and white ruffs. But when it comes to *St Jerome as Cardinal*, twice over, in the National Gallery and in the Frick Collection, it is a picture by a painter of Byzantine affiliation and with innate knowledge of the saints from icons.

His series of apostles and saints at Toledo, in the Cathedral and at the Casa del Greco, are exaggerated and wild of expression and for the most part with excessively small heads. In these paintings again, it is a Byzantinist at work in Spain, and in the result more than a little unpleasantly freaky of effect. But neither is it improbable that he found the task monotonous and uninteresting. His attempts to break from this result in a set of pictures of extreme psychopaths. St Andrew, for instance, on a canvas that must have been painted in a matter of hours, has a long thin face of abnormal vacuity from whom it would be impossible to obtain any kind of sense, and holds on a chain a little personal or household demon of irritating silliness – until one realizes it is something personal one must live with and can never be rid of and that, therefore, there is some sense in it. St Bernard of Siena, also in the Casa del Greco – and how unlike he is to native Italian render-

---

*   Village churches in Crete such as Potamies, near Heraklion, with 'a first rate Pantocrator in the dome and, also, some splendid Emperors and Empresses, all in full fig, complete with haloes'; or Kritsa, 'the largest village on the island', of which church Mr Lancaster gives a colour plate, must be scenes typical of El Greco's Cretan childhood, cf. *Sailing to Byzantium*, by Osbert Lancaster, London 1969, pp. 143–5.

ings of San Bernardino of Siena! – with a heap of no fewer than four mitres at his feet, stands in a hilly landscape, and looked up at from ground level cannot stand less than twelve feet high. The sky at the back of him flashes and coruscates with abnormal lights as if an electrical storm is in progress, and the whole of one side of his monk's robe is outlined by phosphorescent gleams. His robe of course accentuates his height, as does the long Franciscan cord which trails from his waist down to the ground; and above that there emerges from his wide collar an emaciated head, but thin from mental and nervous weakness not from austerity, of triangular shape, and beard and incipient moustache apart, resembling the triangle-head of a praying mantis. It is the head of a man incapable of making any kind of decision, and who must have taken on a monk's robe as the course of least resistance. There are still traces of a life of luxury and fashion about his features, his hair and beard once well cared for, and his weak and melancholy gaze, and he seems unworthy of the electrical discharge and disturbances behind him. It is the picture of a nobleman who has taken to the cowl for the want of anything better to do, and perhaps because of an unfortunate romance in which he could never have been anything other than the loser.

But with El Greco there is always some extraordinary experience in store. The mind can become sated with his paintings in the Prado, but there are ever Toledo and the Escorial to return to. There is *The Burial of Count Orgaz*; while the four finest and most controversial of his paintings, as we have seen, are in the Metropolitan in New York. But for a transcendental experience he should be seen, unpremeditated, and in unexpected circumstances. This happened to me some years ago when visiting Palencia, a town in Northern Spain lying out in the distance between Burgos and León. We had been the day before, I remember, to Soria through Bruegel-like villages of mud huts heaped to roof level with mounds of grain, where everyone, young and old, the women in wide-brimmed straw hats, were all shaking the stooks, or garnering, or working flail in hand, and there was dust everywhere the colour of bleached gold. In midst of all this a tremendous thunderstorm was playing. Lightning struck a hill in front of us and the full artillery of the thunder boomed and rattled. Soria, when we got there, poured with water as if it had lifted itself out of a lake. Its reddish old churches looked as if they had stayed damp since the thirteenth century. And it rained all the rest of the way to Burgos.

Next morning, which was a Sunday, the thunderstorm caught up with us at Palencia. By four o'clock, when luncheon in the new hotel was ending, a leaden darkness had descended, it was pouring with rain, and the electric light had failed all over the town. The cathedral of Palencia was steeped in darkness. We had come there to see the tapestries in the Sala Capitular, Flemish tapestries worked with the arms of Archbishop Fonseca, and reported to be with those of Zamora, of Tarragona, and of Zaragoza, the finest tapestries to be found in any cathedral in Spain. I had seen them twenty years before but could not remember them. In the event they proved disappointing, being late in date; not to be compared to the nine galleons of *Las Naves* in Zaragoza, their subject the improbable fleet of Brutus, nephew of Aeneas, on his expedition to Aquitaine, with horses on board, men at arms, and ladies in tall steeple hats, one of the wonders of the Middle Ages; or to the 'Black Tapestry' of Zamora. We had to see the tapestries of Palencia by candlelight. And then, still holding his one candle, in the deep darkness of half-past four on that Sunday afternoon in mid-September, the priest led us into the Sacristía, next door, where the St Sebastian of El Greco banishes any further memory of the tapestries of Palencia.

If a truly extraordinary picture has ever been painted, it is here. But what is the subject? And, in fact, what is it about? It is a half-length of St Sebastian stuck with arrows, and no one else but him in the picture. So that it is not at all a large painting, indeed little bigger than lifesize. There are other St Sebastians by El Greco, and in those he is feeling his way to this final version. This is his last statement on the theme of St Sebastian. At first glance it might be taken for a myopic condensation or anagram of its forerunners; an anagram, not in the sense of altering the words (or components) but changing their meaning. But it alters nothing. It only strengthens and finalizes its own image. As to the distortion, it must have happened to everyone who has ever looked at himself in a mirror – and who more so than painters who must on occasion have considered their self-portrait? – that there are sideways foreshortenings of the features which can be very ugly. Yet this is as true a reflection of oneself as any other. This angle of view seems to have become somewhat of an obsession with El Greco. It is at work again, on more than one figure in the Assumption, at San Vicente. And it would appear to have been given further force by long study of his lay figures to an extent, almost, which could result in self-hypnosis. Most of the angelic beings in his paintings could well be of this origin and derivation. Their long ankle-length gowns are so obviously the robing of a dummy or lay figure.

But for his paintings of St Sebastian he seems to have had a youthful living model, not the youth holding the plan of Toledo, nor the armoured knight in his St Martin and the Beggar,* and not the handsome acolyte who is one of the principal figures in The Burial of Count Orgaz, but a young man curiously resembling the male models much made use of by Caravaggio, and chosen, knowing that painter's history, probably from the thieving classes. The two painters may have been at work in the same years – their dates are 1541–1614 and 1573–1610 – but it is certain they never met, or saw each other's paintings. It is only interesting to contrast their achievement; how the verismo of Caravaggio takes him in entirely the other direction from the over-excited and passionate mysticism of El Greco. In his long life Greco often repeated the same subject over again, and always in the later version not with more realism but with greater absorption. Nowhere more so than in this hypnotically, and astigmatically distorted St Sebastian. El Greco has often been said to have suffered from astigmatism ('a defect of the eye in which all the rays are not brought to a focus at the same point'), but the more interested he is, the more he shows it. So that it is more a mental than a physical condition; and in as much as it is of cerebral, of mystical origin within him.

* Formerly in the Capilla de San José at Toledo, now in the Widener collection in the National Gallery, Washington, DC.

So this is how in the end the martyred San Sebastián appeared to him. How curious to have seen it in that darkened sacristy by candlelight! And by the flashes of lightning of a summer thunderstorm at mid-afternoon! In a cathedral of Spain where, as a rule, the paintings are nowhere so good as the tapestries, *rejas*, tombs, goldsmith's work, and so on. To be unprepared for a sensation from a painting, and then to see without warning and in such dramatic circumstances, 'one of the most extraordinary pictures ever painted, far outdoing any of the "excesses" of our century, and yet a painting pure and simple'. And what can he have expected its effect to be? To have kneeling women in front of it, day after day, who would never notice the distorted features, and only take it as a long-meditated symbol of divine suffering, but concentrated into something akin to the subject of a fugue. All this from a painter who had tasted the glories of Italian painting, and knew the masterworks of Titian and Michelangelo. Who may have seen himself as a scholar of the lost Byzantium, and therefore the translator of one world of civilization into another; and not to Italy, at that, but further still to Spain. Who saw himself as neither Italian, nor Spanish, but Greek; and whose earliest paintings had been of the Meteora-like, if imaginary crags, above the monastery of Mount Sinai. With great flights or steps leading up the mountain, and as un-Latin as the stone cells of the Irish hermits on the Blaskets, or The Great Skellig.* It is perhaps begging the question to assume that he may have passed through Ravenna on his way from Venice to Rome and seen the mosaics at San Vitale. In which event, he would have seen at first hand the distortions of height practised in mosaic, but he will certainly have been familiar with the device from seeing the painted icons in Cretan village churches. His use of distortion was for supernatural effect, as, also, his luminous and phosphorescent skies, lurid with inexplicable and moving lights. There is no sign of doubt or hesitancy in his acceptance of the supernatural.

No abstract painting in the sacristy at Palencia, by whatever master – be it Kandinsky perhaps the one genius of the movement; how much less still, one of the 'hard' or 'soft edge' masters of the New York school – would have an effect at all comparable to this long evolved statement or thesis of the spirit. How remarkable that it should not have been objected to by the ecclesiastics! Because it must have been an extraordinary moment when the wrappings were removed and there it was in all its ugliness. As uncompromising as one of the pictures, more properly 'mural decorations', designed by Goya for the dining-room of his country house, and of curious purpose because, decidedly, their motive cannot have been to amuse or please. But, rather, they were meant to alarm and frighten.† Which is not at all the motive in the *San Sebastián*. It is an image come from concentrated thinking and from dwelling on the subject until this is all that is left of it.

* This early painting by El Greco, of which a version is in the Galleria Estense of Modena, is surely inspired by early woodcuts of the monasteries of Mount Athos. Neither Athos nor Meteora will have been unheard of to the Cretan population, although they remained Venetian subjects until the beginning of the eighteenth century.

† In the painting of Saturn devouring his sons – he always ate his sons as soon as born, though it is to be noted they are more than half-grown in the picture – the white hair of Saturn has the appearance of cloud nebulae in a telescopic photograph of space.

A young man shot to death with arrows but, in fact, still alive and in a kind of ecstasy of suffering, feeling himself to be one of the glorious company of martyrs. Which may be a sentiment with which it is difficult to sympathize but, then, we are not Spaniards of the sixteenth century. The picture is an image or an icon deduced from these circumstances and conditions. Thought of in terms, not of writing, but of painting. And, therefore, visually, and not to be turned into a poem, a devotional exercise, or dissertation. This is not San Juan de la Cruz, or Santa Teresa. It is a painter who has painted saints innumerable, beyond number, and from all the evidence, believed in and was convinced of them. But, at the last, he must be allowed to express his own spiritual experiences. Which emerge in unfamiliar form but with such force of feeling that we cannot doubt him. It must be recalled, too, that none of the Venetian painters, not Titian, nor Veronese, nor Tintoretto, ever surpassed him in the use of colour. No picture in the Accademia, in the Doges' Palace, or in the Scuola di San Rocco, makes such use of colour as in *St Maurice and the Theban Legion*, or *The Burial of Count Orgaz*. Could it not be said of Tintoretto that he spread himself larger and larger to the detriment of meaning or intense feeling! That Veronese, as was brought against him, painted too many horses, dogs, apes, and German pikemen as accessories! That Titian painted too many official portraits and Venetian senators! In which respect it could be said of El Greco that he was the finest colourist of the Venetian school, except that he cannot have lived for more than a few months in Venice where he perhaps worked a little in Titian's studio.* He absorbed Titian and Tintoretto into his system in that short space of time in Venice, but may have spent as long as six or seven years in Rome whence he emerged, jealous of, but dissatisfied with Michelangelo. And with the great Italian masters in his mind he set forth for Spain.

But in spite of lessons learned in Rome and Venice his pictures painted in Toledo are signed in Greek letters and there was no pretence on his part to be Italian. This left him free to develop in his own directions with even some conscious affectation of Byzantinism such as exaggerated canons of height in his figures, and solid clouds like stage scenery carrying the heavenly hierarchy and nearly touching the heads of human beings. His live men and women were painted with more than life-like realism, while his saints and hierarchs are often studied direct from wax or clay dolls, or lay-figures, and have therefore some of the stiffness, but the very life-like stiffness of puppet-plays, this *San Sebastián* among them, which is really the secret of what is odd and curious about the painting. If this is so, then the *San Sebastián* far from being taken from the living model is, really and truly, a still-life painting. This is the explanation of its mystery, as it is of the *San José with the Child Jesus*, and of the huge kneeling figure in *The Opening of the Fifth Seal*.

* He is thus described by the miniature painter Giulio Clovio in a letter of November 1570 to Cardinal Alessandro Farnese: 'A young Candiote has appeared in Rome, a pupil of Titian, who, so far as I can judge, is unique in painting. Among other things, he has painted a self-portrait that confounds all the painters in Rome.' Greco's curious painting of Mount Sinai was produced either for Cardinal Farnese or his librarian Fulvio Orsini.

It has already been suggested that in at least one land with a civilization sophisticated enough to support a theatre with great dynasties of actors, the drama of puppets or marionettes for a time had precedence over the living theatre. And that their greatest dramatist wrote his plays to be performed by puppets, which later were adapted in order to be performed by live actors. Here, in the *sacristía* of the cathedral at Palencia, we see a puppet or a doll painted with nearly fetishistic absorption and intensity to portray the martyrdom of a saint. Perhaps this would not seem so unlikely were we to look closely from altar to altar of the cathedral, examining the images and opening the sacristy cupboards, where surely there would be robes, or even a change of jewelled dresses for the statue of the Virgin. That, after all, is the purpose of the *camarín*, a peculiarly Spanish feature of churches in Spain, with intent specially to house the dresses for the holy images and statues.

So much was to be anticipated, but not this extraordinary painting. Which could make all other pictures, whatever their merits, only and merely beautiful. For it has a hypnotic purpose, that of a hypnotizing idol or image in itself. Though, at moments, its force is not more than that of one of the wax heads of the guillotined at Madame Tussaud's. To which category at the moment it belongs absolutely. Only to emerge from that in the next moment as among the most peculiar objects our eyes have ever seen. Of magical or talismanic powers, no doubt of that, if such things there be. Whether altogether good, or evil, is another matter for the holy and unholy are not so far apart. But the result of many trials and errors of which this is the end and finding. Something that can be carried and reduced no further. Once seen, at all times not to be forgotten; least of all, here and now in the thunder and lightning and summer darkness. By the flame of one candle, and the phosphorescent lights and hollows in its own night sky.

Note. The reader is now invited to read the paragraph on this painting in the *Note of Explanation*, pp. 13–14, if he has not already done so.

BOOK
THREE

Globe-Trotting

And now, not having worked on it for nearly a year, I must crawl like a worm out of its worm-cast on the wet sands, take a look at my *grande machine* of a book, and give it a heave and a push along before crawling back and burying myself in it again.

It reminds me of something I once saw. Two men, I think they were Australians, rolling a huge globe like a more than life-size terrestrial globe along the street. In St Nicholas Street, Scarborough, my birthplace, outside Marshall and Snelgrove's in about 1910 or 1912.

They were making their way round the world in this manner. Dressed like acrobats, I seem to recall, and handing out leaflets about themselves.

The globe was some eight feet high made, I suppose, of lath and plaster; and did it have a map of the world, with the four seas and five continents painted on its outside? Or was it covered with posters and advertisements?

At any rate it had a door on one side, and the leaflet led one to believe they slept inside it. There may even have been a picture of its interior upon the leaflet. They probably had folding beds and chairs and a table, and must have had other luggage and personal belongings with them.

I think it was somewhere in England, and that they had already walked across the United States. Or had they crossed from coast to coast of India, where, in any case, what with juggernaut cars and sacred cows wandering in the streets, they would not have been much out of place!

I remember thinking they had cheated by crossing the ocean and not going all the way on foot. The whole episode belongs to a time when passports were unnecessary and it was easier to cross frontiers.

At this moment in a street where one saw something ahead of one, and a knot of persons round it. And expected perhaps a barrel-organ, for it was moving, it was moving, it was coming forward slowly in our direction, and giving the impression that it was going somewhere, that it must have some destination!

That it was a piece of theatrical scenery, a prop of some kind, and only being taken for a short journey from the workshop to the theatre; and sure enough they were a pair of acrobats trundling along:

Or some kind of advertisement of a circus turn; or even a pill, a giant 'bolus' to advertise some patent medicine.

Or some mystery contraption, 'looking like' a terrestrial globe, but destined to be lowered into the town drain, or sewer, or let down into the harbour water, and to have in either case cables or wires wrapped round it.

I remember that they were young men of student age. Teaming up to do this turn together much as you take a partner for your 'act' in variety theatres and on the music halls; 'trick' tandem-cyclists, wire-walkers or trapeze artists, turns which when performed without a net below them are no longer 'acts' but deeds. And neither partner must break the contract and leave the other stranded.

The globe having been built to their specifications, and then tried out and found unsatisfactory the very first time they rolled it a few feet backwards and forwards in the yard. Either it would not roll over at all; or showing a tendency to run away with them so that they were nervous of testing it on the smallest declivity.

What brake was there on the terrestrial globe to prevent it rolling down a hill? Or, on the road, if one of them called a halt, just to 'satisfy the needs of nature', what was there to stop it rolling on, and leaving him behind? Like the waters of the Mississippi it would 'just go rolling along'. And he would have to catch up with it like one of the marathon walkers one sees, at the side of the road, strutting along, ridiculously, in shorts and singlet, on their practice evenings.

There was the prisoner who escaped a few years ago, I think from Lewes Gaol, dressed like a marathon-walker; who hurried in this garb through the streets, applauded on his way by the Saturday night crowd, and even having the traffic held up for him by policemen on point duty. That he was recaptured later the same evening did not make his escapade the less amusing.

But, at last, after many delays and disappointments all was ready, though I cannot believe they travelled with it very far in Australia, where distances are huge and there are long stretches of desert. But, rather, that they loaded it at once on board ship for India. Why should I think they had crossed India? It cannot be mere fancy on my part. I believe the leaflet spoke of it. And every mile they walked through Hindustan some persons may have thought the White Imperialists were 'losing face', as the pair of them toiled along pushing the ball in front of them, a mode of progression which has been long, and still is, a form of obsession with Englishmen.

One of the least unpleasant of the masters at my private school told me, when I saw him many years later in retirement, that he was happy watching any form of game played with a ball. H. G. Wells said that visitors landing in England from another planet must think that certain small spherical objects were inimical to the human race, as whenever and wherever seen they were immediately hit, or kicked, or, in sign of their dangerous proclivities picked up, and as quick as possible, hurled back again; while an old gentleman I knew had models of every ball, rugby, soccer, cricket, tennis, polo, golf, badminton, billiards, snooker, baseball, rounders, racquets, fives, croquet, ping-pong, etc. etc., all carved out of ivory at great expense, and arranged over the fireplace in his sitting-room.

Our pair of Sisyphuses could not but come from some offshoot or outpost of Englishmen. And just because it is so much a part of our native temperament, and associated with all our ideas of either private or national enjoyment, I suspect that they must have fared worse here in England than anywhere else for it would be taken as presumptuous on their part to have invented this new thing for themselves which was a form of self-advertisement, and not a game. Neither could win at it, or beat the other. No doubt many persons in the crowd, and not only small boys, would give the thing a push or a kick, not to help them, but the quicker to be rid of them. And the train of thought is obvious enough leading from the pair of globe-rollers, who must have had so much trouble with their contrivance when going up or down hill, to the elephants of Hannibal crossing the Alps on their way from Spain to Italy.

Hannibal marched his elephants into Italy by the Little St Bernard, 'the easiest of the passes, and one of the most ancient', only rising to 7,420 feet. This is but half the height of the Cruz Alto, the pass on the way to Lake Titicaca that you have to cross going from Peru into Bolivia, where I got down from the train at 14,666 feet marked on the station platform, and with halting breath went for a walk along the railway line. But at the top of the Little St Bernard there is 'a fine pasturage on a plain a league long and half a league wide', and at its most elevated point is a circle of stones 'that still bears the name of the Cirque d'Hannibal', where tradition says Hannibal held a council of war, while that he stayed up there waiting for his stragglers is 'an historic fact'. Or is it? For certainly the stone circle is unlikely to have borne that name through twenty centuries and more.

At the opposite end of the plain 'the traveller sees before him the hospice belonging to the Military and Religious Order of St Maurice, dependant on the mother house at Aosta'. In one part of the building 'an ecclesiastic furnishes gratuitous hospitality to needy travellers'; and the other part was in 1859 (this was written fifteen years later) converted into 'a tolerable inn with a very civil landlord where one or two dogs (St Bernards) are kept', the word 'tolerable' in old guide books of the time being always of comical connotation, as when it says of some town in Germany or France 'tolerable German or French is spoken'; and the St Maurice of the previous sentence being no other than the St Maurice of the Theban Legion, subject of El Greco's painting at the Escorial. Of which a smaller and most curious version, probably the *modello* for the larger painting, with the legionaries not in Roman kilts but Elizabethan trunk-hose, was in the former Royal collection in Roumania.

Moving on for a moment from the Little to the Great St Bernard, lying at 8,131 feet, for 'here, in the practice of the most disinterested benevolence, lives a community of Religieux, who devote the best time of their life, when man is most susceptible of his powers for its enjoyment, to the service of their fellow-men, those whose pursuits oblige them to traverse these dreary fields in seasons of danger'. In winter there is seven or eight feet of snow around the hospice, and the drifts sometimes accumulate to the height of forty feet, but 'the convent is warmed with hot air by stoves'; and can it really have been the case that 'the severity of the climate often impaired the health of the monks', and they were driven to retire to a lower and more genial clime, 'with broken constitutions'? For this is not the fate of the managers and staff of Swiss mountain resort hotels.

Attached to the room 'appropriated to visitors' is 'a cabinet of plants, insects and minerals of the Alps, in which a day unfavourable for out-doors enjoyment may be passed with interest and pleasure'; but not the whole of a long day, surely, in looking at such things! While, in the room itself, we would have found 'a harmonium given by the composer Blumenthal, and a piano which was a present from HRH the Prince of Wales' (later King Edward VII), 'and not a little prized', on which to perform – what music? Perhaps the songs of the *lions comiques* of the music-halls?

And back again from the Great to the Little St Bernard whence, continuing into Italy, we would come to the torrent called La Recluse, overhung by the Roche Blanche which is a huge bank of gypsum, 'perfectly agreeing' with the account of Polybius in his *Universal History*, of the passage of Hannibal by such a rock on his way to Italy, and enough 'to force conviction on the minds of unprejudiced enquirers' who, if doubtful, are urged to follow it up – only who is there with the time to do this? – in the examination of the subject by General Melville, in de Luc's treatise, the researches of Wickham and Cramer, or Brockedon in his repeated visits to the Alpine passes.

And going down a little lower (and remembering 'if over-walking ourselves into a state of constipation, to take no physic, but rest a day, drink copiously of water, and eat bilberries',) we would come to the valleys of goitres and cretins, where (ninety years ago) scarcely a woman was free from it, and those who had no swelling were laughed at and called 'goose-necked'. And all the time, except that this was at the other side of steep mountains, we would not be far away from a village of long stone huts, where the church, on a height, 'has a musical peal of bells', and the dark blue dresses of the women, worn on Sundays, 'are made to give great apparent width of shoulder', almost like a pair of wings. 'Kerchiefs and aprons worked with flowers, and white caps are worn', and they ride, two together, astride, upon donkeys which are the beasts of burden, and 'when too old to work are salted down and eaten'.

Which said, we have come a long way from home on this wet Sunday afternoon, to end with a salted saddle of donkey for our supper. All in order to give a push to our project and get it moving.

V.I.P. Lounge

Just a doorway sandwiched between several more doorways in a row. Doors labelled *Personnel Only*, or leading to lavatories or store rooms. Other persons, I don't know who they are, get led there as of right, under personal escort. Some sort of 'grounded' air hostess walks ahead of them.

But there is nothing to feel shy about. Just turn the door-handle and walk inside.

Soft music, and softer carpets. And when the door closes behind you – no one could ever accuse it of 'shutting' – it 'closes' indeed with something of what the poet wrote of as 'a vegetable clang' – you are insulated in a kind of demi-world or world between. 'Insulated' in the old dictionary sense of 'isolated by materials not conducting electricity', the currents in question being every direct contact with the ordinary human emotions.

Or so they think and hope. 'They' being the airport authority. But we shall see!

In the meantime how innocuous the taped music! There is the feeling in all around that everything is nicely under control. And knowing perfectly well the answer we go up to the girl in uniform sitting at a desk and ask her how long there is to wait.

The 'call' will come around six-forty when we will 'proceed through gate eleven and collect our embarkation cards prior to boarding', which makes it sound like hand-to-hand fighting in an old naval battle. Which seats would we prefer?

Meanwhile make ourselves comfortable, and we can have anything we like to drink except champagne. There will be plenty of that on board after 'take off'. At this the automaton who is rather pretty allows herself a trained smile to remind one of the last minute of consciousness in the operating-theatre. 'Just clench the fingers like so! And try to count five!' Then the pentathol and oblivion.

If only it is as easy as that!

We carry our hand luggage to a far corner and sink deep into a couple of armchairs. And the identical young woman comes round a moment or two later with two vodka martinis à la James Bond and paper maple leaves to rest them on.

So we are still here. And we have time, more than time enough, to look around.

It is too comfortable for words. That is to say, there are long curtains – and they must be very tall windows – of expensive material. 'Man-made fibre' of course and not silk, but in the same relationship to that as percale is to linen. And one quickly knows the difference. Of quite pretty pattern, in exactly the same ratio as that of the receptionist at her desk to feminine beauty which is to say a good deal better than nothing, but not the genuine thing.

Too comfortable for words! And in a sense not comfortable at all – were there measures, decibels, ounces, kilowatts of comfort. Yet the chairs are not those of a Harley Street waiting room. Oh! no. They are the chairs of high powered executives' ideal homes. One who has 'been places' and 'knows his way round'.

Look at the landscapes! The accent is on snow scenes and skiing resorts. Not that you see the hotels but they cannot be far away through the pinewoods. And at this moment there comes a roar louder than the crashing of an avalanche, than the grinding and roaring of all avalanches; and the giant metal cetacean is circling overhead and is about to 'touch down'.

Or doing the opposite? Starting off. For it amounts to the same thing. Perhaps the receptionist at the desk, blonde daughter of Erebus and Nox, can tell the difference!

And our eyes are still on the snowscapes. 'They' must have bought up the whole show, 'en bloc'. And what did 'they' do with the rest of the pictures? There is a summer scene in a corner, but not as though the painter had meant it seriously.

It is going to be a long wait. But there are magazines in plenty on a table a foot or two away. *Vogue, Harper's Bazaar*, and so on, both back numbers and up to date, so that one can relax and read of the 'jet set' in this predominantly feminine décor and place of detention.

'People are talking about.' But for how long? With portraits. And by the next issue, naturally enough, 'they' have changed the subject.

Now an announcement, only heard fragmentarily as from the prison governor, or governess's office – or boudoir? – and relayed through the cells. At which the hostess with an air of favouritism – or is it that she senses a neuropath and manic-depressive when she sees one? – comes up and interprets, 'Take off will be delayed for forty-five minutes owing to slight engine-trouble. An announcement will be made later.'

Almost certainly this will mean still further delay. And the hostess, so feminine of a sudden that one wonders if she is male or female, minces off and vanishes intriguingly behind a curtain.

It is time to pay attention to our fellow passengers.

We are to be sent up with them for eleven hours flying time in the metal dragon-fly. When it feels like starting, that is to say.

Opposite is a young woman in a mini-skirt all revealing up to her hips, cigarette in hand, and drinking what must be a gin and tonic to judge by the slice of lemon. She would be here anyway, so that in a sense she is as impersonal as the drapes or carpets, and not here at all.

Her companion is the young man in the advertisement as they sit together smiling up at the steward bringing them their dinners, in a kind of rapture at such generous treatment by the air company. Reserve has broken down under this stimulus and with the free drinks. In another moment they will be telling him every detail of their honeymoon. That is implied in the picture. But in fact married for years, and taking a second honeymoon away from the family because they are so mad about BOAC, Lufthansa, KLM, or whatever line you prefer yourself.

And next time they are bringing the children. But if you listen carefully they are talking Spanish, and probably Mexican, and completely and utterly unreal. Except that they are there just opposite and you could walk over and pinch them.

It happens to one very occasionally to see the live person out of an advertisement walking in Bond Street or Piccadilly. I have passed the bearded Commander Whitehead of Schweppes fame at the door of Fortnum and Mason; and the live man and woman out of a whole run of advertisements for tweed coats in *The New Yorker* at the very moment of their being photographed outside the London Pavilion. It is not the same sensation as recognizing a film star, a famous broadcaster, or politician.

There are as many shades and tones in the real as in the unreal; 57 Heinz varieties, to take the first thing that comes to mind, and the only fault in that instance is that it is a fixed and unalterable number allowing of no further additions or it would break the spell. Something in fact like the Wallace Collection, which is kept static by statute and no new pictures accepted or allowed, compared to the Metropolitan or the National Gallery in Washington, not London, where new accessions are arriving all the time.

To recognize someone you have watched moving and speaking is different from identifying them from a drawing or photographic 'still'. Just to pass them in the street is to see them given speech and movement.

Another announcement. 'Owing to unforeseen circumstances it is regretted that there will be some further delay.' Or that is the gist of it for in the middle of the sentence someone of real, not fictitious importance and worthy of V.I.P. treatment – or so one assumes for we are 'kept guessing' – has arrived.

She has no less than two of the 'grounded' air hostesses escorting her. One to carry her bag, and the other to hold her by the arm. An old lady, sixty, but more likely eighty years old, and quite capable of walking by herself. So that one wonders why she is being looked after with such solicitude.

Of perfectly, indeed uniquely extraordinary appearance. A green toque or turban of nondescript muslin material and macaroon consistency. But mattering not at all in comparison with her face, to which I return in an instant. Green, voluminous, as though padded overcoat, or coats; green knitted mittens and green knitted socks worn over black stockings.

Her face is perfectly enamelled white; the white without the lights or shine of china, and perhaps the *pâte tendre* of fine French porcelain is the nearest approach to it. Upon this she has applied rouge of nearly geranium vividness, but yet rose-like and within the gamut of the rose. It is evident that long ago, despite it all, she must have had a beautiful skin.

Very large black eyes, the disproportionate eyes of shrimps, or whitebait, or even dragonflies; and a most evident and odd wig, black as a rook's wing, but hardly of hair at all in the human sense. More like the cloth wigs worn by the married women in the ghettoes of Cracow and Lublin.

This extraordinary apparition is deposited almost against her will on a sofa, for she is perfectly able to find a seat for herself. The pair of air hostesses put her down there almost with embraces and endearments. And then leave her.

And she begins looking round; just as we are doing. Looking round at her new neighbours. Feeling in her enormous bag for something; and it is obvious, preparing for a long wait.

There is a moment or two's delay, and then I feel her eyes on me. We have met before. We are meeting now. And will meet again.

And now one little mystery is explained.

The resident air hostess, daughter of Erebus and Nox, who disappeared a few minutes ago emerges from behind the curtain wheeling a trolley of canapés or hors d'oeuvres. On the lower shelf are tumblers of different sizes and a row of bottles. It is a difficult, noisy progress for her with all the glasses tinkling and clattering; and the young man, true to his rôle, smiles up at her as he lifts one of the wheels over a fold of carpet, and she smiles back at him.

There are smoked salmon and tinned asparagus wrapped in brown bread. And hot chipolatas, as well, with toothpicks to lift them by. Other dishes have canapés with warm haddock inside; or little rounds of bread with goose liver. There are even squares of toast spread with caviar.

You can have vodka, aquavit, Martinis, 'bloody Marys'; or long drinks, gin and tonic, Bourbon 'on the rocks', or Scotch, or rye. But not too many of any, or of all of them.

'Oblonsky took off his overcoat and, his hat over one ear . . . made his way to the buffet for an appetizer of vodka with a morsel of fish, saying something to the painted, befrizzled Frenchwoman, all ribbons and lace, behind the counter – something that made even her burst into a peal of laughter.'

It is the *zakuska* hour.

And if so, why not the real thing!

'The men went into the dining-room and walked up to a table on which stood half a dozen different kinds of vodka and as many kinds of cheese, with and without little silver scoops, caviar, herrings, preserves of various kinds, and plates with thin slices of French bread.

The men stood round the fragrant vodka and the delicacies' etc. etc.

Time and again in *Anna Karenina*, even in *Resurrection*, there are these accounts of well-to-do Russians feeding from the sideboard before the meal began. 'It is the *Vorschmack* (*Dinette*) of the northern nations'; and one authority mentions raw herrings; *balyk* (sturgeon dried in the sun); raw smoked goose; *rastigai*, patties of the isinglass and flesh of the sturgeon ('very much like muffins with fish'); recommends a glass of *Kümmel* (*Alasch*); or of *Listofka*, 'an excellent spirit flavoured with the leaves of the blackcurrant'; adding that 'the curious may try the other liquors or vodkas which will be served up'; but that the best, however, of all, is perhaps the goblet of cool Lompopo, 'the recipe of which is supposed to have travelled from the Baltic provinces'; and ends with a warning that 'should digestion require it, the Syr, or cheese from the *zakuska*, and even the caviar may be served up again, although it is not customary at a Russian table'.

As against which, a traveller who was kept waiting between trains at the station where travellers got out to dine mid-way between St Petersburg and Moscow, watched the Tartar waiters 'in their bright coloured silk shirts, worn over another garment of equal effect and neatness', giving the last touch to the tables before the express came in and licking the caviar to keep it bright and shining as the hungry travellers poured in.

Surely human hands have never had contact with the canapés served up in the V.I.P. lounge. It is all so impersonal. Behind that curtain there must be the 'de luxe' Gypsy fittings we all know from the galley of an aeroplane. Light metal containers, they look to be; whole shelves of them which pull out, but there are surprisingly few of them for the numbers of meals served. The individual plastic trays are all ready, warm and waiting. But that is if you are travelling 'economy'. The true de luxe Gypsy treatment is for first-class passengers only. A whole saddle of lamb, or baron of beef may be wheeled past on a trolley. And it can be real china and not plastic cups and plates. Where is the hedgehog cooked in clay of the Gypsy camp-fire?

But this is the inside, not the outside of the caravan. Does the bench you are sitting on make up into a sleeping berth? Flying at forty-seven thousand feet with a following wind, at seven hundred m.p.h., so the report says which you hand back to the person sitting behind you. Where are the air crew off to, next? To another continent altogether? I am beginning to think of them as the 'Gypsies' of *Gräfin Maritza* and the *Czardas Fürstin* except that the tuneful music is so old-fashioned.

But we are not up in the clouds. Far from it. We are still grounded. And of a sudden impulse I go up to the desk – and ask the hostess the way to the cloak-room. And she answers with a shadow of pain changing to sympathy and pity in her expression, 'I'm afraid you must go outside. You will find it on the left beyond the bookstalls.'

When I come back, everything as in a tomb-chamber is unchanged. But it is as though I have been away a minute, five minutes, or a hundred years.

There are continual arrivals and departures. But time has become entirely static in the V.I.P. lounge among the V.I.P.'s. This, although the clock over the door has the correct hour to the second and there are planes leaving and arriving all day and all night long.

Static and insulated, but one could catch a cold here, or any other sort of germ, and carry it with one to the furthest ends of the world. Imagine travelling with a disease on oneself at twice the speed of sound! But the microbes are in no hurry. They work to their own timetable and care not if they win or lose.

While I was away those few moments a whole family has settled in. But it makes no more difference than the opening of a vault, the putting in of a body, and sealing it up again. Till next time, which could be now or never.

A family who are archetypal, father and mother and three sons, in proof that it is possible to be extraordinary just in virtue of their ordinariness. Ordinary, that is to say, in the North-American canon with all three sons in absolute facsimile of their father, close-cropped hair, blunt features, and check shirts, but with fantasy footwear; and all four call for 'Coke' and drink it noisily. The mother looking round and interested in the other passengers; the father not at all.

What time is it? the clock marks ten minutes before seven. But time is in relation to each individual and how long he or she has been waiting. When they arrived and when they will be leaving, with that indefinite amount of time ahead which yet is fixed and certain. Already settled although it cannot and will not take place until it happens. But, also, with an eleven-hour flight in front of one, the arrival hour must throw the departure out of reason. In which sense it is absolutely true that the future works backwards and affects the present.

Could we think of this as though it were measurements marked out on a ball of string. On one of those balls of string that revolve as they unwind; a particular theory of time being that it will unwind entirely, sooner or later, and come to an end. But it is just as likely that it winds itself again no sooner than the string has left your hand. So that there are unlimited lengths of it, although it is equally true that its length is entirely finite and could be measured in so many aeons and centuries, or feet and inches.

And I look for the *Fates* or *Parcae* in Dr Lempriere's *Classical Dictionary* only to find in unsuspected coincidence that they were three in number, Clotho, Lachesis, and Atropos, daughters, according to Hesiod, of Nox and Erebus, like the blonde receptionist of the V.I.P. lounge where we are waiting. Clotho, the youngest of the sisters, presides over the moment in which we are born, and holds a distaff in her hand. Lachesis spins out all the events and actions of our lives; and Atropos, the eldest of the three, cuts the thread of human life with a pair of scissors.

Which of the sisters, then, is she? Not Atropos who was clothed in black. But Clotho held a distaff reaching from heaven to earth, and wore on her head a crown of seven stars, which seems appropriate; while Lachesis, too, wore a robe variegated with a great number of stars. Atropos, with her scissors in one hand, held clues of thread of different size, according to the length and shortness of the lives they seemed to contain. Her duty among the three sisters is to cut the thread of life without regard to sex, age, or quality.

The Parcae were generally shown as old women with chaplets made of wool, 'and interwoven with the flowers of the narcissus'. And, sure enough, the receptionist has a vase of daffodils in front of her upon her desk. But everyone of long life lives to be old. It can happen to all of us. And Dr Lempriere ends with the grammarian Hyginus of Alexandria, who attributed the invention of five letters of the Greek alphabet to the Parcae and who, 'with others', calls them 'the secretaries of heaven, and keepers of the archives of eternity'.

At which moment there is a loud clatter of breaking china. It comes from the direction of the receptionist's desk, and it is obvious from her nervous manner that she has been drinking a surreptitious cup of tea or coffee. As though to cover her embarrassment there is a redoubled roaring of aeroplanes overhead. A vc 10 must be coming in to land from a huge distance; direct, non-stop, from the Caribbean; from India; from Anchorage, Alaska, on the trans-Polar flight to Japan. And she begins to tidy the papers on her desk as if to make room for new arrivals.

Things are happening. That is to say, normality is getting out of hand.

The old lady of the enamelled face and black, black wig has at last found what she was looking for in her handbag. It is a cardboard platter. And she is asking the receptionist for some scraps of food.

'Just a little of that haddock out of the canapés, if there is any of it left, and a very little milk.' The hostess sidles behind the curtain again, and comes back with the saucer in her hand.

The old lady is outside the church porch where she goes every day to feed the cats. A big old 'tigress' cat, black and white and yellow, comes up tail in air and rubs herself against the green-gloved hand.

And 'Whitey'? Where's 'Whitey'? And she mumbles something about 'the boys'. 'Why don't they keep them longer in school? They come out, and play around, and look what they did yesterday!' Sure enough, there is a twisted railing near to some tombs just by the church door.

But 'Whitey's' not here today. 'They've driven him away.' And in an instant I am inside, not outside a church when and where something very curious happened to me.

It was late autumn or early winter of 1918 with the war still on, and I was in the army. The *Ballets Russes* were appearing at the Coliseum which many took for a first sign of the war ending. The season began while I was at Albuhera Barracks, Aldershot, early in August or September. As the cold weather began it was announced that the vicar of St Martin's-in-the-Fields had opened the church and was having it kept warm for homeless persons to spend the night in. There was a good deal about it in the newspaper.

My brother and I had been one evening to a performance and decided to look in afterwards at St Martin's-in-the-Fields. We entered, saw at once that the church was apparently empty, and began walking up the left-hand aisle. But as we got nearer we could see there was a woman sitting in one of the pews. I am not suggesting she was not there already when we came in, but it was as if she had suddenly materialized.

I can see her now. She was dressed in a light blue coat and skirt, wearing a hat, but without an overcoat. A stout middle-aged woman between fifty and sixty years old, but I did not want to look too closely at her face. I remember that she was sitting very still and motionless.

We walked past her, not liking to look back. There was, as I have said, no one else in the church; no verger, or other person that I could see. When we got to the altar we turned, and began walking down the main aisle. It was then that we heard yapping, as of a Pekinese, or some small dog, and it was coming from the direction of the woman sitting in the pew.

By now she had disappeared. We could not see her. But the barking or yapping grew louder as we came nearer. There she was in her blue coat and skirt lying face downwards in the pew, and every time there was a bark her body moved. She was either lying on what was yapping; or she was doing it herself. And not liking it at all; still less, wanting to look back, we left St Martin's-in-the-Fields.

The two women, her of the enamelled face and black wig, coming to the church door every day to feed stray cats, and her of Gibbs's fine church in Trafalgar Square, have some sort of affinity to each other. It is of little importance that the familiar was a dog in one instance and stray cats in the other. It is a distinctive feature in stories of poltergeists that animal phantasms when they occur, and they are the supreme manifestations of its powers, 'are objects which could not be real'. 'His sister, who was still living' – we quote from one of them – 'described, without being able to give any explanation of it, an animal that she and her sisters saw in the garden, described as being like a white cat, only larger and with a long, pointed snout . . . She also saw in the daytime a large white cat in the garden. It was larger than a real cat and with a long snout. It appeared to go through the closed garden-door or through the wall into the engine-house, where Mr Proctor, being in the mill-yard, saw it go into the engine-house and disappear as if it had gone into the fire. The cat was also seen by her in one of the bedrooms, going through a closed door.' So much for the hauntings at Willington Mill; the inability to distinguish between a horse and cow, or cat and dog, it could be added, being a sign of mental disturbance, so that if animal phantasms of this nature are of hypnotic origin and derivation they are no less the creations and illusions of a diseased mind.

I have written of the old lady just as I saw her outside the porch of St Sepulchre's, near the old North Gate, at the end of Sheep Street, coming down an asphalt path through the graveyard from the back of the church. I have wondered, and still wonder, about her history. Of what past was her enamelled face the relict? Her feeding of the stray cats can only be a symptom of loneliness, and I picture her living in one room by herself. Or I may be wrong. But I do not think persons surrounded by relations are of the sort to take out saucers of food into churchyards and be teased by school children for their eccentricities. Certainly, if there be such a thing as a lasting, or even irregular and indefinite emanation of a human being, there should be something left of her along this church yard pathway in a Midland town. Something not gone for ever, but which can be recalled.

Come, then, at invitation, and in order to while away for me some of the hours of waiting in the V.I.P. lounge. Wherein few persons indeed are of importance enough to justify their cosseted surroundings; and least of all myself who would be among the very last to be in possession of the necessary, the indispensable credentials. Which are those in nearly every case of material achievement; or would be, if one did not feel certain that all like myself are here on false pretences. It is not good for business that this sanctum should be empty. Or, for that matter, too full, either. There should be a modicum, a half-filling of the emptiness.

For no one would credit how empty it can look in the early hours with dawn coming up and all the lights still burning. Yet perhaps at its emptiest when every seat is filled, and all but one or two are sleeping. When the receptionist is relieved at her post and another of the three sisters, Lachesis or Atropos, sits down at her desk and arranges her papers, pencil and scissors in front of her, in the young and raw morning.

The V.I.P. treatment, if properly administered in its three elements, past, present, and future, would admit of poignant contrasts among the heavy and the weightless. Ramses II of the Nineteenth Dynasty (1292–1225 BC) and his train of attendants in their complex of tunnels and tomb-chambers, their own V.I.P. lounge, huger than the biggest London Underground Station, all in transit, and still waiting. But, also, Napoleon fleeing from Moscow through the snow in the climacteric year of 1812. The door would be open for him, as I think all would agree who have seen the addresses of welcome and farewell from the municipality of Paris to Napoleon and to Louis xviii in the one year 1814–15.*

And, as well, the weightless among whom we would include the beggars of Rembrandt and his *Rat-Killer*; these last a thing unique and extraordinary in all art for how is it that Rembrandt has so 'caught' their stance and attitude that you would know they were beggars just from their shoes and leggings if you could not see their hands? There are some twenty of his etchings of beggars, the one more wonderful than the other in loose point of drawing. In his beggars Rembrandt scarcely bothers about a background. In his *Blind Fiddler* of 1631, the year in which he made most of his etchings of vagrants, there is the fiddler's wife or trull in the background, facing the other way leaning on her stick as if 'working' the scanty audience, and it is enough for Rembrandt to draw her in a matter of seconds, it can have been no longer, to fix her identity. All his beggars, it is to be noted, have wrapped or bandaged feet which are a study in themselves, and indescribable baggy and loose trousers.

But the *Rat-Killer* stands alone and apart. He wears a kind of tall, ragged Hussar cap of rat-skin, and has a tray slung round his neck, resting against his stomach. It is his 'shop-window'; a shelf of dead rats in fact, but on the far edge of it perches what must be his tame rat to show what he can do with rats, his 'rat-quisling' or worse, for he fills the rôle of rat-'provo' or trusted prisoner among the dead of the mass graves and fires of incineration. But, as he can be trained his life has been spared; or is it a mother-rat whom he has 'spaded' so that she can have illicit amours on the deathbed, but no offspring? It is implicit in the etching how many times the *Rat-Killer* must have been bitten. How does he kill his rats? He has no dog with him; and one dog would not be enough in the silt of the water-ways and in infested barns and cellars. Rat-poison will have been primitive enough even if he had his own secret way of dealing with them. It is more probable that he cornered them, shut them in one place, and bludgeoned them to death, having inherited the trade and been brought up to it by his parent. And one falls to wondering who was his mother; and who sewed his rat-skin cap for him?†

There is, of course, a slight shudder and a drawing back of the transit passengers into their seats, who gather their possessions and hand-luggage closer to

* Farewell to Napoleon leaving Paris for Elba and welcome for return of the Bourbon; departure of same and return of Napoleon for the Hundred Days; leave-taking of Napoleon *en route* for St Helena, and the Bourbon back again. Six 'loyal addresses' in all in thirteen months.

† In another larger and more detailed etching (of 1632) the *Rat-Killer* stands at a doorway near a broken rain-tub, and is being paid for his services. But why does the householder turn away from him? Again why does the *Rat-Killer* wear a sword and sword-belt? He has the same high cap, but what is conspicuous is his cloak or fur-stole (of rat-skin?). In one hand he holds a long pole, six or eight feet high, topped by a basket from which dead rats are hanging by the neck. But on the rim of it a live rat is crawling, and there is another rat-quisling upon his shoulder. A horrible child, an assistant rat-hangman, who goes with him and holds a wooden box for dead rats, or whatever, completes the etching. It is more finished, but less telling than the smaller *Rat-Killer*.

them, as the door is opened and such-like are admitted, even escorted into the V.I.P. lounge. It is not unusual for propinquity to the very important to be unpleasant in its consequences.

But where are we off to? For within reason one can go from here to anywhere one wants, even to Samarkand after protracted and quite unnecessary negotiation. There is only one difficulty which is that the tickets have to be paid for. Payment can be made by instalment though this only prolongs the paying.* No one would have got in here without himself, or someone else suffering loss because of it. The *Rat-Killer* is paying for his rat-bites and other miseries. Perhaps, also, for the cruelties he has committed in course of his profession; while both the Pharaoh and Napoleon have much to pay for. The stay here, whether short or long, is both a reward and an expiation. The three sons of the typical American family are paying for their ordinariness, while the lady of the enamelled face is 'checking in' for her eccentricities. The old are paying for being alive still, while the unborn are paying for being born at all.

I have no idea where I want to go for the moment. Having seen most of the fine architecture in the world excepting Khajuraho, the 'Black Pagoda' of Konarak, and the temples of Southern India, though I have leap-frogged that by going one further to Ceylon, I am now more interested in the Solomon Islands, the New Hebrides, Fiji, Moorea, Bora-Bora; and this for the landscape, the flowers and flowering trees more than for any other reason. At that, for a few days only and no longer. For no more time than it would take to admire the oncocyclus irises and the blue bee-eaters upon the telegraph wires in the gentler clime of the Levant. Or, more exciting, to visit the far apart, three or four great cities or rookeries of the flamingos and wait to see them rise upon the wing. In fact, the flamencos or phanoropes of the mud flats and river deltas, which is no more to say than that one could wish to see specimens of all the races of metallic-lustred humming-birds in one and the same garden at the same time.

Every variety of camellia there has been, not singly, but in the profusion of their flowering; and again, the oncocyclus irises, not of Syria and Lebanon but of Turkey, Iran, Transcaucasia, 'immense flowers speckled with dark maroon in contrast to their ivory-white standards; white lilac-veined standards and falls clothed in dense black velvet; or a lake side Iranian', considered by many to be the most beautiful of all irises, 'soft clear yellow and indescribable, crystalline in texture'.† Or, all the roses (the old and not the new); the florists' tulips, carnations and auriculas; the new hybrids of the orchid cactus and Hawaiian hibiscus; but not the rhododendron. In my life I have written many sets of poems about flowers. But upon that, never. The rhododendron is Nature's 'top of the pops'. It does not conform as a work of art, but behaves as though it were an improvisation with no hand to guide it.

---

* While drawing the cheque to the travel agents in the Haymarket for our air tickets to Japan, I looked involuntarily across the street to the cinema opposite, and noticed that the film playing was called, 'Live now, pay later'.

† Elegantissima (iberica) JCA 3263, paradoxa choschab, and Urmiensis JCA from the *The Plantsmen's* list 1968–9, Sherborne, Dorset.

Starting from here we could circle round the Piazzas of St Peter's and St Mark's to the consternation of the pigeons; fly down the gorge of Petra with the shadow of our aeroplane moving parallel to us along the wall of rock; look down on the 'lost' city of Machu Picchu, the Potala of Lhasa, or the glass towers of New York and Chicago. It is all the same to the receptionist sitting at her desk.

The noise of the engine can intrude upon the Mato Grosso, the 'forbidden' spice islands of Indonesia, and the remotest atolls of the Pacific. Or without a second's warning it can come 'hedge-hopping' over the spinneys and fox-coverts of Northamptonshire with a horrifying, head-ducking roar. There is no escaping it, whether in a city of ten millions, or on the lifeless Antarctic of all the ice and snow.

Just now – and heaven knows what time it is of night or day! – there is a piercing revving up of engines. And the moaning of metal coming from another direction is continuous, but as if it were drugged and yet crying out in pain. It could not be with pleasure. And it carries a kind of echo in itself and comes louder. It is indeed nearly screaming at this moment. We can picture it wheeling slowly, so slowly, into position on the runway. Then, standing perfectly still, yet trembling. Rising to an unendurable, even sexual pitch of emotion. Surely it must be 'off' soon and cannot be held waiting any more. No one on board, or within a mile or so, can stand it for much longer. Then, cut off. Absolutely quiet, almost before the sound dies of itself. And now once more deepening into an ear-splitting roaring. It is off down the runway intoxicating itself with its own speed, and at last airborne and coming back over us a few moments later as if to look down and see if we are still here.

A huge aircraft certainly. One of those that on arrival come right in and nozzle their nose against the airport shed as though stabled, and about to feed from a nosebag or manger. And the passengers all leave from the front hatchway and step directly into the main building. This animal tameness and docility from an aeroplane is something new. One has read of, or even seen tame dolphins, and now, it seems, a tame whale in an aquarium. For of all creatures, vertebrate or invertebrate, it is a whale that the newest aeroplanes most nearly resemble. A cetacean, but with fixed and immovable fins, at present, but perhaps for not much longer; and with the flukes of the tail immensely heightened and exaggerated.

A year or two ago at Orly Airport, where we spent one of the most expensive nights of our lives, I watched from the restaurant a huge aircraft provisioning for the flight to Madagascar. At the next table were a bevy of white-clad nuns, but with dark faces, bound for Antananarivo, for Tamatave, or Tananarive. They hurried through their dinner in silence, a little awed by the long journey; and the 'call' came, and they went down the stair carrying their bags and parcels, and emerged a moment later and climbed into the huge aeroplane only a few feet away just underneath us.

It grew dark just in those minutes. The lights went on both in the restaurant and in the aeroplane while the aerodrome transformed itself from light to darkness. A lot more passengers went swarming on board behind them, one or two of them at least in tears from the prospect of the long parting. But they can have hardly settled into their seats before the aeroplane began slowly to move off with lights blazing into the darkness. We drank our coffee and before the cups were finished they must have reached some far corner of the airfield. We would never see the nuns, or anything to do with them again. But how to know whether, or not it was the nuns of a few moments ago as there came a roaring which died into the distance, and another and louder roaring, this time of an arrival, took their place!

There is still a horror and a solemnity about these arrivals and departures. No one watches carefully as the filthy dirty diesel engine draws a quarter-of-a-mile-long train of coaches out of Paddington or Waterloo; or the liner slips away from its berth at Tilbury or Southampton. There is no longer a credibility of the expected. But, curiously, the farewells and agonies of separation are almost intensified and made worse by continual increase in speed. So long as Australia or New Zealand were three weeks or more away by sea there may even have been comfort in that union of time and distance. Once embarked you were 'taken care of' till you arrived. There could be storms at sea but accidents were unlikely. Yet when the experience is squeezed into a few hours, merely, and you only look out onto the clouds, the terrible speed and urgency with the impossibility of stopping or coming down excepting at prepared sites hundreds of miles apart compresses and thereby exaggerates the distance. There are no safe anchorages, or wayside stations for the aeroplane.

We have reached the stage of entire and total metamorphosis when personalities are fluid and interchangeable. Someone has left the door open for a few moments so that the loudspeaker announcements though nearly unintelligible, seem addressed to one personally, and even aimed at one's head. There is 'a spot of bother' as the receptionist, Clotho or Lachesis? – I have decided against Atropos in my mind – phrased it just now, about a Lufthansa bound for Stuttgart, among other places. Eventually, two passengers, a Mr Schliemann and a Mr Meyer, are called by name and requested to report at once to the Information Desk, and the situation is becoming desperate. But might it not be better for them if the aeroplane left without them? This is interrupted by no less than a proclamation, in Spanish and incomprehensible English, concerning what promises to be a round flight to the Spanish Main, and the door shuts. And we are alone again where the announcements are just as urgent in tone but muffled by the carpets and the curtains.

Departure from the V.I.P. lounge when the moment comes is equivalent to stepping voluntarily into a hearse which has been taken over and converted into a coach tour. And from now onward there is no declining. You have got to go. You will be escorted in a group across the tarmac and made welcome on board. Soon over the loudspeaker you will be given the compliments of your captain and your crew who could not care less if they never see you again. But once among the V.I.P.'s even if by accident, you are there for ever and have not left them. It has become inalienable and a kind of birthright like an inherited title which there are legal difficulties in relinquishing.

How relatively quiet it is in here! Reminding one of the joke-quotation, 'Baby!

It's cold inside!' outside the cold store refrigeration centre in our local town. It is in fact warm here, rather too warm and airless, in spite of the air-conditioning; but it is spiritually, temperamentally tepid and almost cold. It is impossible to envisage a hot meal in these surroundings; only sandwiches and warmed-up canapés. The receptionist will give you tea or coffee but nothing to burn your tongue on. It is a half-way house but on the way from where to where? Even the word 'lounge', pejorative in sound and of association, is indicative of neither lying down nor sitting, but just waiting about informally with no set purpose and at no particular time of day. But, also, the V.I.P. lounge is deceptive because by no stretching of the imagination could there be sufficient persons of even minimal importance passing through here every day. It is an honorific but so lax of application that it has lost all meaning. The inmates are the fidalgos among the ordinary passengers, but they have either bought their way here through their first-class tickets, or have got in by subterfuge or by mistake. How often do the authorities know a V.I.P. when they see one, and lead him here with no more ado? How often do they make a mistake and own to it? The posthumous awards outnumber those granted to the living by many tens and tens of thousands. But the one thing certain is that the mistakes will continue. And of course, it would be very irritating to be left sitting with the others like ourselves, and only be recognized and given promotion at the last moment. There are those who would prefer to be lost sight of and ignored throughout.

Perhaps the reason why I feel unhappy here is because I have not yet been elected to it. Having not so far received enough of acclamation to know in my bones I am entitled to it, and feeling therefore unwanted and even a little angry at being here. During their lifetime there is only room here for best-selling authors. A succès d'estime is not enough, and more than one succès d'estime is worse than none at all. It is like the person who writes and telephones persistently for accommodation when he knows the hotel is full. It gives unnecessary trouble and does not make him popular. There is a kind of immodesty in going on writing with no great success.

Ah! Well! We'll listen instead to the music. But it induces a kind of stupor at the thought of it being possible to have such a degree of impersonality and anonymity in, seemingly, endless supply. Music as vacuous as the ms. poems and other writings submitted by yet more hopeless would-be authors to almost anyone who has contrived to get a book published. There is a dreamy continuity of emptiness about it. Never a tune one has known before, but always an approach and withdrawal on the brink of it, which only aggravates. And the irritating semi-luxe, or 'lounge' setting.

Day is night here under the eternal, tasteful lighting. And I suppose those long curtains are only drawn back at off-moments when the place is empty. We are in effect blindfold, all the lot of us, and not allowed to look out, or to listen. It is of course noise which is the enemy. We would not be able to hear ourselves speak, were it not for the carpets and curtains and the air-conditioning. For this last keeps an even temperature, if sometimes that of an ice-house, and reduces the excitement.

Everything is under control. But another reason for all this is in order that we should 'catch' the bulletins and announcements. Which in fact one never hears in entirety, but only thinks there was mention of the flight number, but incidentally, as though in the course of hearing the voice say something else. It is an impersonal voice giving directions to the winds; and carelessly, as if not expecting them to listen. And when it is repeated afterwards in another language it only draws attention to the inhospitality, even the hostility of wherever we are going to. We wish, more than ever, that we had never started on the journey.

Quite a few of the passengers are curled up on the chairs and sofas, sleeping. But, myself, who feels more resident than passenger, stays wide awake. Because I feel I may be wanted. There will be some special message for me, if only I can understand it. At any hour of night or morning, having long since lost all sense of time. But waiting in this purgatorio for the trumpet calls of *Leonora No 3* and delivery from this padded prison. And, instead, the whole episode of the V.I.P. lounge comes to a burlesque ending. I wake up as out of a trance, and hear the voice saying, 'Will Mr Sitwell proceed at once to Immigration Control and take his passport with him.' I gather up my belongings, murmur my thanks to the hostess, and walk off in the direction I have been told to go.

As I pass by, I feel I know her well enough now to smile at the old phantom of the churchyard. Half-an-hour later I am back again. It was all a mistake. It was Mr Schliemann of Stuttgart they were inquiring for, and not Mr Sitwell. I had heard the name wrong. But when I pass where the old lady of St Sepulchre's was sitting, she is no longer there. And by the time I reach my padded armchair I find the papers I've been reading, but cannot remember where I've come from, or where I'm going.

Tropicalia

There is a part of the garden we call the wilderness where I walk every afternoon after luncheon. The name must date from the time my grandmother and her four sisters lived here as children about a hundred and thirty years ago. It is overhung with yew trees and the ivy crawls thick upon the ground. But the beginning of the path has always been called the church walk, and it leads to a door in the wall which I have had bricked up. Wood pigeons fly noisily out of the boughs without warning, and now and then a brown owl flaps off a yew branch into the high trees. More than once an owlet, wide-eyed and steady of gaze as a well-known photographer's model, has looked at me and not believed it, but taken to wing and away. In fact, it is an Early Victorian shrubbery, livelier and perhaps more dangerous by night than day.

Later, there comes a plank laid over what becomes almost a waterfall in spring after a heavy rain shower. You cross the drive, and over into another and more wooded part which in the spring is thick with snowdrops, and up and along and back again by both banks of a little stream. There are no longer the druidic yew trees. Instead, a giant chestnut with trailing screens and fans of chestnut candles stands like a world of its own and invites you to look up high into its boughs. The two or three trees near to it have every year some fifteen to twenty crows' nests in their tops. It is a small rookery.

And the path comes out into the open, leading to where the ground under a great beech tree was white with anemones not long ago, and there were wood violets at the foot of the tree trunk. I walk through the wilderness, I have said, at all times of year; never being sure in my mind which is more propitious for my purposes, a rainy day or one of those rare, hot afternoons when you can wish yourself without much strain on the imagination into anywhere else you would prefer. Soon it will be another winter, and the yew trees will rise like pagodas with the snow outlining their many storeys and lying heavy on their tilted eaves. How to believe this while, as now, the 'lords and ladies' are unsheathing their fourteenth-century green hoods below the same yews!*

In fact, I make use of this wilderness or shrubbery as a kind of forcing-house, though of course no sooner have I reached, let alone neared, the farthest point of the trajectory than I am wishing myself back to where I really belong, and in particular to this dull circuit under the dark yews. Their shade, properly considered, conveys to anywhere one wants to go and as well, to anywhere that one has been. But, in particular, and by the law of disparities, from this little and hedged-in part of Northamptonshire to the Orient, both as it is, and as it may once have been.

* Early in August, the brighter-than-tomato-red and poisonous berry-thyrsuses of the 'lords and ladies', *Arum maculatum*, show up, startlingly, out of the ground ivy.

I suppose a first impression of what is meant by that magical phrase 'the Orient', or even, in little, by the mere word 'Eastern' has come to many persons, as to myself, from early memories of the inside and outside of St Mark's at Venice. Those domes that have some kind of visual association with the howdahs on the backs of elephants; the interior lined with marbles that have the effect of panels of precious silks; the golden mosaics; but perhaps more than all else the pulpits, supported on columns, with bulbous, domed canopies over them, are eloquent of a direction and a point of the compass one has not experienced before. While even at ten years old one is not too young to notice for oneself the turban'd merchants in Carpaccio and in Gentile Bellini's paintings. Too young perhaps to enjoy fully the pictures in the Accademia; but not the unforgettable and magical Carpaccios in the little Scuola degli Schiavoni. Those same merchants from the Orient must have crossed the Venetian bridges and walked along the quays.

I have written before of sitting with my brother at a little window on the stair of the Hotel Daniele in Venice in 1908, to watch the ss *San Marco* cast off from in front of the Doges' Palace and set sail for Dalmatia, and of how we wondered if we would ever reach such places when grown up. I think I already knew that the Scuola di San Giorgio degli Schiavoni had been founded in the fifteenth century for the relief of Dalmatian sailors. That land lay on the far side of the Adriatic and was therefore half in the Orient already. And for more vestiges of the East in Venice? On the far side of the city, somewhere near the Madonna dell' Orto, there are the 'three curious figures in Oriental garb (probably the portraits of Greek merchants from the Morea)', to be seen on the outside of a couple of houses, one of them known as the Casa del Tintoretto. I remember their huge turbans, and the accompanying camel, from a very early age. But why 'from the Morea' where there were never ports of any size and Athens was, then, no more than a village? How much more likely that they were Turkish merchants from Smyrna, or from Istanbul! Or from El-Iskandariya which was Alexandria! Oh! to have seen Byzantium (Istanbul) before it was sacked by the Venetians and the Crusaders under Doge Dandolo in 1204! Where the statues of the ancient world were still erect and standing; but the sumptuary arts, the domes of the churches and the mosaics showed Sassanian and other Eastern influences!

But a very strong impression of an Orient of another sort is to be derived from the paintings and frescoes of Tiepolo. What a wonder it was to have seen this last of the Venetians at the Labia and Rezzonico palaces, and in the church of the Gesuati at Venice; at the Palazzo Pisani at Strà; in the Bishop's palace at Udine; the Cappella Colleoni at Bergamo; and in the Palazzo Clerici at Milan; all of these before I was twenty-two years old, that is to say by 1920, and not later than that.

As a side issue to which study, and for the reason that no one but myself has discussed it in print before, the writer would recall his correspondence with an old lady, now dead, who from long residence in that wild land had made herself into an authority on Albania, alternating her visits there among the tribesmen and their families with looking after her mother in the suburban quiet of, I think it was Wimbledon; and who wrote to me that she always regretted there was no book of good drawings of Albanian costume as she had known it. She wrote to me à propos what I had said somewhere about *Le Grand Gilles*, that most poetical of all paintings in its implication, to tell me her theory about the dress of Pierrot.

This was that during the seventeenth and eighteenth centuries when the Venetians held Dalmatia, excepting for the republic of Ragusa, and their galleons and feluccas called in at every port down the long line of coast from Zara and Sebenico and Traù down to Corfu and the Ionian Islands, Cephalonia and Zante,* a familiar sight to the Venetian sailors must have been the Albanians come down from their mountain villages to find employment, and hanging about the harbour-side in 'zany' character, speechless because they knew no Italian, and wearing their everyday dress of white trousers, long flopping white shirt with huge buttons, and high conical white hat or fez. Was not this, she argued, the origin of Pierrot, for all that he is supposed to have had origin in Bergamo? Not too far, it might be conjectured, from that basement cellar where Donizetti was born, the musician who composed both *Lucia di Lammermoor*, the supreme opera of the whole Romantic movement with its sextet which is a *coup de théâtre* without equal in effect, and also the beggar's songs with hurdy-gurdy accompaniment for *Linda di Chamounix*. But, then, Albanians recruited from the harbours of Dalmatia may well have penetrated as far inland into the *terra firma* as Bergamo, working their way as servants or labourers. Indeed, Miss Edith Durham's theory seems improbable and at the same time convincing.

The appositeness of which last paragraph is in regard to the Orientals in Tiepolo's paintings. Not the old nanny goat Oriental of his drawings who is a familiar figure enough from frequent occurrence, but the aquiline, surely blue-eyed Oriental in striped silk gown and turban, with red hair and moustache, who stands behind the Queen of Egypt in the fresco of *The Banquet of Antony and Cleopatra* at the Palazzo Labia. For he is to all probability an Albanian, and some-one who almost a century later would have been no stranger at the blood-stained court of Ali Pasha of Janina. Thus, too, the mamelukes of Cairo and many, if not all the janissaries of the Turkish Sultans. Thus, we see him in the Labia. We know him by his tall figure and lean features, his red eyebrows, his short, shaved hair. He is always watching, as if his hand were upon the hilt of his sword. At Bergamo, in the Cappella Colleoni, he beheads the Baptist. An Albanian attendant or bodyguard, and, in case of necessity, the executioner. He lands with Cleopatra from her golden barge; and stands behind her at the Banquet.

I can never forget, when little more than twenty years old, and in the first delight of intoxicating myself with these paintings, finding Comanderia, or vino di Cipro, in a wineshop in Venice just near the church of San Moisè. Cyprus being, then, remote, impossible of access, and of a romance which later, it is true, faded the nearer one got to it, to be finally extinguished many years later by the

---

* A dichotomy, or 'continuous division distinguished by contradictory qualities' in those islands, that is further illuminated in the reflection that Zante was the birthplace of Ugo Foscolo (1778–1827), famous as an Italian poet, but, also, of Denys Solomos (1798–1857) who wrote the Hellenic national hymn; while it is written that 'les barcarolles en minore de Zante forment un genre de chansons langoureuses analogues de celles de Naples'.

seaside lodging-houses of Kyrenia, and the lodging-house food. But the memory of those days comes back to me with a vision of the painted 'flats' or side-scenes in that frescoed hall at the Labia; the one with a buffet shelved high with silver cups and dishes, a scullion or kitchen attendant – another Albanian, to judge by his nose and eyebrows – holding a fiasco of wine; or that other with just the mast and side-sail of a vessel to show we are in Venice and that the Adriatic, if not at the door, is at the window but a few feet away. How wonderful, I say again, to have seen such painted halls and stairs! All of which could be accomplished in those days, not without discomfort, on an allowance of three hundred pounds a year. But there it had to stop. And for want of further means all intimation of the Orient ceased at the five red domes and drooping datura plants of the hermits' church, San Giovanni degli Eremiti in Palermo.

Already, and even nowadays, that is a long way away from home. As are, too, the red walls and filigree interior courts of the Alhambra and the whitewashed alleys of Córdoba and Seville. But these visions fade, and I am back again in the shadow of the yew trees which, in fact, I have never left. Shadows that, I have said, are Druidic and owl-infested, as though inviting one to walk among them at the dark of night, or in deep snow. Which I have done, as to the latter; and often and always, as of purpose, it draws one's thoughts to warmer climes. The group, or, indeed, septet of laurels with ivy growing all up their stems, forming a tree-trunk Stonehenge, in fact, a wooden, but a living circle of immemorial antiquity, is probably no more than a hundred years old, but all the past is equally old to us if we were not alive in it. There is something sacred and pagan but a little bad about it, as with the green circle of a mushroom or fairy ring. I must admit to not wanting particularly to be left out in it at night, if for no reason that makes any sense. At this moment with the sun on them, the dying laurel stems with ivy clinging to them could be all that is left of a rustic arbour, like those described and illustrated in Shirley Hibberd's *Rustic Adornments for Homes of Taste* (1857), but a summer house of sinister memory in which some drama with a violent ending was enacted.

But it is another day, and my thoughts are far away on the stimulus of this hot and breathless afternoon. I am thinking of just how long it was after the time I am speaking of before I had any real experience of the tropics or semi-tropics. It did not come from the palm-lined Corso dell' Imperatrice at San Remo with toy railway line below it following the shore, and the gilt domes of the Russian church not far beyond. The magnolias and oleanders of Italy are not in question; any more than the flower-decked terraces of Isola Bella at anchor like a laden galleon rising in ten stages above the lake with the cork trees, oranges and lemons, and the white peacocks, shell-grottoes, arbours, statues, of Mercutio's dew-dropping south. Or than the narcissi growing at the water's edge from the cliffs of Capri when rowed ashore from the little steamer at six o'clock on a January morning, coming from Amalfi.

Much to the contrary, and against all reason, my first intimation of the tropical or nether world came from the hibiscus hedges of Palm Beach – which again is different in intent from the fuchsia hedges of Connemara – and from there being pelicans instead of sea-gulls to flap, heavy of beak and awkward of wing, above the sands. And on the year following upon that we landed late in the August night at Funchal which although this is a flowerless month was a first opportunity for admiring flowering trees. Not entirely, though, for we had seen the jacaranda trees a year or two before this, heliotrope or powder-blue against the azulejo'd or blue-tiled façades of Lisbon. But it was in Madeira that one saw the Uganda flame tree (*Spathodea nilotica*) for the first time, later to become familiar from the Caribbean, but which is beautiful enough with the red-orange 'tulips' in its top boughs, and the look of a park tree but from some celestial game preserve or garden of delights. Another sensation, of which in theatrical parlance this was the première, was the frangipani. I do not attempt to write of it here at length because in an attempt to enlarge the legitimate boundaries of poetry I have written a whole set of poems on the frangipani. Another memorable flowering tree was the bombax with its flower like a rose-pink starfish.

Among lesser and more earth-bound wonders was the yellow allamanda. And in Madeira for the first time the bougainvillea flamed in full glory upon one's vision though in the fifteen years since 1954 doubtless other colours have been added to its palette, there being now for instance a pure white, and a yellow bougainvillea which were not in existence then. The mesembryanthemums were legion, as were the massed brass bands of geraniums and pelargoniums; while the country roads were bordered with blue or white agapanthus and with arum lilies. Perhaps the hedges were most memorable of all for one had never thought to see hedges of blue hydrangeas eight to ten feet high. The climax of the island floralia came on an evening when the night-blooming cereus or Queen of the Night opened one after another its scented chalices, all of which were dead by morning, again offering a theme for poetry more than prose.

But I have come to a part of the wilderness where I had a curious experience a year or two ago. I was walking along when I became aware of a commotion on the path just ahead of me, and what I saw was a snake dancing on its tail and behaving in peculiar fashion. I hit out at it with my stick, catching it on its neck, and immediately a big frog jumped out of the snake's jaws and hopped away, croaking loudly. This was something that would certainly have been taken for an omen in the past and would be supposed to have ulterior meaning. It was where the stream runs out into the garden through a rocky tunnel from the field, and the wild lungwort (*pulmonaria*) shows its flower heads turning their pinky-red of maturity and their oddly spotted leaves.

But my thoughts are far away on this hot and breathless afternoon which will turn into one of those long nights with thunder booming in the distance, and I am at Dakar which is in Senegal. Having arrived there by what is the shortest flight across the Southern Atlantic from Recife (Pernambuco) in Brazil. We got there on an even hotter night than this will be, only to be told at the airport that our hotel reservations were cancelled, and that every bed in Dakar was let because of a state visit of the King of Morocco who had come to open a new mosque. It was a difficult moment to arrive in the dark continent at four o'clock in the morning with nowhere to lay our heads, there were ebon faces all round us, and no one who spoke more than a word or two of French. However, when a half-hour or more had gone by, the same official appeared to tell us that the hotel had honoured our reservations, and off we started on the eight-mile drive to the hotel outside the town.

We got there just as it was getting light, and there sitting on a stool at the top of the hotel steps watching the dawn break, sat a gigantic Negro dressed in bright blood-red. It was only when he stood up that we took in his full height. The giant night porter, dressed all in blood-red like an executioner, cannot have been less than six foot six in height, and big in proportion. Another, only less gigantic Negro came up, and between them they carried our luggage and thence, a little curiously, to the bedroom. For the hotel is built with six floors of bedrooms looking on the garden and down to the Atlantic, alternating with as many floors for lift and passage which look out on the back. Or, in fact, all the bedrooms are on one side and the corridors on the other; and on each floor you come out from the lift and walk down a few steps into the bedroom. The bedrooms occupy all the floor space of each floor, except for a little protuberance high up at the back of each room which is the external passage leading past the bedrooms. It is built on an unique plan which I have seen nowhere else, and that is probably particularly suited to an ultra-hot climate. I may add that Général Oufkir was in the hotel.

We slept late and drove down into the town of Dakar in the late afternoon. But it was the next morning – Friday, which is the Moslem Sunday, when the mosque was to be opened – that was unforgettable. The ladies of Dakar were all wearing their best dresses in honour of the Moroccan King. The Senegalese are the most ebon black of all the dark races. Long before this a French officer in a Senegalese regiment in the Sud-Atlas had told me that it was months on end before he could tell one man in his regiment from another. They all had tribal marks like cicatrices on their anthracite skins. The blood-red 'headsman' of the hotel must, I thought, have been sergeant in a Senegalese battalion. But as for the black ladies of Dakar they were most noticeably good-looking, even beautiful, with straight or nearly aquiline noses, unfrizzed hair, and beautiful smooth shoulders, of which latter they were proud and neglected no opportunity of showing them. Their dresses were not the patterned cottons of Ghana and Nigeria, made in Manchester, but were of the cheapest and gayest organza stuffs, shot with gold and silver for their baggy pantaloons, with the hand of a Schéhérazade to arrange and fold their turbans.

There is nothing of the Berber or the Andalusian Moor in Dakar as there is in Fez, even in Marrakesh. Here, in Senegal, Morocco must be a thousand miles away. This is an ebon metropolis, and it is as noisy and full of life as Naples, than which one could say no more, for Naples is the noisiest and most vocal town on earth. The market-place is nearly indescribable for cacophony and sheer force of sound. A huckster-tailor had taken to the trumpet to advertise his goods. The blare of his fanfares could be heard above the shouting voices and the din of motor-horns. But the ravishment of the dark ladies' dresses outdid all else. What a taste they have in the mere tying of their turbans! They were, nearly all of them, tall and graceful. There were elderly matrons with the mien of Roman Empresses and their maids walking a pace or two behind them. Or standing respectfully, giving their opinion if asked for it, when out shopping.

And it was on that morning we saw the microcephaloid of Dakar. That day, and the next day, and never again, although we looked for him continually in the streets and market-place during two afternoons. He was among the strangest-looking individuals seen in a lifetime. Less than five feet tall, with his begging-bowl in one hand, and a long staff in the other. Wearing a stained white burnouse. The next thing one noticed about him were the spider-bitten bags beneath his eyes, as though he must have had spiders crawling all over his face at night and biting him. His lips were swollen like his eye-bags, and he had a thin tuft of beard. His eyes were in fact glazed over as though hardly opened, or as though he had not begun to see. It looked to me like the sleep of a dead fish, or new-born monster child. But now for his skull for he was microcephaloid; not as the 'mongol' children who, pathetically, are big-headed. But he had a peaked skull, six to eight inches high, and wore a knitted cap round the peak of it to make it higher, thinner still at the cranium where it was no bigger than a two-shilling piece.

He was dark-skinn'd but not negroid of feature, in fact, not negroid or African in the least, this beggar who was like a being from a fairy story, begging in the market-place among a populace of porphyry and anthracite. To my eyes, having lately read of them and seen photographs, he was more like a sage from the Diamond Mountains in Korea. Let us think of him as an anchorite among the Moutan paeonies which have their home there. A reject from the ranks of the straggling-bearded Korean literati in their black top-hats of lacquered gauze and their white gowns, worn till a few years ago but which had been the court dress in Ming China. From the abbeys which may be little more than lacquered pavilions, but the paeonies had been cultivated there during centuries and were planted or grew in pots along the terraces; while the walled parks were habitat for the 'lace-cap' hydrangeas which flourished there in unspoilt perfection. The Diamond Mountains being in fact as well as in imagination places of mystery. He seemed to have no business here in Dakar. Who knitted his cap for him? Who sent him out to beg upon the streets? Even the snapshot taken in that momentary meeting was a total failure. I had even thought of writing to the British Consul to ask if anyone living in Dakar could track him down for this extraordinary creature would be of interest to the anthropologist and to medicine. As much so as that 'missing link' Aiso, the 'homme singe' of the oasis of Skoura, in Morocco, of which its roses are the other fame.* He must be well known to the inhabitants of Dakar. And I pictured him in my mind eating his evening meal and lying down to sleep. Who can have been his family? For his disease or infirmity had removed everything of the African from him, and made of him a figure from Far Eastern, even Korean mythology. But he was gone completely in that moment; lost in the crowd and never seen again.

Two days later there was that other dawn out in the cold air, sister to our arrival at daybreak from South America. With the blood-red porter or executioner

---

* Aiso, 'a degenerate of syphilitic forebears', was another type of microcephalic but, even so, less extraordinary in appearance than the microcephaloid of Dakar.

sitting on his three-legg'd stool at the hotel door, looking out over Africa with his hands upon his knees, both villain and hero of its miseries! And where was the homunculus? Was he awake or sleeping, when we walked out into the morning, and climbed the skies? There could not be a more peculiar human being in all Africa.

II

But, by now, we are along the banks just underneath the trees where the rooks were building. That was where the path a little farther on was a blue haze of crocuses. Why is it they have done better there than beside the path? It has been sprayed more than once with a flame-thrower or weed-gun but, judging by results, this seems only to have helped the crocuses. We could not be farther away from torrid Africa. Though there are, as well, *primavera* moods and visions in the Jasmine Kingdom. As for instance in Morocco when the hills are one fine fleece of marigolds.

But the tropics and semi-tropics were the promise. There are stories of persons who have unpacked crates of china, tea-services and the like, from China or Japan, have discovered seeds among the straw, scattered the seed, even carelessly, and found a growing bamboo hedge next year. Or, in a tropical climate, cut sticks to make a hedge or fence, and the very stalks or twigs have borne leaves and blossomed. It is an unimaginable moment when the full orchestra of the tropics comes into flower, and the only season of spring or *primavera* is in the early morning or the evening; the hour when the humming-bird is on the wing and sipping nectar from the red hibiscuses. But such are the siesta lands, predominantly of Spanish and mock-Indian, or Amerindian accent, which for that reason should come elsewhere in these pages.

And having written enough and to spare of the jacaranda which is among the beautiful things of the world, I am remembering the flamboyants of Aurangabad which seemed to me more brilliantly scarlet than any that I had seen. It is known that this flowering tree (*Poinciana regia*) differs in colour from place to place and according to season. Here surely they sounded a higher, shriller scarlet! This, just as I am walking by the triple sycamore which we see from the dining-room window and that is one of the alas! few beauties of the garden here. Trees, too, which are participants in a mystery of their own for there are only the two trees growing side by side, yet from the windows they are distinctly three stems with the light of summer on them. Till you go right down into the dell, and discover that two of them are the same tree with the bifurcation hidden and obscured by bushes and low branches. How lovely they can look, this trio of sycamores in the fading light!

They are of another speech from the scarlet poinciana that we had seen again and again in Rajputana which is tame elephant country, with for that matter tiger country within its borders. And passing by the sycamores while a wood pigeon flies out of their branches, I remember the wild peacocks of Jaipur, bird-bayadères of Hindustan with tiaras of feathers and long trains, and the hoopoes that preened themselves upon the lawns. But at Aurangabad, where the flamboyants were so brilliant, we were in Hyderabad; and it was inspiring to think of their orangy-scarlet fanfares at the doors, almost, of the cave temples of Ajanta, wherein a dark-skinned Botticellian world reveals itself for it is as beautiful as that, but with the blue lotus for cynosure in place of the Madonna lily. Near, too, to the dance-temple of the Kailasa, not built, but dug down from above deep into the hill. A rock-cut temple like a sacred theatre; with stone scene always in place, stone dancers in bas-relief still in their attitudes, and the pair of giant columns, pillars left free-standing in the auditorium, like the stone bridges which were as gang-planks for the dancers to run along out of the bat-gloom into the glare of India. The Kailasa of Ellora is marvellous in conception, and far greater as a work of art than any of the Egyptian temples in their monotony of hugeness.

Yet the flamboyant, both at Ajanta and at the Kailasa, is a falsification as we find out for ourselves on learning that its habitat is Madagascar, and that local names for it are *framboyan rojo, arból de fuego*, or *guacamaya*, all of which impute to it somewhat of a habanera – save that that is too languorous – say, more of a vibrant and flamenco flavour. But it is curiously apposite that as though in deference to the canon of beauty in the frescoes of Ajanta which are the only great paintings of dark-skinn'd races portrayed by their own hands, the *Bodhisattva* has a skin which is blue in hue and powdered with sandalwood to mitigate its darkness, the women are most admired when they pale into jasmine, and we read that each of the orchid-like flowers of the flamboyant has five petals, one of which is always white or yellow. The East Indian Ylang-ylang or Cananga, the disappointing and drooping yellow flowers of which are so valuable in the art of scent-making, and the petals of which you must squeeze hard between your fingers in order to get the scent, would be more suitable as habitat to these marvellous works of art. But the cananga is in fact dull and uninteresting until you know its hidden properties. The white frangipani, without the flowers of which one can hardly think of the cassia-mitred beauties of the Ajanta caves until one comes to look for it and finds it is not there, but which from much planting has become the 'temple flower' of Buddhist shrines in Ceylon and Thailand and, I would think, in Burma, is Mexican of origin and cannot therefore by any possibility have grown more than twelve centuries ago outside the temples of Ajanta or Ellora and been familiar to its figurants.

I have walked here under the yews with thunder booming in the distance, and the first heavy drops penetrating through the dark spinnate leaves and dead branches, and reaching to the path. And waited a few moments and had to run back into the house, and arrived wet through. Not seldom over the years in high summer with sounds of harvesting not far off which call to mind midsummer thunderstorms in Rossini's operas, in *Il Barbiere*, in *Cenerentola*, in *Turco in Italia*, each subtly differenced, with the thunder and lightning returning when it had seemed to be all over, and the pastoral summer evening come back again from all that time ago and brought to life within the opera house.

How well I remember when the two great trees were felled which grew too near the wall and the road outside and had become dangerous, and the bed of the stream and the bank where snowdrops grew so thick were heaped with fallen trunks and lopped limbs! It was some years indeed before the snowdrops came up again. That night and the next day it was snowing, and in the afternoon we tried at least to lift the smaller branches and the sticks for 'kindling' before the lorries came to cart the trunks away. But it was difficult in the February afternoon to think of anything except that we were to start off next day by air for Bangkok. Coming down at Rome, then Cairo, and then through the night to Dum Dum which is the airport for Calcutta. And a few hours later to this first experience of the Far Orient, and a drive of some eighteen miles to the city.

Where the lift-boy in the hotel asked me in halting English if it was snowing in London, and what it was like to be out in falling snow? Which was obviously to him an inconceivable natural condition; and as unlikely as to find oneself after only a few hours' flight in a city of pagodas built of broken china with dragon finials to their roofs, the white elephant in its stable, monks in saffron robes, and cargoes of pineapples on the canals or 'klongs'. But this Kingdom in South-East Asia can never be the same again after the war in Vietnam. It has been infected and contaminated. What cannot be altered though is the steam heat, and the temperature like that of a stove house to which orchids are as native as the buttercups in English meadows.

It is probably only Angkor that is unaltered. But for how much longer? Where we experienced the greatest heat I have known in a lifetime, and witnessed the break up of it into a storm of thunder among the ruins. It broke late in the afternoon as we reached the temple of Ta Prohm, which has been left by the French archaeologists with the lianas and tree-roots forcing its stones apart in order to show the state of the temples before they were restored. I have never known so loud a rattle of the kettledrums of thunder. What ghosts could one not hope to see in the white blink of the lightning! And how different from the Arcadian thunder of the opera house! Or when walking below the yew boughs! At Angkor, whence the black monkeys are fled,* mostly, there are no flowers, the temples are bat-infested and there is the stench of bats.

Indeed the forest is as dull as the desert, as all travellers in tropical lands have noticed, were it Wallace in the *Malay Archipelago*, or the casual if not unobservant trespasser to the temples of Angkor. Until you reach an oasis, for which the equivalent would be a display of birds-of-paradise in Papua, or, in this instance, a particular flowering tree. Which is more than likely to be a Golden Shower or Cassia; a vision in its day, but which becomes unsightly when the yellow flowers have faded and in their stead are the long black pods, this indeed being the same defect as with the curving brown pods of the flamboyant when its scarlet flowering is over. But the cassia has a special significance and value in Hindu legend and poetry, where we can read:

---

* To my inquiry about the monkeys, the guide replied: 'Ils ne sortent plus', as though they no longer paid calls or accepted invitations.

The god is Krishna in his lovely youth
. . . A youth of Ganges in a yellow robe,
Yellow like gold and garlanded with flowers,
For incense a cassia flower that dangles at his ears
Sheds forth sweet scent on him, shaken by his tread

And later in the same poem:

The gopīs, milkmaids of the herd,
. . . Some flaunt the cassia in their bee-black hair
For fronds of incense, so a mitre of its flowers
Scents eyes and lips, and is their scented breath;
Their limbs and body are the cassia made animate,
That, else, never moved, nor made the signs of love

The cassia, it could be added, being seen to perfection at the flower-fanes of Ceylon. There are cassias, even in the suburbs of Colombo, that make one catch one's breath and that possess the quality of re-creating in and for a moment the classical India of twenty or more centuries ago. Also, they are well and truly indigenous to the scene; and not, unbelievable as it may be, a stranger from Mexico like the frangipani.

The Amherstia, or Pride of Burma, of repute the most beautiful flowering tree of the tropics, is certainly indigenous to the Indies but had to be 'discovered' in a remote part of Burma, which is not the same as if it had been growing near the temples.* Also, it could be said that its vermilion and yellow flowers are beautiful individually, and much resemble orchids, but that for effect they cannot compare to the flamboyant, or the more alluring jacaranda, a flowering tree with power to evoke a languorous music, even a whole architecture of palaces and sacred nunneries contrived and tempered to its shade.

As for the Coco de Mono, Moke, Abricot de Singe, or simple Cannonball Tree, it is of no poetry or mythology but beyond human or aesthetic association, coming from Guiana in South America, strange beyond belief, and with no suggestion to offer beyond its huge and impressive height, flowers that push straight out from the tree bark disdaining the shelter of their own leaves, and ballistic nuts or fruit. It is of no use to imagine anything else for the Koppe Jewadaballi, the Boskelebas, Couroupia guianensis, or Cannonball Tree. Perhaps the only human analogy, in the sense of any possible connection with human beings or human civilization is to the *chaenomeles*, known heretofore more domestically as Japanese Quince or cydonia, of which the fruit grows straight from the twig without stalk or stem, and is to be snapped off with the fingers. But such is a vicarious relationship, of no tie or kinship, and no more than a reminder that there is this memory of fruit-picking whether of apricot or nectarine off the warm walls of summer, for those break off the same.

The possibilities of exotic gardening which have only arrived at fruition, are

* It was found by Dr Wallich, Director of the Botanical Gardens, Calcutta, growing in the teak forests of Burma.

even only beginning to come near to fruition in our time, make a theme remote indeed from those exigencies of abortion, free false teeth and spectacles, and the like, which under socialism malform our island fame. They are as little a part of that as the solar-centred monarchy which could achieve the formal gardens of Versailles. But it is a fresh era in floral gardening when new colours of the bougainvillea which had its origin in the South Sea Islands are to be had from Nairobi; and the ubiquitous hibiscus, rose of the tropics and grown in rose-beds, derives its new varieties from nurseries as far apart as Queensland and Honolulu. The three thousand and more varieties of the ephiphyllum or orchid cactus of the Californian sierra and the Arizonan desert, though their destination be but the windowledge in a flat-iron apartment building are something new in the ant-like march of the human masses before they stifle themselves by mere numbers, even if a personal taste would still prefer the striped tulips of the old Dutch fanciers. But that is because the last-named flower worked to its own grammar and obeyed the rules of taste. This is something wanting in the rhododendron which in its inflorescence behaves as though never in need of human architecture or the human hand. It is self-sufficient, more than self-sufficient, and outflowers all else in sight. And for the same reasons it does not lend itself with grace to being either drawn or photographed.

With but limited experience of tropical or sub-tropical localities, having for instance never seen Indonesia, one must be content with the parterre or quadrilateral of mangoes, the four plots of mango trees round the tomb of the wife of Aurangzeb at Aurangabad – where the particularly brilliant scarlet flamboyant trees have already been mentioned. The mangoes stand in for the ilex or the cypress of more temperate climes. Such shade is inconceivable at near-by Ajanta, or round the Kailasa of Ellora; and not even the change over from Buddhism to the followers of Islam has made it any different. Mangoes, as shade trees, are in intimation of Southern India, that other tropicalia which I have not seen where, too, there is architecture to fit the climate. Where the visual world of nature and of the historical past is not yet in danger. The white sands of Cochin and the coast of Coromandel should be immune during the rest of this century from contamination, and could stay unmarked but for the prows of catamarans and the patterns of the fishing nets.

Theirs is an architecture into which it is difficult to enter in spirit because it is so alien. But it is of natural growth and has adapted itself effortlessly, if with prodigal expenditure of energy in the carving of multitudinous figures and unnecessary ornament, to the climate of the tropics. But we are here to learn not from the temples but the flowers. And at this exact moment I am at the far end of the wilderness where the path turns, and for more years ago than I first remember noticing it there has been a martagon lily growing. There are in fact two others in an altogether different part of the wilderness under some laurels. Heaven knows how they got there, or who planted them! I once read that martagon lilies are often found where there has been a Roman villa; and by odd coincidence the same statement was made about the lungwort (*pulmonaria*) which grows a matter of no more than four or five feet away from the first martagon (Turk's Cap) mentioned.

So, in fact, how did they get here? What is their history? It is true that the Watling Street, most famous of Roman Roads in Britain, running from London all the way to North Wales and to Anglesey passes near here, and that the mosaic pavement of an important Roman villa lies below the site of a farm a mile or two off the Roman road. Towcester, the local town, was the Roman Lactodorum, a name that has milch kine and the lowing of herds barely hidden in its Latinity; but were the foundations of that farm uncovered how curious it would be to find perhaps nereids of the Tyrrhenian, or a satyr of Soracte or from the Volscian woods, under the spinneys and dog-rose hedges of Northamptonshire!

The lilies in question are Turk's Cap lilies, and not so called for nothing. And the name Martagon, taken with no further explaining to mean a Turk's cap or turban? But in any case, they were Turk's caps such as Venetian and other mariners had seen in the Levant and Eastern Mediterranean. And in fact the lilies follow the shape of the earlier form of turban before the greater elaboration and the quarter of a mile of cloth-of-gold of the turbans on view in the Old Seraglio of Istanbul. Later, much later, came the eponymous turbans of the 'Tulip Reign' of Achmet v (1703–30). And it has to be said that while being delicate and graceful the martagons are the least flaunting or extravagant of the lilies. For which, more exotic specimens, one must leave this wood of dock leaves and campions and embark again for the Furthest Orient, and far distant sight at least of the snows. Does *Lilium giganteum*, a veritable thyrsus or rod of lilies for it can grow to twelve feet high and could have been his emblem or pallium when Bacchus invaded India, show itself and drop its trumpet lilies in Nepal near to the Hindu 'monasteries' of Pashupatinath, Kedranath, and Badrinath? The first of which, at least, I have visited, heard the haphazard blare of trumpets, and seen the Hindu *sadhus* striding along trident in hand, and rubbed with ashes. But the others are far away across two mountain chains, near the haunts of the horned pheasant or satyr tragopan, the crimson-breasted, and as though snow-flecked, Mephisto of the woods and Himalayan jungles.

And in the nostalgia of having seen so much, but wishing to see it all, I am transported to the Jain temples on Mount Abu where are ceilings of stone so contrived and carved that they rival the fan-vaults of England, or the Moorish honeycombs and stalactites, and simulate the petals and corolla of some night-scented nymphaea, or the night-blooming cereus, to the extent that it is difficult to believe you cannot pull the huge and defenceless stone flower to pieces with your hands. Thence, for there is not more of interest, to the 'corncob' temples of Bhuvaneshwar, in Orissa on the east side of India. For their towers are segmented like corncobs; or, in fact, one of the temples, the Lingaraja, has a tower of great height more resembling a particular race of cactus. But it is all exterior at Bhuvaneshwar; there are no inner halls or aisles. And for the full maturity of the Hindu temple we should repair to Madura in Southern India which must give some semblance of an inhabited Angkor with temples still intact and in working order.

Here the wonderful features are the gate-towers or *gopurams*. There are four of these at Madura, one to each of its four sides for the whole area is within an immense enclosure, as is the case at Angkor Wat. There are no fewer than seven more smaller *gopurams* within the walls; but it is the four principal and primal of the gate-towers that give the impression of these peculiar and unfamiliar precincts. But whereas the aforesaid 'corncob' temples at Bhuvaneshwar date from the tenth to the twelfth centuries, Madura is a mid-seventeenth-century construction, approximating to the reign of Charles I. How extraordinary must be its gate towers rising a hundred and fifty feet into the air above the fan-fronds of the palm trees! What a fascination to read that in fairground tradition the temple elephants are stabled in the long Angkor-like corridors; elephants that, as Sir Mortimer Wheeler writes, 'are kept for ceremonial purposes, on which occasion they are elaborately painted and caparisoned'. But the 'Hall of a Thousand Pillars' looks dull as can be, and the sacred pool or 'Tank of the Golden Lilies' belies its expectation. It is the *gopurams* that count, compact as they are with all the carved figures 'manning the yard' and 'dressing ship' up to the *chaitya* or gypsy-waggon finish of their roof-line; the *gopurams*, themselves, with their many floors or storeys of carved figures framed in pillars giving the impression of a tower or city, of occupied storeys ending in so many waggon-roofs.

But the temple of Sriringam, not many miles away where Indian distances are in question, stands in a walled precinct three times bigger than that of Madura and has not eleven, but twenty-one *gopurams* 'in descending order of magnitude', the tallest of which, if finished, would have been three hundred feet high. It is at Srirangam that there is the 'Court of Horses', a portico with granite pillars carved into more than lifesize figures of men on rearing horses fighting wild animals or spearing tigers, their horses' hooves upheld on the shields of men on foot beneath them; while in the same Dravidian temple not far away, beyond more temple elephants, until merely a quarter of a century ago there was the *devidasis* or temple-prostitutes offering themselves 'as had their forebears at Babylon and a thousand Asian shrines for countless ages'. In all this group of temples in Southern India; at Tanjore, Trivalur, Ramesvaram, Chidambaram, Tinnavelli, and Vijayanagar, forming a part of the twenty or thirty Dravidian temples in this southern end of the sub-peninsula which, in Fergusson's opinion, rival with any cathedrals of Western Europe, but fall short of them in plan and construction, yet with his mid-Victorian emphasis, 'outvie them in patient workmanship'; it is the *gopurams*, the gate-towers or gate-pyramids that are the extraordinary feature.

So many of them were in association with the vanished Hindu kingdom of Vijayanagar, of which there are accounts by early Portuguese travellers and by the traveller Caesar Frederick, who seeing the city two years after its fall to the Moslems in 1565 describes it as 'being twenty-four miles round enclosing several hills . . . the ordinary dwellings were mean buildings with mud walls, but the three palaces and the pagodas were all built of fine marble'. But above all Vijayanagar was the Kingdom of printed cottons, by the use of which sumptuary effects may have been achieved which would rival with the richest silks and brocades of Istanbul and of Isfahan. Of such were the chintzes or palampores (palagposers) of Masulipatan; and the whole poetic repertory of the names of silks and cottons, the Kincobs (Kimkhwabs) of Benares and Murshidabad, different types from all over India, but the most picturesque of all may have been the chintz-clad population of Vijayanagar. This I write in full memory of the black ladies of Dakar in their nylon gowns and turbans mentioned earlier in this chapter.

But a main reason for taking this opportunity of writing of the unseen Jain and Dravidian temples, and of Madura and Srirangam in particular, is because having written at length of buildings and works of art of like propensity in other parts of the world, I know that these are something I have omitted and that represent a culmination of the same order of mind, if at work in a different and sub-tropical clime. Others, which I have thought more suited to poetry than prose, I have made the themes for long, separate and still unpublished poems. The temples and the orgiastic sculptures of Khajuraho, surely one of the more extraordinary works of art in the world have been thus treated. How curious it is that they should be described in *Murray's Handbook for India* (1905 edition) without any mention of the equivocal nature of the carvings which must have come as a shock to the uninitiated!

It would seem to be high up on the exterior of the Kandariya Temple at Khajuraho that these reach to their climax in a triple band of sculptures, one above the other, showing the *apsarases* in utmost provocation both of attitude and action; and in paraphrase of the poem one could say they are Magian rites of sun-worship, of the fructifying forces of the earth. Which are the carvings? Which the living bodies? For the sculptors had the school of life under their eyes as much as Belsen or Dachau were the schools of death. We see this nowhere else in the world but at these temples. Here we are in the Indian ant-continent, at the other end of the earth from the long saints of Chartres and its wheel-windows, blue roses of the dawn. But we go back to the spires of Khajuraho where the eye ascends the lesser turrets, and down again to the three bands of *apsarases* on the buttresses, between the porches or open balconies. Who could look at them and not feel his heart beat faster, were the choice between them, or a Thebaid of anchorites in the Byzantine canon? Why did the world go that way to the places of dead bones, to Golgotha the place of the skull? Is not the one kind of love, the profane, as strong or stronger than the other? Or is it better to listen to the 'pale Galilean'? Which is stronger in the world? Is it sex; or is it death?

The Black Pagoda of Konarak, on the sea coast not far from the temple of the Juggernaut at Puri, could perhaps be described as not less strong in motive than Khajuraho. But it is wild and poetic in conception; a temple dedicated to the sun-god Surya who in Vedic mythology circled the world in a chariot drawn by either four or seven horses. The temple portrays the sun-chariot about to start off into the clouds at dawn; built of stone brought hither from a great distance, and raised on a plinth or platform sixteen feet high. This 'chariot floor in motion', as one writer well describes it, being carried by twelve huge wheels, their spokes minutely and most erotically carved in red sandstone, while this processional car or chariot of the sun is drawn by seven stone horses at the foot of the temple steps, a point at which the imagery fails a little and becomes unconvincing. But the conception of the chariot of the sun about to rise into the clouds of morning is beautiful indeed, and not even so far-fetched in imagery as we might think for processional chariots in which the images of their gods make journeys are a feature in many Hindu temples. Only as near to Konarak as Puri is the wooden car or rath of the Juggernaut, a wooden chariot forty-five feet high, with sixteen wheels seven feet in diameter, in which the image of Krishna is annually dragged along 'by four thousand two hundred professionals who come from the neighbouring districts, and during the festival live at Puri *gratis*'. Professional chariots in religious ceremonies are a feature in other countries beside India, if we remind ourselves of the dancing towers at the festival of St Paulinus at Nola in the Campagna Felice of Naples, and of the 'floats' carrying statues of the saints during the Semana Santa at Seville. What could perhaps be termed 'Indian' is the improvisatory freedom of conception that allowed of a temple being built in the form of a flying chariot just about to leave the launching-pad. This is something of which we may think the Hellenes for all their invention of poetry to be incapable if only because of their cult of logic and inherent probability.

In which context I cannot forbear to mention another theme I have thought more suited to poetry than prose when, about the middle of March the Hindus, but in this instance it is the Court Brahmins of Bangkok,* observe a swinging festival in honour of the god Krishna, whose image is placed in the seat of a swing and then, just as the dawn is breaking, is gently rocked to and fro several times. It is a pantomime of the yearly arrival on earth of the Hindu god Shiva, and the acrobats and the swinging are in order to amuse him. A temporary King impersonates him, wearing a tall pointed hat and robes that are subtly differenced from those of the real King. With him are acrobats and persons dressed as sprites 'from celestial spheres'. This all takes place beyond the white wall and dragon roofs of Wat Prajohit, where are the teak pillars of the giant swing which I have seen, though I did not witness the ceremony; masts eighty feet high like ships' masts painted red, and crowned with a carved cornice. The three sets of swingers, four to a team, wear naga-headdresses like the hoods of cobras, the game being to catch with the teeth a purse hanging from a bamboo pole, like the trapeze 'artists' of our circuses. They make many feints at it in order to amuse the crowd. At each success gongs are beaten and conch-shells blown. The ceremony which is described as one of the most curious of the Siamese State Ceremonies is repeated two days later in the evening, when the naga-swingers perform a circular dance round the swing, and throw water over each other from buffalo-horns. It is clearly a solar ceremony of ancient Indian origin of which the meaning has long passed out of memory. So let the Brahmins put up their teak pillars and their pairs of posts, and rock to and fro their images of the gods. They have long forgotten it is a solar ceremony;† yet in the Rigveda the sun is called 'the golden swing in the sky'.

* The Court Brahmins are, themselves, of Indian descent from many centuries ago, though intermarried with Thai women and showing no trace now of Hindu blood.

† H. G. Quaritch Wales, in *Siamese State Ceremonies*, London 1931, pp. 238–55, notices the pairs of posts in the temples of Bangkok, 'about four feet high, from which on certain occasions are suspended small swings on which the Brahmins rock to and fro the images of their gods. But the original connection with the sun has been forgotten, and they place in the swing whichever god they wish to placate at the time.'

Why is the sun worshipped, never the arctic cold? Were the sun to rise one morning only a few moments late the extrasensory perception in the birds and animals would warn them. They would stand in consternation, looking into the cloud of darkness towards Tartarus; and turn and flee in terror, burrowing, tunnelling, running into the West. It would be as the warning of an earthquake by animal telepathy which would not happen if all the megaton bombs of the USSR and USA went off at once and rocked the earth, when our four-minute warning system would be as out of date as the one-way singing of the birds.

At which moment I am almost free of the wood and about to tread on a large stone slab that takes up the whole width of the path and must cover a drain where water from a field runs down into the stream. But the interest of it is that it is strewn every day with cracked snail-shells, very small striped or brown-red shells, and always with the snail, itself, missing. For a long time this puzzled me until I found the answer. It is that the thrushes pick up a snail and drop it on the stone in order to break the shell. This is no less than a step towards a civilization; no less so in some sense than the small and rare birds in the Galapagos Islands, lying off and belonging to Ecuador, which carry a stick in their beaks to use as an instrument to open shells.* In fact, they are bird tool-users. But is not dropping something you want to crack or open on to a stone, just as much an instance of making use of a tool or instrument as taking a stick into your beak or mouth in order to effect the same purpose? Yet I have never seen this advanced as proof of a superior cleverness among the thrushes. It was just beyond this that some little woodland trilliums grew beneath the trees but ground elder crept up and killed them. They have never shown their white trilobed heads again. And another rare wild flower comes up in the long grass which I thought might be some kind of fritillary. It is a solitary. There is only the one plant of it, and it seems to show itself but once on an average in three or four years. Now I think I have been able to identify it as 'Star of Bethlehem' (*Ornithogallum umbellatum*) from its glistening stalk and flower-face which seem almost as if they would snap at a touch of the fingers like a stalk of candied angelica, except that the colour of this is more pallid.

What could be further removed indeed from the temples and the flowering trees we have been discussing! Trilliums, white or red or purplish-pink, which grew in the Canadian woods near to a birch-bark canoe, to the moccasin-tread of the Indian, the profiled warriors of Catlin's paintings, their head-dresses of war-eagles' quills and their white deerskin dresses. And the virginal, pale 'Star of Bethlehem' which is like a child too innocently beautiful to live for long. But she survives in spite of this, though inconspicuously, and has outlived the cowslips which grew so profusely in the field just over the fence. But that was ploughed up

* A bird missed, unfortunately, by Darwin when he visited the Galapagos on board H.M.S. *Beagle* in 1839. But it would seem there is another bird-artificer or craftsman. For in a new book on *Birds of Paradise and Bower-birds*, by E. Thomas Gilliard, London 1969, p. xix, it is remarked of the latter that 'some species of bower birds are world famous for their ability to mix and apply paint to the walls of their colourful bowers. An almost unbelievable refinement to their extraordinary painting abilities is their use of a tool, a brush-like tool, to apply the specially mixed pigments.'

in the war when all this part of the county which had been entirely pastoral was turned over to 'food production', and the cowslips have never been back again. How often did the 'green lanes' and even the village street re-echo with sheep-voices talking in multitude as they moved pasture and came by the cottage windows, all clamouring as they went! It was like an army, a very silly army on the march, and even bleating out their marching songs as they went along; nibbling and chewing as they passed by, taking the wrong corner and being turned back again.

Well, I have heard the main body of the Quashqai nomads passing through Shiraz for two hours at least in the middle of the night, and lain listening to the clashing of their camel-bells and the voices of ten thousand goats! I have seen the jacarandas as we came down out of the clouds into Guatemala with their bowers and tents of heliotrope full-pitched and not shedding. I cannot believe that this paragon of trees can be of the same effect in South Africa (except among the vineyards of Cape Province), or in Kenya or Rhodesia where there is no hint of music, no poetry or legend, and no architecture. It only comes into its own where there is a revetment of blue-and-white tiles against its porcelain-blue, or deeper, more mauve pavilions. For myself, it is under the blue-violet flowers of the jacaranda that I would listen to Scarlatti; to the Sevillan guitar in counterfeit and mimed warblings of the great *castrati*, from the quickest, if in little, most scintillating intelligence in all music. And from him a languorous, but brilliant descendence.

But, in the same way, though the roses of Anne Hathaway's cottage at Shottery, near Stratford, still speak of the greatest poet in words that, by now, have become full blown and hackneyed, there is in them yet some hint or echo of voices in the wings, and of drama played in the 'round O' of the London theatre. More still, in not distant orchards, some memory of music, of the apple notes of the clavichord, or other keyboard instrument, notes that are like biting into a honeyed apple, and of the rattle of the lute-string. All of which is in antithesis to the hibiscus and the frangipani. But for those, too, there must be a music of their own, and their own poetry. The hibiscus that holds its flamenco or kanaka flowers for a day only, and has in that some analogy or kinship to Shinto or other temples that are built anew of wood 'of the finest grain' every twenty years in a new clearing in the forest; the yellowish, but above all the white frangipani, 'the white and sacrosanct, of flesh of a cracked claw consistence, of crustacean flesh, soft-shelled from sweet water pools of contentment'; which, Mexican as it may be, should be seen growing among the ruins and the red lotus-tanks of Polannaruwa.

If it be considered an extravagance to think and make invention of the Jasmine Kingdom while walking in the Victorian wilderness or shrubbery at my home, I would argue that every voyage of exploration of Captain Cook's began and ended at Whitby where he was born. My journeys have been undertaken in idleness to look at works of art, but they have brought me to many different parts of the world; and I could as well say that each and every one of them has started and had its end upon the Scarborough sands. It was there, scrambling upon the rocks, that I first began to think, and hear, and see. I live far away now from my early home and birthplace, and the little that I have done since then has been to move the confines of the Jasmine Kingdom to the home that loving hands have made for me. There I have had contentment, time to write, and been able to indulge those dreams which said and done, is my tribute to affection and unselfishness.

ENTR'ACTE
A frieze of pigs' heads

The scene is the High Street of an East Midland town in the week before Christmas, with the crowd so thick before Boots and Woolworths that you can hardly move. Traffic wardens are taking down car numbers as the first snowflakes begin to fall, and the street lights go up. But the scene is too familiar to call for comment except for the extraordinary tableau in the window of a butcher's shop.

It begins high up near the ceiling with a row of identical small joints, so alike that they could be the joints in a doll's shop. Already it is a little 'creepy'. These joints form a sort of frieze or cornice, and the rest of the window below them is left empty. But the whole of the butcher's slab or counter is quite massed with meat. Larger joints, of course, and now we move from lamb to beef. The 'two-somes', once hot, once cold, are replaced by family cuts, sirloins, best ends; then lamb again, neck or shoulder; and back to beef, with a chart on the wall to show just what is what. An Angus steer to judge by his forelock, and not much left of him if cow's heel and calves' foot jelly are what they profess to be. With dishes of 'honeycomb' tripe, pale and gelatinous, in the foreground; ox-heart to remind one of the clown with Elizabethan baggy breeches and traditional hair-do in the Hoxton prints; ox-tongue; kidneys; liver and lights, viscous dark red, and half-congealed; black puddings; faggots which are chopped liver; and nameless substances laid out as for a kit inspection; the *disjecta membra*, all that is left of the slaughtered steer.

But over to another animal. Right down, nearly touching on the window, are a pair of pigs' trotters, slender of ankle but with cloven hoof. And that is not all. There is a pig's head with a whole lemon in its mouth and a tell-tale red mark in the middle of its blank, bland forehead. So the humane-killer has been at work but it has not lessened the horror of its dying. After all Louis XVI was guillotined with a sort of humane killer, and now the pig's head with smiling half-closed eyes looks very like him. It has the dead king's caricatural look of his ancestors, in elephantine facsimile of them without their prowess either of pride or dissipation. It was not his fault. Louis XVI could not help it. But now the pig's head is even more like 'Monsieur', the silly, fat Grand Dauphin, son of Louis XIV, five generations before him. Certainly Louis Quatorze had more of the wild boar than the pig in him. Routing about and rutting, with the tusks bred out in the next couple of generations but reappearing with a vengeance in Louis Quinze, his great-great-grandson.

And now a whole row of pig's heads like a shelf of trophies from the guillotine. All with family resemblance, but differing in expression. All neuter, of course. Not a man among them. Someone else's bachelor uncles and unmarried aunts; their snouts like those of persons recovering from heavy colds. The lip, with one of them, drawn back as if in a sneer, and a trickle of blood oozed from the mouth on to the chin. An extraordinary variety of expression in their waxen masks, of fatty consistency, as though boned yet keeping to their shape. Singed, for there is no trace of hair or whisker; the imberb effect somehow adding to their look of doomed and fatal silliness.

And the butcher has a macabre humour. Not content with the lemon he put into the mouth of one of them, he has written out cards or labels for the rest of them. Propped between the ears of a positive pig-dowager, a card reads, 'I'm Playing Shut Eye'. This, of an animal slumped and abject from that blow between its eyes. It has been stunned, absolutely and for ever. 'A Dish for a King', reads coquettishly, in invitation beside a heavy jaw. This, near to the pair of trotters which perhaps were part of it. While another of the pig-masks just has the notice 'Sleepy Time' hung like a locket, but slipped from its forehead to one side. Another epitaph reads, 'Don't disturb'; and doubtless, had the butcher been a linguist, we would have had 'Nicht Hinauslehnen', 'E Vietato Sporgersi', and probably, 'Prière de ne pas ronfler', and as well, all the catchwords of train and boarding house, thanks be to packet tours, and chartered planes. As it is, we may think he has surpassed himself with the notice, 'Dying to Meat You', at one end of the long line of severed heads.

Pigs' heads, the lot of them, and in their death pains and fatty agony they could be caricature heads of the Twelve Caesars carved in soap or margarine and lightly coloured. Yet they were viceless animals, no worse than gluttons, with snouts for ever in the trough, only a day or two ago. And now on exhibition after a public execution at the time of writing in Damascus or Baghdad! But what a gang were the Twelve Caesars, all allowance made for calumny and exaggeration! There is something horrible in their physiognomy. Beginning with Julius Caesar of whom it was said, and it cannot have been in affection, that 'he was the husband of all the women in Rome, and the woman of all men'. To continue with Augustus, in whom the family were already doomed, for he was publicly reported to be the son of Apollo, and raising no objection to that, 'liked to have it said of his eyes that they possessed some divine irradiation, and was well pleased when he fixed his eyes upon anybody, if they held down their gaze as though blinded by the glaring brightness of the sun'. In just this sense did I hear the inn-keeper on the Wörther-See in Carinthia say he had seen the halo round Hitler's head when he visited the district.

Augustus was succeeded by Tiberius, his nephew and adopted son; the goatish Tiberius who retired in dissipation to the goat-isle of Capri, a relic of whose claustral reign is the number of 'sphintrian' gems found there, to be published in learned and luxurious editions in the eighteenth century, and later.

After Tiberius, his grandson Caligula; and not giving every credence to Suetonius, it was said he committed incest with his three sisters, caused his favourite horse to be made high priest and consul, and intended to build a pier or pleasure bridge upwards of three miles long into the Bay of Baiae.

Then Claudius, who was married to the notorious Messalina, and was poisoned with mushrooms by Agrippina, another of his four wives; who was Nero's mother, Nero being grandson to Germanicus, who was great-nephew to Augustus; Nero of 'the living torches', who watched the Roman games through a cut emerald, and if the historians are to be believed, 'disguised himself in the habit of a woman, and was publicly married to one of his eunuchs'; but later, like the insect-race of the Aphidae who are, indifferently, viviparous and oviparous, and seem to change their sex at will, he resumed the male sex and celebrated his 'nuptials with one of his meanest catamites'.

Nero, most familiar of the monstrous Caesars, was succeeded by Galba and then by Otho, but their combined reigns lasted less than a twelve-month. After which it was the turn of Vitellius, the glutton Emperor, raised, so to speak, at Capri amidst the Tiberian orgies, and who perfected, if he was not the first to practise, the Roman custom of making themselves vomit in order to be able to eat more. Next came Vespasian, concerning whom little that is unpleasant is on record. But Vespasian was lucky to be alive after falling asleep while he was on tour with Nero in Greece, and that ham-actor and would-be-poet-Emperor was giving a poetry recital. Titus, the least harmful of the Caesars, and son to Vespasian, reigned for no more than a couple of years. But he was succeeded by his brother Domitian who conceived the idea of releasing a criminal to be burnt alive on the stage in place of the villain at the end of a genre of popular play, a little resembling our 'Westerns', to the delight of the audience and the approbation of the poet Juvenal. He died in AD 96 and was last of the Twelve Caesars. What a horrible lot they were! The poor pigs, at least, were innocent and harmless, and only greedy.

BOOK
FOUR

Matterig

It is a firm philosophy in life that after a still day without wind there will be
intimations of a storm to come, and it is time now for someone of another tem-
perament and disposition to set foot upon our island shore.

This year (1959) is the centenary of the incident that we are about to narrate.
So long ago was this chapter written. But let us delay for a moment longer with
the name of Matterig upon our lips, for what there is of menace and importance
in the mere three syllables of his name, even in the mouthing and movement in
the letter 'M' at the beginning of it, the two down strokes of the 'M' being stronger
and having more of emphasis to them than the like number of strokes, all of them
upon the slant, in the letter 'W' that so nearly resembles an 'M', only the strength
runs out and is not held there, where it is staked down, as it were, and held firm
in a letter 'M'. Just to think for a last moment of some more names beginning with
'M'; Matterhorn, Moses, Maimonides, Manchester, Metternich, Murcia, Meshed,
with the small 'm' of Timur and Tamerlane supporting the weight of the name
in the middle of it, the strength running out in the double 'n's' of Minneapolis, but
more self-contained somehow in Minnesota; ugly mumblings and mutterings
with yokel undertones in Muggeridge; the steadiness of the 'M' sounds in Sand-
ford and Merton, or in Fortnum and Mason, but a little fluttering and sinister in
Morfa and in Mauleverer, emerging from this thicket or *maquis* of 'M's' to find
ourselves back in the three syllables of Matterig, to the sound of its last syllable
which is like the noise of oars, like the creaking of oars in the rowlocks, and most
appropriate as we shall know in a moment more, to the tide washing something
to and fro upon a pebbly shore.

Mysterious Death at Ramsgate, April, 1859

A very extraordinary case of murder or suicide has occurred at Ramsgate, the
circumstances of which were so mysterious that the opinion of the public
remained undecided until the end.

As a coast guardian was on the look out on the East Cliff on the morning of
Monday, the 11th instant, near the Dumpton Stairs, about 6 a.m. he saw a
boat on the beach. He descended and secured it. About 40 yards further on he
came upon the body of a man, quite naked. It was lying about 8 yards from
the water, and the rising tide was washing over it. A coat, waistcoat, trousers
and flannel shirt were lying about 10 yards off; the pockets of each were turned

inside out. Upon examining the body it was found that the deceased had come to a violent end. There was a wound in the breast, which passed through the chest, the left lung, and the left ventricle of the heart; it was larger internally than externally, as though the instrument had been moved after the blow was given. This wound, the surgeons said, had certainly been inflicted during life, and must have caused instant death. The left hand had been cut off at the wrist, the four fingers were detached from the hand, the ring-finger was cut off between the first and second joints. There was a second cut on the wrist; there were three sharp cuts on the hand, as shown when the fingers were placed in position. The skin of the forehead, head, face, etc. was abraded probably by the action of the water rubbing the corpse against the rocks. There was no cut on either the coat, waistcoat, or flannel, to correspond with the stab on the chest. The collar of the coat showed signs of rough usage. About 70 or 80 yards from the body were found a shirt, the wristbands of which were torn off, and the remainder of the deceased's clothing; and a hatchet, of which the handle had been recently shortened, and the blade sharpened. About 500 feet from the body was a chalk rock, upon which there were four distinct cuts of a hatchet. The pieces of hand and fingers were found about twelve yards, and the hatchet about 200 yards from the rock, towards the sea. It was deposed by the surgeons that the stomach of the deceased presented no signs that he had been drugged; but was full of food recently taken, and which smelt strongly of spirits. The Ramsgate boatmen declared that it was impossible that the deceased could have fallen over the cliffs to the spot where his body was found, nor could it have been washed there by any current of the tide. These are the particulars attending the discovery of the body. The question was, whether the deceased could possibly have committed suicide under such circumstances, or have been murdered and carried down to the beach. The appalling nature of the mortal wound, which must have been preceded by stripping and then by serious mutilation, seemed to render the first suggestion impossible; other circumstances, to be deduced from the preceding detail, rendered the latter improbable.

The appearance of the corpse indicated a man about 35 years of age, and a foreigner; and it appeared probable from the dress, a German. The porter of the Royal Oak Hotel identified the deceased as a person who had come to the hotel about 10.30 on Saturday morning. He had a carpet-bag and umbrella, and a *portemonnaie* containing 10 or 12 sovereigns and silver. He was, also, said by other persons to have had about £40 or £50 in a secret bag about his person. His boots were remarkable. Those produced [at the inquest] were the same, but had been cut shorter in the leg. He wore a gold watch and chain and gold signet ring on the forefinger of his right hand. His left hand was bandaged up. He left the hotel on Sunday morning about ten o'clock. He was next traced to a house of ill-fame, which he left alone about 3 p.m. He was seen on the cliff about 8 p.m., walking with his arms folded and his hat over his eyes; he had his umbrella but no carpet-bag, two or three persons were supposed to be watching him. He was not seen alive afterwards. Thus far, circumstances pointed to murder, perpetrated by persons who had become aware that he possessed a considerable sum of money.

Subsequent evidence tended to alter this view. It was ascertained that the deceased was a German or Dutchman; that he arrived at Southampton, from America, about the end of March, that on the 31st of March he left for London; and on the 7th of April (Thursday) he left London for Dover. A fellow traveller observed that his left hand was bandaged up; he wore a pair of long boots, his trousers tucked inside the legs. On Friday he purchased a hatchet in a shop in Dover, and requested the shopman to cut the handle shorter – the piece cut off corresponded with the handle of the hatchet found on the sands. On Saturday he arrived at Ramsgate and went to a barber's shop and had his moustache and beard shaved off. He then went to the Royal Oak Inn, as before stated. When he left that hotel at 10 a.m. on Sunday morning, he went to Margate, and took dinner between 11 and 12 a.m. at the Elephant and Castle, which he soon after left, taking his carpet-bag, the contents of which seemed to be heavy. He was then seen about the railway station. About 11.30 a.m. on Monday, a person found at the corner of the Royal Crescent wall, two linen shirts, two collars, and other articles. The shirt corresponded with that found on the Ramsgate sands. In the afternoon a boatman picked up from the water, near the same place, a carpet bag open and empty. On Sunday afternoon he was again at Ramsgate, was traced to the house of ill-fame, and was seen late in the evening on the cliff, walking with a downcast air, as before stated.

Some minute evidence showed that the deceased had shown a decided determination to conceal his name and nationality, but some letters which were found scattered on the sands, showed that his name was Matterig, and that he was probably a Dutchman; they indicated also that his supposed possession of money had been grossly exaggerated. These particulars now tended to show that the unhappy man had committed deliberate suicide. But with what strange resolution and disregard of pain! If this conclusion is correct, he must have thrown his money, watch and solid articles into the sea, then stripped himself naked; next, have knelt down and placing his left hand on a mass of rock, resolutely mutilated his hand by chopping off his fingers, and then severing his hand from the wrist, and finally, after enduring so much self-inflicted torture, have stabbed himself by a powerful blow through the chest and heart, giving the weapon a lateral motion before withdrawing it! No knife was found – it had probably been washed away by the sea. The mutilation of the hand was, probably, intended to prevent identification; for one joint of the first finger, and two of the second, had been amputated on some previous occasion. For the same purpose he had probably cut off the tops of his long boots, which may have had his name inside; all the marks had been picked out of his linen, and he had thrown away a German Bible, and some other articles by which he might have been traced. The evidence which could be got together was so inconclusive as to the cause of the death of the deceased, that the coroner's jury returned an open verdict, and the matter remains involved in uncertainty to this hour.

Such is the case according to the contemporary account which leaves it all in total mystery, and at this late date a hundred years after, no more can be done than to offer a few comments on it.

First of all, the boat. We are not told, but have to surmise for ourselves, that the 'deceased' had taken the boat, perhaps cutting it from its mooring with his knife, or with the shortened hatchet. That he had come a little distance by water, arriving, did I not anticipate in the sound of his name, with the creaking of row-locks. Coming stealthily, quietly, with as little splashing of the oars as possible, from behind a corner of rock or a headland (I do not know the locality; I have not been to Ramsgate) like a smuggler into his cove, which has even a touch of the Caribbean to it, and the hinting at a keg of rum.

Unfortunately, police methods were then so primitive that we are told nothing about the boat, or of any traces he had left in it. Did he run the nose of the boat ashore into the sand, and then undress in it, as though for a midnight dip into some phosphorescent ocean? 'About six a.m.' will have been first light on the 11th April, that Monday morning, when the bearded coastguard (as I remember the coastguards in my childhood at a very similar seaside town) 'descended and secured the boat'. And 'about 40 yards further on he came upon the body of the man, quite naked'. 'He was lying about 8 yards from the water, and the rising tide was washing over it.' So that he will have lain some distance from the ebbing tide when it was at its lowest, though the boat will not have moved much but will have kept just awash at about the point he jumped ashore.

We are told nothing of his footprints. The tide was coming in, not going out, and there must have been the entire pattern of his comings and goings on the sands. We could have seen at what point he took off his 'long boots', and began padding round upon his bare feet. About ten yards off, only a few steps away, were his coat, waistcoat, trousers, and flannel shirt with the pockets turned inside out; and then, a longish walk away, were his shirt with the wristbands torn off, and the remainder of his clothing which must surely mean his vest and drawers. A boatman, it is stated, had found his carpet-bag floating in the water, open and empty, while someone else had found two linen shirts, two collars, and other things, at the corner of the Royal Crescent wall, so that even before he had come down to the shore Matterig had begun to jettison his personal belongings. But it is no evidence of clear thinking on his part to have discarded some of his belongings at the corner of the best residential terrace in the town, where it was quite certain they would be found. We may think he was already confused in his mind, and had been drinking. He had thrown away a German Bible, something which must have been with him since he was a child, which surely accompanied him when he went to America (for I feel sure he was coming back from America), and may well have been given him by his mother. But also he had scattered some of his letters about upon the sands, which shows something amounting to a failure of intention or purpose on his part, for it was by this means that his identity was established. It is curious to have taken so many precautions, cut off the tops of his 'long boots', picked all the marks out of his linen, and so forth, and yet left letters addressed to himself to be blown about upon the sands.

We are not told what language the letters were written in. All we know is that they disproved his possession of any considerable sum of money, and showed that he was 'probably' a Dutchman. Matterig is an unusual name. There is no one of that name in the London telephone book; and I have looked for it in the telephone books of New York, Chicago, Munich and Amsterdam, and not found it. So why, 'probably' a Dutchman? It may have been because there were letters written to him in some form of 'platt Deutsch' or Low German, in some kind of German dialect no one could quite read or understand. Then, why had he come to England? And in the next breath one is as certain that he only sailed for England on his way home.

No one tells us if he spoke English with a foreign accent. Or indeed, practically anything about him at all, except that the police appear to have taken trouble to trace his movements, and to have found persons who (it could be) crossed the Atlantic with him, or, at any rate, sat in the same compartment of the train with him between London and Dover, and noticed his 'long boots' with trousers 'tucked inside the legs' and that, already, his left hand was 'bandaged up'. 'His boots were remarkable', we are told again, as though this was something everyone noticed about him. After the passage of a hundred years his 'long boots' bring up a mental picture of a Pole or Russian. Although it was known that he had come from America, there is no suggestion that he was American though Yankees must have been perfectly identifiable by their clothes and accent. The appearance of his naked corpse 'indicated a man about thirty-five years old', and there seems never to have been a moment's doubt that he was either a Dutchman or a German. We now begin to wonder how long he had been in the United States, and whether his clothes and also his 'German Bible' indicate that he had only stayed there a little while, not long enough for it to have been necessary for him to buy new suits. He may have been coming back in just the clothes he started in.

But we will now follow his movements in more detail. He arrived at Southampton about the end of March and left for London where he spent a week of which we are told nothing, leaving London for Dover on 7th April (a Thursday) which perhaps indicates an intention to take the Ostend packet and go from there to Germany or Holland. It is the normal way of going to Germany, or via Antwerp into Holland. But, whatever his purpose, he quickly changed it, or, at least, had made up his mind for on the next day (Friday) he goes into a shop at Dover, and buys the hatchet, asking for its handle to be shortened. No doubt this was for the convenience of carrying it in his carpet-bag.

Next day (Saturday) he leaves for Ramsgate. But why did he come down at all to Dover, and not stay in London? Because he had been there before on his way to North America, and knew it was a town suited to his intention? Had he already begun to pick the marks out of his linen? But it has to be borne in mind that Margate and Ramsgate, with Pegwell Bay in between them, of potted shrimp fame, were the excursion centres of Victorian London. We do not know where he stayed in Dover, or again, why he left it. Because it was not gay enough?

For by 10.30 on the Saturday morning he was at Ramsgate ($23\frac{1}{4}$ miles by rail in $1-1\frac{1}{4}$ hrs by way of Deal, Sandwich, and Pegwell Bay) travelling, it must have been, by the early morning train, and immediately on arrival going into a barber's shop to have his beard and moustache shaved off. He was now nameless, he may have thought, having left behind the most of his identity at Dover. And at 10.30 he appears at the Royal Oak Hotel with his carpet-bag and umbrella, wearing his 'remarkable', foreign-looking boots, and once again, it was noticed, with his left hand bandaged.

He was in the Royal Oak Hotel for long enough to have his *portemonnaie* observed, probably by the waiters, but we have no details of how he spent the day. His gold watch and chain and signet ring on the forefinger of his right hand were noted, as well, probably when he stood at the desk to pay his bill. Saturday was the third night of his little tour of the seaside, and for two nights the hatchet had been in his carpet-bag. 'Tranquillizers' and sleeping pills were unknown a hundred years ago. You either drank a lot; or took laudanum which could be got at any chemist and was considered the panacea for all ills and pains. We conclude that he had several drinks in or outside his hotel; but was it a comforting or a terrible moment when the night-porter handed him a candlestick, and he came along the passage to his room? And put the key in the door, and looked for his carpet-bag, and it was still there upon a chair? And perhaps lifted it up to feel the weight of it, felt that heavy thing of metal in it, and was reassured that no one knew his secret. Impossible not to think of him, standing to look at himself, and leaning his face and head nearer the glass to see that he looked a young man tonight, without beard and moustache. Would Matterig wear a nightgown; or sleep in one of his flannel shirts? We guess the latter; and that as he walked about in the room he pictured tomorrow evening to himself. That night as he blew out his candle, and turned over, and was asleep in his self-condemned cell, he was within sound, we could say, of the muffled hammering as his scaffold was erecting.

At ten o'clock next (Sunday) morning he left the Royal Oak Hotel and went off to Margate which is only five miles from Ramsgate. He walked into the Elephant and Castle Inn where he took dinner between 11 and 12 a.m., leaving soon after with his carpet-bag 'which seemed to be heavy', and was then 'seen about the railway station'. Early on that same afternoon he was back at Ramsgate. We may wonder what made him go over to Margate, the most 'Cockney' of all Victorian watering-places. He can hardly have had time to look at it before he was back again. An hour at most carrying the carpet-bag; and perhaps it was the weight of it that made him take his dinner so early at the Elephant and Castle. It could be that in all three towns, Dover, Margate, Ramsgate, he was looking for the right place, and that he came back so quick because he knew he could not better Ramsgate Sands, under the East Cliff.

Immediately on his return, carpet-bag and all, he is traced to the house of ill-fame which it is interesting to know was open on the Sunday afternoon; and there is the presumption that he knew of it already and had been there on the previous afternoon or evening. Its inmates must have been 'the other persons' mentioned in the report who told the police he carried £40 or £50 'in a secret bag about his person'. In any case, for someone who had hardly spent twenty-four hours in the town, all told, he had found his way to the 'low quarter' of

Ramsgate with remarkable celerity, which induces me to think of him in the less reputable streets of New York, or in the 'Latin Quarter' of New Orleans. This visit to a brothel only a few hours before killing himself, and with his own executioner's knife and hatchet already in his carpet-bag, is a most interesting and curious psychological trait or symptom which only makes the mystery of his death, and the motives for that, more baffling still. Even if he had not the full £40 or £50 upon him, and only the £10 and silver seen in his *portemonnaie*, which was yet a considerable sum of money in those days, worth at least four or five times what it is now in terms of day-to-day expenses, why not go on for a few days longer, more especially as he was evidently the sort of person to take his pleasures where he found them? It is as if he allowed himself no re-trial of his problems, and no reprieve. Not even a postponement of sentence, unless we call that his day-trip to Margate on his last day alive.

He left 'the house of ill-fame' about 3 p.m. and was seen about 8 p.m. walking on the cliff 'with his arms folded and his hat over his eyes', or, as it says later, 'with a downcast air'. He had his umbrella but no carpet-bag. Two or three persons were 'supposed to be watching him'. Because of his foreign clothes and appearance? Or for what reason? Because of something communicable in his mental tension? He was 'not seen alive afterwards'. Where had he been during the five hours between 3 and 8 p.m.? And where had he left his carpet-bag? He must have left it where he was certain it would be in safe keeping. And called back for it just as night was falling. And now to work with many little things to do that he had left till last.

Loosening the boat and jumping into it, having put down the precious carpet-bag, perhaps even fearing the boat and the carpet-bag would drift off without him. Taking up the oars with the carpet-bag beside him. And now a few feet from shore and out to sea, as though the Ramsgate Sands were some tropic isle crowded with cannibals all brandishing their weapons at him. Now safe because he was afloat and moving away from them on another element, and the swarm of cannibals was but the lights of Ramsgate. If we look for it, there is something symbolic in this leaving shore and touching land again, like the passage in Charon's boat and the landing upon the other bank of Styx. But Matterig on his last journey was his own boatman, and here he is emptying the golden sovereigns from his *portemonnaie* into the sea. Dropping in his gold watch and chain after them. Pulling off the gold signet-ring from the forefinger of his right with the doomed fingers of his left hand, and letting that ring fall, too, into the water. Followed by a debris of 'solid articles', whatever those may have been. All of them taking a particle of time to sink down and settle on the sandy bottom. And so round the corner of the headland into quieter water.

But now the mystery of his prodigious actions towards self-immolation becomes really extraordinary. What on earth can have been the matter with Matterig that he did not row out to sea and drop overboard a few hundred yards from shore? Even if he was a practised swimmer he could have allowed himself to drown. Why the terrible and agonizing re-landing? Or why not sever the veins in his wrists and have done with it? And why was it that his left hand was already bandaged? It had been bandaged when he was seen on the train between London and Dover. One would like to know if it was bandaged when he got off the boat at Southampton, coming back from America. What exactly does it mean that 'one joint of the first finger, and two of the second had been amputated on some previous occasion'? It would not appear from the evidence that it had anything to do with this later bandage on his left hand. So it looks like another, and unsuccessful attempt on his part at the preliminaries to suicide. Perhaps on board ship? In mid-Atlantic? Or during his week in London? Which is why he went into the shop at Dover and bought himself the hatchet, so as to have another try.

What kind of curse can have been upon him? Why this fury to be unknown and unidentified? As though some terrible significance attached to the missing joints from his fingers? And as though they would not be found on the sands and 'placed in position' with the pieces of his left hand, which had 'three sharp cuts upon it', and a second cut upon the wrist, as if on that occasion, at least, he had found it difficult to carry out his intention.

The more one considers the manner of his death the more mysterious it becomes. What a strange scene, and one wonders if it was in moonlight under the chalk cliffs! For it can hardly have taken place in absolute darkness. With a stumbling walk, undressing as he went along, leaving his coat, waistcoat, trousers, and flannel shirt about fifty yards from the boat, and if my calculation is correct for the account is a little difficult to understand, about sixty or seventy yards farther on, his shirt with the wristbands torn off, and the rest of his clothing. Then stumbling on, quite naked, for what I take to be another hundred yards or so, this time along the tide's edge where the first heap of his clothes lay, but making for the chalk rocks at the foot of the cliffs, one of them to be his execution block. Carrying all this time the knife in one hand and the hatchet in the other, and at the difficult stages of his undressing having to lay both on the sands. At some point, we may be certain, dropping one or either of them, or tripping up on it for a sharp or dull moment of pain, in eleventh-hour warning of what he had in store for himself, but must dismiss here and now as a mere nothing.

Walking on, naked and barefoot, but fully armed for his purpose, and for those few moments in the moonlight like one of the 'two-sword men', sword in one hand, dagger in the other, on an Italian majolica plate, one of the 'swashbuckler' plates from Montelupo; bravo or swashbuckler himself, indeed, except that those have puffed and striped breeches and fierce moustachios, and that their waspish figures are for ever strutting on a lurid yellow ground. Like a bravo, none the less, for all his nakedness, and for a reason we will soon know; like, also, one of the *samurai* or 'two-swordsmen' of old Japan.

Coming to the chalk rock, or it may be, feeling for it with his hands for it may have been in shadow under the cliff; and then, we know, kneeling, and like another Ravaillac or a Damiens putting out a hand, and thinking he might fail at the last moment, first chopping off his four fingers, and then in confusion from the pain and agony making five cuts in all, three on the hand and two on the wrist, before he detached his hand. Now feeling for them with his other hand to be certain that his purpose was accomplished, and picking them up to look at them for 'the pieces of hand and fingers were found about twelve yards away', and the shortened hatchet another 'few yards from the rock', towards the sea. So that, indeed, what can have been the point of all this self-inflicted agony, unless he had the muddled intention to trudge some distance along the shore and throw hand and fingers into the sea?

Last, walking back 'the five hundred feet' from the rock to where his body was found, 'forty yards from the boat' and 'eight yards from the water', as though he had some other purpose he was too weak to fulfil, perhaps to row out with his one hand holding an oar, and stab and drown himself at sea! But the effort was too much for him. It would be revealing did we but know the pattern of his returning footmarks on the sands, till he came to where he could go no further, and braced himself for his last act. At no determined point, but just at where he cared no longer, and it may have dawned on him that all his concealment was in vain; then, did he kneel once more, we wonder, or was he standing, when he stabbed himself with the knife? Moving the instrument after the blow was given, giving the weapon 'that lateral motion' so that the wound was bigger 'internally than externally' before withdrawing it, resembling most exactly in this the act of *Hara-kiri* except that he 'did not walk into the hall of the temple with a noble air, attired in his dress of ceremony, with the peculiar hempen-cloth wings which are worn on great occasions'. 'The upper garments are slipped down to his girdle, and the willing victim to make self-sacrifice remains naked to the waist'. Matterig was quite naked for his last moments, but had not as in feudal Japan his friend best skilled in swordmanship crouched beside him, watching his every movement, who when he leaned forward and stretched out his neck after drawing out the knife, would leap up and sever his head from his body with one sweep of his sword. A manner of dying that was considered noble, while all that had to do with Matterig's prolonged sufferings is, at once, pitiful and mysterious almost beyond the imagining.

Having given my analysis in full, I feel I have laid a ghost. It is a story that has haunted me for many years, indeed ever since as a boy of fifteen I used to read the shelf-full of *Annual Registers*, up in the balcony of the School Library at Eton. Having thought of it for many years there is little doubt in my mind that Matterig was a madman.

The enigma of his death has long haunted my memory and made him into an archetypal figure for me. What kind of a curse can have been upon him? Why this fury to be unknown and unidentified?

The probability of his being a madman is not even mentioned in the account. Not a single word spoken by him is reported, and it could be said that he gains in stature by his silence. One is led to infer that Matterig was strangely dumb, either from inclination, or because he had no English. The certainty grows upon me that he was tall and big. One cannot see him as a little, fussy man; but is it only because of his axe? I see him with leaning or affinity to the timber-camp. A log-man or lumberman; or, if not that, some employment of chopping or striking, or of proximity to the saw-bench.

But he was not a working-man to judge from his gold watch and chain and signet-ring, and from the inns he stayed at for the Royal Oak Hotel at Ramsgate had a porter. It is persons connected with saw-mills who are apt to lose a finger, even nowadays, and a hundred years ago too much significance, one may think, did not attach professionally to a missing finger joint. I cannot but see Matterig in my mind as someone used and inured a little to this possibility. I do not think it would occur ordinarily to anyone to have the handle of a hatchet shortened. It is something particularized, like asking for a bicycle pump or starting-handle.

Landing at Southampton, going up to London for a week, coming down to the coast, actions ordinary enough in themselves, but in the light of his intentions becoming burdened down with meaning. If Matterig was quick enough in finding himself a brothel at Ramsgate, we may be sure enough he made his way to the 'red-light', gas-lit quarters of London, and we have a vision of him in the Haymarket, or in Orange Street or Panton Street that led to the Haymarket from the nightly lupercalia of Leicester Square.

There must be a purpose when the lemmings swarm across rivers and mountains in order to drown in their thousands in the sea, even if it is a command that they should destroy themselves, an order which is implicitly obeyed. The same fate, or a command issued from the same source, leads human beings to their deaths.

As with the lemmings, so with Matterig, the magnet drawing them is irresistible, unconquerable, and compound of sex and death.

What on earth, under Heaven, or in Hell can have been wrong with the poor wretch, Matterig? It seems to me that he grows to huge stature as one thinks of him, and becomes an archetypal figure like the Flying Dutchman or Wandering Jew. I believe, and with some experience, that it is the most extraordinary case I have ever read of. At times he looms up, stumbling down to the shore as some kind of human scapegoat, taking on and expiating the evils and sins of others. Why, that frightful and frantic wish for anonymity in self-destruction? Why, why, had he chopped off his left hand, having 'had a go' at doing so already to judge from his 'fellow traveller' in the train, and 'other persons' who noticed that his left hand was bandaged? Was it that he could not be sure of cutting off his right hand with his left hand, and so tried the next best thing and succeeded with that?

It must have been cold down there under the cliffs, 'near the Dumpton Stairs', for a naked man on that late April night, or early April morning. Why? Why? What was it all about? What can have been the terrible secret he was trying to hide; and only drawing the more attention to himself by so doing? But, at least he died with it, and left it all a mystery. His Sunday visit to the brothel, the throwing away of the German Bible, his utter and complete silence – not one word from him has come down to us – how telling are these details! And his last walk along the cliff 'about 8 p.m., with his arms folded and his hat over the eyes'! Facing west, perhaps, and walking towards the sunset. Within a few hours of which Dover, Margate, and Ramsgate saw him no more. For, of course, his naked and dead body told a horrible tale but left him untouched, really, and inviolate. The whole story being no more plausible than the Flying Dutchman seen beating up the Channel to lie off the boom at Rotterdam, and gone by morning. Except that of a certainty Matterig died at Ramsgate and his bones must be buried there, though I doubt if we could find them now. It is too long ago.

And now like the snake that sloughs off its skin I must stand up and renew myself. Once more, and for the last time? Throwing away all that I have learned and is unnecessary. No more use of notebooks; not that I have kept any. But the study of living persons, not dead things. Excepting only that the living may be dead bodies. Is not Matterig – I can call him by no other name – more alive to you, I am hoping, than the ticket-collector on the train this morning? Than someone who sat on the seat opposite you on the bus or Underground? Even, now you think of him, larger in vision than persons who are quite an important part of our lives? He is the shadow at the dark end of the passage. Where the dog growls with the hair of his coat bristling, and refuses to budge a step forward; the assumption being that all sensible human beings have long since ridden themselves of such nursery tales and out-dated foibles, though it is true that there is probably not a single human individual who is genuinely and entirely free from them.

But, also, Matterig has another and different importance which is bigger than his physical self. His story which has been known to me, as I have said, since I was a boy at school, is of the nature of a personal belonging. Something one has had by one for years and takes out to look at it again from time to time. When, as we turn it over in our minds, it reverts back to an old interpretation, or takes on new meaning. So that it has many of the totem qualities of an *objet-trouvé*; a piece of worn and decayed wood of whatever size for it need not be small enough to go into a pocket. It can be a whole log or bole of a tree metamorphosed into a sleeping crocodile or marine monster; to the catamaran or outrigger of the isles; or to a standing trunk blanched by lightning, stag-headed, bone dead, but alert as to the horn of Herne the Hunter. It can be a pebble from the shore; or an old bone that the dog has buried. The latter may inspire the sculptor to a huge abstract shape; or the former with its smooth contours be as satisfying as the columns of the Parthenon. One can understand that the garden of huge rocks of Nijo Castle, at Kyoto in Japan, was intended as a tribute to the military glory of the tyrant Hideyoshi. This can be comprehended; as that the water-worn rocks from lake or river beds in Chinese gardens were valued for their fantastic and eccentric shapes which suggested the Diamond Mountains and their temples, the statues of sages and philosophers, or the green hills of Bohea. Michelangelo took inspiration for his drawings from damp marks on the plaster of walls and ceilings; Haydn could be inspired by the angle of poker and tongs in the fireplace, or the arranging and inter-relationship of little objects on his writing table. And an old bone buried by the dog in the back garden can mean to the sculptor a mountain mass with its dread heights, its chasms and gullies; the abstraction of an elemental force given shape for the first time in history; or the contours, but never the features, of a woman's body.

In such senses Matterig, or my tramp acquaintance in Piccadilly, can be moved and shifted about in obedience to certain rules of which they are custodian and repository. But, also, they dictate their own moves and the game is in their hands.

I have used them as though, musically, they were moods of 'couldn't care less' and vagrancy, or themes of fury and despair. Once made use of, they must occur and be employed again. They do not set the whole tone, but are only links or connecting passages, if of as much importance as announcements by fanfare, or the sentries posted outside a door. They make their presence felt and are not to be neglected, being intent to be remembered to the degree that I find them unforgettable myself and am for ever haunted by them. As by others who will appear in their time and place where needed.

Music cannot be all gentleness and melody. It is not all intended to soothe the nerves. The note of terror must be struck again as for dogs and children. There should be hair-raising terrors and excitements that storm the mind. It cannot always be the evening calm. When I say that perhaps the most extreme case of *felo de se* there has ever been, and a story such as that of the *Actor found dead in an empty flat* have been in my mind since I first read of them during childhood, it is only that they have been stored there in the places kept for them, to be taken out when wanted. They are parts, if minor parts in a personal mythology, or the lesser items in one's own collection of *objets-trouvés*.

'Actor found dead in an empty flat'

'Famous actor found dead in an empty flat.'

This is a history piece, as that used to be said of paintings. For anyone who remembers the evening papers being called out with this headline, and buying a paper and reading about it, must be beginning to feel old.

It was in 1910, which is more than sixty years ago.

It is difficult to realize a world so like our own, so near, and yet so distant from us. For they had aeroplanes, in embryo, and almost everything we are used to, whether we love or hate it, except television and the radio. But an appalling double abyss stretches between us and our other selves, which is the disaster of the two wars.

Perhaps there is nothing so intangible as just the time we cannot touch; no figures more ghostly than those we might just remember; or further from us than persons we missed by a few years, or could just have seen.

We might first notice a difference in the ragged newspaper boys, for they were tousled and ill-dressed in those days. But from now on we must belong to both worlds at once. It was, as any contemporary of the writer, then an unhappy schoolboy under the chalk hills of Reigate, will remember, the year that King Edward VII died, that King Manuel fled from Portugal, and that the world passed through the tail of Halley's Comet.

All events that in the past would go for portents. Of what? Ah! that is easier said, as with weather reports, when the hot or cold spell is over. Then, it is a tale of cyclone and anti-cyclone; and the heat wave, never foretold, ends in thunder.

So various happenings, big and small, seemed to point to violence. But, often, in the arts, as in crime, more is to be learned from the lesser masters than from the supreme masterpieces in which all is expressed and nothing further is left to the imagination. Thus, in something little but significant which was sinister and frightening in its day, and in particular upon that evening, we may think we have learned both the design and the direction of an age.

The case of the actor found dead in an empty flat can stand, according to my theory, for a germ or molecule of what is to follow. It is the fore-echo of what was to come. Perhaps the events that it foreshadowed have now happened. We are looking in the years before the 1914 war for premonitory signs of disaster coming.

The generation now in its early twenties, and knowing nothing different, may deceive itself with signs of improvement, for the world, if given the chance, is now recovering a little. Yet, half of the world is gone. The one feature which is incontrovertible, of this century now more than half-way through its course, is that the white civilization of Europe has nearly destroyed itself in two civil wars; in reality one and the same war, followed by revolutions, and in another intermediate outbreak which was the Civil War in Spain.

If two wars so disastrous, this is the argument, and so self-destructive, are signs of a diseased state then the symptoms of illness should be discernible before-hand. Most diseases go through an incubationary and infectious period; or, if not that, at least there is warning. The patient is feverish; or there are certain signals which he should follow.

From the beginning of the century there were signs that all was not well. The abortive Russian revolution of 1905 was one of these symptoms. Another warning was anarchy and disintegration in the arts. The wounds may now be healing. The last third of the twentieth century could be as 'safe' and complacent as the middle-class optimism of Queen Victoria's reign. We cannot tell. It is too soon to know. Crimes and events of threatening nature may be throwbacks and last manifesta-tions of illness, or the 'bad days' of convalescence. Or they can foretell worse things to come.

London was then the modern Babylon of all time, appalling yet fascinating in its mystery and ugliness. With the coming of identity and ration cards most of this is gone for ever. It is now, for instance, very difficult to 'disappear'. Methods of identification are so much quicker. Detection has become, at once, a science and a popular pastime in which the public is asked to join.

The actor found dead in an empty flat seems, in the bare announcement, in the headline as it was shouted out that evening, to be a clue to some deeper mystery. Actors have two, or more, or multiple personalities. From long practice they can obliterate their origins. There is no one more pitiable than an actor in a nervous breakdown. He has lost his identity, while his assumed personalities are no more to him than suits of clothes fallen or thrown upon the floor. There is the agony, too, of lost memory. This must be the recurring dread of actors and of executant musicians.

Wars are the product of jealousy; and it was jealousy that laid Atherstone at foot of the iron stair. He was killed with his own weapon like the half of Europe in two wars. Perhaps he was even slain by someone who had no quarrel with him.

He must have driven there in a hansom. Or even in a four-wheeler for there were few taxi-cabs in 1910. It is a long way from 'theatreland' to Battersea. He would not drive as far as the block of flats for he wanted to cover up his tracks. Probably he drove as far as the end of Oakley Street, and crossed the bridge on foot, looking back more than once to see if he was being followed.

He was found dead in his shirt sleeves. His coat was on the floor beside him. He had taken his watch out of his pocket and put it on the floor as well. In order to wind it? Or because it got in his way? Men, in those days, took off their coats and took out their watches in order to play billiards. Therefore, he was in the flat for some time. He had not come just to look round the flat. He was there for a purpose. Not simply for a change of air from his rooms in Tavistock Square.

So I began to fill in the story from imagination.

And for a long time I could find no details.

But the truth is a little different. T. W. Atherstone was a middle-aged actor, married and with two sons, but separated from his wife. In private life he was Thomas Weldon Anderson. He lived at 17 Prince of Wales Road, Battersea, with his mistress, who had been on the stage, and now taught elocution at a School of

Dramatic Art.* Atherstone was insanely jealous of her. On the night of the murder, 16 July 1910, he was not living in the flat, but had left in a fury a few days before. He had, however, seen her in the interval, and so had his two sons. They looked on her as their foster-mother, and on the night in question Thomas the elder son, nineteen years old, was having supper with her. The father had even said that 'he should very probably drop in too'. She had lived in the block of flats for eight years, having moved up from one of the ground-floor flats half-way through her tenancy because burglaries in the neighbourhood had made her nervous. She now lived on the first floor.

They had just started supper when they heard the report of two pistol shots, one immediately after the other, from behind the block of flats where there was an iron staircase which did duty for a fire escape. The son got up from the table and ran to the window, and looking down saw a man climbing the back wall of the next house. The man jumped down from it, and disappeared.

It was convenient evidence for them, but it so happens that no fewer than three other persons also saw a man running away. A cook, out for an evening stroll in the street heard the shots, and saw a man drop from the wall and run away. A tradesman passing by heard the shots, too, but what he saw was a young man running at full speed towards him, passing him, and running towards the river. A third man, who was a chauffeur, heard the shots, and saw a man drop from the wall and run away. Two further witnesses, making five in all, saw a man drop from the wall.†

None of them, however, could agree on his appearance, or on the clothes he wore. He was described as wearing a peaked cloth cap, no hat at all, or a bowler. All agreed he was small and young.

A quarter of an hour after the shooting a police officer arrived and began to examine the whole building. He knocked at the door of the flat, and Thomas Anderson (the son) and the police officer went out on to the iron landing of the fire-escape. Looking down, the son saw a dark form huddled at the foot of the staircase and drew the officer's attention to it.

The officer borrowed a lamp from the flat, and coming down the iron stairs with the son, found a man huddled there, gasping for breath, and bleeding from two wounds in the face. Holding the lamp to the head of the dying man the son was asked by the officer if he had ever seen the man before, and the son said he was a complete stranger to him. A doctor and a police surgeon came on the scene, but despite their efforts and without ever regaining consciousness the man died, at 10.15 p.m., which was about an hour and a quarter after the two shots had been heard.

Now the plot thickens. The dead man was found to be armed. He carried in one hand a coil of insulated electric cable, looped to his wrist in the manner of a

---

* He seems not to have lived in her flat, but to have been a 'frequent visitor'.

† One of them, a baker, told the police that as he was walking along Battersea Bridge Road, about 9.30 p.m., he saw a man scrambling over the wall on his right-hand side, who, as he alighted on the road, nearly fell on him. But the man got to his feet again and ran off in the direction of the river.

policeman's truncheon. It was wrapped in brown paper and tied with string, so as to look like a parcel, but it was a foot and a half long and a most formidable hitting weapon.

The door of the empty ground floor flat was unlocked. It was in this flat that Miss X had lived for four years, before she moved upstairs. On the mantelpiece, wrapped in brown paper, were the dead man's boots. He was wearing felt slippers.

In his coat pocket were his professional visiting cards with the name T. W. Atherstone.

At about this moment the son, Thomas Anderson, tried to leave the flat in order to go home. A cordon of police was round the building, and he was prevented and told he could not pass. He protested that he had no latchkey, and would be locked out from his lodgings. But the police refused to let him go, and the Inspector came upstairs with him, and at the door of the flat showed him one of the visiting-cards. He immediately identified it as his father's card.

This was the first intimation that the murdered man was his father.

At the inquest the witnesses were all asked if the man they saw running away resembled Thomas Anderson. None of them could agree to this. Miss X, his father's mistress, swore on oath that the son had arrived at her flat at 8.30 p.m., and had never left her for a moment.

The footprints of the running man were closely examined, and were entirely different from those of the son. Nor did the pair of boots found above the fireplace in the empty flat correspond with them. It seems, in fact, entirely impossible that it could have been the elder son.

How old was the younger son? We are not told that;* and we know nothing of the homecoming of the elder that night, or whether a police officer accompanied him to his lodgings.

Atherstone, the reader will agree by now, must have been madly jealous of his mistress. He seems at times to have been nearly insane; and a motor-accident a few months before this when he was run over, crossing a road, and given concussion, only increased his fits of jealousy and the jealous scenes he made. He even demanded that Miss X should only teach women at the Dramatic School. And he accused Miss X of being faithless to him, and committing misconduct with her lover in the flat at Battersea. That was the reason why he left the flat a few days before the murder.

Miss X stated repeatedly that she had no lover, and that it was a figment of his imagination.

What, then, does this entry in his diary mean; and to whom does it refer? 'If he had kept away from her, if he had broken from the spell of her fascination and remained out of reach, this would never have happened. He has no one to thank but himself. We all reap as we have sown.'†

We are to surmise that in his felt slippers he intended to climb the iron stair. And was shot at the foot of that, where he was found huddled, before he had began to climb. By someone who knew that he would be there?

* He was sixteen years old.
† The dead man mentioned the names of four men in his diary.

The footprints of the running man have been already mentioned. It should be explained that behind Connaught Mansions, as the block of flats was called, there were small gardens separated by walls five feet high as far as Rosevan Crescent, which led to Battersea Bridge Road, and so down to the river. There were four blocks of flats in Connaught Mansions, and each one of the blocks had its own garden and its five-foot walls.

There was a double track of the footprints, coming and going, and they were small, and as though made by a person 'wearing pointed shoes'. Plaster casts were made of the footprints. If they were prints of 'pumps' or evening shoes, it would suggest, which is likely enough in any case, that the assailant wore them on purpose so as to move silently. Or that he lived nearby and rushed out of his home in a hurry.

Where was Atherstone living at this time? He had lodgings, we are told, in Percy Street, Tottenham Court Road. We do not know if he lived there with his two sons. Was the younger boy left at home, knowing that trouble was brewing, that night?* Atherstone had to cross London, carrying that home-made bludgeon in his hand.

Both Atherstone and his assailant had put on slippers or evening 'pumps' in order to move quietly. And the person who killed Atherstone came to the fray climbing all those little five-foot walls, like a set of 'obstacles' or hurdles, and left, running, in the same manner, as though he knew the way. He jumped over all the walls, and ran down Battersea Bridge Road towards the river.

But why did he come to Connaught Mansions by this back way? Did Atherstone know that he was coming; and did he wait for him? Did the assailant surprise Atherstone on the look out for someone else? Or was the actor, with murderous intent, about to climb the iron stair?

It was argued that his assailant was a burglar. But, in that era of unscientific larceny, what common housebreaker would be 'on the job' at a block of flats in Battersea at nine o'clock on a summer evening? And why, in any case, should he leave in the same curious manner that he came for the low walls, as we have seen, made it into an obstacle race? He must have come, running and jumping over them, from the direction of the river; and it was to the river he returned, probably throwing the revolver into the water when he crossed the bridge.

The supposition is that Atherstone was killed by his own weapon. It is surmised that he had a revolver as well as his bludgeon with him, that he struggled with his assailant, holding the revolver in his right hand, and that the trigger was pulled during the course of the struggle. The bullets entered Atherstone's face at the right-hand side of his mouth, which is just what would happen if the revolver was in his right hand and the muzzle was twisted round and turned on him. There were extensive lacerations on his face, caused either by fingernails, or by the muzzle or some other part of the revolver as it pressed against him.

There are always inconsistencies in such cases. The bludgeon is variously described as 'looped to his waist like a policeman's truncheon', or 'found in his

* The younger son had been to a cricket match, near Willesden, and returned to his lodgings and went to bed at his usual hour.

tail pocket', leading one to think he wore a tail-coat, which is probable, particularly in view of his profession of actor. He cannot have held both bludgeon and revolver in the same hand; and would a bludgeon 'a foot and a half long', wrapped in brown paper, go into a tail-pocket? It is important. Because on this evidence depends the argument as to whether he wrestled with an opponent who was already armed, or was shot with his own revolver? From the apparent certainty with which the argument of his own weapon was accepted, we may think he wore a tail-coat, and that the bludgeon with loop attached lay in his tail-pocket.

The revolver, too, was fired at the level of his face, and not from a step or two above him on the iron stair. So that his assailant, whoever he was, did not go down to him from the floors above. There could be no question of suspicion falling on the elder son. Miss X's statement apart, who swore that he had never left the flat,* there was the evidence of no fewer than five witnesses who saw a 'young' and 'little' man running away towards the river. All but one of these had seen him dropping from a wall. The son, it will be remembered, saw him clearing the first wall. What a curious leaping and running advance, and retreat from a dark deed!

It is difficult to believe the two halves of that are disconnected. He came leaping and running, and the deed done, ran his course away.

So he came running, it is probable, from the direction of the river; and Atherstone was there already, and had gone into the empty flat and changed his shoes. Atherstone, a 'mad actor', as was Prince the murderer of Edward Terriss, made outrageous statements in his diary and may have been the type of person who bragged to his intimates of what he was going to say and do. So perhaps he told someone of his intention, and it may have been to someone who knew him, and his two sons, and Miss X; and who went there to prevent him doing what he threatened. Who saw him starting off, bludgeon looped to his wrist, and was fearful of the consequences? But that can hardly have been anyone but one of his two sons. Who else was fond enough of him, or of his sons, or of Miss X, to come running to stop him? If it was the younger, would not the elder brother have recognized him from the first floor flat as he scrambled over the back wall? The elder brother, though, a few moments later did not know his own father, but, then, by the light of the borrowed lamp, Atherstone was covered with blood and fearfully injured in the face. What reason could there be why the elder son should, on purpose, fail to recognize, first his only brother, and a few moments later his own father?

Was the wearer of the 'pointed shoes' already on the premises; perhaps already in the empty flat, or in the flat above? But it would appear that Atherstone, having put on his slippers in the front room of the empty flat went into the back room, and waited. Till he heard footsteps coming in from the gardens behind? And went out from the scullery at the back of the flat to the foot of the iron stair?

* Miss X, who took an interest in the elder son and helped him in his studies, had asked him to supper in order to show him passages which she had marked in certain of his school books. There is no reason to attach an ulterior importance to this Paolo and Francesca-like episode.

The footmarks of neither son corresponded to the casts made of the footmarks with the pointed toes. Or it would be possible to imagine a 'family' solution of the whole affair. Yet, was not Atherstone justified in his suspicions? For he came there on his errand and was killed underneath the stairs.

Not a sound of a struggle was heard, except the two revolver shots.

Could the footsteps have been made by a third person who came running to warn Atherstone, or his opponent? But he was seen running away by six persons, the elder son included, within a moment or two of the firing of the shots. Running, as fast as he could go, in the direction of the river. It seems almost out of question that this could be anyone but the killer of the actor. It is not unusual to see someone hurrying, or even breaking into a short run to catch a bus, or keep an appointment. But not a young man running as fast as his legs can carry him, who has just dropped down from a wall.

It would be so simple an explanation that it was the younger, sixteen-year-old come to warn his brother, who met his father on the stair and struggled with him. Except that the footprints were not his footprints, and that Atherstone was on the best of terms with his two sons. Why warn the elder brother if there was nothing to tell him? Except that Atherstone was armed and out for trouble? But it was not the younger son, for those were not his footprints. Yet, why enter the block of flats by that back way; and why leave by the same method, which conduces to thinking that, whoever he was, he knew he would find Atherstone waiting there? Not for him, it may be; but neither was Atherstone 'out to kill' his elder son.

What a mystery! What a strange end to mad suspicions! How fantastic the coincidence if Atherstone should have been waiting in the back room to hear someone coming in by that back way, and it was some stray person with whom he struggled, and who overpowered and killed him. It would be interesting to know if there was any evidence that Atherstone had left his rooms, armed like that, on any other day. Or any evidence that he owned a revolver.

One account of him says 'there were plenty of witnesses as to Atherstone's eccentricities. . . . He was a familiar figure at certain refreshment haunts in the neighbourhood of the Strand'.* Of what did he talk to his bar acquaintances? What had his landlady to say of him? We are not told what was found when his rooms were searched. Perhaps we are not told enough about his younger son. Was the assailant on his way to the flat to give a warning? And did the same person, seeing a dead man, run off as fast as he could go?

But the elder son, entirely composed, and bearing no signs on him that he had been fighting, was seen by the police within a few minutes of the shooting. The younger boy had come back from his cricket match and gone to bed. Every theory can be tested and not one of them is convincing.

We are to infer that Atherstone went into the attack, and was killed with his own weapon. The dead man, in mystery, is always lying at the foot of the iron stair.

He could almost have been murdered by some mythological figure who came running to kill him out of the river, and as quickly ran back again. River gods,

* *Murder of Persons Unknown*, by H. L. Adams, London 1931, p. 74.

though, do not kill with revolvers. And are not seen running, bareheaded, in a 'billycock', or in a peaked cloth cap.

The violent death of this actor in an empty flat seems likely to remain a mystery, now, and for ever more.

Paraphrase on the dead actor

The actor found dead in an empty flat is the actor found dead in his dressing-room. Or found dead backstage. In the off season when the theatre is shut. Having 'broken and entered' for some obscure reason of his own which is best expressed in terms of a power failure or electricity breakdown. In fact, it is impaired or lost magic.

All acting and impersonation being in essence a form of sacred magic; and the theatre its sanctuary or temple. To which the prehistoric cave paintings are allied, whether in purpose, or in the idea behind them. The paintings of live creatures, where human beings had reached to the stage of keeping domestic animals, being in order to bring fertility to the herds, or for a success in hunting. Wherever men are portrayed as animals, wearing animal skins or masks, there is direct line of descent down to the mimetic arts. To be able to draw or counterfeit a human being or an animal being considered a proof of magical powers; as was probably, too, the gift of mimicry or imitation. Which applies to all the civilizations of the painted caves and cliff faces, whether prehistoric or near contemporary; and whether they be at Les Eyzies or Lascaux in the Dordogne, at Altamira, or other sites in Eastern Spain, or are the work of Australian 'Black Fellows', or of the wandering Bushmen of the Kalahari.*

Everyone will have had his or her own initiation into these mysteries. For myself it came with watching the pierrots on the sands. Two or even three companies of them in their theatre booths at low tide, where one could walk later and even see the marks of the trestles on the wet sands. Or on a winter morning or afternoon when there was no sign of them whatever. They might never have existed at all, and their season was still far away. Most exciting perhaps if looked down upon from above along the Esplanade, when there was the extra-ordinary sensation of hearing them all competing with each other, but not being able to catch the music of their songs. In that marvellous amphitheatre of the bay, with the not always inhospitable waters of the North Sea, and the passing of steamers for backdrop. And in the foreground the Grand Hotel which, as reported, there is reason to think inspired Rimbaud's *Promenade*, with the Castle hill rising above that over the fishing harbours. Such was the natural theatre of my holidays from school.

So it was, but never for long enough, only for a week or ten days at Easter, and perhaps for the first week of August, until I was fourteen or fifteen years old. And after that never again; but I have not forgotten it, and still remember

* The Bushman language abounds in clicks, nasals, and 'ejectives', which can seldom be acquired by an adult, consequently the pronunciation of many native names cannot be correct. It has the curious development that specific dialects are attributed to different animals and birds. This fact would seem to have magical, or near-magical connotations.

individuals in those summer companies of more than half-a-century ago. More particularly at high tide when they could not play upon the sands; or on wet days, at the Olympia or the Arcadia along the Foreshore below the Grand Hotel.

I can still see 'the Captain', as we called him, but how far removed he was from the 'Spanish' captains of Callot's ragged *Balli di Sfessania* who, incredibly, were of Shakespeare's lifetime; but this one, being 'male lead' of the company, wore a yachting cap, blue blazer, and white flannel trousers, and sang serious ballads. My companion at the daily entertainments being my old tutor, the 'Colonel Fantock' of my sister's poem, who enjoyed it just as much as I did. Then, too, the 'juvenile lead', harlequin of the company, but with powdered pierrot's face and no patches, who sang in a cracked voice:

> *Have you another little girl at home*
> *Like Mary?*
> *Another little peach upon the family tree?*

> etc.; etc.;

and who, horrifyingly, if still living would be eighty-five years old at least.

But there was, also, the male member of the troupe who took female rôles and was, clearly, a pronounced case of transvestism I think I realized this, then, but without its implications. Certainly my companion never enlarged upon those to me. But we had been told, I cannot now think by whom, that he was a rich man who perhaps even paid to be allowed to perform thus, and had a collection of dresses and a large motor-car. A tall, dark man of about thirty or thirty-five, clean shaven but dark of jaw and chin, with black eyebrows, of Spanish, perhaps rather of Jewish feature. Certainly I remember him appearing in a 'sketch', and to sing a song, in a green evening dress smoking a cigarette in a long cigarette-holder, the audience seeming to 'take it' just in proof of clever acting and impersonation. But, too, we had the excitement of recognizing him in his motor along Westborough, just at the corner of the Londesborough Theatre, with the cracked voice 'harlequin' and another person on board. It was an open car, and an expensive one at that, and its occupants did not look like ordinary persons. Nor, clearly, did they feel they were. They were determined to be seen and noticed by just the slightest extravagances of manner and behaviour. A little more pallor, or, maybe, the opposite of that, and the traces of greasepaint but, anyway, they were conspicuous in the motor, to be known in that moment and recognized. And we saw them at least once again walking in the town. How much I would like to know their history! What had happened to him during those years of pre-World War One, and after? Where can he be now? Almost certainly he is long dead.

This experience of the seaside pierrots, though so slight and transitory, was equivalent to a full-scale immersion or baptism into the magic and mystery of the theatre. And with intimations of other things besides. Though I am prepared to believe that such equivocal persons are no strangers to towns like Brighton or Scarborough, or indeed to the villes d'eaux of any clime or land. Who was that 'foreign nobleman . . . who had a big yacht lying out in the bay' and who was 'fleeced' to the extent of nearly five hundred pounds by a singer and comedian at the Aquarium? More than once I have thought I was on the scent of this prince or count and could give his name. Then, too, there was Lord Arthur P . . . C . . . , one time Member of Parliament for Newark, who figures in *Bad Companions*,* and had given concerts at the Spa Theatre with his friend and female impersonator Ernest (Stella) Boulton; thereby causing, one would imagine, a certain amount of discussion and controversy. That had been in the 'seventies'. One may be reminded of the equivocal performances of the novelist Colette and the Marquise de Belboeuf in the theatre at Dieppe under the eyes of M. Willy, Colette's energetic and voracious husband.†

The thought of such summer seaside entertainment leads naturally enough to the great castrati singers of the Italian eighteenth century of whom much has been written. They may have been the most finished and perfect, if exaggerated, of all singers there have ever been. Their warbling was of sounds to which our ears are not attuned and which they are not likely ever to hear again, while their affectations and show of temperament were of the gilded opera house as to the manner born. It was no more to be expected of them that they should give a naturalistic performance than it was implicit in the golden caryatids and gilt theatre-boxes and balconies of the Old Bedford, the Holborn Empire, and other Victorian music-halls that the comedians and 'lions comiques', often billed and labelled as 'eccentrics', should perform otherwise than with a fantasy and touch of the sacred frenzy. I think all would agree who carry some memory of them in their minds. Of George Robey with his long coat, red nose, and battered billycock, in his unfrocked parson, dipsomaniac-bachelor garb, with aggressive manner, not a person to be mocked at the street corner, or behind the engraved plate glass windows of the saloon bar.

Or so many others; T. E. Dunville of the staccato machine-gun delivery, and more than a little frightening in spite of the obvious and hopeless pathos of his attitude. Little Tich, who was entirely different for there was nothing pathetic about him; who was well able to look after himself and who would 'look after' you, too, if you were not careful. With some malevolence about him which, being small, was his protection, and a warning. A grocer before a drop-scone of Holborn Viaduct with all its lamp-posts, as I watched him at the Holborn Empire, but from some small and eccentric concern of his own, no chain store or Co-op. As a dancer, Valentin-le-désossé of the Moulin Rouge may have been his only rival. But Valentin was probably the greatest eccentric dancer there has ever been. It will be recalled that Little Tich was extremely popular in Paris where he often appeared, and I have seen the outside of a theatre in the rue St Honoré covered with posters and photographs of him. He was sinister, as well as funny, as a Spanish dancer in high comb and mantilla, in which rôle he resembled a picture by Zuloaga; though we may be sure that Goya or even a greater and older name than his would have painted him. As himself, so to speak, he was at his best

---

* *Bad Companions*, by William Roughhead, London 1930.
† The Marquise de Belboeuf was the daughter of the Duc de Morny, half-brother of Napoleon III and son of Queen Hortense, by Princess Troubetzkoy.

in a check suit, hands in pockets, in the immensely long boots in which he danced – standing upright in those boots which seemed nearly as long as skis, and longer and more important than the shovel hat of Don Basilio, and there came the moment when, standing in them, he was able to lean down and bang his head upon the boards. This slightly horrific genius in his kind, who appeared as a child when the Tichborne case and claimant were still fresh in public memory, was friendly with the more misshapen, but of course greater genius Toulouse-Lautrec, and Walter Sickert has told me of meeting and talking to them both, when walking together at Dieppe and on Brighton Pier. It is of interest too, that no sooner than arrived for his pre-war seasons in London, Nijinsky would ask to be taken to see 'Littler' as he called him; not only for his dancing, but as a master of make-up, the other actor Nijinsky most admired being Chaliapin.

Another music-hall artist who, on this analogy, we may be sure the great Russian dancer would have appreciated, was Nellie Wallace. It was enough to see her fingering the limp feathers in her hat, then dancing a few steps of the Charleston. Her boots were inimitable, and a comic 'prop' of importance, as were her unique clothes and hats, and her mingled pathos and gaiety, so that one did not know whether to laugh or cry. For neatness of dancing and wild, if in her case unscheming gaiety, she compared to Groucho Marx whose dancing has been over-shadowed by his other comic gifts. Ella Shields of the 'Burlington Bertie' song and Vesta Tilley were of the *travesti* tradition, with its long stage history going back to Peg Woffington who excelled in men's rôles; with counterpart in opera from Cherubino down to Linda, the little Savoyarde, and her songs with hurdy-gurdy accompaniment or imitation in Donizetti's opera, and to the principal boy of Victorian pantomime.

To be included with the latter all the wonderful scenes and persons to be read of in Blanchard's theatrical memoirs, from diary entries such as '2 October 1859. Flexmore (clown) calls for annual song and spends afternoon', to 4 September 1860, which reads 'Flexmore comes in chaise with Mme Auriol about pantomime'. Flexmore being one of the most famous of the English dancing clowns who burlesqued the great dancers of the Romantic Ballet, such as Perrot,[*] Carlotta Grisi, and Cerrito; reviving for instance *Esmeralda* which is still, a hundred years later, in the repertory in Russia, and producing in 1849 the skating ballet *Les Patineurs* to Meyerbeer's music from *Le Prophète*. Then there was George Wieland, the imp or sprite, whom Blanchard thought to be the greatest exponent of the dying art of pantomime, who took the part of Asmodeus in *The Devil on Two Sticks (Le Diable Boiteux)*, the old ballet in which Fanny Elssler, as Florinda, danced her famous cachuca. Both Flexmore and Wieland died young, from their over-exertions, there can be no question. And Blanchard has wonderful tales to tell of Tom Ellar, the harlequin who died in his lodgings in Lambeth, 'leaving a wife and child totally unprovided for'; and of James Barnes, the pan-

---

[*] Jules Perrot (d. 1892), with Auguste Vestris and Vaslav Nijinsky, one of the greatest male dancers of all time, who appears in many prints of the Romantic Ballet, makes a late appearance as the old ballet master in more than one of Degas' paintings of dancers in class.

taloon. But having been rebuked by a 'famous critic', for having referred to previous works of mine in a footnote, my reason being that so many of them are out of print and not likely to be printed again in my lifetime, I refrain from informing the reader where he may learn further of such matters, though they may possess their own aesthetic values and are surely more than the mere dross of poetry.

The music-hall I am thinking of was that of the years between the two world wars when it was already dying. Having been a cockney art form deriving from Hoxton, Lambeth, Bermondsey, Brixton, and so forth, and at its best between 1860 and 1890, as we see it in the music-hall song covers, of which minor art an Irishman, Alfred Concanen, was the master. At times it is a single figure of the singer or comedian with no background at all; or, at greater expense of lithography, he is shown against the scene of his act or song. And in another, and third category of song cover, not on the boards but in a true to life scene taken from the words or action of the song. Thus, in a 'turn' about, let us say, Brighton, the Marine Parade is the background, or, perhaps, the Chain Pier. They vary very much, but out of the hundreds of Concanen's lithographed song covers let us suppose a couple of dozen to be works of art.* And there are of course the many hundreds, and probably not as many dozens of good song covers by the lesser men.

Unfortunately there is less evidence, and indeed little more than the posters to tell of the splendours of the old London pantomimes. It was left to a Frenchman, Francis Wey, to mention them as among the wonders of the modern Babylon. He says that the Christmas pantomimes, especially at the old Surrey Theatre, were upon a scale of splendour and fantasy that was the pleasure or hallucination of the poorest fog-bound slums of Lambeth.† With, it might be added, the portraits of the Archbishops in their full-bottomed wigs and leg-of-mutton sleeves never far away in Lambeth Palace; and for a time, William Blake in his lodging at the 'House of the Interpreter' in Fountain Court, likewise in Lambeth. These London pantomimes were of the fifties and sixties, long after the time of Grimaldi, but in the days, or, rather, matinées and nights of Dicky Flexmore, Wieland, Tom Ellar, and Jim Barnes the pantaloon, in a very different theatrical world from that of the music-halls. The serious London theatre was still under the spell of the acting of Edmund Kean (d. 1833), of whom Coleridge wrote 'to see Kean act is like reading Shakespeare by flashes of lightning'. There are many portraits of Kean among the tinselled Hoxton prints, which were again a minor and Cockney art form. But for all their crudity in colour, we may assume these 'penny plain, tuppence coloured', to be imbued with the tricks and gestures of his acting. One could be justified, too in thinking that the 'obscure actor' in a London theatre who inspired Delacroix to his lithographs of Dr Faustus, during his stay in England in 1825–6, belonged to Kean's school and style of acting. In

* *The Age of Paper*, followed closely by *Kleptomania* and *The Bond Street Beau*, are the best song covers by Concanen that I have seen.
† *A Frenchman sees the English in the fifties*, translated and edited by Valérie Pirie, London 1935.

the lithographs there is some indication of the scene painting, and not only of the acting.

How much one would have liked as a noctambulist to have seen the theatres! And hardly less so, the Christmas pantomimes with scenery by the Grieves brothers, and the unprecedented and spangled splendour of their harlequinades. Between which and my own person there is but the tenuous link that at the Drury Lane pantomime in which I saw Dan Leno in 1903 or 1904, myself aged six or seven, there were still some members of the Vokes family dancing with contorted, twisting legs, whom my mother told me she remembered as a child in the panto-mimes of the seventies (she was born in 1869). How many were there of the Vokes family? Where did they come from? How did they come by their strange legs and arms? What was their history?* The mere photographs of this peculiar family with their goatee-bearded father or brother is equivalent to an initial draught or intoxication into the wonders of the theatre. In the *musée imaginaire* which collects and forms itself all through one's life, how much one regrets the absence of other witnesses who could tell one more about such things!

There are, to be sure, the lithographs and caricatures of dancers and opera singers by A. E. Chalon, an excellent artist though scarcely mentioned, if at all, in the dictionaries of painters. But one would have wished for outside evidence. And to have imported, though the basic facts are a little against its historical possibility, if only by a few years, the draughtsmen specializing in actor prints from a kingdom, or indeed, an empire at the other side of the world.

II

Just the information, as to the author of one of these prints, that 'in his early years he worked as cartoonist in the tea-house of the Niwaka theatre where he painted caricatures of the actors on the promenade fans of the theatre-goers', being enough to show their degree of involvement with the stage. As is, too, the number v after the actor Danjuro's name, and the formidable woodcut portrait of him wrapped, cocoon-like, in an, apparently, free-standing cloak of the terra-cotta family colour, with the huge square pattern or crest upon it. And, as well, to be told that this particular woodcut master, Katsukawa Shunso, published in 1770 a book which showed on white fans the coloured half-length portraits of Edo's (Tokyo's) most popular Kabuki actors against a blue background.

To judge from the prints by these artists which served as placards or theatre posters, they were all capable of catching the ferocious airs of Kean. One master, in particular, Toyokuni, who is a few years later in date, almost defies description in his prints of Kabuki players, and might have made the greatest poster artist

* Jessie Vokes was four years old when she first appeared at the Surrey theatre; Victoria made her debut when but two years old; Rosina was even made use of in long clothes; Frederick Vokes was a sprite. Jessie Vokes had been taught dancing by the Misses Gunnis, and by the great clown and dancer, Dicky Flexmore. The Vokes family had, indeed, their own and peculiar, or, indeed, inimitable style of dancing. It could have been one of the three sisters who had been pupils of Dicky Flexmore, whom I saw at Drury Lane. She need have been no more than fifty-four or five years old at that time.

there has ever been. But it would need a theatrical tradition lasting some two hundred years, and eight or nine generations of actors of the same families, to get the public used to posters of so violent a nature. For instance, one of Toyokuni's series of 'large heads' of actors, shows a furtively mouse-like looking individual hunched up in a muffler-like garment which has a form of the squared family crest of the Danjuro dynasty upon it, while his outer robe has a carp swimming up a waterfall upon one shoulder, and coming down it on the other shoulder. He has Mickey-mouse-like puffs of hair or ear-protectors, a bald blue patch upon his cranium, with a clown-like, what appears to be a feather sticking up from out of it, and a kind of grid of brick-red lines imposed upon his pink skin which must have been specially 'pinked' for the part he was playing.

Another print is of a melodramatic nature unsurpassable, and depicts such a villainous character as can never have existed, save that in the tradition of the Kabuki he may have been hero, not villain of the piece. Yet another theatre poster by Toyokuni has for subject a ferocious swordsman with both hands on his sword, and a fat man naked to the navel behind him, expostulating with outstretched hand. The pupils of the eyes of both actors are strained to the utmost for dramatic effect – this is a stage trick acquired by long practice in the Kabuki theatre since early youth – and both men have hair of another quality from the first actor described, not mouse-like, but looped over the bald cranium and below the ear with the strands separate, as though for more emotional effect.

Perhaps the most extraordinary of all Toyokuni's actor woodcuts depicts a pair of actors fighting and scowling at each other. It can be no mere interchange of courtesies. They appear to have descended on each other, and to be hovering no more than a foot or two above the ground like a pair of exotic birds. That squared family crest again – they still sell handkerchiefs and objects with the actors' crests upon them at a stall in the Kabuki-za Theatre in Tokyo – but the crest takes up about a quarter of the whole woodcut, only ending where the lower of the two curious creatures has tied a kind of blue rope in odd fantasy below his chin. The 'grid' of red lines is marked all over his face, reminding me that I once read of actors of the old school, but they were the ageing ones who 'played' the English provinces, looking in backyards and demolished houses for a piece of red brick of the right colour for their 'make-up'. Hair, black as black, and like the corner of a wind-vane; top knot receding, and stuck with what look to be the paper windmills sold in childhood at the English seaside, but without the sticks they blew round on in the sea breeze. His opponent bearing down upon him with narrowed pupils and terrifying leer, red 'grid' in place like a visor – both actors have their mouths distorted like a badly tied boot-lace looping at one end – an enormous built-out ear, tufts of hair, not two, but four of them, where beards should be, or whiskers; and greatest anomaly or paradox of all, in his right hand a fan, of all things, but it could be a 'war-fan', as they were called. Or is this just a courtship dance, or mating ritual? Is the upper one the hen bird; his upper garments float out above and behind him almost like a pair of wings? And for crowning fantasy he has a knot of the same blue cord as his rival or enemy underneath his chin. They are characters who cannot get away from one another, and have to wear items of the same clothing or uniform as though they are at the same 'prep' school.

The *onnagata*, male actors who take the female rôles in Kabuki dramas, are marvellously portrayed by Toyokuni, likewise by Shunsho, author of the wood-cut of the actor Danjuro v in his terracotta cloak with family crest. But never so well as by the outstanding genius Sharaku, whose career is among the most extraordinary of all recorded in the human arts. He may have been, for nothing is certain about him, a Nōh player who offered his services to the famous print publisher and patron of Utamaro, Tsutaya Jusaburo; and in fifty days he made the drawings for twenty-three large woodcut portraits of Kabuki actors, often with silver or mica backgrounds. But they failed to sell, and his career ended after some ten months in 1794, during which time he had produced a total of a hundred and forty-five woodcuts. After which he disappears from history, although a list of Nōh players for 1825 mysteriously contains his name. It is Sharaku who can reproduce the peculiar, cringing walk of the *onnagata*, and their sham femininity so that we almost hear their high, but stylized falsetto voices. But I make no further attempt to write here of this extraordinary genius, having tried my best elsewhere to transfer him for an episode of the universal *musée imaginaire* to design posters for the bull-ring in Spain. It is at least remarkable, in conclusion, to what degree the preliminary drawings for the actors if preserved, which is rare indeed, and transferred to woodcut, approximate to the Shakespearean features in our harlequinade.

Thus, in the woodcut reproduction of a sketch in Chinese ink attributed to Sharaku, you can almost hear the sweep of the actors' voluminous robes as they recoil backwards, one of them with his immense sword in hand balanced by the scabbard rising up behind his crouching figure. They could be two turkey-cocks, bustards, or who knows what pair of huge cock birds, defending themselves. This must be a drawing roughed out from a sketch made upon the actual scene, it being obvious that the draughtsmen would be given special facilities for taking the preliminary drawings for their prints. But this drawing could so easily in attitude, in diction, as it were, be of English warriors on the eve of Agincourt, rehearsing their dire deeds for the morrow. But in the plays; not on the battle-field.

While, in a Chinese ink sketch for an actor's portrait by Toyokuni, which can have been the affair of no more than a few moments, the eyes, the very shape of the head, and the ruff-like folds of the garment round his neck, might well be a sketch done of Grimaldi, or another of the famous English clowns, James Byrne, or W. H. Payne; the clown's dress being traditional and little changed, if at all, from Elizabethan times. Being a brush drawing, it has a broader line than had it been a preliminary sketch by Cruickshank. It is in fact more in the technique of James Gillray.

If there could but have been an interchange of theatrical draughtsmen! To have had woodcuts, by the artists named, of Astley's Equestrian Drama when *Timour the Tartar* was on the programme; prints, too, of the pantomimes, and of the great clowns and harlequins and pantaloons; of the dramatis personae of the tinselled and spangled prints, rendered with all the pluperfect refinements and finish of the Japanese wood engravers, their *gauffrage* patterns which were pressed into the paper from the back so that they stood out in relief; with background for the actors' heads of mica, of metallic colours; or sprinkled with gold dust for the skies, or to give the designs on dresses, and the lights on arms and armour.

And in reverse, let us imagine for ourselves impressions of their great actors, the aforementioned Danjuro v, for instance, and of others of the great dynasties of Kabuki players, by Delacroix and other painters susceptible to the Romantic drama, who would have found for themselves another world of wonder in the Kabuki and the Nōh plays. So often there have been living parallels in the history of the arts, but it is the law of nature that they never meet. It being a temptation, therefore, to pinch them so that they come together in the middle.

Finding myself back again where I was left at my own wish, at the summer theatres along the sands, or on the Foreshore below the Grand Hotel. How difficult it was in the short winter afternoons to believe they had ever been there at all! There was no trace of them upon the tidal sands. The next stage in my education, once out of the Army in January 1919, being undertaken largely in Italy. In this manner, on not much money, travelling ever second class and staying in uncomfortable hotels, whereby I was enabled to see much of Italy when I was young, in supplement to my childhood memories of Venice and Florence, Bologne, Lucca, and Milan. But remembering particularly, even before the winter of 1922, the Lion of St Mark's in the piazzas of so many towns of the terra firma, Verona, Bergamo, Brescia, Padua, implying the Venetian dominion and the feel of Venice.

But there was, also, the Russian Ballet of Diaghilev of which the influence even now is not fully appreciated at its true value. In the end it may prove to have been at least as fruitful as that derived from Ruskin and William Morris and the English Aesthetic Movement. It was above all the music, and the scenery by Bakst and Derain and Picasso that interested me, and not so much the dancing, or, then, the ballerinas. But I remember seasons of the Ballets Russes in no fewer than six London theatres; and I am not forgetting the *Actor found dead in an empty flat*. Or that part of London round Drury Lane and Covent Garden, the first of which pair of theatres seems haunted, in so far as it is worth believing in such things; and in fact one of the dressing-rooms at the Theatre Royal, Drury Lane, is said to be haunted by the ghost of Dan Leno.

There should, and there must be haunted theatres. For they have had their dramatic moments, connected, or unconnected with the play. The theatre must be the most dramatic of all settings for assassination. Consider, for instance, the murder of Abraham Lincoln at the Ford's Theatre in Washington, in 1865. Lincoln had shown signs of a premonition of his end. Had he perhaps received secret warnings? His assassin John Wilkes Booth belonged to an old and famous family of actors, as well known in their day as the Barrymores, a fact which adds tremendously to the dramatic possibilities, all of which, and more, were fulfilled and played to capacity on the night in question. The actor-murderer had been specially to the theatre on that morning to review the scene and mentally rehearse the action. The performance opened, and when his moment came Booth entered the box on some pretext, and with no more ado, and not a word spoken, emptied his pistol into the seated figure of the president. He, then, vaulted over the ledge of the box onto the stage, thereby breaking his leg, despite which he contrived to run out through the wings in the confusion and uproar, and was only caught and arrested some days later.* A good deal of mystery still surrounds what happened subsequently, attended by the discrepancies which still attend political assassination in the United States. There is a gruesome photograph of the hanging of six men and one woman who were found guilty of conspiring to commit the murder, but in all probability it will never be certain what were the true facts.

Or there was the murder of the Russian prime minister Stolypin in the opera house at Odessa, which was the prelude or curtain-raiser to the attempted, but abortive revolution of 1905. The Tsar and Tsarina were in the royal box, and Stolypin with other ministers was sitting below them in the stalls. The theatre was in darkness. The performance had begun. The assassin came down the aisle to Stolypin and fired point blank at him. All the lights went on again, and in full view of the audience and of the Emperor and Empress the dying man looked up at the royal box and at the moment of death made the sign of the cross. A shudder of horror went through the theatre, for that gesture seemed to contain in itself the direst of warnings and a prophecy of the troubled and fateful years to come.

Of that other sort, directly connected with the play, there was the death of Kean, his last performance at Covent Garden, on 25 March 1833, when he was playing Othello to his son's Iago. By this time Kean was crippled with gout and rheumatism and may have suffered the consequences of other illnesses as well. Besides which, he was an alcoholic on the verge, or over it, of delirium tremens. He had now the appearance of an old man, and greying hair, although he was no more than forty-five years old. He always kept loaded pistols by his hand and, also, invariably, a bottle of brandy. His son must have led the most peculiar life with him; being roused up at all hours of the night to go for a headlong drunken gallop on horseback; or spend the day watching him drink and rave in a darkened room with the blinds all drawn. His clothes were in rags. Financial affairs were in a hopeless tangle. He could not be relied upon to get successfully through a performance, but he was still capable, perhaps more than ever, of producing the most violent effects of genius in horror or terror. On this last night of his career, in the fourth act he reeled and trembled, and fell into the arms of his son, muttering 'I am dying. Speak to them for me!' He was given a glass of warm brandy, and driven to his cottage which was next door to the Richmond Theatre, where he lay for a few weeks between life and death. So died the greatest of English actors there has ever been. Somehow, that lingering for those two or three weeks, when it would have been so much more dramatic to have died in full view of the audience upon the stage, approximates to the fatality of the *Actor found dead in an empty flat.*

* Booth shouted the words, 'Sic semper tyrannis. The South is avenged', from the stage, and then ran out through the wings. Twelve days later he was shot in a tavern near Bowling Green where he had concealed himself.

Or there are the deaths of two young dancers, Kate Webster and Emma Livry, both fatally burned during performance. Clara Vestris Webster, who was only twenty-three years old, and 'the most promising English dancer of the Romantic Ballet', during a performance at the Haymarket Theatre on 14 December 1844, inadvertently touched with her skirt the naked flame of an oil-burner. Her dress flared up, and the audience rose to their feet in horror as she rushed panic-stricken about the stage, her costume blazing. A stage carpenter caught her in his arms and beat out the flames, but she was fatally burned. It is pathetic in this era of first aid and ambulances to read of her being driven to her lodgings accompanied by a doctor and by her lover, a young officer in the Brigade of Guards. She lingered in agony and delirium for three days and then died. The case of Emma Livry is more dreadful still. This dancer, the twenty-one-year-old illegitimate daughter of a member of the French Jockey Club and a sixteen-year-old member of the *corps de ballet*, during a rehearsal of *La Muette de Portici*, went too near a gas flare, and again, her dress caught fire. She died in great agony as long as eight months later, but hers was an even greater tragedy than the death of Clara Webster for she was the star pupil of the great Taglioni, and was said not only to have a *ballon* and elevation rivalling that of Taglioni, herself, but also, to have had imparted to her by her teacher the unique gift of hovering, or appearing to hover for the fraction of a moment at the height of a leap, and then coming down slowly, in apparent contradiction of the laws of gravity. The only other dancers having ever possessed or practised this beside Marie Taglioni being Auguste Vestris; and it was the gift, also, of Nijinsky. When questioned about this mysterious effect, Taglioni, who taught it to Emma Livry, is reported to have said that it was simple and mainly a question of breathing. Such are tragedies built into, or a part of the fabric of the theatre and in ratio, therefore, with the dramatic action.

But there are other happenings exterior to, but not the less connected with the theatre. I have not in mind the murder of the Swedish dramatist-King Gustavus III by Anckarström, on the night of 15 March 1792, at a masked ball in the great theatre at Stockholm; or the bomb attempt on the lives of Napoleon III and the Empress Eugénie by Orsini outside the Opéra in Paris. In the ensuing carnage the intended victims of course escaped unhurt, while fifty-six of the crowd of onlookers and the military escort were killed and injured. But a blood-bath is not necessarily more impressive because of its cubic-capacity and size. Everyone, again, must have his or her experience of something with its own unforgettable, and vastly extended dramatic possibilities. The *Actor found dead in an empty flat* was something only read about, but which seemed to be possessed of key significance as if it were the clue or opening to many secrets and unsolved mysteries. But there was something else which happened many years ago; impersonal, in the sense of its being connected with persons unknown; but yet, archetypal, a word that implies pattern-forming, and certainly of theatrical connection and implication.

This was the burning alive of an old actress in her caravan on Eckington Common when I was ten or twelve years old. It was in the summer holidays, somewhere round 1908 or 1910 before the First World War, Eckington being my native village in north-east Derbyshire. Was it, one might wonder, really an accident? In the sense that it may have appeared to be accidental but was, all the time, pre-determined to be her fate. Just as much as if she had been killed by a train going off the line. So perhaps such things are inescapable. Ah! everyone was born once, even the most unlikely ones, even the bony hand picked out of the molten slag-heap, and all the rest a mystery; a woman's hand, but no rag, no shred of skirt or dress; even the old actress who was burned alive in her caravan! Oh! how those two things frightened me when I was a small boy! Eckington Common was a piece of waste ground not far from our gates, strewn, as I remember it, if not thickly, with bits of paper and old tins. I do not think we had noticed there was a caravan upon it. In any event it was probably in the far corner near some houses, and we had only just arrived home for the holidays. Her caravan, we were told, had been there all the winter through. Months ago she had sold the horse that drew the caravan. So she was stuck there, and could not get away. I knew her name for many years, and remember reading of the inquest on her in the Sheffield newspaper. There was some idea of her having been known in the district through appearing in the local theatres, but I am not sure of this. It was said she had been starving all the winter. This may have been exaggerated, but there were no old-age pensions, then. Probably she had overturned a lamp and set fire to the caravan. But nothing was certain. It could have been intentional, and a case of suicide. And of course at that age I was discouraged from asking questions.

But why had she chosen Eckington Common of all places on which to hitch her waggon? It can hardly be said to be on the way to, or from anywhere. It is just incidental and happens to be there, outside a village, or, in fact, a small town in a coal-mining area. And why a caravan at all? What got her on the move, and started her travelling? I remember people who had talked to her in the door of it, or seen her coming down the steps onto the ground. I am not sure we were not told she was an old woman with red hair. Of course we began to credit her with having played in Shakespeare. But perhaps her real background was the circus tent, and not the stage. This would explain her living in a caravan. But, in any case, the mystery of the poor old woman was in my thoughts for days and days, and I could not help thinking of her while falling asleep.

Oh! how those two things frightened me; the old actress found dead in her blazing caravan, and the bones of a woman's hand found in the molten slag-heap, and here I am remembering them years later, as I remember the words and rhymes scrawled in pencil by the young colliers upon the white paint of the bridge over the trout stream in Eckington Woods, and it was my first intimation of love among the bluebells, of lying down among the bluebells to be a satyr in the flowers; meeting on the bridge, their postern into the blue woods, there to lie with their sweethearts till dew was upon the wild garlic and the red campion went pale in the wet evenings. And another afternoon I saw a stallion come down the steep field and cast the shadow of its manhood on the grass. It is true, about then, I saw the Gypsy woman suckling her babe under the long wall at Reigate Priory, and it appalled me when I was a schoolboy for I did not know that human beings were but animals.

But away from the Gypsy caravan, if it was that, and back into the theatre of the golden caryatids! Of which sort there are many; it being the only true theatre except for the stone auditoriums of the Hellenes in their landscap'd settings. The finest and best preserved of those being at Epidaurus; at Taormina with snow-capp'd Etna for backdrop; and at Aspendos in Asia Minor. Such theatres of the Ancients are of the open air, needing but an awning or velarium to draw over the audience when the sun is overhead, and maybe, no shadow nearer than the fig-tree's shade. They are ruins; if still inhabited in poetry by the two stone figures of satyrs 'from the Roman period' in front of the proscenium at Segesta, in Sicily; and by the very classically-minded proscenium of Aspendos, which has two orders of columns, the lower Ionic, the upper Corinthian, and in the centre of the colon-nade 'the figure of a female springing out of the calyx of a flower, and holding branches of foliage in her hand'. Nothing could be more different from the fair-ground caryatids of the typical old London theatre. The more *mondaine* and essentially Gallic version of whom are to be admired *in excelsis* at the Paris Opéra, with the rostral columns of its exterior, naked lamp-bearing nymphs, crowned N's for the be-laurelled *Empereur des Français*, and sloping carriage entrances, now too narrow and winding for any motor-car to negotiate and therefore unused and obsolete.

It is the unfailing and unquenchable optimism that this is the one and only language of decoration that is so remarkable about both the exterior and the interior of the Paris Opera House. And this confidence extends to its dependen-cies as anyone would agree who has ever worked in the Bibliothèque de l'Opéra. It is the Opera House of the nineteenth century *par excellence*, attuned to the music of Gounod and Meyerbeer, and temperamentally incompatible to the music of the future. Begun in 1861 and completed in 1874, 'there is hardly a variety of marble or costly stone that has not been used in its construction', the windows of the loggia have balconies of green Swedish marble, while the hand-rail of the grand stair, or *Escalier d'Honneur* – and what a staircase it is! – is of Algerian onyx, but work on it was necessarily interrupted during the 1870 war. It suffers in consequence from the dichotomy between a Second Empire and a Third Republic, while still being, and much too much so, the grand opera. And yet this style, just because it is creation and not imitation, is to be preferred to the sham Louis Quinze of the Ritz Hotel and pre-war Atlantic liner. Garnier is seen to more advantage in the beautiful golden theatre in the Casino at Monte Carlo. Also, I have been told, in another golden theatre that he built at Homburg.†

The *Actor found dead* and the actress burned in her caravan will have played in

---

* Compare the *Escalier d'Honneur* of the Paris Opéra and the mid-Victorian Gothic staircase of Manchester Town Hall or of the St Pancras Station Hotel, London. It is the same temperamental difference as that between a Paris gendarme and a London or Manchester policeman.

† The style of the Second Empire is, or was, to be seen at its best in the dining-room of the Hotel de Noailles at Marseille. And of the Third Republic, at the Pont Alexandre III (1896–1900), the four 'massive pylons' at the ends of which, surmounted by gilded groups of 'Pegasi led by allegorical personages', are not without merit, if of a meaningless and inflated kind.

third- or fourth-rate theatres which does not mean they were not beautiful theatres in their kind. As with so much of the past, and an increasingly fewer number of contemporary things, nearly every theatre built up to the end of last century had its beauty and its theatricality, in comparison to which the interior of for instance the Royal Festival Hall is like the vastly magnified interior of a typewriter. No body of man or woman found dead in the Royal Festival Hall could have its due of drama or mystery about it. But perhaps the Hayward Gallery next door, except that even the word 'door' has something of human comfort and propinquity about it, has attained to the outer limits of impersonality set out and expressed in ugliness. It is in truth a cement wilderness at its worst on a wet and windy day, difficult even to locate in that monotony of reinforced concrete which imitates, idiotically, wooden posts and paling, almost totally unsuited to its purposes, and dull, dull to the point of utter blankness. It is ugly enough now. What will it be in a few years' time? But, at least coming out from it, thankfully, and looking for the way, one can lift one's eyes across the river to the dome of St Paul's.

There were beautiful theatres, mostly destroyed now, in so many of the provincial towns all over England. But of what theatres have been, and could be again even in altered conditions, there are the prime examples. To no more than mention Palladio's masterpiece, the Teatro Olimpico at Vicenza; or the Teatro Farnese, by Aleotti, his pupil, in the Pilotta or Royal Palace at Parma. But those are the grandest things of their kind, and for present purposes the little, white Teatro Regio or Opera House at Parma built by the Empress Marie Louise, the widow of Napoleon, with its white 'Empire' exterior, column'd foyer, rows of boxes, and orchestral pit where Paganini presided on occasion, is more to the point. I own a copy of the Court Almanac of the Duchy of Parma for 1842, printed at Bodoni's press, giving Baron Niccolò Paganini as her Court musician. So his bony frame and emaciated features are at least in association with its pillared portico. This little theatre at Parma is of an elegance perhaps exceptional for its time; but it has its rivals, the Teatro del Giglio at Lucca built when that was a principality under Napoleon's sister, Elisa Baciocchi; and above all the Teatro Grande at Brescia with its foyer or ridotto, a model of its kind and fresco'd in the manner, if not in person, of Alessandro Longhi's carnival scenes on the stair of the Palazzo Grassi, on the Grand Canal at Venice.

Yet theatres by the great Bibbiena dynasty of theatre architects and scene painters, with one exception, are curiously disappointing. The Teatro Comunale at Bologna is by Antonio of the name; the Teatro Filarmonico at Verona by Domenico; and the oval theatre on the ground floor of the Palazzo Pubblico in Siena – of all unlikely places! – is by Antonio Galli da Bibbiena. Their family relationship is difficult indeed to disentangle and to reconstruct; and none of the theatres mentioned retain anything of the pompous magic of their scenic drawings. The one exception is the Old Court Theatre at Bayreuth by Carlo Bibbiena. But neither can it be said that such other buildings as still exist by them – the church of Sant' Agostino, or Pantheon of the d'Este family at Modena, according to Burckhardt, 'one of the most fantastic flat-roofed creations of the Baroque style';

the Jesuit church at Mannheim by Alessandro Bibbiena; or the boring and uninteresting Memoria church at Belem, outside Lisbon – make any further contribution to the family fame. That must come to rest upon their scenic drawings. And yet, only lately to visit again after many years the once famous landscap'd park and castle of Schwetzingen, the former summer palace of the Electors Palatine, and find that one of the Bibbiena family worked there, revived the old interest and excitement.

The surprises of Schwetzingen, the beautiful park with its platoons and parterres of ancient trees apart, being the pair of semi-circular wings stretching out to right and left of the castle, and the theatre, by Pigage, not by Bibbiena, in the south wing. But it is the 'north circle-house', so called, which was built in 1748–9 by Alessandro Galli da Bibbiena and which is reputed to contain 'the two most spectacular rooms' in the castle. And they were inaccessible, closed for repairs and not due to re-open for at least a year, or more. So one came away unsatisfied from Schwetzingen, disappointed, too, at having missed seeing again the sixteen or more 'festival hunting' pictures in a room upstairs which I remembered from years ago with their unmistakably sadistic undertones as among the *curiosa* of the entire eighteenth century. These 'festival hunts', or holocausts, which were as though all the forces of the Inquisition were let loose upon wild animals, could be ranked, scenically and dramatically, as theatrical entertainments, but heeding the friendly critic's censure, I forbear to tell the reader in a footnote of where I have written of them elsewhere.

And so away from Schwetzingen no wiser than when I went there before in 1923. And indeed how much can one learn and forget in a lifetime? Or not be able to understand, but not from being stupid. And yet without a clue to the motive of the event, on which this is the paraphrase; a word defined in the dictionary as 'the meaning of a passage in other words ... or the explanation of a text or passage in fuller and clearer terms'. So perhaps it is less a paraphrase than a parable, or 'story told to point out a moral'. But, certainly, there is no moral in it. It is more, just the extension of a very extraordinary and inexplicable happening. And no more than music, whence I have borrowed the term, has it a definite or assured meaning. It is but a reflection upon a theme or subject. Because an empty theatre must for some reason always be more interesting than an empty church, and a dead actor in its dramatic import more promising than a dead clergyman. And yet, without descending to the absurd, is it not also the case that a clergyman found dead in an empty church is less dramatically interesting and appealing than an actor found dead in an empty flat? The one is a diminishment of rôle, the other a magnification. The one is a pathetic story, while the other has inherent drama.

No less so than the stranger or foreigner of whom little more than the name is known, found dead on the shore; having made every effort to conceal, or, indeed, obliterate his identity, then, chopped off his left hand, and stabbed himself, fatally and determinedly. His being dead for more than a hundred years, and forgotten now by everyone but myself, making his end but more mysterious and horrible. How extraordinary indeed would be a film taken of his last day, and night; recording his every movement, his hesitations and re-resolutions!

Or of the running and leaping the low walls from the river to the block of flats in Prince of Wales Road, Battersea, and back again, by a young person wearing 'pointed shoes'. And of what happened between his coming and going. If indeed, it is any more of a mystery than how we get our limbs to move, or make our eyes to see. For it is all inexplicable, as is one's own identity. And the past and future are no more of a mystery than is the present. It is all without explanation, and one might think without design or purpose. Unless it is set in motion by a chain of events on which we have a little control, both by decision, and by indecision. In which event we are half, but only half-masters of our destiny, and the rest is left to chance. Which is insensible; but no more so than to be born, and live, and yet have to die.

A breath from the Jasmine Kingdom

'Girls . . . wearing the loose jasmine-hung bodices of their trade' . . . not long down from the mountain villages, and standing in their doorways at the torrid hour, by now priestesses of the Jasmine Kingdom. The words between inverted commas being a quotation, of which I have lost the rest, but have tried to make the phrase into a sentence by filling in the sense. And given those first few words, where is the scene? It is certainly not Britain, which is so much better and more truly named, England, Scotland, Wales and Ireland. It is not even in Italy, though I have been surprised to read that at either Marsala or Trapani, I forget which, at the far corner of Sicily, water ices are to be had flavoured with jasmine. This sounds like the start of it, though I would be nervous of the water supply. And of the Mafiosi, and of other things as well.

Just as decidedly, it is neither in Germany, nor Switzerland. Still less in Belgium, or in Holland; Benelux, as an entity, is inappropriate to it. The nearest we have come to it is Sicily which has Arab or Moorish undertones. With Tunisia, not far away, which one might be tempted to consider the prelude or anteroom to the Jasmine Kingdom. It was in a villa at Hammamet that one was handed every afternoon a little bouquet more like a child's top, formed of the petals of jasmine bound together into a long stalk or handle with green skeins of cotton, which bouquets were made by the Tunisian women during the long hot siesta hours when it was easier to stay indoors out of the sun. Just before the war began these toys of jasmine were on sale in the streets of Paris, arrived overnight by aeroplane. Further than this, there were scent distilleries – roses, orange-flowers and jasmine – a few miles away at Nabeul; while at Tunis, itself, in the *souks* which are the best in the Near Orient after Damascus and Aleppo, there was the stall of Mohammed Tabet famous for essence of jasmine, in the Souk El Attarine.

If Tunisia, then one might guess Morocco, as much, or more so? But this is not the case, despite the roses of the oasis of El Golea in the Sahara of Skoura, and of the valleys of the Dra and Dadès in the Anti-Atlas, veritable 'roses of the south', of which useful manufacture was made after the Bulgarian attar was no longer available, and the Valley of Roses at Kazanlik no longer sent its products to the west.* Moroccan roses, then, but not jasmine in this far west of the Orient that

---

* *cf.* the chapter on *Roses of the Desert* in the book on *Old Roses*, by Mrs Nancy Steen, London 1966, pp. 234–40.

personal experience makes one associate in memory with the spring meadows outside Tangiers, quite blue with the native iris *I. tingitana*; or the long sloping Moroccan hillsides entirely yellow with marigolds, and the clouds racing over them, or lying like an ewe and her lambs upon the meadows.

The Jasmine Kingdom is dead in the other direction and there is no place for it in Africa. But neither does it bring us much nearer to say that it is in no way involved with the finding by someone of a half-acre upon a hillside covered with flowering yellow Crown Imperials looking down upon the blue domes of Isfahan. That was an experience that should have befallen the architect of the Masjid-i-Shah who might, then, have dreamed of domes and minarets of rose-pink tiles, like the rose-morning or a moment of it; domes like the Turk's Cap or fritillary, 'lilies of a rose or lily-loving Tamerlane, each lily as lovely as a pleasure dome, and senseless as a sacred college'.

Instead, it is in India. In Hindu India, lost somewhere in the huge sub-continent. Where there is more than enough room for it; and where a kingdom, let alone a largely imaginary one, could be interpolated upon the map some while before any notice was taken of it.

BOOK
FIVE

Flight of the Dragonfly

Lord Russell, just dead, who was a greater man in many respects than Sir Winston Churchill, if no less liable often to misjudge of things and make mistakes, but this must be understood and condoned as occupational hazard – whether with statesmen and national leaders or with philanthropists and great philosophers – it was Lord Russell who towards the end of his long life became more and more obsessed with love and overwhelming pity for his fellow beings. Pity, which can be as strong an emotion as love, and indeed the strongest factor in that, or, at least, in the permanence of human love which is different from its more transient phases.

Have we not all seen a pair of dragonflies in their joined flight over a pond or sheet of water after mating, and probably wondered at it during childhood! This phenomenon, not to be disassociated in mind, now, from the refuelling of aeroplanes in full flight, which latter could be described as supremely typical of the technological age in that it is lacking in all the elements of pleasure and enjoyment, is no less of a symbol for the swifter passages of love. Only for a short moment in the few days of the dragonflies' life as they career in mid-air above the pondweed and the yellow waterlilies; and they dart away still in tandem into the willow boughs. To disengage; or do they die after their nuptial flight? One would hope not; and that they can and do repeat it many times over. I do not know and must find out. One thing is certain. Their electric brilliance is given them, or they have achieved it without ulterior aid, for the one purpose and the big moment, whether or not they come to it again.

What is the purpose of the scent in flowers? Why have the roses different shades in scent, and not all the same? Are they not competing deliberately in this? It cannot only be in order to attract the bees and other insects for purposes of pollination? There must be deeper reasons. Could it not be in part for their own pleasure? Otherwise, why do the invisible scent-chambers in the rose petals shed forth, beside the true and authentic rose-attar, all the other rose scents. One does not have to be a rosomane of long standing to distinguish between those proffering the satyrous rasp of the raspberry or blackberry bowl, and those others suggestive of the pagan deities of the cream jug. There are rose-hearts smelling of sun-warmed peaches, these being among the most delicious of all; while others, less ambitious, whiff and almost taste of lemon, of oranges, of cloves, of lilac, and of peonies. There is even a rose that could be a camellia that had the smell of roses.* Those smelling of green apples are the sharpest, sweetest, most poignant, redolent of the ne'er encountered, apple-cheeked hamadryads of the green tree stems and green bodies; if best of all is not the dark red rose smelling of roses, dark and Circassion-looking enough to be the rose for Schéhérazade's hair. And as well, of course, there are the magical rose-stalks and the thought-provoking mosses of the old roses, all of which have their distinctive ichors which stay upon the fingers.

Is it, or is it not, verging more on the animal than the vegetable or arboreal, to know that there are various sorts of pears and apples that require the services of certain other kinds for successful pollination? That they can express in fact a choice or preference? And why is this selection confined to these certain sorts? Why, if they do not self-pollinate do they not mate, indiscriminately, polygamously, with the nearest other pear or apple tree? What part does the scent or structure of the blossom play in this? Is it a mere chemical appositeness or affinity? Or have they gone out of their way to make themselves irresistible to each other in this sub-section of the arboreal world?

Is it true, then, to veer away from roses, that the uniform plumage of the tribes of birds – of the families or septs, that is to say, within each nation – is thus ordained just precisely in order to prevent hybridization; that the Great Bird of Paradise (*Paradisea apoda*) should know his kind and not try to mate with a hen bird of Wallace's Standard Wing (*Semioptera Wallacei*), or of the Twelve-wired (*Saleucides nigricans*)? Which argues a certain corporate family purpose, and an instinct perhaps as strong as that of avoidance of danger and self-preservation among animals.

It could be advanced with reason that the humming-birds, the birds of paradise, and other families of birds, parrots for instance, and sun birds, have gone to positively unnecessary lengths in devising ornamental plumage for themselves; 'a pair of long white feathers coming out at right angles from both shoulders, making four plumes in all, which can be spread or lowered at will' (the aforementioned Wallace's Standard Wing); long streamers with what look to be enamelled plaques of brilliant blue, only they are head and not tail streamers, and can be erected or depressed according to whim (the King of Saxony's, *Pteridoptera Alberti*); with even more incredible diversions and divagations for the humming-birds. It is only reasonable to think that an even greater amount of resolution, and of mutual, if unconscious will power has gone into the evolving of the humming-birds' iridescent gorgets, the mock wings on their chests given them only for pleasure and display, and their pectoral shields of plumes that they can hold erect as fans. Nobody, on beholding these wonders, could hesitate as to their purpose, or what lies behind them.

In that extraordinary corpus of little glittering forms bedecked with every conceivable far-fetched and fangled extremity of bird fashion there is almost visual evidence of a master mind at work. But we must not deceive ourselves. It is the corporate body of the humming-birds that has evolved these ornaments in

* *Bourboniana*, 'Boule de Neige', 1867.

response to their own demand and in accordance to their wishes, and otherwise it would not have been. Just as certainly it is a more agreeable and pacific philosophy and purpose of life than that which prompted the shark and the hyena, and shaped them to devour and kill. In essence, the extraordinary embellishments of the humming-birds can only have been designed to please and can only come of some compulsion within themselves. It is not their wish to repel or frighten, and their armoury is free therefore of all the appurtenances of fear.

But were they always so down through the ages? Certainly they did not come into the world thus apparalled for the opening chapter of *The Book of Genesis*. Would it not have been possible to intercept them half-way in their development, at some halt in time? Surely it will have been a slow approach to the glories of their full plumage; or did it come to them with a sudden rush, as when the hand of the human hybridizer got to work upon the tulip and the iris. By which time it was perfectly possible for a human being to live surrounded by beasts or flowers of his own handling, as a creator on a minor scale among his creatures. With the courtship rituals of birds, and such extreme instances as the dancing floors of the lyre birds, it is difficult not to see the beginnings of aesthetic feeling.

It has been argued that at certain stages in his evolution primitive man had only to pick up a piece of coloured stone or tufa and he could draw upon the cave wall or cliff face as no man in ten thousand, trained or untrained, could draw today. We are to suppose that there was nothing unusual in this skill or talent, and that it was as normal as being able to whistle or sing. Thus, the men of Lascaux and Altamira, and the Bushmen and Australian 'black fellows' of today; and we have arrived at the first of those stages when the hand of man could not go wrong. Of which there have been many, and until not so long ago, but the fear and the dire probability is that there may be no more.

How many thousands of years later came the age of Fergusson's *Rude Stone Monuments*;* his supposition, which was certainly a false one, being that the stone circles and other cyclopaean remains were co-aeval and works of the same culture. But the men of the dolmens and the cromlechs, of Carnac and Stonehenge, were not capable of building a stone room of any size for they could not contrive the roof or ceiling, though they had abundant labour to drag huge stones over great distances and pile them one on another. And yet! It is difficult to believe that there was not even in the far Hebrides, to which this culture extended, some rumour of a hotter land with huge temples, and that these were not crude imitations of the pyramids of the Pharaohs. But this proto-civilization, for it was no more than that had, by then, lost the skill of the 'hunters' of Les Eyzies and Altamira and there is no carving or drawing of a human figure anywhere among the stone monuments. They were as incapable, or as nervous of ornament as the epigoni of today's office blocks and towers of flats. No art movement to come from them, but only card houses of giant stones! They had lost the natural gift or dispensation, if indeed, they ever possessed it, to be able to draw almost without thinking, and were but barren masters of the monolith and megalith.

They must have lived in huts of reed and wattles with mud walls at foot of the

* James Fergusson's work of this title appeared in 1872.

stone circles. And knowing so little, with not even a clue to their racial origin or language, we have only the visual image of their flocks moving over the downs, or among the scattered stones and little pools of the Outer Isles, as if they were shadows of the clouds out of that innocent and unencumbered sky. Smockless shepherds, though dressed in fleeces; but priests and caciques of the golden torque, as that one I remember of British or Welsh gold which a farmer in Flintshire had bought from a Gypsy, and used as a catch to keep a gate shut; and the Gypsy had found it a hundred years ago under the rose-hung hedges, where it had hidden its glitter for how many centuries!

The slow, continuous evolving of the species and the choice and rejection exercised among them, whether of themselves, or in obedience to some code of laws or rule of reason, argues the existence of some natural system akin to the theory, if not the practice, of self-governing soviets. They have evolved or been started off – when, and by whom? – and left to fend for themselves as best they can. The responsibility is in their own hands, and if they fail it is their own fault and no one else is to blame. But work is always in progress. This winter for instance has seen the evolution of a new virus of Asiatic 'flu, resistant to the antibodies of inoculation, and as its victims know to their cost, with boomerang propensity to return and strike a second time, a germ which certainly is not from the stables or *atelier* of 'le bon Dieu'. And to whom, then, does it owe allegiance? One might be tempted to say, if not the USA, it must be the USSR – if it be as simple as that? For, decidedly, there are two opposing bodies, the one inimical to the other, and each plotting and planning the other's destruction, with no uneasy lull or truce between them.

The plain question, therefore, is: are there two studios or one? Do both sets of plans come from the same drawing-board? Is the energizing force – of the existence of which we are not in doubt – indifferent as to which side prevails? There is no reason to think it is all for the best. On the contrary, as with the human incidents of daily life, there is a vicious propensity for everything to go wrong. Fundamental good is less in evidence than evil. And there is always death which is the unreasonable opposite and antithesis of birth. Or is there no point to the one without the other? Without death there would be no life, and vice versa. They are the negative and positive, and the one could not exist without the other, any more than there could be good only and entirely without evil. So that they are as parents one of the other. The one, a nymph or pupa, that is to say, a chrysalis; and the other a larva in the caterpillar stage, undergoing metamorphosis which is the change of shape and substance, and the emergence into something different. Both being in the embryo stage before the time of parturition with, as yet, no finished form evolved which is decidedly the truth as to human beings, though it is less true of the world of nature. Eagles for instance are eagles, and tigers, tigers. But within the span of this living generation, who have made ourselves masters of the airs, we have abandoned balloons and heavier than air dirigibles in favour of every conceivable form of propelled flight and have in fact done everything but grow wings, which is beyond us. But not beyond the slow evolutionary crawling of the lizard; and there must have been that first day when some creature, between bird and lizard, glided from the bough with leathern wing, or took a little assisted leap from branch to branch.

But, also, evolution is so torpid in movement that we cannot keep track of it within the span of human life. We are not to suppose nature was different in the time of the Roman Caesars; or even thirty centuries before that in the first dynasty of the Pharaohs. Too short a stretch of time is involved. Some species will have disappeared, but that is happening all the time, as now. Not a year passes but some bird or animal has gone, never to return again. The evolved or set forms were long ago unalterable; or the clock-hand moved so slow and imperceptibly that the difference was not visible.

The pace of evolution has been quickened by the breeders and hybridists as the speed of supersonic flight compared to the two miles per hour of the lumbering ox-cart; but it has been an artificial, not a natural acceleration. It has not been allowed to find its own way as, after torrential rain, a stream will do through a meadow in order to join its waters with the roadside ditch. But is that necessity, or is it instinct? Is instinct, indeed, involved in it at all; or does it work out, simply, as practical mathematics, and merely a question of running down a slope, then welling up and running down again? Where the land lies suitably, and with no choice at all. In which instance necessity is the same as instinct, and no different.

It would seem that where there is growth there is freedom of direction. Except, again, that water only runs because it cannot do otherwise. It stands till it must overflow, and after that it has no power of choice. It moves only by the pressure of its own numbers so that to some little extent it has a will of majority and acts in obedience to its own powers, and is not irresponsible as the winds and airs. Or as the mountains which are fixed and immovable though, maybe, they were molten once and pushed up from below in their pangs of birth. Then, allowed no choice but to stay there.

Not that nature, should that be the name for it, can be credited with aesthetic, or anything but haphazard workings. The fine plumes of certain families of birds as compared to the utility robe of the sparrow, or even the dark suit of the blackbird or the nightingale, must be the project and the achievement of those families themselves in response to their unconscious wishes and requirements; just as much as those plants that are fly-traps in their purpose may have been started on that path but they have progressed along it and perfected their machinery for so doing. They cannot have been brought into the world as trained fly-trappers, and must have changed since then. Instead, they must have started somewhere with the first fly trapped, perhaps with primitive stickiness and no hinged chamber, as now, or perilous reception parlour, but allowed, or taking for themselves, a minimum of choice or opportunity compared to that of human beings.

For how much longer will we ignore the truth that the god is in ourselves, and not outside and above us? It has been a waste of time to think otherwise. And it has been time wasted through all sentient time, ever since human beings have seen death at the end of life and hoped because of that for another life to come. But the thing given is worth more than that which is taken away. It could be here and nowhere else at all, which would be enough to make one believe in some special dispensation. And whether that, or it be in augmentation beyond the powers of imagining, it is the opportunity and we will never have another. Which has been taken in the past but ever compensated for in other ways, as though inevitably; but this is no reason for accepting it. Though this applies only to human beings, and there is little evidence that the wonderful creations of nature have suffered for their pains.

The pool of all talents and all mysteries is the grand consensus which is the sum of human knowledge, and religion plays no part in this for it is but speculation of the unascertainable and unknown. All its efforts in all its different kinds have brought the truth no nearer. It is but the vapour of breath, and yet it is the most potent and habit forming of delusions, and humanity has found it difficult to live without it. Much hardening of the sensibilities is needed before one can face the truth which is that there is nothing there. No hope of another world, or of renewed meetings. There have been the chances of making this world more equable and beautiful, but generally in small communities. Even the optimist could have little hope of New York, Tokyo, or Chicago, excepting for the study of human character which in cities of that size must always be, as, or more, interesting than its architecture.

But the grand consensus is not so much a museum as a studio – the repository of all knowledge and the fountain of all ideas. Herein is the only immortality for there is no hope of being remembered elsewhere. Holiness in itself counts for little if there are not other things to recommend it. Not that there is bodily tangibility, or any form of hierarchy; for it is no more than the thirst for truth which is knowledge feeding itself and never satisfied. The god is in ourselves if we would only allow of that and admit him to be mortal. Dead, but ever reborn, which is the only immortality. It is creation that is important and paramount, and not mere appreciation. Is this what painters lived for, to have their works hung in museums? Or as in Italy, to hang for centuries in dead churches? Or, if you were a composer, to have your music performed in the Salle Gaveau, Carnegie Hall of New York, or the Royal Festival Hall?

But the studio, it is obvious, is in no hurry. It has more patience than Hitler, and can wait longer than the Vatican. Perhaps it is even shut for the summer while the artists are on holiday. For a sabbatical year lasting for a century or more, for that has happened, though there is ever something in progress somewhere. But the staff can be sent away while so little is going on, and there are only a few assistants left to answer questions. And that may be just the moment when they are taken by surprise. But it seems unlikely now. Until human beings have settled their population problems which may not be before disaster overtakes them. Till there has been a culling of their numbers, and maybe a non-human agency will have lent a hand.

In fact how much of what has been painted, or composed, or built, or written in this century will be remembered in another hundred years from now? Who, indeed will be the Luke Fildes, and Alma-Tademas or Orchardsons, as against the Rothkos and Jackson Pollocks of our day? And will there be much difference but in degree of dullness? As in pop music, so in poetry, too. With the hundred and twentieth Canto finished, and all said, at last, of T. S. Eliot. By then, the immortals will be more immortal still, and but to be approached on hands and knees. Lond dead and receding into time. With the clock stopped, and maybe, not wound up again.

So that there is much to celebrate in the past, and some of that not so long ago either. And the glory and wonder of having been alive. The eighteenth century, its brutalities apart, being a time of enlightenment in every country of Europe, as witness the architecture left behind it to which there is no parallel since the long centuries of the Pax Romana. But, also, France of the Third Republic between the wars of 1870 and 1914, during the age of the Impressionist and Post-Impressionist painters, of Mallarmé and Debussy, and of the burgeoning of the Art Nouveau, had its advantages of living, the ugliness of nearly everything visual apart; and it was like no other age there has ever been. Can the same be said of the zenith of England which was the Victorian age? There were the Pre-Raphaelites and the aesthetic movement – and no wonder! – and Ruskin and William Morris. And there is the nostalgia of our own time for its monuments which were the marks of our greatness as world rulers; such being Waterhouse's Assize Court and his new Town Hall at Manchester; villas and terraced houses innumerable; a hundred Victorian Gothic churches all over England; Gilbert Scott's indisputable St Pancras Railway Hotel of the incredible pinnacles against the foggy sunset; and most extraordinary of all, if by English architects, the semi-Parsee Gothic buildings of the cotton-boom at Bombay. Whether, nostalgia apart, all things considered this was a happy or beautiful time to be alive in must be left to everyone to decide from his own conscience. Personally, while understanding and sympathetic to the nostalgia, I would say it was a very ugly time indeed. In fact the very point of it is its ugliness which is forceful and uncompromising, but commends itself and even comforts in its way. Certainly it is not to be despised. In any event, what right have we to criticize, who have lost the self-confidence to express ourselves in any idiom but that of the steel and cement grid! Little wonder that the green copper-capp'd tower of the Imperial Institute is now considered a minor masterpiece, and that Waterhouse's yellow terracotta-fronted Natural History Museum, in the Romanesque of all styles, has its admirers. Yet the last-named building on a rainy afternoon in the Cromwell Road, even on an evening of spring is anything but beautiful. It is ugly and rejoices in that, loud-voiced as the Rev. Ian Paisley, and as unrepentant.

But let us forget all that. For I hear, or think I hear, distant music, and am looking for an exeat to this chapter. Like the fumes of religion it should float its false clouds before our eyes, deceptive as the Delibab or Fata Morgana of the shepherds, seen about July or August over the immense, treeless, grassy plain of the magnificent sunrises; and from the shepherds' huts in their small groves of acacias, later in the evening and far into the night, you would hear violins playing and the glissandos of the cymbalom. Whence, at long remove, to the Gypsy violinists of the restaurants. And from those, in theory at least, it is short distance to the studios. Where, rather than in *The Book of Genesis*, were the stirrings of life and the, heretofore uncontradicted, hours of trial and error.

The Workroom

'The workroom of an artist; room where photographic portraits are taken; a building or room where film plays are staged; a room in a broadcasting station used for transmissions'. So reads the dictionary, and it is to be noticed how the interest diminishes with the coming of modern times. Rembrandt had a studio; so had Ingres and Delacroix, and certainly Cézanne with plates of old apples, and indeed, decaying apples everywhere. But, already, 'studio' has begun to mean something different. By now it is a room where a man with a camera on a tripod and a black hood over his head takes photographic portraits; and of course the camera, unlike the painter, 'never lies'. In fact, it is the biggest liar of the lot, and hardly ever tells the truth. You cannot trust a camera.

In the next stage it is a film studio, which is a further distortion implying either that painters were never artists, or that actors and film-crew have usurped their title. And, lastly, it is 'a room in a broadcasting station used for transmissions'. Or, in other words, it is the place whence the 'slanted' news emerges and the fount of swollen reputations, exaggerated to gargantuan size and out of all proportion to their merit. They have the most powerful weapon of education ever wielded in their hands, and they only use it to further criminal instincts, to instil non-music, and for football matches. It is all day and night pop-music and football in the place of 'bread and circuses'. Where is the wisdom in this? And who is the better for it?

It is hardly necessary to add that studios were once used for nobler purposes. But now they are almost exclusively inhabited by 'television personalities'. It is worse, because less transient than the padded uncomfort of the V.I.P. lounge. There, at least, you are either arriving, or going away. But, as to the public, there are persons 'glued' to the television screen for as much as eight hours a day, and I use the term, 'advisedly', because it is very different from the dedication of an old-fashioned bookworm if indeed such exist any more. But the addicts referred to are as flies in the lampshade, or wasps upon a jam pot. They cannot get away, but not because they really want to stay.

Yet it should be perfectly possible to educate them and hold them there by other means. For two hours, or so, at a stretch, for that is long enough. And perhaps an interval, and then on again. If they are pandered to, to the extent of some ninety per cent of the programme space from dawn into the middle of the night, what other can the result be? It is a foregone conclusion but, unfortunately, a conclusion that is only a beginning for it is likely to get worse and worse. Of course there is good entertainment from time to time, plays beautifully acted, nature talks, travel talks, good comedians, Frankie Howerd, Harry Worth, Derek Nimmo, with others, and old films disinterred and performed; but a little, just a little more should be done to educate the public. And that particular public which is ripe and ready to take it should be separately considered and provided for, and above all made to feel important.

And so we move away from the sandwich bar, with soft drinks but no soft music, through the uterus-interior of a high cavern, more like a salt-mine than the 'blue grotto' of Capri, hearing, as we go, the fading echoes of Dusty Springfield, can it be? Sandie Shaw? Lulu? Cilla Black? all crooning their girlish griefs and intimacies into the chained 'mike', mingled with hoarse roarings from the more than 'million-pounder' Tom Jones in hysterical sob-coma, deserted again, or successful, it is all the same in sound.

But away from it all into the bird-song hour and the early morning of the world. With, alas! some names that need not have been mentioned still dying on our ears. For there will be others like them, and they will be forgotten in a few months or years. But may one not pick up a book to squash a mosquito? Is that forbidden? For it is not forbidden to the animals to kill each other. There were flying lizards with leathern wings, sabre-toothed tigers, and giant pachyderms like huge lumbering tanks.

But it is becoming interesting. The steatopygous Venus of the Hottentots makes appearance, waddling and disquieting. Or is it the huge woman of the Hypogeum, for it is difficult to be certain in the demi-dawn? The Hypogeum being the extraordinary three-storey temple of the Stone Age in Malta, and the lady in question a mere statuette five or six inches long, of a woman of enormous proportions lying on her side. She is not sleeping, or dead, but in a trance; under hypnotic influence; or has taken some intoxicant, or drug. Or had the Stone Age men of Malta discovered the properties of wine? It has been suggested before that the magic of the Beaker Age, as this culture is called from its multitude of drinking cups, lay in what was in the beaker.

Moreover, at Tarxien, another temple nearby, and above ground this time, is something more extraordinary still. The lower portion, only the feet and legs, of an enormous woman five or six times lifesize. Her body and head are missing. The huge creature wears a knitted skirt hanging in pleats, of the same woollen material as worn by the reclining lady in a trance. No giant stone statues have been found in Sardinia, where the *nuraghi* are of the Bronze Age and a millennium later in date. And at neither Carnac nor Stonehenge is there a representation of a human being. The woman of Tarxien is the only giant statue of the Stone Age. What a tragedy that her head and the upper half of her body are missing! But there is always the hope that a complete statue may still be found in Malta.

A giant goddess, we are to presume, and when intact she must have stood some ten or twelve feet high. No sex-appeal, as had the Venus of the Hottentots, who had all, and more than all, 'that makes a member of one sex desirable to a member of the other', to quote the staid definition of sex-appeal from a dictionary.

Just an enormous woman in goats' or sheep's wool, and probably a fertility image for her shadow to follow the flocks along the cliffs, where I have seen the little yellow irises opening, not more than an inch or two high, in the cropped grass. And looked down into the water where the *lampuki*, as they are called now, all dolphin-snout and flukes and tail, came leaping in from sea, one behind another, playing and jumping out of the water and damaging the nets. But did the Stone Age men have fishing nets? I would doubt it, yet, certainly shepherds or goatherds must have looked down and even copied the scudding leap of the dolphins to one another while they trampled on the irises.

How, and when did human beings get to the islands? And what language did they speak? This, no one will ever know. Nor what was spoken in the *nuraghi* of Sardinia where was another culture altogether; neither is it known what language they talked at Carnac, or at Stonehenge. Nor on the cliff-ramparts of Dun Aengus, 'the most magnificent barbaric monument now extant in Europe'; a huge fortress facing, mysteriously, the full Atlantic, originally oval in shape, 'and having acquired its present form from the fall of the precipices into the sea'. When can have that been? Who were the enemy they expected to attack them? Coming in from open sea with the nearest landfall three thousand miles away, to invade the Aran Islands off the west coast of Ireland! It is all a mystery.

And while pondering upon it we have the painter's vision of two huge women racing happily, hand in hand, along the seashore, their black hair streaming out behind them. Their free arms, as though jointless, flung into the air. Jewellery, or accessories, rings, ear-rings, bracelets, necklaces, crocodile shoes or handbags, and the rest, they have none; they run, barefoot, and their dresses are as simple as that of the giant woman of Tarxien. They have not even so much as a little phial of scent to dab on behind their ears. Woe betide him who gets in their way as they leap and bound upon the shore! And one may well wonder what language is spoken by the two big women! Where do they come from? Not from a hotel bedroom, a circus tent, or bathing hut. It is in fact Picasso's curtain for *Le Train Bleu*, painted in 1924, and bought in 1969 for the proposed National Theatre Museum for 69,000 guineas.* Nothing could have been in greater contrast to the fashionable *plage* of Monte Carlo, the scene of the ballet when the curtain lifted, or to the dancers supposed just to have emerged out of the train from Paris, and all dressed for the beach by Chanel.

But it is a lesson in what is possible and impossible. The figurants on the stage may have been good to photograph, but they were not for painting. The canon has been lost, or gone wrong, and in order to get it right we have to go back to Rubens. In default of whom, it is the giant women of the Hypogeum and of Tarxien, identified in ignorance by the one great genius in painting of our time. No doubt there were loud guffaws of laughter as the curtain was revealed, and persons in the audience who felt they had been insulted.

But no painter could have made anything of the dancers on the stage. Dresses for dancers are notoriously more difficult to design properly than dresses for ordinary actors and actresses, if only because they are continually in motion and must move with the music. The chic and fashionable has always been an enemy to painting through all the centuries, that is to say, so long as painters aspired to representation. And it would require genius of a high order indeed to achieve such effects in the non-painting of abstraction. The huge ladies of the curtain

---

* Not, in reality, specially designed as a curtain, but enlarged from a small sketch of Picasso's by Prince Tchervachidze, who was scene painter to the Russian Ballet.

are no less impressive and awe-inspiring, now, than when they first came out from retirement to race along the seashore nearly fifty years ago. The scale of their limbs, apart, and their exuberant abandon, it is their expressionless features and egg-cup eyes. They are monumental, that is certain, and this effect is more than the cleverest painter could have got from using fashionable models. The beautiful young women of the fashion magazines, and they are more beautiful now, to be sure, than any of their predecessors, and there are more of them, do not 'lend themselves' to be made into works of art, as do the huge ladies of Rubens and of Tarxien.

But sit down beside them and you will find them more difficult to talk to! Even with a translator who knows the language that they speak. It would be women's talk about children, housekeeping, and so forth, though as to the latter, out of their beehive huts they are beachcombers and tend to make for the oyster beds. Hence, their leaping and running along the margin of the sands. While, as to the fat ladies of Flanders, they may still be seen eating gargantuan luncheons on Sundays at Mechelen or Malines, which is half-way from Antwerp to Brussels. And there, or to the midden-heaps of the salt shore, should the painters go to pick their models.

What a sight would it be could we go back to the days when the steps of the Piazza di Spagna in Rome were crowded with artists' models from hill-top villages in the Abruzzi, come to hire themselves to pose in studios! That was in the middle of last century, and how bad were the paintings done from them! And could we, instead, crowd those self-same steps where now are flower-stalls, with the huge women of Tarxien, female counterparts of the Sumô wrestlers of Japan! What themes there would be for monumental sculptures, to be known at least for human beings, and not two-piece, three-piece, disjointed bones of dinosaurs. Strolling among them would be like taking a walk in a breeding-colony of seals, having to jump over their prostrate bodies and brave the animosity of the bulls. This, on some Arctic ice-floe, not among the violets and tuberoses from the Alban Hills.

It would seem from the findings of archaeologists that the aboriginal studio or workroom of *homo sapiens* was somewhere in East Africa, in the Kenyan uplands, or thereabouts. Was it there that human, as opposed to animal relationships, first evolved? And was it, as well, the fount of all the arts? However that may be, those seem to have had an effortless beginning. In the sphere, at least, of drawing. It was sufficient to take in the hand a chunk of yellow or red ochre and you could draw an antelope or hippopotamus hunt, untaught, and with no previous lessons. Except, of course, that those who drew would be those who wanted to draw, and soon found it amused or interested them to do so. In the same way, boys who can mimic easily make themselves popular at school. But it is a talent born in them, they do not have to learn it. They teach themselves, and can imitate perfectly at ten years old. If looked at in that light, the phenomenal talent for drawing on the part of some primitive races becomes less mysterious. Conversely, if told that some highly evolved intellectual type such as Einstein was a superb mimic, would one not be a little surprised and inclined to attribute it to a childish vein in his nature? But it could indeed be the most human side in him.

The drawing gift dwelt humbly in the 'semi-civilized'. In the Bushmen and Hottentots, in the mysterious races of the painted caves of north-east Spain and the Dordogne; reaching to its height on the cliff faces of the Sahara, and still a living force among the Black Fellows of Australia. The much more 'civilized' Maoris of New Zealand never possessed it, neither did the Polynesians, both of which races, it will be remembered, took a lively interest in the first white men arriving in their sailing ships, while the Australian natives hardly looked round, but went on with their beachcombing, uninterested and undismayed. The more primitive the greater this particular talent, it would seem, and that it inhabits a special strata of human being who is, otherwise, ungifted. But ask this of the most profound human intellect and he would probably be unable to comply. It is, therefore, no sign of especial talent to be able to draw, except in so far as drawing happens to be the particular talent of the person concerned; and for the rest, you might as well expect any ordinary individual to write fugues, or play the piano without having had lessons from a music teacher.

It is a talent, and it implies no more than that. There have been weakminded persons who could draw and paint. And there have been such phenomena as ready calculators who cannot read or write; and in the case of one completely illiterate individual from Barlborough in Derbyshire, of whom there is a portrait in my old home, he was even consulted in the eighteenth century by the Astronomer Royal to assist in mathematical calculations concerning the weight of stars. More mysterious still, this particular mathematical 'kink', if it is that, sometimes deserts its host and leaves him half-senseless in other and more ordinary ways. We have to assume that it is this same phenomena of the coming and going of talents that gives a clever person stupid and untalented children; and that can desert and bring down an entire civilization, as that perhaps of the Ancient Mayans. And if this did not happen, then all the world would have talent, which has been the case with some little particle of truth with the Bushmen and similar races, but has failed completely with the great masses of human beings.

At the moment the white races in Europe and in North America may have the greatest mechanical and scientific, technological, if you will, genius there has ever been in human history; in fact it is the only civilization of the sort there has ever been, when we consider that human beings depended upon animal transport by land, horses, oxen, camels, and so forth, until little more than a hundred years ago. But, now, when we have landed on the moon and are reaching out, if tentatively for the stars, there is no great portrait painter – and there have been dozens of them during the last five hundred years – I would deny the title of poet to most of the poets; those who say there are great living composers of music must know perfectly well that they are exaggerating when they say this; and there is an almost uniform ugliness in nearly every artifact made by human hands.

Something has gone wrong, and no one knows how to put it right and get it started again. Appreciation of works of art has never been at such a scale as at present; neither have the arts of restoration, of pictures, furniture, old buildings, etc. ever been brought to such a pitch of perfection as now. Both of which are bad portents. For a great age in the arts has always been wasteful of what has gone before it. As soon as it saves up every little scrap of the past the signs are bad. Now, in the prevailing anarchy of styles, but with destruction going on, as well, as with the demolition of the Georgian Squares in Bloomsbury by the London University authorities, and unremitting vandalism in nearly all provincial towns and throughout the countryside, we have the destroyer and the perpetrators working hand in hand. And the careful restoring and preservation of what little is left only gives deeper accent to our impoverishment. All factors considered, one might guess that it would be several centuries or more, if ever again, before any state of cohesion and uniform is reached. Or, in fact, never. So the only sensible procedure is to make the best of it, and enjoy ourselves from past and present experience while we can; even if, principally, it is from the past.

Probably the crassest political fallacy of our time is equality of opportunity. That is the sure path to destruction from inanition. It is to set the same pace for everyone which will be, inevitably, that of the slowest, not even of the medium-paced. How is it conceivable to speak of 'the white heat of the technological revolution', in that fatefully stupid and notorious phrase, when given this rule with which to start the race. A finance minister who can write optimistically of the possibility of abolishing all inherited wealth within the space of a human generation is cancelling all human incentive. The ideal of a four or six-roomed house near the supermarket, the cinema, and an arterial road, is too bleak and drab to contemplate. Of course, large fortunes, inherited or self-made, are too large by far but all human idiosyncrasy must not be trimmed down and cut to uniformity.

As for 'jumping the queue' far from that being discouraged, it should be the first reward for talent, and the most lasting. Even in Russia, heroes of the Soviet Union, wearers of the Red Star of Lenin, and so forth, take first place at the ticket office, the food store, and in the fish queue. It is the young talents and the old veterans who should be privileged. So long, though, as it does not come to that, for this kingdom is not really adapted or suited to an ant-like population. The dreariness of their tired feet dragging round the china bowl, 'follow-my-leader' for hours on end, because no ant has the initiative to change its course! So talents are to be set back and dress their ranks, but this will never do. They should not be allowed to waste their time but should be forwarded in all possible ways.

Is it 'jumping the queue' if you are old and ill, happen to have a dislike of community companionship, and by hazard can afford to pay for a bed by yourself in hospital? Must you wait your turn to have an aching tooth pulled out? Is it only to be pop-singers and cabinet ministers who have chauffeur-driven cars? The welfare state, like all others, has its aberrations. For a prime minister to have breakfast with a famous broadcaster and 'television personality' puts the renown of both of them on the same level. Who, then, of the two is condescending to the other? Or, if both are equal, things transitory are not made permanent. If you ask why the guest of a broadcaster, and not for instance of a famous actor or opera singer, the answer, as such, is the popularity and the distorting lens, which is both a powerful and a dangerous weapon.

Surely it is the lowest denominator outlook and point of view which is the fatal mistake. No civilization can be run for and on behalf of its invalids and aged, its mentally retarded and handicapped, or even, only and entirely for its working classes. The express train as a symbol of progress counts for more than the slow train which stops at every station to take on passengers. The pace of civilization for sure is not that of the richest for money, as ever, gets more often than not into the wrong hands. But I have to admit that my ideal is not that of philanthropy, nor that of redistribution after redistribution, just for the sake of ironing out and levelling, of the money in other people's pockets. My own interest in a civilization is in terms of its arts without too much regard for the political system responsible for it. That, I think, is the scale of measurement to be applied to it and the terms by which to judge of it in history.

There is, of course, the anomaly of a culture producing the best and the worst, both at the same time. Conspicuous instances of which were the French Second Empire and the Third Republic. Baudelaire, Flaubert, and the Impressionist painters, Manet, Degas, Cézanne, and others lived under this dispensation, if they did not exactly flourish, while official art was ugly and dull beyond description. Outside France it was no different. The rooms in which Wagner, Liszt, or Tchaikowsky lived are almost painful to look at in the photographs. But the instance of France is the more conspicuous because of her great painters. Queen Victoria, King Edward VII and Queen Alexandra lived in hideous surroundings of which they were unconscious. And the rooms of Ruskin, of Walter Pater, of the aesthetes, were no better. Comfort was perhaps an English invention. The French houses were not even comfortable, while the Villa Wahnfried and the house at Klin were monumental in their ugliness. Sympathy for their inmates is only tempered by still greater pity for King Ludwig II in his megalomaniac settings.

But the same disparity or dichotomy has prevailed at other times. It was not the monopoly of the nineteenth century in general, and of the Third Republic in particular, in France. It, also, affected some of the great epochs in Chinese art; and is to be seen simultaneously at its worst and best in Japan. In this latter, at its richest but, also, at its most restrained; as for instance in the shrines of Nikko which for all that are most captivating in their bantam quaintness; and in the Katsura Palace and Garden at Kyoto which are the very height of aesthetic simplicity for all the ages, and have been attributed to the famous tea-master Kobori Enshû (1579–1647). There was more of philosophy in the tea-ceremony than in all the sports and athletics on which the Occidentals waste their time and run through their lives.

The best and the worst, in fact, can be coaeval and flourishing in the same time and place. And the worst ruffian is as likely as the benevolent despot to be inspirer and patron of great works of art. Saintliness is not next to godliness. But neither is it necessary to 'live dangerously' in order to be interesting either in yourself, or to anybody else. But dangerous silliness is deadliest of all. Of which there are pernicious instances in every direction; in the 'entertainment world' particularly, but, also, in poetry, in fiction, in music, sculpture, painting, and in all the arts. The distortions of fame can never have reached to such heights of absurdity before. A 'pop-singer' of a few months' renown, for it never lasts, can have greater popularity than has ever been accorded in their lifetimes to the greatest of human beings (and their number does not include Hitler or Stalin). How much better to work and be forgotten, than remembered in such company! For the minority are inarticulate in face of the immensity. They are outnumbered and surrounded on all sides. And the silliness can but increase. To what heights will it be reaching in a few years' time? Lunatic prices paid for paintings are but another symptom which equate a Renoir or a Rembrandt – and mark the difference! – with a single year's earnings from popular recordings.

The barbarian invasions must be coming soon. Or are they to be vertical, coming up directly from below, not from outside? Which could easily happen not a full night's flight away. Or could cripple itself in bloody retribution against those wronged in the first place and reduced to slaves? And with their decline the West would be wide open. But those others have their troubles, too, their internecine hatreds which could 'loom up' and end in mutual destruction. The toys in the nursery were not intended for ornament. They must be played with one day; and the dawn following on that would be ominous and lurid. The sky lit up with fires; and more than one mock-sun, momentarily, in the heavens. And green rain, that is it! I was told that at Hiroshima. And the blasts of scorching air.

Or you may stay quietly on the green belt somewhere, living in hopes of having a poem published. In the New Statesman or Times Lit. Suppl. and going to London to join in marches and demonstrations. There are enough to choose from to suit all shades of opinion, and the only innocent sufferers are the police force who have their Sundays spoiled for them. But persons who disapprove of bull-fights should not hit and kick the police horses. It is illogical. And 'peaceful demonstrations' ending in violence are not the way to end wars. Demonstrations are nearly always for the right ends but in the wrong places.

All is not lost. There has never been such a public, as now, for the music of Bruckner and of Mahler; or, not that there is the very slightest resemblance or line of connection between them, for the poetry of T. S. Eliot and of W. H. Auden. There are shelvesful of books on Pound and Eliot, and young persons of both sexes as far away as Japan 'majoring' or trying to write theses on them both. How much will, or can they make of it? And to what purpose? Would they not be happier with Keats or Herrick? Appreciation of poetry is rare indeed, and it would seem a mistaken policy to start students from a culture so far different from our own on two of the most difficult writers in the language, simply because the poets in question are contemporary and living. The dust has not settled yet, and no one can say how much poetry will be left. Could it not be the extraneous matter, often misunderstood and misinterpreted, that so many books have been written about? On poetry that is in quintessence there is little more that can be said.

Rapidity of communication has become in itself its own worst enemy. In that an item of news, the assassination of a president, the death of a racehorse owner, can be bounced off a satellite in space and carried in a few seconds to the far corners of the world. But it goes so fast there is no time to think, and one knows that no message of more than factual importance can get through. Time for a Hitler to say his patience is exhausted, but no coherent message from those whose voices we would want to hear. The great sages of the human race would be all but unintelligible in this medium, which has found its own elysium in the chatter and silly games inside the lunar capsule. It would 'boob', in the vernacular of the politician – 'I made a boob with teeth and spectacles'* – if confronted with anything other than the straight news. Certainly the landing on the moon was an extraordinary and historical event of the highest drama, but they played it at the nursery level. It was a grave mistake to let the astronauts overtalk and play down to the public. We may be thankful there is no cine-record of Cortés meeting with Moctezuma, or Columbus landing on Hispaniola. In brief the pabulum of television is the variety programme, and their best they give grudgingly as though ashamed of it.

The greatest novelist, author of *War and Peace, Anna Karenina,* and *Resurrection,* with Voltaire and Goethe one of the sages of the modern world, as he grew older became more and more distrustful of the arts. His scathing description of a ballet in *War and Peace* will be remembered. It could be rejoined that neither Voltaire, nor Tolstoy made any pretence to be art lovers. And it is indeed possible to know too much and have too good taste, both of which things are in some sense the enemies of creation. In parenthesis, we need only recall that it was often noticed about Redouté, the flower painter, famed particularly for his exquisite paintings of roses, that he had such exceptionally large and coarse hands. This always struck visitors to his studio as being unexpected. Tolstoy, to climb back again on to the bigger scale, was at the same time conscious but almost proud of his stumpy figure and coarse, peasant features which were in contradiction to his aristocratic origin. No more than Beethoven, or Rembrandt, did he pretend to elegance. In the painting in Dresden of Rembrandt holding a glass of wine, with Saskia on his knee, painted in the year of their marriage, his sword, fine sleeves and feathered hat are in almost serio-comic contrast to his blunt features.†

Tolstoy seems to have felt that all forms of art were but make believe, the very art in which, typically enough, he was probably the most supreme practitioner there has ever been. But, then, he was a writer, and not a painter or musician. Perhaps he distrusted anything he could not do himself. His disbelief and contempt for music come in *The Kreutzer Sonata.* But substitution of a faith in the basic human virtues for all the pleasures, sad or gay, from works of art is the council of despair. Neither, it could be added, are there enough good novels to repair this. Perhaps he would have one read and read, and neither look nor listen except to woe and misery. For he was no present optimist in the conditions of his time. At the start of *The Cossacks* does not the hero keep his coachman waiting outside a club all night till early morning before he emerges, at last, and they start off on

* The Right Hon. Richard Crossman, MP.

† Compare, too, his self-portrait at fifty-seven years old, holding his palette, in the Iveagh Bequest at Kenwood, and his self-portrait painted shortly after his bankruptcy, in the Frick Collection at New York. No paintings are more marvellous than these; the latter almost surpassing his *Polish Rider* which hangs near it.

the long drive to the Caucasus? But was Tolstoy, himself, particularly considerate to his servants? It seems unlikely. And he was certainly unkind, cruel and thoughtless in his married life. He thought himself above, and exempt from, the doctrines he was preaching. And, of course, he was right in this, in virtue of himself, but it illumines, and yet tarnishes his image.

It is perfectly possible to reach to a mood or state of mind when all paintings are illusory; and when it seems only too obvious, granted the deficiencies in the Latin temperament, that many of the greatest of them should be the work of Italians. It is typical of them that they should have the ability to pick up a piece of charcoal or a brush and draw or paint upon the wall. This is something you could expect of the inhabitants of Naples or Venice, and which you would not anticipate in Oslo or in Aberdeen. Not simply because of pre-knowledge and historical fact, but in view of climate and the mere visual look of things. Further than this, it is only too like the Italians that they can carve in wood and marble, and build huge town 'palaces' and the flamboyant fronts of churches. Should one love the Italians for this, or despise them? For there are, or have been, the opposing points of view. And what can have come over the staid Dutchmen that they produced perhaps some hundreds of painters in a single century? In a climate too, that is almost identical with that of East Anglia! Where there were painters, also, but no more than two or three; say, in all, perhaps a dozen of them. And the balance begins to right itself again with a view by Pieter de Hooghe of a quiet backyard in Delft or Amsterdam, on one of those long afternoons when you would remember the impact of a bee upon the windowpane, so little else was happening.

Also, and I hate to admit it, the orchestral repertory is fast fading. After long familiarity it is difficult to listen to the four symphonies of Brahms, to the *St Anthony Variations*, or his double concerto for 'cello and violin. Much pleasure is to be got though from his Hungarian Dances; and from the finales to the violin concerto, the second piano concerto, and the two string quartets op. 25 and op. 26, all of which are in Hungarian rhythms. Also, from the *Liebeslieder waltzes*. Beethoven's symphonies, alas! I know too well now, but how wonderful they are still, and how wonderful they have been! Tchaikowsky's symphonies are feverishly tedious, though one can never tire of the genius and invention in his ballet music. *The Sleeping Princess*, even *Casse Noisette*, are surely immortal in their way, but in the theatre not in the concert hall.

Having been an admirer of Mozart almost since I can remember, I now find his texture thinning. The marvellous promise, elegance and high spirits of his early maturity,* now that I am getting old myself, I find too unbearably sad to listen to. *Così fan tutte* I find tiresomely artificial, despite the wonder of its orchestral accompaniments. The whole of *Figaro* and much of *Il Seraglio* are among the beautiful things of the world; as are, too, about a dozen or even fifteen of his piano concertos, many of them written for himself as soloist, and which surpass

---

* His five violin concertos, quintet for piano and wind, two piano and string quartets, trio for clarinet, viola and piano, etc. How dearly I loved them many years ago! So much so that I cannot hear them again.

his symphonies in sheer beauty and variety of invention.* But his piano sonatas, lovely and elegant as they may be, must pale in the end beside the beauty and rapidity of thought in Domenico Scarlatti. Had he not the quickest and most brilliant mind in music? His melancholy, depth of feeling, and again, his brilliance are unmatched in music. There is sufficient in his five hundred and more short pieces to last a lifetime.

If a few more remarks on personal taste and predilection may be tolerated, the results of a lifetime of listening to music, the twelve Grand Concertos of Handel are to be preferred to Bach's Brandenburg Concertos. Because they are looser in structure, more urbane, and of more worldly experience outside the organ-loft. And for the very inverse reason to this – because Bach's mental and physical experiences were inner and spiritual and unworldly, seeming at times to demonstrate and explain laws that are outside and beyond the cosmos – his organ preludes and fugues, toccatas, fantasies and fugues, and other organ works are upon a scale to which Handel could never attain, despite his mighty fist and stately step, which were no less splendid when he lowered his stature a little to suit the public taste in his Organ Concertos, descending majestically, a step lower still for his *Fireworks Music* and his *Water Music*. On the 'Forty Eight', it is impertinent of any writer or critic to remark further than that there are forty-eight of them, some of them of such incredible, far meaning beauty that they outreach the others; and that this greatest of musical geniuses may be more relaxed and no less wonderful when he puts off his armour and gets down to less formal clavier works, among which, in incredible proof of his supreme genius, should be numbered the forty-minute-long *Goldberg Variations*, the *Chromatic Fantasy and Fugue*, the Toccatas, and the *Italian Concerto*. Alone, and by themselves, the sarabande movements in his *English* and *French Suites* for harpsichord are a cosmogony, a term interpreted as meaning 'a theory of the universe and its creation', and this in the form of a solemn and grave dance. Into his hundred and forty and more *Chorale Preludes* for organ, and between two hundred and fifty and two hundred and seventy-five *Church Cantatas*, I venture nothing in my ignorance – which it is too late now to repair and put to rights.

As against the orchestral repertoire which is fast becoming worn and thread-bare, and is not amenable to much augmentation, from the point of the music-lover equipped with gramophone and television there is endless pleasure from opera. There are the dozen and more operas of Verdi, from *Ernani* and *Luisa Miller* to *Otello* and to *Falstaff*. There is the reviving fame of Donizetti after nearly complete neglect. He had lyrical qualities which were not in Verdi, as evidenced in *Lucia* and in the less romantically beautiful *Lucrezia Borgia* in which

---

* How to differentiate between these wonders which are utterly and entirely impossible to describe in words! But one could mention the first movement of K271, an early initiation into this world of beauty; the second movement of K450 in the form of variations on a marvellously beautiful theme; the finale of K491, again in variation form and in certain touches as though Mozart had already the wedding march of *Figaro* in mind and the mock departure of Cherubino to the Elysian wars; the writer's own and eternal favourite which is K503 in entirety; and the scarcely less beautiful K537, penultimate of so many wonders. But, then, there is the paragon K451 as well!

the aria and cabaletta in the first act are so lovely in the old Italian manner as to cause one to catch one's breath, as at this composer's 'moments' in *Don Pasquale* and *Elisir d'Amore*. Other *opera seria* by Donizetti, *Roberto Devereux*, *Parisina*, perhaps his penultimate grand operas, *Dom Sebastian* and *Maria de Rohan*, must have beautiful solos and ensembles in them, if both of them are haunted by his wretched, oncoming insanity. It is possible, too, that more comic operas by him may be there to be resuscitated and make him the equal of Rossini.*

Turning to piano music, one can never tire of Chopin's *mazurkas* even if one does not want to hear them all the time. For it is a question of mood; and when in the mood, one would wish to listen to nothing else for a few days on end. There is nothing in all the arts that remotely resembles them. They are nostalgic, and not maladif, which sets them apart from some of the rest of his music. The flashes of fire in a few of them are dazzling and stir the blood. Elsewhere in these pages there is mention of his *études*; and having loved his music, unquestioningly, while young I think one returns to him when one is older. How beautiful are his *Polish Songs* in Liszt's piano settings! One would wish to know more of the words of the songs in order fully to understand them. But to anyone who has ever seen Poland, how evocative they are of its fields and woods and villages; even more so than the mazurkas which, as to many of them, seem interiors in mood and not Mazovian or Sarmatian landscapes!

If another personal note may be allowed, ever since I became seriously interested, which was at about twelve or thirteen years old, I never remember a time when one tired of Schumann. Of certain pieces by him. This is not true of Chopin for he can 'go out' for months at a time, but has returned now, and remains. The pieces by Schumann in question are the *Fantasiestücke*, his *Novelletten*, his *Arabeske*, the *Toccata*, *Carnaval*, *Papillons*, and of course much else, nearly all of it written before he was thirty years old. All of these have some quality difficult to define; but they suggest being in the company of a number of young people, girls and young men, of romantic tendencies, in a never-ending summer. Hence, his *Arabeske* than which nothing could be more beautiful when properly played, and which could suggest walking by a waving cornfield in just such company; and the marvellous, poetically evocative *Des Abends*, *Aufschwung*, *Warum?*, *Grillen*, *Traumes Wirren*, all of them from *Fantasiestücke*. What do they mean? Who that ever heard them, at fourteen years old, played as encore pieces by Paderewski, could ever forget them? But to have heard Liszt play *Carnaval*! As against such bonds of love and affection as there were between them, it is hateful to make any

* Possibilities among these latter being the two-act *opera buffa*, *L'Ajo nell' imbarazzo*, first produced in Rome in 1824; the two-act *opera buffa*, *Il Burgomastro di Saardam* of 1827; the one-act *farsa*, *Le Convenienze ed inconvenienze teatrali* of 1827, with a part for an old woman played by a *basso comico* in travesty, a little opera much admired by Berlioz during a visit to Naples in 1831; and the three-act *opera semiseria*, *Il Furioso all' isola di San Domingo* of 1833, of which interesting accounts survive. *Il Furioso* and *L'Ajo nell' imbarazzo* seem the most likely of Donizetti's comic operas to be successful in revival. They may show his lyrical and comic genius at its finest inspiration. Autograph scores of these operas are preserved in, respectively, the Naples Conservatory Library; the Ricordi Archives, Milan; and the same again. *cf. Donizetti*, by Herbert Weinstock, London 1964.

criticism of Clara Wieck, with whom Schumann had fallen in love when she was seventeen, and they were married when she was twenty-one.* But her influence, and an injury which he did to his hand trying to improve his finger technique, combined together to impede and thwart the virtuoso in him, and perhaps changed the character of his compositions into other directions, giving more accent to the domestic, and indeed Biedermeyer side of him, as opposed to the German Romantic. Granted his shy, introspective temperament and long silences, it is typical of him that on his wife's instigation he should have distrusted 'the tinsel' in Liszt, whom he knew well, while nothing disturbed his admiration for Paganini whom he had heard play, but never met. But what a personal and distinctive feeling develops in listening to Schumann! Of an intensity of feeling rivalling that to be induced by reading Turgenev! And particularly in *Carnaval*. One might think that Tchaikowsky was conscious of this when he brings in the *Grossvatertanz* into the first act of *Casse Noisette*. If, in *Carnaval*, it is 'in caricature of the Philistines', in *Casse-Noisette* it is in evocation of the Christmas-tree party of President Silberhaus, and the arrival of Councillor Drosselmeyer in this old German home, as described in E.T.A. Hoffmann's fairy tale, no less appropriately than in Delibes' or Offenbach's musical settings to Hoffmann's stories.

Of Liszt's piano music, which has been written of at such length elsewhere, it is both unnecessary and inappropriate to write here, beyond remarking once more that in Domenico Scarlatti, as in Liszt, alone, there is more than enough to last one lifetime. And now that virtuosity is returning to the boards, and it is not considered enough, and at the same time to have been too much, to hire the Albert Hall, as did Schnabel, and play nothing else for hours on end but Beethoven sonatas, there is increasing opportunity to widen the concert repertoire. There is no precedent or reason at all to allow the 'pop singers' and drummers and guitarists, fearful as they are, to enjoy and dispense all the pleasures of music. But neither should the 'sacred trance' of music to the flute of Krishna:

> *Flute-player, reed-blower, soother of the shadows,*
> *To whose every step the forest trembles*

be allowed to degenerate into scenes resembling those at the last night of the Proms. It is only a plea for more diversified programmes and a more receptive audience, anxious to hear and appreciate things they have not known before.

It is possible, if you love music, that music is more easy to spoil and demolish than painting. Because, for one thing, there is a much smaller quantity of it in circulation. There are, let us say, ten or a dozen first-class orchestras, and about that number of Hermitage or Prado-level picture galleries. But even if the galleries feature the same painters in general, they are putting on show different pictures by them, and not ever and always the same symphonies, symphonic poems, and concertos. At least, you have to go to Venice to see Carpaccio and Veronese, to Florence for Botticelli and Fra Angelico, Madrid for Velázquez and Goya, The Hague for Vermeer, Haarlem for Frans Hals, and so on, whereas Haydn and

* Clara Schumann 'already a remarkable pianist at nine years old', developed into a famous player of quietist category, but with a faithful following.

Mozart, Beethoven and Tchaikowsky, you can hear in most of the big cities in Europe, and from a dozen or more orchestras in the USA. It is only a question of choosing between the wind and string instruments, and the conductors.

The decease of music can come from over familiarity. Even so, there is the anomaly that you can hear the same piece of music fifty or a hundred times more often than you can read the same book. Except for certain poetry; but then lovers of poetry are as rare as toxophilites, or pteridologists.† Not only are they rare, but likely to diminish still further in number, and before long be extinct. Whereas the musical public, and the quantity of persons deriving pleasure from paintings and from architecture, should be capable of almost endless multiplication. Will the Minister for Fine Arts ever be as important as the Secretary for War? It seems unlikely. Why not, indeed? For that is as it should be. Perhaps the truth is that it could only be with a diminishing world population, when some sort of Utopia might come in sight.

But is the whole world, then, to be let in to the secrets? To be allowed to share the privileges without undergoing the attendant pains and troubles? There have been musicians and musical thinkers, the great virtuoso Ferruccio Busoni among them, who have held a different point of view. That it is a sacred, not in the religious sense of the word, but an enclosed or hermetic art, keeping its secrets to itself and not sharing them with the public. And there can be no doubt that the first intoxication of music when it was no longer a matter of home or amateur performance on the early pianoforte, or by a trio or quartet of local talent, but by a modern orchestra with a conductor of the calibre and generation of Richter or Hans von Bülow, or played by such virtuosi as Liszt or Anton Rubinstein, must have been an excitement beyond parallel. Dating back, now, we must remember, for more than a hundred years – Liszt gave his last public concert in Russia in 1847 – while we may consider that the great period of the virtuosi ended when Anton Rubinstein gave his famous series of 'historical recitals' in St Petersburg, London, and other cities in 1886, which was the year, too, in which Liszt died. During this period, and perhaps extending it a little to cover the Paderewski furore, the public were subjected to musical experiences they had never had before, and that they will never have again, sensations which have now descended from the gallery to the gutter with the non-music of the Rolling Stones, The Pretty Things, The Monkees, The Who, and all the *olla podrida* of the 'mike', the banjo, and the guitars. There is certainly no reticence in their performances.

But Busoni had grown to hate playing in public and to detest his life as itinerant virtuoso. He wanted time to compose. In his letters he tells how he hated making records for the Welte-Mignon and the pre-electric gramophone.† In the result they show his fatigue and lack of interest and are very different from those made by, for instance, Josef Lhévinne, and are not a fair recording of his genius. But the marvellous pianist in question had no aspirations as a composer, and did not feel that it was a waste of time. The flood of music-making which came in with

---

* Lovers of archery, and fern collectors. The terms are used purposefully, for reason of their rarity.

† *Ferruccio Busoni*, by Edward J. Dent, London 1933.

broadcasting and with the improvement in recording not long after Busoni's death in 1924 would, we may think, have bewildered him. Because it removed the sanctity and inviolability of music. But by now, despite early failures and disappointments, it has attained to dimensions when it is certainly more effective and important as an influence than the Church of England, and has surely a larger number of devotees, the potentialities are enormous and inexhaustible, and out of that surely some good must come. But it is creation more than mere audition that is important; and there again a too ready access to all forms of music removes and dulls initiative. There must be effort; and it had best be a huge effort against circumstances and environment to obtain knowledge. If it is made too easy, the results may be of no use at all. It is necessary to make a fight for it when one is young, or it is not worth getting.

The late Sir Thomas Beecham, who prided himself on having at one time or another during his long career performed almost everything in the orchestral repertoire that was worth playing, once said to me that while he was a young man, Brahms, Puccini, Dvořák, Sibelius, Debussy, Richard Strauss, were all composing. Then, something went wrong. And it went wrong just before the First World War, like a premonitory sign of disaster.

This is not at all impossible. The birds and animals know before an earthquake. There are many stories that go to prove this. If only, and how is it, that after a war more male children are born, to compensate for the lives lost? Also, when some particular race of animals has been over-persecuted by human beings they lose the will to live and die out of themselves. There are problems of instinct and of the mass consciousness that we do not understand. But of which there is more than enough evidence to convince even the sceptic. Are we to suppose that Napoleon died a perfectly natural death after five years on St Helena; or that Wilde should have lived happily for years after he came out of prison! The fallen Emperor and fallen arbiter had this in common. They both died of failure and disappointment.

Now, a quarter of a century after the second world cataclysm and disaster, as far as the musical world is concerned the curious situation has been reached that there is a bigger public for music than ever before in history. But the ghost has fled. In England we have musical virtuosi such as we have never produced before. But as the music they perform almost without exception was written before they were born it is equivalent to having in our midst not great living architects and craftsmen but the most competent and trained restorers. They can bring back the past again, even the recent past, and make it look as good as new. As to the 'new' music it has yet to show its powers of survival; in any case it is indisputably new, unlike what there has been before, and calling for other qualities both of performance and of appreciation. Perhaps it is not music in the old sense, but another art of sound and auditory sensation. The two arts could become in time perfectly distinct and separate arts with their own particular audience and performers.

It is arguable that the same situation, but with a considerably lesser degree both of involved genius and of acquired skill, is overtaking the other arts, not least, the more tactile art of sculpture. Here, too, there is likely to come a sharp division between lovers of the old and new. The problem is really quantitative as much as it is comparative. A sculptor for instance of the individual quality of Giacometti is to be appreciated when put on exhibition with the work of other sculptors. But a huge display only of his works, room after room of them, as was the case a year or two ago at Zürich, with the option of that city buying the whole lot of them as a memorial tribute, raised its own problems of sameness and monotony. Based, in principle, on the sculptor's personal canon of ragged contour and attenuated stature which becomes rather more than merely an irritating affectation when applied in the end to nearly everything to which he put his hand. The whole wing of a gallery devoted to this, even with the assistance of Giacometti's drawings, might become more of a burden than a sinecure in the years to come.*

On the other hand what wit and what a display of genius in Picasso's sculptures! The exhibition of these at the Tate Gallery, only a few years ago, must be something unprecedented in the career of any other painter or sculptor of whatever school or time. There can never have been such an exhibition. It was predominantly funambulist in mood and character. That is to say, prestidigious both in conception and execution and, withal, of deceptive simplicity. That an artist of his inventive skill should have contrived a few objects of this nature for his own amusement and as a pastime is understandable. But such works in quantity are dazzling, yet but the by-play of the prodigy of the Catalan cafés; of the master of the *époque bleu* and *époque rose*, of the harlequin paintings and early dry points; the practitioner of the different phases of cubism and neo-classicism; the curtain-painter of *Parade* and of *Le Tricorne*; of the Cassandra-like Guernica; of the hundreds of classical line drawings and engravings, of every inspiration from Ingres to Flaxman, and from Etruscan mirror-backs to the *Lysistrata* of Beardsley; of the ceramics of Vallauris, alone and by themselves; of the master of the toreros, the picadors and dying horses, and of the round 'O' of the bull-ring; and at eighty-nine, not it is to be hoped in finale, the three hundred and sixty and more drawings executed in every form of engraving during a few months in 1967. For once, it is to be admitted grudgingly, the public estimation has been correct and Picasso is the genius of the age. Not in many respects an agreeable one, but he is the genius of it.

From acknowledgement and recognition of which in reluctance to the public taste, it was some palliation to be admitted to this secret arcana of sculptures which the artist had kept so long to himself. In what contrast, too, to the weight, pure and simple, of another show at the same gallery, of intermediate-state *homo sapiens* inspiration, ignoring all experience or lessons learned since then, and without a smile on any face of stone or metal. But, there, in this other and make-shift world of funambulist affinity where part of a bicycle, the mouthpiece of a telephone, or anything else that comes to hand can be assembled and formed into an object of amusement, and more often of beauty, the wit and wisdom of the Mediterranean races are not thrown aside and left to waste. Picasso is well capable

---

* A sculpture by Giacometti was sold recently for £43,000. It seems a lot of money to pay for a very ugly figure of a woman, nine feet high; and one out of an 'edition' of five, worth, presumably a quarter of a million pounds in all.

of ugliness for its own sake which is the age-old Spanish anarchist at work in him, but at least it is always purposeful and not involuntary. It can be done in order to delude and lead into a cul-de-sac where the followers and devotees are left to find their own way out, while he moves onto something else. But, also, there is a streak of the gamin and of the clown in him. Grock – and who could have known more about the subject than he? – said that 'If Italy was the land of tenors, Spain was the land of clowns'. Hence, his love of wearing masks, funny hats, etc., and there were items in the exhibition of his sculptures at the Tate Gallery that could only have come from someone who not only loved the circus but was almost a part of it, himself.

Most certainly he stands alone and there is no one else to take his place. When he goes there will be no one who is both an innovator and an old master. To the extent that others, even, have but doubtful credentials, and are not over anxious to emerge from self-imposed obscurity and abstraction in order to show themselves. Braque was the one other master, and the inventor of pre-conceived but non-existent forms in which just the quality of the paint in itself is an aesthetic pleasure. The ceaseless invention without repetition or redundance but only in variation upon itself, and once that problem solved, the dauntless start of new adventures into the unknown and untrodden was wonderful with Braque, as was his creation of a classicism of his own with its own governing laws of surface and proportion.

ENTR'ACTE
Le Grand Gilles

This page is written in 1969, the bicentenary year of Napoleon I. And without the wish to strain after an excuse or a parallel in the first thing that comes to hand it could be remarked that there is some little similarity in the self-assumed rôle of his nephew Napoleon III and the fate of our actor found dead in an empty flat. That there was not the slightest physical resemblance between uncle and nephew proves nothing. But was he in fact the nephew, for we remember that his mother was the beautiful and unpredictable Queen Hortense, married to the dullest of Napoleon's brothers, Louis Bonaparte, King of Holland? After all, even if he never met Morny, his half-brother by Flahaut and Queen Hortense, until just before the *coup d'état* of 1851, the third Napoleon had heard about him and must have known of his mother's excursions out of matrimony. The Second Empire, therefore, was so much play acting and imposture, or, at the least, impersonation, with its chief protagonist for leading actor, who in his turn, even now after a hundred years has not been forgiven for the disaster and humiliation of Sedan.

It was a civilization of cafés and flashy uniforms, and crinolines. The Paris of Baron Haussmann and the 'vespasiennes'; of Offenbach – why was not he, too, made a baron? – and of the fiacre drivers with white bowler hats. All of the army, to judge from prints of the period, wore waxed moustaches and little pointed beards or 'imperials'; the restored eagles of the Empire were on their standards; the cavalry had the imperial crown with 'N' beneath it on their saddle cloths; but, of course, it was with the twenty-two battalions of the Garde Impériale that para-military fantasy reached to a climax. The little pointed beards that were so typical of ordinary Frenchmen of the Second Empire, and so unlike the 'Dundrearys', or the beards and mutton-chop whiskers of middle-class Englishmen, being in themselves no new departure in trichology but only a revival or imitation of the wispy beards worn by Frenchmen under the Valois Kings.

The illusionary reality, but improbability of the age shows clearly in the drawings of Constantin Guys, Baudelaire's *le Peintre de la Vie Moderne*, who was the most reliable witness or reporter of its extravagances. We know of him that he came home and made his drawings late at night from memory.* Can the carriages

---

* It was Campbell Dodgson, a late keeper of prints and drawings at the British Museum, who told me he had bought drawings by Guys in the Charing Cross Road, never paying more than ten shillings each, for many years before he knew the artist's name, or had any clue as to his initials.

of the countesses and courtesans have had that marvellous floating lightness as they passed him in the Bois or along the Champs Elyseés? It was the great age of carriage building and this showed, too, in the liveries. The cocottes and the ladies of the Faubourg St Germain were rivalling each other in their horses and the smartness of their equipages, and the ignorant could very easily mistake the one kind for the other. Written accounts of this concourse of painted carriages show that Guys was not exaggerating the beauty and fantasy of the passing scene.

But the pinchbeck Second Empire was already losing its false glitter. What a dreadful night it must have been for the defeated Emperor, a few days after Sedan, when he was removed as a prisoner of war to the Château of Wilhelmshöhe, outside Cassel, and given a state room with a lifesize portrait of Madame Mère, mother of the great Napoleon, hanging over his bed! For this formidable old lady had been the active principle from whom the family genius was derived. He may have wondered if her portrait was oblivious of him in his humiliation. No actor found dead in an empty flat can have been more pitiful; and his waking, were that the word for it, from half-sleep, incredulous of what had happened, must have been worse still. Or we can think of the first night, and first awakening in Reading Gaol. That, too, has elements of the same kind; particularly, if we consider the wit and fallen arbiter drinking his brain away in shabby cafés in the inferno of his after-imprisonment.

As much as Thomas Weldon Atheretons of the empty flat in Prince of Wales Road, Battersea, probably shot by accident, or by a person unknown, with his own pistol, it could be said of Napoleon III that his defeat and even his death less than three years later were brought about by false intentions. Probably Napoleon III was hated just as much, and no more nor less, after the disaster of Sedan than he had been esteemed when most of France voted him in as their Emperor at the plebiscite. His starting off for the war from the palace of St Cloud with the four-teen-year-old Prince Imperial for his 'baptism of fire', and being seen off by the Empress surrounded by the Cent-gardes in their pale blue tunics, white breeches, and horse-tailed helms, was the last throw of an old and ill actor who knew by now that he was no longer what he had once pretended to be. The bedroom at Wilhelmshöhe under the portrait of Madame Mère being in effect the empty flat he died in. It, and its aftermath of humiliation in defeat, were what killed him. He had only embarked upon the war in fear of the greater humiliation of refusing, and not foreseeing the surrender of Sedan – where the Emperor, though not in command, gave up his sword to the King of Prussia, together with one marshal, thirty-nine generals and eighty-three thousand men, this, after only three weeks of fighting, on 2 September 1870; followed on 27 October by the surrender of the fortress of Metz, by Marshal Bazaine, with two more marshals, fifty generals, and one hundred and seventy-three thousand men taken prisoner; and the siege and fall of Paris and the horrors of the Commune still to come. It is after such crushing defeats and failures that the Second Empire seems in retrospect to have been hollow inside and like a gilded shell, and its whole achievement like the interior of a golden theatre, empty and lightless after the play is done.

I suppose that it must be in getting away from the truth of things, and interposing another and fictitious personality to cover oneself and to hide in, that the fascination of acting takes hold both of actor and audience. It is this that gives the sacred tingling of the skin which is the descent of the god, and is the mark of music upon mankind. Of which the most appalling instance one can think of is the Aztec god Xipe, or the 'Flayed One', dressed in a human skin 'to represent the new covering of vegetation with which the earth clothes itself each spring'. The priests of Xipe, at the ceremonies in his honour, put on the skins of freshly flayed captives and danced in them. They are shown thus in Aztec sculptures, the true import of which has to be explained, unless one is forewarned by reading of it.

For what one sees is a rounded face, more moon-faced than with the ordinary Mexican Indian, and then one notices something curious about the mouth and eyes. The eyes are double-rimmed, with two sets of eyelids one within the other. Or is it just that they are swollen? But the lips are odd-looking, too, as though doubly rouged with lipstick, perhaps from short-sighted eyes. In fact, the inner mouth shows inside the other. And now we may be beginning to wonder, or suspect something. We turn the half-length stone figure round, or walk behind it. This is what we see. It has bows or knots of skin up and down its back where the priest stepped into it, or got inside it, and had the freshly flayed skin of the dead man 'done up' where his hands cannot reach to it. As, indeed, a woman has to ask for help with her zip-fastener or the topmost hooks and eyes. They are neat bows, not more than three or four of them, tight little knots of skin. And the final note of horror is his hands, for he has four of them; his own pair, and the other hands dangling from his wrists as if they were a pair of gloves. As he danced they will have flapped against his hands. Doubtless he would have worn the dead man's feet, as well, were it not that they would trip him up in dancing.

The priests of Xipe lived and slept in the skins for weeks on end, until, or even because, the stench became unbearable. This was their equivalent to the wooden or leather masks of the Greek tragedians; and indeed when the day came that a fellow priest cut the knots and they came out, their naked skins scabbed and black with dried blood, their hair clotted with gore, they will have looked to be worthy sons or brothers of the Atridae. What had they been doing in the dark corners of the pyramids, and on the high platforms and terraces, but acting? No less so than when Lady Macbeth 'enters reading a letter'; the weird sisters have all-hailed her 'Thane of Cawdor' and soon 'light thickens and the crow makes wing to the rooky wood'.

All of it is but the amplification and extension of children's games, just as no form of cruelty or unpleasantness but had its counterpart in the English private schools. Those, before mollification set in, were the places in which to study primitive tribal customs without incurring travel expenses, as if in fact the pupils were so many stone age tribes with taboos, puberty rituals and initiations, and the rest of it. If those represent a freeing or release of the libido, 'the emotional craving which is said by psychoanalysis to lie behind all human impulse', then how much true this is of both audience and actor. Alike the villain of melodrama, and to only lesser degree the school bully, is scapegoat of the public who both takes on their sins and expiates them.

The great brute and monster of the all-in wrestling match who is hissed and booed, who shakes his fist at the public, calls to heaven for justice, and insults the referee, is of course semi-hero of the entertainment. For the appeal of the theatre, as of the wrestler's ring, is divided between whom you'd like and whom you'd hate to be. But all-in wrestling is already stylized. One could almost, if not quite, be watching a Kabuki play, or the Sumô wrestling in Japan. Not all the villain-heroes are beetle-browed and menacing. All-in wrestling has its comedians, too; who may climb into the ring wearing gold lamé 'trunks' with back hair in a queue like one of Nelson's tars, or a torero of the bull-ring, and show disdain for his opponent. He will even stand with his back turned, blowing kisses to a lady in the audience, for a few seconds after the bout has begun. And will mince away after a minor success, rubbing his hands as though having disposed of his foe, for good and all.

There are those who will proffer a hand to shake in camaraderie and good fellowship, only to land the unsuspecting victim with a stomach butt, or a drop-kick to the face. There are all the tweakings of muscle and sinew, and sudden spring-like release from hopeless posture to somersaulting onto the feet again. The 'bear-hug' with hands to the throat and chest so that the agonized victim cannot breathe, but despite grimacings of agony continues to do so. The hideous pouncing on the weak points at every chance, so that when released by the bell the victim rubs and tries his arm, or limps painfully to his corner waggling his head; or is hurled again and again to the canvas with his victor sitting on him after each fall, and even jumping with all his weight on an injured arm or ankle. The wrestler lying prone on his back and banging on the canvas floor with both hands, which is part of the ritual, and one of the moments when all-in wrestling seems near to Sumô and to flamenco dancing. The humiliating face-slapping of a tiring contestant; the bare fist hitting of back or chest – one of the few moves which perhaps are not as painful as they appear to be – and the vicious, nasty tempered last kick after the bell has sounded. The refusal, probably wisely, to shake hands; followed in spite of this by an agonizing handgrip; the hurling of the opponent across the ring who smashes against the corner-post and slumps to the ground; or, surely, unnecessarily, as if this is one of the tricks, turns and rushes back and they meet with sickening impact. Or, even, run twice or more times hand-in-hand with comical effect across and across the ring, heading for disaster against the ropes. He, who seemed to be winning, may be hurled through the ropes into the audience as though from long practice at this form of diving, and emerge unhurt and climb back into the ring.

The 'half-Boston' looks painful enough; and the half-Nelson scarcely less so; but there is the more sensational 'aeroplane-spin' when the seemingly helpless victim is lifted bodily above the head, whirled round several times, and thrown crashing to the floor. How is it they break no bones? Or, in matter of minor injuries, do not have slipped disks? But, as in the puppy games of dog with dog which also have their rules, one will artfully lie still as though vanquished, and in their convention, feigning dead, while he is in fact just resting, taking it easy. And all the time his opponent must know the trick. Surely he cannot be taken in by it!

But the trick works; one can only think by mutual consent of both of them. The underdog rolls on top again. Tempers are frayed, or seem to be. The bell clangs. 'Seconds out.'

And the last bout begins in fury, on both sides. There is an undoubted comic element about all-in wrestlers' laced boots, especially in a heavyweight contest, when one bearded giant may turn the scale at nineteen stone. Their boots are like a babe's bootees, and so are their tantrums, if not their deep bass roarings. By now, the hero of the hour is staggering, thrown five times to the floor with great violence; then sat on, and his left arm where he has been hurt before, wrenched wickedly. 'Ten seconds to go.' Everyone is shouting, and there are female as well as men's voices. He is seized, not altogether unwillingly, and sent running wildly across the ring. His opponent charges him, and misses, and lands himself with great force against the ropes. But, in the last few seconds, with a head butt to the chest brings him to the floor as though never to rise again. It is a knock out in the sixth round, and he still lies there in agony with trainer and referee trying to get him on his feet. The hero-villain is booed to the echo. He expostulates and shakes his fist. The other is on his feet at last, but will not shake hands. And one, and then the other, climb through the ropes and jump down to the floor. The radio voice says, 'Happy Thursday, Friday. See you, Saturday,' and all-in wrestling is over till next time.

Probably had we known the actor found dead in an empty flat we would have thought nothing suited him so well as his end, so perfectly was it in character with him. As, also, it was perhaps not necessary to be either clairvoyant or chiro-practitioner to foretell what would happen to the winner of the plebiscite and victim of Sedan. As, too, the wearer of the absinthe-dyed, green carnation who cannot have been a difficult subject for the fate-foreteller. Ill fame and fortune can circulate in the very air we breathe. There is the old stage tradition that the play of *Macbeth* is unlucky to the players. The young actress describes in her memoirs* how she came home from the theatre to find Dan Leno waiting in her flat to tell her of his miseries – he was in the latter stages of acute melancholia and to die before long in an asylum – sitting, if I am not mistaken, in the darkened flat in a pool of moonlight, in that theatrically near immortal part of London, the purlieus of Drury Lane and Covent Garden. What an extraordinary experience! Indeed, nothing stranger or more haunting could happen to one in a lifetime. And what a subject for a painting, did painters but essay such themes! But they are intent, one and all, on illusionist fantasies for the nursery wall; gridiron patterns that change and interlock with each other as you come towards them; the simplicity of the dartboard and the dazzlement of the box of toys. No history; and above all no humanity.

One does not have to be a phrenologist in order to see a physical resemblance in the features of Buster Keaton, the 'dumb' film comedian and the person portrayed in Watteau's painting of *Le Grand Gilles*. Except that the young man of the painting is no actor. He is the son of a friend of the painter and wearing, pre-sumably, clothes borrowed from an actor. His coat is too loose and his trousers

* Miss Constance Collier, *Harlequinade*, London 1929.

are too short for him. But the clumsiness, almost doltishness, only increases his sensitivity. In the same way, the supreme pathos about young children is that they have not chosen their clothes. Those have been chosen for them, and they have to wear them. They are helpless and at the mercy of all and sundry. Gilles, in the painting, looks incapable of acting, or doing any of the things expected of him.

Which is in a sense exactly the rôle of Pierrot, and the reason why Watteau should have painted him as Gilles. He is the young man presented with difficult situations, who is dumbfounded by them and yet solves them by his kind of natural magic. A strong aura of poetry attaches to him enhanced by his diffidence and awkwardness which are at the same time his acrobatic ease. The dolt or zany of this company of actors, for Mezzetin and others of them are in the picture, but below him with only their heads and shoulders showing – and he stands there with hands to his sides as though suddenly materialized – is mercurial of temperament and agile as quicksilver once he gets moving. All this is expressed in his attitude, in his round, moon-like countenance, and in his eyebrows. Those are the key to his unexpected character.*

And everything that has been said here could be applied, as well, to Buster Keaton. Even his face, seriously considered, was sensitive and beautiful. As a small boy not more than three or four years old, and from then onwards till he was about nine or ten, Buster Keaton was literally thrown about the stage by his father, who was an acrobat and comedian; and on occasion rolled up like a ball and kicked along the boards. There are early photographs of him undergoing this strange apprenticeship or training, which was not cruelty for the sake of cruelty, but only his schooling for the theatre, or, more properly, the circus tent. That his physique was not seriously injured is remarkable, though he must have been to some extent permanently cut and bruised. But it was the academy of experience through which many great artists have passed from tender years, and it must be more valuable than any school of dramatic art. They are taken young to it before the time for 'O' levels, or anything of the sort at all, and have not to wait for school-leaving age before they can begin. It is a career that for better or worse is out of question in the welfare state, and its disappearance has probably retarded or removed the highest talents.

From the painting of *Gilles*, now shown in all its poetic glory in the Grande Galérie of the Louvre where, of late, hung Leonardo's *Mona Lisa* and his *Virgin of the Rocks*, it is an easy transition to the theatre proper. Not that it can be thought that, even with paintings by Claude and by Poussin in aid, the French school holds its own with the Italian, but the contrast between them is interesting.

* 'Que Pierrot serait content s'il avait l'art de vous plaire' was chalked across the stomach of Gilles during the time that this marvel of painting was exposed to the elements for some three years outside Meunier's shop in the Place du Carrousel. Eventually Vivant Denon bought it for 150 francs, though he was attacked by the painter David for doing so. This poignant anecdote concerning a great painting I owe to my friend Mr Francis Watson. I would like to add to this the remark of Chagall that 'the pants' of Watteau's Gilles 'made him want to cry'. What a subtle and beautiful compliment from one painter to another! The present writer has thought differently of Chagall since he read this.

The world of Watteau, and of his master Claude Gillot, has an ever recurring nostalgia of the theatre, but its underlying melancholy is as the music of Couperin le Grand or of Rameau, stilted, not so free moving, with its not infrequent *bourdon* or bagpipe drone and imitations of the hurdygurdy, compared to the climatic ease and intelligence and clattering brilliance of Domenico Scarlatti.

BOOK
SIX

'Say, what is love ?'

'Say, what is love,
Pray tell me that, MacGregor'*

Is it the three hundred or so girls and young women with whom Lord Byron had 'affairs' during his three years' residence in Venice? Not a few of them were the daughters of gondoliers.

Was it the three hundred or more boy victims of the country vicar who was sentenced at the Assizes a few years ago? He wrote down careful notes of it all in his diary, and had worked much with youth clubs.

The hundreds of wives and concubines of the sheikhs and kings of Araby? The ninety-nine daughters of the McNab, in the portrait by Raeburn, and at last a son?

Was it Queen Elizabeth I who never married and had no children? But who loved admiration and amorous dalliance. Or the Empress Catherine the Great who had the brothers Orlov, Zubov, Potemkin, Saltykov, and lovers innumerable, and named one of her children by these unions Bobrinskoy because he resembled a baby bear? What a strange world in which a reigning Empress and widow could have illegitimate children without prejudice to herself or public comment!

In *The Present State of England* by Edward Chamberlayne, a regular yearly publication (first edition 1669), it is remarked of the reigning monarch King Charles II: 'His Majesty hath natural sons, servants in ordinary above stairs, all educated and fitted for martial employment both by sea and land, who may one day be of great use and ornament to this nation', a pious exhortation which it cannot be said was satisfactorily fulfilled. Even less so in the instance of his brother James II whose natural son by Arabella Churchill, the Duke of Berwick, fought against England under the flag of Louis XIV. A state of society in fact in which polygamy had virtually been accepted as long as practised in the highest circles, and which prevailed for the best part of another century, with brief resuscitation for the reign of the third Napoleon, when at big receptions at the Tuileries, or at house parties at Compiègne, a high proportion of the persons present were not, paternally, or maternally, who they purported to be. But, of course, this situation

---

*   Phonetically translated by Edwin Evans for Poulenc's music in *Les Biches*.

was most pronounced of all at Versailles, 'the capital of the civilized world', in the time of Louis Quinze, 'le bien aimé', when the Queen Marie Leszczynska lived in one wing of the palace, and Mme de Pompadour had her apartment and her salon of scarlet lacquer *vernis Martin* upon the ground floor. And later, when both the Queen and the Pompadour were dead, the King installed Mme du Barry just above the *petits apartements* of himself and his daughters. There was nothing cynical about this. It was the undisguised truth.

It is a long way removed, at least, from the amours of the animals. From mere creatures, like the species of spider that is seven times larger than her mate and devours him at once after copulation. What kind of relationship is that? For how long do the most affectionate of animals retain their love for their offspring? Do dogs after a few weeks or months know their own puppies as any different from other dogs? Is it true that wolves keep back their eldest daughter in a litter to help them with next year's family of wolves? Is there love among the fishes? It is at least very highly developed with the whales and porpoises, who are born of their mothers, who suckle their young, and are not fishes at all but mammals. After which it is but cold comfort to learn that dolphins are amenable to training and may prove useful for submarine and mine detection.

Was it less, or more ignoble during the youth of space travel a few years ago when pigs dressed in khaki uniforms were sent up for experimental purposes into the stratosphere? And rhesus monkeys, strapped down onto their couches as in a nightmare version of sessions with a psychoanalyst, and with instruments inserted into their brains and hearts, were rocketed up into outer space and back again? How many thousands of rhesus monkeys killed in a year in the course of scientific experiments, the point and purpose of which is that they should end in death? The fact that a rhesus monkey is a little homunculus in the shape and form of man being about the nastiest feature of the scheme. Should not their propinquity to human beings have been allowed to save them? But this did not spare the black men in the holds of slave ships. In fact, it could be said that it was just because they were like white men, only stupider, and black, that they incurred the penalty.

It might be asked, and with reason, where love comes into all of this? And, of course, the answer is only as surely as all positives are followed by a negative, or day by night. That there have been affirmative times in human history is not to be denied, any more than that the golden reign of nature is vitiated by microbic infections, parasites, and beasts of prey, the creation and living habits of which it is difficult for any human religion to account for, or explain away. It could be that they are possessed of extranational or extramundane rights; but based on what argument, and by whom accorded? This could not be *pro bono publico*, or to the public good; or to take only individual human tragedies, and not wars or plagues or general disasters, Beethoven would not have been suffered to go deaf, or Keats or Mozart to die young. Yet from the point of view of the powers of evil, if such they be – and it is difficult in this context to think of them as anything else – how sickening, and what a setback, that they should have been allowed to go as far as they did, or be born at all.

Yet it is of no use to force the issue. It would probably be possible now for medical science to keep those human geniuses alive and in health, but that is only half the problem. Disease sharpens some talents, and it could be that human beings have to meet their fate; that if it is altered for them, it is to their detriment in other ways. Prevention, not cure, therefore, must be the answer. In which field the war is against the law of numbers. The swarming must be prevented, if it is not now too late for that. The pullulation is continuing and must come to its own climax. Already it is reaching to the point when in any painting or old engraving it is noticeable and enviable how few persons there are about. The poetic tranquillity of Vermeer's *View of Delft* derives from the handful of persons that there are in sight. And in Bruegel's peasant scenes the crowd is only such as would attend a crowded church service or village fair. The camera came in at the beginning of the human swarming, and accompanies and records its progress to destruction, which seems inevitable but could be averted.

But, again, it is not love that is concerned with numbers. It is not through loving that there are four hundred million in India, and maybe double that number, or even more, in China. There are other names for it than that. It should by now be obvious to everyone what the condition of the Indian sub-continent, and of the constituent coloured parts of the Commonwealth in Africa, is likely to be within a few years' time. The arming of the Arab states by France and Russia is a public danger, and not least to themselves as they cannot agree among each other.

When human beings are on the point of discovering the ultimate secrets about the universe, and about themselves, why cannot they control their numbers? It is no impediment to sensual pleasures.

Perhaps no one can understand the population problem who has not seen the Indian cities, albeit those are a stagnation, as well as an explosion problem. Or Japan. But it is different with them. The Japanese, by now, are masters and not slaves of the machine. The yellow ants are workers and not drones. Because, if born an ant, it is better to work hard and earn good wages. There is nothing disgraceful in the ant's status. The workers are out for the benefits and are getting them. They have certain innate talents which are not dead, but still alive in them. If their arts recover from the anarchy of modernistic imitation they will have much to teach the world, perhaps more than all Europe, or than North America. Whereas Italy, once the most fertile soil for the arts in the past now lies fallow. Or, in effect, the Italians have ploughed the soil without sowing it. And their past, it could be said, keeps on coming back and hitting them. What are they doing putting up that tin advertisement for Cinzano by the side of the tomb of Virgil at Posilippo? Or is there nothing wrong with that? There are posters, too, along both sides of the Appian Way. Where ten thousand of the followers of Spartacus, the 'Thracian shepherd' and escaped gladiator from the dreadful training pits of Capua, were once crucified by the Romans, in warning, along both sides of the road. What sort of a people could they be, wrote Gustave Flaubert of the Carthaginians, who crucified a lion? It was Marinetti, the Futurist, who urged the Italians to bomb their own museums though, in the end, it was the Allies who bombed their cities for them.

Of Sacred and Profane Love it is the first that is dying, dying, and all but dead and gone. But what a wonderful world could be dawning if there are not too many hundreds of millions to enjoy it! And so long as the mother of the arts is not allowed to be the BBC or its equivalents. By whom all the values are altered and personalities are swollen up and distorted. Who have the opportunity and the occasion and have let it drop. If they ever and consistently appeal to the lowest denominator in the public they will forfeit the power to rise, and lose him too. It is always the vulgarizing, and almost never the touch of good sense and sensibility. They build up a huge musical audience, and then wantonly let it go in favour of more sports news which is a clear case of pandering to the public and not helping them to other things.

The pop-singers, male and female, tied, or rather, chained to the 'mike' and ot knowing what to do with it, or how to manage it, are a pathetic phenomenon of our time. They cannot dispense with it, but have to manoeuvre that truncated abbreviated stalk of a thing as though it were truly and really their life-line, and the umbilical cord connecting them with the audience and the big money. Shouting and yelling into it, or cajoling it, while gesticulating with the other hand, brings them to the same level and displays their universal and unexceptional lack of all talent. Their microphone is as the asp in Cleopatra's bosom; they cannot conceal it, and it will be the death of them in the end. That is to say, there must be a revolt against this hideous and hardening contrivance to project the human voice. It is as though a dancer had a lasso looped round her ankle without which she could not move across the stage.

It is certainly true that popular music is no longer professional, but amateur. The mere earning of tens of thousands of pounds on a tour, or selling a million copies of a record does not confer professional status. On the contrary it is the almost certain sign of sickening sentiment, embarrassing lyrics, and musical inefficiency. It need be no better than a popular novelette, and is but another instance of the jerking into a magnified and false focus which is the illness and malady of the mass-media age. It confuses and dazzles the retina, and makes mistakes and misjudgments in both directions; allowing of a Van Gogh, a Gauguin, or a Modigliani to have the greatest difficulty in selling a painting during their lifetimes; and of the BBC 'scrubbing', i.e. destroying in their archives, the recorded voices of Yeats and of Arthur Waley reading their poems, while promoting the sales of disc-jockeys and ladling out vast sums to pop-singers and other noisy nonentities, male and female. There is far too large an educated public now for this sort of thing to be allowed to happen. And yet it continues. There is all the hope and expectation, and but little of the fulfilment. I do not care how popular they are, or how many records the pop-singers sell, I do not believe in them. The rat-like squealing of the girls and women in their audience is revolting and unedifying. It is not in association with music, and music is not to blame. But, rather, like paratyphoid, paranoia, or other words with the same prefix, it is a side or parallel phenomenon with a few, but only a very few in this instance, of the same ingredients and effects. Thus, it is played with musical instruments which on occasion, and with certain groups, are purposely broken to pieces as part of the process. But even mere guitar-twanging or drum-beating is not the height or power of music. It is paramusic with none of the technique of musicians, and failing in all but the most rudimentary effects of music. It has therefore nothing to do with the jazz age of great song writers like Irving Berlin, George Gershwin, Cole Porter, Jerome Kern and others, who were phenomenal in their especial line. It needs much more than talent to write tunes as they did and give character to an age. Musical chaos with a sexual kick of primitive sort and kind is no substitute for what is lost and gone.

Moreover, as someone who has an intense personal interest, both in the history and trappings of fanaticism and in virtuosity, *per se*, that is, in the virtuoso as virtuoso in all the human arts, I condemn their long hair. Driving round, as ever, in a 'chauffeur-driven Rolls-Royce' and often on the way to or fro from the law courts because of some drug offence, is not enough to make an artist or a musician of someone just simply because he has long and untidy hair. They have usurped the long hair which was the prerogative of the nineteenth-century musician, together with some of the oddities, but none of the values, of the Indian *sadhus*. When one thinks how fearful and awe-inspiring a great many of these may have been over the centuries, it is apparent that they have laid their hands on this and spoilt it, too. It was a transitory fashion with the richest of them to sit at the feet of a Hindu teacher or *guru*, imbibe the 'wisdom of the East' and return after a few weeks, no different but in length of hair and beard. Doubtless the more interesting and unusual appearance of the Indian sitar players who have come to England has influenced this short pilgrimage to the Himalayas.

The *sadhus* may have had as much as thirty centuries of experience behind them, rascally and vagabond as many of them must always have been. The temples of Bhuvaneshwar, of Konarak, of Khajuraho, with others long forgotten and lying in ruins, must have seen some most extraordinary ascetics. Then, too, there were the missionary Brahmins accompanying the mysterious 'King of the Mountain and Lord of the Isles', the Hindu prince from Southern India who set forth in the eighth century to conquer the world, and like a second Alexander subdued Java, Sumatra, and the Malay Peninsula. Because of the Indian laws of taboo his name could not be pronounced, and is not known to this day, but his contemporaries called him Sailendra, or 'King of the Mountain'. He, surely, must have had some fearsome *sadhus* and Brahmins in his train. It was Sailendra or his successors who built the great temple and stone mountain of Borobudur in Java, second only to Angkor, and it was he who sent a relative Jayavarman I to rule in Cambodia; hence, the Khmer temples of Angkor. If, in the decline of spiritual and aesthetic values, anyone should be sceptical of 'the wisdom of the East', let him visit Angkor. If it still be there!

But as well, and over a long period there will have been *sadhus* and ascetics who came down from the Himalayan monasteries, as we would think of them, into the plains of India. Over the centuries what extraordinary appearances of fanaticism and solitary meditation must have haunted the stone, nenuphar or lily-ceiling'd Jain temples of Mount Abu, or other shrines all over the vastness of India! That there were, also, extraordinary and magical musical virtuosi, more particularly from Southern India is, also, historically certain. We may think that the hermits of the Thebaid, the anchorites of the Nitrian desert, the holy idiots of Russia, even the Syrian and Georgian stylites or pillar hermits, ghostly residue of a millennium of classical building of pillar'd porticos and colonnades from before the age of Pericles to after the reign of Justinian, were but the pale shadows of their Hindu forbears and brothers. After which genealogical table of long hair as an attribute of gifts or natural talents, religious, musical, or otherwise, it is merely silly to leave the Assize Court wearing *eau de nil* trousers, a pink shirt, perhaps, and a fur coat, to a girlish chorus of 'Isn't he gorgeous!' and be driven away in a white Bentley.

As against this, there are the streets of red brick houses to forget, and the hideous uniformity. I remember thinking when I was young that masculine dress, men's clothes, were fixed and immovable and would never change. One of the tests being a photograph of the dinner scene in *Lady Windermere's Fan* (1893), with the men, of course, all wearing tail coats, white waistcoats, and white ties, and after the passage of half a century the only difference was a slightly higher collar. But this is from the point of view of the Savile Row tailor, who does not come into it at all. Sartorial change for one of the first times in history has come to London from the North and Midland towns, the uglier the better, and has spread across the world from there.

It has always been the case that the uglier the town, the friendlier its inhabitants, as though from inborn desperation; and now they are, as well, the more talented. London lies fallow of talent compared with Lancashire, and the North and Midlands. Just when one might be thinking that brains and talent would never emerge again from the diminishing countryside it appears in the big towns, and proves that all is far from hopeless. Even with the James Bond 'novels' selling a total of seventy-seven million copies in all languages? And the Bond films besides? For that is the conundrum and the terrible absurdity. Are there, then, that number of adult persons with the IQ level of a twelve-year-old child? And a nasty child at that! But such, apparently, is the shaming truth, and it is nothing to be proud of.

So let the long-haired ones run to seed and be forgotten. They will leave little to be remembered by. We are only alive once and let us make it worth our while. The wonders of the world are in part of human creation and the rest was there already. We have to guard the one, and work at and increase the other. It is only necessary to be shown a close-up photograph of the lunar surface to appreciate how beautiful our world is. In which human beings have perpetrated terrible cruelties and crimes on themselves, and on the animal creation which after all is not so innocent as all that. A total destruction or 'final solution' to all house flies and mosquitoes would be no crime against the animal world. It is not the same as the slaughter of the 'blue' whale, largest of all mammals; or the killing of the last oryx, supposed prototype of the unicorn, and to make that worse, by an Arabian oil sheikh from a speeding Cadillac.

The largest aerodrome in the world with the longest runways, V.I.P. lounges, cafeterias, magazine stalls, duty free shops, and all the rest with, as is said in house advertisements, 'all usual offices', does not compensate for a few green fields. With a jumbo jet arriving and disgorging, or departing loaded to the gills, every few minutes all day and night, bound for a land that should of right, by all the laws of nature, be a night's flight and not a mere two hours away. The simultaneous telescoping of distance so that far continents become within an airborne mealtime of each other, while the population, and particularly the coloured population, hums and buzzes inarticulately and begins to swarm below, is but one of the problems. Already a medical authority has suggested that it would be sensible and economical to pay five hundred pounds to a man with more than two children to have himself sterilized. What are we to think of the medical history of a Victorian family like that of Edward Lear, a person of talent and charm and geniality, but an epileptic, and one of a family of twenty-one children? How many of them died in infancy? Had any of the rest of the children any talent at all? Was it all, in fact, or any of it, worth while? One would like to resuscitate the mother and ask her opinion. But this was a lower middle-class family with some degree of comfort as the Victorians understood that. Let us not think of Seven Dials, of East London generally, and of the blackened and awful industrial north. For the sins against which we are still, and will be for ever suffering, because countries like Sweden or Finland with no industrial past and no industrial deserts and waste-lands can be true welfare states, with all the lesser ills and ineptitudes and lassitudes which that implies, but it cannot be here because we cannot pay for it, and must still further impoverish ourselves by trying to attain to it.

But the wages of sin are no longer death. That, at least, is something, though achieved not so long ago, as lately indeed as the discovery of salvorsan which was only a decade or two after the implications and consequences implied in Ibsen's *Ghosts*, from some of the projected shadows in which human beings are still suffering.* Next, after the abolition of the wages of sin and the devils driven away, so to speak, with overlong pause between, comes the all-permissive age in which anything and everything is allowed and there is entire licence. 'The permissive society is the civilized society', but that depends to some little degree on who says it, and on what is meant by 'civilization'. It decidedly does not only mean the abolition of all censorship. And as to its other meanings and interpretations it certainly leaves much to be desired and a great deal more to be explained. The 'civilized society', to begin with, is outside and above politics, has no interest in vote catching, or in the manoeuvring of tax-levels for political purposes; but it includes all the population and is a matter really of increasing the audience, and has nothing whatever to do with adding to the number of voters, very doubtfully, by lowering the voting age. That could be, like the asking of other boys at your school whether you are popular, almost fatal, and indeed highly dangerous and revolutionary in result. There are questions that are better not asked, and this is one of them.

* But it is reported that '"Even nice people get VD" was the comforting [*sic*] slogan broadcast nightly on American TV last week', and it has been announced that in Britain venereal disease is now second only to measles as the most widespread infectious disease, and that cases among the under-sixteens have risen by 10 per cent in the past year.

Increase in appreciation, which should be a principal aim and purpose of the 'civilized society' is more than a mere question of school education. It is the self-educated who should inherit the earth. More was ever learnt out of school than in it, whatever the socialists may say. It was at least the good point of my public school, and I rather doubt if this obtains or is possible at any other school, that having fulfilled the modicum of what was considered necessary, I was left alone to do my own reading. This was due to my tutor,* and I spent all of my time in the school library, and none, if I could help it, on the 'playing fields'. I had begun writing poems before I left school. Speaking from my own humble and far from satisfactory record, for my career as a writer has been very far from being the success that it might have been, I am altogether against all children being subjected to exactly similar systems of education. I am entirely, that is to say, in favour of specialization. A boy who shows particular talent in drawing or in music should be encouraged in this to the utmost, and not be forced to take all manner of unnecessary exams. Our great actors in the past, be they tragedians or 'comics', generally made their first appearance on the boards at three or four years old.

One life is too short to be even moderately good at everything. There will be the lapsed prodigies, the failures and the 'drop outs', but the risk is worth taking. And there will be those anyway. I am all, therefore, for privilege; but of talent, and, decidedly, not of birth. The talented should be forwarded at all costs, even in a career as unprofitable and unrewarding as that of poetry. But, of course, it is necessary in this to have a sure idea of what is poetry, and what is not. And opinions may differ as to this. Of the poet who has had more books written about his poetry, before and after his recent death, than perhaps any poet there has ever been, a recent author concludes her second chapter by examining his objective correlative to another, named, poet.† Does not this jargon betray itself and prove that a number of writers and critics are engaged upon their project for reasons other than poetry? What can an 'objective correlative' have to do with poetry? The arid desiccation of such language is the death of poetry.

Judgment is precarious, it seems to me, and far from trustworthy at the moment in painting and in sculpture, too. But those with talent for drawing will not be content for ever with entire abdication of the gift born in them. The human theme must return again and form the language and grammar of the arts. The eyes will not be content for ever, or even for much longer, with what is too often a subterfuge for incompetence. The dry desert of abstraction will not beckon for evermore.

But how much time is left? We are told there are eight hundred million Chinamen and that the population will double itself in a generation, which means sixteen hundred million Chinese by, or even before, the year 2000. Decidedly, that will be no moment for the dilettante. Nothing but a cataclysm could forestall this swarming, even if there has been miscalculation, as is more than probable, and

* C. W. Headlam, to whom I shall always be grateful.
† *Times Literary Supplement* for 1 August 1970.

there are only six hundred and not eight hundred millions. Therefore it must come to a climax, or an anticlimax. And there will be not far short of that number in India, as well. And Brazil? And it is said there will be eighty millions in a South American republic like Columbia, by then, So it is no use worrying. For there is nothing we can do. But let us appreciate and enjoy the world we live in while we may. And the anticlimax, which will be more welcome than the climax, could be surprising when it comes. There might be food enough for everyone and a decline in numbers. It is not time yet to listen for the locust and for the darkening of the skies. If the swarms attack each other that is their own affair.

There seems to me but little difference, and again, and this is its importance. all the difference in the world, between the parading of giant rockets on May Day through Red Square in Moscow and the Dionysia at Alexandria, in the time of Ptolemy II Philadelphus (d. 364 BC), successor to the Egyptian Pharaohs, as told by Athenaeus, after Callixenes of Rhodes. He tells of ten or more huge sacred chariots passing in procession before the pavilion of Ptolemy and his sister-wife according to Ptolemaic custom.* Among a crowd of thousands there passed 'a veritable army' of Sileni, Satyrs, Ithyphallics, and Maenads following the statues of the gods and the *tableaux vivants* hymning his praises. There followed an Indian 'Triumph of Bacchus', Alexandria 'being the port where the commodities of India are brought'; and now the climax of the Dionysia. Amid the clashing cymbals of the Bassarids there came a chariot bearing a golden thyrsus ninety cubits long and a silver lance of sixty cubits, a cubit being half-longer again as many feet, and therefore longer than any vehicle we meet on the arterial road with motor-cycle escort. The silver lance being another symbol of Dionysus, and lying on the same chariot beside the golden thyrsus, if, that is to say, you call a 'chariot' a float or car drawn Indian-fashion by many hundreds of devotees.

And after it, another chariot with a gilded phallus a hundred and twenty cubits long, 'all covered with engravings and hung with gilded streamers, with a golden star six cubits in circumference at the end of it'. The phallophoroi walking to either side, their heads crowned with ivy and with violets; noble virgins carrying golden baskets full of flowers; and others with white striped garments reaching to the ground, and on their hands they wore gloves composed of flowers; all walking beside the closed wagon or van of Bacchus which held his mysteries. These at least, are fructifying forces of the earth, not death, for all the decadence of the Ptolemies of Egypt; the Dionysia of the Greek being no different in kind from him who would pray to the pear tree on the wall, or bow to the shadow of the moon upon the waters.

But for the sensation of this year's parade in the Red Square there appeared a truck, a thirty-two-wheeled truck, scurrying like a centipede across the square, supporting a gross and fearful parody of the human weapon and instrument of procreation, with intent to rape and burst the calyx and wobble the earth upon its axis, their best, thus far, show of 'rocketry'.

* This lady was worshipped after her death, as Venus Zephyritis, and her husband-brother began to build a temple in her honour in which was to be a statue of the Queen suspended in the air by the means of lodestones.

It seems to me that the world of the Ancients during the two or three centuries before the birth of Christ, and perhaps for as long after that, say, for five or six centuries in all, was faced with the same problem of over-population. Cities like Rome or Antioch or Alexandria, with a million, or even two million inhabitants, had better methods than ourselves of employing their leisure. I am not thinking in this of the Roman games which are the hideous and lasting shame upon the Romans. But they had a multiplicity of religions, as in Japan there have been Buddhism and Shintoism; while beyond all comparison their great cities were more beautiful than ours. Not darkened with factory smoke. You could choose your god to worship, and presumably, change him if you wished to. There was slavery, it is true; but was this worse than working in the coal-pits, or the bestial horror of the London slums? Anyone curious enough to have read of the 'White-chapel murders' and of Jack the Ripper will have formed some picture for himself of the Victorian poor.

The conditions of living there were sordid and horrible beyond all imagining. From evidence given at the inquests on the Ripper's victims some strange details emerge. The eighties of the last century were a time of unrestricted emigration into the East End of London from Russia and Poland owing to the pogroms, which, of course, to some considerable degree altered the cockney characteristics of Stepney and Whitechapel. Females, to use the old phrase, 'of doubtful reputa-tion', when, so to speak, off duty, thought nothing of paying visits and calling on each other in their lodgings, which were rented single rooms, at one, or two, or even three o'clock in the morning. This, although they were born Londoners, but it reads like a custom from a warmer country, perhaps the Ukraine or Southern Russia. Cries of 'murder' rising from the darkened courts were apparently no cause for concern and did not interrupt these after-midnight conversations. There were always late-roaming drunkards and the brawling, or worse, was blamed on them. It may be recalled by persons who have read the trial of Stinie Morrison for the mysterious murder of Leon Beron on Clapham Common, at a much later period (1911), that the victim and his brother would spend all day from eleven or twelve o'clock in the morning till late at night in a café, at a total expenditure of 1s. 3d, or 1s. 6d at most, for dinner, tea and supper. Most of the persons involved in this case, were also, Russian Jews, the all-day café habit being certainly not of British origin. It may be added that the bad characters, male and female, in the 'Ripper' cases were of English or Irish origin, the Russian-Jewish inhabitants of Whitechapel in contrast keeping to the Rabbinical laws of family, however, odd their social attitudes.

During the span of years between the publication in 1861 of the first of the four volumes of that extraordinary and wonderful microcosm of Victorian Lon-don, Mayhew's *London Labour and the London Poor*, and the Whitechapel Murders of 1889, the great change which had come over the East End of London was this influx of refugees from Russia. From the different hours they kept it may have seemed like a colony or hive of nocturnal beings in the midst of the more stolid, gin-drinking Londoners of tradition. Incidentally, and for what little it is worth, having been interested in these murders for their sinister undertones since

I was a schoolboy, I feel convinced they can only have been the work of some local person well acquainted with the dark courts or alleys. How could a veterinary student with rooms in Mornington Crescent; a well-known London doctor; the latest suggestion, a Wykehamist and graduate of Oriel, later become a barrister; or even much more illustrious suspects than those mentioned, have found their way about the rookeries of Whitechapel without long training? He could have been a sailor, or a ritual slaughterman of Russian or Polish-Jewish origin, but nothing more interesting than that.

It is to be emphasized that the 'horrors' of Mayhew's *London*, in so far as they are horrors, are horrors of London origin, and the concomitant and derivative of Hogarth and of Cruickshank's London. They are the inevitable outcome of Hogarth's *Beer Street* and *Gin Lane*, and of his *Four Stages of Cruelty*; and of Cruickshank's forgotten masterpieces *The Bottle* and *The Drunkard's Children*, all of which should be studied in this connection. The most rabid of anti-Semites could find no evidence attaching to his bugbear in these various works, and sadly and unfortunately the blame for these horrors is all-British. The conditions of life preluded in the works of these two great philanthropists, for both Hogarth and George Cruickshank certainly qualify for that to be said of them, would shame an island or hinterland of painted cannibals. Gin-sodden prostitutes, their evening's earnings gone on drink, would roam the streets hoping for a late encounter to earn them the threepence or fourpence needed for a bed, and at that, in a doss house, in a so-called dormitory of wooden sheds. Lowest of all, and only in order to get indoors from the rain, was to pay a penny and stand up with a rope to hold onto. Amours at the threepenny or fourpenny level were in the backcourts, on the rubble or the paving stones; giving at least a touch of the native refinement and luxury in little details to the women we read of in accounts of the Yoshiwara of Japan, who waited about the alleys for prospective customers carrying a rolled up mattress which they would unroll on request. And from them upwards in the hierarchy to the expensive beauties of the Green Mansions to be admired if, for ourselves, hardly to be recognized, in prints by Utamaro and other masters of the 'Floating World', with their elaborate coiffures and patterned kimono, compared to whom their contemporaries, the crinolin'd and bedizened pedestrians of the Haymarket, and inmates of the 'night houses' or 'dress houses' (brothels) of Panton Street would be, one may think, but poor and illiterate company.

An East End music-hall song, quoted below:

> *My first was a cornet*
> *in a regiment of dragoons;*
> *I gave him what he didn't like,*
> *and stole his silver spoons*

reads like a hideous early oleograph of semi-prostitution, as sung, no doubt, with leering insinuation, to a theatre of threepenny or fourpenny admission into the gallery. It is, also, a pitiful and awful cry of doom from an illness, lightly considered then, but for which there was no cure. What a hideous life foreshadowed and forsworn! What a vocalist and what an audience, unless we are to think that the implications in the verse were taken to be more serious than mere badinage! Anyway it is a slum song, if ever there were one, contemporary one would suppose, to the shadows projected in Ibsen's *Ghosts*, shades that are still abroad after eighty years and have not yet shot their bolt; or, better put, entirely dropped their green rain. It is almost worse to think of the song being written than of the song as sung. In a room, or corner of a bar with a decrepit piano; the incidence of the tune, and the process of putting words to it which would amuse the audience. If that was their idea of a joke! And the song must after all have been printed, or it would not have survived. So, then, the music – awful thought! – must still be living.

Is it only because one is an Englishman, oneself, that one feels these awful conditions of life, if indeed it is even worth calling it that, were worse in London and in the industrial North than anywhere else in Europe? I think not. Because the industrial age was the invention of Englishmen, and it was here, first, that it was put into practice and achieved. Spain and Italy were in innocence of these horrors; Naples, to be sure, had its dark rookeries, its basements inhabited by whole families; but not Berlin, nor Vienna, nor St Petersburg, had the fogs and slums of London. It is in respect of this that the classical world in spite of some loathsome features – the slave system and the gladiatorial games – still keeps its pre-eminence. And its aesthetic predominance most certainly. Where public buildings are concerned, in the sense of temples (churches), theatres, baths, forums, triumphal arches, aqueducts, and so forth, it is of no use to compare any city of the modern world to Ancient Rome. A seaside or summer resort of the second order like Pompeii makes ridiculous any comparison to Deauville or Brighton or Monte Carlo; more so still, maybe, to towns like Las Vegas where the riches and faults of the contemporary world foregather. Probably the greatest revelation would have come from the towns of North Africa and Asia Minor, where the talent was still more Greek than Roman; cities such as Ephesus, or Antioch, or Alexandria. Which is the reason why the Dionysia, as celebrated in the last-named city, was chosen to contrast with the parade of rockets through the Red Square in Moscow. Because that expresses and displays the differences. In the Ancient World, as has been said, you were at liberty to choose, and change the god or goddess you worshipped. But by, say, the third or fourth century AD how many serious pagan worshippers were there? Christianity was coming in to alter everything. The religion of the Ancients in its totality of gods for which there is no name, no genetic term like Buddhism, Shintoism, or Confucianism, had lasted by then for some twelve to fifteen centuries at least, taken over by the Romans from the Greeks, and by now beyond the energies of a holy war, a crusade, or any show of force and resistance. It was no more than an excuse for public festivals and enjoyments in a monumental setting for which we have no parallel today.

The never more than partially explained successes of the Arab conquerors who overran the Middle East, Spain and North Africa in the seventh and eighth centuries, when hordes from the Yemen, it would seem, surpassed all that the other barbarian invaders, Goths, Vandals, Huns, had inflicted on the dying Pax Romana, were due in some little measure to the inborn Semitic distrust and hatred of the graven image. But there can be no doubt that the multiplicity of statues, sculpture being the art of the classical world, outraged the puritanical precepts of these warriors from the desert. To set foot in a colonnaded city adorned with statues of naked youths and Venuses must have badly shocked their susceptibilities. Perhaps worse still, the statues were raised on pillars to show them to the best advantage and advertise their wanton wickedness. It has to be conceded that these cities of Roman institution, but Levantine or semi-Oriental habit, with classical buildings of the order and quality of Baalbek or Leptis Magna, which is to say, of an architectural luxuriance not found in Rome itself, may have been the most splendid cities of the Western world. Mediaeval, or even Early Renaissance towns, Florence, Siena, Venice, individual churches and palaces apart, can have been no match for the ordered splendour deriving from seven or eight centuries of siting and planning since the age of Pericles in fifth-century Athens. Not that the *souks* of the eternal Orient will have been absent from the purlieus of Pergamon or Alexandria; but there were, as well, the baths, forums, theatres, temples, of the classical world and of a richness, when it was a question of the Asiatic Greeks, not equalled in Rome, itself, or elsewhere in the Roman world. The rich citizens of such cities, which were regularly built, often colonnaded, and always with streets intersecting each other at right angles, would have recoiled in disgust from the narrow and tortuous lanes of mediaeval Paris. It may have been a vitiated civilization given over to pleasure and worshipping the wrong gods but, at least, it was not necessary to invent the term 'Gothic' as a name by which to describe it, and it kept its pillared statues and its colonnades.

The wages of sin were not death in that world of the Ancients; it was twelve centuries before venereal disease came back from South America with the first Spaniards. It was an uninhibited and permissive society in the full sense of the term, but reserved especially for the rich. There was very little by that time that could have shocked the Alexandrians, though this held in itself the seeds of its own decay. When the statues were toppled from their pillars the next occupants, in theory at least, would be the pillar-hermits. A phenomenon, to be exact, of Syrian origin in the person of St Simeon Stylite; the Egyptian hermits being desert dwellers from the communities of anchorites in the Sketian and Nitrian desert, religious 'drop-outs' from thirty centuries of hermetic civilization under as many dynasties of the Pharaohs, followed by the Second Empire licence and debauchery of life under the Ptolemies, to end, typically, with the brother-sister reign of Ptolemy XIV and his sister Cleopatra. The 'hippy'-pattern austerities of those shaggy, satyr-like beings, for there is little to choose in the end between austerities and excesses, being still there to read of in the *Paradise* of Palladius. *The Temptations of St Anthony* (of Coma in Middle Egypt), the first hermit, 'the portrayal of whose contests with his demon-tempters was a favourite subject with fifteenth and sixteenth-century painters', and who 'fixed his hermitage in the mountains to the east of the so aptly-named city of Aphroditopolis', being now available to all and sundry, it could be added in a footnote to the history of our own times.

For the permissive society is here of official announcement, and also, there is evidence enough that the wages of sin are no longer death. It was not death under the Roman Caesars because venereal disease had not arrived yet, and it is death no longer because it has been conquered together with other forms of death. Therefore, within the span of a single generation and in a lifetime, we have reached a situation that was attained after natural growth over many centuries in the Ancient World. Just before the coming of Christianity when no one any longer believed in anything at all, which is a state of incredulity or indifference natural to a certain degree of material prosperity that is not identical with what civilization could imply and mean. It has been attained by human cleverness in the field of science which is more likely to deny than confirm all religious feeling. Neither the discoveries of science, not archaeological 'finds' are going to support biblical theories of the origin or creation of the world. Stories of virgin birth and of the raising of the dead which are common to most religions are disputed and not believed in, when, in fact, it would be a greater help to human beings to know we are all, himself included, human and within finite limits of life and death. That he suffered in order to help other human beings like himself puts him among the immortal spirits; but in the transition of remembering him and not by magical and illogical means. His mother is as the mother of Beethoven, the peasant and real mothers of Leonardo in his mysterious painting, or the princess-mother of the 'Lord Buddha'. Nothing more to it than that. But it is nearly all of everything.

We are in the permissive society with no strings attached, and for how long will it continue without disaster? Will it be swarmed over, in parody on itself, by long-haired and bearded 'drop-outs' from the caravans and camping-sites? It is not to be denied that 'pot-smoking' has a certain bearing on this. Or are we to think that Sir Walter Raleigh, who died in the Tower, let loose as bad, or worse a plague on us with the discovery of tobacco? It is too early to know yet. It could, it might be leading, now, a whole half-continent to destruction. Where the cannabis or 'giggle-weed' grows wild, and has spread over two or three southern states of the USA from Mexico, more thickly than poppies in the August cornfields. Or is it no more harmful than the tobacco leaf of Virginia; and much less so than alcohol? Which last, I am more than accustomed to, myself, and would hate to be without. Which I have known to kill people; but to keep others alive and make their lives worth living. No half-continent, nor yet half-Kingdom, after all, has yet died of drink.

Is it to be overthrown from within itself, or from outside? Or can it go on its way? And if so, what happens, then? Certainly it is a revolutionary change; if not, so far, a revolution by force of arms. Why Che Guevara should be considered a hero, and acclaimed a few months ago by *The Listener*, the BBC Journal and in a sense, therefore, to some degree a government-financed paper, as 'Man of the Year' is difficult to understand, unless indeed there are forces working within that paper for their own destruction. And granted the general silliness that is not improbable. Anyway, Che Guevara who was singularly unsuccessful as a revolutionary, was the icon of the year 1969. André Malraux has said that it is one of the greatest revolutions since many centuries, but a revolution 'à base d'érotisme'.

This would seem to be very near to the truth. Another authority, but this time a fashion designer and not a famous philosopher, says that no young man who now wears his hair long will ever wear it short again. It is a great physical change or transformation of the sexes and in no sense comparable to the 'hirsute adornments' of Victorian men. Old persons who recalled those days have said that one of the things they remember about it was that the men of all classes had such quantities of beards and whiskers, of every shape and form from the pomaded, drawling elegance of 'Lord Dundreary' to the 'mutton chop' and the 'Newgate fringe'. But it did not make them any different in sexual approach; it only reinforced their masculinity and made them more the same.

Again, the huge periwigs that were the fashion for half a century from 1660 onwards were an accession to, or even an artificial masculinity, though I have often thought that, with the wigs off, the fine ladies in their curtained beds might have been in the arms of as many clowns. Later, the white wigs of the eighteenth century were a prolonged masculinity, as it could be, an attempted eternal youth, giving, they hoped, no clue as to their real age. But, now, and probably for some years to come it is an invasion by hordes of mock pop-singers disguised as hobos or *sadhus* with the hypnotic trance as sexual approach and means to that supreme end. A produced hypnosis, at that, and placing reliance on new methods of self-intoxication. With music, but only the worst values of music, and the abrogation of all musical sense and melody as secondary weapon of approach; and with mass hysteria as nirvana, which is no help to music but only brings it into disrepute.

It would seem indeed that it must destroy itself from within. But it may not be allowed this opportunity. There are other races in their millions reaching out for food, and swelling their own numbers at the rate of compound interest. Other races that are basically antagonistic to each other, and from whom there will be no mercy for they have long been, or consider they have been, exploited and enslaved. And that is only danger from one quarter, though it could come from different directions. For there is another part of the world that has been its own slave master over the centuries and wishes with Messianic fervour to impose its slavery on the rest. And, as well, there are the hereditary, natural militarists who twice within our lifetimes have been not the least dangerous of the lot. And the entire inertia of ourselves, and of the others, who do not appear to mind whether they are destroyed, or not. Perhaps for the reason that they are destroying themselves in any case.

And if it continues? Without molestation, or interruption? For the one lot might attack the other which would give a lull. But lulls do not last for long and are soon over. And in the meantime? If things work out peacefully and without violence? The sexes will certainly be huddled in one long embrace, and it is not so indiscriminate as all that. But let the place, at least, be tidied up for them. Beginning – why not? – with the hippies in their camping-site on the 'island' round the statue of Eros in Piccadilly Circus in the summer of 1969 – Eros, we remember, was the god of love, and the Erotia was the festival held in honour of him. It was their Île de Cythère, but it cannot be said they were a good advertisment for London. But neither could it be said that the Lord Mayor's Show passing on a November morning along the Strand compares in any way with the Dionysia at Alexandria under the Ptolemies.

So let the young enjoy themselves, and probably never before or since will there have been such facility of pleasure, but only in certain directions. Not in all. At least they are proving it is not necessary to have money in order to give, and be the recipient of pleasure. I would not like music to be too popular and familiar, for it must keep its magical and hermetic secrets. But there is little likelihood of that happening. What must be done is to mark the difference between music and the anti-music of some of the ranters and screamers. Let it be awarded some other name than music! And the same thing in their different spheres is applicable to a number of paintings and objects of sculpture. As to the former, it is a game played with pigments, of some degree of virtuosity, but no more than house-painting does it qualify as art. And of course a lot of sculptures betray their ugliness and ineptitude at the first glance and have no ultimate or deeper secrets to reveal.

It is necessary now to consider some of the splendid new buildings in New York, or other city of the USA. The best of them are the finest buildings of our time, just as New York is at once the wonder and the despair of the modern world. Typical are the Seagram Tower, the Steuben Glass Building, or the General Motors Building; the last named shooting up vertically to a dizzying height, so that it really hurts to look up at it, on Fifth Avenue. These, and others, are the undisputed masterpieces of their sort and kind; the best of which the most skilful and experienced architects of our day are capable. But they dare not attempt ornament. The day will come when something has to be done about that; and what will it be? Within the next twenty-five years, at most, or, say, by the year 2000, if the city is still there, someone, or even a group of persons, will need to be commemorated by a portrait or a statue. And then what happens? Faced with the physical portrayal of a great man – if such there continue to be – either in bronze or stone; or else in painting? A 'blown up' photograph is not enough and would be too much of a betrayal of self-confidence, and an abandonment of all the past. Or are we getting to a time when all representation of human beings and animals, except by camera, is taboo – and not from puritanism, as with the Moslems, but as the result of deliberate losing of the skill? But the Muslim had their genius, and it is not likely we will achieve the filigree courts and half-honeycomb ceilings of the Alhambra, the white phantom of the Taj Mahal, or the blue domes of Isfahan. Yet now the great painters of Paris are dead, and Pablo Picasso is ninety-one, architecture in only a few hands is the living art. Not in London, where there are only pathetic copies of the New York buildings. But the new skyscrapers are wonderful in point of engineering and, also, beautiful but abstinent, or teetotal, as though afraid of one side of their nature and of the excesses of the past for which they have certainly no responsibility. It is true that a portico or colonnade on a building eight hundred feet high would be out of scale, but they must invent for themselves. One cannot believe that a revived Ictinos (architect of the Parthenon), a Bramante, or Brunelleschi, or fifty or a hundred names from the past, would fail of ideas and stay his hand. Buildings of steel and glass are more than card-houses, and have their own philosophy and way of life which can be learnt and then improved upon.

Love, which is something other than concupiscence, will ever be the stronger of the two. But though it has permeated the building of a temple, a mosque, a cathedral, or even a palace, and a private dwelling, it is difficult to find it in a block of offices, or apartment flats. It is the sad touch that nearly everyone now dislikes the work that he, or she, perforce is doing; the exception, being those few persons who from childhood have wanted to act, or dance, or play the 'cello, and find it in their power to do so, with, or without opposition. The 'drop-outs' who want to do nothing, and succeed in that are nearly as much to be envied. They come, at least, before those who dislike every day of their own working lives. Of whom the number must be steadily increasing nearly everywhere except, it may be, in ant-like Japan. There, they become involved in the factory, or whatever industry, almost to the point of becoming part of it; hence their vast industrial progress and more than satisfactory balance of payments.

But would one sooner that, or be sitting at foot of the statue of Eros in Picca-dilly Circus with nothing to do all day and evening, the near-by Tube to shelter in if it showers, and the Park to shamble off to when it's time to sleep? Maybe the London *lazzaroni* are not so spineless and weak-willed as that. One has only to study the engravings done just before the French Revolution – but chiefly the aquatints by Debucourt, the *Promenade de la Galérie du Palais Royal* of 1787, and the gardens of the *Palais Royal* of 1792 – almost to recognize some of the types and faces of today. Debucourt, who lived in the Palais Royal for twelve years, had the chance of studying them in the arcades and gardens which were to the Paris of that day a mixture of Bond Street and of the Piazza of St Mark's. In this latter print, the King and Queen were still alive but the Terror was already approaching, was already darkening the sky. We see this, I think, in the insolent and sprawling attitudes, even in the angles of the empty chairs. These are characters, as to some of them, thrown up in the surf of revolution and likely not to be seen again but to disappear by violent means.

Hark! hark! the dogs do bark.
The beggars are coming to town

have in fact already arrived, and in many of the big cities are making it dangerous to walk about after dark. And soon it will be as bad in daylight. Or, indeed, they have not in any sense 'arrived' for they were before but have now collected together in numbers. A lot of them look like Ancient Britons, or Danes, or Saxons, or yokels from the Middle Ages, but one has learned it is becoming dangerous when too many of such persons are seen about. Once, not long ago, a solitary individual of them would have been looked round and stared at. Now, they are swarming, and it is the ordinary person who must not look round and stare. Or he will get the worst of it. I have been told by Russians, Serge de Diaghilev among them, that persons of this sort were always to be seen about before serious political and revolutionary troubles; and it was he who said to me that no Russian of his acquaintance had ever heard the names of Lenin and Trotsky before their emergence into Russia out of Germany in 1917. So the names of the future stokers and masters of the furnaces could be entirely unknown, and this does not make it any the less alarming.

Of the lighter or sexual side of love there will be more and not fewer Maithuna couplings. Or there is a great reaction coming, and probably from an unexpected direction, that of the aggressor. But permissiveness has advanced too far now to be halted and put into reverse. Though it is to be noticed that the menacing and minatory majorities with the huge populations, as to two of them, at least – for the third with its pious exhortations and preachings of austerity is too flower-like and ineffectual even to be dangerous – are wholly drab and puritanical in outlook. So that the revolution in permissiveness is one-sided and not likely to taint its conquerors when they swarm over it. The decontamination measures would be instant and too rigorous for that to happen, and the infection would be stamped out before it had even started.

But unrestricted amours are what we disputed and called in question by the quotation from a French nursery rhyme which is the heading of this chapter. There is an almost complete collapse of the old moral values, with new ones to take their place not even formulated and the loose ends left untied. The moral laws are valueless in the multiple change of partners. Female virginity which once was beyond price is at a discount; and where the young girls go out to work like young men and have to earn their living, this is no matter for surprise. Let us say that after a certain age they have the same rights and liberty as young men for that is only fair. The deviationists are forgiven and no longer ill treated, and the high dramas and tragedies are for them and not for ordinary men and women. It will not be long before breach of promise and alienation of affection are allowed among them. By which time marriage between the sexes will be old-fashioned and impracticable, if only in order to avoid joint taxation.

The world we live in is beautiful and inexplicable, as yet, but made ugly by human beings and especially during the last two centuries. Yet the Paris of Baron Haussmann who pierced through the old city with his 'grand boulevards' is more congenial than Welwyn Garden City, where an avenue of Japanese cherries does not compensate for lack of human interest. The worst of the industrial age in England may be over, with smokeless zones, with the monstrous streets of brick houses and outdoor lavatories, back to back, for the most part, but not all of them yet, pulled down,* and with proper wages paid. But the horrors put up instead of them all over England, and particularly on the moors outside Sheffield are the towers of flats. These vertical slums of twenty or thirty cement floors, all in exact facsimile of each other – some of the most awful of them are in the suburbs of Paris – must be more heartless to live in than any community dwellings yet devised. The indispensable 'elevator', and possession of a television set, cannot make all that difference where every landing is the same, and the towers in dumb

---

* Of which the most shameful instance known to me is Arkwright Town, only a few yards from the Palladian façade and vanished 'Venetian' interior of Sutton Scarsdale, which is just off the M.1 road, about opposite the distant view of Bolsover and Hardwick Castle. But perhaps there are as bad, or worse, red brick towns or villages in Co. Durham.

rehearsal of what may happen one day without warning, begin to nod and sway towards each other in a high wind.

What is inexplicable in the world is how, and when, and why it came about. And every human being holds no less of a mystery which is that of personality, and our not being all alike as rats or mice. Yet another problem is why the predatory animals, the sharks and birds of prey, the noxious snakes and insects, and so forth, when the world could do perfectly well without them? But this is to postulate that there are good and evil which is obvious enough from human history. So each for himself; and there must be a law for the eagle and another for the sea-anemone, even if it is equipped with electricity and can give out electric shocks. Birds are 'of a feather' in order not to interbreed and keep their race, or there would be universal miscegenation. It is the beings of light and intelligence who are the living wonder and may, or may not, have their counterpart elsewhere. If they are unique here, then, indeed, it is extraordinary and might lead one to belief in some especial dispensation, some licence or exemption. Or it could be conceivable over the centuries to send and receive signals, and eventually to understand them. And eternity would be like an unbreakable sheet of glass between us.

If there is anything there it seems more and more probable that it lies at a safe distance. For the sake of all of us, or by chance; and it would be interesting to know the answer? If there is one? For there are things that are unreasonable and beyond explanation. Death, for instance, unless it is only in order to reduce the numbers. And that life must have its negative or opposite. And they could be in a sense the parents, the positive and negative. We are born from one and go back into the other. But only for that once and never again. But what an elaborate life cycle the butterfly has evolved for itself; birth from the egg, the caterpillar, the chrysalis, and then the winged butterfly! Could one say that it is one life, or two, or three, or four? It has some degree of sensibility in all four stages of its life. Not less, but more fierce and masculine, the dragonfly. How well I remember, in the boat-house on the lake, the dried up old husks like sheaves of straw which were the discarded coverings of the dragonflies; any number of them on the wooden walls and rafters of the ceiling on a hot August afternoon. A little creepy and horrible to the touch, the dead integument or carapace! And when poling the punt out and about to hoist the sail, the sudden whirring, and a splendid fierce creature with long body and heavier than air flight would hover and whirr with its wings and dart away. There were dragonflies, with bodies the colour of light through red Bohemian glass; and electric blue, smaller ones; and green dragonflies; and sometimes a huge brown-yellow one, the heavy carrier not the attacker dragonfly. But, always, as tropical as humming-birds, and as improbable as that, near the bulrushes and yellow waterlilies, with the panting engines and the collieries in the distance. The dragonflies are insects, after all, and one might conjecture that if they have those changes and intermediate stages there could be something in store for at the least those human beings of light and intelligence. Except that one may feel the secret would not be so easily revealed. It has either to be taken on trust innocently and stupidly from whatever religion, or waited for interminably at the laboratory door. And when it comes, if it ever does, delivered in lecture form with diagrams, the news could be disappointing and unsatisfying.

So it is better not to think too much about it, and to have no dread or horror of it. But it is the separation and the parting that is terrible. Of which there was the first forewarning when going back to school, if it was no more than the taste of one's own salt tears upon the tongue. That was the first and the last parting, all together. But one returned, and this last time one remains. And it is obliteration; final and entire extinction. No one, soon, to know one's voice. By which time grief, if any, will be over. But there is, also, the parting from the wonders and miracles of the living world, in respect of which it was a mark of favour to have been born. And to have had propinquity through seeing or reading, or listening to what has been. For it was over, or nearly over, not so long ago. Or it could come again. But with less probability, as time goes on, owing to the ant-like swarming. There is no more to come from a city of ten million inhabitants than from the hotel with ten thousand bedrooms. Better the fallen column, where there was malaria, and the fig tree's shade. The cavern of the anchorite and the coral strand, in early times before the package-tour.

It is too late to stop this. So everyone to his, or their 'bed-sitter' and those are lucky with no experience of that. And the dragonfly to the boat-house where its progeny undergo and emerge from metamorphosis. Which will always be the fate of a few human beings. Of some few bright spirits who will probably lead difficult and unhappy lives.* Yet it is as obvious that a number of them have greatly enjoyed themselves, even in their misfortunes, and have made the most of the gift of life. They are those to be envied; to have had that, and to have been born into a propitious age. With a settled grammar and vernacular which, for an example, allowed of Haydn writing a hundred and four symphonies, seventy-seven string quartets, thirty-one trios and fifty-two piano sonatas, with little monotony and a seldom failing originality; whereas his pupil Beethoven was at much greater pains because a much deeper mental effort was required of him owing to music's change of tone and change of purpose, and to the more serious and epochal times he lived in.

At the moment it is difficult for anyone however gifted to write poems, paint, sculpt, or compose music, without looking nervously over his shoulder to see what everyone else is doing. Happy those few who would sooner go their own way, not try to catch up, and prefer to be left behind! The only facility now in any of the arts is in writing novels.† That is in part because the language has still to be intelligible, unless the appeal is only that of obscenity; there have still to be characters and a plot, and a personal and recognizable style of writing. Lack of talent in the other arts is more easily hidden under a load of nonsense.

When the time comes to say farewell to it all, there is the mere having been alive to be thankful for. And for the marvellous and transcendental experience of

* Though there are the exceptions, Sir Peter Paul Rubens being one of them.
† Mr Graham Greene has a dozen near masterworks to his credit. It is a record scarcely to be equalled in any other of the living arts. This is not to suggest that it can be easy for him to write as he does.

the arts of nature and of human beings. It would even seem that they compete and vie with one another; for not the panorama of the Himalayan mountains from an aeroplane flying to Katmandu, the capital of Nepal; not the extraordinary sensation of flying over Lake Titicaca above the Altiplano or mountain uplands of Bolivia and Peru, neither of which experiences could have happened to an earlier generation of human beings; not yet the Lofoten Islands, unfolding like a hundred-mile-long drawing of mountain peaks by Leonardo, as the ship moves up the narrow 'canal' between those islands and the Norwegian coast, is more wonderful or more awe-inspiring than many of the works of man:

Than the Kailasa of Ellora; than the octagonal interior of San Vitale at Ravenna, its basket capitals as of plaited palm fronds, and mosaics of Justinian and his circus-Empress Theodora with the priests and courtiers and eunuchs of fifteen hundred years ago; than the Ducal Palace of Urbino, palace of all palaces, with wooden doors inlaid with maidens in long fluttering dresses from designs by Botticelli, opening into a high room with vaulted ceiling, above the running-game or tug-of-war of *amorini*, white on a blue ground upon the chimneypiece. . .

But this has gone on too long already, and everyone will have his or her own ideas upon the subject; and their own comparisons to make. I must come to an end of it with a last memory of the greatest scholar, and the person with most understanding of all the human arts that I have known in my lifetime, who was Arthur Waley, the translator above all of Chinese poetry and of *The Tale of Genji*. When he lay dying from a broken back and from cancer of the spine, and in very great pain, but refused to be given any drug or sedative. He had the courage to do so because he wanted to be conscious during the last hours of being alive, the gift which was ebbing and fading and could never be again. In this way during those few days he listened to string quartets by Haydn, and had his favourite poems read to him. And then died.

ENTR'ACTE
À la Japonaise

It is another winter picture, as now at five o'clock in the morning upon the frosted windowpane. But I see an end to it all from the other side of the world, and set off upon a pre-dawn view of Hiroshige, the master, by elimination, not only of the snow, but rain. Beginning with the latter; but remembering, first, his most famous woodcut of a wooden bridge, a bridge more of utility than ornament. Not like the five-arched Kintai-bashi or 'Bridge of the Brocade Sash', which in all things was more 'Japanese-looking' than anything imaginable. With wooden spans, all five of them of different sizes, entirely of carpenter's work and put together without metal joints or nails. Where, no sooner have you climbed one of the arches, than you have to go down the barred slope of that arch for the crossplanks are laid down like little bars of steps, and begin to climb another; and where the bed of the river between the piers has been laid with pebbles so that the water moves over them with a gentle and flowing music.

That is the Kintai-bashi. But the *Bridge at Ohashi across the Sumida river*, the subject of Hiroshige's best-known woodcut, by contrast, is a wooden trestle bridge with wooden, not stone piers, sturdily built, but of the cheapest possible construction. The woodcut is in fact nothing but wet wood and rain. And the rain is pelting, is even to use the Hallamshire expression, 'siling down', the long lines of it pouring out of the leaden cloud overhead and crisscrossing themselves in their descent, to end with no perceptible splash on either bridge or river, and be just absorbed into more water. The lines of rain are rendered in a technique particularly adapted to woodcut and which it would be difficult and laborious to produce in any form of painting. Because it consists mainly of long vertical lines scratched into the block of cherry wood and drawn with a knife point, or any pointed instrument. Six persons, no more, are staggering through the downpour holding their waxed paper umbrellas, or with coats over their heads; and the long lines of rain are emphasized and made to look longer still by the immensely elongated raft which one solitary boatman in the rain is poling along. The far bank of the river rises away on an arc, and over there it is absolutely and entirely in a shroud of rain.

There is another print by Hiroshige in which there is a stone island, an artificial island of neatly piled up stones, with stunted trees and a small temple standing upon it, but the whole scene is really one gigantic pine tree rising to a great height, and of which the side branches are supported by poles standing in the water. This pine tree is obviously an object of veneration, but the curtain of rain comes down from the clouds and hides all of it from us except only its outline. The rain comes down in such an outpour that it has not even time to entangle its strings and skeins. It just falls bodily out of the dark cloud of solid water at top of the print. We hear its hopeless jangle where it drops; and, meanwhile, the masts of a fishing boat or two by the side verify the not impossible scale of the giant pine tree. A gale, in the sense of a storm of wind, forms another subject. One such, bending everything before it in its path, and with people running to take shelter in some lattice-sided shops or tea-houses, gives all the fury of a sudden storm. This time, the rain is all blown in the one direction without confusion, out of a livid sky, but soon over and forgotten.

And the master of mist? For this was the special gift of Hiroshige. There is his bridge-scene with a horseman, obviously a personage of only minor importance, a lesser samurai or country landowner, riding along in the mist of evening with two servants, one to lead his horse, the other for his luggage. The bridge, the travellers, and the hill behind them, are all in silhouette, as are the trees on the far river bank. The foreground is in colour, with two children playing with dogs; but the drama is in the evening emptiness. Yet another woodcut shows a family crossing a rustic turf bridge. The poverty of their patterned dresses only giving force to the trees and river bank to which their backs are turned, and which in the moonlit winter evening are shown in silhouette like a green cut-out or stencil but, seemingly, of polypoid, sea-anemone or houseleek substance; or like the lobes, one could say, of a mesembryanthemum. And the receding bank, winding behind that, shows dimmer and more colourless still, as of another world at back of and behind the moonlight. With but a solitary inhabitant out in the night air, and making for a haystook-shaped object which must be his home.

Wonderful, too, are Hiroshige's flights of birds. On one of his fan-shaped prints we see a soaring and simultaneous or regimented 'touch down' of wild geese, coming down into the marshes in their squadrons and escadrons, and at both ends of their trajectory already in the reeds and shallows but, also, still high in the evening sky over far off Fuji. Their flights are used by him to give scale and distance as, on occasion, but a gaggle of geese in momentary zigzag across the moonface. It is a device that Hiroshige uses as often as the sails of his fishing boats, smaller or taller as they come up towards us from under the horizon. But you can hear the peculiar honking of the geese and the whistling of their wings; their under-carriages are out, the lowermost as they skim just above the water hold their feet out ready for landing. How Hiroshige would have loved the RAF Show at Farnborough, or other event of the sort! How he would have delighted in the display of aerial acrobatics when they fly in formation and change pattern and direction as quickly as the starlings rising up from the stubble; and what prints he would have made of the newest and most whale-like prototypes of future aeroplanes to come! Surely, too, he would have drawn cloudscapes as seen from the portholes of an aeroplane!

Nevertheless, it is in his snow scenes that he is unrivalled, in all the different depths and kinds of snow. For example, in the well-known print of the forecourt of a vermilion-painted temple with a huge paper lantern hanging overhead, larger than life. The snow is falling, but there is not a footmark, it is coming down so heavily. There are several of his woodcuts in which the snow is falling, a feat only once attempted by Pieter Bruegel in his *Adoration of the Kings* (now at Winterthur in Switzerland), 'his last attempt at creating a new kind of winter picture',* and in fact the falling snow in his painting, as here, is muffling and obliterating the action. It is becoming impossible to see owing to the thick snow. Great must have been his labour in adding the descending snowflakes to the thick coat or couch of snow already on the ground and lying heavy on every object. In none of Bruegel's other five or six winter paintings is the snow falling. It is always deep winter with a permanence of snow, as in his famous *Hunters in the Snow* at Vienna.

In woodcut the process of rendering a snow shower was quicker, and the details of it could be left to the printer and engraver. There is Hiroshige's fan-print of *A lakeside in the Hakone mountains*, where a sufficiency of the falling snow for his purpose is shown by a countable quantity of white blobs against the blue of the water. Another, and beautiful instance of his incomparable skill, all allowance made for the proficiency of the craftsmen in the printer's workshop, is the wood-cut of *Snowfall at the Gion Shrine* where all is deep in snow, up to the stilted shoes of the ladies sheltering under their umbrellas, and where the grey stone of the torii arch and fence show blue against the snow.

But Hiroshige's snow scenes are innumerable; only to include the snow switchback or *montagne russe* in the Kisokaido series,† with wide-hatted coolies on a swept pathway between high snowbanks in front, and to both sides; and his *Evening snow at Kambara* from another series, which portrays black or ageing snow in all its sadness and depression. It is late evening, and there is nothing for it but to huddle in front of the brazier and try to forget the outside cold. But his few masterpieces in the genre are of a quality to which a painter of skating scenes like Hendrik Avercamp could not aspire. Among these is *A Mountain Stream* in snow from the *Illustrations to Chinese and Japanese Poems*, an extraordinary evocation of deep winter with the effect of its having been blown or breathed upon the paper, so delicate are the gradations of its white masses which have scarcely an outline against the darker, snow-laden sky, and only reveal themselves as mountains by the four jagged, wind-blown fir-trees that mark the edge of the hill against the other hill that stands behind it. There is a bridge deep in snow, and a solitary individual crossing that with bowed head towards the snowy outline of some buildings. And the blue, but snow-flecked stream, and two more skeletal trees clothed on their windward side with snow: and nothing more.

---

* *The Paintings of Bruegel*, by F. Grossman, London 1955, p. 200. The author adds, further, that 'snow showers were painted before Bruegel in the calendar illustrations of Flemish *Books of Hours* (which were among his main sources of inspiration)'.

† The Kisokaido and the Tokaido were the two principal roads from Tokyo (Yedo) to Kyoto. It was along the former that the daimyos (nobles) made their solemn progresses from the old to the new capital, there and back, once a year. Hiroshige made sets of woodcuts of *The Fifty-three Stages of the Tokaido* and *The Sixty-nine Stages of the Kiso-kaido*.

But there is, as well, his great snow triptych of *Mountains and River along the Kisokaido*. This masterpiece of elimination in its uninhabited desolation curiously recalls the more than inhabited, the even overpopulated painting of *Hermits in the Thebaid desert* by Gherardo Starnina, in one of the first rooms of the Uffizi. A huge land mass of snowy mountains with a blue, blue river flowing, unfrozen, from end to end of the triptych is the subject; but Hiroshige has heightened, and as it were, thickened the hills by the quantity of observed detail in the river bed and the absence of anything but two or three trees upon the mountain side. Now on closer scrutiny, there are the signs of habitation; a wooden bridge carried on high trestles in the right-hand panel of the triptych with even it could be a minute human being no bigger than an ant upon it, and in the corner of the left-hand panel another and smaller bridge leading, even, to three or four shacks but they are far, far, perhaps some miles away, deep in snow, themselves, and are almost inconspicuous upon the snowy mountain gorge. The central panel of the triptych, at least, has no sign of a human being in its haunted, but uninhabited Thebaid. It looks to be a day's journey, or more, from end to end of this snow scene; and now there is something that could be the figure of a man in the right-hand panel where the path winds up beside a waterfall. He is the only live being except the frozen and sleeping trees, and the water which is still flowing.

Such is this great master of the woodcut resumed, or, at least attempted, in the span of a few pages. Just, as, in fact, the thought of him filled perhaps an hour or two in the middle of the night, and was proved and took shape in the morning. I have known and loved his woodcuts since I was a schoolboy, and have still by me the books on Japanese woodcuts I bought all those years ago at the bookstalls in the British Museum and at the V. & A. They are works of art, once seen, always remembered, which have a place in the memory and come to life again. As one grows older and the nights get longer but, by the same token, are gone into nothing by morning, they feed one's wakefulness and keep one happy, with other and unhappier thoughts waiting their moment, which can drag out into hours. They are a panacea depending upon mood, and not always effective. So that one must have others. Of which I have several, if not too many.

Nor is this all. For I must complete the entr'acte, and fill the sleepless hours. Fairly often, in order not to forget them, I try to memorize the temples and gardens I saw ten years ago during nearly four weeks in Kyoto, the old capital of Japan, and thus make myself familiar once again with Kokedera or the 'Moss Garden'; known, also, as the Western Paradise, or Saiho-ji, with its billowing hummocks of mosses – more than twenty, some say even fifty varieties of mosses growing there* – and the huge 'garden stones' dug from lake or river bed. Incredible as the date may seem, this has been attributed till lately to the Zen priest Mosu Kokushi (1275–1351); but, even more astonishingly, it is now supposed to have been already a hundred and fifty years old when the Zen State Priest came to add some small touches to it, and to have been laid out between 1190 and 1198. There

---

* 'But a booklet, given out by the temple, lists the botanical identification of at least nineteen species,' quoted from *The World of the Japanese Garden* by Loraine Kuck, New York and Tokyo 1968, footnote to p. 395. *One Hundred Kyoto gardens*, 1936, is by the same author.

is, it appears, a record in the contemporary diary of a Prime Minister, of a visit to the Kokedera by an ex-Emperor in the year 1347, when the cherry blossoms were at their best, and to view them better the party took to boats on the pond. Later on in the evening, we are told, everyone came ashore and the Emperor took his seat under one of the blossoming trees. It is still indeed a place of magical beauty, perhaps unlike anywhere else in either Orient or Occident. The author of the superb book mentioned in our footnote speaks of 'the translucent azure light over certain patterns of mosses'; while mentioning other sorts 'that are coarser in texture and a full two inches high, like tiny conifers'. The Kokedera was a new experience in aesthetics to someone like myself brought up by his father, no mean authority, to admire above all the moss'd Atlantes of Villa Lante.

And I can see again Ginkakuji, the 'Silver Pavilion' with its lake and garden stones, and its two mounds of sand for moon-viewing as the moon comes up to time, never a moment late, just as in mid-fifteenth century, from behind the wooded hill. But how intriguing to learn that it is just as likely they were simply two heaps of extra sand, put there to be used when wanted and then left so long that in the end they became a feature of the garden with a legend attached to them! Perhaps the most fascinating detail of all concerning this garden of Ginkakuji is the attribution of its stone arrangement, to quote the same authority, to a certain Zen-ami, 'the old riverbank workman', spoken of in his day as 'the greatest in the world in stone placement', who lived to be ninety-seven. And I try to remember, as well, Kiyomizu on its baulks of timber built into the hillside, and its fiery maples and azaleas. Such colours, again, are something new to our eyes, for whoever thought to see a mediaeval temple against a falling foreground of yellowing or reddening maples!

Not forgetting, too, the wooden cathedral-abbey of Higashi-Honganji and its fifteen or twenty rooms with wall panels and sliding screens painted with such unfamiliar themes as monkeys and ceremonial flower-cars, willow trees under snow and silver pheasants. Not only these, but also white peacocks under double-blossoming cherries, horses and cypress trees, and even a little room painted with musk cats and fern palms. Two theatre stages there are, as well, in this Buddhist monastery for the performance of Nōh plays, a feature to tally in imagination with the 'sacred theatres' in that incomparable pair of Rococo abbeys, Ottobeuren and Zwiefalten. And where else but from this Zen abbey could have been the provenance of Ogata Korin's famous iris screen painted with blue irises, the *I. tectorum* or roof-iris of Japan. There is nothing to compare with this in the monasteries and nunneries of the West.*

Then, also, there are the Katsura Palace and Garden to the designs, it has generally been assumed, of the great tea-master Kobori Enshû (1579–1647), though now it would seem, *pace* the authority just quoted, that he did no more

* One of the curiosities of painting in this and other temples in Kyoto are the 'imaginary' blue-eyed tigers on the prowl through bamboo stems or flowering peonies, always on a gold leaf ground; the Japanese artists never having seen a live tiger, but crediting them by instinct with the blue eyes and white or silver stripes that have only occurred of late in the domains of an Indian rajah. A specimen of which race of tigers is now in the Bristol Zoo.

than offer friendly advice and had no actual part in it. The palace, itself, is well described as the most aesthetic of buildings there has ever been; while the lake at Katsura, which is a masterpiece of landscaping, is in the 'walk round' style with the view from every footfall studied and considered; a multitude of bridges of all sorts and kinds; a few wonderful stone arrangements by obviously a master hand in the art; and islands planted variously with maples, bamboos, cryptomerias and more tropical-looking cycads in order to give interest and variety.

The most beautiful flower paintings of the world are to be seen at the Chishaku-in temple by the painter Hasegawa Tohaku (d. 1610), which were removed hither from another temple, built by the tyrant Hideyoshi. Tohaku, unappreciated until a few years ago, was at work during Shakespeare's lifetime. He had been known before only for his ink drawings in the style of the fifteenth-century master Sesshu, which in its turn was derived from Chinese landscape painters of the Sung dynasty. Tohaku working in this manner is to be seen in his screen of *Pine trees in a fog*,* an unpromising theme, but at his hand it achieves an epic emptiness to the degree, even, that two of its six panels are left bare of anything at all but the tag-ends of a couple of fir boughs. The rest is fog and damp, and yet another masterpiece of elimination. In his other manner Tohaku may be perhaps the greatest decorative painter there has ever been, surpassing even Eitoku, Sanraku, and others of the Kano School. This, at the Chishaku-in at Kyoto, in a pair of folding screens of a *Pine tree and grasses*, and a four-panel painting of *Flowering Cherry*, all these on a gold ground.† The room of *Maple Trees and Flowers* is another revelation, the more extraordinary because of Tohaku's different mood of evasiveness and reticence. Here, the full orchestration is quite overpowering and an aesthetic sensation not to be forgotten.

I have left till last the most controversial work of art of all, the 'flat' garden of Ryuan-ji, a 'garden' of fifteen large stones and raked sand, occupying a space a little bigger than a tennis court. There could be nothing less like the conventional views of gardening; and it came as rather more than a shock to the writer, having imbibed the Italian at an early age. It is possible to attach all shades of meaning to it, just as certainly as it is among the most uncompromising and original of all works of art. According to mood, its mere sand and rocks are meaningless. Or it can take on the importance of a divinely inspired planetarium.‡

And it is the same problem with the Raku tea-bowls which change hands for huge sums of money, indeed for higher prices than any ceramics in the world's markets. The Japanese esteem them as much as they do their most precious paintings. But to Western eyes they are uncouth and ugly, and among the strangest of all objects ever to become the cult of aesthetes. Perhaps again, as

* In the National Museum at Tokyo.
† The *Cherry Blossoms* panels are now attributed to the son of Tohaku, who was called Hasegawa Kyuzo (1568–93); or father and son may have worked together on them. *cf. Far Eastern Art*, by H. Herl-Kunze, in the *Dolphin History of Painting*, vol. VI, London 1969, p. 111.
‡ It is tempting to credit the suggestion that Sesshu (1420–1306), one of the greatest of Japanese painters, after his journey to China, may have 'placed' the stones at Ryuan-ji, or given at least his advice concerning them.

with the garden of Ryuan-ji, it is all or nothing. Not every Raku bowl is black in colour. Others are rufous, or turkey-wattle red; with black treacle-lip; or splashed with white as from an eagle's droppings. When properly understood they become works of art.

Why is there not time for more about Kyoto? For another garden in the same compound of temples as Ryuan-ji, that known as Daisen-in which is in fact a Sung landscape painting portrayed in 'L' shape out of the choosing and rejecting of many hundreds or even thousands of individual rocks and stones, round two sides or a temple drawing-room? For Nijo Castle, the palace of the Shogun Ieyasu, wherein can be seen the entire range of Japanese decorative painting in its golden age? Which is in fact the Elysium of the gold-leaf screen. With cyclopaean walls, and garden of huge rocks intended as a tribute to Hideyoshi's military glory. There should after all be, basically, no more difficulty in achieving this, in what is really abstract sculpture, then in contriving the same effects in the sister art of music.

Or for yet another temple, Sambo-in, outside the city, with to my taste the most beautiful of all Japanese gardens. The lakes and islands are an enchantment, and the arrangement of 'garden stones' superlative even to the most casual of observers. In fact, another 'riverbank master', Kintei, again according to the most recent authority, spent no less than twenty years in going over, moving and arranging, rejecting and at length settling the stones in place.

It was at Sambo-in, that Hideyoshi, in the year of his death (1598), held his great cherry-viewing party, pendant and companion piece to that fête he gave in the dry river bed of the Kamo river, when he invited the tea-masters and their pupils from all over the country to bring their choicest bowls and utensils to a great outdoor tea-ceremony, and went round the four hundred guests, from group to group, talking to them, and admiring and comparing the treasures they had brought with them. Inimical as I am, myself, to 'parties' of more than six or eight persons, how much I would have loved to attend both, or either of these entertainments! Kyoto is, indeed, a world of wonders, big and small. There is, even to this day, a 'doll temple' where dolls are mended, and a 'fan temple' where fans are repaired and sold.

BOOK
SEVEN

'I came sad home':
Disintegration of places,
persons, things

The phrase which forms the title for this chapter is from a letter of a dear friend, a Spaniard, on parting from my wife and myself after a holiday spent in Tuscany in a house, and under circumstances never likely to be repeated, during the lovely September and October of 1969. The mere repetition of the five syllables of which the name of the house is composed bringing back pitiful memories of persons dead and gone, and of the changes that can and do occur in them during long illness when a lifetime, or what one had thought to be a lifetime of affection and long loyalties, can succumb under pressure of failing faculties and infirmity to other and alien influences. But so it is; and I must try only to remember the cypress trees, the headless and broken statues, and the slow tread of the pairs of white oxen pulling the tumbrils of ripe grapes to the wine press. And forget the rest. Not that it is easy, after friendship with the family of *contadini* who live there dating back to 1909, for more than sixty years, and to four, now even five generations of this same family – if with long intermissions due to other, if similar influences of like origin – but it all ends, as with so much else, in sadness.

Having been disappointed, even cheated of the one thing, one might have thought to have found the other in Rome despite the narrow pavements, the overlarge population, and incessant roar of motors. The most splendid sight of the Renaissance city being the interior court and upper passages or corridors of the Palazzo Farnese, the work, surely, though it be disputed, of a giant hand, that of Michelangelo, and a sight nearly to put all the rest of interior architecture to shame. This is static splendour, incomparable in scale, of a frugal, sometime frowning mind, where Bernini's elliptical colonnades to St Peter's, of four rows of Doric columns of travertine, are the work of an easier, more flowing, more acquiescent, in short, less troubled mind. For the rest, remembering Rome, its ancient remains apart, as preeminently the city of façades, I now thought those architectural frontispieces less inventive and imaginative than its assembly or array of domes which are no less than the predominant feature in any view of the city, whether from far or near. Ignoring the most conspicuous of which, and the multitude of others, it being not possible to overlook the pair of domed churches that stand next to each other beside Trajan's Column. I have never entered either church, but have admired time and again their entire harmony with the Roman triumphal column of fifteen centuries before. And a little further back, just across the road – but what a road! It is the broad avenue or boulevard driven through the ruins to display the temples and *fori* of the Caesars – is another domed church no less in keeping with its situation. These are everyday, if lesser things that remain in mind after a stay in Rome.*

But, even while I am writing, this whole episode and everything connected with it, falls to dust. It is impossible to visualize, or even think of anything at all that does not turn sour and leave a bad taste in the mouth and in the mind. Every human relationship lies in dust and ashes. There is no reliance in anything at all, human, or even animal. It has all failed and is hopeless. There is nothing left to rest one's mind upon. But neither is the damage done by night repaired by day. The dreadful hours between three and six have worked their worst. The truth has fallen, dropped from everything. Human, even animal affections are all perished. Spiritually, they move around and leave behind them but the bat-like ammoniac aftermath of themselves, as do musk-oxen, civet-deer, of all shades of horrible animal intimacy from fox to skunk; and in night hopelessness and torment I turn from persons to things, only to find them emptier still.

Where to turn next? But even out of the emptiness my spirits are rising, and I embark in the darkness upon a pre-dawn or pre-auroral tour of Le Nôtre parks and gardens, most of which can be reconstructed in the mind's eye from engravings; and think of the avenues, the fountains and cascades, the water organs and *buffets d'eaux*, and the parterres of cut box and coloured pebbles. Such were the old French gardens; though I would sooner have seen them when those same green barricades and tunnels were not new, but already full grown – avenues, no less than Roman roads being difficult to obliterate and be rid of. But the old fashioned, stilted choreography, as never that of Petipa himself, palls upon one. For it is very near to that, this green architecture of parterres and clipped trees.

The shallow, attenuated façade of the château of Versailles seems about to collapse from both ends and fall in upon itself like a house of cards. The meanness of the entrance court disappoints and oppresses. How could *Le Roi Soleil* have his bedroom looking towards Paris at so low an elevation, with no external magnificence and no sense of scale? This is what is lacking in the French taste. On longer reflection through the darkened hours nothing but the double flights of steps, the masterpiece of Jules-Hardouin Mansart, leading down over his Orangerie to the *pièce d'eau des Suisses* has life and movement. The rest is static; and more particularly the terrace that is like a broad platform immediately in front of the château.

* Such as the marvellous play of light and shade, particularly by night, on the pillars and shadowy recessions of Rainaldi's façade to Santa Maria in Campitelli, and the three or four façades of churches by the painter-architect Pietro da Cortona, especially his hemi-cycle-portico'd and winged frontispiece to Santa Maria della Pace, at back of the Piazza Navona. In the city of façades this may be the most beautiful and imaginative of all.

And the garden statues? Their precision, even machine-finish altogether lacks the poetry of the Italian garden sculpture. How could one compare the Bassin de Latone with its gilded lizards, frogs, and tortoises spouting water to the fauncaryatids of Caprarola on the terrace looking towards Soracte! Or the inchoate and mixed mythology of the Bassin de Neptune, 'statues of Neptune and Amphitrite by the elder Adam, of a dragon bearing a cupid by Girardon, of the Ocean by Lemoyne, and of Proteus guarding the flocks of Neptune by Bouchardon', all afloat in shallow water like toys in a child's bath, to the Isolotto of the Boboli Garden with its capricorn-crown'd pilasters that guard the causeway leading to that marble island, with its pots of lemon trees round the circle of the balustrade, and statue of Oceanus in the middle in heroic pose, as in Giovanni da Bologna's other fountain of Neptune in the centre of the town square!* The comparison is impossible; and the only feature in the park and gardens of Versailles that is in scale with itself is the cruciform Grand Canal which is a mile long and must be some sixty to seventy yards wide;† to be the more appreciated in winter when the accompanying avenues are leafless and the static choreography of Le Nôtre's parterres and bosquets distant and no longer able to impose itself and dominate all that is in sight. In conclusion, despite the classical theme of its sculptures there is certainly nothing pagan about the gardens and avenues of Versailles.

But this is something that the Italians achieved at times, perhaps in relief to have escaped for a little from the rigours and reminders of religion. Nowhere more so than in the gardens of Caprarola and of Villa Lante. The pagan sensation is overpowering in both gardens.

It could have been on climbing to the terrace of the upper casino at Caprarola, during her stay there, that Queen Christina of Sweden 'made the strange comment, "I dare not speak the name of Jesus lest I break the spell." '‡ And indeed the pagan world could vanish on the lily-scented evening to a flash of lightning and a crack of thunder, with nothing further happening than a gentle rain blowing in from the Ciminian hills. To be back again in the next moment until the spell once more is broken.

The gardens of Caprarola and of Villa Lante are a world of their own, with but changeling-sisters in enchantment, the Kokedera or 'Moss-Garden', aforementioned, and their part-equivalent in music, work of a sixteen-year-old genius, never further fulfilled, and written, oddly, in 1826, a year of the domed and howdah'd Pavilion, the Chain Pier, and the stucco squares and terraces lying open to the salt sea. In this music, while the elves dance in the moonlight of *A Midsummer Night's Dream*, there sound not once but twice, those two curious notes of warning, in comment that all may vanish. What a stroke of inspired genius, if

* In the Piazza del Nettuno at Bologna.
† The only true comparison is with the canals or moats of Angkor Wat that surpass even the waters of Versailles in scale; and of the two Angkor Wat is incomparably the greater, because more mysterious work of art.
‡ Information from Miss Georgina Masson who quotes it in her *Italian Gardens*, London 1951; *cf.* also, her biography of Queen Christina of Sweden, 1896.

ever there were one! And what exactly do they mean? The youthful Felix
Mendelssohn may not have known, himself. But they warn; they give warning,
that it is going, going, gone. They seem to say, 'And, then?' And again, that
second time, 'And then?' The elves, the lily-proffering children, proffering,
even forcing their bunches of lilies-of-the-woods into our hands, are gone. And
to the same mysterious syllables, the faun-caryatids of Caprarola, with the smile
still upon their saturnine lips, would fall from their pedestals in dust and
fragments.

II

But now the disintegration of ideals sets in again. How typical it is of all that is
worst in the temperament of the Italians that they should have been great painters,
Illusionists, ever, and presenting the picture of things as they have never been
and never could be! Incapable of facing the truth, and past masters of improba-
bility! How can one doubt that the Christian religion stifled the painters of Italy
as much as it inspired them! The Church may have been the greatest patron of
the arts but it was, as well, their tyrant and dictator. It being the body general of
all the saints that smothered, first the Eastern, then the Western Church. The
oppressive catalogue of martyrs, and the mere monotony of so much Mario-
latry, affording themes in perpetuity but only yielding full results in the case of a
naïf or innocent like Fra Angelico who would be categorized, now, as simple
minded, if with all the simplicity of genius; while there were other painters who
could so enlarge upon their theme that the appurtenances and the exterior, even
extraneous detail grew to be more important than the theme itself.

Fantastic and meticulously rendered buildings of no direct import to the
subject, even the shadows on the walls of propped-open shutters in the Adriatic
sunlight, garlands of fruit as for a harvest festival, but tied together with bands of
linen, the stray pear or apple, here or there, on floor or window ledge, the irrele-
vant child spectators in pictures by Crivelli; paintings of *The Agony in the
Garden* by Mantegna and by Giovanni Bellini, both of them in the National
Gallery in London, the latter being painted in rivalry or emulation of the former,
and the real motive in either case being to depict the light of early morning upon
the hills and clouds; Paolo Veronese's elevation of the actors in the sacred drama,
however improbably, into personages clothed in silks and satins, with attendant
dwarfs, monkeys, horses, pages, greyhounds, Negro servants, halberdiers and
musicians! It is the rendering of the flowers, even the weeds in a painting by
Carpaccio or by Cosimo Tura, that hold the attention and stay in memory. And
the main altar-painting once achieved, the delight of the earlier masters was the
little subjects forming the *predelle*, which could be termed their parachute or
safety line of descent to where they could divert themselves, and perchance for-
get the sacred boundaries and limitations.

Painters of the Italian Seicento, on the other hand, we have to think of as
trained to embark upon a subject much as though they were opera composers
called upon to provide a solo, or trio, on occasion, even a quartet or quintet of

voices to meet a given situation. Painters with the supreme competence of Guercino, Luca Giordano, Solimena, or some fifteen or twenty others of whom the number increases as they are more studied, painted on cupola, or wall, or canvas, as though for the *stagione*, the winter opera season at the San Carlo or Fenice, and could work to any story or sentiment they were given to express without unnecessary redundancy of detail, or any of that irrelevance which makes the poetry of earlier painting. It was all a matter of competence and continual practice; and as to their degree of interest and involvement it may be doubted if they were often 'carried away' by the subject they were engaged upon. How uninspiring was their anthology or catalogue of martyrdoms and miracles! Classical mythology, by contrast, stale as it may have become in the course of ages, had at least its origins and its roots in poetry. Ten centuries, more or less, was the length of time it lasted, and the inventiveness of a celibate clergy during double that length of time is not likely to have surpassed the creations of the Hellenes who were the first poets.

Is there any serious lover of works of art who is not disappointed by Michelangelo's fresco'd wall and ceiling at the Sistine Chapel? Are these really the greatest works of art of the Western world? His *terribilità*, and use of quasi-orchestral forces in Richard Strauss's *Heldenleben*, *Tod und Verklärung* scale, as if works of art became great works of art in ratio to their size and violence! But neither can it be said that, architecturally, the Sagrestia Nuova at Florence, where are the Medici tombs, is successful. Is there not too strong an emphasis on the pilasters, the canopies and cornices, which same faults of overstatement are glaringly conspicuous in his portico and staircase hall to the Biblioteca Laurenziana? Contrast to this the peace and calm of the Cappella Pazzi! There is no touch of the frowning brow, the *furioso*, in that marvellous, spatial calm of Brunelleschi. But, then, the Cappella Pazzi is one of the 'beautiful' works of the Early Florentine Renaissance, more than a hundred years before the working life of Michelangelo, and lyrical beauty had not at that time given way to suggestions of forcefulness and over-exaggeration. There are the same blemishes of inward struggle and exasperation, but without the breathtaking beauties and emotional progressions of Beethoven, to be observed in Michelangelo, there being many points of temperamental identity between the two men; and of the two it could not be denied that despite the appalling handicap of his deafness, his shorter life – he died more than thirty years younger than Michelangelo – and circumstances, not more, but that much less propitious in the instance of Beethoven, he was in spite of everything the more successful in the works of art he created. With Michelangelo there are his failures to point to; and in the case of Beethoven a number of trivia, but, at the least, he never over-reached himself, nor did he leave so many works unfinished. The very ubiquity of the Italians was – for now, decidedly, it is past and over – their aesthetic downfall. They were everywhere – and willing to undertake anything and too often, everything. The over-finish is symptom of their decline; from the intarsia of a Milanese cabinet, or the elaboration of a suit of Milanese armour, down to the Victor-Emmanuel monument in Rome, or the statues in white Carrara marble in the Campo Santo at Genoa.

But there is so much more to think of and try to remember. And not only in Italy. The Cairene mosques of Sultan Qualaun, of Qait Bey, El Mu'aiyad, El Mardani, Sultan Hassan, and Sultan Barquq; the thurifer or incense-shedding, incense-spreading – in the look of them, their pierced apertures and openings – minarets of the Mamelukes! Under Saladin (1169–93), and for two centuries after him, when Cairo was more, not less civilized than London or Paris of the day. No town of mediaeval Europe has churches or other buildings of a comparable grandeur and beauty of design. What reason is there to think that had the Moors under Abderahman defeated Charles Martel at the battle of Tours in AD 732 – only a hundred years after the Hegira, which is not the least astonishing part of it – and most of Europe become Muslim in respect of that, which could have happened, there would not have ensued a civilization as fine, however different, as that which was to produce the Frankish Reims or Chartres!

On the second occasion when Europe could have fallen – and it does not need much prescience to know whence and by whom the next opportunity will come – when the Turkish hordes besieged Vienna in 1683 and their raiding parties reached nearly to Munich, the Turks, who in the sixteenth century had been the greatest military power in either Europe or Asia, were still dangerous in point of savagery but in their decadence and nearing the burlesque, basso turqueries of *Die Entführung* and *L'Italiana in Algeri*, and the turbans of the 'Tulip Reign'.* Having lapsed in their history from the silken, satrap luxuries of Solyman and Roxelana to tiled turbehs (tomb chambers) and kiosques of china. From, too, the mosques of Sinan (b. 1489), their great architect, which show like giant kettledrums on and below the skyline of Stamboul seen from the Bosphorus and Golden Horn. Here, again, as at Cairo, there are five or six of the chief of them, that of Suleimaniyeh, the mosque of Solyman the Magnificent, standing upon the third hill of this, the second Rome; of Bayazit below that on the same hill; of Mohammed the Conqueror, or the Fetiyeh, upon the fourth hill; of Sultan Selim upon the fifth hill; of Shahzadeh, one of the most perfect of them all, as I remember it, shell-like in purity of form; and the Mosque of Yeni Cami low down by the Galata bridge, with its dome and minarets coming up out of the smoke of the modern town. What a site for a world capital, with all of Asia and Europe opening before you along the narrow waters! Some half-dozen of the Imperial mosques of Istanbul to tally with a like number of mosques that I have named in Cairo!

Then, too, the half-dozen medersas (sacred colleges) of Fez, with their interior courts, ceilings of inlaid cedar wood, and honeycomb'd stalactite arches! Are not these as beautiful, even in their monotony, as anything in Rome or Venice? How lovely are their very names, Medersas Attarine, Bou Inania, Cherratine, Seffarine, Sahriz, and Mesbahia! How can one ever forget that first moment of entering their cedarn, stalactitic gloom from the sun-striped, torpid street outside! Is not the general, overall impression that of a mediaeval civilization as strong there as in the two Italian cities named? The Muslims to whom the portrayal of human, or even animal forms was forbidden, seem to have been

* The 'Tulip Sultan' was Achmet III (1703–50).

content with their stucco'd or tiled intricacies and abstractions. But was it more, or was it less restricting for them, to have to invent for themselves, the elements, not to say the alphabet, of abstract ornament? There being no direct reference or representation of what they were working for except, maybe, an evocation to the prophet in a stucco arabesque, or the cedar beam of a ceiling. Endlessly repetitive ornament being, also, incidentally, the Semitic element in flamenco song. The truth being that the more gifted and intelligent races who embraced Islam found inspiration, but after a generation or two exhausted it and let it lapse. Indeed, in its different forms it was static and not capable of further development. What Islam produced was marvellous enough and perfect in its way; the Mezquita of Córdoba and the Alhambra of Granada; domes, one might say, in their clones and cultivars, inlaid war-helms, ribbed canteloup or netted melon of the Tombs of the Caliphs outside Cairo, and again, there, of Qait Bey and Sultan Barquq; or blue domes, more feminine and mamillary in shape, of Samarkand, Meshed, and Isfahan; the swan-like Taj Mahal; and stalactitic vaults and interior cool of the Andalusian Moors.

In contrast, Venice, the incomparable treasure of its paintings apart, has St Mark's which is unique and beyond compare, but only the mediaeval churches of the Franciscan and Dominican monks, of the Frari and Santi Giovanni e Paolo, on a scale to contrast with the mosques of Cairo and of Istanbul. Rome of the Middle Ages, its early basilicas not in discussion, has its trio of mediaeval splendours, Santa Maria del Popolo, Santa Maria sopra Minerva (of Bernini's elephant obelisk in the square outside), and Santa Maria in Aracoeli, these three, and in fact no more than these, while Florence, looked down on from the Piazza Michelangelo in that world-famous view, has the Duomo – which is dull, indeed, within – and once more the Franciscan and Dominican churches of Santa Croce and Santa Maria Novella, and we might add to these the earlier San Miniato on the hill above where we are standing, looking down on the city across the river Arno. No one of these cities, Venice, Rome, or Florence, has buildings of the Middle Ages finer than the best of Cairo, or other Muslim cities.

I do not believe that anyone interested in such things can fail to be disillusioned by the aforementioned pairs of great churches in Venice and in Florence. In the latter city there is the undisputed fact that the marble façade of Santa Croce is mid-nineteenth-century from a design 'said to be by Cronaca' and 'at the expense of a Mr Francis Sloane' – the façade of the Duomo, no less, being by an architectural nonentity Emilio de Fabris (1875–87), which rather impairs the validity of both exteriors – that of Santa Maria Novella, at least, being genuine fourteenth-century work, yet on an aesthetic par with its marble companions. The plain truth being that the Italian temperament was not suited to this play of polychrome marble, hence the incongruities and discrepancies of Tuscan Gothic. In Venice, in contradiction, they are great brick churches, wonderful indeed in their contents, their tombs and paintings, but uncompromisingly, boringly brick, with little trouble taken as to the firing or colour of the brick, and not comparable to the rose-petal interior of the great church at Delft, or such Northern marvels of their sort as the brick Marien-Kirche of Lübeck, or I would imagine, in *absentia*, not having seen it, the Marien-Kirche at Danzig. Personally, their contents apart, I would give all four churches, two in Venice, two in Florence, for the Grande Mosquée or Mosque of the Ommayads at Damascus. But, then, its Caliphs were rulers of half the known world as far as distant Córdoba in Spain.

The ratio is no different in the rest of Europe. There are the three Nuremberg churches of the Middle Ages, the Lorenz-Kirche, the Liebfrauen-Kirche, and St Sebaldus, which are for those persons who can get pleasure from the German Gothic, the spiky intricacies of which never seem far removed in spirit from the instruments of the torture-chamber. Moreover, the churches of Nuremberg are in that unpleasant medium, pink sandstone. Cities more lastingly and unbrokenly mediaeval in content, Siena or Toledo, can be the project and occupation of three or four days, no more; the one for the opportunity of seeing paintings by Matteo da Giovanni, Sano di Pietro, or others of the Sienese school, displayed to more advantage in their natural environment than in the cold seclusion of the museum; the other city for the few pictures by El Greco suffered to remain *in situ* – and I would say they are less in number than when I first went round the churches of Toledo looking for paintings by El Greco which was in the spring of 1919, directly the war was over – and for the reward of finding for oneself *artesonado* ceilings and fragments of Mozarabic or Mudéjar workmanship in church, or former mosque or synagogue, in this polyglot city of Castilians, Moors, and Jews.

III

But there is the disintegration of persons as well as of places. Which happens, and is happening all the time. All said and done, will human beings never succeed in leading civilized lives in controlled numbers for that is essential, but without religion, knowing that the godhead is in themselves for good or evil? But it is lost – no doubt of that – lost this time again, and will not recur till very much more has happened. All, or most of which, will be to our detriment and destruction, and perhaps could have been avoided, but given sentiments and qualities that are unattainable as things are at present. So that it was unlikely, and perhaps out of question, being better in the planning and in the possibility than in the realization. And as it could be, and has so nearly been, the taste and the flavour of it still remain. Of times when it all but happened which amount to a few weeks, no more, in a lifetime. Or has occurred in a country for some few years on end, only realized when old men recall their youth for it may have seemed in its day only to be hard and unremitting work. And in fact is ever the result of that and not of inspiration. Though there may have been times when it flowed effortlessly, but after deep application and unconscious thinking, if coming apparently for no reason. For that is how it can arrive, and even quicker than that depart and be gone.

In the course of living one loses nearly all one's ideals and illusions. In any case, I am no longer interested in myself, or in my own reactions, and only want to find the key to certain mysteries while there is still time. The world has been beautiful enough in all conscience, but it is the mess that has been made of it by human beings! Only to think of one or two instances on this glorious June evening while the immortal birds are singing! How is it conceivable that they should do such fearful things, should wreak such frightful vengeance on each other!

There is the Epilogue to *War and Peace* in which Tolstoy seems intent on unmasking and destroying the characters whom he had created and made use of in his masterpiece. Seven years have passed, and in the hundred pages of the Epilogue an unendurable flatness has set in. It is even difficult to persevere to the last page. Natasha is married with the three daughters and the son she longed for – the accumulation of children and cessation of all other activity is in itself depressing – as though the beauty and romance in young women is only devoted to the one end – marriage – and then it all stops and is over, and never comes again.

Natasha 'has filled out and grown broader ... her face had lost the ever flashing, eager light ... very seldom now was the old fire kindled'. All this in only seven years of marriage. And after only fifty of the hundred pages of his Epilogue conversation has run out and his characters have no more to say. Tolstoy, it may be added, had a worsening, pejorative view of the worth and spiritual value, if any, of all works of art, which is made evident in his very funny, if 'Philistine' account of the opera-ballet in *War and Peace*; with the reprobate, but handsome Dolohov, 'leaning back against the orchestra rail in a Persian dress, his curly hair brushed up into an enormous shock,' standing in full view of the audience, never taking his eyes off the Rostovs' box where Natasha was sitting. And of course, Tolstoy being Tolstoy, there is appreciative, if feignedly disapproving mention of 'bare arms and shoulders', 'her slender arm bare to above the elbow', 'the half-naked women in the boxes', and 'all the women with precious jewels on their bare flesh'. While, of music itself, without the adventitious aid of singers and dancers, and an audience of rank and fashion, Tolstoy thought little better, as witness *The Kreutzer Sonata*. Nor is it much different in the ending of *Anna Karenina*. In the last fifty pages, forming practically an Epilogue, the tremendous force of the novel has run out, culminating in the heroine throwing herself under the train; and after that, all, as if on purpose, is flat and lifeless. Tolstoy is no longer interested. Vronsky, the hero-reprobate, we part from in the train on his way to Serbia, 'taking a squadron at his own expense' to the Russo-Turkish war of 1877, and smitten with appalling, agonizing toothache. And that is the last we hear of him. He is unimportant and no longer matters.

In our lifetime there have been holocausts and hecatombs; but though these have been upon a scale never before achieved or perpetrated, they have not been in the name of religion, or in the name, at least, of any god. Does it make them better, or worse, than what has been before? I do not know. I only know that it is no good to call upon the name of god. Because there is none. Or perhaps it is only that this is not the right name for it. Certainly Hitler and Stalin, but not Napoleon, were evil as any false god could be. But if the past repeats itself, the coming age has its precursors, too. For example, the Anabaptist regime in Münster. The Anabaptists under their three 'Kings', John of Leyden 'the Tailor

King', Krechting, and Knipperdollinck, had seized this town of gabled and half-timber'd houses in 1534, and held it for two years. Fanatics from Holland, Friesland, and Westphalia flocked to this New Jerusalem mentioned in the prophecies. They were a revolutionary sect, in other respects, too, in advance of their time, who believed in adult baptism, proclaimed a community of goods and of women, and attacked all constituted authority as the only means of rooting out evil from the earth. The breath of anarchy was in the air, just then, – as now – for witness the Spanish Comuneros of 1519–20. But the Anabaptists of Münster were in a sense precursors of the French Commune of 1871 and of the six hundred Communards who 'perished to a man' in the burning of the Hotel de Ville in Paris, though there was this difference that the French Commune had no background of religion, and it may be thought doubtful if Frenchmen would have thought it worth the trouble to legalize polygamy. Yet the Anabaptists, as suggested, were ahead of their day and would be likely to recognize their kindred sprawled round the statue of Eros, 'the messenger of love', in Piccadilly Circus during 1970; or at the Fontana di Trevi, the Piazza Navona, or on the staircase of the Piazza di Spagna, their trio of gathering places and vantage points in Rome.

And the fate of the three Anabaptist 'Kings' of Münster after law and order were restored? As to Knipperdollinck, most hated of the three, the executioners, we are told, first enclosed the 'King' in a collar of iron and bound him to a stake; whereupon they seized glowing pincers and 'fettled' him on all fleshy and other parts of his body for upwards of an hour. Knipperdollinck sought to strangle himself with the collar that bound him to the stake, seeing which, the executioner tied his head fast to the stake with a cord that passed through his teeth. Finally, he and the other Anabaptist 'Kings' had their tongues torn out by the roots, and they were pierced to the heart with a dagger. Their bodies being, then, fixed upright in iron cages and suspended from the tower of St Lambert's church in Münster.

And there, on the tower of the Lamberti-Kirche, true to national instinct and tradition, and despite of the tower having been 'rebuilt by Hertal in 1887–98', the three iron cages in which the bodies of John of Leyden the 'Tailor King', of Krechting, and of Knipperdollinck were hung in 1536 – the cages, but not, for a wonder, the remains of their bodies or skeletons – can still be seen. I have, myself, seen the cage or cages high up on the church tower. Whether the cages still hang there, or were brought down by aerial bombardment, I do not know.* Knipperdollinck, which is a name of the same furious obscurity as Schickelgruber! Now there is nothing left of the latter, and much greater monster; not even an iron cage for his skeleton, but only his problematical false teeth or dentures, or what is left of them, in an old cigar-box in the drawer of a desk somewhere in Russia, most probably within the Kremlin.

Doubtless, Knipperdollinck and his companions were monsters of their kind. But if the reader can stomach another paragraph of horror, but in the heroic vein, let us remember the persecution under Louis XIV of the Camisards or Protestants of the Cevennes! The body of Roland, one of their leaders, killed in combat in

* The three iron cages are still there (1970).

1704 and his body dragged at the tail of a cart to Nîmes, consumed on a fire, his ashes thrown to the winds, and his five companions who were captured with him broken alive on the wheel round his funeral pyre. This was in the Place de Boncairie at Nîmes. Or the fate of two more of their leaders, Catinat and Ravanel. They first suffered the torture of 'the bones' (said to be the most exquisite of all tortures) – the victim is laid in a wooden, coffin-like box with holes in it through which long poles or spikes are hammered in to break the leg-bones. While this fiend-like punishment was going on, the scaffold and the pile of faggots were raised to conclude the scene, but Baville, the appalling and monstrous judge in charge, concluded it was too late to finish with the victims that night, so with their bones partly crushed they were taken back to their cells. At ten o'clock next morning an iron chain was fastened round the necks of Catinat and Ravanel, and so they were bound to the stake, and to each other, back to back in chairs, and burnt alive, while their comrades, Jonquet and Villas, were broken on the wheel and then burnt.*

What happened next? As always, nothing, nothing. There is no god, and never has been god. It is all illusion. The 'god' is mortal and is in ourselves. There is no more to happen to the dead. One has only to see a dead sparrow to know that it is dead. Or a dead bird fallen from the nest. Another life, it has been said before, is but the sweet a mother puts into her child's mouth to make it sleep.

---

* Was it any better here in England? The brothers Robert and William Kett, leaders of the 'Norfolk Rising' of 1549, were hung alive, in chains; William from the steeple of Wymondham, his birthplace, and Robert Kett from the walls of Norwich Castle, 'until his body completely disintegrated from corruption'. *cf. The Companion Guide to East Anglia*, by John Seymour, London 1970, pp. 181–5.

'For want of the Golden City'

> *The wind, the wind, the wind blows high*
> *The snow is falling from the sky*
> *Maisie Drummond says she'll die*
> *For want of the Golden City**

I

What next? And, then? And, then? What happens next, in the instance nearest to me, has been the conspiracy of silence. The taboo upon mentioning her name who had been so famous. And while she was 'swept under the carpet', those who had most praised her looked the other way. Another time it will happen again more quickly and easily still, because the prospective victim neither minds nor cares, and was never the recipient of adulation.

'And, then? And, then?' What happens? No one knows. So why worry? And, indeed, no one really cares. 'If R.B. were to walk into this room now, one wouldn't know what to say to him.' This said, sitting at supper after an evening at the opera, of a friend who died during the Second World War; who was torpedoed somewhere off the coast of Morocco in 1942 or 1943, nearly thirty years ago. Of course it would not be the same thing had one just not seen him for some reason or other during all that time. He would know something, at least, of what had been going on. He would not have 'missed out' on absolutely everything. When I think, too, that I had school friends, quite a few of them, but two in particular, who were killed nearly thirty years before that! How curious, indeed, had one been able to introduce one, or both of them, to each other! Were they to meet in the form of their own ghosts!

There have never been holocausts on this scale in all our history. In the Peninsular and Crimean Wars there was no comparable slaughter or culling of the young. No one, who did not want to, got himself involved in those. Yet, two of my four great-grandfathers fought in Portugal and Spain. They were of the sort, presumably, of those who were killed in our two wars. But this was not demanded of them and they survived. They were not wanted. Or for some other reason which could be no more than chance. The 'chance' to get yourself killed in peace time in a motor-race, or win the football pool. A chance either way, in fact. But the tags had lead upon the ends of them in both World Wars. The dice were heavily 'loaded', and it could be said the 'chips' were down. Six weeks, no more than that, was the expectation of life for a 'young officer'. So it was said, whether truly or not, I know not. What a world to be born into, and removed from so suddenly!

* A children's song admired by the scholar and poet, Arthur Waley.

And now R.B. appears in the doorway facing me and catches my eye, knowing me at once of course. With nothing, evidently, no time lapse between this and our last meeting. As though it had been yesterday, which it most certainly was, only more so. Still argumentative, I could see, but I believe thinking that nothing much had happened to him. That he had been concussed, or stunned, and had just 'come round.' 'Passed out for a moment', and no more than that. And of course just its utter impossibility made it easy to begin talking to him. Not that much difference in the rest of us except that we are all that much older, which I can see him beginning to realize and take in. Of course there are friends to ask for news of, and so on. And I remind him of our meeting when he had just come back from Mount Athos, and from seeing the churches in Salonica, at the older and much nicer, then, Grande Bretagne at Athens, where I remember the bullet-headed, 'cannon-fodder' German or Swiss manager and the head waiter, and our diurnal inquiry as to whether wine had come in from Samos or Santorin. And so it goes on, agreeably enough.

But this other who has been dead much longer; who was killed, in fact, on 17 October 1915, shortly after his nineteenth birthday. What was one to say to him? My brother, who was in the regiment, but not at school with him, as I was, died in 1969. He has two sisters living. His nephews and nieces would mean little to him. He was dead before most of them were born. There is not much to say to him after so long an absence. But he always had a quick eye, and now I believe he began to notice something about our clothes. But it is as though he came into the room holding his own skull in his hand. By which I mean that the signs of time passing were only too evident in nearly everything.

And now it is in the restaurant. In the restaurant looking down Charlotte Street, which is still a restaurant but it has changed its character, as no wonder in so long a time. The perspective of houses is much the same, and the slight muddle and difficulty in coming in at the door. Where we all dined together, two nights running, in the early days of August of that year (1915), my having escaped for the first time, in the sense of having gone down to stay at *The Complete Angler* in Marlow, near where my brother was encamped with the regiment, for a couple of nights after the summer holiday had begun, until recalled home by a telegram from my father. How well I remember on both mornings, walking on the hills in the August heat, wondering if I would be able to write poetry when I was older! An ambition that has been fulfilled, and the poems written. But, then, what is poetry? All I know is, that I am not to blame.

The mornings were spent, thus; or in the hotel garden at Marlow thinking and listening to the weir. And on both evenings we went to London. To the restaurant which, did one wish it, could have its fill of ghosts. The resort of painters; with Walter Sickert, whom I knew so well: with whom my brother and I used to breakfast in his studio in Fitzroy Street, and he dined with us in Swan Walk and in Carlyle Square. And so many others sitting at the tables, all dead now. Nina Hamnett, who was to give me the letter to Modigliani when I came out of the Army and went to Paris in February or March of 1919, and then for the first time to Spain. The genius manqué who wrote *The Apes of God*, a tome the size of a telephone book, time-bomb'd to explode in 1926, and meant to kill, but that is nearly fifty years ago, and it failed. Nearly all those portrayed in it are dead, now, it is true, but from natural causes. Augustus John, come all the way across London from Mallord Street in Chelsea, and who had been a draughtsman and painter of great promise till within a year or two of 1915 – he died in 1961 – was there, and had a kind of aura and a beard-blown, if blue-eyed Gypsy arrogance which was peculiar to him.

All of these, and others, I was to know later. Only a year or two after this, in 1917 and 1918, but it seemed much longer than that. On those two evenings I am writing of, two young girls, Nancy Cunard and Iris Tree, both of them poets, and to both or either of whom I was too shy and nervous to speak, were at our table. Both were young and beautiful, and both wrote poems which made it doubly difficult. But now this feeling and first intimation of poetry, and of other things to come, takes entire possession and I can remember nothing more. I am no longer in the friend's flat where we were having supper after the opera only two or three weeks ago in this June or July of 1970. I can only think of those two August evenings, fifty, no! it is fifty-five summers ago – and of that feeling of imminence; of everyone leaving school and going into the Army, or being in it already and in likelihood of being, at best, wounded, or else killed.

I can remember no more in detail, but only the atmosphere of the time, which was, distinctly, that of Russians being the artists and innovators. I had been two years before this, in the summer of 1913, to Drury Lane to hear Chaliapin in Mussorgsky's *Khovantchina*. I can still hear in memory the blaring and snarling of his brass instruments, of which with Berlioz he was the supreme master. And in that, or the following year, just before the War began, I heard Stravinsky's *l'Oiseau du Feu*. Strange indeed, that Stravinsky should at the time of writing, in the summer of 1970, be still alive! I had seen Nijinsky dance in this and in *Spectre de la Rose* on the same evening.

I think that owing to this predominance of Russian music in London, thanks to Sir Thomas Beecham and his father, and to early reading of the novels of Tolstoy and Dostoievsky, there was a feeling that a great art movement was in progress in Russia. Whatever could have been, this was all shattered within three or four years and its protagonists had vanished, or were homeless refugees. The War had been on for a full year by the autumn of 1915, the Russians had already suffered enormous losses, but this feeling still persisted and persuaded one to look for poetry and romance in the nearest spiritual territory to Moscow, or Kiev, or Kazan, which would be in the mean houses of Whitechapel or the Mile End Road. Might it not be that, as in the last named of the Russian cities, there could be, if not a Kremlin, at least, a Tartar quarter and a Kitaigorod or China Town! And because of the drama and the music of *Petrouchka* one had an affection for circuses and fair grounds, and preferred the music of steam-organs to the symphonies of Elgar. This was tinged again with early reading of Rimbaud's *Les Illuminations* which I certainly knew by 1917, if not by 1915; and indeed in June 1918 when *The People's Palace*, my first book of poems, was published, only a week after *Clown's Houses* which was my sister's second book. Aldous Huxley meeting me for the first time, flattered me, needlessly, by asking if I was not 'le Rimbaud de nos jours', an honour and an appellation to which my talents, such as they are, could never possibly have aspired.

The sound of a barrel-organ in those days was a transmutation of the London air into poetry, and the churning of its metal tongue worked magic, even in mean streets. The *Eiffel Tower* with its steamy windows giving on to the long vista of Charlotte Street could have been made for barrel-organ music, which was certainly the case on one of those two evenings though I do not pretend to remember what were the tunes. Nevertheless in imagination I can hear it still, as distinctly as the waters, aforementioned, of the weir at Marlow; and now I know how 'old fashioned' would be the taxis, let alone the clothes and dresses of the time.

At a table near by was sitting a young woman, I suppose of twenty-three or so, with short 'bobbed', pale yellow hair. This was Carrington, known by her surname, according to the Slade School custom, and who was the first girl to wear her hair cut short. There was certainly an aura attaching to her, too, and one cannot but have every sympathy with the painter Mark Gertler, who loved her perhaps even at that time, and could not understand her devotion to the freakish and anything but kind-tongued Lytton Strachey who, as his biography proves, had something unpleasant to say about every one of his contemporaries in turn. The whole of life and of intellectual experience were for Strachey one long and high-pitched 'giggle'. It was in just this spirit that John Lennon and his fellow Beatles swarmed into Buckingham Palace to collect the decorations they had so inadvisedly been awarded. The two or three paintings that Carrington left behind her reveal her talent, and her personal touch shows in her letters. In her distinctive, yet classless appearance, she epitomized those few months or years of her own youth. A current in time which is captured and recorded, for those interested enough to seek it out, in Albert Rutherston's coloured drawings for an edition of Maeterlinck's *Blue Bird*, though the young woman featured in them was not Carrington but the wife of the painter.

After which we return to our lives and deaths. My school friend Yvo Charteris whom I never saw again after that evening, and in fact he was killed some eight or nine weeks later; and Robert Byron, a friend, though I was older than him, of my own generation and present at the first, but not the second, of these evocations of the lost and dead. It is but as though, in both cases, they got up and left the room and might, or might not, be back again in a moment. But it is all the contact we can have, and at that, a slight one; little more than a shape and a memory, and a few words to put into the dead person's lips; no more than, at most, a life-like mimicking or imitation. And they are gone, and it is over.

And the point, now, is how much would they mind? Would they, indeed, care about it in the very least? How much would they want to 'come back', to put it in a trite phrase? That depending upon how deeply we believe they have been here all the time, and have never been away. A belief which is beginning to wear a bit thin by now, to express it in the plainest language, because it must be perfectly obvious that they are gone beyond recall. We would not know what to say to them; still less would they know what to say to us. There is not the faintest hope under heaven or hell of meeting with them again. They are gone, gone. No longer there, or anywhere else at all. In the instance of being killed shortly 'after your nineteenth birthday' it is an irremediable disaster and worse, even, than dying at nine months, or nine years old. The other, drowned in the Second World War when thirty-seven or thirty-eight, was, at any rate, about twice his age. He had lived, and had time.

But even were there something, which we may be sure there is not, there is little likelihood they would wish to return from it. The dying may want to come back to us, as they are dying – and not all of those, at that – but not the dead. We are therefore missing something abstract, for there is no life in it, which does not miss us in reply. Which only makes it all the sadder. Which only lies there, for one cannot think of it as sitting or standing, for all eternity. And all the Indians, five hundred and fifty million of them, to date, including Pakistanis, to quote from last night's television programme? – and the Chinamen? Where will they be going? Or is there no meaning – perhaps there is not! – in mere numbers? The creator, if there is one, has to select among his creatures. And the only justice is that there is none.

But we must have our gods and they are human. Therefore not infallible, which is the humanity in them. Few, if any of them, are in power politics. Some may be humble indeed; though all told they outnumber those in the Ancient or the Hindu heavens. The godhead may descend in human form for a short time. The tragedy is its transience. Its shortness of tenure and, being human, its uncertainty. It comes and goes, and often does not return again. The god was in Van Gogh when he drew the cornfields of Saint-Rémy and made the painting of his old boots. Is there no limbo in which lovers are reunited and the murdered can ask questions of their murderers? The babes in the wood are back in the brambles and dead leaves; where they went hand-in-hand into the wood to play at 'Indians', lay huddled to each other in the cold and were turned to skeletons. At least no monstrous hand had throttled them, and they kept their innocence in the shallow grave.

To have been alive and sentient is the grand experience. When we think of the dead, and of that silence, deafness, dumbness, blindness, which cannot be far off, and comes ever nearer, remember only the fine hot days that they have missed! I thought of that when we drove past the war memorial in the village in Gloucestershire, some years ago, and read the names there. Impossible, then, not to remember the weir-waters and hanging woods at Marlow, the now dying or extinct voice of the barrel-organ, the sunset street and that sight of the young girl with the sad and strange history ahead of her. And the god comes down into one with a tingling of the skin, and while the past lives again in that moment I cannot move or stir. It is some kind of foretaste of the 'Golden City'.

II

It is a fine hot morning of cloudless sky, and this afternoon I shall sleep for thirty or forty minutes just out of the sun, moving my chair perhaps once or twice as the sun comes out again from behind a cloud. This is one thing they missed, perhaps, because they were hardly old enough to enjoy it; though, thinking again, I am sure this would not apply to Robert Byron. But, anyway, they have lost a lifetime, two lifetimes of this pleasure; and, also, its alternative or opposite which is to lie warm in bed on a winter night of full moon when it is so quiet you may think you can hear the frost outside. I shall never forget one such night this last winter when, on opening the front door to look out, two owls were calling to each other from some way away in the tall trees, or even from the elms half-way down the field. Then, again, with uncanny nearness out of the moonlight invisible, but out of the heart of moonlight, and its answer from farther away. An exaggerated, extraordinary performance, as of unearthly singers and lovers, moonlit and transcendental, and of theatrical, Italian schooling. And long after I had got into bed I could hear them calling to each other across the moonlight out of the tall trees.

It is the luxury of lying awake, or, still more, of awakening to this world of wonders and forgetting its sadness and horrors. But dead persons know of neither. No more than the coffin or urn is sentient; or than there is feeling in the shroud or winding-sheet. So that it is of no use to credit those with sensibilities they possess not. The only sensibility is in ourselves in thinking of them, and the living thought goes of course when we die ourselves and that is the end of that. The dead are all dead together, and it is our destiny as well. There is a consistency in this, that there is no use in thinking too much about it. Or I would be writing here with a skull on the table in front of me.

But all history is of the dead when they were living; while, of all artists in all the arts, it is their works which live, and in which they seek life or death. We can think of them, therefore, as being dead and not having to die; not having to face that ordeal of transition from something into nothing for a second time. If one could forget the miseries and think only of the splendours! But the two are inseparable and nearly related to each other, the existence of the one being in fact impossible without the other. It is the dust of the millions and millions of the poor. Palpable but invisible, and buried anywhere, or nowhere, which is not less impressive in bulk than the tunnelled tomb chambers of the Pharaohs hewn into the hills. To be interred in a man-made mound or tumulus with a four-horse wagon and even when found, the skeletons of its horses, as were the spangled chieftains of the steppes with how many slaves and women slain to keep you company, is of no more help than the rag-doll put into a dead child's hand. All such are mistaken in purpose, and but postpone the thinking and the knowledge.

The answers are self-obvious if we can but face them. There is nothing more in store for us. It is over, once and for all time. There is no more to come. Which is enough to make the poor break into the rich men's houses and destroy them. It is the last and permanent injustice, and one that cannot be condoned and forgiven. But there are too many sheep to graze the fields. The blessed emptiness is gone for ever. The end of the virgin soil has come. No longer, as I was told the other day of someone whose brother I knew well, can a man cross the Ocean, travel to railhead, buy himself a horse and saddle, and ride for two days until he found a piece of land he liked the look of. Then ride back to town and buy the land, come out to it next day, start to build himself a log cabin, and spend the winter in it, only going into town twice a month to buy food. And when winter was over have just money enough left to start life as a small farmer. What a change from a Derbyshire mining village; and from their house just inside the park gates at edge of the grime-darkened woods, with ironworks and collieries near by, but within sound on Sundays of the Salvation Army band! The days of virgin soil are over and can never come again.

In the literal sense, but it has other meanings. What keeps one young is curiosity and the longing for knowledge. In which sense the world of human beings is but in its beginnings. And the more one knows the more one is lost in wonder and astonishment. At the follies and cruelties but, also, at the miracles achieved, not only of creation but, as well, of incident. It was Dr Johnson who said, 'he who tires of London, tires of life itself'. Then, it was the horror of the modern world, preluded by Hogarth and illustrated in all its enormity by Cruickshank and by Gustave Doré, with the attendant satellite slums and 'rookeries' of the industrial North. But it will not be denied that the attractions of London as a modern city are fast fading and now dying if, always, with a city of seven million inhabitants there must be something left. Although in London there are places for the 'performing arts', there are no other arts visible, architecture least of all, which is something not true of New York where are the only good buildings of the modern world, and where you have at least the feeling of living in the last decades of the twentieth century for good or evil. They are, maybe, the only works of art of capitalism, more impressive, certainly, of rocket ascent and cliff-like fall, than the workaday triumphs of Socialist Realism. The assembly of sky-scrapers down at the end of Madison and Fifth Avenues must be how much more impressive than were ever the 'hanging gardens' of Babylon, prototype of New York in the ancient world. One can understand, both those many who would like to leave the city for ever because of its noise and the vertical horror of its walls of cement and glass, and the few who cannot separate themselves from this hive of human character, presented here on a polyglot scale never before attained in the history of human beings.

Not that character increases in ratio to the size of the population. In Vermeer's *View of Delft* there are but the few persons visible among so many buildings, but in this land where one cannot understand a word of the language but that has as much of personal individuality as had pre-revolutionary Russia, or that there is still to be found inland away from the coast in Spain, one knows what characters would come pouring from the gabled houses at the call to arms. The Haarlem of Frans Hals had not a monopoly of besash'd and genever'd arquebusiers. The tippled companies of marksmen or 'town archers' were common to every town in Holland, and in their more aqueous, sister climate to our own, strong drink had helped them to repulse the Spaniards. By now the danger was over, but they were still celebrating the victory. It is in such tight-knit communities that character flourishes and grows until they become stale and sterile, which probably strikes them in the second or third generation. This is the golden age of the Dutchmen, if it is not the 'Golden City'.

But it is difficult to deny that title to small towns where nearly every building is still beautiful, and where the population are all contemporary to each other, in the sense that a race of birds or animals are all alike and 'birds of a feather', as that could be said of rooks in a rookery or of herons in a heronry. And with the sort of person in mind who is likely to have written the poem at the head of this chapter we transfer to places which would be strange to her, but not entirely alien and beyond her range of sympathy. To the region, or Arcadia of rich farmers and peasants, that fulfils the stage direction for the first act of the old ballet, to wit, 'a square in a little town on the borders of Galicia', which is much the same as Shakespeare's 'Bohemia. A desert country near the sea', for the opening of *A Winter's Tale*. Or, in other words, it leaves a lot to be filled in by the imagination. One of the mysteries bearing on this Arcadia, imaginary or not, being that there is little evidence of its existence before the latter part of the eighteenth century, and that it reached to its height early in the nineteenth. The old toy-maker of the libretto would have been at the age we see him in about 1820–30. And this is exactly right. The great blooming of sunflowers before the wooden houses of Sasbachwalden, to name a probable village, was just then. As, also, of the petunias in the window boxes and the fruiting or harvest of the vine-clad hills. I have said that the inhabitants should be as 'birds of a feather', and in all that region and for many miles round the plumage is exceptional.

Not only that, but it varies from village to village. And in the next valley they may speak an altogether different language. They are all minority populations, more or less. A vast and neglected region of the picturesque lasting, as usual, for some two or three generations from 1820 or 1830 until 1914, and even later. It is only a wonder that no painter, or painters, if admittedly not of the first order, was willing to devote a lifetime to recording this extraordinary diversity of human beings, their dresses, their houses, and their customs. I have tried to point to this omission in more than one place in my writings. And it is too late, now, for it is of course gone for ever.

Capable, too, of almost endless extension into the distance. As far as the little isle of Castellorizo or Castel Rosso with its small population of 'sponge-fishers and pirates' (as late as 1878), and its distinctive red costume. And if as far as that, why not a little farther to the mainland, and to the ladies of Lebanon with their conical headdresses in the form of 'horns of plenty'? Or even further still, to Nazareth where, till but a few years ago, the Christian farmers' wives wore the wimple and line of dress of the Crusaders' women and went on riding-camels to their festivals and weddings. The sartorial past of Europe which is something else fast disappearing from the modern world being evident in an account of Trieste – of all places, if you have been there! – from a handbook to Southern Germany, of 1843, where it says, 'the real Albanian capotes are to be purchased here. A native of Joannina makes them. They will keep out any rain, and are very warm. The best cost from 23 to 28 good gulden.' The tailors of Janina were famous all over the Middle East, and their handiwork was to be seen in its splendour in the time of Byron with the Albanian costumes at the court of Ali Pasha.* Luckily a young Frenchman, a pupil of David, came in time to this curious court and made drawings of the old monster, attended by his 'long-haired Ganymedes', floating lazily in a caique on the waters of Lake Ochrida.† This is almost the only responsible account by any artist of Albanian costume, and then only in two or three lithographs although, doubtless, it was the best subject of its kind, and the absence of a work devoted to it is a serious loss.

But if the tailors of Janina were famous, every written account agrees that Scutari, on the Adriatic coast, was the place of places in which to observe the costume of the Balkans; a peninsula of which it could be said, taking it as a whole, that costume was *par excellence* the art of that whole area, in contrast, that is, to those other peninsulas of Italy and Spain. The sartorial interest, in fact, was greater than that of the architecture to be seen. Very special to Scutari were the red cloaks of the Christian women, of which the writer has seen a surviving specimen, but the dresses of the Albanian mountaineers must have been splendid indeed. Of all of which only slight traces are left now, when the occasional local dress is seen in the traffickless streets of Dubrovnik, once more famous as Ragusa, or on the quays of Traù (Trogir).

But neither must the 'Golden City' be confused with the 'Heavenly' or 'Celestial City' which is another concept altogether. Were we looking for that, the specifications are, or used to be before they were spoiled by tourists and summer visitors, nearly fulfilled in the Grecian isle of Mykonos with its dozens of blue-domed chapels, whitewashed cubical houses, and flights of marble steps. This may be a first experience of the only lately recognized and admired 'Greek Island' style, though expert opinion might prefer the isles of Sifnos and Folegrandos in the white cubist style of the Cyclades. The metropolis of the 'villes blanches' of Greece being near by at Syra, or Hermoupolis, capital city of the Cyclades, where the cubical houses are mostly less than a hundred years old, but all the better for that, and the town is an extraordinary vision at night with its two conical hills above the harbour terraced from top to bottom with white houses, and glittering with a myriad electric lights.

* The merchant tailors of Janina were famous throughout the Middle East. Thus it was that Ali Pasha, 'in whose time 1,200 needles were busy at work', was able to establish the workshops which supplied capes, cloaks, gold-embroidered coats and costumes to the whole of Albania and the Balkans as far north as Bosnia, as well as to Egypt and Tunis. 'Even today in Epirus people speak of someone coming from "a family of tailors" when they wish to describe a man of illustrious birth. The art of the Greek tailor and embroiderer was so renowned that they were still making the gold-embroidered robes for the Emperor of Abyssinia and his Court as recently as 1900 and even later.' This account is abbreviated from the *Introduction* by Angeliki Hadzimichali to vol. 1 of the splendidly illustrated *Greek National Costumes*, edited by Antoine E. Benaki, Athens 1948–54.

† Louis Dupré, *Voyage d'Athènes a Constantinople*, Paris 1823 – As late as the *Guide Bleu* for 1911, it is remarked, 'de Dodone' (of the doves and pigeons) 'gendarme ou Zaptié nécessaire'. It was only in the following year (1912) that Janina was lost to Turkey and became a part of mainland Greece.

Yet neither Mykonos nor Syra is the ideal. The one is too rich with visitors and tourists, the other too prosperous and mercantile. Perhaps the 'Celestial City', if that is what we are in search of, is the whitewashed town of Thira on the volcanic isle of Santorin. The whole island is a volcanic crater out of which a corner has been blown by eruption, in the vast cataclysm which according to recent theory may have overwhelmed Knossos and the Cretan civilization by earthquake and tidal wave thirty centuries ago. The island is now shaped like a sickle or a crescent moon some twenty miles long, and in the centre of it, upon three hills on top of the red tufa cliff, stands Thira with its flat-roofed white houses, and again, a multitude of chapels with blue or whitewashed domes. The red rampart of the cliff once climbed on foot or on donkey-back, and I have accomplished both, there is another, not less astonishing view, down over a sloping plain of vineyards, out to open sea. The isle of Santorin, and its town of Thira, are a natural wonder taken possession of and improved by man.

This is the 'Celestial City' of the Byzantines, with the domes and flat roofs to be seen in mosaics and frescoes in the Kariye Djami at Istanbul. And, no doubt, could be studied in quantity whither it transferred and prolonged itself for centuries with the blue or golden onion and shallot domes of Moscow, the 'third Rome'. There must be marvellous 'Celestial Cities' of the imagination in Zagorsk, Suzdal, Vladimir, and the multiple-domed wooden churches on islands in Lake Ladoga and the White Sea. Whereas the cubical, barrel-roofed and whitewashed houses of Capri and of Amalfi and its district show Moorish influence in addition, but bear a resemblance which is more than a mere identity of circumstance to the white villages of Santorin or Mykonos in the Greek Islands. There must be some definite link of connection between them. As, also, to the 'villes blanches' of Andalusia, those small towns of dazzling, lime-kiln whiteness, fascinating in themselves to fill the leisure hours of a lifetime, and that connect again across to Morocco with the whitened alleys and the veiled and Cyclop-seeming women of Atlantic-washed Sallee.

A theme, it has been said, that is capable of endless variation and extension. Stretching from Alsace and the Black Forest, wherein lies Sasbachwalden of the window boxes, until it reached through Bavaria to the Bohemian border; and then, Moravia, Slovakia which is its real beginning, and thence into the heart of the Arcadia, which was Hungary and Roumania. The minority populations could be Wallachian, Moldavian, Ruthenian, Saxon, Suabian, Szekler, Slavonian, what you will! And there could be, as well, Poles, Masovians, Polesians, Hutculs or Houtsoules; Matyos – as of the long gowned, surpliced men and women with headdresses like horses' manes of the village of Mezökövesd – who are probably Tartar of origin; full-blooded Magyars; Armenians; Gypsies in plenty in their different tribes, Oursari or bear-leaders, Calderarii who were tinkers, Ferarii, and others who are ironsmiths, flowersellers, or makers of pitchforks and of wooden spoons; and small towns such as Sighetul Marmaţiei which are, or were, entirely inhabited by Jews. All of which I have dwelt upon at some length, for together with other and less interesting communities it is part of a huge belt reaching from Transylvania into the old Baltic republics and even as far as Sweden.

One might be inclined to advance the same reason for its existence as has been argued for the uniform plumage of the different tribes of humming-birds or birds-of-a-paradise; that it is to prevent them from hybridizing. As though the unconscious, general council of each such division of birds convened itself and promulgated this unwritten law for the general weal and well being. In which case we would have to equate or parallel the different degrees of family mourning* with the permutations of moulting and of adult plumage with for example the parrots, and more particularly the lories, of Australia and New Guinea. What other purpose than pleasure and delight in ornament lies behind those permutations? Are they not, like peasant costume, the pastime of dull lives?

But, as with all else of the kind they are disappearing fast, and soon will be no longer seen. To take one or two instances; the beautiful Dalecarlian dresses to be seen in the nineteen-thirties on Sundays at Leksand and Rättvik on Lake Siljan are no longer worn, and the huts behind the church where their horses were sheltered during service now stand empty. And it is the same over nearly all of Sweden. Gone, too, are the *bragou bas* and the long hair of the Breton peasants, though the women still wear the high lace caps. As late as 1926 Andalusian dress was almost universally worn in Granada, and I remember the milk being delivered at the hotel by a horseman *à la Andaluz*. As late as 1947 the *oorijzer*, or golden casque of the Frisian women was still to be seen, if rarely, in the streets of Leeuwarden though the old women in an almshouse, a few miles from the town, all wore it, and upon Sundays you could see a bonnet of jet and feathers worn upright upon the golden helm. Now, I believe this sign and insignia of the fair-haired Frisian women is gone for ever.

But there have been villages and small towns even in England of which the setting and the inhabitants must have formed a select company. It is difficult, as I have said, to deny this about small towns where every building is still beautiful, even in town-villages not far from where I write. The village street of Wendover, in Buckinghamshire, is a case in point; and I am thinking, hackneyed though it may appear to be, of small Cotswold towns, Burford, Broadway, Chipping Camden, now given over to tea-rooms and antique shops, but where an exceptional level must have prevailed at one time, say, between 1680 and 1760, for the inevitable two or three generations, if no more than that. And they were 're-discovered' about ninety years ago, largely by Americans come to settle in Europe, who may have found in them some semblance in spirit to the white bargeboard houses of villages and small towns in New England. The row of almshouses at Chipping Camden, and the buildings and the number of little, they could almost be called Palladian, bridges over the stream at another village, Bourton-on-the-Water, argue a high level of sensibility and civilization. The effect, if not the truth of it, depends more than a little upon the warm-hued

---

* For near relatives the people of the Island of Marken, in the Zuyder Zee, wore mourning for not less than five years; and it was this long, one could say, before their costume returned to its full plumage. In the meantime it went through all shades of half and quarter mourning. There were no less than seven degrees of mourning in the small town of Hindeloopen, opposite, across the Zuyder Zee.

stone. Other towns, Stamford in Lincolnshire, for instance, though as full of fine old houses, are built of a grey stone which has not nearly the radiance of the Cotswold stone.

Suffolk villages, such as Lavenham or Long Melford, despite the beauty of their Perpendicular churches of striped flint and white stone, have not the corporate effect of the streets of stone houses in the Cotswolds, which is that of a small town population all contemporary to each other, in exactly that sense I have suggested of a race of birds or animals all alike within their own category, but inside of that, possessed of their own character and individuality. The country in Suffolk is wooded, with gentle hills and cornfields, the very landscape of Gainsborough's early painting of Squire Andrews and his wife, which landscape setting gives it the advantage over heathy, sandy Norfolk however unexampled in splendour and diversity the Norfolk churches with their panelled flushwork of multicoloured flint and their 'angel ceilings'. They are a wonder little known to the world outside, unredeemed by landscape, and stretching across an extremely dull and flat country for the most part. And it is true to say that there is still an ambivalence between those persons who know East Anglia in detail and those others who prefer the West Country. Few, indeed, are those who know both in detail.

That is as it may be, and is dependent upon personal taste and affinity; but the extreme melodic beauty in local architecture in England where, that is to say, it has the perfection of line and form of folksong is to be found, surely, in the Perpendicular tower of Mells in Somerset. And doubtless in its sister towers in that countryside, as at Wrington or at Evercreech, a few miles away; though I would somewhat mistrust that southern congery of towers round Taunton, Bishop's Lydeard, or Kingston, which are of red sandstone. Others, belonging to another group, Kingsbury Episcopi and Huish Episcopi, a pair which are but a mile or so apart, are of blue lias, but it is the pale golden stone of Mells which is unsurpassable. The church tower is indeed a thing of wonderful beauty which would be famous were it in any other country but in England. There is certainly no minaret, and I have seen most of the famous minarets of the Muslim, to compare to this. Its only sisters in beauty being the other Perpendicular towers to be seen in different parts of England, but it would appear that the finest of them all in effect of serenity and peacefulness are in Somerset. The architect of Mells, whoever he may have been, was the master of elegiac repose and calm, the attributes most needed in a living monument to the dead, if a church is to be something more than a mere charnel house of bones.

It has been said earlier that the village street of Wendover is admirable in its way of a community of agreeable building; and if this be allowed it is hard to deny it to Norman Shaw's red brick cottages and white-painted dormers and mullions of Bedford Park, it being in accord with the spirit of the poem at the head of this chapter that the 'Golden City' must be seen in the light of what it may have seemed to be, then, and not of what it looks like now. At the time this first of garden cities was built in the early eighteen-seventies, now a hundred years ago, in the very decade of Gustave Doré's slum drawings of London – drawings that can have been but little exaggerated or heightened in horror – these quiet houses standing under fruit trees, and the rather aesthetically inclined residents, must have seemed to be paradise indeed. Probably more than one comedy could have been written about the 'artistic' inhabitants of Bedford Park; but it would have its touches of poetry, as well, coming from young men and women long dead now. Of course, the unconscious, instinctive practice of such ideals is more attractive because of its sincerity, if less entertaining, maybe, in retrospect and in perspective. But there are, or there have been, as I hope to have shown, villages and small towns, of which the setting and the inhabitants, as certainly, must have formed together a select company.

III

So in the end, the 'Golden City' means no more than somewhere one has been happy. More probably still, somewhere that one had the chance, or had thought it was possible to reach into that frame of mind. Which has happened to many, but by no means to all. And is, therefore, both tangible and intangible, even if one has attained to it, because one can never reach to it again. So that everything to do with it has the aura and flow of what is personally sacred. As though I could come back to it from the nineteen-twenties and only put my hand upon the windowsill and do so again, alas! how improbably! in ten years from now. As though the white-painted windowsill was sentient, even though cold and heartless as a geiger-counter that given contact with any substance, wool, or hair, or fibre, that has ever had life in it, or just been in derivation from something living, can tell the date of it, but only within a span of – is it two hundred, or two hundred and fifty years? – by which time anything and everything personal to one in the sense of all one knew or loved would be gone from all knowledge. The traveller in time could come back to an old house, or a cottage, and make himself known, forward or backward in time, to his relations. But such is a perquisite and an anachronism as rare as the ceremony of the keys performed nightly for how many centuries at the Tower of London. A performance as extinct as the dodo, but surviving as curiously and unexpectedly as the coelacanth to confound the sceptics. Only the privileged can hope for it, though the individuals concerned are as indifferent and uninterested as that prehistoric saurian, for it looks less fish than reptile, brought up from the ocean depths off Madagascar, or the Comores. As an individual it is ignorant of its historical importance, and would go back to the glaucous deep as gladly as the recruit to his bed in barracks.

But to the four-roomed house, 'two up, two down', with grandma lying upstairs! Hearing nothing? Noticing nothing? Not even on the night they made the tape-recording? There were often children in the house whom they met at the market and brought home with them. Is there no memory of all this left in the bones of the house? Or its soft places? Nothing? Nothing? By day, or night? Then, there can be nothing left, either, of the places where one has been happy. And there is no hope of leaving one's shadow of person, or personality behind one. The inarticulate in their hundreds of millions are lost and gone for ever. The privileged are those few who have left, as it were, the shreds of their clothing as with the public exposition of a dead body. But such is the genius of *homo sapiens*, who in his entity is the only god, but mortal, and only immortal in totality, that his relics can be more important than his person, or than he may have seemed to be when living. Instances of this are too innumerable for it to be more than mentioned. But which is worse, to die famous and soon be forgotten, of which probably the most trenchant example is the composer Meyerbeer who was often compared in his lifetime to Michelangelo, a comparison dependent on mixed metaphors in any case, and who almost as certainly cannot wholly deserve the oblivion into which he has fallen. Which is worse? Or to begin famous, and end in growing obscurity and gloom? Is it not rather more than coincidental that both Rembrandt and Beethoven, also, two of the great geniuses among human beings, should show every sign of ending their lives as heavy drinkers? They were not drinking, we may feel certain, just out of high spirits. They may have felt confidence in themselves, but the reason was poverty, loneliness, and the growing impossibility of their lives. As one grows older oneself it is only natural that one should have more sympathy with the failures. One has seen too many of the graphs of the rise and fall of human beings. It is the more agonizing because of the certainty there is not another life, and that posthumous awards and honours are not even cold comfort to the dead. It is wiser not to have wanted those, and to have been intent on enjoying the wonders of the living world. Only for this once, and never again; there being in high probability nothing in all the rest of creation to vie with it, or match its miseries and splendours.

Of which I have tried in my life to gain as wide a knowledge as possible and pass on the experience, though its meaning is a mystery, and indeed there is so much mystery of which there is no explaining. Why, and how it happened in the first place, and with what intent? Or by mere accident? For that, too, is how things happen. And is there a chain connecting them; or is it all haphazard? Is there design; or does it only improvise and not think ahead? For it is easy to get both impressions; of a purpose, and of mere whim as to what follows and comes next. Certainly there is instinctive purpose; and, as surely, none at all. And as well, the death wish, *course à l'abîme*, the swarming of the lemmings, call it what you will. There would seem to be more of a plan, or a settled motion, in the celestial bodies, and little of helter-skelter compared with the little world of animals and human beings. Or is it just that erratic movements are hardly visible against the infinity of time? That there has been time for hardly more than a handful of visible planets since recorded history began? That the huge births and explosions are few and far between; but in their time-currency may be continuing all the while.

Will it ever be determined what an ant thinks of a human being? They are certainly conscious of our presence. But the smallest human dwelling is to them the height of the Andes, or the Himalayas. And they can climb it? Did ants not appear out of the bath-room wall six floors up in the hotel in Rome? And some instinct told them of the box of chocolates, and within two hours they had swarmed in this, to them, sugar island of the Antilles. The sperm whale, the biggest living mammal, is ninety to a hundred feet long, about fifteen times the length of a tall human being from which we may, or may not, compute the scale of a termite in comparison with, say, the Seagram Tower, or the General Motors Building in New York. All of which details are reduced to absurdity by the grand mathematics of astronomy to the extent that they could almost be in themselves the secret or the source of life. At least there is no room in them for sentiment, and indeed their entire impersonality is what is terrible and frightening. After which it is comforting and reassuring to find some small familiar object still in shape. This is part of the solace of old buildings that they are still there. That they come out of another world altogether and have survived into ours. Which is of another order of feeling altogether from reading an old letter for that belongs to a dead world within ourselves. And about which there is nothing whatever that can be done. For it is gone, gone. One cannot even bring back yesterday. It is too late. After one has reached to a certain age nearly everything one can think of is either pitiful or poignant. Because it is all in the same predicament that it has happened and is helpless. It cannot reach to you even if it wished. It is caught there and whirled away. It may seem static, but only too soon so far out of touch that it is as though you cannot discover whether it is alive or dead, just as there are persons of whom one does not know if they are still living. Or whom to ask, and how to find out. More dead, then, than the dead, of whom that at least is certain. And it is definite, and that is where they are and not in limbo.

Ofone thing we may be certain. The 'Golden City', wherever it be, and if it exists at all, lies nowhere near a motor-road. Max Beerbohm wrote that when he was a young man, London, when spoken of, was always referred to in the feminine as 'she', but now – and this was in the nineteen-twenties – the 'she' was referred to as 'it'. There were fewer motors, then, and no noise from aeroplanes. There were rows of houses much too near the trains and main London railway stations but, at least, the trains went past at long intervals and were not continuous. We have to conceive, now, of families living in the front rooms because there are no backs, with their windows as little as eight feet from the new by-passes and fly-overs; and children and grown-ups alike subjected to non-stop roar of traffic, petrol fumes, and neon-lights strong enough to pierce the strongest curtains. They are in as bad a way as the white-clad pavement sleepers in Calcutta or Bombay. Los Angeles has permanent smog over its houses and highways. Tokyo with ten – or is it twelve million inhabitants? – has streets with no names, and houses numbered according to the order in which they were built. If invited out, you have to go to the nearest police post and get them to help in puzzling out the address, in this human ant-heap where students are hired to push passengers in and out of the commuter-trains. As late as the nineteen-twenties Vienna was the theme of a popular and rather pretty song-hit. Much has happened since then to make this unlikely of repetition. One can perhaps still sympathize with the boulevardiers of Paris who were unhappy if away from the French capital for more than a few days. But that was in the heyday of the Second Empire, a spectacle that dazzled all beholders, even the disapproving, and that can never come again. We have but to remember written accounts of the painted carriages of the ladies and the demi-mondaines, or look at them in the drawings of Constantin Guys, remembering that Haussmann's Paris was the first city of restaurants and cafés and imagining for ourselves a few minutes' existence in the 'fourmillante cité' in order to watch the crinolin'd ladies and perhaps an officer of the *Guides*, the fashionable regiment,* or baggy-breeched, antochthonous Zouave of the Garde Impériale in his tassell'd cap, hoping the door of a café may swing open, or that we may even pass a theatre and hear only a few bars, no more than that is necessary, to know the music is of Offenbach and this is the Imperial capital in all its gaslight and glitter.

In fact, a period of great ugliness, with most things gimcrack, of fairground loudness, but redeemed by the ladies who were as improbable of dress as in woodcuts by Kiyonaga or by Utamaro, and a night and day in which it must have been most wonderful to use one's eyes. And perhaps that is the last that can be said of the great cities, though if one reads of the coaches of the peers with their bewigg'd coachmen and footmen in state liveries in the family colours arriving at the Abbey for the coronation of King Edward VII in 1902, which was before anyone could be sure of arriving anywhere by motor-car,† we could be back in the day of George IV and his coronation in 1821, at the very least, if not earlier. I can remember the women's dresses of only a very few years after 1902 – having gone to school in 1905 – and they were not beautiful. It was one of the ugly periods in dress like that of Henry VIII or James I, the more hideous where they had the best tailors and dressmakers as in the Paris of François Premier or Henri Quatre. But the contemporary Paris of portraits and drawings by Boldini and Helleu, as, less so, the world of J. S. Sargent, is endeared to someone who can remember his mother looking like that and dressed in that manner.

There are always beautiful clothes, perhaps more so now than ever before, just as there are a larger number of persons with looks suitable for wearing them. It is not human beings who have deteriorated, it is their environment and what they have perpetrated on that and permitted to happen to that. There is a bigger public for things of the intelligence than ever before in history, and at the same time a larger number of ignoramuses. But creation has not kept pace with education which is an unhealthy condition. Rather, it should have the public following after it and not leading it. Because the Impressionists and post-Impressionist painters were so unappreciated while alive – Van Gogh not selling a single picture in his lifetime and so on – it does not follow that every painting in a series of pictures of soup-tins or soup-cans is a work of genius. Any more than this possession of genius is confirmed by the fact that the Dutch little masters practised their talents upon a jug, a dish of oysters, a piece of glass or

* Rossini is said to have written a march for the *Guides*, though there is no mention of it in any list of his works. He may have recaptured the time and place in this as magically as in *La Danza*, the tarantella he wrote in the manner of Lablache, the great basso singer, which so marvellously evokes the Naples of Ferdinand II and the Parthenopaean city of the time.

† It is unusual to number Oscar Wilde among the pioneers of early motoring, if only as a passenger. But he undertook the journey by road to Paris from the Riviera in 1899 with Harold Mellor, someone long dead and forgotten.

silver, or other object of everyday life. It is true that in Holland in the seventeenth century, it amounted to a positive, if inexplicable epidemic of painters in a light and in a climate, if anything, worse than our own, and without the conditions being particularly hopeful or encouraging. Why this should have happened has never been explained. There must have been as many, or more, painters to a town than there were butchers or bakers. Everyone must try his hand but, in the result, if many of the Dutch painters are dull, there are fewer demonstrably bad painters than with the Italians. Or is it only that the Dutchmen were less ambitious? In any event there is not the acreage of indifferent fresco and dull board or canvas. It is in the future surely that there will be the real holocausts of bad paintings when 'pop art' and much else has outlived its brief day! No paintings at all and bare walls would be no bad convalescence and recuperation.

Does anyone feel sad any more at parting from the big cities? Who would not sooner live outside, than inside Rome or Florence? Manchester and Liverpool, New York, Chicago, San Francisco, it is all the same. Perhaps it is only in Paris there is not the same feeling. Did not a Paris taxi-driver say to me in the first week in May, 'Regardez les châtaigners! Ils sont magnifiques', rather as one of Napoleon's marshals might have watched his troops advancing. But, then, the deepest compliment a Frenchman can pay to a celebrated view abroad is to say he is reminded of somewhere in France, 'On dirait le Provence, Les Baux', and so on. It is only in the poorest, meanest parts of London that the cockneys, if there are any left of them, would prefer to stay and not be 'evacuated' down to the country tedium and quiet. Who does not long to move out of the vertical slums, the towers of flats, and get underneath the trees? It is the heartlessness of the new, as of a rising generation who do not listen and have no patience. What heart is there in the arc-lamp burning all night long just outside the window? What heart is there in the cement path leading to the garage? There is more of warmth in the senseless chirping of the sparrow. There is more comfort in the rain falling when one can stay indoors and not have to go outside. But one must keep young and not have an old person's feelings. There is enough of interest to fill a hundred lifetimes. Ah! until something happens! And, then? And, then? Nothing can go on for ever, except entire negation and nothingness itself. Which has no beginning and no end, and therefore no existence and no being. But it is there, yet, and all the time, although you can neither see, nor hear it.

The beautiful solitude is going, going, gone. What is most to be envied in old pictures is their notion of a crowd. In Guardi's or Canaletto's views of Venice, or Pannini's paintings of contemporary Rome, there is no crowd to compare with every evening's rush hour on our London underground or tube platform; while in Altdorfer's *Battle of Arbela*,* a painting of Alexander's victory over Darius which was so much admired by Napoleon that he had it hung in his bedroom, the wonder of which picture is the immense number of combatants and the tremendous vault of sky, the crowd is no greater than at a 'demo' in Trafalgar or Grosvenor Square. The invisible mobs are more awful than those that can be seen and smelt. An unseen public of how many hundreds of millions for the oafish

* Altdorfer's *Battle of Arbela* is in the Alte Pinakothek at Munich.

World Football Cup, relayed by satellite; and in miniature, an audience of how many millions to bring in, if this is true, a million dollars, £416,000 each, to Richard Burton and Elizabeth Taylor for every film they make together? There could scarcely have been a bigger 'assistance', granted all modern facilities of communication, for the beheading of Charles I or Louis XVI, or for both of them together, if only that could have been 'screened'. This is the contamination of the crowd, of the char-a-banc and camping site; of the Jewel Tower, and the isle of Capri, and Ann Hathaway's cottage, all reduced to the same category. And no doubt before long Bora-Bora, and the 'dream island' of Noumea which lies opposite Tahiti. So that the only solitude is in one's own home, and all adventure and experience are to be had within oneself, and there is little point in going outside that. The few become more important every day before the steam-roller of the 'comprehensives' which will obliterate and pulp the masses. And why are music and ballet the only 'priorities' to be favoured and helped along? This is the more aggravating only because it is part of the truth and not the whole truth. The rejuvenation of the English, if ever, will not come through dancing and play- ing the violin. This is not in our national temperament. We have many and more serious talents, now dormant, but which may flower again. Poetry among them; and who was ever taught to write poetry? Equally, no poets have had pupils; they may have had followers and imitators, but no poet has worked with success in the 'studio' or workroom of another. Perhaps, in my own case, I was as much a pupil of my sister as any one poet has ever been of another. She was ten years older than me, and I remember her reading poetry from my earliest years. Surely in its beginnings it is an instinctive art which requires an especial 'touch' or 'hand'. If this be lacking it is probable that it was hopeless from the start. The maturity of poets is often between eighteen and twenty-three, which happens but rarely in the other arts. Yet, where that has happened, it is more instinct than inspiration, the two being quite separate identities not related in any way, and the latter a preposterous boast that seldom justifies itself, or descends again into the person.

Who can it have been who wrote the little nursery song at the head of this chapter? She may be still living. Is it 'Maisie Drummond', herself, who wrote the poem? That would seem probable for the poem has some of the quality of a 'primitive' ex-voto painting of the sort to be seen on the walls of some miracle- working shrine. Its four lines are certainly a *cri de coeur* and of high precedence as a work of art. How do such things get themselves written down? It is no less mysterious than the birth of school slang or prison jargon. Who first coined the prison word 'snout' for tobacco? How did the 'chain-gang' songs get written? Probably more than one convict prisoner had a hand in those. But 'Maisie Drummond' must be the work of a 'solitary'. And there is far more to it than its mere four lines; and more, again, than can have been the intention of its creator. It is the lament of town for country; and not less the sadness of a country person at not finding the streets of the city paved with gold. Immaterial, not material gold of the sort that is weighed in the scales, but the gold of dawn and sunset and of the high empyrean.

In the mind of a person coming to London for the first time; or arriving there, or anywhere else, to make his or her career. Or, even, in anticipation, of the youth of seventeen in the restaurant, under the hanging woods of Marlow, or listening to the weir; and wondering all the while whether he could write poetry. And now the time has nearly come to know, one way or the other. I can hear the churning, churning of the barrel-organ in the street outside, and am young again in that moment of a terrible time in our family history in view of what was to come to us in November of that same year, which was to tie the three of us together, two brothers and sister, in our determination to live, and leave a mark of some sort or kind. And the time has, as certainly, arrived to offer thanks for having lived and been alive. I do not think I knew at that moment what was coming though there had certainly been warning enough in the preliminary law suits. But it was to precipitate us into action, into taking pen in hand. A strange, strange moment; and the first poems I wrote were written in that same month of August when I reached home. I have still the first drafts of them, as of those I wrote a year or two later while at Chelsea Barracks, and at Aldershot. A climacteric evening when much was decided. The building is still there; but I cannot think of a single other person dining in that restaurant who is alive still. They are all dead. And I suppose the barrel-organ was wheeled away into the sunset of that late evening with the man and woman, or whoever they were, looking up into the windows, as they used to do, to see if anyone was throwing money down. Long, long ago, they turned the street corner and were gone from sight and sound.

Since when, the 'Golden City' has been found and lost, not once, but several times. Over and over again, indeed. It was there this morning, early, but now a mist has risen out of the orchard. Or it is an autumn bonfire; portending October, November, and that amount of it lost and gone for ever, which cannot come back. And it is like arriving on an evening when the restaurant is shut; and there has been a muddle, and how are we to arrange to meet, and it must be somewhere else. No more than that, but it is for a long time, longer than we thought. A lifetime come and gone, and what comes next?

Persona perturbata

After two years of personal sadnesses and disappointments, into the details of which it would be ignoble to enter, I have found as often before the only release to be in reading. And no doubt like many others before me, have re-discovered happiness and comfort in reading Trollope. A wide choice and variety of his novels, including such lesser masterpieces as *The Vicar of Bullhampton, The American Senator,* and *The Small House at Allington*; being in the fortunate state of knowing no novel of Trollope at all until three or four years ago, this treat being thereby reserved for me till I was no longer young. But *Can you forgive her?* – or am I wrong, and should it be *Phineas Finn,* or *The Duke's Children,* or *The Way We Live Now?* – seems to be the most balanced and perfect of his novels as a work of art. What peaceful and unending enjoyment one owes to him, once his books have fallen into one's hands! And how did he contrive to write so much and at such a sustained level of excellence through, alone, those two mid-Victorian decades of the eighteen-sixties and seventies while, also, carrying out his official duties at the Post Office,* sitting up late playing whist and, as well, hunting on so many winter days a week?

There is hardly mention of either music or painting in his novels; and his characters when they go abroad notice little, if anything at all of their surroundings. The very word or meaning of 'technique' may have been nearly unknown to him, and certainly cannot have applied in his own mind to the writing of his novels. Yet how beautifully 'managed' is the chapter, *Dinner at the Bear Garden* in the *Duke's Children,* where Lord Silverbridge in a weak moment finds himself dining at the club with his father, the Duke of Omnium, and his racing crony Major Tifto to his horror and consternation comes up and introduces himself to his father! How touching the passage in *The Way We Live Now* where Lord Nidderdale, hearing of the suicide of the swindling financier Augustus Melmotte from Melmotte's daughter Marie, goes to her in spite of his father's advice to the contrary. Her note ran . . . "'I do not know who to send to. Will you come to me, only for a few minutes?" But Nidderdale's better feelings would not allow him to submit to this advice . . . He had been engaged to the girl. At any rate for the time the heartlessness of his usual life deserted him. "I couldn't refuse her", he said over and over again. "I couldn't bring myself to do it. Oh, no; – I shall certainly go" . . . "You'll get into a mess if you do" . . . Nidderdale simply shook his head as he took his hat and gloves to go across to Bruton Street.'

This episode I find to be more true and genuinely moving than most things in Dickens; Lord Nidderdale is portrayed by Trollope as the archetypal, drawling Lord Dundreary of fiction, though there are others, too, when one comes to

* A little, nearby, relic of Trollope's unfailing industry and invention is the pillar letter-box designed by him, and still on duty near the railway station at Banbury. I believe one other of these is still in use somewhere else in the country.

think of them, 'Dolly' Longestaffe for instance in *The Way We Live Now*. And in passing, if we look for a drawing of him we have it to perfection, the lisping, languorous voice and manner, the whiskered, pomaded, top-hatted, young dandy of the sixties, in *The Age of Paper*, Alfred Concanen's masterpiece out of his many hundreds of music-hall song covers of just that period. It must be the portrait drawing, one imagines, of some actor playing just this part, and how well! upon the stage.

But at my climax of sadness and depression I think I was saved by re-reading *The Duke's Children*, and finding myself fascinated and spell-bound by Trollope's description of fox-hunting, having never, myself, hunted or ridden to hounds, though I have enough relations who have done this. There are the couple, Mr and Mrs Spooner, who make their appearance in only two short chapters, or some twenty pages and no more of this novel. Mr Spooner is silent and port-drinking. But his wife is a virtuoso of the art of fox-hunting.

'The fox never went into Grobby Gorse at all. I was there and Sappho gave him a line down the bank.'

'I think he must have gone into the gorse, my dear,' said her husband. 'The earth was open you know.'

'I tell you she didn't. You weren't there and you don't know. I'm sure she was a vixen by her running.'

... 'Thirty-two minutes up to Grobby Gorse. The hounds never hunted a yard after that. Dick hurried them into the gorse, and the old hound wouldn't stick to her line when she found that no one believed her.' ... 'We chopped one at Bromleys,' said Mr Spooner.

'When a man loses his hounds in that country, he ought to go direct to Brackett's wood,' said Mrs Spooner.

... 'We've had it a little faster once or twice,' said Mrs Spooner, with deliberation, 'but never for so long. Then it was straight as a line, and a real open kill. No changing, you know. We did go through the daisies, but I'll swear to its being the same fox.'

'... I'm afraid we shan't have anything like that today', she continued. 'The wind's in the west, and I never did like a westerly wind ... I always know what a west wind means.'

'... We shan't find them at Grantingham. They were cutting wood there last week. If I were you, my Lord, I'd go away to the Spinnies at once.'

This is what Silverbridge and Tregear, two young men in the novel, have to say of her.

'I wonder what you'll think of Mrs Spooner?' said Silverbridge.

'Why should I think anything of her?'

'Because I doubt whether you ever saw such a woman before. She does nothing but hunt.'

'Then I certainly shan't want to see her again.'

'And she talks as I never heard a lady talk before.'

'Then I don't care if I never see her at all.'

'But she is the most plucky and good-natured human being I ever saw in my life. After all, hunting is very good fun.'

And as Lady Chiltern says of her, 'She will talk hunting too. If Chiltern were to leave the country I think they ought to make her master. Perhaps you'll think her rather odd; but she really is a very good woman.' This is, apart from a word or two, almost all that Mrs Spooner has to say, and it takes up little more than a page of print. It is not conversation by any standard at all, but it shows what can only be called expertise and discernment; and in the same way that Simenon, a notable writer in his own line, amazes by his knowledge and participation in life on board a Norman or Breton fishing boat, or of barge life on a Belgian or French canal, so the tactical and working knowledge of the 'odd-looking Mrs Spooner' in some curious manner at the same time informs and warms the heart. And of course the hunting scenes, here, in *The Duke's Children*, as in *The American Senator*, and elsewhere in Trollope's novels, are of an exhilaration that makes it impossible to lay the book down and put out the light. This, as I have said, to someone who has never hunted in his life, to some degree disapproves of certain features and formalities connected with it, but must have some atavistic tinge of low percentage in his blood. Such passages are irresistible; they are so technically perfect in what they set out to do, and have so high a degree of spirit and *élan* in their handling.

Trollope is an acknowledged master, and if I compare him for this moment with a forgotten theatrical draughtsman like his contemporary Concanen it is no belittlement of either of them for Concanen at his best, I feel certain, would have had appeal for artists like Degas and Toulouse-Lautrec, or in our own age for Walter Sickert. But in a time of acute personal worry and sadness when all effort seems useless and owing to entire disillusionment one loses all faith in oneself and in any help and comfort to be drawn from works of art, it can happen that one is brought back again to one's senses by some little technical display which whets the appetite. This is no time for the 'Appassionata', or the Sistine ceiling, but for some humbler thing that has a life and being of its own, and it was a happiness to read and read over again just those hunting scenes from *The Duke's Children* for they are so perfectly achieved and done.

It is to be supposed that religious-minded persons must experience similar, or worse, losses of faith. But their effect is to bring us back to our beginnings and to our youthful memories, and in every category of artist, be he painter, writer, or musician, it must be to the birth of ambitions and ideas. This is long ago in my instance for I claim to have been interested at thirteen or fourteen years old in just the things, in principle, that still interest me now. My horizon has of course widened, but I think that anyone who remembered me, then, would know me now as the same person. Such thoughts, going back as they do from the past to the present tense, bring the feeling in me that I have cheated myself, and been cheated, of my birthright, not once, but twice over. And I have suffered enough from it, myself, though dependent upon it for the mere possibility of being able to write the kind of books I write, to know the weakness and inherent wrongness of inherited possessions because of the misery they bring. So what is the answer? That the world is better without the poet and dilettante, in the old and real sense of that word?

But, mainly the problem has been that owing to circumstance I kept myself, or was kept away from Italy. And instead I went to Spain. But now I am thinking of the years after the ending of the Second World War in 1945. Before that, I could not have conceived of a civilized world of the past without Italian painters and architects, and saw Italian influence everywhere and in everything, to the degree that in the absence of that all things pertinent were invalidated. I had thought we would be going often to Florence, where I had been so much as a child before 1914 and between the years 1919 and 1939. But the legend of devoted families in the context of brothers and sisters is disproved, and becomes sadder still when another and younger generation, coupled with unworthy and alien influences, who know and understand nothing of past affections, become involved, or involve themselves in it. And so the legend dies and leaves its survivor unhappy who had thought it was otherwise, and who must continue for what little time is left in the knowledge that much was false that he had thought was true; or only the weakness of infirmity and illness under influences alien to all the past, and as well as evil, uncomprehending. I had never thought when young not to have gone often in future years to Italy, and in particular to Florence. But I was never there between 1939 and 1965, for twenty-six years, long enough for some young genius to be born, and live, and die. Or for oneself, with all one's own stupidities and failures, to move from middle age to something even more unpromising than that. But one cannot go where one is not invited. So legends die; and that is the end of that.

What I would wish to remember are the early years, passed in large part in the town where I was born, and where the house we lived in has been turned, grotesquely, into a museum for stuffed birds and animals, and on a recent visit I found glass cases of owls, seagulls, and such like, in no fewer than eight rooms in which I remember sleeping; though it is true one large room has been kept as it was and is full of books, photographs, and other relics of my family. None the less, it has been a drastic change, calculated, too, to make one look back on one's childhood as being even longer ago than is really the case. They are all gone now; my mother's family who spent a few weeks every summer in the house next door, and had strong local ties at one time, and my father and mother and brother and sister. All gone. And it certainly seems to be a long time ago. When I was a young boy, or, indeed as late as my first year or two at Eton, when there were hansom cabs in London, and one took a hansom from Paddington Station though there were already a few taxis. Or to take but one other memory, that of the cabmen several of whom I well remember personally and by name, coming out of their cab rank opposite the Grand Hotel into the raw cold and swinging their arms to keep warm, just like the droshky drivers in *Petrouchka*. Yes. It must be long ago. The older persons I remember, my grandmothers and uncles and aunts, and dozens of others, must have been familiar with life just exactly as it was lived in Trollope's novels, though not in this same part of England. Hence, I think, the therapeutic and restorative effect on me of reading *Phineas Finn*, or *The Duke's Children*, in a time of sadness and depression.

But no more of this. It was all to be the excuse for writing about Florence, and for an entr'acte on something Florentine. What a wonderful transition from those winters of the last few lines, and from the endless Augusts and half-Septembers spent at my old home of the high rooms and, of occasion, shuddering nights! Of the yew pyramids and green terraces, and the lake and woods, with collieries underneath it all! I loved that, too, and forswore my right to it. But now find myself in the flower market with my mother buying tuberoses. The cabman's fur collar is odd-looking, and he has a huge green umbrella. But how small his cab is compared to those huge Scarborough 'four-wheelers'! We are in the narrow streets of Italy at any time, one could almost say, between 1846, or so, when railways began, and 1925 or even 1930. Visually, conditions can have altered but little during that time. Perhaps trams and the cocoon of tram-lines round the Duomo were the main innovation. My Florentine memories of that date were of my father, who did all he could and was 'out', as it is said, to awaken one's interests, and was by no means so 'difficult' and laughable as he has been portrayed, though it is becoming late to redress the balance. Perhaps he was gentler and more affectionate on all counts than his portrayer. And of my mother to whom I was devoted. I find it not easy to write of her without emotion. She was in her late thirties and beautiful, and I have most touching memories of her childish nature and her affection. But those are my personal possessions and I would share them with no one else.

I was old enough to be taken by my father to Lucca and to Bologna, and on more than one occasion to Venice. Then my Easter holidays in Italy seem to have lapsed for a year or two by which time I was thirteen or fourteen, or older, as I have said, and had decided interests in paintings and works of art. After that came the War, and when I went out to Italy again it was as a young man, and it was still for a few years more the old Italy but everything else had changed. Then it was that I went down south and found Naples for myself, which gave me a subject for my first book.

Meanwhile, my father after endless manoeuvring was about to move into the house in Tuscany which he had bought in 1909, and which had already therefore been in his possession for ten years. He was, by now, though not more than sixty, certainly 'eccentric', though not improbably so, all things considered, for he and my mother had been victims of an arranged marriage. She was seventeen, still in the schoolroom and, I was told, had met my father twice at luncheon. They can never, I take it, have been alone together for more than a few minutes before marriage, and now after more than thirty years of married life they had not one single interest in common. This drove him in upon himself and made him solitary, though, in any case he had no need of friends. And she, finding herself in another world of antiquities and old books and genealogies to that in which she was born, where the horizons were limited to hunting and to shooting parties and to London 'seasons', developed extravagant habits, albeit on a fairly modest scale considering her husband's income, most of the surplus of which he spent on collecting Italian furniture, and 'went to moneylenders', with disastrous results due to one ruffianly character, in particular, who was a semi-criminal of strange origin and intimidating history. As the result of all this, both of them, my father and my mother, were the wrecks by this time of each other and of themselves. It should be added that she was entirely uneducated, having, as I say, left the schoolroom and the nurses and governesses at the age of seventeen when her allowance of pocketmoney had been eighteen pence a week; she could not add up, could very decidedly not subtract, and I think had only the mistiest notion of who Julius Caesar was, or the meaning of the Napoleonic Wars. But she had great humour, beauty, and human understanding. I was devoted to her until I was fifteen, or older, and always loved her. Perhaps being the youngest child I had the best of the love and affection of both my parents, difficult as they became; and they had their own troubles and difficulties. Probably it is to the good to have had a positive and a negative for parents, though I would be unable to decide in my own mind which was which.

For all these reasons I grew up familiar with the huge rusticated boulders of the Palazzo Pitti, the Ponte Vecchio, and the porphyry statue on its column in the Via Tornabuoni. These I remember for as long as I can remember anything of aesthetic interest except perhaps the garden my father made at my old home. Santa Maria Novella is the first church I can remember in any detail, apart from the chapel at my private school. Giotto's Tower and the Duomo, too, are early memories, and in fact I knew them too well to find them interesting; and only realized the full beauty of Brunelleschi's dome, on a spring evening not so many years ago, when I caught sight of the huge bulk of it with a horned moon in the empty sky above, from the upper cloister of San Lorenzo. Then one saw its iconic importance as symbol of Florence, and wondered no more at how much it had been admired. It has been there, and is still there despite wars and floods; while the little landmarks of life come and go, or, almost worse, are changed and lose all character, like Doney's, my beloved sweet shop of childhood, with its *granita d'arancio*, and *chocolat Péruvien*, this latter to be eaten from its box with a little wooden spoon in its lid, both of such treats now gone for ever and never to be again, and a part of childhood Florence.

Even the paintings of Fra Angelico I remember from childhood, and certainly from the time I was seven or eight years old, because my grandmother – who was a lady of much character, but of pious proclivities and potentialities as powerful and tyrannical as any form of drug addiction – in passages and bedrooms of her houses at Gosden and at Scalby, had those early coloured prints of Fra Angelico – are they lithographs, or not? – they were, I believe, published by the Arundel Society in the forties and fifties of last century, I doubt not under the auspices and encouragement of the Prince Consort who was one of the first to appreciate the early masters. There were the prints, and I think, also, actual painted copies of small figures, trumpet-blowing angels and the like, out of his paintings in San Marco. All these, when I come to think of it, must have been relics of my grandfather and grandmother's honeymoon tour of Italy in 1858. My aunt Florence, I may add, in whom the religious propensities had reached to pathetic and serio-comic limits, as I remember, had pale golden hair of a naïve and holy innocence that must have been touching and beautiful when she was a child and a young girl, and was very like, even when I remember her, to an angel in almost any one of Fra Angelico's paintings. How clearly I recall being prayed for by her for playing with matches and setting a hearthrug on fire in my bedroom! We knelt together, I would like to recall, in the little window looking into the conservatory – which in my grandmother's time, while she lived there, had been full of tropical birds and flowers – from that library in the house at Scarborough that is preserved in its original state as some sort of little family museum. It is an odd, if touching memory, that few of the present or coming generations will have experienced! But how often it must have happened in the past!

The fair-haired, trumpet-blowing, azure-robed angels of Fra Angelico were therefore no strangers to me. But in the second and happiest phase of my Florentine association which was in the years just after 1920, his place in my admiration and affection was taken by Benozzo Gozzoli (1421–97) who is thought to have worked for a time as his assistant in the cathedral at Orvieto. Probably at the start, because his landscape backgrounds in the little chapel of the Palazzo Riccardi nearly resemble the cypresses and stone pines, or the fields of vineyards and distant buildings upon hills round Montegufoni, the villa my father had bought in Tuscany. And immediately I wanted to see all other works by Benozzo; his scenes from the life of St Augustine in Sant' Agostino at San Gimignano of the many towers, and at the little hill town of Montefalco; even becoming curious about the manuscript of Virgil said to have miniatures by him in the Biblioteca Riccardiana at Florence, an inquisitiveness not yet satisfied, but I think the miniatures must have been wrongly ascribed to Benozzo, or more would have been seen or heard of them by now. But of course Benozzo's masterpieces were at Pisa, on the walls of the Campo Santo. Indeed these frescoes, and Signorelli's marvellous painting of *Pan and Apollo* in Berlin, were the worst casualties where pictures are concerned, of the Second World War.* Luckily for myself, I often saw his frescoes at Pisa, have written of them, more as a poet than art historian, and, as well, of the earlier *Triumph of Death* by another and less-known master, and can never forget them, but more especially the Benozzo of *Noah's Vintage* which was beautiful and inspiring beyond words. How terrible that it should have perished! The wild flowers and small birds, the mongrel dog playing with two small babes, even the loose pebbles and bits of stone had life in them, as had the wooden beams of the vine trellis. And as for the young maidens carrying baskets of grapes upon their heads, the dangling grape bunches, and the treading of the grapes before that immortal landscape of little hills and cypresses and small farms and villages, immortal, but gone in a moment, this fresco by itself out of some two dozen

---

* Another casualty of the Second World War, it could be said cynically, was, or is, the Church of Santa Chiara at Naples, 'restored' in a single night by the American Air Force from being an eighteenth-century ballroom with painted ceiling by Sebastiano Conca of *David dancing before the Ark* to its original state, more or less, as built by the Angevin, Robert the Wise, King of Naples, early in the fourteenth century.

frescoed scenes by Benozzo was indeed beautiful beyond imagining. Not upon a heroic, or gigantic or cyclopaean scale, but beautiful; beautiful as such a poet as Robert Herrick is beautiful, and one need say no more!

Curiously, although Benozzo gives such intense pleasure he is relegated to the second or third rank of Italian painters, from which one may think he would be too humble in character to emerge as the result of his own complaining. The, otherwise, excellent *Penguin Dictionary of Art and Artists** gives five lines to him; a like amount to an obscurity like Dirck van Baburen, and twenty-one lines to Hendrik Terbruggen, the two of them not particularly interesting followers at a becoming distance of the great Caravaggio, and members of the Utrecht School. Much depends of course upon what is the latest talk among the *cognoscenti*. It seems only fair that appreciation should be weighed and measured in units of enjoyment and pleasure given. Happiness, and the radiance of being alive in a living landscape should count for more than tenebrism and 'a predilection for strong contrasts of light and shadow'. Pinturicchio, on the other hand, is allowed thirteen as against Benozzo's six lines, Pinturicchio being generally not much more than a good story book illustrator as may be judged from his frescoes in the Cathedral Library at Siena, though it is only fair to add that this view of Pinturicchio alters considerably on seeing the chapel in Santa Maria in Aracoeli, at Rome, frescoed by him with scenes from the life of St Bernardino of Siena. One would never think from the Piccolomini Library at Siena, from the Appartmento Borgia in the Vatican, and elsewhere, in the Cappella Baglioni in the cathedral at Spello, that Pinturicchio could attain to such heights of fantasy and poetry. He is in fact a yardstick by which to assess and judge of Gozzoli.

But the Florentine empyrean too soon darkened into twilight. Having lasted, it is true, for some two centuries and a half, but it was over and finished soon after 1500. There may have been an endemic strain in the Florentine blood inimical to conjugal life and its procedures and consequences. The signs, and the report or sounds of this are in their greatest geniuses, in Leonardo and Michelangelo, in Botticelli and in Benvenuto Cellini. But there is no noise of it among Venetian painters, and it is typical and could give credence to this theory, that while Venice had great painters, Mantegna, Carpaccio, Cima, Giovanni Bellini, contemporary to Botticelli, Filippino Lippi and the best of Florence, painting in Venice was not nearly at an end. The Venetians had still Titian, Tintoretto, Veronese, to come, not to mention the finale and curtain to Venetian painting in the eighteenth century. It could be, also, that the fact that Tuscany hardly had credibility as an entity and an independent state – in comparison to the authority and pomp of Venice, great upon the mainland or *terra firma* and ruling the Adriatic, and beyond, with its galleys, being the only independence in Italy to emerge since the fall of Rome – that this may have imparted strength and more lasting power to the Venetian painters.

Long association with the English since the time of Sir Horace Mann, the friend of Walpole, or even earlier, had given some sort of false affinity with the English so that one could think the young women in Botticelli's *Primavera* had

* *Penguin Dictionary of Art and Artists*, by Peter and Linda Murray, Harmondsworth 1959.

taken it upon themselves with the passing of the centuries to look English in order to please. There is – if it is still there – a wayside shrine or tabernaculum at Prato, by Filippino Lippi,* in which the Madonna is so much of this appearance that an absent-minded savant or stray spinster, if such there still are, might start talking English to her. Or it is that our young people for a generation or two, and under the influence of poets and pre-Raphaelite painters, began to look like this, for there is no sign of it whether in Elizabethan or in eighteenth-century portraits, least of all, in portraits by Van Dyck, in Peter Lely, or in Kneller. And as surely, under other influences, it has died out in the present generation. There were the expatriates living in Florence, usually for cogent private reasons of their own, as had been the case since the middle of the eighteenth century, and there was still the dying whisper of Vernon Lee and Mrs Ross and Henry James in the air. Not so much in the narrow streets as in villas on the hills above the town. Then came the moment when my father moved into the house he had already owned for ten years and we were marooned out there with him in full eccentricity, by then, though not really as recorded by my brother for he was much kinder and more affectionate than he is portrayed. But the house was on a little-frequented road, quite out of the way of those going to Siena or on the way to Rome, and the better for that. If you went from Florence to Siena by train, I may add it being still necessary until the early nineteen-thirties to change twice, at Empoli and at Poggibonsi, which made the journey of some sixty miles into a minor experience. And by the same token, how many villagers I remember at Amalfi where I spent the winters from 1920 to 1925, who could not read or write. Old 'Barbanera' for instance who brought the letters up the steep flights of steps to the Cappuccini, and his wife Fortunata who were surely born, both of them, well within the time of the Bourbon Kings of the Two Sicilies.

The effect of many springs and autumns spent in and near Florence with intermissions, during the twenty years from 1919 to 1939, was to over-familiarize one, if that is possible, with the contents of the Botticelli room and of the Tribuna at the Uffizi, particularly, too, as I remembered them well as a small boy before the First World War. I found myself, not preferring certainly, but more interested in the, then, forgotten gallery in the Palazzo Medici painted in 1684 by the Neapolitan Luca Giordano with 'the Medici as gods of light among the deities of Olympus',† or in neglected Florentine painters like Giovanni di San Giovanni (1599–1636). More interested, because I felt that more could be done with them. And before long I was able to follow this same Luca Giordano to Naples, his birthplace, and admire him in the Certosa di San Martino above the town and the Parthenopaean Bay, where he painted the ceiling and cupola of the Treasury as the final *tour-de-force* of his old age, non-stop, during forty-eight hours. This is the stupid sort of feat which has harmed his reputation and caused him to be nicknamed 'Fa Presto'. But of course he was a much better painter than this

---

* 'To the left at the end of the Via Santa Margherita, close to the Bisenzio (Key at the house, No. 293)'; Baedeker's *Northern Italy*.

† This painted gallery in the Palazzo Medici is in the same building and under the same roof as the chapel frescoed by Benozzo Gozzoli.

implies, and his frescoes at the Certosa of Naples are inventive as ever and beauti-
ful in colour. The churches of the town contain many paintings by him which,
with others of the school are beginning now to receive their due of attention.

During this period in my life when travel, I suppose, cost a quarter or even a
fifth of what it is costing now, among much else of more importance and greater
interest, I was enabled to see the frescoes of Luca Giordano, this *coryphée* of the
East', as Professor Justi calls him with Teutonic humour – coupling him in the
same sentence with Tiepolo and with Raphael Mengs – in the grim setting of the
Escorial, upon the vaults of the church, and on the frieze and ceiling of the grand
stair. But, also, on the ceiling of the Sacristía at Toledo Cathedral, in the crumb-
ling hall of the Buen Retiro at Madrid, and in the camarín of the remote monastery
of Guadalupe in Estremadura. It is the *modelli* of Giordano, of Solimena, di Mura,
Corrado Giaquinto, Paolo de Matteis, and other painters of the Neapolitan school,
that are now so much sought after by museums and collectors. In those days, if
and when found, they could have been bought for a few pounds. But they have a
much greater decorative value than the huge canvases of the Bolognese school,
and the painters named have, each, his character and individuality. For a quick
sampling of their work in its best, the sacristy of San Paolo Maggiore at Naples
should be seen. Here, in decaying splendour, are Solimena's frescoes of the
Conversion of St Paul and the *Fall of Simon Magus*, and it will no longer be a
mystery why Fragonard should have made a drawing of one of them for the
Voyage Pittoresque of the Abbé de Saint-Non (1786). Solimena, who had been
dead for forty years, was to sink into oblivion by the end of the century, but up
to the time of Fragonard had been a part of civilization, and one of the painters
of Italy and therefore of the world. As such, it was only natural that Fragonard
should admire him. And indeed an affinity with the French in their grand
moments of drama links him with Delacroix who is much akin to him, as has been
remarked before, in his *grands sujets* or *grandes machines* of painting.

To return to Florence, those persons interested should make a comparison
in their minds – if such mental games are permitted, or even physically possible
for much longer – between Luca Giordano at the Palazzo Medici and Giam-
battista Tiepolo on the ceiling of the Palazzo Clérici in Milan, painted in 1740.
Here, Tiepolo's theme is *The Course of the Sun* – the chariot of the sun with
Mercury for charioteer crossing the continents of the world – and it will be noted
that the nereids and mermen of Giordano with sprigs of coral in their hair, or
indeed his cupids or merboys, trident in hand, sitting on a bank or reef of coral,
while a triton sounds his conch-shell close by, if not as physically beautiful are not
less full of invention than the like figurants of Tiepolo. And if the wonder of this
painted room at the Clérici is the quadriga of the sun and its white horses passing
through the clouds in the centre of the ceiling, then again in the Palazzo Medici,
but along the edges of his ceiling, Giordano has painted the chariot of Neptune
drawn by piebald horses. In the end, Giordano is not inferior in handling and in
imagination, but only in poetry and in the physical beauty portrayed by the great
Venetian. The Luca Giordano fresco was painted, as has been said, in 1684, and
the Tiepolo in 1740, after an interval of forty-six years, which is salutary to think

of. For what would be said now of a painter in 1970 at work in the mannerisms of 1924! But it requires more than one lifetime, and more than one generation, to perfect an art and bring it to fruition. This has been proved over and over again in the past, and it is no less true of the present.

In the end it is inevitable to return to Italy. One has never, in parenthesis, heard of anyone who felt he must live for even a part of every year in Holland because of the great Dutch painters. The school of Paris is over and finished. There are all the other reasons for going to this most beautiful and interesting of modern cities, but no longer, as was the case till not long ago, that it is a living, and live art centre. But there had been the expectation, long a certainty, that my wife and I might live our last years in Italy in the house that I remembered since I was twelve years old. This ambition fell to the ground, and was altered, in strange circumstances and in secrecy, in the last six months of his life and only revealed to me the night my brother died. So our long family association with Florence is to end in sadness and humiliation. There are things one never thought to happen, and that do happen; and it is the same with long loyalties and affections which do not stand the stress of time. So stories are born, and so legends die. And in the shock of that, spread needlessly over some eighteen months and made horrible by every unnecessary annoyance, it became impossible for me to write the book I had intended to write, and had been waiting to write. From which I salvage the one chapter, and place it here for entr'acte or interlude to ease my mind. It being mpossible to continue with this present and longer work in which it now features and not think in sadness of what could have been. Having hoped to come back to Italy where I learned everything, and now the hope is gone.

On Luca della Robbia

Florence, in virtue of its name, claims some special favour of the world, has been given it by acclamation and general consent over several centuries – has kept that, and not lost it yet. It is still the 'art city' of Europe, that is to say of the Occident, as Paris is the fashion and luxury centre of the world. But, as is inevitable with an 'art city', the dust is settling on it fast. Better, perhaps, to lie in ruins like ancient Athens; and be judged by your bones, not by the ageing flesh. Yet what other city has induced parents of different nationalities to call their daughters by that city's name? Not New York, certainly, nor London; nor Vienna, though 'Wien, Wien' comes enough into popular songs; hardly yet, Venice, although there may be one 'Venetia' to fifty or a hundred 'Florences' in four or five tongues, no less The custom is proper and peculiar to Florence; to Firenze, once Fiorenza, from the Latin Florentia or 'town of Flowers', so that it would seem the Romans had noticed the beauty of the Tuscan landscape, and perhaps admired the *primavera* and the coming of the first flowers of spring. Not that in fact those are remarkable to the point of being sensational in the countryside round Florence. But they flower, as it were, upon the senses and obtrude themselves gently upon you. Perhaps a white, a bluish or greyish-white iris growing on a bank beside a path, the *Iris fiorentina*, in pattern of the lily-towers of Florence. Or, a day or two later, walking beyond the cypresses and stone pines, below the vines, in a little wood, treading on white anemones with every step, there was of a sudden the sensation of trespassing in an entire conservatoire of nightingales, the young ones trying out their scales, and the parents correcting them, at times singing a whole passage over again and making the young nightingale repeat it after them, note for note. A few weeks, or a month or two later, you could hear them evening after evening, fully rehearsed and singing perfectly, but that earlier experience had been the *primavera* when they had been little more than fledglings trying out their voices and testing, too, their wings.

A countryside, then, where the early spring is of exceptional beauty and delicacy, and suggestive of immortal youthfulness. It has not the full and fierce orchestration of the tropics though that has its softer and more lulling moments in the mauve, the powder – or even porcelain – blue of jacaranda trees – that are surely among the beautiful things of the world – but neither, in another key altogether, has the Tuscan spring any effect to surpass the positive, the nearly metallic clangour of a buttercup meadow in full cloth-of-gold, lying out as far as the distant elm trees and half-hidden church tower in a full and blazing noonday in June.

But, also, the *primavera* is and should be Italy before the coming of the orange and the lemon grove, before the wistaria trellis, and in innocence of the cactus and the prickly pear. It has the stone pine and the cypress, which are enough and more than enough with the flowering meadows of the early masters. With wild flowers sometimes not readily identifiable in the foreground, and the sunlight, undiluted, falling upon rose-petal walls and the very simplest and most primitive of roses and other flowers, not fully domesticated yet, or sporting and performing as they will before many human generations have come and gone.

Tuscany, thought of in this context, becomes for about the span of two life-times one of those rare communities in which the hand of man can scarce go wrong. Not, that is to say, in what they inflict on each other, but only and simply in the work of their hands. It may well be concomitant with much cruelty and poverty, but doubtless it was one of the flowering periods in the arts of man. Were they aware of this, themselves? It would seem unlikely, because it came freely and was not forced. Nor did it end in extravagance and ruin. It just came and went, and had passed by. The *primavera* was followed by the dog-days and the dull heat of summer, like every other summer.

So, now, in this 'city of flowers', to the flower market, to which I was so often taken by my mother, but the best time was on Thursday mornings. The Mercato Nuovo where is the bronze statue of the wild boar, and there are the flower-stalls under the arcades where is the very epicentre or the hub of Florence among the tuberoses and carnations. And indeed no more than that. For it is a dead city: a city of dead souls. No more will ever come of it. It had been dead from the neck upward long before the Medici became Grand Dukes of Tuscany in 1569, when it could still move its limbs and was not quite swollen and hyper-trophied; as, witness, the Medici treasure in the ground floor rooms of the Palazzo Pitti which is a collection of freak objects in precious stones, agate, lapis lazuli and the like, engraved crystals, baroque pearls, gems shaped into dwarfs, into heads of Negresses, or chimaeras, in fact a treasury of the fantastic with only the 'Green Vaults' of Dresden for its peer. Such was the *brutto seicento* in apogee; the 'August, or pompous, high meridian' of the arts, when the arts had little more to do, and nothing more to say.

Such is the later Florence of the Medici Grand Dukes with their Habsburg features and 'Alfonsine' chins; of the Cappella Medicea, most depressing of all tomb-chambers for it lacks both the authentic gloom of the Escurial and the funereal genius of Guarini at the Santo Sudario at Turin. It is the Florence of the Medici busts that awaited you at top of the Uffizi stair, and have now been stupidly removed to the ground floor where they make no effect at all; among them, the half-Habsburg Cardinal Leopoldo de' Medici, more Spanish than the Spaniards, founder of the Uffizi and one of the greatest art collectors there has ever been; down to Gian Gastone, last of the Medici, crapulous and gluttonous and highly unpleasant in his tastes and appetites. Also, it is the Florence of so many buildings in the local green stone, with the bat-wing volutes under their windows which are characteristic of the age of Jacques Callot and of Stefano della Bella in their fantastic frontispieces for court masques.

And now having the feeling of Florence in us, whether from early childhood or but new arrived, we are on the narrow pavement at touching distance from that most typical of Florentine palaces, the Palazzo Strozzi, hardly able to move ahead in the jostling crowd and at the same time in danger from cars and 'Vespas' if we step down into the gutter. The huge stone cabinet of a palace, of which we can touch the ramp with our fingers, was begun a year or two before Columbus went to the New World, and is on a massive, a cyclopaean scale for a town house. Its huge rusticated individual stones look indestructible; and above them is the celebrated cornice which is an enlarged copy from an antique fragment of cornice, but certainly worked upon or adapted by a giant hand. The whole is intensely satisfying to the eyes as are, also, the arched windows with columned openings set in the building, and the flat 'eyebrows' above them of the same stone. And there are, as well, the dragon link-holders and the corner-lanterns or *fanali* which are by Caparra, a famous ironsmith, the masterworks of their sort and kind. The snakes or dragons of the link-holders look to inhabit the rusticated stones upon which they are set; while the *fanali* have as much of the message of Florence in their design as the halberd-prow or *ferro* of a gondola has to tell us of the back canals of Venice and the warning cries of the gondoliers. How better to design a corner-lantern then here at the Palazzo Strozzi where with lavish Italian hand the ironwork rises at the corners like climbing or aspiring flames made permanent, or like the generous wasting of the coils and fronds of their favourite *pasta*! The Italian canon of scale – perhaps with road-making their one trait inherited from their Roman ancestors – is in all and every detail of the Palazzo Strozzi, and this is a characteristic of which the French taste was not capable. They had never the bold or giant hand of the Italians; not anywhere in their post-Gothic architecture; save perhaps in the crowded roof-line of Chambord and with the double stairways of Mansart's Orangerie at Versailles. But it is manifest in the Palazzo Strozzi; and eloquent in its massive bulk of an intention of permanence that proves itself in the phenomenon of the nearby Palazzo Rucellai, another and still earlier town house of mid-fifteenth century by Bernardo Rossellino, still inhabited by the Rucellai family, and by other town houses in Florence still in like condition, such as the Palazzo Pucci.

But such buildings are reticent and have to be searched for in the narrow streets. The visual impression of the city comes from the polychrome fronts of the churches which are far from beautiful and as to the two chief of them, those of the Duomo and of Santa Croce, are nineteenth-century reconstructions. Is Giotto's Tower beautiful? Has it the hues of dawn and sunset, as these are to be seen in dove-throat softness on walls and buildings in Fra Angelico's paintings? It is for the reader to decide for himself. At least the Piazza del Duomo is no longer, as it used to be, a trip-up spider-web of tramlines, and one can look up at the windows of the tower that Ruskin so ingenuously admired. And the other, and ineradicable impression of the city – the memory of the sculptures apart that stand in the

Loggia dei Lanzi and in the Piazza della Signoria, statues by Donatello, by John of Bologna, by Benvenuto Cellini, such an assembly of sculptures standing in the open air as cannot have been assembled since the time of the Roman Emperors, or since the fall of Constantinople to the Crusaders in 1204 – derives, I think, from ceramic reliefs by the della Robbias. Of which one may not be directly conscious in any one instance; unless it be with the medallions of children between the arches of the Foundling Hospital, or Spedale degli Innocenti. There are a pair of typical *brutto seicento* fountains and a bronze equestrian statue of a Medici Grand Duke in the piazza in front of the hospital, and one has probably passed through the square on the way to see the paintings by Fra Angelico in the Convento di San Marco. That, I think, is where an impression of the della Robbias is born; but the medallions of children at the Foundling Hospital are in fact by Andrea della Robbia, who was nephew to Luca, and not the great man of the family.

The uncle, who was born in 1400 and died in 1482, at some early date in his career discovered a method by which he could combine the lead glazes used in pottery with sculptures and bas-reliefs in terracotta, or, in fact, produce vitrified or enamelled sculptures. The basic della Robbia – whether by him, his nephew Andrea, or his great-nephews, by which time it had become a family industry – is a white pottery Madonna against an almost sky-blue background. The Madonnas of Luca della Robbia are of exceptional physical beauty, as beautiful though very different in type as the peasant-women Madonnas of Giovanni Bellini, and this of course has been a reason for the popularity of Luca della Robbia. It would seem impossible to reproduce a physically beautiful and life-size human being by ceramic process; not even Franz Anton Bustelli, the famous modeller of Nymphenburg porcelain achieved this, though he came near it in certain little female figures from the Comédie Vénitienne. But Luca della Robbia was able to accomplish this practical impossibility, and there are Madonnas by him in the Bargello which are as facially beautiful of feature as sculptures by Donatello; in particular the lunette from the former church of San Pierino; a Madonna and Child with two attendant angels and surrounding wreath, described by one authority as 'abominably put together, with no regard for direction',* the result of unskilful restoration but, in truth, it is beautiful enough with its separate bunches of flowers bound or trussed up with blue ribbons, and consisting of white lilies, roses, and olives, with leaves of all colours from robin's egg blue to dark green.

Even lovelier is another lunette in the Bargello, which was formerly above a door on the outside of a house in the Via dell' Agnolo. Here the Madonna is beautiful indeed and the epitome of a clear-eyed, beautiful young Tuscan woman. The angels at each side of her hold pots of white lilies, while the surrounding wreath of bunches of roses and lilies with, again, leaves of robin's egg blue and yellow and green, is better composed. The child is fully clothed in this lunette, and not naked, possibly, as the same author suggests, for the reason that he stood above the entrance to a convent where young girls went to school.

Florence must have had an additional fascination to its streets when there were

* *Luca della Robbia*, by Allan Marquand, London 1914.

the lunettes, and often a *stemma* or family coat-of-arms by one or other of the della Robbias on the walls of the houses, as was the case until about the middle or end of last century when many of them fell to pieces or were removed or sold to private collectors and to museums. Such coloured terracotta reliefs represent of course the fatal charm and facility of Italy, and up to this point are of the aesthetic value of a beautiful Neapolitan song from the festival of Piedigrotta. In poorer examples of more sentimental appeal it is the eternal Italy of '*O sole mio*' and '*Santa Lucia*' with the roses and mandolines of Naples and the carnation terraces of San Remo never far away in spirit. But this is not so in such lunettes as this pair by Luca della Robbia in the Bargello, where the direct, unfrightened glance of the Madonna is something without precedent and wholly redolent of the Florentine spring time in the arts.

What force and authority of vision can be given to a mere coat-of-arms is to be seen in the *stemma* of King René of Anjou, now in the Victoria and Albert Museum. This is a masterly and superb affair of huge size, and of as much authority as the iron *fanali* of the Palazzo Strozzi. It is circular or medallion-shaped, and contains the King's shield in the middle, quartering the arms of Hungary, Naples, and Jerusalem, to the thrones of which he was claimant, together with the arms of Anjou, his birthright, and of Aragón (to which in fact he succeeded and held Sicily, but could never enter Naples). This travelled and peripatetic sovereign, much beloved in his native Anjou and in Provence,* had visited the Pazzi family of Florence and stayed with them in their villa at Fiesole. Hence his *stemma* from the Loggia dei Pazzi.

A pair of flaming braziers stand at each side of his shield-of-arms in its mantling embroidered with the lilies of France and lined with ermine, and the blue-purple flames from the braziers fleck the green ground of the medallion. Over the shield is a splendidly bold helmet under a *fleur-de-lys* which could signify both France and Florence; and springing from each side of this helmet a pair of dragon wings stand for Aragón. It is the wings with their ten pinions to a side that give character to King René's *stemma* and that fill the medallion. The other feature of which is the circular wreath or garland surrounding it. This is composed – though it is true that their recognition demands the degree of botanical knowledge that can disport itself, with the aid of field glasses, on the roof bosses of Lincoln, or among the stone capitals at the chapter house at Southwell Minster – of seven varieties of fruit, pines, pears, lemons, plums, quinces, grapes, and cucumber, each variety of fruit appearing in multiples of four bunches, all differing from each other – and this, even if on occasion such as this it could be less trouble by far to let each bunch be different and not slavishly the copy and facsimile of its neighbour.

Another of Luca della Robbia's *stemmas*, and of the same Pazzi family, has a garland of pine cones, grapes, oranges, apples, and in succession, grapes, cucumbers, pine cones, and apples moving round 'in the direction of the hands of a

---

* King René of Anjou, as quickly known from his features as his contemporary Duke Guidobaldo of Urbino, appears with his wife Jeanne de Laval in the painting by Nicholas Froment of *Moses and the Burning Bush* in the cathedral at Aix-en-Provence.

clock',* or, following your whim, anti-clockwise, according to which way your eyes pursue them round. While another *stemma*, of the Serristori family, and better preserved, has a garland of grapes, citrons, pine cones, and apples, with the addition of oranges and of *zucchini* or gourds, this time arranged on purpose to go round widdikins, that is to say, in the opposite direction to its companion *stemma*. So much play, then, can be had of the arranging of bunches of fruit or flowers.†

Yet other *stemmas* by Luca della Robbia are to be seen, but not easily, on the outside of the church of Or San Michele. But they are the *stemmas* of the Florentine guilds, of the stone masons and wood carvers, the silk merchants, and the chamber of commerce or *mercanzia*; the surrounding garland of which latter is composed of sixteen bunches of flowers; citrons, beans, pomegranates, chestnuts, 'followed' – clockwise or widdikins? – by 'apples or quinces', doubtfully, thistles or artichokes, *zucchi* or cucumbers, pine cones, quinces, plums, grapes, poppies, oranges, figs, pears, and olives, all with their proper leaves, 'and with white and violet-red flowers freely interspersed', as though left lying carelessly in casual abandon upon the different kinds of fruit.

Such are the lighter or lyrical moments, the *lieder* it could be said, of Luca della Robbia, but he is to be seen – when the church is open again after the disastrous flood – in more solemn mood in the tomb of Benozzo Federighi, Bishop of Fiesole, in the church of Santa Trinità in the Via Tornabuoni, a monument that, anyway, is now at its third removal from church to church, and not likely to have benefited as well from the recent tragedy and destruction. The effigy of the bishop is a little dull and conventional; still more so, the figures of the Virgin, the dead Christ and St John, on panels above the recumbent figure of the bishop. The winged angels below him holding the wreath around his epitaph are adequate; but the beauty of his tomb is the polychrome frame surrounding it, formed of flowers in coloured terracotta. It is indeed a glazed pottery mosaic, uninteresting as that sounds but beautiful, and much admired by Vasari, who wrote of it 'questa opera è meravigliosa e rarissima'; a pattern most complex in the planning, so that its repetitions should not come too near each other, and composed of his usual flowers, roses, lilies, pine cones, pomegranates, and olive branches with addition, somewhat surprisingly, of morning glories. What could be termed in abrupt phrase another of Luca della Robbia's 'fruit friezes' is to be seen in a church at Impruneta, the suburb of Florence known also from Jacques Callot's etching of the *Fair of Impruneta*; though the *baldacchino* of which this is part has an overloaded gilt cornice that prevents appreciation of the grapes, citrons and quinces in groups of four apiece, as they issued from the kiln.

But a work of the greatest beauty by him is his ceramic cupola to the Cappella Pazzi at Santa Croce, where he must have worked in close association with Brunelleschi. In the centre are the arms of the Pazzi, two dolphins standing on their tails and five crosses on a violet-blue field with surrounding garland; and

* Allan Marquand, *op. cit.*
† Both *stemmas* are in the Palazzo Serristori, one of the town houses in the old part of Florence lying between Santa Croce and the Duomo.

round this central medallion are three circles of sixteen medallions in each row, which circles grow bigger in their turn as they fill the cupola, to end with an outermost row of half-medallions; all and every one of which medallions having a yellow flower on a blue ground, with a white circular frame round it which carries a wreath or garland of green laurel. The interstices between these rows of medallions, alike large and small, have yellow flowers on a ground intended for red porphyry and green serpentine. This is polychrome architecture as it is found nowhere else; and the whole circle of the cupola touches on the edges of four cockle shells which come out from the corners and complete the ceiling. This is merely the porch of the Cappella Pazzi. The chapel itself has four coloured medallions of the Evangelists in the spandrels of its cupola; and here perhaps Brunelleschi imposed his will upon della Robbia, because the medallions though well suited to their purpose are flat and entirely lacking in Luca della Robbia's powers of invention and imagination.

There is no other completely integrated architectural scheme carried out and by him, while I am debarred from writing of his most famous work, the Cantorie or Choir Galleries of the Duomo, removed years ago to the Cathedral Museum, because of a dislike engendered during childhood in Florence for his groups of singing and dancing children. I must admit, too, to having dismissed over a period of years such stray works by the della Robbias as one comes across casually in Florence without looking for them, just as I at the time disliked and despised the operas of Puccini. But in the end one repents of one's own sillinesses, and begins to wonder at the beauty and fluency of his Madonnas; all and each one of them physically beautiful; a Madonna for instance in his usual cowled hood or head-covering with naked infant, and the child has his finger in his mouth and is evidently teething.* To look through a collection of photographs of his Madonnas is to admire as many beauty queens in succession, but all of them radiant and not vulgar, and as intensely pleasurable as listening to Italian singing.

The art of the della Robbias fell into decline in the hands of the nephew and great-nephews. Blue skies still predominate, and there are the white clouds of early spring. But what a variety of pose Luca della Robbia achieved from the simple theme of mother and child! There are the Madonnas and child, half-length in niches, as in a half-shell, with the curve of the child's body and its left arm round its mother's neck, face against face, and with left-hand pulling at his mother's headdress where the folds of that touch on her chin. Always the Virgin's hands are of utmost beauty as they hold his body. Sometimes the child is standing; sometimes, sitting in her lap; or being carried, often on her left hip as though she were walking, or standing still to talk. He is a small naked baby of a few months; or, again, a two-year-old boy in a shift with long sleeves down to his wrists. But, always, he is intelligent and human; on occasion, enough so to help and comfort by his glance. Again, he leans his head on his mother's chest and has his eyes open as though thinking. The cares of the world are on him already and keeping him awake. Mother and child are people of the enlightenment, not of the Middle Ages; not Florentine aristocrats, nor yet, exactly, peasants, but townspeople with

* In the former Kaiser-Friedrich Museum in Berlin.

perhaps a summer *villino* or farmhouse in the country a few miles from the city.

The portable nature of the ceramic works of the della Robbia family, for all they accomplished could easily be packed in its separate units and assembled again, has had the effect that quite a few of their works have been moved from the places originally designed and intended for them. For instance in the church at Peretola, which is a village on the road to Poggio a Caiano, there is a marble tabernacle by Luca della Robbia which was moved thither from a hospital chapel in Florence.* For its early date (1442) this is an astonishingly sophisticated work when we consider the England of Henry v, or contemporary Germany, or France. The elegant, fluted and acanthus-capitall'd columns that form the frame of the tabernacle with its marble figures, and the sky-blue background to the relief above that of the Pietà; more so still, the coloured frieze of winged cupids' heads, with the green garland uniting them with its roses and morning glories, has the authentic breath of the early and pure Renaissance.

Then, again, the fact that such pieces could be carried away and put together again has resulted in works by the della Robbia family being found not only in near-by towns like Prato or Pistoja, but as far away as Venice (San Giobbe), Bolsena, and even far off Aquila, in the Abruzzi. Perhaps an altar or a relief by the della Robbias, even though not of the first quality, can never look to better advantage than in some hilltop church in Tuscany. This is because its colours take the hues of the landscape and the skies; the figures portrayed are those to be met with in the lanes and by-paths and standing in front of their houses engaged, as likely as not, in straw-plaiting for the *fiaschi* of Chianti wine, or to make the wide brimmed, high crowned hats of Tuscan straw. There must be reliefs and altar pieces of this nature in so many villages and small towns like Radicofani and Santa Fiora on the slopes of Mont' Amiata; perhaps better still at Stia and other villages in the Casentino. Their blue and white colours are perfectly habituated to the sky and the clouds, and their green garlands to the cypresses and country flowers. But it would seem that the reliefs of the della Robbias are at their greatest beauty at St Francis's convent of La Verna with its three churches, where no less than fifteen works by various members of the family are to be admired. Probably the balsamic air of the beech and pinewoods has helped in this, and has kept their bright colours untarnished for five hundred years.

The *Florentine Entr'acte* is now accomplished, it having been something I set myself to learn about and try to understand, having till now taken the della Robbias that are so much in evidence in Florence for granted. Or, in other words, gone by and never looked at them; being even faintly disinterested and bored. As by the Madonna lilies in a cottage garden that are always there, five or six stems of them, every summer; and one never remembers to ask whether much care is taken of them, or if they just come up out of the soil with their green points showing after an early summer shower. Whether the one, or the other, they contrive somehow to be there again, and so it is with the reliefs and medallions of the della Robbias.

* A crutch which was the emblem of the hospital appears on little medallions in the spandrels of the tabernacle.

It is now for the third year running that I have tried and failed to get plants of the common iris of Tuscany (*Iris fiorentina*) from which the orris-root is made, and each time the stock has failed and no other nursery can supply it.* I had forgotten from long absence how beautiful it can be, seeing it again after so many years growing by the roadside under the cement posts of a vineyard; or, better still, in full light which it softens incredibly as though to its own requirements. What a marvellous moment, that of this soft blue, slate grey-blue iris, semitone of the blue flag-iris of the sedges and damp places, heraldic counterpart to the lily-towers of Florence, that of the Palazzo Vecchio but, also, of the lost, humiliated and forsworn castle above the bastions and the cypresses! Better to forget it, as with that other lost house above the collieries and the woods of bluebells, and never set eyes on it again.

* Obtained at last, after much time and trouble, but it flowers here much more pallidly than in Tuscany where the bluer forms predominate.

BOOK
EIGHT

Concorde and Concordia

And now there is not much time left, but time enough. It being a commodity which is at once transitory and eternal. So that one could feel one has had enough of it, and in the next breath call for more. As of something exquisite and delightful of which, when one comes to think of it, there has been plenty and to spare. But there are other angles of approach to it, mortal and perishable sensitivities that fade and vanish with the person. As of the dear old Concordia at Bamberg, which I saw again one morning less than a month ago, not having seen it for nearly a lifetime, since 1922 or 1923.

The Concordia is an old club-house of 'William and Mary' date, were it in England, down on the riverbank opposite the fishermen's houses where the boats are tied up and the fishing-nets spread out to dry under the windowboxes of geraniums. It was a delight to see the Concordia again after so many years, gaze at it and its terraced garden across the river, and take in once more and probably for the last time, the impression it gives of happy afternoons and convivial evenings. Could we but join the old friends there for a few moments, and not having seen the Concordia for almost a lifetime, this did not seem entirely out of question, they would be sitting in their long wigs drinking the Franconian or Stein wine, to which they are welcome and it is their birthright.*

When I was in Bamberg all those years ago we stayed for two or three nights, and looked at the Concordia and admired it every day. Because of its pleasing name and sensible, dignified appearance. But Bamberg on all counts is one of the oldest and most interesting towns in Central Europe, coming second only after Prague from which and from the frontier of Bohemia it is not far away. Several days could go by in Bamberg, seeing the treasures in the cathedral, the poodle-like portraits of Holy Roman Emperors in the Residenz, with their huge periwigs and Alfonsine chins, the old Town Hall with its fanciful and lovely balconies built on a bridge over the river, and walking about looking for the old houses in its narrow, winding streets.

But now I discover, what I did not know before, that E. T. A. Hoffmann (1776–1822) lived for five years, 1808–13, in a little house in the Schillerplatz, almost opposite the Concordia, 'in two small rooms one above the other, com-

---

* The Concordia at Bamberg is probably by one of the Dientzenhofer brothers, a family of architects who, also, built churches and palaces in Prague. It is a little later than 'William and Mary', building having begun in 1716.

municating through a square opening in the floor which allowed Hoffmann sitting up there under the roof to talk with his wife in the room below, during which years he was working in the Town Theatre which had just been built. How much I wish I had seen this old theatre in 'classical style', and its stage door through which Hoffmann must so often have come in and gone out! Hoffman, like his contemporary Paganini, being a character of intense and special interest whom one much admires, even without the wish to read or have heard everything that came from his pen. But not knowing a note of his music, at least he was the inventor of Swanilda and of Doctor Coppelius, and deserving of much credit just for the creation of their names. How much in his vein is Bamberg even now!

There is that extraordinary old house in the Judengasse – word of forbidding implication for the future – a strange, nearly topheavy building with hugely heavy dormer windows on its roof-line, and great centrepiece of doorway carried up as a feature for two storeys of windows, with herms and caryatids and what not; in fact, the town house of Hofrat (or Councillor) Ignaz Tobias Boettinger. And now it appears that the Concordia was never a club-house, properly speaking, but the 'summer residence' or Hofrat Böttinger, or Boettinger, whose winter home in the Judengasse was but a few hundred yards away, the Concordia incidentally being by far the better building of the two. But it makes no difference; the purport of the Concordia remains the same. It was for convivial gatherings, and where he entertained his friends. Hoffmann must have known and admired those two old houses that are so strangely near together. At a time, too, when the Hofrat had not been dead for so long, and there may even have been persons in the town who still remembered him.

Hoffmann's own narrow and curious habitation, you can hardly call it a house, is almost at the end of the street from the theatre where he was working; and one member of the audience will have been the philosopher, Hegel, who was living impecuniously in Bamberg, meanwhile editing the local *Bamberger Zeitung* and engaged upon his *Phenomenology of the Spirit* which first made his name. It was probably at Bamberg that like Kant, another German philosopher in a parallel stage of his career, Hegel first awoke from his 'dogmatic slumber', which same phenomenon, so aptly described, and still in full potency, has descended also upon those old houses, as though they held opinions that nothing on earth could make them alter. It is this indeed which is beautiful and endearing about them.

With no shadow of doubt we are in the world of Dr Coppelius and Swanilda, and have no need to travel in imagination as far as 'the square in the little town on the borders of Galicia' which is the stage direction. It is not even necessary to have read *The Tales of Hoffmann* to see the old toy-maker coming out of the doorway where he went every week to wind up the automata and the mechanical clocks. Up that grand stairway, open to the public now from 9–12 and 14–17 hours – and how I wish I had seen it! – and some moments later down the stairs again. And Hofrat Böttinger, or Boettinger, much to his displeasure, did he but know it, is becoming indistinguishable from Dr Coppelius; like a different actor or dancer taking the rôle, and that is all.

What was I thinking about all those years ago while I was walking about in this old town? Of course I do not remember in detail, but it was much the same, probably, as today. Except that, then, I had ambitions and I have none left now. One cannot have ambitions after writing books and poetry for more than fifty years. Of course there is dissatisfaction because they could have been better. And one goes on working for the sake of working, and for self-satisfaction, however seldom satisfied. Certainly I realized the Hoffmannesque properties of those old houses and their former inhabitants. If I had not read Hoffmann, I, at least knew George Cruickshank's magical etchings for Grimm's *Fairy Tales* and for the *Peter Schlemihl* of Chamisso, in all of which there is some approximation or affinity to Hoffmann. A Swanilda, or an Olympia, I knew not, then, or ever. Or not till later, when they came before my eyes in doubled or alternate presence. It was something then lacking in my life.

But one may have thought, even so lately as this present year, of seeing Coppelius coming out of a doorway at Sasbachwalden, of previous mention, that village of timber-frame houses and petunia'd, zinnia'd balconies, in the Black Forest. But no Swanilda looking from a window, where we first see her, and a moment later coming out of the house and looking up at a window opposite, 'where a young girl sits apparently reading a book'. This latter being the doll Coppelia, probably from an automata-maker of Nuremberg, which is not far away, though Hoffmann who was born at Königsberg on the Baltic and spent his youth among Balts and Esthonians and others who from the inherent difficulty in pronouncing their names had Latinized them, thought otherwise for Coppelius and sited him far to the east of Nuremberg and Bamberg. But it could equally, as I say, have been Sasbachwalden below the fir trees and the sloping mountain meadows. Or, inded, at Neuweier, only a few miles' walk or ride away, where the landscape is quite changed for the hills are quilted from top to bottom with vines in the autumnal, clear brightness of that air. But no sign of Swanilda. She is not there. That was long ago. Another, and substitute ballerina is taking her rôle. And that is all.

So back to the Concordia and to Hofrat Böttinger. Which being in Franconia is in another Bavaria altogether from that I have frequented in the past, of the brothers Cosmas Damian and Egid Quirin Asam, and the other pair of brothers, Johann Baptist and Dominikus Zimmermann. Only to add for the mere sake of their names, Johann Michael Fischer, Balthasar Neumann, and more bucolic-sounding, however naïvely sophisticated in action, the Schmuzer brothers and Peter II Thumb.

That other world of the Concordia is solider, less brilliant, while being neither peasanty, nor aristocratic. Indeed, the Hofrat's two houses are, typically, 'burgher-palaces', as they are known locally. There could be no better word for them. And the Concordia, of them both, now, as it did then, gives out friendly feeling and conviviality. How delightful it is to think that Giambattista Tiepolo, the last lion and paragon of Venice, during the two or three years he was at work on his frescoes in the prince-bishop's palace at Würzburg, not many miles away, abstemious as we may be sure he was like most Italians, may have had this same wine in its flask-shaped bottles to inspire him. It will have been while Hofrat Böttinger was still alive. And when the Teutons were still in their proper divisions before they became dangerous. Since when, the world has changed, no one would deny that; and the world has become better in some ways, and much worse in others.

Concorde and Concordia, and what a difference between them! We are spending seven hundred and fifty millions* and in the end probably nearly a billion on the Concorde, we were told last night in minuscule coincidence by the BBC. And where is the good of that? It is enough to sour and turn any mind politically. All for the sake of arriving an hour or two earlier at plutocratic cost for the individual passenger, when another continent, in fact, the New World, should and must be more than a night's flight away. Or it is sheer madness! Only to think what the income of this sum, merely invested at ordinary rates of interest, would bring to hospitals, and schools, and old people! And just a fraction of it to spend upon music and the arts! While everyone must have his own projects as to the disbursing of but a thousandth part of it. I would sooner, for myself, spend seven hundred and fifty pounds on my unpublished poems, worked on intermittently for twenty-five years, 1946–1970, which so far have been refused by eight London and New York publishers. I take that as a good sign. At least my mss. and note books are in the University Library at Austin, Texas. But I cannot get my poems published. My first prose book came out in 1924 after I had paid the publisher Grant Richards fifty pounds to have it printed, and when the manuscript had gone the round of nearly every publisher in London. And I can see that it will end as it began, which may be a good sign too.

I know that what keeps one's mind and spirit alive is technical interest and curiosity. That is why famous musicians continue to give performances after it is no longer necessary, either financially or for their reputations. It is because they enjoy doing so, just as, in modesty, I know that I revived myself, when dejected, by writing of the della Robbias and returning in that to the world I hoped for and had in mind when young. Perhaps there is nothing so destroying to the soul as broken legends. And the only cure is to continue in them for oneself, and for oneself alone.

The soup of the day thickens and needs salt and pepper. It is no case of seasoning to taste. The flavour is there already. But to take two more instances, or items of news. From two successive days. Ten thousand children in Tees-side have nits in their hair; this in the land of a free health service and compulsory schooling. And when, in re-reading Tolstoy's *Resurrection*, one is appalled at the 'hero', Prince Nekhlyudov, visiting the prison in Moscow, and 'his attention being riveted by a large, dark grey, many-legged louse crawling through the hair of another prisoner, the nice-looking stonemason's cheek'. And that, in a novel about the horrors and injustices of 'Holy Russia' before the turn of the century, some seventy or eighty years ago.

Or that other newspaper-heading on the next day to this: 'Inquiry planned as

---

* Now, less than a week after writing this sentence, the cost is estimated at eight hundred and twenty-five millions. And since then it has risen still further.

sewage talks fail.'* With headline sequel, a little incredibly, on the very next day, 'waves of sewage hit Sydney harbour', like some form of tidal echo reaching even to the Antipodes. Newspaper captions that make the Three Witches as topical as tonight's evening papers. What is it but soup of the day that the three Witches are stewing and boiling in their cauldron? It is as though they have been invited over or 'borrowed' for a gourmet week-end at a hotel. Bringing with them their *batterie de cuisine* and kitchen assistants, and some of the local delicacies one cannot get in England. And how approximately it reads, in *Macbeth*, 'Fair is foul and foul is fair. Hover through the fog and filthy air,' because as the gourmets can generally get abroad for themselves for their spring and summer holidays, the tendency is for the gourmet week-ends to be arranged and take place in winter. How apt, too, for soup of the day, is that direction of the *Second Witch*, 'Cool it with a baboon's blood; Then the charm is firm and good.' Or, if not a baboon, why not a rhesus monkey, which are smaller, go easier into the pot, and are brought over in their thousands to take part and be the victims of astronautical 'tests' and the 'experiments' of vivisectionists. Those of them, that is to say, that do not arrive in the aeroplane dead already. Or, finally, for the aftermath of banqueting, the First Witch speaking, 'Sleep shall neither night nor day, Hang upon his pent-house lid.' Thus, the Three Witches in *Macbeth*. 'The weird sisters, hand in hand, Posters of the sea and land.'

In these quotations, as so often with Shakespeare, there would seem to breathe the authentic voice of prophecy. As in foretelling the experiments with monkeys; in the Nostradamus-like mention of pent-houses, as though with pre-knowledge of the millionaire, top-floor flats of the 'chain' of Hilton, and other luxury hotels; and in the phrase 'Posters of the sea and land,' which uncannily puts the 'trendy' and correct phrase into the Witches' mouths.

And the week finishes and is complete with another mass-murder in California, this time of five persons including two young boys, and the arrest of the suspected murderer, a 'hippy-type' young man living in a shack in the woods, three-quarters of a mile from the house, over a ravine a hundred foot deep crossed by a rickety wooden bridge: 'Sitting alone there he studied his fortune-telling tarot cards and had visions of changing the world single-handed. Above the bed where he was found asleep there is a sign painted in green with the one word, "Fun".'† No green light for safety, this! And so autumn fades to winter.

And back again to the Concordia for happiness and good humour, even if it be true that the huge Renaissance château at Aschaffenburg, a town between here and Frankfurt, 'a favourite residence' of the Archbishop-Electors of Mainz, in the form of a hollow square with lantern towers at its four corners, was built from the confiscated estates of persons, men and women, burnt for witchcraft. There had been a veritable epidemic and orgy of witch trials at that time in this part of

---

* Coupled with warnings from the police about the danger from dustheaps in Soho during Guy Fawkes Week from small boys playing with matches and setting fire to their 'guys', and from football fans up in the West End for Saturday night 'after they have had a few drinks'.

† Ellsworth Jones in *The Sunday Times* for 25 October 1970.

Germany, and it is not a pleasant thought as one sees the towers of Aschaffenburg from a train window. But, then, we are in a land where the last person to be broken alive upon the wheel suffered as late as the year 1826. At the same time, persons with murderous instincts, probably in a drugged condition, and considering themselves to be at war with the rest of the world, cannot be allowed to take the law into their hands, and 'execute' at random.

How is it that human beings can do such appalling things to others, to each other, and to themselves? Where is the sense and mercy in the world, on either side? And is it necessary, is it really necessary, to have a religion and to 'believe' in things that are logically nonsensical, in order to be fair and have a balanced judgement? For how much longer is the deception to be practised? It has given happiness and comfort to millions, but it is simply not true. It has, also brought great miseries and hideous persecutions. Surely human intelligence has now reached a stage where we can face the truth and do without it. But death is the enemy in face of whom human beings, and even the animal creation, it would seem, have to be doped and anaesthetized. And as a doom, and an end to everything, it needs some explaining.

The best in religions has been in the buildings that they have left behind. But what comfort can that have been in their last moments to victims of the Inquisition, to martyrs of the Marian and Elizabethan persecutions, or to their relatives and friends. Works of art are the luxuries of religion? Nor has the Christian faith the monopoly of such things. The earth is littered with them; from the Pyramids of Egypt, hugest and heaviest, if simplest of monuments ever raised on behalf of the dead against death; and from the temples of Karnak to the tombs of the Pharaohs in the Valley of the Kings. If we believe in one religion it would be as sensible and as well to believe in all of them, and take them all on trust. For their abiding cause and purpose is identical and the same. In most, if not all, there has to be divine birth in order to explain things that, otherwise, are inexplicable. And there has to be promise of an afterlife, but only, so to speak, to ticket-holders; and those who have issued the tickets reserve the right to cancel them with or without notice.

Or, if the promise is not of another and eternal life it is of something that, yet, is very different from death. It is of oblivion, which is beyond death, and not being dead is substantive, in a nothingness brought conscious, were that conceivable, by unconsciousness. Buddhist services, it may be added, as those may be seen performed at one or other of the wooden cathedral-abbeys and Buddhist temples of Kyoto, are very strikingly similar to high mass in a cathedral in Italy or Spain. There must be some liturgical chain of connection between them which has been forgotten, or purposely ignored; or perhaps their historical origins are the same. This might be denied in Catholic circles but it is evident enough to an uninformed observer. It is the same story, everywhere, of the fear of death; but the great ones of the world have made their own arrangements and are on special terms. In some religions it has been an industry, almost, and a lucrative one at that, to arrange that their sins should be forgiven, by intercession, in order, so to speak, that their passports should be visa'd and in order for the day. But forgiveness should be on earth and not from heaven.

There is no reason to think that any power or influence outside this world has the very slightest interest in our deeds or misdeeds. It is our world by inexplicable circumstance for which there must be cause or reason. But we are responsible only to ourselves, and have to be ashamed only before ourselves, and no one else. There are races who have worshipped the human past, and ancestor worship at least demonstrates of what human beings are capable and sets up measurements and standards of achievement. Some form of respect and deference for the past seems to be sensible, but only if history is rewritten and it is decided who were the great men, and who were not. In the same breath there were monsters and ogres who created great works of art; Tamerlane ('Timour the Tartar') for an instance, to whom are witness the mosques and medersas of Samarkand. But benevolence is not everything. There is little enough, historically, to show for benevolence, alone, and in itself, *per se*. That is the weakness in mere kindness. The beggar begging in the street, where there are still beggars, is ever a more interesting figure than the old lady giving alms. It has always been so, and will always be the same. But the beggars will still be there long after the old ladies of the western world have 'gone to their rest', and disappeared.

There could be a parallel to the Marxian call of 'Workers of the world unite', which would put the importance of the arts and sciences before the extinction of poverty and the freedom of the masses. For the Marxian Utopia, which could never be true to its own precepts any more than the Christian religion can ever have borne resemblance to its original teaching once it was exported from the Palestinian scene and Galilean shore – the Marxian Utopia has no place in it for music, poetry, painting, writing, architecture, still less for what the proletariat would really miss, which is sport – yes! sport, relayed by satellite and giving un-Marxian prominence to 'heroes of the people' who in this case are genuine and whom the 'plebs' revere. So this was but another theory turned inside out by time, and left facing the wrong way round. The sciences in this context being what I would call the arts in science, comprising medicine, scientific discoveries, useful inventions, historical research, many sorts and schools of investigation into human and animal life and its infinite possibilities, but not increases in noise, speed, pollution, and additions to the general ugliness due to the proliferation of engines and machines.

Have there not been enough, or nearly enough 'inventions'; and is not the thinker more important by far than the inventor? We would wish the world of human beings to grow larger again by restoring distance and giving it back its dignity and poetry. The world has shrunk to the size of a withered apple compared to the genuinely infinite horizons of a pre-(both) World Wars childhood. The sixty-mile-an-hour railway train was fast enough; and that New York harbour and the Statue of Liberty should be four or five nights away by sea. That the Atlantic should be flown in two hours and a half at fifteen hundred miles an hour advantages no one except those flying to a deathbed, and if they missed that they would be spared the pain. It is too much for any sense to have a satellite circling the globe so many times a day, and an eye for ever watching us, day and night. But it is not the eye of god; not even the eye of 'what the butler saw', from the slot-machine on Brighton Pier. It has only a dumb interest in what it has been told to do, and the topical computer brain. The computer can already 'compose music'. But what music! The music of a schizophrenic typewriter, were that a possibility, and one in permanent need of a new ribbon. The satellite relays information, but would never have told us from its shifting stations in the empyrean where a Beethoven or a Mozart was born. Those being strictly human questions which yet partake of the divine. Nor could it tell of the plague, or of waves of terror; and would to all probability have left the French Revolution unreported, while telling its little tales of minor battles and troop concentrations. In short, the most inhuman of machines to report on humanity and enhance our troubles.

It is our machinery that is the main enemy. That causes all the noise and all the oil fumes, and makes the night incandescent and impossible to sleep through. How appalling to have your bedroom, on, or below, or above an arterial road with a lamp-standard a few feet from the window! With that indelible, dead white, or mock-orange, at your blind or curtain all night long. And the car-lights like astral stalking-horses, racing, racing, on their courses along the mini-empyrean of the bedroom ceiling, with noise and roar not as 'all the stars singing together', but with ceaseless surf-like nervous thunder, as waves breaking on a beach, never gaining foothold, but just coming, coming past, and never stopping.

Worse still, to have traffic lights outside. Which change; but what 'change' is there in something that only alters in order to come back again; and ever and always, each time, mechanically the same. And every fiftieth, or hundredth time, you are deceived and taken in, and the lull lasts a long time; then, mercilessly, begins again. But during the interval of a few seconds, each hundredth, each five hundredth time, from sheer fatigue you relax, almost, not absolutely. And it is only that much worse when the engines 'revv' up again and roar away. The ills are artificial light and the noises of machinery and machines. It is only, I suppose, in the last few decades that a light shining all night long in a prison cell has been one of the torments inflicted on a prisoner, shining directly upon the prisoner's face and straight into his eyes. Now there is ceaseless, or intermittent noise laid on as well. There is, and has long been, for it was in use in the Moscow prisons at the time of Tolstoy's novel, *Resurrection*, a little observation window for each cell. 'On both sides of the corridor were padlocked doors, each having a little hole in it about an inch in diameter, called a peep-hole.'* Now, if perhaps not in Tolstoy's day, the sentry with heavy tread, on duty in the passage, looks through the peep-hole every few minutes to be sure the prisoner is still there, 'all present', and whether both hands are outside his sheets, however cold in the unheated cells. Scalding-hot food, with only a few minutes to eat it in; or with so much salt that it is inedible, are other, reported mini-torments of the prisons.

The appalling dungeons in which prisoners and lunatics were confined until a century or more ago, lying on straw, in darkness, with no lights at all, alive with cockroaches, and with water running down the walls, had, at least, none of the trappings of civilization, and were uncontaminated by science. It was naked

* Quoted from Tolstoy's *Resurrection*, translated by Rosemary Edmonds, Harmondsworth 1966, p. 231.

barbarity; as against the electrically or chemically-heated clothing of the space-men, and their self-imprisonment in the new medium of speed, which has its own dangers, and could end in a deeper, live loneliness than has ever been before. And naked barbarity, horrible in itself, is no better and no worse than much that has happened during our lifetimes in 'civilized' countries that have aeroplanes, anaesthetics, motor-cars, all the trappings of the age.

Is it too late for human beings to come to their senses and stop this sort of thing? But all the signs are bad. Society, in the meaning of centres of power and human population, is at war within itself. And what was only obvious in so many directions is beginning to come true. 'Black Power' could have been prophesied in the time of Wilberforce and of Mrs Harriet Beecher Stowe. A huge India, huger China, and black Africa were clear as day. The two World Wars, it seems to me, were not so obvious and were more the result of misjudgment and muddled thinking. In other words, they might have been avoided, whereas it is impossible and out of question to prevent, or even delay, the swarming of the coloured races. Birth-control and the 'pill' have halted it a little, but at such a staggering sum of millions that it is too late. And all the rest has followed as though according to plan, except for the one invention and discovery which is that of town guerrilla fighting.

This, with its aids and auxiliaries of kidnapping and hi-jacking could be as decisive as the atomic submarine. For no power dares make a massacre and blood-bath of its own students, particularly if some proportion of those are not male, but female. The assailants, therefore, have many advantages upon their side. They can shame authority into action, and then silence and humiliate it if it attempts reprisal. They can always carry things their own way, just far enough, and no further. For this once, and then try again another time. The anonymity of a huge city, despite the police, the reporter's camera, and the television screen, is a safer place to hide in than the pampas or the jungle. It is not so easy to drop napalm bombs on a whole area of city as it is to defoliate a forest. A whole street cannot be 'sprayed' as easily as a native village. There is a social conscience that forbids this. Enemy and ally, if ally he be, are racially indistinguishable from each other. and this is an instance of anonymity, which has two faces, working the other way. Human beings have got their affairs into an awful muddle. I dreamt, not long ago, that the Chinese took over the Isle of Wight, arguing that the British had already been in Hong Kong for over a hundred years.

It must be realized, and taken into consideration, that the lightning speed with which news is conveyed to all quarters of the world, and even visually reported in 'full colour' – together with 'instant' news-cooking on the mass media, so called – have conspired to magnify, and at the same time make everything, whether large or trivial, of equal importance. It is like a glass which magnifies and distorts, but by applying the same lens or scale to everything has the effect of minimizing, by making equal, even while it magnifies; e.g. a television personality, cup-footballer, sport commentator, or whosoever, has, overnight, the fame and notoriety of a film-star, or of some African dictator. But are any of them of any importance, that is the question? It is all too obvious that persons of real interest may not, once in their lifetime, make headline news. And when world fame descends deservedly, as to Stravinsky, or Picasso, it sickens and stultifies by over repetition, and ends by boring. With others, but not those two mentioned, it is the same story as with the exposure or unmasking of a poltergeist. The child who may have had uncanny gifts, and has become the centre of attention, begins to lose his powers. Fame has come too late to him, and he is soon, and perhaps undeservedly, forgotten.

Instantaneous 'newsflashes' could conceivably antedate their own happening. This is already so where the 'date-line' has been crossed. As, for instance, you may leave home in England on a Monday, and arrive in Japan or in Australia on what is already Tuesday to you, but is Wednesday according to their reckoning, so that you have 'missed out' on all Tuesday, and it is lost and gone. But it makes no real difference; it is only through measurement of something immeasurable which is time. An arbitrary division, with no beginning and no end, reigning and in force over most of our world, but having started at no settled and defined moment; and in any case only in our own time currency, not negotiable in other solar systems, but only in our 'one-horse' system which is harnessed to our sun. Therefore, things can happen in the Antipodes and be reported here before they happened, in this fictional time scale, which is either true, or untrue, in two hemispheres at once. It is further complicated, too, by flying 'into' and 'out of' time, for of course on the return journey you gain a day. Leaving Australia on a Monday, you do not arrive here in England on a Tuesday, but you get here on the same British Monday which is almost too convenient, for it is in theory the same day, though you spent all the previous night that, by then, had presumably reverted to Sunday in the aeroplane. While, if making the return journey by rocket, which will happen ere long, you might literally arrive here before you left.

The two, we could call polar caps or hubs of time, are when the event in question happened, as related to where you, yourself, chanced to be. But any single event, or train of events, is in this same relationship to all other events or persons wherever they are; so that no event is an isolated happening, but a continuous happening in continuous time. It is a movement and a countermovement like going in a boat upstream. Your speed is not the real speed that it would be on land. Flying into time, with time behind you, not in front of you, is like moving downstream, or coming in upon the tide. In any case, wherever you are, time is moving about and around you, and is in perpetual motion. It, at least, is never still.

But now we ask ourselves whether in this era of the Concorde with all its detestable attributes, the spirit of the Concordia as manifest and made visible in a beautiful old building, can ever be again. And the answer is, 'No. It is not possible.' Those are beauties of a world only to be played over in mind like a piece of music by J. S. Bach. It is of no use to wish or hope for it again. Its horrors, which were many, are forgotten, as are his hindrances and frustrations while he was alive. But J. S. Bach was a North German; and Bamberg, it has been said, is near the border with Bohemia. Of one of its Prince-Bishops in the sixteenth century, Georg III Schenk of Limburg, 'who maintained an extravagant court', it is said naïvely, that 'constantly in his company could be found such men as Ulrich von Hutten and Joachim Camerarius', whoever they may have been; but, also, 'among his guests was included Dr Faustus'. This is interesting news indeed, and fits in marvellously with the thought of the years (1808–13) spent in Bamberg by E. T. A. Hoffmann, in what must still have been a German city of the Middle Ages, despite the Concordia and the other later buildings. But a mediaeval town of extreme beauty and romance, which I can only qualify in my mind by saying that I always coupled Bamberg in my mind with Dinkelsbühl – Dinkelsbühl of the vistas of mediaeval streets opening one after another like shutters, or as the 'flies' or side wings of a stage, and of the marvellous old church with its tall rows of columns, bare as the trunks of beech trees and not unlike those in colour by the last light of evening – as compared to Nuremberg, a town which had old churches before it was 'blitzed', and it was the city of Albert Dürer – but I always link Nuremberg in my mind with the quaintly interesting, but far from beautiful Rothenburg-ob-der-Tauber.

The news, for this was the first intimation of it, that Dr Faustus had been a guest of the Prince-Bishop of Bamberg, puts the history of that city into a yet higher romantic category. Had Dr Faustus ever, indeed, been appointed Rector of the University of Wittenberg, in succession, oddly enough, to Dr Wagner? But the very little of fact that is known about Doctor Faustus reads curiously, and is a little sinister. Was he not finally disgraced, and categorized in the sense, almost of a police description, as 'blasphemer, sodomite and nigromancian' which last word reads frighteningly, if only in the sound of it, while the epithet preceding it rises in horror to the nigromancian level in the Italian word 'sodomitaccio' that Benvenuto Cellini in his *Autobiography* says was hurled at him while he was working on his bronze statue of *Perseus holding the head of the Medusa*, now in the Loggia dei Lanzi in the square at Florence. And did Hoffmann know of the sojourn of Faustus in the Alte Hofhaltung, or Alte Residenz, up above the town and facing the cathedral? There is something in the old German towns, in Regensburg (Ratisbon), in Goslar, in Hameln, in Bamberg, which is like nowhere else in the world. And it is this that inspired Hoffmann to invent inhabitants worthy of them; 'a Germany made up of an agglomerate of little kingdoms and autonomous duchies, of palatinates and prince-bishoprics, bristling with battlemented castles, and preserving even in the Gothic character of its handwriting, the imprint of the Middle Ages', in the words of someone, a musician (Saint-Saëns) who remembered it like that. Later on, it developed along lines of fantasy that are unparalleled. I am thinking, now, of its eighteenth-century churches and palaces – but the solid, burgher houses of Hofrat Boettinger are the expression of lives that must have been well worth the living.

We will never know that species of calm as expressed in the very stones; not in our urbanization, or conurbation, which sounds like, and is, a nasty habit of living brought on and compelled by planning,* mercilessly, and without respect

---

* *cf.* the proposal to 'bi-sect' the ancient and beautiful town of Bury St Edmunds with 'a four-lane motorway with three flyovers' (*Daily Telegraph* for 3 November 1970). But this, at least, in a townscape unadorned by modern sculpture. Or the town clerk of Bath's remark that 'we want our kids to have the same chance as the kids in Liverpool'. This in defence of the proposed desecration of some of Bath's fine Georgian buildings.

of persons and enlivened, where possible, by hideous, unforgivable works of sculpture. Oh! for a statue of Queen Victoria, the Queen-Empress, and Widow of Windsor, rescued from some land where it is not wanted, dragged here and set up again! Now gone in time; and as far away, as improbable and remote from ourselves, as the portraits of Habsburg Holy Roman Emperors at the Neue Residenz at Bamberg. Or on wall or ceiling of Kaisersaals in all the monasteries along the Danube; and at that 'uncomparable pair', of Ottobeuren and Zwiefalten. For all is, frankly, very, very ugly now.

The word 'Concordia', if it stands for any special concept at all, infers control and in particular a controlled population. Were we to inquire into that in detail we would find that at the time in question they had enormous families of children of whom certainly thirty or forty per cent died in childhood. As well, there was a shorter expectation of life; and these two factors together achieved the balance of nature. But it is now in our power to attain to this and in permanence, without pain or trouble. How often on going into an old church, but this seems to apply particularly to Northern Europe, there is a tomb with sculptured rows of children on its base, sometimes, boys on one side, girls on the other, and on occasion the armoured, or doubleted and ruffed progenitor lying on the slab above, with a wife to either side of him. The children may number anything from ten or twelve to a couple of dozen,* often with a chrisom babe or two, in swaddling clothes, clasped in its mother's arms, or neatly coffined by her side. The inference of the two wives being that both were killed by constant childbearing, and that the innocent but uxorious husband had slain them both, one after the other.

Thus, the 'balance of nature'; and if only the scales could be evenly balanced it might be thought probable that many other blessings and benefits would ensue. For one thing, that we might again have settled art-forms changing with the human generations, and enabling artists in all the arts to fulfil themselves in their lifetimes. This has always been a difficulty in a population with volatile and quick-changing minds. In fifteenth-century Tuscany, their two greatest painters Botticelli and Piero della Francesca had become old fashioned and not much thought of before they died. And we may be certain the same kind of thing prevailed in Periclean Athens, where it is probable that quick intellects and the arts of conversation with their humours and attendant dangers first came to flower among human beings, it being doubtful if there was anything of the kind in Pharaonic Egypt or elsewhere in the ancient world.

To produce a working man with nine children to complain about the cost of living in a television programme is to underline the stupidity and carelessness of such a course of life. In a sensible world such a situation would be impossible and out of question. The unnecessary pains and troubles of the past are terrible to think of. That Edward Lear should have been one of twenty-one children, for

---

*   e.g. the nineteen children of Sir William Pelham at Brocklesby, Lincolnshire, 'but if we really wish to see the ravages of infant mortality we must go to Tettenhall, Staffordshire, and note the twelve dead chrisom babes round one sixteenth-century tomb, and nearly as many on other Tudor tombs in the same church', quoted from *English Church Monuments* (*1810–1840*), by Katherine A. Esdaile, London 1946.

instance; that someone of my acquaintance, from New Zealand, should have been one of twenty-four children, by the same father and mother; such things grow, mercifully, less and less credible. And the balance is likely to be achieved within two generations, probably by the end of the first quarter of the next century, say, in fifty years from now. But, in the meantime, nothing, nothing in the world, will stop the growth in Asia, in Africa, and in South America. And, therefore, the inbalance will continue with the scales weighed down disastrously for the future of human beings.

All talk to the contrary is Utopian, or, which is worse even if it is pleasanter, Arcadian. The Utopian is a Butlin holiday-camp conception, a wonderful improvement in itself, if not for the dilettante. While, as for the Arcadian, it is sterile and not life-enhancing. A working and dedicated life, if little profitable, has been the personal alternative. And that, if for not much else, in order to celebrate the splendours and miseries of having been alive. Having experienced worries, and bad ones at that; but certainly not miseries, though one is aware of those at an early age, at school, as school used to be not so many years ago, and which I hated from the age of seven, when I was sent to a boarding-school at Folkestone, until I began to hate it less at Eton when I was about sixteen. These are unhappinesses that are spared to the present generation. Those apart, one is only too soon conscious that all is far from well with human beings. That this is nothing new one knows at seven or eight years old from Cruickshank's wonderful illustrations to *Oliver Twist*, and for some time after, and in consequence of those – and I am almost ashamed to say, too, of the outline drawings to *Little Arthur's History of England* – I was ashamed and frightened by anything that was old. The workhouse master in Cruickshank's etching in the first-mentioned book, and the beheading of Prince Llewelyn in the other, seemed quite appalling. And I think it was only a few years later at my second school at Reigate that I began to know the safety and comfort of most things that are old, that have seen the ills of the world and are still there in spite of them. Even so, I found the woodcuts to early volumes of the *Illustrated London News* dating from the eighteen-forties, which were in the school library, more than a little alarming, whatever the subject. That phase of my life began in 1908, and the earliest of the dusty volumes, dating, I think from 1843, was already sixty-five years old. Let the reader work out for himself how much older they are by now! How much I, then, loved my mother and my brother! It is all gone now, and with both happy and unhappy memories.

Since which, or once the war ended and out of the army, what a glory it has been! I have enjoyed every moment and every hour of perception of the wonders human beings have created for themselves in this world which is ours, and ours only, though we are but animals, superior animals, and no more or less than that. Which is why we must be forgiven, by ourselves, but must also be praised. We have lifted ourselves out of the swamp and snow and forests, while the rest have done no more than make lairs or build nests up in the trees. It is one thing to praise the bees or termites, and wonder at their ordered lives; but quite another to envy their six-legg'd scurryings and antennae'd recognitions and inquiries. Or to believe the bees are not just at labour loading themselves at the nectary from the flower-mouth, and are universally happy in their apiaries. Such, or no better, are the only civilizations other than our own. Yet all have their own rules, and some sort of consensus, or general council, even if it is instinctive and unconscious. They have evolved of their own volition. The sparrow has decided its practical, dull clothing over the ages, and without thinking. Any more than the peacock its sistrum-tail; or the satyr tragopan its pair of horns and crimson, snow-flecked breast. All these they have thought of for themselves without thinking, but with their own and no one else's guiding hand. That it is part of some general, positive assertion, and a will more than a permission, is true; but it is true, also, of the germs of cholera and cancer; and of the eagle's beaks and claws. Such things are difficult to balance; and they make an unsatisfactory equation, unless we think that good and evil are the same and indivisible, and all parts or limbs of the same force. This seems to be about in the world at large; and so ubiquitous that it is clearly obvious the one could not exist without the other. They are in a sense parents of every-thing; the aconite and the thundercloud, the maelstrom and the sea-anemone, and are as though sexually opposite, or even male and female. They are the worries and frustrations that build up obstacles; and the bitter-sweet fruits, also, of success.

We have everything except the cataclysms of nature in our hands, and can deal with all things except disease and death. Those two are the root-causes and reasons for religion; and with no more belief or need for that, we must decide for ourselves from past experience what is good for us and what is bad. We must decide, also, what is ugly in all senses and what is not, whether in human behaviour or in what human skill can work at and achieve. The true and reformed Socialism which should be the universal political creed must recognize that the relief of poverty and care of the sick and old are necessary indeed, but not paramount, and that there are other considerations just as important for the future of the race. Among these limitation of the population takes first place. But this elementary step towards wisdom is likely to be practised among the white and mixed races every-where before the end of this century, except perhaps in Latin America. With a controlled population and the balance of nature restored, were this ever possible, then a beginning could be made. That is to say, the right priorities would be asserted, and the arts would take their rightful place again. It is because of the near impossibility of this happening that the culminating, if long drawn out tragedy hangs over the human race. It may be delayed, but it is none the less inevitable; often prophesied, but now almost certain to take place. Not in punishment for some, but in retaliation for having been, at once, too clever and too stupid. And, as always before, but in the past on a lesser scale of world wars, revolutions, and the like, because the faults were in ourselves. Not divine justice, in fact, but as of catching a foot in our own carpet, and crashing down, with some months or centuries in hospital and little or no progress made. Another Dark Ages, but only the darkness of machines; and without the mind and skill of which human beings are capable. And have shown their hand over and over again.

Not least in a good-looking, sensible building such as the Concordia of Bam-berg. In the comforting precincts and surroundings of older churches and houses with which it is in entire time and harmony. Of which I have attempted to paint the picture, if with divagations, and with a trial of higher and more important things that as one grows older are never far from mind. The mere conjunction, if with some three centuries between them of Dr Faustus as guest of the Prince-Bishop and of Hoffmann in his 'one up, one down', attic dwelling, being enough to demonstrate how time ran slow before it started on its vertiginous, near-twenty-first century career, if even it reaches that without intermittent, or grave engine-trouble, *en route*, and as it roars down 'boom alley' on the way to, maybe, a new and altered destination, not on the time table, or mentioned whether by 'news-flash', or on the bulletins.

ENTR'ACTE
Triptych

I THE UGLY DUCHESS

Having been in proximity, if only by mention, of Dr Faustus, there are the other legends, the *Pied Piper*, the *Wandering Jew*, the *Flying Dutchman*, and there seems no reason why audience should not be requested of the *Ugly Duchess*. Destination, then, a castle in the Tyrol, though already it looks to me less like the Tyrol than one of the 'Saxon' towns of Transylvania. I know the landscape, having been there myself. The population are Saxons who, according to tradition found as early as the sixteenth century, claim to be descendants of the children who followed the Pied Piper when he had freed the town of Hameln of its invasion of rats, but had not been given his promised reward! The local story goes that many young people were sent away, with no hope of return, to colonize far away lands to the east. It is the Saxon or Transylvanian 'tract' of stormy mountains breaking the horizon and with the crests of the Carpathians ever in view. There is the whiff of Count Dracula in the air, and it will be no different when we reach the castle.

For all I know we could be on the way to the castle of the chieftainess Tamara, in the Caucasus; and at our peril for we know the legend, and can even hear in the music the thundering waters of the river Terek. But what is the name of the tribe of mountaineers who have moustaches like Edwardian Guards officers, and dance like eagles, long cloaks and bandoliers flapping, upon the points of their toes? This, too, at the Albert Hall! And I am left wondering about them for a moment with the music of the *lezghinka* in my ears.

It is of course an experience the preliminaries of which I am sublimating in every direction, and I look up 'to sublimate', not being certain of its precise meaning, and it expresses just what I wanted to convey: 'to heat into vapour and allow to solidify again'. Or, more comically for my purpose, 'act of sublimating; in psycho-analysis, an unconscious process by which the repressed energy of sexual impulses is de-sexualized and directed into ways of cultural and social development'. How, more expertly than in these words, could my intentions be set forth and explained? But this is nothing mutual or reciprocal, no 'moving backwards and forwards, or giving in return', to quote from that encyclopaedic authority again, except that on taking leave from so exalted a personage one should perhaps take a step or two backwards before I leave the room.

And with no more ado for it is a private audience, I am in the presence. The lady indeed is furiously, energetically hideous, and her very appearance sends a shudder down one's limbs. Her 'pocket-mouth' takes up more than half of her whole face or countenance; her short nose and eyes and forehead being those, surely, of a hauntingly ugly man. She has bat-like ears, and it could be a flattened bat-face from out of which some squeaky, but low basso twittering should emerge. Her hair, the little there is of it, is a man's hair. Her cheeks, horribly wrinkled, are aids and helpmates to her hideous mouth. Her high peaked forehead, too, is masculine; and perched on her cranium is her 'pikehorn' or bi-corn headdress of some green and red material, with linen veil coming down from the crown of it where it touches on her forehead, and a horrid brooch on the napkin part of that where, in coquetry, should be her 'widow's peak'.

The awful creature, who has been looking steadily away as though sitting still to have her portrait taken, now turns in my direction, letting the linen folds of her veil play upon her shoulders. Can it really be a woman? She is already eyeing me in menacing, unpleasant way, mouthing, and lifting and letting fall that upper lip of hers in anticipation, and I am dreading that in a few moments I shall be summoned to dance with her. For the band has 'struck up' though it is not the dance music we are inured to listening to, but a sort of plain-song played on early instruments, to which one could do no more than lift one's feet and put them down again, bowing formally the while, with more or less of emphasis and discretion, as in films of the courtship rituals of the birds in which, notwithstanding, there are the elements or bases of classical ballet.

And her mouth! That mouth which is avid of kisses, which horrifies and inspires pity. For the purpose and machinery, or workings of which, I have to resort to an obscure and sinister page in botany. This concerns the pitcher-plants or *nepenthes*, 'the nearest thing in reality to those figments of the imagination, man-eating plants, though their "prey" is seldom larger than a cockroach or a beetle.' These carnivorous plants are generally vines or epithytes, and can climb as high as sixty feet into the trees. The lid on the inside of the pitcher, corresponding to that upper lip of the Ugly Duchess, and as well the leaves and tendrils of the plant, have nectar-secreting glands to attract the insects. 'Attempts by flies to stride along the rim of the pitcher usually result in downfall [into the pitcher], and the same fate awaits ants which try to walk on the waxy inner wall. Cockroaches probably fall into the pitcher from sheer clumsiness, and crawling insects tend to be caught more frequently than flying ones ... Juices secreted by the glands below the waxy zone inside the pitcher aid the digestion of the drowned insects.'*

And the tale of horror is finished with the information that 'inhabitants of the pitcher include certain spiders, insects and aquatic micro-organisms which are found nowhere else in the world' – what a habitat! – and that 'the Malays used to

---

* Quoted, with permission, from *Wild Flowers of the World*, painted by Barbara Everard, with text by Brian D. Morley, London 1970. The passage quoted is from the text opposite plate 111. It should be added that the sixty or seventy species of pitcher-plants or *nepenthes* have their centre of distribution in Borneo, but extending to Madagascar in one direction and to New Caledonia in the other.

pour the contents of the pitchers over the heads of the incontinent. The efficacy of the cure is hard to estimate, but since the odour of a soup of partly digested insects is thoroughly disagreeable, the cure was probably more objectionable than the disability.'

One wonders how the iconic significance of her ugliness has persisted so that after one glance there is no mistaking her. If asked for an explanation of Quentin Matsys's extraordinary, if imaginary portrait of her, I would suggest that he had seen this actual freak at a fair or peepshow, a 'man-woman' in whom the genes had gone very wrong indeed, perhaps dressed up as a grand lady in that fantastic headdress, had painted her portrait from memory, and called it after the legend, the *Ugly Duchess*. It is the face of the coarsest female impersonator; of a relapsed barefoot friar who has taken to the boards and performs in beer-halls and low estaminets. A freak or oddity; and something as evaluated or developed in the horror scale as the Elephant Man of Sir Frederick Treves.* The eyes, though, are perfectly sane and cunning, if of animal more than human calibre and meaning.

Yet she was woman enough, to judge from the lurid stories of her nympho-mania. Her divorce suit from the youthful Prince of Bohemia, heard by the Bishop of Coire or Chur, which ancient city is capital of the Canton of the Grisons, brought to light details that made it the most sensational case of the age. Two historians, Stegerer and Ignaz Zingerle, have left, we are told, very curious accounts, but these have not been translated from the Mediaeval German-Swiss and are therefore inaccessible to me.

For Margaret 'Maultasche', or 'pocket-mouthed', was an historic personage, Duchess of Tyrol, and of repute the most ill-favoured princess in all history. We all know Tenniel's drawings of her in *Alice in Wonderland*; and as well as her portrait in oils by Quentin Matsys, who incidentally can never have seen her because she died nearly a hundred years before he was born, there is a very similar and perhaps earlier drawing of her at Windsor Castle, attributed, doubt-fully, to Leonardo.

Her mother was daughter of the King of Bohemia, and she was married at only twelve years old to the still younger son of the blind King of Bohemia who was killed at the battle of Crécy in 1346. The Black Prince after Crécy, it may be recalled, had taken the crest of the three feathers and the motto of 'Ich Dien' from the slain, dead king, and adopted them for his own insignia and that of succeeding Princes of Wales; while his nephew Richard II married Anne of Bohemia who is supposed to have introduced into England the very same 'pikehorn' headdress to be found on the tomb of noble ladies, and that we see tilting, first to one side then the other, from the forehead of the Ugly Duchess. She must indeed have been aunt, or more probably great-aunt, of our King Richard II's Queen, Anne of Bohemia.

Looking at her, trying to see the nicer side of that face, and wondering meanwhile how to speak to her, I would think that, in essence, hypothetically, of

---

* cf. *The Elephant Man and other studies*, by Sir Frederick Treves, London 1923, and an article on *The Ugly Duchess* in the *Burlington Magazine* for April 1921 by W. A. Baillie-Graham.

course, she listens in to every David Frost programme, this by way of 'the Social and Cultural Development' that are so important in our lives; that like myself she is an addict of *Dr Finlay's Casebook*; and that she attends the bouts of all-in wrestling on Wednesday nights and has her favourite among the heavyweights: 'Happy Thursday, Friday, see you Saturday,' goes the slogan.

So the Ugly Duchess was a historic personage as real and genuine as the Black Prince, or John of Gaunt. And Margaret 'Maultasche', or 'pocket-mouthed', is a fine name for her, though we are not to suppose that a mere nickname can have moulded the enormity of her features. She has grown into a legend like the Flying Dutchman, or the Wandering Jew. And in the same context how satisfactory it is to read that at Hameln, the old town on the river Weser, the rats are still to be seen in many shop windows in the form of sweets and souvenirs in memory of the Pied Piper, that 'mysterious character in the multicoloured clothes'! How satisfying, too, in the same vein of fantasy, that Theophrastus Bombastus von Hohenheim should have been the full name of the physician and alchemist Paracelsus. Names have certainly a physical and nervous effect upon their owners. Neither myself nor the books I have written, I say in all humility, would have been as they are, had I been called 'Tim' or 'Eddie'!

II 'A FROGGY WOULD A-WOOING GO'

We could be foreign envoys just about to set forth to present our credentials, a carriage has come from the Palace to fetch us, and soon we will be seen in it trotting down Pall Mall. There is nothing so very peculiar about this. Railway trains and steamers apart, draught animals were the rule down to the beginning of this century. And not so long before that, at about the same distance in time, human beings depended entirely upon animals for transport; our only rivals in the domesticating of other creatures being the ants who keep and breed *aphidae* or greenfly for their milch-kine. But, in fact, alike the diesel train dirty and ugly, rushing through a railway station at eighty miles an hour, and the jet plane with the streamline beauty of shark or other predator of the seas, but with fixed wings or fins, sleepless cetacean of the clouds and skies – both are no more than beasts of burden, than the humblest ass or donkey, which at the least can lie down and die.

It will be a carriage, one would imagine, from about the only Royal Mews left in the world. But once it was not so rare. My mother used to tell me that her father, who had beautiful horses and carriages and lived in a big old house in Berkeley Square, drove out to dinner in his coach with a coachman on the box, and a pair of footmen standing at the back holding long staffs, all of them in livery and wearing three-cornered hats and wigs of spun-glass. And this latter detail I never quite believed until this week when reading a book of memoirs,* where the author remembered in the seventies and eighties seeing carriages waiting in Charles Street, round the corner from Berkeley Square, with coachman and footmen wearing wigs of spun-glass, and on occasion a coach standing at the door with postilions in blue silk jackets and white beaver hats.

* *Romantic London*, by Ralph Nevill, London 1928, p. 19.

Perhaps the texture of a wig of spun-glass was a little like the solidified foam of Badedas, the green stuff you squeeze out of a tube into the bath, turn on the water, and in a moment it has become a foam-bath. Odder still, it contains, apparently, a special extract of horse-chestnuts. In any case, wherever or whenever, a spun-glass wig is as remote and far away from us now as Cinderella's coach; the Ugly Sisters, Clorinda and Thisbe, daughters of Don Magnifico; and Dandini, the harlequin, quicksilver valet. Except of course, when, incredibly, they are to be seen upon the stage, at no farther distance than the Coliseum, post-war home of Grock and of Diaghilev's Russian Ballet, in Rossini's *Cenerentola*!

But now there comes a furious blaring and whinnying of trumpets. Fanfares are sounding with every pomposity of announcement and arrival, but irregularly and badly blown. A virgin queen, or her like, is borne past in a litter, and it is of no use in face of what we see now in our own lives, day by day, night by night, to think that such sights and persons have never been.

It could be when the frog-prince came a-courting, whom she christened 'My Frog', and wore always a jewelled frog in her bosom in compliment to him. Whom his mother, the Queen-Mother of France, hoped might come to enjoy living in a court of ancient ladies 'with cheeks sugar-candied and cherry-blush't so sweetly', and wearing 'nosegays of yellow hair on their furious foreheads' and 'glorious borrowed gleaming bushes'.*

By whom inspired, as ever, for catalyst, albeit through a second person, we are in that other presence, of an immense openwork starched ruff, with sticks or spokes to it, bigger in circumference than any bicycle-wheel, wide sleeves curiously embroidered with roses, pomegranates, carnations; with very long thin, scented hands and a spouting whale or sea-monster on her hooped farthingale. And from the midst of this – icon-like, expressionless, with red eyebrows, aquiline nose, small mouth, and red hair, or frizzed red wig – Parthenia, our Virgin Queen. We hear her voice – her huge father had a high-pitched voice – hear her breathe, and hear her small movements as of so many slats, pearls, bobbins, rubbing together and making a jarring, rustling, and as the flicking and shutting of so many fans. Her 'Frog Prince' is nineteen years younger, and not the descendant of Titian's François Premier for nothing. Dark-eyed, heavy eye-brow'd, and as typical a Frenchman to look at as Monsieur Pompidou. But all else is drowned in heavy scents, 'knock out' scent, and the throbbing, clattering of lute strings.

She has sent her 'Frog' a basket of ripe apricots as a present. Which fruit is very typical; and it is only a pity that her age missed the 'black' apricots that were grown in a later time by Sir Joseph Banks, the explorer and naturalist, who discovered the yellow Banksian rose and the *nelumbium*. For the Elizabethans would have delighted in a conceit of this kind, as in any direct contradiction or antithesis to something they knew and admired already.

Thus, to have a herd of unicorns, not milk-white as of legend, but with sable

---

* Thomas Nashe, *Pierce Penilesse his Supplication to the Diuell, describing the ouer-spreading of vice, and suppression of vertue...*, London 1592, and *Christ's Teares over Jerusalem. Whereunto is annexed a comparative admonition to London*, London 1593.

skins, for they could be things of the imagination, their reality was of no moment. And knowing their music and their poetry, a herd of them, skewbald, feeding on the scythed lawns below the battlemented towers. But to conclude the incident of the apricots, 'she sent them in one of her own little work baskets which always stood in her cabinet, and desired the Earl of Leycester to send it to him with her commendations, that he might see that England was a country good enough to produce fair fruits'. Pears or apples, whatever their flavour, lost now after centuries one might like to think, or with new and sappy flavours still to come, were too ordinary. As would be a gilt basket of ripe strawberries, where in the reply, it was wished 'that the grafts from France might, in good time, produce fruits even more perfect'.

One of the reasons why apricots were preferred to the rosy-cheeked or peasant fruit, or the green-cheeked hamadryads of the orchards, 'nymphs who lived in the country, and presided over the trees, with which they lived and died', being not only in their taste, but in their skins. Nectarine complexions, in contrast, were of the nymphs that sleep indoors in heated glasshouses or conservatories – and whether the Elizabethans had those or not, I do not care! – with this thought added, that conservatories are for music and not for tropical flowers and that in Tuscany below the cypresses down in the wooded valley, there are the afore-mentioned conservatories for young nightingales where in the springtime I have heard them practising their notes with parents or relations to correct them. The apricot-skinned, to finish with those, being that of nymphs-in-waiting, as Sir Walter Raleigh found and Aubrey narrated, to be enjoyed up against a tree with result of stammering and slurred speech.

From which I come to the lute music and the madrigals the latter being for three or four voices sung round a table, and therefore like a game of cards with points for poetry, though we might find the high thin voices of the counter tenors whom they so much admired more artificial and curious than beautiful. But that they pierced through and attained to particular kinds of poetry must have been the case. It will have been in exultant or else unrequited passion, akin to the serenades and tenor airs which are the lyrical heights of the old Italian operatic style:

> *The swans, whose pens more white than ivory,*
> *Eclipsing fair Endymion's silver love,*
> *Floating like snow*
> *Down by the banks of Po,*
> *Ne'er tuned their notes, like Leda once forlorn,*
> *With more despairing sorts of madrigals,*
> *Than I,*
> *Whom wanton Love hath, with his gad,*
> *Pricked to the court of deep and restless thought.*

So runs one of the most beautiful of English madrigals by Roberto Greene, and there could be no more lovely expression of the game that 'Cupid and Campaspe played, at cards for kisses'. Such is the essence or distilled spirit of the madrigal when in the right hands.

And the lute music was the attuned product of the same poetry. The line of Swinburne's will be recalled, of 'leaves trembling like lute strings, or like fire', a wonderful touch of genius from a poet who was completely unmusical and could not tell one tune from another. For in it he achieves, and almost certainly without knowing it but only for his own pleasure in the simile or image, the very sound of lute music, as distinct from the guitar of the Spaniards, or the Neapolitan mandoline. This is not music of the wineshop and whitewash'd patio, nor of the narrow streets and Parthenopaean bay. It is the plucking of strings, neither strident and plangent, nor metal-thin, and it is the apt and proper accompaniment for poetry, if at all the distance in the world from the metal guitar and the microphone; but if the truth must be out, a little boring and monotonous, and perhaps too easy a vehicle for preciousness and affectation. Swinburne's line describes lute music as it could be heard on some inspired occasion.

We get that Italian tenor-like extremity of passion in the miniatures of Nicholas Hilliard and Isaac Oliver. The young lovers have frantic and mysterious inscriptions in the background, and romantic feeling is wrought to the highest possible pitch of excitement. One might think these could not be the portraits of young Englishmen. The Elizabethan gallants who live for us in Hilliard's miniatures linger eternally in the flames, or on the rose-briars 'die of a rose in aromatic pain'. That poetry and that music are the expression of the same exuberance and over-perception that were characteristic of the age. But it was a time in which poetry was on the wing and need hardly put out a foot to touch the ground.

It was an age in which nearly everything north of the Alps, except in England – but there, too, on occasion, as at Wollaton or Burghley – was ugly and exasperating. As witness, in any general account, the castle at Heidelberg and the over-praised châteaux of the Loire; but making exception for the Place Carré of the Louvre, now restored from the soot and grime of centuries so that the sculptured caryatids and bas-reliefs of Jean Goujon in their Cellini-like finish and precision can be admired again in their daffodil-hued stone. On a fine or even a wet day, screened and shut away from the noise and traffic of the city, this is to experience again the poetry of Ronsard and du Bellay as one did when reading it at eighteen years old. But what a hideous age for dress and costume! How absurd must have been the wasp-like 'mignons' of Charles ix and Henri iii! How ridiculous their pretentions and affected manners! To have heard the high voice of the Duc d'O, and observed his sinuous and curvaceous movements who was, not surprisingly, the last of his family!

For whom it would not have been practical to have effected an audience with the Ugly Duchess for their lifetimes were not coincident, and she must have been coffin'd a century and a half, or more, before the Duc d'O was born. Whether her tomb is still to be seen I know not, but it should be possible to find out where she was buried. There could lie a feast there still for the phrenologist, and maybe, the student of acromegaly. It is probably within some tomb-cluttered chapel in the Tyrol or the Grisons. With the Pied Piper, the Wandering Jew, the Flying

Dutchman, it is otherwise; as with Dr Faustus, they are not coffin'd, but ever on the road, or abroad on the high seas.

III   PRINCESS OF THE APHIDAE

But now my thoughts alter and transform into the princess of the aphidae. By whom I intend a very different figure from the preceding, which could in this passing moment be that of my dead sister when I was a young man. I would wish to attempt one more sketch or description of her before it is too late. Of the aphidae I call her because of her tall thinness in her youth, and the suggestion of long waists and wimples, long thin fingers and pointed feet. Of virginal beauty, as should be a young abbess or palatine, not sexually, but poetically and spiritually beautiful; some kind of 'throw-back' from being the child of a mother who was not yet, or scarcely eighteen years old; so that I have often wondered, never having seen anyone at all resembling her, whether there may not have been nuns like her, one or two of them, maybe, when princesses of English descent and origin brought their ladies-in-waiting with them as nuns to Spanish convents like Las Huelgas, which is outside Burgos, in Castile. More than once I have felt that little note of affinity, which must come out of the very distant past, as though there had been young women there much resembling her, to whom indeed one could, but they were strictly cloistered, have talked of poetry and other kindred things. It may even have made the nunnery of Las Huelgas more romantically interesting to me than it really is, although one could scarcely exaggerate the effect of that wooden floor of wide, huge planks as though from some untouched forest, or Armada shipyard, with the stone coffins resting there, and the thought of the dead kings and queens and Infantas in their endless sleep enclosed within them.

When I was seven or eight years old and she was seventeen or eighteen, and already copying out poems and reading them to me, I remember she had two or three little carved sandalwood boxes on her dressing-table, of which she was very fond and in which she kept her rings and earrings. I suppose these sandalwood boxes were of Indian origin and of the humblest description, but they remind me of the wooden doors by Moorish craftsmen and of the stucco vaults and arabesques of the Mudéjares in Las Huelgas. These were more appropriate to her than the fourth-floor flat in Moscow Road where she lived in needless near-poverty for eighteen years. I cannot think there has been any other feminine influence in poetry of like calibre and potency for a very long time, or such a sure hand for what is poetry and what is not. Rarer still to have been, herself, a poet and not just a lover of poetry; and having known her one might conjecture that her person, like such a poetess as Christine de Pisan (1364–1430) went back to the handwrriten, before the printed, page.

Of the female vehicles of poetry I have had knowledge, they being more often to be met with than the fount or clear spring of poetry mentioned; such, or their like, being certainly the aboriginal inspiration for a lot of poetry, the inspiration, that is to say, if not the authority and the guiding hand. The essential virginity in the first place having been the magic and the touchstone, and often the poetry has gone once the object taken and achieved. For the lasting magic in which, witness the inspiration proffered and accepted over the centuries by Mariolatry, or the worship of the Virgin Mary, the innocent mother of Christ, ideally, having been almost more important than Christ, himself, as a theme and embodiment to be worshipped.

BOOK
NINE

The Green Boy and Girl

After degradation and death comes rebirth.

This is a miracle common to all religions though no more miraculous than the green buds pushing out of the earth in obedience to laws they know not, but which are instinctive to them.

Where is it to be? For there has to be a legend.

Dawn came at five o'clock that morning in an empty firmament, except for the Milky Way crossing the heavens and thought to point to somewhere at the far end of the world, unknown to the reapers. It is the land of warrens. One warren alone sends forty thousand rabbits in a year to the London of Dick Whittington. There is even a particular warren famous for its rabbits which have valuable silvery-grey fur. This is the district of the 'brecks', wide open fields mixed with warren and sheepwalk, and the haunt of the great bustard taken by greyhounds in the days of Charles the Second, and which according to Gilbert White 'when seen on the downs resemble fallow deer at a distance'.

Here, too, are pits of the flint-knappers, which is a prehistoric industry. Diggings or passages have been found eighty feet deep, deeper than any warren, dug into the land; and sticking in the side of one of them, a pick-axe made of a flint fastened to a stag's antler. There are ancient pits or ditches in all directions. Some, which are as much as forty feet wide and twelve feet deep, have been paved with flints 'in a bowl shape'. They must mark the settlement of an earlier population.

The miracle is to take place early on this August morning, at the same hour that the little shepherdess rubs her sleepy eyes and sees the Virgin standing before her; the hour of little Bernadette of Lourdes, or of the three peasant children of Fatima. A vision looking into the rising sun with the light behind it.

A morning of hallucination, not at all an ordinary morning, for, already, all is still as glass, or as a death pool under the trees. There is not a ripple, not a breath. Ghosts could come out of every wood and spinney. We have to look, and look again, under the lone oak trees. There are haunted corners of fields, and small quick sounds behind the hedges. But no Gypsies. For those still lived in Little Egypt.

Absolute stillness and no movement. This is an important point to establish because few persons have been witnesses of a miracle, and we could be much questioned about it later.

Two or three reapers in blue smocks come over the brow of the hill with the scythes on their shoulders showing like sickle-moons against the sky, behind their wide-brimmed summer hats. They walk softly in their shoes of skin, with exaggerated, hallucinatory slowness, and not speaking.

After them some young women come up as though climbing a flight of steps into the sky, or mounting from the back upon a stage; and as soon as they are entirely visible down their short skirts to their feet, fade back in the half-light as though going back into the earth.

The morning strengthens but is still wet with dew. A fungus or toadstool is as a pagan statue that has lain for centuries under the water, it is so cold to the touch. And soon the sheepwalk, as we go along with the harvesters, leads down to the cornfield, pale flaxen as the hair of children, but now mostly stubble, with the shocks or cornstooks pitched in long lines like wigwams or bivouacs.

Look again at the cornstooks! They are trophies of pastoral warfare captured and heaped into piles; or even, prisoners bound and shackled.

Just at this moment a hare runs out of the uncut corn, and doubling on its track runs in and out among the stooks as if lost in a maze, or as though enchanted. Round and round it runs, not scurrying as does a coney with little white scut showing behind it as it goes, but running more like a small deer or antelope in ever smaller and smaller circles till a harvester hits it with a whetstone as it runs near him.

The animal turns over and over in agony, rolling to its feet as though beseeching him to kill it; he hits it with a stone and lifts it up, bending back its neck and breaking that, and now throws the dead hare on the ground.

The hare was a witch running out of the cornfield. Someone had to kill it.

Down in the valley a steeple rises out of the pastures like a witch's hat. It is, at one and the same time, a morning with a spell cast upon it, and the sum of all the harvests that the oldest men and women can remember; not 'once upon a time' as in all fairy stories, which means upon a day there can never be again, but the story says 'out of these trenches there once came in harvest time', which has another meaning. For this portends that it once happened, that there was the instant before and the moment after.

Now the women put down their bundles and baskets of food. The reapers lean the handles of their scythes upon the stubble, take their whetstones and sharpen the curved blades. This, leisurely, as though there is no defence against the flail. For their enemy is but of straw.

The uncut corn stands like a platoon of pikemen with erect lances in an old battle engraving. But their ranks have been cut into just as you would cut into a honeycomb with a spoon; playing with it and whittling round its sides, leaving an island of corn and a main body, and here a straight edge of cornstalks, and there a bow or mullion with a swing of the scythe, or a corner cut off, as though to shape a hexagon or octagon out of the cornfield, all done last evening in the failing light.

The only sound is the whetstone going 'schresh', 'schresh', and 'schresh' again upon the harvest blade; and another down at the corner of the harvest field, and more if you listen for them far and near.

We could hear in imagination the hammering of the scythe-blades, a memory of childhood at Slitting Mill, beyond the Eckington Woods, beside a millstream, where scythes have been made and beaten into shape for many hundreds of years since the Middle Ages. But no time for that.

The battle begins after a lull of silence. A child with a little scythe fights his way towards a clump of poppies hiding in the corn. Each harvester to his task. The women follow behind and bind the sheaves. It is the women who truss the helpless prisoners, kings and men of straw, whole dynasties and populations, once green as the leaf, now golden, and to be ground to grain.

So the women follow over the battlefield and lay out the dead. They are peasants and nearer to the animal. Being brutish they treat nature as a tamed animal that they must curb and conquer. The scent of the beanfield is their aphrodisiac. Who does not know that they make love lying upon the haystacks, during hay-harvest, looking down as though from clouds or golden castles?

Is there none among the husbandmen who, walking alone at the edge of the wood, has stopped to listen and put his ear to the tree stem?

At which moment, the curious odd silence and stillness falls, as though it were the putting of a patient into a trance. It grows darker and darker as if with the twisting of a screw; and a phenomenon that is always noticed, a little colder, like a little cold wind blowing upon wrists and forehead, but not troubling the leaves, except for the spinning of a poplar leaf so peculiar and inexplicable that it could be taken for an oracle.

The reapers look up into the sky for thunder, but not a drop of rain falls. There is an empty shuddering, whether far or near it is impossible to tell, but more like a noise from very far off felt behind the ears. All objects are so still and static that they look as if they may move violently; the trees as though they may bend down suddenly in a rushing wind; there is a snap or blink of the air which could be lightning – and out of one of the trenches no deeper than a gravel pit, near a crab-apple tree, the Green Boy and Girl come up.

They rise behind the blackberry hedge; where grows the deadly nightshade and children are forbidden to touch the blackberries, close to a wood which is the only place in this neighbourhood where grows herb paris. The manner of their arrival is that of coming up on a lift or trap from below stage, head first, then shoulders, waist and legs, and as soon as they are level with the earth they set foot upon it.

The Green Boy and Girl are as creatures that can walk as soon as they are born.

But their first tread is upon the golden cornstalks.

They are green as the caterpillar. You would think that privet and hornbeam were their daily bread.

At the moment they put foot to ground a loud noise like the ringing of bells comes up out of the earth after them, so loud that the reapers look up from their work. It is a greater mystery, even, than the Green Boy and Girl.

It could be that this ringing was in order to 'cover' their coming up out of the earth into the cornland, though we know it was as much of a mystery to the Green Children, themselves, for we are told that 'after hearing a loud noise like the ringing of bells all at once they found themselves among the reapers in the harvest field'.

By the time the reapers look again the Green Children are standing hand-in-hand.

The Boy is half a head taller than the Girl. They wear short tunics 'of some unknown stuff'; but only unknown in the sense that silk from China was unknown to pre-Columbian Indians, Arctic furs to the Africans, or, it could be said, 'mixtures' like Aertex or Viyella to the Ancients.

The Green Children wear tunics with belts or girdles round their waists, and well-worn sandals. They have come up into our world no differently from the French boy who went rabbiting with his dog during the War, saw his dog had disappeared into a hole in the ground, and found himself in the cavern at Lascaux with mammoths and wild horses painted on the walls.

The Green Children are born again.*

Till they are old enough to rebel children must wear the clothes their parents give them. These wear their hair short, and the manner of their dress and general appearance suggests that they are the children of food-faddists and nature lovers. They are Adam and Eve; customers of the Health Food Centre, probably vegetarians and eaters of wholemeal bread.

Their parents may have been 'delicate'. The children are certainly robust.

'They were caught and taken to the village', so it is evident they tried to run away.

Did they separate and go in different directions as ducks do if you chase them on a pond? Or run away together still holding hands?

But the curious point is that they made no attempt to go back into the trench. They had no wish to return into the womb. New-born babies weep, not because they are sorry to leave their mothers, but only of instinct to expand their lungs.

They ran away, awkwardly, as would children who are not good at games, and the village children ran behind and in front, teasing and imitating them. So do rooks and starlings circle round any strange bird that comes among them, and drive it off.

But the children were caught and taken to a cottage, where 'they gradually lost their green appearance, and the boy soon died'. The girl survived and was married to a man of Lynn who courted her at the Michaelmas Fair, when she went to

---

* The source of the legend of the Green Boy and Girl is William of Newburgh (Hist. Anglic., Lib. i. c. 27), and the scene was the village of Woolpit, or 'Wlfpittes' in Old English, which lies in Suffolk. 'At first they could speak no English; but when they were able to do so they said that they belonged to the land of St Martin, an unknown country, where, as they were once watching their father's sheep, they heard a loud noise like the ringing of the bells of St Edmund's monastery (at Bury St Edmund's, the chief religious centre of Eastern England, whither even King Henry VIII walked on pilgrimage, barefoot). And then all at once they found themselves among the reapers in the harvest field at Woolpit. Their country was a Christian land and had churches. There was no sun there, only a faint twilight; but beyond a broad river there lay a land of light. The bell ringing, the river, and the green colour of the children all belong to the true old fairy mythology.' cf. Murray's Handbook to East Anglia, 1875, pp. 175, 176.

market carrying a green goose under her cloak. They had no children, and you may look in every churchyard in Lynn, and not find her tomb, or hear mention of her.

The Green Boy and Girl were a seven days' or even seven months' wonder, but now they are forgotten. No one has heard of them. We are not even told their names.

Born Again

But time returns.

Why should not the Green Children come up out of the trench once more at harvest time, while we hear the honking of the combine-harvester, and all is mysterious in the early mist and dew, and the newspapers carry stories – or did – of 'flying saucers'? Or now, only a year or two later, of American or Russian Astronauts.

It is no more of a mystery than the green buds coming up out of the earth, only it happens but once in nearly a thousand years instead of every February or March.

Again the shuddering emptiness and stillness, the sense of waiting for something to happen, the blink of lightning, and the Green Boy and Girl coming up into the harvest field, but the 'loud noise like the ringing of bells' is drowned by the roar of an aeroplane overhead. It is a bomber of the US Air Force from one of the air fields in East Anglia. No one bothers to look up, they are so used to this, but the crew have 'seen something' for they keep on circling round and flying low.

But now it appears that no one else has noticed anything. The combine-harvester turns and comes down the cornfield as though nothing has happened. It is only for ourselves and no one else was interested.

The two visions fade into one another. We are back in the harvest-field a long, long time ago, or now, this very moment, it matters not which, but the bell ringing dies in the air and we are in the kingdom of deadly nightshade and herb paris.

The Green Boy and Girl are standing with no one to chase or catch them.

Adam and Eve, we are told, were born without 'original sin'. But the Green Children pick the berries of the deadly nightshade and put it in their mouths.

At that moment in their green tunics they remind me of the 'lords and ladies' growing in the April woods. Green cloaks and hoods a month after the snow-drops are soured and muddied. At the hour of the cuckoo and the kingcup.

Ah! but it is more mature to come up into the cornfield. Autumn days are longer and the mornings mistier. We only need consider that mushrooms come up how many months after the fading of the snowdrops! There is room in the world for both, but not at the same time. One looks wicked and the other innocent; or it is only the more innocent season of the year? Is it wickeder to be born from spore like the fungus; or of spawn as are the frog and toad?

Snowdrops come of a bulb or sow themselves from seed. The most immaculate birth of all is from the eggshell. The swan is born of that. So are the eagle and the satyr tragopan. How many human beings were begotten in drunkenness? Yet all have intelligence, or the rudiments of that, which is something other than natural grace, even though born of an act that was nothing else than original sin.

A crab-apple drops from a branch and we see the glistening spider's web among the blackberries.

Green Children! you continue to eat the deadly nightshade. You have slanting eyes and cheeks that are like green apples. Let me look at your high cheekbones!

Now disconcertingly, the Green Boy and Girl turn round; and the Girl holding a handful of blackberries to her mouth spits out the blackberry pips. At which moment you can see in either of them any resemblance you choose, and they are like everyone else there has ever been.

There is everything in all human beings. It is but a question of how fate works in them. Some have no chance; others are eaters of deadly nightshade and it does not harm them.

I look at the Green Boy, now, and can see the suicide's best friend in him. I see him tip-toeing in the shuttered room after the post-mortem, tying labels on bits of furniture and getting ready for a move. And where he is going to will be quite different, and yet just the same. It is no good hoping to reform him. You cannot turn a butterfly into a bull-dog, nor a moth into an owl. He has no sting and does no harm. But he is weak and silly.

Does one turn green from an overdose of veronal? It is so out of date a sleeping-draught that, may be, only the curator of a medical museum would know the answer.

Green as the caterpillar that gnaws the leaf. Green in the old fairy mythology being the colour of changelings and visitors from the underworld. You must not give them presents, or leave out food for them, or you will offend them and they will never come back again.

But the Green Children are beginning to lose their colour. Again, one of them soon dies. The genius goes out of him. And the Girl loses her genius when she settles down and gets married to the man of Lynn.

We are to imagine that her talent has forsaken her. The Boy, had he lived, would have been another Infant Roscius. But the Girl, who survived, was as someone who had powers once as a medium and has lost them. The genius goes with puberty. Not enough is known about such mysteries for it to be possible to explain them. But there are, certainly, mysteries. And no one of them is more mysterious than puberty. It is as great a mystery as life or death. Or is it not the deepest mystery of all?

It is two hours after sunrise and in broad clear light.

The Green Children have come up into the world and turned their backs upon the shadows. Those have hidden themselves until another darkness of the spirit, which is of a different creation from the starry night. That is for melody and sweet reasonableness, the terror of its immensity apart. And upon a still night you may listen to the stars singing.

But the shadows have crawled into the ditches and shady places, which is not to say that they have laid down their functions, but the horrors and terrors are abated. The mysteries of death are of no more moment. There is no longer some-one in the passage outside the unlocked door.

Instead, it is the land of green fingers and the hour of growing. That is why we put it at two hours later than sunrise after a warm night. For it is during the mild nights that there is growth, and if we but knew the meaning of it I could find no more wonderful name for what I am attempting than 'the land of green ginger', pretending that there is magic in the morning air and that it is an epoch when the hand of man cannot go wrong.

Who that reads this page has known the golden light of Rome – the tawny apricot light of the Campagna where the aqueducts cast broken shadows; the light of the peninsula of Sorrento with its short yellow cliffs; of the *latomia* of Syracuse which are but golden quarries; of Olympia and its balsam-dropping pines; of the *aprica littora* of Tarragona – will know my meaning for a yellow light as of the level beams of sunset seems to attach where there are the remains of classical antiquity as though in visible sign of a declension from a golden age. Were not the poems of Horace 'afternoon poems' in their epoch, to be read, metaphorically, before the air grew chilly and it was time to go indoors. It is in this sense that the Pax Romana, which lasted for nearly four centuries, was a late evening of the spirit, shading imperceptibly into the night of the Dark Ages. It is out of that long night that the Green Children came. When a new consciousness was stirring, but men and women were still afraid of the dark corners of a room, as are those persons who like myself were brought up by candlelight and 'night-light' and told ghost stories by the nursery-maid. As a result of which I find myself even now lying awake listening for noises in the old house.

There are mornings and midnight of the spirit, according to whether that is in ascension or in decline. But the period of the Green Children is the early morning.

Yet what is certain is that on a day not very long ago, between the wars, they had vanished.

Where had they gone to? There are stories of this nature from all over the world. But, of course, it comes as a shock to be told of this happening in a parish in East Anglia, so near to the new aerodromes, in a countryside where there are always American airmen driving about in jeeps. Not only are our own County Constabulary continually patrolling the roads, night and day, but there are US Army Police, as well, and you would not think there could be an occurrence of this sort without some warning.

Remember that there is no bell-ringing without permission of the Vicar. There is also practice which takes place at stated hours, and of course the bell-ringers are well known in each parish. The harvesters say that the sound seemed to come up out of the old pits or trenches, reach to a pitch of loudness, and die back into the air. They first heard the noise of bells ringing under their feet, as it were. Two or three of the reapers state that they noticed the ringing from far away, coming nearer quite slowly at the speed of an aeroplane, but not a jet-plane, as one of them put it, and the moment it was just below them there was a peal of thunder from overhead.

One harvester, an ex-service man who had fought in Burma, said that it re-minded him of the 'afternoon earthquakes' that he and his mates grew quite accustomed to, for there was a little shock nearly every day at about the same time and always it was accompanied by a rumbling sound, underground, coming from far away. When it reached them the earth trembled and at the same time a peal of thunder came from immediately overhead, and then the rumbling died away into the distance. A point worth noticing is that the older harvesters seemed less susceptible to the sound. One or two of them even said they had heard nothing more than a loud chirruping or chirping which could have been the noise made by a large flock of starlings; like starlings when they perch on every branch of a tree and then suddenly take to flight and manoeuvre in strict formation, making dives and turns over the stubble.

At least two of the reapers heard nothing and did not notice anything extraordinary. But, then, as the church organist remarked to a reporter who was quickly on the scene, there are people in every walk of life who are tone-deaf to many other things as well as music. A woman, and the mother of twins, who was standing, talking, at the edge of the field says that the few moments of uncertainty and queer feeling before the Green Children came up into the cornfield reminded her of some of the sensations she had experienced during pregnancy.

And about half-a-mile from the harvest field a Gypsy woman, Mrs Lovell, suckling her child at her breast, felt strangely ill when the sound reached her and had to be helped into her trailer. Her husband, and an elder child, a daughter, 'did not like the feeling' and stood quite still, listening, until the sound died away into the distance. Children, on the other hand, only thought it was some kind of loud speaker 'gone wrong' on one of the Yankee aeroplanes. 'They are always trying out new gadgets, and we thought it was done as a joke to frighten us on our way to school.'

A postman who is a bit of an amateur scientist and spends his Sundays and half-days in his 'laboratory' which is an old converted air-raid bunker, stood and listened intently, looking into the sky. He was starting on his round, and although he did not hear the sound of bells, saw or rather felt that snap or blink of the air and expected to hear the two loud reports which mean that an aeroplane has broken through the sound barrier. He heard the one clap of thunder, but nothing more happened. There was not the noise of broken panes of glass falling from windows, which he had anticipated, and he continued on his round determining to ask householders if they had heard or noticed anything.

The whole occurrence seems for once to have been something for which no lucid explanation can be offered. The authorities are frankly puzzled by it. It is suggested that the identity of the Green Children is perfectly well known and that it was to the advantage of certain persons that they should leave one particular neighbourhood and make an unheralded appearance in the guise of vagrants and changelings in another. A pair of unwanted children cannot be kept in the dark for ever. Even their green colour has been put down to long seclusion in an underground cellar, or in some attic room with boarded windows.

So simple a happening has upset the laws of logic and the rules of reason. It is as though nature lied to the camera. For the machines have grown to expect implicit obedience of man. But what if the film is exposed and the lens in order, and yet the image will not take? If the Vickers-Viscount breaks its moorings and runs whinnying down the tarmac to its bearded pilot? If the keeper of a car-park complains that he is overwhelmed with attentions from a motor side-car; or the waitress working in a milk-bar with a road-drill tethered at the door, is found strangled with her own nylon stocking? Her body is fearfully injured, and the police suspect foul play and are looking for a maniac who throttles women.

A mad world, all 'commencing' with that morning when there was a loud noise like the ringing of church bells, and the Green Children came up out of the earth among the reapers in the harvest field. Clergymen, and others, have expressed the view that their coming has upset the balance of nature.

In the meantime the Green Children are to be issued with ration books and National Insurance cards. When old enough (I was writing in 1953 – but a similar state of affairs may recur again at any time) the Green Boy will of course be liable for National Service in any of the three branches of the Armed Forces, unless he claims deferment for medical, agricultural, or other reasons. His sister is expected to apply for work in the aluminium factory. She has already made up her mind never in any circumstances to enter domestic service. Young girls prefer the fixed hours and half-days on Saturdays; also, a fortnight's holiday with pay and railway-vouchers, 'becoming overalls' provided free, and in a choice of colours, and cheap and plentiful meals in the canteen.

There is only one difficulty. How to enter their parents' names in the space allotted in the insurance cards? She has told her friends that she would like them to call her 'Wendy'. The boy has expressed no preference, as yet. In any case, this is all premature as inquiries are not yet completed. Both children are living at the moment under the care of foster parents in a good home chosen for them by the Welfare Officer, and the address is being kept secret.

* * *

Or we could put it a little differently.

Were the Green Boy to write home while on holiday in Eire, which seems an appropriate spot for him, his letter would come with *License your Radio Promptly* stamped upon the envelope. The banshee and leprechaun have not paid for their licences, we may be certain of that; and over another matter the Irish police are of the opinion that those two and their relatives, if any, could assist them in their inquiries.

A temperance hotel overlooking a little harbour is the ideal holiday place, but the drawback is that too many Catholic priests come here to rest, and walk reading their breviaries along the rocky coast. Long ago, but not so long ago as all that, a mermaid was washed ashore and found fainting on the sands. She was taken into a cabin; one of those with fuchsias growing at the door, where she died the next morning.

But there are old people who say that she did not die at all, and that the son of the lobster-fisherman loved her and carried her on his back into the soft ling or heather. A little girl looking out of the window over a stone wall saw him walking away with what she thought was a huge fish lying across his shoulders. She looked again and saw the mermaid's breasts and golden hair. As she went she was thrashing with her tail. He brought her back that one time, but the next day the pair of them were gone for good. The little girl is now an old, old woman in the next village; and you can ask her, if you can make her hear, for she is stone deaf.

Others say that the mermaid and the fisherman's son lived for a long time in a cave. He could be heard singing when it was low tide. In the end his clothes were worn out and he was dressed in seaweed. They would come out of their cave in the moonlight and lie upon the shore. Legends are beginning. There is a story that one day he walked into the Post Office, which is the general store, and bought needles and thread and was gone before they recognized him. He was sewing a cloak for the mermaid and it was made of bog-cotton. Another time he came at night and stole the priest's umbrella. There was a great hallo'ing heard the next evening, rather late, and it was thought some of her relations had come back for her. It is well known that the mermen blow into seashells to make themselves heard above the waves. But a week or two later, there she was combing her hair and sitting on a rock. Of course he had bought the comb for her, probably in the next village where he is not so well known.

The fisherman's son must have been telling her about pocket-mirrors. Because, one day he came into the store with no money and wanted to bargain for a looking-glass with two handfuls of little pearls that he had found in oysters. But it explains what food they ate. And it is plain, too, that they collected samphire, and that other seaweed off the rocks. And caught little fishes out of the rock pools with a bait cut out of pearlshell.

One day he borrowed a bicycle which had been leaned against a boulder by someone who had come down to the shore for a swim, and she came to the mouth of the cave and called after him and was not happy till he rode back again. It was no good her trying to ride a bicycle because of her forked tail. And the two of them surprised a pair of lovers who were strolling on the cliffs by walking towards them, hand in hand, and she waddling forward on her tail. They were almost making an exhibition of being in love, themselves, he with a flower of red campion stuck behind his ear, and the mermaid with little daisy chains upon her wrists. As they passed by, they were singing together, and she had her arm round his neck. The couple let them go by, but looked back after them, and saw them lie down together in the heather.

What is certain is that on a day not very long ago, between the wars, they had vanished. Like the tinkers who, one fine morning, will strike their tent and be gone along the rose-hung hedges. The tinkers seldom, if ever, stay in the same place for more than two nights or three, though they may come back to it. You find the ring of ashes where they had their fire, near the sacred thorn-tree, at the parting of the roads. They will have tied another rag for luck to a branch of the blackthorn, and passed on in their two-wheeled cart.

But, at least, if you looked for long enough you would find them. Whereas these two were gone absolutely. All that was left in their cave was a bed of seaweed and a mound of empty mussel-shells. Where are they gone to? Will they hear a loud noise, one day, like the ringing of bells, and almost at once find themselves in the harvest field among the reapers? For it much resembles the story of the Green Children.

But the stop press is that 'Wendy' has run away from her home and that parties of searchers are looking everywhere for her under the direction of the police. Tomorrow morning, if conditions allow of it, a 'frog-man' is to descend into the waters of a disused quarry. Abandoned mine-shafts are also to be examined. Detectives have taken away particles of soil for examinations from the backyard of her home, 419 Sunbury Road. There has been an all-night conference at 'The Yard', and cups of tea and plates of eggs and bacon were taken into the conference room just before midnight. But Mrs Goodfellow, her foster mother says: 'Wendy won't have gone far. She was always complaining that her shoes were hurting her.'

After the first few days' story of the Green children the girl has become known as 'Wendy' to the public. She is, already, as famous as a film-star; or as Princess Margaret. 'Wendy' is an attractive brunette of fifteen. Char-a-banc loads of visitors came to the village every day last summer in order to see her, and parties were taken round to her home by the vicar and by the Wesleyan minister at a shilling a head in aid of local charities.

But is 'Wendy' in fact a brunette? For her colour is continually altering. Mrs Goodfellow told a reporter that 'Wendy' had changed into a red-head when she came down to breakfast that morning about a week ago. 'I didn't like it so much,' her foster mother says. 'Wendy has not got the right eyes to go with that colour hair. My husband says there is something funny about it all, and he can't get to the bottom of it. I think I agree with him. Except that she's such a nice, natural girl, and never any trouble. She has no boy friends.'

But 'Wendy' has gone completely. No trace of her to be found anywhere. She was lost, like you can lose a sixpenny bit in the corner of your room. And it may turn up, years later when they take up the floor boards. Foul play is no longer suspected. A 'Yardman' says she is unlikely to have left the country. For she was never issued with a passport. In any event, what motive can she have for leaving Britain? She had no friends abroad, or overseas. But Mrs Goodfellow is keeping the Green Girl's bedroom just as it was in case she should come back again. 'I want "Wendy" to know she always has a home here. She can walk in at any hour of the day or night, and be welcome.'

But no more was heard of her and it remains a mystery. The Green Boy did not survive long. He died, to be exact, on Friday, 14 November 1949, at about 4.45 in the afternoon, just when people were pulling down their blinds. He had been discovered, or had first appeared, only just over eight weeks previously, on that early morning in the harvest field. He had gradually lost his green colour and was beginning to eat cooked food. The doctor's diagnosis disclosed no extraordinary feature at the autopsy. He was backward, even when it is taken into consideration that the ordinary intelligence tests could not be applied to him. Doctors doubted if he could ever reach the nine-year-old standard, lower than that of the average American GI according to some authorities who rate our army recruits considerably above that. He only learned a few simple sentences to cover his daily wants, and of course could neither read nor write. 'He was,' one of the doctors remarked, 'what we call in medical language "an extreme isolationist case" – as with the, so called, Indian wolf-children of whom there are stories from time to time in the newspapers – of a child who has known no other children except his own sister, and has not the normal reflexes and reactions of a young boy of his age. He never would have improved to normal standard, and our system of education would not have helped him. The exact cause of his death remains uncertain though there are many theories to account for it. In my opinion he died because he was unable to condition himself to his new environment. If we could go back to where he came from it is probable that many of us would do the same.'

Morning Glory

There remains one thing more. It is the ending of one book and the beginning of another. Now the doors of purgatory are shut and barred not otherwise than as if the shutters are down and the staff and inmates away on holiday. Or do some few of them still wander round, bored and disconsolate with nowhere to go, the *boulevardiers* and *flaneurs* of the underworld who must stay up and cannot go home and early to bed?

An attraction of another sort has come to town and it is a circus tent. Striped blue and white like a convolvulus flower or 'morning glory'. The motor caravans and trailers arrived last night – but was it yesterday, or tomorrow evening? From the air the tent looks more like the paper rosette worn by prize horses and cattle at the fair. Or like a paper 'windmill' bought at the seaside. But, really and truly, as we shall see, it is a 'morning glory'.

It took the whole night to put up the tent. First the poles have to be erected. They come on special vehicles and they are in galaxy. North and south poles, for there is arctic and antarctic in every temperament and metabolism, and magnetic poles, and poles of 'inaccessibility' and of 'loneliness'. How many in all one does not know but they can be counted. Shall we call it a nebulous number and leave it to those who would count up the chromosomes in a rose, or look for traffic lights and road signs in the Milky Way? As if it is not enough that the one is a brook falling lazily through a meadow of daisies, and the rose is a rose.

But I am nearly forgetting the excitement, amounting to intoxication, of their arrival. Early in the evening; at sunset, just at the hour when one longs to hear music in the air. Only last evening it was as if a new world were born. Or they brought a new world with them.

The first person to get down out of a trailer was a young girl in a blue gown with long straight hair. Next, several children, but they must be her brothers and sisters. She is too young to be their mother. After this a pair of young girls who must be acrobats, for they have a more sophisticated air and one of them is smoking a cigarette. In old days they would have paraded round the town in Roman chariots in their tights and spangles. But there is no need for that.

During the six days' wonder it is a marvellous spectacle all day and into the night. The vehicles of creation dwell in the motor-trailers. More than one woman is with child. There are flowering window-boxes on the caravans. Every hour is magical, and there are extraordinary beings but walking across the fair-ground.

A youthful genius looking like an archer with nose and forehead in one line, and his wife and children. Or, another time, twenty-eight points of light – are they stars? – in the form of a goat, always appearing in the same place in the night sky, and when old enough we are told it is Capricorn, believed by the ancients to be the goat which fed the king of heaven with her milk. One legend is as good as another; much later in the Middle Ages, the East Anglian countrymen thought the

Milky Way in the heavens pointed to the shrine at Walsingham, while in Spain it led to Compostela and was called 'St James's Way'. Of a certainty these molecules of light and huge constellations are moving to some purpose and have direction, and there must be an order in their grand interludes and processions.

Trailers and lorries are parked all round and the convolvulus opens its blue trumpet-flower. The steps are put down, and the invitation is to pay at the door and come inside. One is pushed into the world puking and crying and is allotted a seat. Or for some there is only standing room. In the confusion others go to the wrong row of seats. But if the house is half-full they will let you stay where you are and keep your place. If we are lucky we will be able to see both the old actor rehearsing and the live performance. Both of them being transitory, in a sense, and ever on the move. Indeed all is ready late on Saturday night and they are off on Sunday, as if only to prove there is no fixed point in time. No truth in 'The World created in the 710th year of the Julian period, year 4004 before Christ'; though indeed many persons in full possession of their senses were prepared to believe that, and more still, as late as two years after Queen Victoria had begun her reign.* The circus tent, striped blue and white like a convolvulus flower or 'morning glory' is ever on the move in its own 'orbit', a word defined as 'the track of a heavenly body, or the cavity holding a human eye', though differences have to be allowed for between a year of *Le Roi Soleil* in his golden youth, dancing as the Sun God in the royal masques and ballets, if with none of the born dancer's 'ballon' or elevation, or, again, a year of his old age with all its sadness and ennui; or either, or both of these clocks of time compared to the years of a convict in the hulks, or sentenced to the galleys. Time, indeed, has different signatures and meanings, though at least the circus tent may return upon its tracks and come back again another year.

But now for the old comedian or clown; and I have to admit that a good photograph of Grock, or any one else of the famous fraternity of clowns or comics, is as impressive as any portrayal in painting of the Creator. And not less frightening. They have it in them to suggest that they are not to be trifled with, or made fun of. You do that at your own risk and danger. Such, too, is the tramp or vagrant's self-defence. He may look funny enough in his rags, but it is a warning to be careful. The facial expression of nearly all comedians, even of Buster Keaton, is more than a little menacing and dangerous. They may all turn nasty at not even a moment's notice.

The reason for his huge stature, for he is now in transcendence like one of the giants in Goya's etchings, whether an illusion or not, is that he is a kind of human ghost or emanation. A spiritual embodiment, and a being as universal as the crowd at a football match. All laugh with him, the babe-in-arms and the intellectual. So that he is all himself and yet a part of everyone. And it comes from that,

* As on the first page of *The Chronological Table* from the Creation of the World to the Fall of the Roman Empire in the West, and in the East, at the start of Dr Lempriere's *Classical Dictionary*, 1830 edition, which Chronological Table 'has been compiled with great accuracy, and chiefly extracted from *The Chronology and History of the World*, by Dr J. Blair, 1754, and Archbishop Usher's *Annales Veteris et Novi Testamenti*, Geneva 1722.

that he is bigger than himself and in transcendency over his own person. He is beyond his own physical limits because he has become a part of everyone, which is irrespective and regardless of what he is, himself. He is in everyone, and everyone is in him, which is all any artist or any human being can attain to. No one can do more than that. He is sent to us, and we are given to him. But he is not a person to pray to, and he demands no sufferings or privations. He is human as we are, and mortal, but living for the moment, and when we laugh at him we are laughing at ourselves.

It is a human being he sees in his looking-glass, who looks at him. They are one and the same person, but who can say which is the real and which the false. The one looks at the other and both are living, but you can only touch the one of them. The other is but the living image, 'image', indeed, because it is flat on the surface of the looking-glass and you cannot make contact with it. You can breathe on it in order to hide its face but that means interposing your own image, and you cannot get near to it without having the reflection of any object that touches it thrown back at you. You are touching it without having the feeling of it at all for there is nothing there. Yet there is most definitely something there, watching for what you do next, unable to take its eyes off you.

Now we have the feeling that it is not his farewell performance but any and every appearance. But certainly he is an old man. He opens his mouth for convenience of dabbing on the paint and his tongue fills his mouth; fills it so that you cannot see his teeth. Perhaps he has no teeth. He is old and toothless. And suddenly we know the truth. He is an old man and a little child. Indeed, a babe in its cradle. Before a babe teethes, and when he cries, and has stopped crying and his tongue blocks and fills his mouth and he is tasting the salt in his own tears. This old actor 'making up' in front of his hand-mirror is no different at all from a baby crying in its cot.

This is what I have been looking for, and found at last. Having gone from one end of the emptiness to the other, and it is now filled. Filled and overflowing. He is a human being laughing and weeping. We are back in humanity and out of the demi-world. If the old man can laugh and cry he has a heart and soul. The old man 'making up' for his performance has the countenance of god. Looking at him, you do not know whether he is crying or laughing; still less, whether to laugh or cry with him. For there should, it is certain, be sacred weeping and sacred laughter, this latter being something now gone altogether from the world, though there have been times, the Bacchanalia, Dionysiac festivals, and the like, in which it has been practised. In probably the last instances for this ever to happen, it may in the result be more like a sacred theatre or celestial dancing floor; but the confidence of spirit is irrepressible and the inspiration too happy to be serious minded. A comparison now suggesting itself between, say, the glorious cheerfulness and gaiety of the Wieskirche, 'the dancing floor of God' and the masterpiece of Johann Baptist and Dominikus Zimmermann in the sub-Alpine meadows, and the interior of St Mary's Cathedral, Edinburgh, of the Scottish Episcopal Church, 'a fine E. E. edifice, generally considered the masterpiece of Sir Gilbert Scott, built between 1874 and 1879 at a cost of upwards of £110,000'. 'Take your choice,

Gentlemen,' as Sir Thomas Beecham said at rehearsal when the orchestra was tuning up and the oboe-player gave the note with too much vibrato.

And yet how deceptive can be appearances in the sacred theatre. Outside and beyond the world of Christians, there is at Polannaruwa in Ceylon, a wonderful and most sacred place of ruined temples; a mile and a half of ruins, with whole monkey-families leaping in the rocks; or, as the guide book says in comic terms, 'certain to be seen crossing the road in large troops', with an artificial lake or tank where a huge red lotus grows in profusion, the descendant of those 'once grown for use in the temples and palaces', in this place deserted since the end of the thirteenth century. What use, indeed, can there have been for the red lotus except to be held in the hand? But farther down, down below lotus-level, past a round building like a stone gasometer open to the sky; and down below that, farther down again, there are rock-cut sculptures, a cross-legg'd Buddha and a reclining Buddha with Ananda, 'his cousin and favourite disciple'. The reclining Buddha, indeed, is not asleep but in Nirvana, in oblivion which is beyond death, but not being dead is substantive. And it was there, 'above that holy place brought conscious with his unconsciousness', that we saw the yellow-flowering tree. Only here in the sacred park of Polannaruwa, did we see it, and nowhere else in India or Ceylon, and we were never able to find its name. A tree of yellow cups with but few leaves held near the sky; their petals holding, yet spilling down the glorious sun-wine and ichor of the light. Here, also, near the statues, the white frangipani grows in unforgettable perfection. The broken petals were littering the ground, with whole unbroken flowers of the yellow-flowering tree among them, the two sorts lying together.

It was not difficult, lifting some, rejecting others, to find a perfect flower like a yellow grail-cup. The white frangipani is of particular association with Buddhist temples, to the extent even that it is called 'the temple flower', and has become a part almost of Buddhist legend and mythology, though it is of origin in Mexico. But looking up at the brother-flowers of that yellow-flowering tree and taking in the ecstasy of scent out of that grail-cup, we seem to see the saffron robes or petals of the early Buddhist monks, though this prince of Nepal or 'Lord Buddha', did not claim to be the son of god, but only mortal like all other men, which in itself is something salutary and exceptional among religions. And for nearly ten years I have wondered and wanted to know about this yellow-flowering tree, only to find within the last few weeks that it is *Cochlospernum vitifolium*, of origin from Maryland, USA, much planted in the latter part of last century at Polannaruwa and at Anuradhapura, another Buddhist site in Ceylon, 'where its beautiful yellow flowers grow from bare branches'. And where it has mastered, as it were, another landscape and another language, and transformed them into its own.

It is before the yellow-flowering trees of Polannaruwa, as nowhere else but at the blue roses, three rose-windows of the dawn, at Chartres, that one is attuned to spiritual messages and emanations. These things become credible in front of such manifestations of the mortal and the immortal. It is the thought in particular that the Lord Buddha did not claim to be the son of god, 'but only mortal like all other men', that excepts the miraculous and makes all things possible of human beings if only they will try for them. There is nothing, good or evil, of which rational human beings, the only reasoning creatures, are not capable. But we all must die, and there is not much time. That is the message. This present book which opens with the *Death of a Flie* carries that warning, which is no worse for the smallest insect than for the most wonderful of human creatures. And no better, either. It is the inevitable, the unavoidable truth but, also, it is the appetite and the spur of life. And that we are mortal, always have been and always will be, is the infallible, the transcendental truth. In face of which one might feel in favour of some form of sanctity attaching to human achievement for there have been miracles that are real enough, but in the arts and sciences, not in religion, almost never in politics, still less in war. As to the practicality or the possibilities of which coming to pass, they are as unlikely as that the millennium should begin tomorrow. For the history of civilization would need to be re-written, or, in truth, written for the first time, and from a universal and unbiased point of view, while judgment changes and alters too quickly for there ever to be even an approximation to a permanent and lasting truth.

Vaudeville of the Living and the Dead

Let us go back, rather, to the blue circus tent or 'morning glory'. For it is there that creation is ever in progress, or it could be said that 'something is always going on'. As to the potentialities of which, listen to what Jules Clarétie, for many years Director of the Comédie Française, has to say of the first night of Offenbach's *La Vie Parisienne*,* which he attended. He declared that the third act made him laugh so much that somebody might have been tickling the soles of his feet, and added that the effect of this scene was as if the whole house had been taking hashish. It is of course a masterpiece of comic humour, and withal so haunting and nostalgic a picture of its moment in time that the intrinsic beauty and poetry run out if it is not 'revived' with the greatest delicacy and lightness of hand. But in ideal performance, obviously, in the theatre on that autumn evening of 1866, one can well believe it had the described effect upon the audience. It was the descent of the god into the sacred theatre, but another god altogether from that worshipped in Christian churches in the last two thousand years. The comic genius of Offenbach at his best was closely akin to poetry as was the case, too, with Rossini at other minor god-like inspirations of his humour.† But the laughter of Offenbach is not as kindly as that of Rossini, it is goat-like and *endiablé*, the butting laughter of the horned god or billy-goat; and it is not without reason that we noticed the constellation of twenty-eight points of light in the form of a goat, always appearing at the same place in the night sky above for present purposes the gas-lit Paris of the Second Empire. For they are in emblem of Capricorn and the horn of plenty, which horn in classical mythology 'had the power of giving the nymphs whatever they desired', and no zodiacal sign whatever could be more appropriate to those courtesans and *hetairae*, probably the most numerous and strident assembly of the sort there has been in history.

Would that the mere list of their names, Cora Pearl, Léonide Leblanc, Silly, Anna Deslions, Léontine Massin, Caroline Letessier, Giulia Barucci, Constance Rézuche, Marguerite Bellanger, Adèle Courtois, Rose Thé, Humberta Ghinassi – and how ugly they are, always it seems with the exception of Cora Pearl, in their photographs! – would that the list of their names were card index to their carriages and parasols, and crinolines! For they rivalled with the Duchesses and Countesses of the Faubourg Saint-Germain in their equipages, in their horses, their coachmen in livery, and the diminutive English 'tiger' sitting beside the coach-

---

* 30 October 1866 at the Théâtre des Bouffes-Parisiennes.
† For instance, the '*zitto, zitto*' finale to Act II of his *Cenerentola*, the 'chitter-chatter' ensembles to *L'Italiana in Algeri*, Almaviva's serenade to guitar accompaniment in the *Barbiere*, where humour is mixed with poetry, and at many other moments.

man, arms folded, upon the box. Constantin Guys, as remarked by Baudelaire in his essay *Le Peintre de la Vie Moderne*, 'draws and paints a carriage, and every kind of carriage, with the same care and ease, with which a consummate marine painter treats every kind of craft'. He was the master of the calèche, chariot, daumont, clarence, coupé, britschka, grand duc, or grande coureuse, but what is missing in his hundreds of sepia or pencil drawings is the pattern of the dresses. In a book that appeared as long ago as 1929 I quoted with approval from a commentator who had written of fashionable ladies of the 'sixties', 'who were seen in military coats of yellow velvet with Chinese embroidery, in red velvet mantles trimmed with black lace, in black tulle dresses with gold lace. They went back to the caracos of their great-grandmothers and chose to have them of flaming red satin studded with gigantic steel buttons, or hung with cut glass; they wore the Diana bodice which left one shoulder uncovered; and, added to this, their hair had to be red like a cow's tail and curled like a lap-dog's, *en bouton frisé* or *en caniche.*'

To do justice to which theme, time itself must needs be travestied, and we would have to imagine a painter of the 'green mansions', an Utamaro, perhaps better still a Kiyonaga, imported from his native Japan to work for a few years in Paris of the Second Empire, bringing with him the craftsmen to cut the blocks of cherry-wood and take the prints from them. Both artists having made just those very circles in Japan their particular subject. Utamaro, in especial, because of the grace of his elongations and distortions and to whom the crinoline would have made fantastic and extravagant appeal as, also, the extraordinary headdresses and 'hair-does' depicted by Compte Calix in the fashion plates to *Les Modes Parisiennes* all through the eighteen-fifties and sixties; and Kiyonaga, whose woodcuts were particularly beautiful because of the pattern of the Kimono, a detail to which he always paid great attention, and for the care which he lavished on the women's dresses. The suggestions where both artists are concerned being implausible and complete anachronisms, Utamaro having died in 1806 and Kiyonaga in 1815; but their mere impossibility makes them the more fascinating, and we may be sure that had this confrontation taken place the success would have been immediate. The Japanese craze had already taken root in Paris of the sixties though it was only the tag-end of the Ukiyo-e masters that reached France from the newly opened ports of Japan. Woodcuts by Kuniyoshi, Kunisada, and the like; and in rare instance a Hokusai, or a Hiroshige.

Had two great masters of the school, an Utamaro, or a Kiyonaga, established themselves and worked in Paris in defiance of the rules of time an extraordinary chapter would have opened in the history of the graphic arts, and we may be certain they would have gravitated towards the gay quarters of the French capital. And the beauties of the tea-houses and 'green mansions' would have been recognized in their Parisian equivalents of the 'floating world'. We have to imagine for ourselves triptych prints, for which Utamaro was famous, of the paragons of fashion on the summer sands of Trouville; at the *Longchamps fleurie* of the valse by Waldteufel; or of the friends of Swann and members of *Le Jockey*, as in Tissot's group of them but in another rendering; of the procession of carriages, in the named varieties, along the Bois and up and down the Champs-Elysées; in the green room of the Opéra, the top-hatted gentlemen talking to the dancers; or of ladies entering the Café Riche or Maison Dorée with the waiters bowing. Scenes of boating, too, and the *déjeuner des canotiers*; and of skating in the Bois on winter afternoons when 'le lac gêlé se transformait en grand salon'. And for the rival artist, Kiyonaga, more attention paid to what Guys for all his minor genius can never give us, the too daring, clashing colours of that worst epoch in taste, which just for that reason must have made so extraordinary a spectacle for those persons who could use their eyes; dresses 'of shot taffetas, damask reps, clouded, spotted, checked, and marbled *merveilleux* at sixty francs a yard, gold and silver brocade from Lyons, figured with bunches of flowers in coloured silks, lampas figured with golden palms, brocatelles embroidered with flowers in gold and silver thread'.

Tunes that have descended, come down to the circus, like the valse *Les Patineurs*, like *Estudiantina*, like the can-can from *Orphée aux Enfers*; that dance of *bordelle* origin pushed up in the world by the noise and glitter of the revived Empire, with the six strident 'call-notes' of *le grand écart* when the dancers come down one after another in 'the splits' and the music, poodle-like, for it has the gibber-movements of performing poodles, hurries and hustles on, and hops ahead. Now but a circus fanfare, and meaning nothing; with no meaning whatever to the extraordinary beings just now walking across the fairground, who have heard it all their lives and been brought up to it from the blare of the steam-organ, now 'on tape' alas! and robbed of course of any history or meaning, yet still haunted like the equivocal room on a first floor which must have had a past, but no one remembers and it is no use asking.

To know nothing of the past is like the younger generation who neither drink or smoke. Those are not vices to them, but merely silliness that costs money and a waste of time; and they have started their adult lives when very young. At an age when young people of my day were troubled by a number of problems, they are living together without fuss or bother. And if it does not suit them, they move on and take another partner. Nearly always they come to rest after an experience or two, and often it is at the first trial. Money is not so important as all that, and the more sensible of them do not read the newspapers. They are perfectly well informed in consequence, but not stuffed full and forcibly fed with nonsense. But, in truth, I am interested in neither beggars nor aristocrats except in so far as they form a theme or subject of which although one lived for centuries there need never be an end. As for instance the *vice solitaire* of church-viewing and comparing in Lincolnshire and East Anglia, there being sufficient in that part of England alone; and then as well, there is the West Country from Worcestershire to Cornwall. Or, more lively in character, the pursuit of the Baroque and Rococo in Austria and Bavaria as discussed earlier.

For those who are not creators there is much else to do, and there are pursuits and hobbies which amount to a form of creation, as in plant-collecting and hybridization. One is ready to envy even the persons who spent their leisure, years ago, in searching the remote parts of Brittany for surviving specimens of the little fawn-coloured, Breton basset hound, whose bigger forbears Shakespeare writes of in the lines:

> *My hounds are bred out of the Spartan kind.*
> *So flewed, so sanded; and their heads are hung*
> *With ears that sweep away the morning dew;*
> *Crook-knee'd and dew-lapp'd like Thessalian bulls,*
> *Slow in pursuit, but matched in mouth like bells,*
> *Each unto each.*

Or going from village to village in the most inaccessible parts of Mexico looking for the Mexican hairless dogs called 'sholos' or in the Nahuatl language, Yoloitz-cuatli, ghost-like creatures the more spectral for their playfulness, with the curiously high body temperatures, as big as Labradors, and with nothing whatever to do with chihuahuas. I contrived to see some while in Mexico City.

Or in minutiae of theme, but of extreme labour and difficulty in the finding, such a search as that for paintings of archangel-musketeers, marksmen in Court dress of the reign of Louis xiv; embroidered surcoats, elegant shoes with red heels, long breeches, huge pair of wings, and plumed hat. Of whom a couple of inspiring specimens are to be seen among the paintings in the new museum at Lima, in Peru; the one, loading his arquebuse, and the other musketeer actually taking aim and shooting as we look at him. Which paintings are in a category to themselves, derived from some seventeenth-century book of engravings of marksmen, but given full rein of fantasy, and coming from churches in distant regions on the Altiplano of Peru and Bolivia, to which they are indigenous and to be found nowhere else. Only a year or two ago an Englishman appeared with photographs of some dozen, or dozen and a half of these angelic musketeers, quite dazzling in their finery, and like some long lost shooting-party of guests of King Florestan, awoken to find themselves on the high plain among the *chulos* and *mestizos* of the Andean villages. How desirable that there could be some excuse for publishing these unexpected and strange works of art! Who could have painted them, in some remote inkling or hearsay of *le Roi Soleil*? But the mysterious traveller took them away with him, leaving no address, and maybe has gone back to the region of Lake Titicaca to look for more, which is a very long way indeed from the angel ceilings of East Anglia.

Both sorts of angelic visitors, the armed and the unarmed, pertaining though to the same faith or religion which is a salutary thought, and if one searches the world over everywhere there are these insurance policies against death. It is a thing human beings cannot fathom or understand and that hangs like a dark cloud over our heads. There is nothing, nothing we can do about it, except perhaps postpone the evil hour. We should be perfectly satisfied by now that neither a virtuous life, nor a wicked one, has any bearing on it. The rewards and penalties are on this earth and not in heaven. The one prime difference is between the living and the dead. The holocausts and the hecatombs are at back of us and in front of us, and there is only breathing space between.

But the living are humming and buzzing, and there is so much to see and listen to, and try to understand. More particularly if we label as living what the dead have left behind them. Once again and for ever, it is humanity that is both the wonder and the shame. According to the original meaning we are both our own gods and our own evil spirits, and for present purposes for all it matters there is no reason to think there have been any others. In which case we are responsible only to ourselves and to no higher being. There are neither rewards nor retributions after death but only changes of opinion. And those will come too late, they can neither flatter, nor even hurt our feelings.

That there have been god-like human beings is true, but more often in what they accomplished than in what they were themselves. That is why the pursuit of technique as technique is more satisfactory than the study of human behaviour The trivia of personal habits are unlikely to make heroes of those one most envies or admires, yet they have not to be disembodied in order to be understood. The removal of the brain and viscera made mummies of the Egyptian Pharaohs, and left but a gilded and painted chrysalis with no germ of life inside it. Under all the scented bandages is the pitiful skeleton, no happier than the other skeletons in the charnel-house. Even the macabre gaiety of the German *Totentanz* is forbidden to them; no bony fanfares and rattlings of dead bones, they are waxed and sealed up, wingless in their pupa-cases, embalmed and immobile, unable to join in the dance.

That they were the first great men is indisputable, even if the new dating of the green hill of Silbury and the Avebury stone circle is to make them contemporary with the Pyramids, in which case they are redoubled in their mystery. That all of them were achieved with forced labour detracts nothing, but only adds to the solemnity of the hedgeless downlands which have an antiquity more real than Toltec or Mayan temple. Of their own boasting, Assyrian Kings with their trail of blinded captives were the first monstrous beings in history, and founders of a tradition that has been maintained into our own times. That human suffering, even proportionately on a greater scale, has been and is accompanying the egalitarian revolutions that are proceeding under our own eyes is no mitigation of the horror, and there will not even be left as memorial the bas-reliefs of the great king standing in his chariot, lion-hunting, with unguent-dropping beard. The Moscow Underground is no substitute for the temples of Thebes and Karnak, any more than the dividing wall between West and East Berlin with control point at 'Check-point Charlie' can stand proxy for the Great Wall of China. Absolute equality cannot be otherwise than featureless, even if it soon succumbs to the same vices as its predecessors. History repeats, and contradicts itself, at the same moment and in the same tone of voice. It is at the mercy, or seems to be at the mercy of individuals, but in reality they are powerless and it runs away with them. There is no stopping a tyranny with kindness, or changing a deathbed into a coronation scene. The lion and the lamb do not lie down together without a disastrous end for the innocent. There are indeed no fairy story endings in human history.

Jewelled Skeletons

No! No! It is impossible! It will not do! It is not enough that we are not intended to know the answer. We are alone here and left to our own devices. There has never been, and there never will be divine interference or interposition in our affairs. Put here by whom and for what purpose? But why should there be a purpose? The mystery only deepens and grows the more mysterious. And if there is a mystery there must be an explanation; even if it is no more than an algebraic figure which could be written in chalk on a blackboard, a successful formula which allowed of life to begin. A secret which may be found one day in a laboratory, and we will be none the wiser for the discovery. And once found, the scientists will transfer it to their test-tubes where, intrinsically, it will be no more interesting than moondust.

Such would seem to be the most likely explanation. And that it was an accident, originally, more than an intention. To have come out of absolute negation is not credible, however near that is to the Nirvana of the Buddhists. A molecular, or mineral, or gaseous parenthood is probable. The animals understand implicitly, unquestioningly, because they do not reason. They have their own corporate body, the 'soviet' of the rats or of the ants, that protects their interests and that works on instinct. They adapt themselves as do the lichens and the mosses, the microbes and the micro-organisms. But human beings are baulked of an answer because they can think and reason.

The animals have their collective instinct which for the most part is no less afraid than we are of dying. Who that has ever seen a scorpion, the *toro bravo* of the world of insects, stay still on wall or floor and hold his ground, waiting to be killed, will understand the scorpion knows what is coming to him. This is something more than the bluebottle that knows not when to stop, and yet is too stupid to be frightened. That 'takes evasive action' and flies off again and again, but more from mischief and playfulness than from fear of death. The bluebottle, rich, well fed 'bourgeois revisionist' of his race and kind, shining sutler of the summer winds, not the humble, nuisance-housefly whose deathbed we attended in our opening pages. The obsequies of the former must needs be grander, if no less humiliating.

Or it could be that things have gone further now than was intended. If there was even an intention; or anything more than the mere drift or current of there being life, and of being alive. And having once started, there is no stopping it, unless we do something very silly ourselves, because we are our own masters. If we tried hard enough we could even rock the earth on its axis, and it is 'anyone's guess' as to what might happen then. Indeed, the stupidest reply would probably be the correct answer. But, as just said, it belongs to us and we are our own masters. 'The world is our oyster', and we have to swallow it whole while it is still alive. And supposing it is dying, dying; or just simply moribund, in fact diseased?

What, then? For we are working as hard as we can to kill it, and what we have done in this direction in little more than a hundred years is remarkable.

Are we being watched, or any notice whatever taken of us from outside? This is very doubtful. The supernatural does not exist and there have been no miracles. And one day the whole edifice of all the religions put together will collapse and there will be nothing to put instead of them. The proofs will be there, as plain as the notices outside a police station or ticket office, but it may be a long time before people trouble to read them. Yet nothing is ever going to prevent children, and not only children, myself included, from being frightened of the dark. Most persons have known the uncanny experience of a dog being terrified, the hair of its coat standing on end and it refusing to move a step along some dark stretch of passage, or crossing a dark room. Could it be that the dog is afraid of a ghost dog? Which is a little worse than were it frightened of a ghost human being, for it means the dog has some instinct going beyond death, and dying.

So it has all been a waste, but what a glorious waste of time! But no more so than building a beautiful house which will lie empty, or even be lived in by your descendants on your death. Such things are not achieved only for yourself, or even for posterity. They are achieved on their own behalf, or, in fact, they build themselves. But there must be an overwhelming will power and an insistence.

And when the incentive wanes and withers? The horned moon has its phases, but it returns. It comes back again. To be seen in its youth climbing the evening sky; next, at the owl-hour rounding and swelling in the branches; then, rising replete and serene like a pastoral mask, of moon-like enigmatic smile; and now dwindling and diminishing to an empty rind. But replenishing and returning which is something we cannot even attempt, though someone else perhaps not in our race or time can do this for us though we will not know of it, which is little comfort. Or perhaps once is enough, and there is no appetite for more. In any case it is too late and there can be no answer. Which has never been a negative for the great builders, or the other practitioners and achievers. Who have continued in spite of themselves, and even because of the difficulties that have beset them. Just so the ant continues on its path, but making use of its antennae; and the riderless racehorse runs on after how many others have passed the winning post! The greatest artists in the arts have been both the most famous in their lifetimes and the most obscure. It is the mediocrities that have come between, and earned a decent living. So that it is, in a sense and to great degree, all or nothing. And if everything between those two extremes were destroyed and swept away, what remained would be the best. Unless one distrusts that and would sooner the safe and middling.

But in the end it is all for our own enjoyment and not to the glory of god. Which comes to the same thing if, as is the fact, the god is in ourselves for good or evil. It is only the cirrhi and cumuli, the sum of vapourings of conscience in the face of Judgment Day that impede and obscure clear thinking. And if there is really nothing to fear it has been so much misspent energy. The mosques and churches and temples of the world are no different in intention; it has all been to the same purpose, to ask for forgiveness and for another chance of life, but of preference in another sphere. Why is the humblest of creatures afraid of dying? As though life is to be held onto because it does not come again?

It could even be that the sun rising every morning and going down at night under the horizon or below the mountains pointed to this difference. The light is born again in youthfulness and is immortal. Neither sun nor moon, it is to be noticed, has found favour as a place for the immortals. Because the sun is too hot; and the moon too near to earth on a fine night when its bucolic mask like the ageing of a beautiful woman into something too round-faced and absurd is too plainly visible. The heavens have had to be sited further than those two luminaries, male and female, up in the true regions of the immortal spirits. We have to consider nights in the far distant past when there was no interior light but firelight in order to appreciate the daily miracle of sunrise and the importance attached to the meanings and movements of the stars. The first learned men, alike of the Mayans and of the raisers of the megaliths, builders of Carnac and Stonehenge, were students of the stars. And after them, at least, in the western hemisphere, the first artists were the bards or poets.

For we had not the carved stelae, or stone monuments to astronomers, or calendars – if that is what they are? – of the ancient Mayans, and there were not the tail feathers of the quetzal bird to inspire our ancestors, whose wealth was in the flocks that wandered like the shadows of clouds upon the downs – if even they are our ancestors and we are in part descended from them. There is never a human figure among the stone monuments, for lack of which the great stones might have raised themselves upon the plain without the help of human hands. Not so the fluttering caciques, for they are all feathers and flattened foreheads, on the stelae of Tikal and of Copan. We are left in no doubt that they are the work of human hands, unlike the anonymous, faceless tilters and raisers of the megaliths upon the bustard-haunted sheepwalk of the Wiltshire downs.

But the motive ever and always has been the same. It is the wonder of living and the dread of dying, and in order to bridge the gulf or pit of time. Not only so as to be remembered and not forgotten but also, in order to probe and attempt to understand. For the mysteries are overwhelming, and the greatest mystery of all the orbiting drifting lights over our heads, with now and again a comet crossing the heavens with its tail of fire. A messenger of something? And you can think you hear its rushing passage through the night, of which the utter silence is no less a mystery with so many moving lights.

At both sides of the world the early thinkers and night-watchers were at work. With the Mayans in Guatemala and Yucatán; and at the stone clocks, sun-dials, orreries, or call them what you will, of Carnac and Stonehenge. This was something not attempted by the Egyptians for all their greater sophistication in temple building and the attendant and, in the main, mortuary arts, for their minor arts were, by and large, those of the mortician. They were preoccupied with death yet without making deep inquiry into it. But for a millennium, or even as much as two thousand years before the Mayans of their first period in Honduras and Guatemala, the builders of the megaliths were studying the stars, and must have been obsessed therefore with the mysteries of time. They, at least, were looking for a meaning. As now at this moment of writing, with the launching last evening of Apollo 14, and 'touch down' expected for a week on Tuesday. Yet so far only to the moon and no further. And one would think this may be the limit to 'manned research' in space, though instruments may send back messages from farther afield, out of the polar cold or burning furnaces of other surfaces and landing-stages. And an end to it all because of the expense when so many human families need rehousing? Or because it is realized the distances are too immense, and that there could be some plan or intention that this should be so? There is no knowing; this in the final, irrevocable meaning of that phrase.

And an end to reaching for the stars could be the first step down the ladder out of the light into darkness. As at about the year AD 475 with the abdication of the too aptly-named Romulus Augustulus. But civilization continued elsewhere, in the Eastern Empire; it was not all finished. Yet in the succeeding fifteen centuries of the Christian religion it has been the serious thinkers who infringed the rules, and more often than not who paid the penalty.

Theological disputation marked no step forward and is no key to wisdom, any more than the wise men of the world are the saints and athletes of religion. Their self-inflicted sufferings helped no one. In contrast to which, how many centuries of patient watching and observing must have gone into the making of those stone monuments and temples of astronomy! When there was no alphabetical system of writing; and how did they retain and take down note of their observations? Which, presumably, would have to be learned orally. Calculations that it would appear are correct down to the smallest particular. It was the rising and setting of the celestial bodies over a lifetime as marked against the hills and trees with the acquired knowledge of where to expect them and take notice of their returns and exits, which does really seem nearer to wisdom than mere saintliness even though, like that, it avails nothing.

But it is time spent in watching the supreme mysteries, and in looking for an explanation, which we are still doing thirty or more centuries later, and of which we have scarcely begun the understanding. Of their beliefs and superstitions we know nothing, which is the saving grace, and only makes them the more interesting in our eyes. And it could be that to consult their wise men and ask their opinion would be to learn some part of wisdom.

In the same way that a considerable body of sense together with the results of long experience are to be found in the remedies of folk-medicine, this could be true also of those first explorers and watchers of the night skies, and of their theories as to the effects, if any, upon human and animal creation and upon the world of nature. They must in simple words have had their own opinions as to what it is all about. Surely in any case they would be nearer to the truth than the priests and monks who inquire no farther than the clouds.

* * *

Or there is a book still to be written about the jewelled cadavers of the saints and martyrs. Of nuns stooping their paled faces to the embroidery of pearls and coral for the robing of the skeleton. Of the half-mummy at the fittings, armed into his long-skirted coat, in Spanish Court dress of the seventeenth century, and made to lean upon an elbow as though reading. His skeletal digits in jewelled gloves; a rapier at his side, and shoes with ribbons and red heels. Such a gallant as ever nun dreamed of, and must tell to stand back that night from her bed-curtains, or put her crucifix into his hand.

As now in the hot golden gallery of mirrors, with old ladies looking on, and the première calling out the numbers, where the changeling of the jessamine, half-Siamese and half of Portugal, moves in mannered walk to show off the dresses. But that other, the gallant in the glass case, had but his death's head for a face, his death's head gone further than the head dropped into the basket beneath the guillotine; that other, all the others, like bones that a dog has buried, or left upon the altar. There is no more to them than that. Had but a vulture picked and dragged the bones. For there is a nobility, almost a poetry to that. As, for contrast, in the metaphysics of old bones, the sheep or pig's jaw with the teeth still in it that lay on the path where the dogs had dropped it, at Ciudad Rodrigo where we saw it but two years after our war had ended, on the green slope of the castle hill; one of the grinning masks of war, it seemed to me to be, but not the flute made of an eagle's wing.

Such jewelled skeletons as those just spoken of had been seen by the poet, open-necked, with hair cropped short, *en toilette de guillotiné*, whose opiate fancy would take delight in the *apsarases* of Khajuraho, had he but seen or even heard of them. At that time when all men were whiskered and bearded, if it were no more than the pointed 'imperial' and waxed moustache-ends of l'Empereur, and nearly every career soldier in the French army aped him and wore them in his pattern, it pleased Baudelaire to have his head shaved, almost, and his shirt open at the neck as in the condemned cell. What he intended by this it is not difficult to imagine for in fact he was already doomed and threatened with aphasia or loss of speech, and hemiplegia or semi-paralysis, the effects of syphilis. In his *Mon Coeur mis a Nu* he already writes on 23 January 1862: 'Aujourd'hui j'ai senti passer sur mon front le vent de l'aile de l'imbécilité,' first symptom of the pitiless illness that was to destroy him.

It was however four years later in March 1866, having in the meantime gone to live in Belgium because of his debts and of lack of appreciation from his own compatriots, that Baudelaire in company with the etcher Félicien Rops entered the former Jesuit church of St Loup at Namur, was greatly impressed by just these glass coffins and jewelled skeletons of which the like are not left in France, and expressed his intention, then, of writing of them. But in this same church within a few moments he had his fatal fall and paralytic stroke from which he never recovered.*

* Baudelaire died at Paris in the arms of his mother on 31 August 1867 after a long agony, having never recovered his speech properly, but with his memory and intelligence, it would seem, unimpaired and uninjured.

It was the first time that Baudelaire had come into contact with such things, having never been to Germany, or Italy, or Spain; and it is deeply to be regretted, marvellous art critic that he was, that he did not write about them. And the Jesuit church of St Loup at Namur need only have been the beginning. One could wish that he had been able to see Zwiefalten, and Vierzehnheiligen, and Ottobeuren; but perhaps in particular Weltenburg, of the Asam brothers, on the river Danube, where the equestrian statue of St George, a knight in golden armour on a silver stallion, rides out over the high altar in a nimbus of light, and slays the dragon and frees the maiden, who holds up her hand before her eyes at this blinding vision. At that date now more than a hundred years ago such were themes which he would have had entirely to himself. No one having looked at them critically much later than the middle of the eighteenth century, or, for that matter, for at least another half-century in time to come. From the midst therefore of a century and a half, or more, of complete neglect and oblivion. This might have been a wonderful extension of his talents, too often constrained and confined by the paintings of which he was compelled to write appreciations in order to gain a living, as was only too evident in the Baudelaire exhibition in his centenary year in Paris in 1967. The paintings were there in plenty; but in pitiful sign of his poverty were the few photographs by Nadar, his letters, signed copies of his books, busts of Madame Sabatier ('La Présidente'), his walking-sticks, and the few other personal possessions of the poet who, all his later life, had only one room in a second- or third-rate hotel to live in.

Now, even the jewelled cadavers of which so sinister and haunting an anthology or catalogue could have been compiled, are in danger. It will not be long surely in this present climate of Papal authority before the edict goes forth and they are removed or interdicted together with the saints' days, now that the Pope is no longer carried in on the *sedia gestatoria* by a dozen footmen in red or green velvet coats and kneebreeches to the waving of ostrich-feather fans and the blare of silver trumpets, but walks from the sacristy into St Peter's, it being in retrospect no more than a century ago, no long time in Papal history, since there were eunuchs singing in the Sistine choir.* He walks into St Peter's, but flies all over the world in his yellow-painted 'executive jet,' never stopping anywhere for more than a few hours like some high powered oil-tycoon, one of the company of private 'jet' owners, and in this manner all the mystery will have flown to the winds in the space of a single lifetime.

Having once attended a ceremony in St Peter's when the skull of San Luigi Gonzaga was reunited to his skeleton I became interested in the jewelled cadavers, the quest for whom would have taken one to all sorts of strange places, from Goa, where lies the body of St Francis Xavier to Mexico, and of course to convent churches over much of Catholic Europe. Essentially, it is the work of nuns, forming a curious and concluding chapter in the history of costume; in appendix, as it were, to Court dress and to theatrical costume, by both of which it must have been influenced. The skeletons with their exemplary histories could have made a

* There is even a gramophone recording of the last of the Papal nightingales in faded, if full song.

volume which would have been extraordinary indeed, probably the most macabre collection of its sort ever put together within the confines of a book. A funeral masque of gigantic importance and implication after the compiling of which the author or artist by a way of a restoration of normality must needs undergo perhaps a 'refresher course' at an undertaker's.*

* The reader's attention is drawn to the skeletons in 'Spanish' court clothes, lying in glass coffins in the St Peters-Kirche in Vienna, just off the Graben. They are fine examples of their macabre genre; as, too, are those to be seen in the church at Hall, a few miles from Innsbruck, where there was formerly a Salesian *Damenstift*, or nunnery for noble ladies.

ENTR'ACTE

Grand Pas de Deux from Tchaikowsky's 'Casse Noisette'

Opening with a rocking, lulling movement over the full orchestra, a promenade or slow progression on arpeggios and glissandos up and down upon the harps, of grand dramatic flourish and excitement portending that a pair of extraordinary beings are about to make their entrance upon the stage, and since this tension cannot continue, with the crescendo or screech of trumpets, the clashing and clang of cymbals foreshadowed for not far ahead in time. A waving of huge wings to this moment but, also, a winnowing in a warm wind as of the bowing and obeisance of the fan-palms that I saw just now for the first time in the hotel garden on the Pacific shore of Mexico among the apartment buildings and the nightmare blocks of flats on Acapulco Bay. Palm trees fifteen or twenty feet tall, and formed of separate fronds like the slats of a giant fan. But of these later, for now the music settles into its pace which is that of these beings of a nightly immortality, for indeed they are made immortal in these few moments; and now they come on with easy quick walk and little bird-like steps to take up position. Both of them small even to insignificance on the huge stage of lights, but growing under our eyes, according it could be, to the laws governing the Golden Section or Golden Mean, 'a name given to an irrational proportion known at least since Euclid, which has often been thought to possess some aesthetic virtue in itself, some hidden harmonic proportion in tune with the universe'.* Whatever the explanation, the mystery only deepens as the dancers dominate and seem even to create and shed light around themselves.

The marvellous, glissando-propelled, gliding yet perambulating music of their entrance ended, and it moves in stately step at only half the pace at which they walk or almost run onto the stage, there is now more serious intention and purpose in the music. But with deep-drawn sighing and longing for some far-off object or purpose, distant and unattainable in the past or in some Elysium, or pantomimic make-believe, the legend of a Tulip Sultan, or earlier Timurid of domes of turquoise and of lapis, for such there have been; and in extreme physical

---

* *The Penguin Dictionary of Art and Artists*, by Peter and Linda Murray, Harmondsworth 1959, pp. 135, 136. And the entry under this heading ends, optimistically: 'It may easily be discovered in most works of art.'

and sensual longing for what is unimaginable, almost, yet expressed and satisfied in the music, and transferred bodily into this celestial, but ethereal pair of beings. And the music continues with its alternation of gliding arpeggio and glissando, as of immortally beautiful wire-walkers upon the harp strings, all sense, all probability abandoned, yet with the sighing and lamenting on the wind-instruments for some object dangerous and unattainable to the point of hopelessness. This said, aware of the preferences and proclivities of the magician but finding them muted, neutralized as between male and female in the wonder of the moment.

And this passage ended, it is as though the music is walking round looking at itself, delighting in the wind-instruments and leaving the dancers to themselves, while the genius at this genre of music thinks only of himself and of his sorrows and tragedies of conscience which he has no other means of telling. But returning again in full fanfare with climax and apotheosis of unfulfilment not far away, and yet more emphasis upon the bird-walk of the dancers, their climbing upon one another in ritual courtship, with all but wings to leave the wooden boards and lift into the flies.

To the sweeping of the harps, and as it seemed to me, the genuflection of the fan-palms, just seen and new to experience, being vegetative equivalent to the naga rails or cobra heads on the balustrades of Angkor. But in simplicity, having but the fan shape of the seven-headed naga, and being nothing more than a palm tree in the form of a huge fan. The fans of ostrich plumes carried before popes and other potentates, but lacking the overlapping filaments of the feathers and trimmed, as it were, to leaf shape, a palm tree of individual fronds which yet is one huge fan. It is nearly inconceivable there should be such a palm tree, as though waiting its chance to be in escort to a pearlshell princess, daughter of Nautilus and a nereid of the coral seas, and be carried before her and whatever rarefied being she chooses for her lover.

Which, the unisex of the dancers once established, is exactly the meaning and message of the music, now failing in itself and growing desparate. And now one hears on the brass instruments the descending steps into the abyss, a familiar musical figure from his symphonies, faltering steps, too, which seem to plunge before the end. But he recovers himself for the last and transcendental moments in exaltation of the glittering and ethereal pair in their ritual dance of courtship, and to prolonged rolling on the drums and despairing fanfares on the trumpets the music ends.

BOOK
TEN

À la Mexicaine

Having come so far in belief and in disbelief the time comes near for a credo and an affirmation, whomsoever it may offend or please. It can be no more than an expression of opinion, but for once young and old are in agreement and those are few indeed who live content and satisfied. It is the despoiling of the world, our world and the only one we will ever know, which is imminent and hanging in a suffocating, obnoxious smog over our heads. Self-engendered, too, and we have only ourselves to blame, *homo sapiens*, as such, being hero and villain of these histories. Yet what a world of wonders, and what a dispensation to have been born with eyes and ears, and a hand to hold a pen! Many of the uses for which are beyond my powers and capabilities. But I have been drawn to the bright colours of the world and to the darker mysteries, as to the latter of which there is almost certainly no mystery at all and only eternal nothingness, which only makes the more wonderful its opposite, the living world and supreme mystery of mysteries.

And with no more ado, since this is in part a factual account of the days in which it is written, and of our world-wide daily fare of successes and disasters, I am decided to 'hot things up' and put 'a little something' into the *sopa del día* or the *soupe du jour*; a touch of red or green pimento, or a drop of chilli sauce 'scorching as a scorpion's tail' with the hot, or, at least, heating taste of chocolate never far distant, as in the popular dish *champurado*, of cornmeal-mush mixed with chocolate, and we are back in Mexico from which I only returned two weeks ago.

This transition because in the daily pabulum of perpetual strikes in every branch of industry and the public services, and the constant harrying of the public here in England with threats to their light, heating, telephone, petrol, newspapers and letters, with special torments practised on the long suffering tens of thousands of commuters, it is a relief to turn to a land of heat and light, on which it is true there lies one large blot which is Mexico City with its six million population and its pall of smog, now already creeping over the mountains in the direction of Cuernavaca which is some seventy miles away.

It can be argued that the, by now, predominantly Indian inhabitants of the capital do really appreciate the noise and the rush of traffic. Probably they even enjoy the all-night-long neon lighting of the main streets and arterial roads into the city. Certainly the hotel staffs are still in a state of pleasurable excitement at 'all mod: con:' and are willing slaves of the bath-tap, ice-box, the hoover or the floor-polisher. It is noticeable how much they jog and sway to the music of the hotel band, even to taped music, and while handing round dishes or making out the bill. It is as though they have never been exposed to it before which is probably the truth. Mexican popular music and their marimba bands, in particular, being a perpetual disappointment. Not only the waiters but the persons at the desk are in nightly entrancement, as are the lift boys torn between the pleasures of shooting up to the fifteenth floor and that happy moment when the lift-doors open of themselves and they can hear the band again. Even at petrol stations along the roads the mechanics are not yet disillusioned, though more under the thrall of the big lorries and less interested in private cars.

Such child-like innocence of course cannot continue, and one would think may last for another ten or fifteen years, no longer. It is true that many of them not long ago were living in their villages on incomes or pay-packets about equal to those of Hindu-Indians, and that the increasing and air-borne proximity to the USA with its hugely inflated incomes *per capita* are slowly altering things to the advantage of the peons. They are resurgent, coming up in the world, and very different from the sullen, apathetic and hopeless, coca-sodden Quechua and Aymara of the Peruvian Altiplano, for whom there seems little or no future. But nature is not so kind to them as to the Mexican-Indians, and those quasi-Tibetan altitudes are pitiless and inhospitable.

Nevertheless, the typical Mexican landscape for most of the seven hundred miles between the Texan border and the capital is desert-like with tawny mountains, shallow salt lakes and endless distances, of an aspect that cannot have been unfamiliar to Spaniards from Estremadura or High Castile though they would not have known they were climbing to twice the height of their native plains. It is often in fact of Spanish austerity, if made more menacing and exciting by the clumps of organ-cactuses, but where it relaxes it can be of paradisal beauty and entrancement owing to the flowering trees. For a taste of which it is not necessary to proceed further than a score or so of miles from Cuernavaca which, itself, is much more a 'city of flowers' than was ever Florence. Of flowers, and of a benign climate, but of little other interest compared to what more there is in Mexico, but redeemed by the flower-market and by the beauty of the jacaranda trees which were in full blossom. If these are not lovely and breath-taking there is nothing beautiful and god-sent in a godless world.

This is in the Mexican State of Morelos, and of what other country in the world, one may ask, could one read that 'it is celebrated for its exquisite fruits; Playacopan is renowned for its delicious plums; Totolopan for its *chirimoyas*; Tlalnepantla for peaches; Jonacatepec for limes and *pitahayas*; Yautepec for *mameyes* and oranges; Oaxtepec for bananas; Tetecala for coconuts; Jozutla for melons; and Cuernavaca for mangoes and guavas'. How delightful in themselves are just the Mexican village names! The lesser and out-of-the-way roads lead to valleys of a fertility and luxuriance beyond experience, and as sensational as any oasis arrived at out of a desert. The prosaic reason may be a plentiful water supply, and it must have been in respect of this that every few miles we passed a sugar-mill in a large old building with crumbling walls surrounding it. And always in every instance, and it happened perhaps four or five times during the morning, behind those high walls there was a church tower with a main building and the local equivalent of barns and outhouses, and it will have been a monastic grange or *hacienda* chosen with their ubiquitous feeling for its amenities, in this case of shade and water. And here for three centuries until the confiscation of their estates in 1856 the monks must have regaled themselves on bucolic plenty. Here, too, for the willow trees beside little winding streams and the apple orchards of such a monkish paradise as parts of Worcestershire and Gloucestershire with their Benedictine abbeys, the unit of vegetation, one could say, is the banana palm. Its wide and lush fans of leaves are in place of elm, or lime, or sycamore. Perhaps a vineyard was the one thing lacking in this bucolic luxury, and that could only have been because it is unsuited to the grape.

The one or two small towns had their house walls painted in the water-melon pinks and reds of which the Mexicans are natural, if unconscious masters, with proportion of moonlight blue walls among them, with oyster-white and the faded white of Le Grand Gilles' worn actor's old coat and trousers. Each town has its plaza with clipped trees and a bandstand; but the townsmen are Mexican, and so are the fruit stalls and the tropical trees; and to this moment it is only 'le douanier' Rousseau who painted them, who served in Mexico in the French army under Marshal Bazaine at the time of the Emperor Maximilian. Even the rickety motor-buses in the square antedate their real age by a century and seem to date from then. I do not think it is known which parts of Mexico Rousseau visited as a soldier, but the evidence of his paintings would seem to point to Tehuantepec where the presence of the French troops is supposed to account for the beauty of the women, and also to Oaxaca which is really and truly in the semi-tropics. Decidedly his two or three years here as a conscript left a strong impression on 'le douanier' to judge from the two or three 'jungle' pictures that he painted, which are entirely in the gamut of this forgotten and obscure valley leading in the end to a thermal resort, but that is out on the plains again and up in the hills where in fact at the beehives beside the road – such is this land of Mexico – they sell radio-active honey.

What, then, of further countrysides 'embowered in flowering fruit trees and flamboyants' (*Delonix regia*), where in their season 'the country for miles around is flecked with their scarlet scimitars'! For myself, only a day or two later, it was an extraordinary excitement to be starting off for towns I had wanted to see, and been waiting to see for so many years. This, in spite of having been three times before to Mexico, but then it is a big country; though much huger still when it included Florida, 'which the Spaniards conquered and controlled for two hundred years', the whole of Texas, New Mexico, California, and at least in theory extended to the site of Chicago, and to Kalamazoo on the eastern shore of Lake Michigan!

It is just such a desert I have described that we had to traverse on the way to Querétaro, but this was the main road from Mexico City to Laredo on the Texan border and has an excellent surface. As the result of which, and having started early and come through the smog of the capital with little loss of time, we reached Querétaro at half-past twelve; and this, locally, and for present purposes, was an ill-fated hour. Ah! but the excitement of getting there at last after all this time! And off at once in the blazing noon to find the convent church of Santa Clara. Down the arcade of a big square, looking back under its arches at what must be San Agustín, but not having a moment to spare for the statues of plumed angels at base of the blue-and-white tiled dome, 'like Indian caciques performing a dance in honour of some old pagan divinity', still less for the caryatids on the cloister arcade 'which seem to be making the signs of the deaf-mute alphabet with their huge uplifted hands', all of which I have been longing to see for nearly three-quarters of the time I have been alive.

And now was the chance, but the immediate problem was to find the convent-church of Santa Clara. By which time it was apparent that Querétaro, far from being the dusty and endless suburb into which we had arrived was an old town with straight streets and many fine old quasi-palaces, for they would have been that in Italy or Spain. But, also, it was midday, and just come from Canada and the worst winter in living memory with more than twenty-three feet of snow by the time we came away, the heat was nearly incandescent. One became aware of the palaces, they did not obtrude themselves; they had fine doorways often with elaborately carved wooden doors and a view of interior courts, though in the heat we missed the most important of them, that of the elaborately named Marqués de la Villa de Villar del Aguila with its cusped Moorish arches in the patio.

Indeed the beggars were more obtrusive than the 'palaces'. Two or three of them we met again and again; Indian beggars, that was the difference, not Neapolitans or Sicilians. And there were Indian women with tortillas for sale, brittle, dingy-coloured sherds, you could not call them crusts, paper-thin, heaped untidily in baskets, all acrawl with flies. But fine houses, good shops selling textiles and pottery made on the premises, straw hats, and, curiously, doll furniture for which the town is famous, and *molinillos* or 'chocolate-whirlers' to remind one, should one forget it for a moment, that we are in the streets of a Mexican provincial town. And now after many inquiries we are told with certainty that Santa Clara is half-way down the street, and brushing past a man with opals for sale in a piece of cloth we are in a small square in front of a pretty statue of Neptune with attendant, columned arch behind him, as in a porcelain table centre-piece, but set at an angle in the square as though, which is the truth, moved here from some former location. Beyond and behind this pagan interpolation stands the convent church of Santa Clara with carved frontispiece richly worked in stone of 'Indian' intricacy, but like a tabard or even a padded waistcoat hung on the church wall. But of Spaniard inheritance, none the less, and at long remove from the Isabelline or plateresque church fronts of Salamanca. Above are the dome and tower of Santa Clara; blue on yellow tiles for the dome, and a tiled tower with cupola of blue and white and yellow.

And the convent-church was shut! It had shut at midday which was not more than ten minutes or a quarter of an hour ago. This was what I had come all this way to see, and the sacristan must have locked the door almost as we arrived in the town. Worse still, it was one o'clock by now and Santa Clara would not open again until five o'clock at earliest. We could not wait till then. It would mean arriving late at night at San Miguel de Allende where we were to sleep. I would never see the nun's tribune or latticed opera-box above the doorway leading to the sacristy and into the nunnery, its supporting gold woodwork and the shell-like ornament over and above the grille, or the six golden retablos crowded with figures and towering like the floats or chariots of a juggernaut procession, as I wrote of it in a book published in 1924, and in a passage written as long before as 1920 because for a long time no publisher would take the book. So after the passing of half a century I had got here to the church of Santa Clara and could not get in.

And the only thing to do was to set forth in the midday heat in search of the other convent-church of Santa Rosa di Viterbo, in case there was the bare possibility of that being open. It was a walk no less exciting after the incipient disappointment, and the more so because in no circumstances would one ever come here again. It was now or never, with the negation of all the years between. The high red façade of a barbaric, ugly-looking church undergoing repairs, or more likely being pulled down, seemed, almost visibly, to be trying to compensate me for the disappointment. And in a welter of new directions from passers-by, some few of whom had never heard of Santa Rosa di Viterbo and knew nothing of its whereabouts, we came down long street after long street leading out of the town, and at last there it was before us in a dilapidated, dusty square, to be known at once by the inverted arches or buttresses on its outer wall, a bold feature in the manner of a rhetorical flourish, and by its being not so much a façade as a breastplate of carved stone. And below it, once again, another locked door.

The cloister in aggravation lay open and to all purposes uninhabited, with a great stairway backing on the church, and not a soul to be seen. Even the plaza outside was empty and lifeless. It was as hopeless to try and get into Santa Rosa di Viterbo as if it had been arranged beforehand in the knowledge that we were on our way. It seems for that matter a remote and far-fetched allegiance and act of homage from Querétaro to Viterbo; to a sainted young virgin 'who lived only for a morning, the lifespan of a rose', dying indeed in 1252 at the age of seventeen.* We would have had to remain another five hours in the town, at the least, in order to enter the church, and motor after that deep into the night.

It would seem that neither church, not Santa Clara, nor Santa Rosa has a large interior. How, then, all that about Santa Clara 'having sheltered upward of eight thousand nuns'? The conventual buildings have been pulled down, it is said. But Santa Rosa 'has a small interior, now narrowed to a single nave without aisles'; while Santa Clara 'has an interior which is smaller than that of Santa Rosa,

---

* Santa Rosa of Viterbo 'had urged the people to rise against the Emperor Frederick II', and her blackened mummy is still to be seen in the church of her name, where a great festa is held in her honour every year on the night of 3 September, and her image is carried by eighty men on a wooden tower, the Macchina di Santa Rosa, sixty feet high, from the Porta Romana to her church in a blaze of lights. How many of the inhabitants of Viterbo, though, have even heard of her church in Querétaro?

but is equally rich in its decoration'. We saw neither of them; and missed in Santa Rosa the grille in front of the nuns' choir 'with cupids at the side pulling back a stucco curtain, and the space over this formed by a number of portraits of saints, all separately framed, but coalescing together into a golden reredos, above which the screen has been given the handle and slats of a huge openwork fan'. The screened balcony for the Mother Superior also we never saw; nor yet, or ever now, the 'bizarre' confessionals with canopies in the form of gilded shells, 'and the cabin inside like a sedan-chair painted with flowers in carefree, light-hearted mood'. Or, on the wall of the sacristy, the fresco of the Hortus Conclusus or Walled Garden, with the Virgin sitting in the foreground within the gateway of the garden with cupids hovering over her and lambs playing at her feet. The lambs are receiving white roses from her, which they carry to the crucified Christ in the foreground of the garden, where they are turned red by the blood from his wounds. It is in part, therefore, the legend of Santa Rosa. As backcloth to it all there is the far wall of the Hortus Conclusus, with recessed arches and urns on columns; there is the parterre, and there are the fruit trees of the walled garden. And in the foreground, in their habits and coiffed head-dresses, the nuns of Santa Rosa and their pupils working in the garden; one of them with a parrot on her shoulder, and another resting a water-jar on the painted balustrade. It must be a beautiful theme, at least within the mediocrities of the Mexican school of painting.

The visit to Querétaro was now becoming like a strange kind of ghost story, and one with haunting implications. Here I was, for I must put this in the first person, having let my enthusiasm run wild when writing of them in 1920–21, and now standing in front of both Santa Rosa and Santa Clara, fifty years later, but without any hope whatever of getting inside. We would have had to start at about six o'clock in the morning in order to get here in time. Would I be here again in another half-century waiting for Santa Clara and Santa Rosa to open their doors for me, and what would have become of the world by then, in 2020 or 2021? Or here all the time and never far away? Which is nearer to the truth, perhaps. Having had a predilection for convent churches; but to name Santa Chiara and San Gregorio Armeno at Naples; the Descalzas Reales in Madrid, which miraculously survived the Civil War with its treasures intact, where Infantas and Queens of Spain retired to end their days as nuns; the convent chapel of Santa Clara at Oporto, and that of the Convent of Jesus at Aveiro. Of all of which I have written for I find them inspiring as a subject; but additions to the series are coming in even now. As with the oval chapel of San Bernardino at Orvieto, in pale blue and white and gold, organ-case with female caryatids, and golden-latticed opera-boxes to either side of the high altar; this, when I thought I had seen, or knew of, everything of the kind in Italy. And, even as I write this, news of the opening of the Convent of Santa Catalina at Arequipa in Peru, with the last few of the nuns still living in their apartments with their own furniture and servants, 'now open to the outside world for the first time in four hundred years'. The earthquake prevented our going to Arequipa when we were in Peru in 1959, and the Convent of Santa Catalina in any case was both unmentioned and inaccessible until 15 August 1970.

But we had seen at least the exteriors of Santa Rosa and Santa Clara, and there comes a moment when refusal and negation hold more promise. At least, now, like a genius who dies young it could not prove disappointing; and so these paired or twin inspirations of my youthful days remain unspoilt for me. I will always be sad though to have missed them, and would like to think that now and ever they are waiting for me. And so away from Querétaro with a last look at its tiled domes and towers which I will never see again, and in a few moments there is not even the mark of them upon the skyline. It is only about three-quarters of an hour farther on to Celaya, another Mexican town which was much in my thoughts all those years ago because of its churches by the local architect Tresguerras, to whom it was then customary to ascribe everything; but it now appears that he had nothing to do with either Santa Clara or Santa Rosa, the latter of which was finished in 1752 when he was only seven years old. Tresguerras was in fact a neo-classical architect of no great distinction, and he even expressed his disapproval of the side altars in both chapels for 'their intemperate extravagance'. But it is just exactly the golden altars that give the distinctive 'Indian' air to these Mexican interiors. Tresguerras, then, is but another illusion gone and it was no particular disappointment to admire the towers and domes of Celaya from the distance and go no nearer to them.

But the laws of loss and compensation had been at work that morning. And we soon came to Irapuato, a town I had never heard of before, in an area 'where the soil is several yards deep and of a rich black like the alluvial deposits of the Nile'. With surprising results, for Irapuato and the surrounding district are famous for strawberries, 'which are of such good quality that not only are they shipped as far south as Mexico City', but they travel air freight to Covent Garden and are sold in London. And not only this, but for several miles on end stalls are set up beside the road for the sale of strawberries and cream, the latter perhaps entailing a health risk because it must be doubtful if the milk is pasteurized. But there were the strawberry stalls, and great sale, too, of jars of strawberry jam.

In what contrast though to their brother and sister strawberries on sale in England! At Wytham for instance, 'known in Oxford as the strawberry village' – but one would guess all that is forgotten, now! – and the author from whom I am quoting adds that 'nowhere, unless it be in Kent where the flavours of various kinds of strawberries are discussed with as much nicety of knowledge as our fathers showed concerning vintages of wine, does the strawberry flourish more abundantly, nowhere is it eaten with so much of abandon as at Wytham'; adding further and most appropriately that 'it is probably due to the deep alluvial soil', and that 'in the season the whole village is entirely given up to providing that fruit. The strawberries grow here in great profusion, and in almost all the gardens of the spotlessly clean little cottages are arbours of honeysuckle and creepers, with tables for the accommodation of visitors. Strawberry picnics are made from Oxford – the distance is but short for a summer walk; or, if it seems more pleasant, by boat to Godstow and thence you may walk, leaving your boat at the inn – and strawberries are eaten systematically out of clean white bowls with heavy stemmed wine glasses to pound them.' And most aptly he ends that 'neither mango nor mangosteen, neither persimmon nor custard apple, neither guava nor banana, possess a taste so clean and unquestionably delicious as the strawberry of England at its best.'

Or at Irapuato, where surely should be an experimental station for all kinds of strawberries, and already it has strawberries nearly all the year round? And where we stopped for a sandwich – I am ashamed to say – and there were posters, I could hardly believe it, to advertise the coming Strawberry Feast to take place in the last week of March, with competitions, flower shows, dancing to marimba and other bands, and bull-fights as climax and big attraction. I had never thought to see *toreros* in their 'suits of lights' risking themselves, as on all bull-fight posters, for a strawberry feast or festival, and felt almost disposed, other attentions lacking, to take it in compliment to a strawberry feast of poems that I have written. I took it, too, in balance and in compensation for the lost convent churches of Santa Clara and Santa Rosa di Viterbo. But we drove on, still having some distance before us, and looking back regretfully at those roadside stalls for Mexican strawberries and cream. I had, I was remembering, inadvertently attended a white truffle feast only the autumn before at Alba in Piedmont, where the best of the *tartufi bianchi* come from, 'ses délectables truffes blanches', as the *Guide Michelin* for Italy puts it, 'qui sont detectées par des chiens diplomés ECTR (École de Chiens Truffiers de Roddi, au Sud-Ouest d'Alba)'.* And a truffle feast it certainly was at this town in Piedmont, which is scarcely like Italy at all, on the green foothills, with banners across the streets, galaxies of lights, and *Taviolini tartufalba*, *Fonduta tartufata* and the mysteriously named *Crema Santa Teresa con tartufi* on the menu. And why so particularly of Santa Teresa? Probably only some veteran Bollandist would know the answer. Well, Alba and its white truffles are as far away as the strawberries of Wytham. Far in theory and further still in practice, and we are on our way now to Guanajuato, this, too, being the fulfilment of an early ambition.

Which in the event was very unlike the preconception. The desert approach to it being not unfamiliar, and that of the central tableland of Spain but at twice that altitude, a town like Ávila on its boulder-strewn escarpment with the snow-capp'd Sierra da Ávila at back of it and the sempiternal cold of its streets and passages giving the impression of lying at a much greater height, where it is in point of fact at only half the height of Guanajuato. This is not the landscape of the humming-bird. Although, none the less, it is!

But more than most other towns I have been to, Guanajuato gives the feeling that you are never going to get to it. Turn after turn of the road postpones the moment so that when reached it must almost certainly be disappointing. Then comes a largish village which as often on such occasions is the decoy or 'mock-up' of Guanajuato and another interminable series of twists and turns, and we have arrived. This must be the silver-mining town and its truths anticipated. Upon which we plunge without warning or even hearsay into an immense chain of tunnels, their darkness made blacker still by the bright sun outside. It is as

---

* 'The delectable white truffles of Alba, which are nosed out by dogs with the diploma ECTR (School of Truffle Hounds at Roddi, south-west of Alba)'.

though the centre of Rome between, say, the Piazza di Spagna, the Piazza del Popolo and the Piazza Navona, were honeycombed with tunnels by a population despairing – as they may well become! – of circulating in the streets above. Presumably the tunnels were formed from mine shafts connected together and formed into subways underneath the town. Already we had passed great ore-heaps in evidence of the deposits of gold and silver within these hills; but the tunnel approach to Guanajuato is impressive, and metropolitan in the sense that it arouses expectations which it intends to satisfy. This must be a little centre of civilization with fine buildings, and this is only the truth. The unexpectedness lies in finding them in this remote place so far from Spain. One never ceases to wonder at the control exercised by the Spaniards from it could be as far as a six months' voyage away. But, then, as has been argued before, no place is remote to the persons born and living there. The Eskimo feels as strange in Paris as the Parisian in Baffin Land or Thule. But the secret of Guanajuato is simple enough, that the Spaniards had trained the 'Indios' to work for them not only in the silver mines but on the façades and golden altars of the churches.

And on emerging from the Guanajuato underground system, which is sensational enough in its way, we found ourselves in the centre of the city and in a traffic-jam worthy of the last experiment in conurbation. Moreover, it was the delayed luncheon 'rush hour' of about half-past two. How far away the rustic strawberry-stalls of Irapuato as we kept on at a snail's pace passing building after building! Of course the riches of the gold and silver mines were responsible for the fine churches, and one may be wondering, meanwhile, why they have not their equivalents at Klondyke, on the Australian goldfields, and the South African Rand? But there is an answer, or half-an-answer from the goldfields of Brazil, where the Rococo churches of the Minas Gerais were due, not to the monks and nuns who were forbidden to set foot within it, but to the lay-confraternities of the Franciscans and Carmelites, which if it is not quite the same is at least the next best thing.* Religious sentiment apart, the buildings of Querétaro and Guanajuato are due in very large degree to the religious orders, and to the fervency of their 'Indian' converts.

The veins of silver running under the town came to the surface in the three mines of La Valenciana, La Cata, and Las Rayas, the last of which had, for bonus, a stratum of amethysts in crystal form. And soon the boom-village of Guanajuato had seventy thousand persons living in it, the palaces of the owner and the mud huts of the miners standing side by side, near to the ore-heaps, and at the heads of the shafts into which the miners had to descend to fifteen hundred feet. The town is all at different levels owing to the excavations and upheavals, and it was absolutely necessary to take a guide on board, in addition to which we were now involved in the 'rush hour', ourselves, in the determination after having missed seeing the interiors of Santa Clara and Santa Rosa not to be baulked of the 'lion' of Guanajuato which is the church of La Valenciana.

* The most beautiful building in Ouro Preto among the goldfields is the Church of the Rosario, with *bombé* front and double oval plan with curvilinear walls, built by the lay-brotherhood of that name, to which only Negroes were admitted.

The churches of the three silver mines are, or were, outside the city; one of them, that is to say, that of San Juan de Rayas having been removed most improbably, stone by stone, from where it stood at the mouth of the silver mine, and rebuilt, half a block from the main street, by the Rotary Club of Guanajuato. But which was San Juan de Rayas, and which the church of La Cata, third of the silver mines? And, as well, there was the Jesuit temple of La Compañía and the church of San Diego. I felt that I should know the former of these by instinct from having seen the Jesuit church of La Compañía in Cuzco, and its sister church of the 'scarlet lacquer' interior – but it is not quite all that the term implies! – at Quito in Ecuador. And sure enough a large, important building of suspect date was La Compañía; but more interesting by far were the façades of two or three other churches in which the 'Indian' craftsmen most clearly showed their hand. I take it that one of them was San Diego, of which the carved front was of utmost delicacy and cut in a reddish stone several shades lighter in colour than the red tezontle, or 'porous amygdaline, stained a light red', of the two façades or pair of frontispieces to the Sagrario of Mexico Cathedral.

But, then, again, we passed what was certainly the transferred or transported church of San Juan de Rayas with its obelisks or *estipítes* and flaunting its *espedañas* or tail-feathers of stone against the skyline, to apply local or etymological terms to what is certainly a localized or native hybrid of what is essentially a Spanish style. A Spaniard may have drawn the plans, but it will have been 'Indian' craftsmen who did the detailed carving, and it is far from clear as to the working method. Did the 'Indians', or *mestizos* they may have been, work freehand without close and detailed preliminary drawings? It would seem that this was so, as with the most elaborate of Oriental carpets. In any case this façade of San Juan de Rayas, all pedestals and medallions, is of marvellous technical virtuosity as is that, too, of San Diego. And there is the other mining church, that of La Cata on the way out of the town, which we saw, at last, but again for a passing moment owing to the late luncheon hour, of an intricacy beyond belief and reminiscent of the temples of Halebid in Mysore. Where else have been such fluttering cornices, and fretted pilasters that seem to turn slowly and revolve of themselves as you try to hold their outline?

We were on the way to La Valenciana outside the town, and not only that but far above it in a mining landscape of shafts and slag-heaps with views down to Guanajuato which in these desert surroundings had all the appurtenances of a small capital or metropolis. The church must be a good thousand or twelve hundred feet above the town making it, I would think, all of eight thousand feet above sea-level. And now at last it was in sight with a crowd of persons on the steps up to it, and in the market place in front of it – and wonder of wonders it was open and we could go inside! It is still much frequented and can no longer be in the charge of one solitary, plain-clothes priest. It was built by the Conde de Valenciana, owner of the mine; but, also, by the miners who gave part of their wages for the purpose. One of the two towers is unfinished, and the façade is disappointing in spite of its grand terminal position at top of the hill above a flight of steps. The interior, too, is uninteresting but for its three towering and glittering altars, crowded and manned, as it were, by a multitude of saintly personages, male and female, and *amorini*; and as ever in these churches like juggernaut floats or processional towers more than static *retablos* or altars. Having at long last reached Guanajuato and seen the church of La Valenciana it would seem on reflection to be less of a semi-tropical, yet altitude-conditioned *tour de force*, than the three churches of San Juan de Rayas, San Diego, and La Cata in the town below it which, as to their façades, out-Churrigueresque anything of the kind to be seen in Spain, and are virtuoso feats of high calibre and virtuosity, but with little or nothing at back of them for their interiors are all spoiled. Nor does it compare to advantage with the church at Taxco. Indeed, like many things at length attained, it is a disappointment. Not so the three churches in the town below with the humming, spinning of their ornamentation in that hot midday sun.

And leaving Guanajuato by the panoramic road high up on the hills past the dead or dying silver mines, and deciding to ignore the mummies of which horrifying postcards are on sale outside La Valenciana, we were soon back among the strawberry stalls of Irapuato with hallucinating memories of pre-World War One strawberries and cream, in 1913 and 1914 on the Fourth of June, and walking down to the river to watch the fireworks from underneath the trees. The last of the rustic arbours was soon gone, gone for ever, and we were passing Salamanca, 'a characterless Mexican town' – and which can be worse, on occasion, characterless or characteristic? – But only in the last year or two, and on the recommendation of one writer,* it has become known that in the church of San Agustín there are four golden *retablos* of utmost splendour. There is documentary evidence that they are by the sculptor Pedro de Roxas, who carved the altars in the convent-churches of Querétaro. The high altar has gone, but there are the four side altars, two of them surmounted by huge golden crowns, and this would seem to be the moment to make a census of the golden altars that form the Mexican *chef-d'oeuvre*. It is a mistake surely to speak of them as Arte Colonial, but then the word 'Indian' is untrue and ineffective though a substitute has never been found for it, and yet these golden altars, all of them, are almost certainly the work of craftsmen with a strong, if not total infusion of native blood.

There are these four of the *retablos* in San Agustín at Salamanca; the array of six at Santa Clara, and others at Santa Rosa, both in Querétaro; and no less than twelve of them in the church at fast-spoiling Taxco, for ever doomed and fated to tourism with the proximate opening of a hotel that is to have its own aerodrome and landing-ground. But perhaps the most dazzling of all are the five golden *retablos* of Tepotzotlan, in the novitiate or seminary of the Jesuits, with the octagonal *camarín* or chapel of Loreto, which has much red in it as well as gold, to one side of the church. Let us say, some thirty in all of the golden altars still existing. The number of these altars that were destroyed and melted down just for their gold content alone all over the country must be considerable, the French soldiery, as ever, having done their share during the Mexican adventure

* *Arte Mexicana Epoca Colonial*, by Pedro Rojas, 1963, p. 100. One of the golden altars of San Agustín in Salamanca is illustrated on pl. xxii.

of Napoleon and his half-brother, the Duc de Morny. Probably those remaining
are a good deal less than half the body total of these altars. These places named,
Tepotzotlan, Taxco, Querétaro, Guanajuato, are where the golden altars *in
excelsis* are to be seen in all their glory and, also, the twisting, coruscating
Mexican façades which are their contribution as a nation to the Churrigueresque
style that spread from Spain to Mexico. Alike, these Mexican altars and the
igreja todo de ouro which is typical of Portugal,* are the direct offspring of the gold
mines of Mexico and Brazil. There is no other such gilding as in these churches in
direct contact with the gold mines of the New World. And if we add to these
golden interiors the tiled domes and façades of Puebla, in and around which city
there is a definite Poblano style, and, also, of necessity, for it is most original of
all, the scarlet shark's skin or shagreen front and white towers of the Santuario
de Ocotlán, we have in essence everything that is Mexican and pertaining to *le
style Mexicain.*

Meanwhile there is more desert to traverse on the way to San Miguel de
Allende over a vast plain with troops of half-wild horses cluttering the road,
and the only human interest a bus-stop every few miles, merely a shelter of palm
branches in which to hide from the sun and wind, and maybe two buses a day
in each direction with hour upon hour to wait. Or the bus-arrival, and the wonder
it arrived at all such was its state of disrepair, with disembarkation in order to
leave the road and start off over the hills for some invisible destination in the far
distance. The flea-infested buses travel very noisily and at tremendous speed,
they are difficult to pass on the road, and as crowded as a trainful of refugees. It
seems curious that in this vast, thinly inhabited country there should be so many
travelling. Going to market must be the main reason, and that there is a market
every day of the week within a radius of a few miles.

The interest or point of San Miguel de Allende is much enhanced by its
extreme improbability when approached from the north. There is no indication
whatever that a town is near. The sign with the name of the town on it comes
before any of the houses can be seen, and then suddenly there is a dramatic break
or fall in the landscape, and we begin coming steeply down. It is a precipitous
descent into San Miguel de Allende. There are cobbled streets and many flights
of steps, and now the better buildings and many fine old homes. At the bottom
of the hill below the town is the most darkly umbrageous of public gardens, of
nightingale-dense shade and with camellias and magnolias in evidence. All of
San Miguel de Allende is on the steep hillside, and where there is room for them
are the good buildings. A church with fretted jigsaw façade in the fine manner of
Guanajuato; and a very ugly red Gothic church built in the last century by an
untrained 'Indian' who has left a heavy blot upon his native city. Perhaps there
may be as many as a score of fine old houses, and this in the knowledge that they

---

* As for instance the interiors of São Francisco and of Santa Clara at Oporto, the chapel
'rutilante de dorures' of the Convent of Jesus at Aveiro, or the tiny golden chapel of São
Antonio at Lagos in the Algarve. Two or three of the churches of Recife in Brazil, but
none of those in either Rio or Bahia, qualify for inclusion among the *capelas douradas* of
Portugal.

are better inside than the exterior would suggest and have pretty interior courts and patios, thus lending themselves to becoming an artists' colony. In brief, San Miguel de Allende has been 'discovered', but not much more than thirty years ago, which at least means that it is preserved in some sort of order, if with the recurring threat of tea-rooms, boutiques and lending libraries. It has become an associate member, so to speak, of the group which includes Broadway, Chipping Camden, St Ives, Clovelly, Positano, San Gimignano, and the rest of them all over the world from Capri to Guatemala. It seems, at the least, blessedly far from both railways and aeroplanes. The view from above the town over the sunset is limitless, and the nearly full moon shining at a dizzying height in the empyrean, and round as an arc-lamp took one's breath away.

That Mexico can be dull was made manifest next morning at Morelia, a town which could be a Basque town in Northern Spain, near San Sebastián; or where it is greener in Navarre which is like Spain with chlorophyll added to take the taste away. Morelia has wide streets and faceless buildings, the phrases 'the location ensuring excellent drainage' somehow expressing its dullness and lack of character. 'Indian' tribes seem as remote from Morelia as they do in the Eastern Townships of Quebec, or, I presume, in New Brunswick or Nova Scotia. Yet they are not far away and are in fact very near. It is the Tarascan 'Indians', chiefly, who inhabit Michoacan of which Morelia is state capital, of whom we read that, of old, 'they flattened the head by binding it and filed the teeth to represent swallow-tails', and that 'they took the femur bones of enemies captured in battle, notched them, and made them into flutes and whistles', neither of which customs speak nicely of them.

More agreeably, it was the Tarascans who were expert at making feather tapestries of the wings of humming-birds, and we are on our way now to Pátzcuaro, on the lake of that name, which once was famous for these tapestries. One or two such pieces sent home by the early Conquistadores to the Emperor Charles v are still in the Schatzkammer or Imperial Treasury at Vienna; notably, a headdress of feathers of the spoonbill, the 'lovely' cotinga of purple and cerulean blue plumage, the quetzal, and another unidentified bird; and a circular shield with a blue and white coyote on a salmon-coloured ground. The feather mantle of Moctezuma, it will be recalled, was made of tail-feathers of the quetzal. These feather tapestries were made a few miles across the lake from Pátzcuaro, at a village called Tzintzuntzan, a name which in Mayan dialect means 'tresses of the day-star', while a word more local to Pátzcuaro, and onomatopoeic as its alternative, is huitzitzilin which portrays, as certainly, the hovering whirring flight of the humming-bird. In the church at Pátzcuaro to complete the picture – and it should be added that the wings of the humming-birds were attached to a web or fabric of maguey fibre – there was, or there still may be, an image of the Virgin made of cornstalks, very light in weight, and glued together with a substance obtained from orchids, as was the glue used by the Tarascans in their feather mosaics.

Lake Pátzcuaro, in the meantime, has come in sight but as quickly disappears again behind low hills. And indeed the town is a mile or two inland and not, as one might imagine, on the lake shore. We had no time to visit any of the twenty Tarascan villages round the lake; to see their dugout canoes and butterfly fishing-nets, or set foot on their islands. And had we done so would we have been that much the wiser? Neither did we see a living specimen of the axolotl or larval salamander which has the peculiarity, at Lake Taxcoco and nowhere else in Mexico, of never transforming into an adult yet becoming sexually mature while still in the larval condition at six months old; a similar condition, it could be said, ironically, being not totally unknown among human beings, both male and female, though at a later stage in life. The Indians eat the axolotl; and we at least ate the *pescado blanco* or white fish of Lake Pátzcuaro which is excellent eating and appears on the menus in restaurants in Mexico City in the form of *Blanco de Pátzcuaro pané*.

The town of Pátzcuaro has its old houses and plazas of clipped trees and is a hillside town of cobbled streets after the fashion of San Miguel de Allende, but much more remote, while the lake resembles a mini-version of Lake Titicaca. Never have I felt so far away except at Puno on that other lake and near the border of Peru and Bolivia. At Pátzcuaro one feels to what an enormous distance the early Spaniards travelled four hundred years ago. To think that the first bishop, the saintly San Vasco de Quiroga, personally chosen by the Emperor Charles v for this mission to the 'Indies', arrived at his diocese in Tzintzuntzan in 1538! When there were already twenty-eight Castilian families living in the place! But I have said before, and repeat it now, that no one who has seen the house of Pizarro, the conquistador of Peru, at Trujillo in Estremadura, 'a little roofless cyclopaean hovel with an enormous round arched doorway', will wonder any more at his leaving home to seek his fortune in the New World. It is true that compared to him Hernán Cortés was as a knightly paladin, but there would be time to think of Cortés next evening when we were back in Cuernavaca among the flowering trees.

One Town: One Voice

One could guess that the prime aim in life of a museum curator must be to get away from the objects committed to his care? Of a clergyman to escape betimes from his care of souls? Of a prison governor from his prisoners? And so on. And saving a physical presence in human shape, which is a presumption on the part of human beings, should there be a creative force of higher and more sensitive intelligence than a gaseous body, mere chemical substance or 'active condition of the molecules, or of the ether round them' – which is electricity defined, if demonstrated more excitingly as 'the force which shows itself in lightning' – then we have to concede a presence more often disinterested and absent-minded over our affairs. Or, at least, away on holiday and not available for the time being. Of late, indeed, it has been more of an absence than a presence.

But not always and in every instance.

When, then, all the care lavished upon this one planet? As though it were the particular hobby or interest of someone. A model farm on which to breed live-stock, or, in fact, start things living. And now it has been allowed to run to seed as though the millionaire proprietor has been murdered by the Mau-Mau! For that could be one way of explaining what has happened. In spite of World Wars One and Two the population is now really and truly swarming, and, if we listen to what we are told, within the lifetime of the present generation there will be barely standing room. Or everything is perfectly all right and there is no need to worry? But the owner has disappeared, packed up and gone overseas, and probably to some country with which we have no extradition treaty. In which case he has forfeited his legal rights and cannot press his claims against us. Or it could be also, that we have failed him badly. We were given the opportunity and neglected it. The whole outfit was stocked and in working order, and look what a mess we have made of it! Now it has run down nearly to the point of no return.

And are we to suppose that 'nature' exists only on our five continents and in the oceans, and is unknown elsewhere? That there is probably only molecular or gaseous 'life', scarcely deserving that term, outside or beyond this? 'Nature', indeed, being something of a free accommodation and convenience in an other-wise inconveniently arid world. And put here for our sake? Or with its own ends in view? Because it could not be haphazard and by chance. Or, were that so, the whole of creation could have been the result of accident.

We have only to look at the bleakness of the other planet men have set foot upon to feel happy at a blade of grass growing in an asphalted backyard. It makes a hanging garden of the lolling snapdragon, and turns a plant of groundsel into a tree of lilies. Such is the dead dullness of our only satellite that we have to drag round with us wherever we go.

Not that we have any choice in the matter, but they were experiences of another sort for Columbus and for Hernán Cortés, who were the real explorers into another world. There can never again be such an encounter between disparate human beings. That moment when Moctezuma in his cotton robe, sandals with golden thongs and soles, both his cloak and sandals 'powdered' with pearls and emeralds, and wearing a long trailing, prototype 'Red Indian' feather headdress of green quetzal plumes, got down from his litter and leaning on the arm of his brother and his nephew came forward to meet the white man, was one of the extraordinary moments in all history.* It will not be surpassed in excitement with the first astronaut to stumble on a weed or come across a crawling insect. And if, as is likely, the exploration is done mechanically by remote control, that first meeting will be less interesting still, and indeed banal.

But it is a fine sunny morning, the world is still young, and how many barriers have been lifted! Who is there who would go back wilfully into the past? All of music, painting, architecture, are going cheap – if we can afford the fare, that is to say! – and are at our finger ends to touch, and see and hear. We are at real last the heirs of all the ages; inheritors of the green hill of Silbury and the stone circle, not a mile away, which is as old or older than the pyramid of Kheops; part-sharers, too, if we will, in the thousand-odd stone heads and torsos on Rapa Nui or Easter Island, two thousand three hundred miles to the west of Chile, with the nearest landfalls in the other direction thirteen hundred miles to Pitcairn and sixteen hundred miles to the Juan Fernandez islands. An island indeed of tremendous mystery deep out in the Pacific main. The prehistoric inhabitants arrived there, it would seem, in the eighth century AD. And whence? And how did they get there? It is all a mystery.

Those too, who can pay the air tickets may see the pyramids of the Mayans; four of them at Tikal in Guatemala, with temples and roof-crests on top rising above the jungle like the cones of volcanoes; and the carved *stelae* at Palenque in Chiapas where the 'Indian' physiognomy is most marked and which Stephens noticed immediately, commenting upon one bas-relief in which 'the principal personage stands in an upright position and in profile, exhibiting an extraordinary facial angle of about forty-five degrees . . . The upper part of the head seems to have been compressed and lengthened. The head represents a different species from any now existing in that region of country; and supposing the statues to be images of living personages, or the creations of artists according to their ideas of perfect figures, they indicate a race of people now lost and unknown; the head-dress is evidently a plume of feathers.' In those few sentences is all the mystery of the Amerindians or mock 'Indies'.†

To have seen some few of these ruins, and those of Angkor at the other side of the world – while there was still time as to these latter, and they were still

*

Their encounter is curiously underplayed by Prescott, *Conquest of Mexico*, who merely says of it, 'Their interview must have been of uncommon interest to both'.

† J. L. Stephens, *Incidents of Travel in Central America, Chiapas and Yucatán*, 1841, and *Incidents of Travel in Yucatán*, 1843. The two double volumes are fascinating to read, and the little less than marvellous plates accompanying the text are by 'Mr Catherwood', who in another and unlikely incarnation had been a friend of Keats.

there, for it seems inevitable they will be badly damaged if not destroyed in the not remote future – is the measure of being alive in this time of history. And to have seen as well a Greek temple, perhaps at Segesta or on Cape Sunium, let alone the Parthenon; and out of the rest of the world the octagonal marvel of San Vitale at Ravenna with its marbles and basket-capitals and mosaics, like another vision of a vanished race; and perhaps the Ducal Palace at Urbino for its fluttering inlay of Botticellian maidens, and room with high ceiling above the running game or tug-of-war of *amorini*, white upon a blue ground, where cupids stand sentinel at the obelisks upon the corners, and the hood of the fireplace climbs high into the ceiling.

For we are three-quarters of the way through the twentieth century, and why must we go back to the fetishes of New Caledonia or the Congo, or make a painted replica of a row of Campbell's soup-tins, a sheet of stamps, or 'great stacks of Brillo soap-boxes', when the originals of all or any of these can be bought for a few cents or new pennies, and they are far from beautiful in any case? Outside the purlieus of the New World there is nothing to be ashamed of in our aesthetic ancestry, and it is all a lot of nonsense when there are authentic paintings and works of art around, though of course where these mechanical copies of hardware and other industrial products originate it is only possible to see or encounter works of art inside museums and outside the immediate environment. This is no moment for making rude faces at the past, our own, or anyone else's.

We may not want to go back into it, but we want to enjoy ourselves in this wonderful liberty of knowledge. There is universal access to almost anything under the sun, in the immediate sense that there were as many as eighty-five Bach *Cantatas* advertised for sale in the USA Schwann catalogue of long playing records as long ago as March 1969, and by now there may well be as many as a hundred;* and that in bookshops in country towns in England there are books for sale on Modigliani, and Paul Klee, and Jackson Pollock. Whether this facility of knowledge is good, or it would be better in the result were it more difficult to acquire, is a question that it is still too soon to answer. It is certainly a most extraordinary change and advancement. In the present temper of opinion, will a book on Paul Klee have a bigger and quicker sale than its companion volume on Raphael? Or the book on Miró or on Mondrian 'go better' than the one on Mantegna or on Fra Angelico? One might think this probable; while sympathizing with the preference for Piero della Francesca or Botticelli over Raphael.

But there can be moods in which it seems that the rows of books and shelves of records can do no good, and if they add to appreciation it is only annoying. Is it even desirable that there should be a much bigger public? The bleat of approval can be irritating. It is like universal tourism in another medium. For an innocuous beginning, bus-tours to Palladian villas in the Veneto; but, now, trips to Easter Island, as lately announced, and tours to Afghanistan, Sikkim and Bhutan, and Katmandu, and a 'garden tour' of Japan. And static musical touring round areas previously inaccessible; worse still, to private and personal possessions

* The Bach *Cantatas* that survive are 206 in number, and no less than another 89 are lost. His total production was at least 295 *Cantatas*.

shared with no one else before. To do with forgotten painters, authors, even book-illustrators. Upon whom it would be possible to write at length, and mainly for one's own pleasure; as, also, of towns and palaces, villages and monasteries, a few of which are famous by now, while others may stay hidden for a little longer if they are but kept secret. For the true luxury is to have something of one's own, as exclusive to oneself as some small piece of private property. Many a village in England has more to give than all of New York and Chicago put together. It is doubtful how much can ever again come out of a town with even a quarter of a million population. We had best remind ourselves at this moment of Aristotle's ideal for the capitals of the Greek states.

II

The ideal of Aristotle for the capitals of the Greek States was that they should be cities small enough for the voice of one herald. And we can take his ideal literally, or as we like it.

Because there are times when William Blake, some of whose utterances and apophthegms are second only to those from the mouths of Shakespeare's actors, sounds like the one sane voice of the first quarter of the nineteenth century – the years of the industrial age and of the Napoleonic Wars – transmuting the hideous slums and 'rookeries' of London as much as he obliterates its dying elegancies. And coming out of the very heart of the poverty and pollution, from the pair of rooms in Lambeth that his painter-disciples, Samuel Palmer and Edward Calvert, called 'the House of the Interpreter' and looked upon as the fount of all wisdom.

While, for its other meaning, in the north sea-coast town of my childhood there was a human phenomenon in the form of a fish-wife whose voice could be heard all over the town. A city with a north and a south bay, esplanades and terraces, hotels and lodging-houses and a winter population of some forty thousand, but this woman could be heard crying her fish from end to end of it. From outside the terraces of the South Cliff and under Oliver's Mount; and nearer, outside the red brick house of Dr Dale who drove to see us in his brougham, wearing his frock-coat, as did the other doctors in the town, and with his stethoscope coiled like a snake inside his silk-hat; over or under both bridges across The Valley; floating above the Spa and outside the Grand Hotel where Verlaine and Rimbaud, it seems, had walked one day and looked up into the windows; over Huntriss Row and Newborough to Falsgrave and the Cemetery; and to the bleak houses on the North Cliff below the green-baize Castle Hill. I wonder sometimes if anyone else still remembers her voice which I have ringing now in my ears.

*   *   *

And immediately the first cockcrow of particular and clarion sound. Such are a literal and an imaginative interpretation of Aristotle's ideal, including the assurance from personal experience that the capitals under discussion could be cities of some size. As large, maybe, as Agrigento, the ancient Acragas with nine temples, more than any other centre of the Greek world, and 'the most beautiful city of mortals', according to Pindar. At Agrigento, at least the siting of the temples is exemplary in that tawny landscape, and one must extend some licence in his language to the poet – if one can forget and it is not easy, but neither is it the fault of Pindar, the pulmonary poverty and phthisitic horror of the gaunt dark modern town, its tall narrow streets of houses half-slipping down the hill, damp and cold in winter, and tossing as with fever through the nights of summer.

But the situation of the temples? It is that which is truly marvellous. It would seem that the Hellenes had a genius for siting. From the temples on the Acropolis of Athens to Segesta in its loneliness, and to Selinunte in the cornfields; and from Bassae in its Arcadian setting, if only from hearsay, where the temple is by Ictinos, architect of the Parthenon, to the temple of Poseidon on Cape Sunium. Which last, whether approached by land, or more dramatically from the sea, is never to be forgotten. Even a relic of the Hellenes of no more importance than the theatre of Taormina, which by and large is a Roman restoration, is enough to show their hand and the incomparable gift they had of choosing the site and enhancing the landscape by their building; in the instance of Taormina by contriving the view of snowcapp'd Mount Etna, of hidden fire and lava, to be seen as backdrop from the auditorium above the pillars of the proscenium.

And yet even about the Hellenes there are doubts that linger. As to whether any or all of their temples can have looked to be more than dolls' houses put down upon the hills, among acanthus and asphodel and dwarf palmetto? It, at least, is architecture, but is it beautiful? And the chryselephantine statues of the Hellenes, of ivory and gold? What can they have been? This is something we will never know.

With the Hellenes it could be argued that their poetry was more perfected than their architecture. There is beauty in their poems in the sense of absolute beauty, at perhaps its earliest appearance in the world of human beings. Certainly beauty is not an epithet applicable to the temples of Ancient Egypt, that impress from accuracy of calculation and of finish, or by size and mere antiquity, which is to say, aesthetically, for most if not all of the wrong reasons. Poetry was something of which the Egyptians were not capable. The first poets, then, were the Hellenic poets. And their poetry entered into and permeated their lesser or minor arts, such as jewellery; their rings and bracelets, necklaces and earrings. Their votive offerings, such as the pair of golden wheatstalks found in a tomb in Northern Greece, and probably a tribute to a local corn goddess; the leaves like broad blades of grass, the wheatears each wired into its stalk, and the 'silk' of the wheatears, of filigree wire, of gold, too, but like spun glass. Where are to be found, anywhere, objects more beautiful than these?

But, also, when the Attic potters, and later those of Southern Italy, of Apulia, Campania, Lucania, were not thinking monumentally in terms of their red-figured vases and 'took time off' for a pottery oil-lamp – the only artificial illumination in antiquity but that of firelight – in shape of a Negro's head or satyr's mask, their handiwork has the poetical force and pungency of a distich or an epigram, while the poetry runs dry upon their painted pots and amphorae. Is not Greek pottery in this day and age the deadest of all dead artifacts? Deader by far than Italian majolica in our time, which prefers humble Staffordshire lustre-ware to the 'lost' metallic carmine of Maestro Giorgio of Gubbio.

Who does not prefer, now, the Korai, the Hellenic maiden chorus in statuary, to the canon of Phidias or Praxiteles? What, then, had happened to the Hellenes? Those young girls in procession, redolent not so much of the peasant as of the small country town, with their long pleated woollen dresses, their hair plaited with utmost care into corkscrew ringlets that touch upon their shoulders and reach down nearly to their waists, their youthful but swelling breasts like the ripening and swelling of pears or apples, their straight noses and hieratic, even mascara'd eyes; young women carrying perhaps a lamb or a kid its feet tied together, across one shoulder; what had become of them by the fifth century BC? Certainly the race of them was not extinct, but still to be found and met with at only a mile or two outside the towns. But their day was done. The boring athletes had taken over; 'youths who stood under the stone pines with their trainers and admirers, their skins oiled and powdered with red or yellow, or others of the five kinds of recommended dust', and the young girls were neglected in their favour. Perhaps the same thing, or something similar, happened in fifteenth-century Florence and brought the early Florentine Renaissance to an end. The spring was over and done with and the summer flowers were eyeless and had run to seed. Their progeny was Mannerist and childless. Or it could be that this was bound to happen and could not be prevented since all living beings carry within them the seeds of their own decay.

*   *   *

And we hear the herald again from all over the town. Or it is the second cockcrow of the morning.

*   *   *

Dawn comes in with the trumpeting or crowing. They are the voices of the Nanagako-dori or long crowers; 'very few in number and preserved for many centuries for the purpose of announcing the dawn'. Of three breeds; brown in colour, with a shrill plaintive tone, the length of the crow being generally seven to eight seconds; black in colour, the highest and clearest, from five to ten seconds; and brown in colour, a deep solemn bass, the longest crow taking sometimes as long as twenty seconds by the stop-watch. They lift their voices for an hour before the rising sun. We hear their crowing and wonder at them, till they flutter down like clockwork figures and go back into the little room behind the balcony.

At this moment while I have it in mind it is like that little instant of theatrical magic when the curtain rises in *Coppélia*, and Swanilda appears at a window and a little later runs on to the stage, looks up at a balcony opposite where another young girl, the automaton, sits apparently reading a book, tries in vain to attract her attention, and now the waltz, the mimosa-laden waltz begins.

The familiar music is only, I am thinking, in order to put it within my reach and give it back to me. Like a memory of childhood in this particular town that, I cannot help it, haunts me with many things dead and gone. Even a little clockwork peepshow in the railway station, of all places, with little figures of a *corps de ballet* that danced as for the csárdás or mazurka in *Coppélia, ou la fille aux yeu d'émail*.* Or the Spa Theatre shut, empty bandstand, shops closed, palmists and clairvoyants gone, though perhaps still in the town, and nothing but the wintry seas and bare and empty sands.

And we are back to where the fanfare ends.

* * *

It has been no more than a stage announcement of how beautiful the world has been, and could be again. For there are times when the hand of man can do no right, and times when the hand of man cannot go wrong. And for the sake of sanity we have to believe in good and evil. It is not necessary to be religious in order to believe in this. It is perfectly evident if we but use our senses.

But of what use is this proclamation of the dawn over a small and sleeping city when there are already three hundred million too many Indians in the Indian sub-continent, and perhaps as many as six hundred million too many Chinese! And they do not see why they should not live as the rich Americans have lived. But of course, the one sub-continent is not regimented as the other and bigger one; and ask yourself therefore which is the greater danger. Happily they are not within marching distance, yet. So do not let's run out of the theatre to where the crowd waits. But, instead, we will stay inside. It is as much a sacred precinct as any monastery of the Dark Ages where learning and the arts were kept alive. But if it happens again there will be no religion to pull them through. That is the danger.

No matter what happens, and which of the many catastrophes are impending, nothing is going to halt the advance of science. It will proceed whatever else has ceased to be. How long for instance before the Russians have a permanent monitoring station, 'keeping an eye on us', and patrolling overhead? Round and round again before there is time to finish dinner. After which, really and truly, no one will be able to say his life is his own. The Russians are of course only collecting scientific data and taking meteorological records, but are we really to

---

* *Coppélia, ou la fille aux yeux d'émail*, to one of the 'tales' of E. T. A. Hoffman, libretto by C. Nuitter and Saint-Léon, and to the ever-enchanting music by Delibes, from the moment the curtain rises and we hear the strangely evocative fanfare, as of early morning on a propitious and sunny morning with the breath of magic in the air, to be succeeded in a moment or two by that mimosa-laden waltz – but it is so much more a 'valse' than 'waltz' – which sounds so flowing and easy, but it caused the composer a great deal of trouble. It is interesting to recall that the première of *Coppélia* on 25 May 1870 was the last gala performance attended by Napoleon III and the Empress Eugénie, and in a sense therefore the last fête of the Second Empire. How lovely the experience though, then, as now in our day and age, to be hearing the music of *Coppélia* for the first time!

believe that it is little more than a weather station? It is not the same thing as the vicar taking notes and looking morning and evening at his rain gauge. It was about his only hobby, except watching billiards a little improbably in that hall in Leicester Square.

Incidentally, there remains quite a lot more to be done with the weather. It should be possible before long to cut off the rain supply of quite a large area of country simply by moving on the clouds and altering their rate of precipitation. The cloud effects or cloudscapes may become thrilling, and there can be more to it than that. Already in Vietnam they have had a lot of experience with defoliation, not that it is quite the same thing, but it is a step in the same direction. Interference with nature it could be called. And towards what end? Towards making the earth, where needed, permanently and for ever infertile and incapable of bearing crops. In fact, a form of abortion but upon a global scale.

As regards the living there is the chatter of too many voices all speaking at once in too many different tongues. And no one set grammar or lifelong syntax as that which enabled Haydn to compose, *inter alia*, thirty-one piano trios, eighty-three string quartets, and one hundred and four symphonies. Now, as there is no one language of period or style, there are more opportunities for the untalented in all the arts than ever before in history; and by corollary or natural consequence that number the fewer, in proportion, of persons with true talent; all in accordance with the unwritten law of diminishing return. The reason for this being nothing other than the swarming of numbers and multiplication of the drones. But we can live it all down so long as there is tolerance from the other side. Let them have sportsnight all day and night and every day so long as watching games is not made compulsory as it was at school. The 'follies of youth' were not all upon the youthful side.

And what a waste of time it was! Belonging to a generation that endured torment at nine-years-old and upwards from Greek grammar, but worse still from the problems of Euclid, 'a mathematician of Alexandria who flourished three hundred BC' (Dr Lempriere), together with other discrepancies and anachronisms of a so-called classical education, so nearly alike according to their own lights to those for which we deride and denigrate the 'mandarin' Chinese and their state examinations in the 'classics', I am probably not alone in being left wondering what it was all about. The Ancients for instance had their religion, but what name to call it by? There are Buddhism and Hinduism, there are the Shinto and the Muslim, but the classical past has been so much the focus of emulation and attention from the fifteenth century onwards until the nineteenth century and later, that as with some familiar object that has been constantly under observation since childhood we may have lost the power to distinguish between real and false, or in fact to see it as it really is. The failure or the inability to detect the mote in one's own eye being further exemplified in discussing as a mediaeval anachronism the rule of a priest-king or Dalai Lama in Tibet while ignoring the nearly similar status of Papal Rome until September 1870; and in the accounts of Royal marriages in our 'national' newspapers which treat of all such occasions as absurd and out of date in every country but our own.

It is even doubtful now how much can ever come out of a town with more than a hundred thousand population. London, Paris, Dublin, Vienna, Venice, every city one can think of, had a larger number of craftsmen in all the skilled arts a hundred and fifty years ago than now. And a hundred years before that a larger number still. If that be denied, look only at the buildings; palaces, churches, streets of houses! This continued until the end of the first quarter of last century, which is about the time steamboats and railway trains were introduced. It survived, the wars of Napoleon notwithstanding. Look at the crescents and terraces of houses, at the printed books, at even the caricatures of fashion, and see if this is not the case! The vitality of the age is still alive in the jagged, nervous line of Cruickshank as of one accustomed, as I am afraid was the case, to draw the semi-starving in the poverty that so appalled Géricault, Gavarni, Gustave Doré, and every sensitive foreigner who came to London in that time.

At least in the fashionable part of London the painted carriages in their elegance, cleanness of outline and glitter of detail, may have given a pleasure to the spectator with which motor-cars now they have become a mass-medium and diesel engines, no longer wearing the bright liveries of the private railway companies, cannot compete.* Now, if we come to think of it, there is little left. No good posters – even the lubricity on the moving stairs is photographically reproduced – no music-hall song covers, no painted engines or other vehicles, not even the pierrots on the sands, and certainly little pleasure from looking up at the Trident or Jumbo-jet passing noisily, and half-empty, overhead. Compare the scene at Paddington, or the Gare du Nord, or at any railway station, *ad. lib.*, with the Royal Academician Frith's admittedly grouped and static painting of 1867; or at an airport, Orly or Heathrow, John F. Kennedy or Miami, and the loss in mass personality is at once apparent. It has been the acceleration that started the dying and the falling off, and nothing now can halt that. There is something wrong, very definitely wrong with the world where a pop-singer, as announced last week, is to make forty-two thousand pounds a night; and another has an income of more than a million pounds a year. It is useless to invoke the names of Mozart, or Schubert, or Beethoven. For who cares? But a world that allows these contrasts is a sick world, has been so for a long time, and can but get worse.

* * *

And it is like being ill in bed, as I was in the early spring of 1921 in the town where I was born, and so nearly died. Ill in bed there, on a morning of spring, and hearing that voice calling out from all over the town on a spring morning of low tide, which, as everyone knows who has lived there, means that one can walk to unfamiliar rocks and rock pools far out on the sands.

I find it difficult to realize that when I came out of the Army in January 1919,

---

*   That the building of carriages was an art of astonishing elegance and finish as late as 1859–60 is to be seen in the coloured plates to *The Carriage Builder and Harness Makers Art Journal*, a production one would have liked to have fallen into the hands of Baudelaire who of a certainty could have ill-afforded to subscribe to it.

and went two months later to Paris with a letter in my pocket to Modigliani from, I think, the painter Nina Hamnett, for, also, it could have been from Jacob Epstein, I do not believe that there can have been as many as a dozen persons in England who had ever heard Modigliani's name. This is not the place to tell at length how I bought two full length oil-paintings by him for four pounds each, one of which is now in the Tate Gallery, and several drawings for a pound apiece, which drawings were later, and not by myself, packed as wrappings for my shoes in the hotel at Biarritz. And how on my return to Paris three weeks later from Madrid and Toledo, Modigliani was dead, his mistress Hébuterne who was with child had thrown herself out of the window, and his dealer and friend Zborowski offered me the whole contents of his studio, with twelve large nudes, sixty to eighty paintings, and many sculptures and drawings for a hundred pounds.* I was twenty-one years old, had no money of my own, and could not prevail on my father to lend it me. It was a strange moment, of which only two repetitions, or similar experiences *in diminuendo* have offered themselves in my lifetime. But the senseless and lasting shame of it is that Modigliani, who was obviously dying, would have liked twenty or thirty, let alone the equivalent of a hundred pounds, and it would have made a difference to his last days and perhaps made him feel his whole career had not been a total failure. It is of course fifty years ago, but the acceleration in knowledge and in appreciation has been prodigious, perhaps in the nature of a hundred-thousand fold, and to have watched this incredible multiplication of numbers with one's eyes and in one lifetime has been a curious experience.

A haunting and odd experience.

And like the legendary feelings of a drowning man everything I have known, or that has happened to me, flashes through my memory. I am for ever in a top passage where was a rocking-horse, outside the North Bow room, which is, I suppose, my earliest memory. But I want somewhere to myself that no one else remembers. In the empty house which is now a museum.

What did the dying fly think of, or remember, as it was dying? When it longed to crawl into a corner, but staggered to its six feet and died out in the full white glare.

*   *   *

And once more the voice rings out, from quite near this time. It is the past come back in the winking of an eye. It was like that, and was no one's fault. But all gone before the voice has done.

And away to a happier present in the darkening world.

---

* Just one of such paintings of Modigliani, similar to the pair I bought from him for four pounds each, was sold this summer (1971) at Christie's for one hundred and five thousand guineas. This thought is quite revolting in its injustice and cruelty to the artist.

ENTR'ACTE
Pourriture Noble

In considering all this let us remember that thing called *pourriture noble* or 'noble rot' (*Borytris cinerea*) which a well-known oenophilist or connoisseur of wine describes as 'a parasitic fungus that attacks grapes with the result that they develop grey rot and spoil, while in others the *pourriture noble* produces some of the greatest white wines in the world'. In Germany it is known as *Edelfäule*, a word which has the same meaning, and is responsible for the rare, and still rarer Auslese, Beerenauslese and Trockenbeerenauslese wines of the Rhine and Moselle, as well as for the Hungarian Tokay. In a word, *Borytris cinerea* or *pourriture noble* 'is a grape fungus which in sweet white wines becomes a virtue.*' And something not altogether dissimilar to this seems at certain times to have affected human history, and more particularly human beings as they impinge or touch upon the arts. In the sense and to the degree, that is to say, in which they offer or lend themselves as theme or subject. And it is a phenomenon like the *pourriture noble* that covers only some areas of history and is of no validity in others.

It is the 'noble rot' that gives the flavour, and even a distinction in flavour that is not to every taste. It is the 'noble rot' that makes a hero of a highwayman but falls short of a car-bandit or a bank-robber. Even though both are equally bad and there is nothing to choose between them. But the *pourriture noble* is in the one and is not present in the other. In its literal meaning *pourriture* is of highly disagreeable imputation. It is given in *Larousse*, as one might have guessed, as 'état d'un corps en décomposition: sorte de gangrène qui était jadis commun dans les hôpitaux des blessés', and finally, 'maladie cryptogamique commune à divers végétaux'.† But *pourriture noble* has finer shades of meaning.

In the aesthetic and literary context it has its picaresque and tatterdemalion connotation. 'Noble rot' is of course a bad and misleading term; and it would be better translated a 'noble decay', or 'poverty', or even 'noble deliquescence'. In which sense it would apply to the hypersensitive paintings of Picasso's *époque rose* and *époque bleu*, his pictures of half-starving beggars and harlequins, and

---

* *cf.* Alexis Lichine's *Encyclopaedia of Wines and Spirits*, London 1967, pp. 149 and 381.
† 'State of a body in decomposition; a sort of gangrene formerly common among the wounded in military hospitals'; and 'a cryptogamic disease found in various vegetable growths'.

marvellous dry points and etchings by him such as *le souper maigre*. It attaches to *Le Grand Gilles* of Watteau, but not to his *Embarquement pour Cythère* which is for ever spoiled and tarnished by a line of Baudelaire. But it inhabits as of preference Jacques Callot's woodcuts and etchings, Rembrandt's beggars and rat-catchers, the ruffianly panders and cut-throats of Caravaggio, would have been at home in the studio of Cellini, and lurks in the murky corners of the *tenebristi*. *Pourriture noble*, again, is of another intention and meaning from the trite and repellent *faisandé*, a term that applies as if by patent to the chamber of horrors of the Musée Wiertz. And there let it rest, in that dark gallery in Brussels, unless it sorties of its own volition to attach to recent one-man exhibitions at the Tate.

The drawings of beggars and cripples by Hieronymus Bosch are of the noble decay or deliquescence. He seems to have had a permanent repertory, long memorized, of the halt and maimed; while no one who has seen it could forget the little painting of beggars by Bruegel, which is in the Louvre. There are five of them hobbling on their stumps and crutches for all five are legless; and it is only lately that they have been identified as lepers from the fox-tails sewn on the fronts and backs of their clothes, which emblem or insignia of their disease they wore for the lepers' processions on the Monday after Twelfth Night, and during Carnival. It would not be fair to equate this wonder of pitying observation to the gin-sodden boors of Adriaen Brouwer in the next century, most of whom it has been suggested are in a stupor from nicotine poisoning. But the inspiration of Bosch or of Bruegel persists in full Middle Ages with the leprous and/or syphilitic demon in the corner of Matthias Grünewald's altarpiece at Colmar, in Alsace, 'a little hopping fellow like a toad, with a hood over his neck and shoulders, half-shut eyes as if to cry out, and scars and pustules on his stomach and legs that have come to a head and are like poisoned and inflamed nipples', to amend a previous passage in which I attempted a short conversation with him. For we have met before.

From whom at long remove to the banditti of Salvator Rosa round whom romantic legend persisted down to the *Orgie de brigands* of *Harold en Italie*, the viola concerto commissioned from Berlioz by Paganini, in whose skeletal form, ravaged by disease, noble decay or deliquescence, the concept of *Mens sana in corpore sano* receives a final and lasting contradiction. The bandits of the Abruzzi being in concept a minor contemporary art form comparable to the parts played by the heroes and villains of the early 'Westerns'. And an art form this latter has remained when it can produce a film like *Butch Cassidy and the Sundance Kid*. There is a convenient vagueness about Salvator Rosa, to return to him for a moment, which made him suited to operatic and balletic treatment. In the sense that his is a famous name, but those are few who could name a painting by him. Calabrian bandits and the *lazzaroni* of the Bay of Naples are at least hero-villains, and in that lay their fascination.* It is a virus, if it can be called that, which affects

---

* As witness, the operas *Fra Diavolo* and *La Muette de Portici* (*Masaniello*), and their ballet equivalents of *Marco Spada*, *Le Tarentule*, and *Caterina, ou la fille du bandit*. The music for both operas, and for *Marco Spada*, was by Auber.

whole periods of history and in the absence of which history dulls and makes bad reading.

Mid-sixteenth-century Italy was a period in which it was rife. There was all of the ruffian and bravo in Cellini, as to which 'he makes no bones' in his auto-biography; and the same thing could be said, though he does not say it himself, of Caravaggio. Both of them were lucky not to have had their departures 'brought on' or hastened, and to have died natural deaths. The bravos are to be seen in full panoply and braggadocio on the 'swashbuckler' plates from Montelupo; in their slashed doublets and plumed helms, musket on shoulder, but more often a rapier and dagger, or a pair of daggers in their hands, and nearly always against a ferocious and jaundiced yellow ground. And as though the bravos were not enough, the Italians were plagued, too, with the Swiss *landsknechts* for whom in very truth Italy was a stamping ground; their mercenary ferocity recorded and participated in the drawings of Urs Graf (1485–1528) of Basle, a fearsome and vile ruffian who it is thought took part in the sack of Rome.

The decline of the human warrior into a mere mud-stained, mechanized automaton is illustrated in the impossibility of making anything at all in the way of a work of art out of subjects connected with either of the Two World Wars.* Already, by the time of the Franco-Prussian and the American Civil War, it was becoming impossible, but now it is entirely hopeless, which one must suppose proves the efficacy of modern warfare. The *Edelfäule* or *pourriture noble* has departed from it. Gone with 'the captains and the kings'. Already it had begun to grow nastier during the Napoleonic Wars, as witness Goya's *Dos de Mayo* and his *Desastros de la Guerra*; and ignoring the patriotic nonsense of David's painting of *The Emperor distributing the Eagles*, or of le baron Gros at *Napoleon crossing the Alps* or on the *Field of Eylau*, both latter paintings, admittedly, being emotionally inspiring at sight of the young Alexander in his war tracks.† Less than a decade later he was a prisoner on St Helena, but no less of a legend, and no less, still, of a nuisance.

The faster the world grows in population the more quickly and completely it can be stupefied, eight hundred million Chinamen for an instance; and the voice of their Chairman not being that of the herald whom Aristotle spoke of for the Greek cities. No such adulation has ever before in history been addressed to a human being in his lifetime. Though, up to this present, whoever has been so incontestably right is generally proved wrong in the ending.‡ He has imposed a dread uniformity upon his devotees. But the civilizations of the West have depended upon the individuality of the person, and in the decline of that they are fast weakening.

* The residuum of both World Wars being *Strange Meeting* and a handful of other poems by Wilfred Owen.
† It is typical of some phases of French history that Gros was made a baron by Charles x for his dome of the Panthéon, which had been intended as an apotheosis of Napoleon and had to be converted into an apotheosis of the Bourbon restoration. cf. *A Dictionary of Art and Artists*, by Peter and Linda Murray, Harmondsworth 1959.
‡ Compare the inscription *Il Duce ha sempre raggione* on walls in every town in Italy during the Fascist regime.

As to those luckier periods, which were not necessarily happier, it is a truism that it permeated into the smallest details and that there was an attendant splendour even in their worst moments. The groan which went up from the crowd on the beheading of Charles I at Whitehall cannot have been the same in timbre as that which greeted the guillotining of Louis XVI or 'l'Autrichienne', Marie Antoinette. At the start of her ride in the tumbril she had asked whether she was likely to be torn to pieces by the crowd; but we may guess that no such thought had occurred to the Stuart King, who only hoped his shivering from the cold on that January morning as he stepped out of the window onto the scaffold would not be mistaken for his being frightened. Even the most sordid things of life take on some sort of dignity in a period of great language, and this was within the lifetime of the younger Elizabethans. This is not to say that it reduced suffering, but only that it has a deceptive gloss upon it which is conspicuously lacking during the industrialized nineteenth century when the smog was already lowering upon the factory chimneys. The fearful but wonderful drawings of London of that time by George Cruickshank and by Gustave Doré are as though the draughtsman had dipped a finger, or, in the case of Cruickshank even drew with his fingernail dipped into the soot and mire. Of the earlier period there was still poetry written and fine architecture in a golden age of language, and it is hardly an exaggeration to say that this penetrates into the written accounts but, also, even into deeds and actions described and done.

That is to say, some pollen or debris of the *pourriture noble* appears to cling to them and there is not the sordidity in reporting that spoils even the most interesting murder or other cases in our 'national' Sunday papers. If no more than a sentence or a phrase is set down in print it has the 'ring' of a great age of spoken speech to its turn of phrase, however coarse or vituperative its purport and intention. The two extremes of language being the speech of the Queen, who wore a silver *corselet* over her white velvet dress and held a truncheon in her hand, to the assembled troops at Tilbury on the eve of the Armada, and the no less proud and vaunting language of the beggar's song, Tom o' Bedlam, which, too, has 'the heart and stomach of a King', but of a King o' the beggars, not a King of England. Who indeed could have written this poem? An observer of the scene like Jacques Callot, although he is said to have joined a troop of Gypsies and travelled with them; or a true and born participant like Villon? One would guess it is of the former, not the latter; that it is a work of art, or artifice, and not of nature. It is nearly inconceivable that in the other category it could have been of more than a stanza or two's length. No untried hand could have sustained it. So it could well be that the theme or the inspiration came from the first few lines found scrawled on a fly-leaf or scratched upon a wall, and that the finder took them away with him to set to work. The poem is a mystery of mysteries, in little, and one might guess that it could only have been written by someone used to the roystering life, who had travelled on the muddy roads and slept beneath the stars. And in the same breath it is no more mysterious than many other of the ballads, and only exceptional because of its inordinate length.

The gift of tongues, if it can be called that, persisted through the seventeenth century, but the talent for using it may have been more manifest the lower the social order of the speaker, in that the fops and persons of fashion in Hogarth's tell-tale series of paintings spoke an affected and less vigorous English than that of the poorer classes. Or, in fact, fine language was dying at the top but still strong and supple at its roots. The vocabulary or phraseology of the slums and in the prisons will have been of a strength and pungency never attained before or since, and all for the reason that it was a golden age in decline and that sparks from the finest poetry ever written were still flying around and about and starting little fires. That flickered and soon went out, but in settings and circumstances of a new savagery and horror. Because the towns were growing and there had never been big towns before, the London population by the turn of the century being estimated at between six and seven hundred thousand. The Great Fire of 1666 may have done more good than harm by destroying many of the worst quarters between Old St Paul's and Wapping Stairs, but by fifty years from then there were new and worse, low dens and rookeries to add to those already there.

That there was a kind of ferocious aesthetic attached to the age makes itself felt both in incidents, and in the language made use of to describe those happenings. It is the stuff and material of drama; whether of the fiercest and most melodramatic of Kabuki players where we could find ourselves on the left-hand side in the stalls near to the *hanamichi* or gangway from the back of the theatre to the stage, along which the actors 'come on', sometimes on horseback, or in the *aragoto* which are plays of particular violence and dramatic action, wherein the actors at times advance in great leaps along the gangplank, and even mouth 'meaningless words which have been concocted in order to give an effect of force and strength'. It is the stuff of 'Westerns' which are an art form, if only a mimetic art; and in real life alike of the bull-ring, and of the bare-fist boxers of 'the fancy' or PR (that is, the prize ring). The combat for instance between Ben Gaunt and Bendigo that took place in September 1845 at Lillingston Lovell, a village a few miles from where this paragraph is written – the ugly features of both men 'darkened by the astringent pickle with which prize fighters' hands and faces were treated to toughen the skin and minimize bleeding', and which was won by Bendigo in the ninety-third round both men by then having broken knuckles and badly damaged forearms.* Impossible in this context not to recall, too, the passing mention of the bare-fist pugilists in Borrow's *Lavengro*, and the passage in which he describes Thurtell, the murderer of Mr Weare, crashing on his horse through the boughs and sticks to the tent door of the Gypsy, Jasper Petulengro to whom he spoke in his 'strange tongue', 'this horseman of the lane, of half-jockey, half bruiser countenance'. That it may have been Borrow who 'wrote up' some of the murder cases reported in *The Annual Register* for the eighteen-thirties and early forties accounts for the lasting impression they made on a schoolboy reading them eighty years later in the school library at Eton.

It is the Regency 'sporting world' of Pierce Egan, of his *Life in London*, 1821, with aquatint plates by George and Robert Cruickshank, to which a key and a

---

* cf. *The Victorian Underworld*, by Kellow Chesney, London 1970, pp. 267–276, for a lively description of the contest.

'vocabulary of Flash and Cant' was later published, and of his *Life of an Actor* with circus and theatre scenes by Theodore Lane, an artist who died tragically young. It was Pierce Egan whose knowledge of low and sporting life enabled him to contribute the slang phrases to Grose's *Dictionary of the Vulgar Tongue*, 1824.* Of this sporting, half-criminal world Thurtell may have been a typical member, where we leave him as seen again by Borrow, dashing through the rain and thunder, splashing and scattering man, horse, and cart to the left and right, in his open barouche, drawn by four smoking steeds, with postilions in scarlet jackets and leather skull-caps; and the Gypsy foretelling 'a bloody dukkeripen', fulfilled fifteen years later beneath the gallows before Newgate prison.

The tradition of violence, and the glorying in that, had persisted one may think since the high tide of vagrancy, for no particular reason save the simple one that they had begun to swarm, which was a phenomenon in the reign of Henry VIII. In proof of which it has been put forward that no fewer than two thousand vagrants, beggars, and thieves were hanged for every year he was upon the throne, to the tune in all of some seventy-two thousand, no more, no less. It will have been during those years that the vocabulary of cant and slang began to grow, reaching to its climax towards the last years of the next century. Merely to compare the list of cant names of vagabonds and criminals given in the one book with the eight-page glossary of colloquial and cant words in the other, is to know a fall in value can be brought about in the value of words as fast as in any commodity upon the money market.† In the latter list though there are still words of Gypsy or even Skelta origin, and many relics of the earlier age, Americanisms have begun to creep in and tarnish the aboriginal Cockney that may have had its roots in the remote past of Chaucer's London. Rhyming slang, versatile as it may be, is no match for real creation and invention.

What are we to think indeed of a city wherein there were more than three-hundred and fifty offences punishable by death, as was the case in London for the forty years between 1680 and 1722! Is it any wonder that a kind of desperation in literature grew up from and around this for it is of a degree of danger and violence akin to the expectation of life for an officer, an NCO, or a private soldier in regiments during the First World War. Hairbreadth escapes and jail breaks are the warp and web of drama. Is it possible to conceive of anything more dramatically moving than the history of a child later to become a famous highwayman, James Dalton; who at the age of five had seen his father hanged – 'indeed, his father had carried the boy between his knees in the cart to Tyburn so that he could watch'. And James Dalton, transported twice, and celebrated enough to be alluded to in Hogarth's *Harlot's Progress*, impeached fourteen of his accomplices in the game of deadly ninepins the characters played with each other's lives, and was in turn impeached and hanged. As companion piece to which there is the thief Roger Johnson who appears in books and pamphlets by both Fielding

* cf. *Aquatint Engraving*, by S. T. Prideaux, London 1909, pp. 305, 307, 308, 335; and for Theodore Lane, pp. 308 and 365.
† cf. *Thief-taker General: the rise and fall of Jonathan Wild*, by Gerald Howson, London 1971, p.24; and *The Victorian Underworld*, pp. 377–384.

and Defoe, and who impeached his own mother for coining in order to save his own life. She was committed to Newgate, but died in prison before she was put on trial; while her son, one of those whose lives were more perilous by far than those to be read of in the Spanish encyclopaedia of tauromachy, escaped the gallows and survived.

But what a world to live in! And conducted for the most part, if not engaged in robbing on the turnpikes, in areas of London where the 'rookeries' and human cess-pits jostled for place with the houses of fine brick with fan-lights over their doors and torch-extinguishers for the linksmen. But with slum areas of hoary age, with secret cupboards, sliding landings, and as many trapdoors as ever Lupino Lane jumped through in his harlequin performance. Roger Johnson who impeached his mother, to return to him again, had on one occasion been arrested in Newcastle and conveyed thence all the way to London, double-ironed, and chained under a horse's belly. What a journey that must have been! For we are to realize that it may have taken fifteen to twenty days, and what a horrendous sight to pass upon the road; at the end of which in the Hold of Newgate, 'the stone floor was deep with dead cockroaches, whose shells crackled under the feet, while fat white lice crawled all over the prisoners' clothes'.* After which, for this is but a misty condensation from Mr Gerald Howson's wonderful but terrible recital of human rights and wrongs, one can but quote the quatrain from *Les Phares* where Baudelaire apostrophizes the sculptor Puget (1620–94).

> *Colères de boxeur, impudence de faune,*
> *Toi qui sus ramasser la beauté des goujats,*
> *Grand coeur gonflé d'orgueil, homme débile et jaune,*
> *Puget, mélancolique empereur des forçats:*

a quatrain of which I will not attempt a translation, but only with little more in some sort than a schoolboy 'crib', and the hint that 'goujat' in slang or 'argot' infers a low sort of ruffian or even cut-throat, while 'forçat' is a man condemned to the galleys. It could be said that Baudelaire searching about for names that act as 'beacons' or 'lighthouses' for the human spirit, and among the immortal apostrophes that he addresses to Goya and to Delacroix (the latter still living!) may have found himself at a loss for a French sculptor. One must suppose that he rejected the more obvious Jean Goujon as too sensuous and decorative – but without knowing perhaps very much about him. Baudelaire touched upon the appropriate name with Pierre Puget. For Puget, unlike the majority of his contemporaries, had gravitated away from Paris and worked in Italy, but above all in Genoa and at Toulon. In this latter city he carved the Michelangelesque caryatids of the Hotel de Ville, but worked mostly in the shipyards where he must have had a studio wherein to sculpt the figureheads of the galleys, for which many preliminary drawings still survive. Those wooden and gilt carvings are in some sense a caravan or fairground art transferred from the open spaces in or out of towns to the treacherous and saucy fields of Arethusa, but Puget had a huge

* *cf. Thief-taker General, the rise and fall of Jonathan Wild*, pp. 28 and 289.

hand and worked outside and beyond the ordinary curriculum of the ship sculptor's trade.

There was precedent enough for the use of Turkish or other galley-slaves as models, in for instance the 'Quattro Mori', the four Turkish slaves in bronze at the base of the statue of Grand-Duke Ferdinand I of Tuscany, at Leghorn. This is by Pietro Tacca (1571–1640), a Florentine sculptor who had been a pupil of John of Bologna; and there are slave caryatids or 'stand-ins' in Bernini's fountain in the Piazza Navona, at Rome. Later, these figures of galley-slaves were to become a commonplace in memorials to admirals or generals who had fought the Turks, and are to be found all over Europe from Malta to Sweden, and from Seville to Budapest. They are to be known by their shaved heads and the tufts of hair upon their foreheads, and became as much a part of the sculptor's jargon as death's heads or faun caryatids. They are to be observed on the tomb of the Margrave Ludwig Wilhelm in the Pfarrkirche above Baden-Baden; in Austria; in churches in Warsaw and in Cracow, thanks to Sobieski; and in nearly every Christian country in Europe except in Holland and in England. The 'mélancolique empereur des forçats', be it Pietro Tacca or Pierre Puget, had many subjects of mixed nationality, autochthonous as well as foreign. Perhaps a majority of the *forçats* whom Puget must have watched at work in the dockyards at Toulon or on board the galleys will have been French criminals assigned to this dreadful fate. One has only indeed to pay a visit of a few days to Malta to become aware of the full horror of a galley-slave's life, whether in their barracks at the Fort of Sant' Angelo or 'on caravan' as it was called when the galleys put to sea. The lot of an ordinary criminal condemned to hard labour did not cover the same hideous extremes of physical exertion as that of a galley-slave pulling at his oar. Perhaps in all its dreadfulness it was only equalled by transportation to Port Arthur, Port Macquarie in Australia, or, worst of all because of its quasi-lunar isolation, Norfolk Island, a thousand miles from the nearest point of land in Australia, and some three hundred miles from the most northerly cape of New Zealand, where there was a penal colony from 1788 to 1813, and again, before those ghosts had time to settle, from 1823 to 1855, during which latter period it was even worse than it had been before.

No wide stretching of the imagination is required in order to include the inmates of Newgate and the other English prisons within the cloak of an 'Empereur des forçats'. Like the inmates of the concentration camps there was this much in their favour, for what little it was worth, that death was always no further than round the corner. Not only that, but almost certain in the end to catch up with you and finish you. It could be put in this way, that when you could be hanged for stealing a handkerchief or for a simple case of pocket-picking it was indeed a career of dangerous living, and it gave a desperate levity even to their jokes and bawdy scenes. There was no *Beggar's Opera* to be written a hundred years later round the tattered wretches of Mayhew's *London*. The *pourriture noble* had rubbed off long ago by then. And by the time of Gustave Doré's *London* in the early seventies it was simply and entirely out of question. Read this:

In four small cottages, with two bedrooms each and with two rooms on the ground floor, there was an average of 188 persons lodged; they had a small yard, and the remains only of what had been two privies, all the ordure being in the open yard. In this yard was also a building, in a loathsome condition, occupied by a man, his wife and child, and one female lodger, the dimensions of the room on the ground floor being 6 ft. 2 in. long, by 4 ft. 4 in. wide, and 5 ft. 4 in. high. This has been a nailer's shop and the walls and floor were jet black. In the same yard, in one bedroom, 8 ft. 9 in. by 9 ft. and 7 ft. high, lived a husband, and a wife, and six children. In another lodging house near, there were three small rooms upstairs: in the first were 16 men, women and children, lying together on the floor; in the second there were twelve, also on the floor; and a third room upstairs was used as a privy, the boarded floor being literally covered with human ordure. In the same yard at the same time, but in another lodging-house, in worse condition than the last, there was a bed in the house-place, on which lay a woman in the pains of labour; by her side lay a man apparently asleep, and ten other men, women and children were in the same room. This was at 2 a.m. In a back place, with the window out, and used as a receptacle for the filth of the house, lay three little children in some shavings. In the room over this lay six women and children on the floor, and in the front room were four beds on the floor, filled with men, women and children, carrying from 2 to 6 in a bed.

This is not from Engels' *Condition of the Working Classes in England in 1844.* It is in the words of the town clerk of Macclesfield, in Cheshire, who took officials of the new Local Board of Health around the town one night in 1854.* That these horrors should have been co-existent with the period of our widest territorial expansion and greatest material prosperity is perhaps the supreme paradox of modern history. Not that it is fair to blame the one upon the other, or to argue that the riches were in fact paid for by the sufferings of the poor. Or even to say in excuse that though the sun is shining in one part of the country it may be raining or snowing in another. For it is beside the point. But that the one condition must be in some sense and to a certain degree in relationship to the other is unarguable, although the lines of consanguinity be remote and difficult to trace.

And I am led back to Nova Scotia Gardens where most certainly I have set foot before. Where the children of Bishop, one of the Bethnal Green 'burkers', who sold their murdered victims to the anatomy schools to be dissected, were seen playing with a pair of white mice. This being in 1831, only a year or two after similar professional deeds by the more famous and eponymous Burke and by Hare in Edinburgh; and the white mice having been the property and means of livelihood of 'the little Italian boy', probably a Savoyard, Carlo Ferrair, last seen in Regent Street by an Italian organ-grinder about a fortnight before the day when his corpse was taken round, shortly after midnight, and shown to the night porter at King's College. He is described as being dressed in a blue smock, with a sort

* Quoted from *The Victorian Underworld*, pp. 104, 105, and derived from *Parliamentary Papers* 1857, 2nd Session, XLI, Reports on Common Lodging Houses, 23.

of flat fur cap upon his head, and having round his neck a cage 'that turned round', with two white mice in it. He, also, had a tortoise ... Then we hear of his being seen near Bishop's lodging in Nova Scotia Gardens; and a little boy who is six years old, describes looking out of the window and seeing a boy, older than himself, with a cage of white mice round his neck, and being taken away from the window by his mother and told not to look because it was a waste of time ... and later a flat fur cap and a blue smock are found in Bishop's lodging.

But Nova Scotia Gardens, twenty years later by Mayhew's time, had been themselves anatomized, as it were, and an enormous stinking rubbish pile rising higher than any of the nearby houses, was instead of them. The slums were getting steadily worse, not better. Perhaps it is only necessary to quote from Mayhew's description of one figure in a lodging-house near the London Docks where he had decided as a macabre experience to give supper to the inmates. In the end the number of guests swelled to fifty, all feasting on 'beef, potatoes and materials for a suet pudding', but Mayhew could not forget a figure on a form at the end of the kitchen, whose squalor and wretchedness produced a feeling approaching awe. 'His eyes were sunk deep in his head, his cheeks were drawn in ... while his dark stubbly beard gave a grimness to his appearance that was almost demoniac; and yet there was a patience in his look that was almost pitiable. His clothes were black and shiny at every fold with grease, and his coarse shirt was so brown with wearing that it was only with long inspection you could see it had once been a checked one; on his feet he had a pair of lady's lace-sided boots, the toes of which had been cut off so that he might get them on ... I never beheld so gaunt a figure of famine. To this day the figure of the man haunts me.' And it should be added that the charge at this house was twopence a night, which could be paid up till eleven p.m., when those who had not paid were turned out and no further applicants admitted. Half the lodgers were thieves; a quarter dock labourers; a few living on parish relief, a few who collected old bones, and a 'pure finder' or two who collected dogs' faeces which were used for tanning leather.

It would appear from Mayhew's pages that threepence or fourpence a day was just sufficient to keep alive on. It would buy a pair of herrings and a cup of tea, and in fact Mayhew mentions the inmates of this lodging-house kneeling in front of the fire and toasting herrings. This kind of hell-kitchen had an unboarded floor, and was lit by the flare of 'a rude iron gas-pipe' standing in the centre of the room, which of course will have burned the night through. A further twopence, we have heard, was needed for the night's lodging, so that life could be sustained on fivepence or sixpence a day, but it is difficult to think of such a living and not be seized with horror. How could that scarecrow with the lady's lace-sided boots, and the toes cut off, ever go out into the daylight? Were these, then, but his bedroom slippers in which to sit beside the fire? Something tells one it was his only foot-wear, and that since he was reduced to this he could not venture out. There are rainy days enough in London in the nineteen-seventies, and what must those winter nights have been in the eighteen-fifties! Mayhew further tells us that this hellhole lay off a fairly big slum court cluttered with coster carts where a number of pros-

titutes of the poorest sort lay sleeping. These carts, then, would be tilted and stand-
ing on their shafts, and one wonders for how many months or years that kind of
professional life could be endured, in just this decade of the 'covered waggon' of
the prairies! As for him of the lace-sided bootees he was immobilized, reduced to
doing absolutely nothing at all, all day long; but anything, anything was to be
preferred to the workhouse or infirmary. How, though, he contrived the sixpence
a day that this required is beyond thinking!

The final pitch of degradation is immortalized in Gustave Doré's London
drawings. That he spoke little English, and had to have the meaning of things
explained to him by his night companion Douglas Jerrold, who wrote the text,
only perhaps further intensified his response to the scenes of misery. The number
of little girls each holding a child scarcely smaller than herself are a conspicuous
feature in the drawings; as are the general listlessness of the figures of young and
old standing in doorways; while the number of starving Jews in his Whitechapel
scenes is remarkable, and this was before the pogroms in Russia and in Poland had
driven large numbers of them to seek refuge in the East End of London. And the
top-hats! There is a peculiar and extra horror in this insignia and emblem of solid
respectability worn sleeping out on the Embankment, huddled in misery under an
archway of London Bridge with feet practically in the muddied river tide, or
sheltering in a street doorway as though doomed to stand all night!

Cruickshank is no different from Doré in the misery he depicts. But Doré was
a stranger, and Cruickshank a Londoner if not a Cockney. By the eighteen-forties
he was already a survivor from an earlier period and another world of extravaganza
as shown in his *Monstrosities of Fashion* and his coloured plates to *Life in London*
and other pictures of the 'sporting world'. Also, in the multitude of his coloured
caricatures which were in the vein of Gillray. But it is to be noted that his palette
darkened at the incoming of the industrial age, and he had become a black-and-
white draughtsman by the time gaslight and the steam engine were established.
Or is it only that the technical processes had changed, and etching and steel
engraving had taken the place of aquatint and the handcoloured plate? If it is only
that, and no more than that, the loss of the bright colours of the Regency is
symptomatic and the change over to the soot and murkiness of pollution. No
more timeless picture of London has ever been drawn than his *Early Morning*, in
Sketches by Boz (1837), where the little chimney sweep and his master on the way
to work are drinking at a coffee stall, and no one else is about except the police-
man tired from his beat and leaning against a street post. Even the lamp-post could
be nowhere else than London. The inexhaustible vitality of Cruickshank never
runs dry for a moment in the many numbers of his *Comic Almanack*. But there
is a darkness, a darkness over all.*

Probably this was nothing other than the darkness of London itself; and the
pall hung as well over the industrial cities of the north. To which there are
contingent witnesses. It will be remembered that Ruskin in his declining years
complained that there was never now a good sunrise or sunset, and that the cloud-
scapes of his youth were gone. This has been taken as evidence of his mental

* *The Comic Almanack* was published yearly from 1835 till 1852.

disturbance, but it is just as likely to have been his understandable exaggeration of the truth. It could be, too, that the preternatural brightness of the colours in pre-Raphaelite paintings – in early pictures by Millais like his *The Blind Girl*; in *The Pretty Baa-Lambs* of Ford Madox Brown; the *Stonebreaker* of John Brett; *April Love* and *Amy, or the Long Engagement* of Arthur Hughes – are instances of this combative and self-assertive brightness in sign of a new age and the hoped-for dispersal of the fog and soot. Cruickshank lived on into those years. He only died in 1878, by which time he was all but forgotten. A young Frenchman, Octave Aubry, who came to London to write on English caricature, has written of meeting a tall thin old man with an aquiline nose whom he often passed on Hampstead Hill on his way to the Reading Room of the British Museum, and who looked at him as though he would have liked to speak to him. This was Cruickshank, whom Aubry had thought long dead. Cruickshank, himself, has written of his pencil lying idle, and of how during the sixties he could not get work to do; his fame in the meantime going back to about 1812, and his name being in some sense a 'household word', owing mainly perhaps to his drawings for *Oliver Twist*. But he must have hated and disliked the pre-Raphaelite painters, and did not in all probability have the slightest wish to be relieved of the Cockney gloom of mid-Victorian Islington and Bloomsbury to which he was accustomed and had grown to love.

All, or most of which, may have been upon the same site as what has gone earlier, but the spirit is altogether changed. It had altered from what someone of Cruickshank's generation could remember; within whose mature years the hansom cab, funereal black like the Venetian gondola – and as much a master-piece of obtrusive unobviousness as the top-hat and frock-coat of all but the poorer classes – had darkened the London streets and pavements. The middle-aged city man riding on horseback to his office in mid-Victorian times, a practice which continued until at least the eighteen-eighties,* will have noticed the increasing drabness compared to the London of thirty or forty years ago.

Only this morning on the day this is written a postcard comes from a friend who has been in Nardò, a small town in Apulia, between Lecce and Gallipoli, telling me of its fourteen quite splendid seventeenth-century Leccese churches; and that Monopoli, another little town farther north on the Adriatic coast, was 'another delight and equally unspoiled as far as the old town is concerned'. This is only quoted in evidence that it was a wonderful flowering everywhere, not least in this remote part of Italy which I have made bold to call The Third Sicily.† But where London is concerned, look only at the steeple and portico and side walls, all cleaned lately and looking now their best, of St Martin's-in-the-Fields, a splendid masterpiece by Gibbs in the midst of London; repeating again what has been said of it before, that 'if we look at this dispassionately, we may not feel certain there is a finer building in all Rome or Venice'. Lovers of quietist architecture, for which Holland was the other centre and alternate studying

---

* Mr Bravo rode into London from the Priory, Balham.
† Naples under the Spanish Bourbon kings until 1861 was known as the Kingdom of the Two Sicilies.

ground, would have noted the extraordinary contrast in London between the fine streets and squares of brick houses and the plague spots of the London slums. Impossible to see the one without the other for they stood cheek by jowl. They were round every corner, at less than a minute's walk from the just mentioned St Martin's-in-the-Fields; and at the same distance from every landmark, and from each one of the fifty and more City churches that were designed by Wren after the Great Fire of London. But according to our creed and if we have a belief in such things, and it should have all the force and strength of a religion, a fuller life is led by all in such conditions. In the same sense that one could say, and without affectation, that it was better to live, more interesting and a finer experience, in fifteenth-century Florence or Venice than in mid-nineteenth-century Hudders-field or Elberfeld; and in whatever circumstances, save those of extreme physical pain, to have lived in Bernini's Rome than in Seven Dials or Bluegate Fields which were two of the worst Victorian slums. The Cockney inhabitants would not agree but it is no less certain for that reason.

For the most wretched and depraved of Londoners of that earlier generation had tasted, if but tasted and no more, the deliquescence or the guttering of *le pourriture noble*. Their nerves were not shattered by our noise and speed, while what was visibly fine came as if of nature with no hesitancy and no excuse made for it. The swarming was but in its beginning, and the population of London somewhere between six and seven hundred thousand. Compared to life in London at that day there was nothing whatever of *le pourriture noble* attaching to gang warfare in the Chicago of Al Capone. Again, it would be rather more than an affectation to say that what was missing with the Mafia gangs were Gibbs's steeples to St Martin's-in-the-Fields and the two churches in the Strand. It would be tantamount to saying that none of that would have happened had the two, and now three glass towers of Mies van der Rohe been standing along Lake Shore Drive. But the hoodlum shootings and the ensuing gangster funerals were flat and discordant without even the debris of anything better than themselves upon them. The clipped, ice-creamer, or 'hokey-pokey' jargon that they spoke, and their 'bar-b-q', cheeseburger nicknames are their all. There is nothing more.

Whereas something, and a good deal more than that attaches to the saloon bar of the 'Western', let alone the stage coach arrival in the veranda'd town, the mountains and the *hacienda* and the semi-Mexican detritus, the clatter of the 'shoot-ing up', the horses and the wide-brimmed hats; and always the hope of 'Indians', to whom some little of the 'Redskins' of George Catlin still clings as anyone will remember who as a child, or much later in life, held the *North American Indians* (1841) in his hand and read his accounts of the Mandan or the Crow chieftains; of the rattle of their war crests made of the plumes or quills of the war eagle; of the chief of the Crows who had the longest hair of any man in the nation, 'who on any great parade or similar occasion let it drag behind him, some three or four feet of it spread out upon the grass, and black and shining like a raven's wing' – of the Mandan chieftain, of whom Catlin remarks when he came to have his portrait done, 'that no tragedian ever trod the stage, nor gladiator [nor matador let us add!] ever entered the arena, with more grace and manly dignity.'

Such, I have said elsewhere, seeming to be the equestrian or circus qualities nurtured in the tent. They have the *pourriture noble* upon them, whether of the noble savage, or of the sweepings of Moctezuma's robe of green quetzal plumes. At a millennium or an astronautical remove from the Chicago gangs; but coaeval or equal in dramatic worth and as subject for legend and song to the chiefs and highwaymen and transportees, whether 'returned' or not, and thus living dangerously twice over, of the London 'stews', who have the dust and the 'flash' or 'cant' speech of hundreds of years of history behind them. But they end in violence. And often a woman hangs with them, with her hands likewise tied together in front of her, but for some reason it is particularly horrible to see a woman hanging up in a skirt. As for the men, they dangle on the gallow's tree and some of their bodies have turned round in their strangling agony. They might swing a little in a sudden gust of wind, and are petty thieves hanging for a stolen shilling. But, at least, their bodies are soon taken down, whether, or not, to be anatomized. The greater heroes are hung in chains, and sometimes in pairs, near the scene of their robberies, in front of the Two Fighting Cocks tavern in Southwark Mint, in one notorious instance. The clanking of their irons may have been audible now and again in reminder. Or they were hung within sight of other dead criminals on Hounslow Heath, or Kennington Common, or similar open spaces all over England, and left to rot in their iron bodices until they fell to bits.*

---

* A drawing by Thomas Rowlandson, *Visit to an Old Acquaintance*, signed and dated 1819, could make a postscript to this chapter. Two ruffianly horsemen have reined in their steeds and look up at the gibbet. There hangs a hardly recognizable half-skeleton, dangling from an iron ring driven into the wooden beam above him. His corpse is sheathed, more or less, in irons as for some terrible surgical correction of the spine and leg-bones. The corpse must certainly have swayed and clanked in the wind. And the two horsemen turn their horses, and one would like to know their thoughts as they rode away. Criminals hung in chains on the high roads appalled foreigners who came to England; while travelling Englishmen complained of like or worse sights abroad.

BOOK
ELEVEN

Personalia

I WESTON

For all that, the *pourriture noble* is not a nice idea. Yet the dust from it falls even upon the nymph and the river god who wait together beneath the cloud stair at Würzburg like a parable and commentary upon youth and age. This is one of the passages 'of sublime poetry' on a painted ceiling. She, a potamid near to her brake of reeds or bulrushes; and he, an old whitebeard with one arm round her naked waist and the other hand upon his urn. Their legs and feet come out over the parapet and are painted into the architecture. Only to remember the glorious masses of white cumulus and the three white horses of Apollo's chariot banking down and out of that into the blinding light. Ah! but the painter was the last lion of Venice, slowly declining even then into the Adriatic.

But it is not to be like that at all.

Because it does not follow that I like best what I have written about most. All of that is for writing, not for living. I do not wish for instance to have a painting by El Greco in the 'bedroom' where I do my writing. I would sooner no pictures at all; though it so happens that for want of wall space in a small house there is over the bed a copy, in reduced size, of Bruegel's painting of *The Triumph of Death* which hangs in the Prado. Many persons would not like to have this in their bedroom and directly above the bed, but I find it comforting to think that it may, or almost must have had contact with the painter and been copied in his workshop. And I find that it even gives me a kind of vicarious relationship, not of blood, with Philip II of Spain, who had Hieronymus Bosch's triptych of *The Millennium* hanging in his bedroom at the Escorial, which, if not one of my places of predilection, is among those that have left the strongest impression. To have seen the Escorial twice in the snow is never to forget it.

Too fine a view from a window would, also, be an impediment to writing. My window looks out upon a lawn and on old trees. There should not be, and in any case there are not, too many flowers. The room, it is true, is much too small, but I am used to it. Since we came to live here in 1929, having spent some four to five hours every day, during seven to eight months of every year in this room, writing. From quarter or half-past nine to half-past twelve, and again from five-o'clock to seven. Every week day, on Christmas Day, Easter, Whitsun, all public holidays, and '*always* on Sundays', which works out at about seven years on end here, 'in solitary' in this room, working and looking out of window.

Where the most interesting sight are the birds on the lawn; young jackdaws who live in the old chimneys; wagtails after a shower of rain darting about like young ballerinas practising upon their points; rooks out of the tall elms; now, after long absence, a green woodpecker, or 'yaffle' or 'eccles' in local dialect, tapping invisibly, or flying with hysterical laughter across into the trees; and once, long ago in wartime, a hoopoe for an Oriental visitant and nostalgic reminder of the turban'd East.

Also, towards the end of June or early July, a sparrow-hawk, which makes pretence of joining the young jackdaws feeding where the grass is mown, appears to pass unnoticed among the other birds like Achilles among the women, then takes to the wing with long rudder-tail predominant, and treacherously 'dive bombs' the jackdaws, achieving several near-misses only a few inches above ground, then off with no word of apology into the trees. All of these, and now and again a stray dog from the village, or feral and young bird-devouring cat.

And in my room itself no 'coffee-table' books, only guide-books and books of reference, and a few personal treasures of no value at all, such as prisoners 'on life' are allowed to have in their cells. For in very different circumstances that is what it comes to; one cannot get or keep away from it except when ill; or during absence, when it seems impossible one should ever be able to resume or get it going again. So that it is a form of imprisonment, and one comes to dread the day of eventual and permanent release into the uncomforting, and cold world. May that be delayed for a little longer!

Only one picture in this room, as described, but with two horrendous shelves of books of my sister's and brother's and my own writing. Not nearly complete, at that, but there they are! With so many of my own which I know will never be reprinted. But this, far from being sad, is rather a nice feeling. Never having hankered after the Bible-reading – in numbers! – equivalent to the public of the Rolling Stones, or Beatles.* I would wish – and the wish is granted in advance without even having to ask for it – to have few readers, not even as many as the inhabitants of a small town, though more, I have to admit, than the population of the village where we live who are three or four hundred no more, in all. To come at the tail end of a family of writers has not been easy; for this is written in the wake of not one, but two powerful personalities who have preceded me, and I am still riding the waves and down in the trough behind them. Moreover, misleading labels are on the luggage of anyone who has travelled much and reached out far from his home. They are stuck there and they never get removed. Worse still, one is too quickly known and identified by such labels. I have said that the

---

* The seventeenth-century mansion of Mick Jagger is announced as 'To Let' in today's papers at £2,500 a week, the rent to include the use of a recording studio and the services of a *cordon bleu chef*. It has twenty bedrooms, turrets, battlements, and a minstrels' gallery. Though his brother Chris (23), at the mansion as a caretaker, says: 'There certainly isn't a *cordon bleu* here at the moment. All I've got to eat at this moment is toast and cheese, and the toast isn't very hot.' *Vide Sunday Express* for 27 June 1971.

one painting in this room is here for accommodation more than by choice. I would prefer no picture at all; or it could become a museum of little drawings and reproductions not much bigger than a postcard.

Not so long ago, and until they were swept away in one general holocaust of tidying, the mantelpiece had four coloured drawings of Welsh costumes of about 1840. They were the 'originals' for the steel-engravings on writing-paper, sold by a stationer in Chester to Victorian travellers returned from, or about to set out for a trip into Wales. Within the last few months a similar drawing, almost certainly by the same hand, of a market scene with the Welsh women sitting or standing by their stalls, and a curious interest given to it by the different levels of their tall hats, has been sold in a London saleroom for several hundred pounds and attributed to that painter with a tragic history, Richard Dadd. Next to these drawings, and for cogent reason, a coloured postcard of the almswomen of Castle Rising in Norfolk, in their red cloaks with the Howard badge, of Henry Howard – the learned and eccentric Henry Howard, Earl of Northampton – and the high peaked hats of James I's time, a costume which 'probably' – and one may say now, with certainty – 'survives in no other part of England'.

Upon the walls of my 'cabin-cruiser', as one might call it, was an enchanting lithograph by J. Brandard of Miss Farebrother, as *Aladdin* in *The Forty Thieves*, 'the principal boy' of pantomime *in excelsis*, in her Albanian dress with false 'imperial' and mustache. This is one of the most beautiful of the lithographs of the Romantic Ballet, although this lady who later left the stage to become the morganatic wife of the Duke of Cambridge, Commander-in-Chief of the British Army during the half-century between the Crimean and the Boer Wars, perhaps hardly qualifies for inclusion among the great dancers. And on the other walls, lithographs of the Garde Impériale of Napoleon III, all of them, 'to a man', with the waxed moustache and 'imperial' of their master; with more than one lithograph of the Cent-Gardes, the personal bodyguard of the Emperor, in their breastplates, pale blue tunics and plumed helms that were designed by Eugène Lami. And nearby on a bookshelf my two unfolding panoramas, the larger of them well over eight feet long, of the *vivandières* of the Garde Impériale, in female travesty of the lancers, chasseurs, above all zouaves of that transitory and in the end ill-fated phase of the French army.

From all of which, and there could be a good deal more, it should have emerged that the present writer would have had no talents whatever as a decorator. And this although no small share in the little renown he has acquired is for 'writing up' churches and palaces in Southern Italy and Sicily, together with buildings and interiors of extreme fantasy in Southern Germany and in Spain and Portugal. Yet I would prefer to be found to have other and different qualifications than only these. In my time and age, when young, there would have been little point in trying to acquire a literary reputation of original sort by writing of Botticelli; or even of the then – for I am thinking of the early nineteen-twenties – much less admired and loved Piero della Francesca. One aspired to the fame of a writer, and therefore in some sense an artist on his own credentials, and not merely an aesthete and art-historian. Much research was still in progress, then, on the Sienese painters, but it was not enough to devote some years of a lifetime to Sassetta.

It is true that only now within the last year or two has a study appeared on the four great pulpits and other sculptures by Nicola and Andrea Pisano, an omission that it is difficult to account for.* But the work in question is by a writer already well known as author, sculptor and draughtsman, and it is doubtful if a writer, however talented, could now leap into fame on the strength only of a book on Andrea and Nicola Pisano. Such is a rediscovery and a reappraisal but it is hardly an opportunity for writing, and an author must needs find a more sensational theme to write upon. Taste changes, and the time is over when a writer of Ruskin's force and genius could carry the public with him on a protracted tour, wet or fine, of the exterior of Amiens; or along the upper arcade or loggia of the Doge's Palace to examine, one by one, the sculptured capitals of the corner-columns, that under the Adam and Eve at the S.W. angle, 'in the workmanship and grouping of its foliage' etc. 'being on the whole the finest he knows in Europe,' etc., etc. Thus far, and no further, in *The Bible of Amiens* or *The Stones of Venice*. All the work possible upon the capitals having been done by the fifteenth-century Lombard sculptors who carved them, and there being little left for even the fieriest and most convinced eloquence to say. Or is it only that taste has altered, and taken to the plaited palm-frond capitals of San Vitale, or to the marvellous bestiaries of Souillac, Moissac, and Santo Domingo de Silos ? It is that touch of the Orient in the places named that conveys and takes away from the cold limestone of the Northern quarries, even though these be sub-Alpine and within view of the Campanile of St Mark's, and of other and lesser towers of the lagoon.

But Ruskin wrote not really having seen that very much. He never ventured to Southern Italy, probably regarding the Bourbon Kingdom of the Two Sicilies as wicked and pestiferous in the Gladstonian tradition; and where he writes of 'the finest that he knows in Europe', never having set foot in Spain. Had he penetrated as far south as Monreale or Cefalù and seen the mosaics and twelfth-century cloister, or the Cappella Palatina at Palermo with its golden walls and Saracenic ceiling, he might have altered his opinion and changed his views. But he seems to have felt content that he had seen all there was to be seen, and is therefore a guide to be trusted in his convictions but not from his experience. Had he been told the mosques of Cairo with their melon domes and fretted minarets, or those built by Sinan, the Turkish sixteenth-century architect, are as splendid and serious as any buildings of like purpose in mediaeval Europe, we may feel certain he would not have believed it, if only because both architect and worshippers were Muslim and not Christian. It is on the other hand his dogmatic blindness to objects outside his own direct range of vision that makes him fanatical and wonderful as a writer, however obstinate and wrong-headed; though right in heart and feeling.

Our world is not so confined and small as that, nor yet so huge and over-whelming. Ruskin's love of *trecento* Italy and of French cathedrals, but less,

* *Giovanni Pisano,* by Michael Ayrton. Introduction by Henry Moore, OM, London 1971. The pulpits by the Pisano family are at Siena, Pisa and Pistoja.

typically, of Chartres than of Rouen or Amiens, blinded him to anything savouring of Louis Quatorze, worse still the French eighteenth century. Impervious as he was to paintings by Claude – he took exception, it will be remembered, to Claude's rendering of leaves and boughs in his *Liber Veritatis* because of his loose and free handling – we may imagine with what contempt he would have regarded Watteau's *l'Embarquement pour la Cythère*, Fragonard's *l'Escarpolette*, or the room Fragonard painted for Mme du Barry, now in the Frick Collection in New York. The vestiges of *la vieille France* still persisting in Ruskin's day; the fountains and ironwork of the Place Stanislas at Nancy, the little formal park or promenade at Avallon, the clipped trees before a bishop's palace here and there in the provinces, or other traces of the king's garden-choreographer Le Nôtre, he paid no more attention to than we do to the Victorian relics of our great ascendancy that, not without increasing protest, are disappearing every year. Ruskin was single-minded; and in the at the same time bigger and smaller world in which we live – as the scope increases and communication gets quicker still till all the world will be within a night's flight, but more and more of the world becomes politically inaccessible – there is that much the more to take the measure of and try to understand.

One could become a polyglot of the arts of the world in an hour, or even after a few minutes one day a week, in a branch of W. H. Smith & Son in any country town in England. This, because of the proliferation or swarming of illustration, a mathematical increase which is only paralleled in the swarming of the human population. And of course any good gramophone shop fulfils the same function. As to what good this does, that is another question. For it is bad that it should be made too quick and easy. One does not want to be told too much about where one is going before one gets there. It must end, almost certainly, in disappointment. The element of surprise is removed, which is equivalent to some natural deficiency regulated, and therefore no longer missing. One is told, or is beginning to learn for oneself, that food never tastes so good when no longer eating with one's own teeth but using dentures. That is to put it brutally, but it produces the effect of over-illustration.

Speaking for myself, it is not so long ago that I could get to sleep, or stay happily awake, in thinking of and trying to remember in detail the little paintings by Carpaccio in the Scuola degli Schiavoni in Venice which, thanks to my father, I have known and loved since I was ten years old. Now that one can buy for as many shillings, or fifty 'new pence', a booklet with more than a hundred colour plates of nearly every Carpaccio painting in existence, it is not the same thing. To buy postcards when one is there and bring them home that, somehow, is different. But the universal accessibility is soul-destroying and altogether too easy and complacent. What does all this mean to the Venetian family living in poverty next door to the Scuola degli Schiavoni? With a couple of churches round the corner that have paintings by Giovanni Bellini and by Cima da Conegliano that would fetch at least a million pounds in the sale room? It means less than nothing; and only matters to the few hundreds of persons who have seen the paintings of Carpaccio and Bellini.

Or for another device, whether awake or sleeping, a voyage up or down the Grand Canal by gondola, or, quicker and cheaper, by the *vaporetto*? Omitting the rather uninteresting straight stretch of canal after the Rialto, till it curves again about opposite the Palazzo Rezzonico? When it becomes wonderful indeed, and unequalled by street or thoroughfare anywhere in the world, and this said from wider experience than was possessed by Ruskin.

There are scenes and places one would like to be kept in touch with if only because there may not be time to see them again. The roses of February in the Plaza de San Fernando in Seville, seen in the spring of 1925 with friends, three of them dead now, and with so many wonders to look forward to; the Barrio de Santa Cruz, 'a whitewash'd labyrinth of narrow alleys and hidden patios lying in a sempiternal moonlight of its own'; the cathedral of cathedrals with its court of orange trees, and huge iron and copper *reja* or choir-screen of Armada bulk and weight; the old Infanta, one of the daughters of Queen Isabella II, in her box at the bull-fight, immensely popular, 'amid the plaudits of the crowd'; with wonders to come of a first visit to Granada, which is an experience one is unlikely to forget.

So many immortal memories for it is impossible they should die out and be forgotten, they surely must have made their little mark upon the landscape. To lose all this and, as well, every memory of person and of affection in the oblivion to come – unless oblivion like empty space is substantive to the degree, at least, that it has mathematical and theoretical entity – is large part of the bitterness of death. But, of course, it is not so. It all goes. The coming into, or driving out of Florence on the road, always in both senses to Cerbaia. That warm wilderness of cypress and stone pines of almost animal heat after a long hot day, in the valley below Bombici, where it is thought Michelangelo designed the loggia, or was it perhaps the *cortile*? – but the arches of the loggia show but little of his giant hand – and then the landscape opening and unfolding in immensity into the distance with the farms and villages of the Arno valley. And now it is vines and a long yellow villa with Bombici left behind; and the next sensation is that first moment of coming down over the hills and seeing Brunelleschi's dome like a huge red lid or snuffer put over Florence, with no tie-ropes, not likely to have them loosed and lift into the skies – disproportionate – but, now, after many years and nearly a lifetime of familiarity, lying and floating there like the marvellous work of art that it is.

Meanwhile, the monastery of the Certosa is immediately below us on its hill of cypresses, and comes nearer with every turn of the road. As a child, half of the beauty of Florence seemed to lie in its cloister and long, mysterious, underground passages. And the return journey probably late in the evening, never to see again that first view of the tower, and the stone lion and leopard of the ramparts. An experience which at least could be, for it is still physically and visually possible; but not of my mother and father, brother and sister, all once part of it, now dead and gone.

Two wonderful experiences in my life came at long interval apart. In the winter of 1920–21, penetrating for a first time into the architectural deep south and seeing the palaces and churches in Naples, finding therein a theme to write about and, as well, the little world apart of Amalfi and Ravello where five winters from November to March or April were spent, writing, or trying to write, poetry or prose. Always upheld and encouraged – it could be depressing there! The waiters had taken to putting the clocks on by half-an-hour in order to get down earlier to the town, so that we dined every night at seven-o'clock knowing only too well that it was really only half-past six, and there was nothing whatever to do after that! – by the thought of unknown and forgotten works of art, both paintings and buildings, near at hand in that vanished kingdom of The Two Sicilies which, like Burgundy and like Poland, had been a historical entity but had vanished altogether from the present. Writing about that during the next couple of years was like a succession of intoxicating draughts of poetry but taking shape in prose.

And the other and rather similar experience was in arriving in Japan, all but forty years later, in August 1958, where the effect was of a like force and intensity but with another cast, as it were, of dramatis personae, a different company of actors. Only new to oneself, for it had been familiar enough to how many other writers since Commodore Perry reached Japan in 1853! But I do not believe that any one of them can have enjoyed himself more than I did in going there a hundred years later. It was like arriving in Italy or Spain for the first time.

The only comparable and parallel experience would have been in flouting all possibilities of person in order to arrive in Russia while it was still a hermetic kingdom in the middle of the nineteenth century, constantly grumbled at and reviled by its intelligentsia – but would they think it that much the happier, now, after fifty years with the Revolution in full power? – and when it had the greatest novelists there have ever been; promising musical composers; when Petersburg, few of its buildings more than a hundred years old, may have heen architecturally, organically, the most beautiful city in Europe; and the older capital, Moscow, an inspiration of another sort from its golden onion domes, instead of steeples, and those in multitude, as many as nine to a single church, with floreated crosses rising from them, or hung with glittering veils or nets of chainwork – torrid summer nights, fur-clad Muscovite winters. Tartar overtones and undertones and Gypsy bands. Something gone and vanished, too, like that other lost Kingdom of Naples, and only to be attained in the imagination, which I attempted, myself, in the account of a ball at the Winter Palace in St Petersburg, never having been to Russia, but undertaken as a holiday task and published in 1941 in the middle of the war.

In the continuing philosophy of which there is attachment to things or places never achieved, which is different again from those wholly imaginary and that never had existence; as for instance that Mozart and da Ponte as librettist made that other play of Beaumarchais into an opera with result that there are more encounters with Figaro and Count Almaviva, with Susanna and the Countess and Cherubino to look forward to, and those ultimate felicities of music are not at their end but increased and replenished. Or, in the other category, that one had been permitted by some chronological alchemy to see the Trianon de Porcelaine, of blue-and-white pottery, and as though washed in the summer rain; or the main building and twelve pavilions of Marly in full occupance by the Sun King and his train of satellites; or even a safe permit and 'laissez passer' to the *domus aurea* of Nero. Everyone will have his or her preferences in this matter, and it is unnecessary to be dogmatic.

But, necessarily, there is so much one would like to see that one has not seen. And the same with music unheard, and books unread. Never having been to Conques in the Rouergue to visit the eleventh-century church of Sainte-Foy and the statue-reliquary encrusted with gold and jewels in the treasury – though I saw this statue when exhibited in Paris in 1965 – and not likely to get there because my travel routes do not seem to lie that way. This is the trouble, that there are omissions it is difficult to repair now. As indeed with other Romanesque abbeys and churches in many parts of France: Beaulieu (Corrèze) for an instance, and Saint-Benoît-sur-Loire which is near Orléans, and there are many others.

But, more contingent to my purpose, we should have taken the aeroplane to Vilna when in Poland in 1937 for that indeed was an occasion that will not come again; just as, when in Budapest on the way to Roumania in the autumn of that same year, the opportunity should have been taken of going to villages like Baldög or Mezökövesd, but it was neglected because in comparison with Roumania it seemed that Hungary was not so far away but, in comparison, almost near.

The attraction of this pair of villages being their Matyos inhabitants who are different, ethnographically, from the Magyars and probably of Tartar origin. In the last named, the married women wore caps or helmets with a crest of short red ostrich feathers, but more often black feathers to match the blackness of their dresses; which in a curious manner suggested an equine ornament, as though the women, in symbol, were mares. They were, in fact, maned headdresses which could have been taken from the fringe of hair between the ears across a horse's head; while the men wore long white gowns like surplices, with laced sleeves, and shirts thickly embroidered with roses and tulips. An equine civilization of the Hungarian plain, parallel to that of the gauchos of the Argentine pampas; or of the Appaloosa (or 'spotted horse'), the name derived 'from a breed developed by the Nez Percé Indians in the Palouse country of Central Idaho and developed primarily for war uses' – how fine that rings! – or of the Pinto or 'painted horse', 'which was always a favourite with Red Indians for war and ceremonial uses', and known to all readers of stories of the Wild West.

The Matyos, being of distant affinity to the horsemen of the Mongolian Steppe, and to be found in that ethnographical cauldron between the Balkans and the Black Sea! Or I could have gone then without let or hindrance to Sub-Carpathian Russia, inaccessible now, and but another Arcadia of the rich peasants demolished and destroyed. There were villages like Detva, 'with a strong admixture of Balkan blood', whence Brahms and Liszt derived many of their 'Hungarian' tunes; and it is some such place we should have in mind when listening to the furiants or sousedskás of Dvořák.

Plougastel in Brittany is another enclave or entity that I would have loved to see. But it is too late. It is all extinct and gone now, being too near to the naval part of Brest, a few miles across the bay. But as late as the time of Augustus Hare he was able to say of it that 'of all isolated sea-coast populations that of Plougastel is the most curious. Till recently the men all wore Phrygian caps, the women a headdress like that of the goddess Isis; country people call them "Les Galiléens"; and they have always been a colony living apart like Jews, intermarrying with each other and keeping up all old customs. They are said to be emigrants from the Troad.' And Hare quotes from a book, *Autumn in Western France*: 'If the weather is wet – and more rain is said to fall in Finistère than in any other part of France – wait; if you are bored to death in your hotel, put up with it, if your time is limited, relinquish everything else, but on no account omit Plougastel.'

Not only were they a population of fishermen. The whole south side of the promontory of Plougastel was 'almost entirely covered with strawberry gardens, and a *Liqueur des Quatre Fruits* also called *Vin de Plougastel* was obtained from hence'.* There could be some possible doubt as to the shape either of a Phrygian cap or the headdress of the goddess Isis, but Hare gives no further detail than that 'the very beautiful costume of the women of Plougastel has become nearly extinct in the last few years;' yet in a book of costumes drawn from dresses in Breton folk museums, a farmer of Plougastel is dressed in the brightest and most vivid red. Not a fisherman, be it noticed, but a farmer or 'agronome'; why not a strawberry grower? 'Dressed like a red dahlia, in the vermilion of the petal', and belonging to 'that Mongol-Oriental strain which some authorities profess to find among the Bretons' – just as we read, elsewhere, that 'the romantic notion got about during the eighteenth and nineteenth century that the fishing communities along the Portuguese shore, north of Oporto,' – portending Povoa de Varzim and Viana do Castelo, but not Nazaré, therefore – were partly Phoenician mixed with Norman blood.†

At Plougastel, to return there for a moment, all accounts agree that the population seems to have been a race apart, as much so as the inhabitants of the Claddagh which was the fishing quarter of the town of Galway, where the dress of the women – 'a blue mantle, red body gown and petticoat, a handkerchief bound round the head, and legs and feet *au naturel*' – was very peculiar and imparted a singularly foreign aspect to the Galway streets and quays. Now the Claddagh is gone, too, idiotically pulled down from the Irish point of view for it had the largest Erse-speaking population of anywhere in Ireland, and instead of its whitewashed cabins they put up new cottages like those of a Nottinghamshire mining village. The world, in short, grows smaller as it gets bigger, and more ugly when it should be becoming more beautiful.

And here am I, regretting the hundred and one thousand things there will never be time to do or see, or read or hear! The little thing I have in mind at the moment being the street of old houses in the town of Tønder in Denmark, down near the German frontier, and which I feel sure must be the prettiest place in that

---

* *cf.* Augustus Hare, *North Western France (Normandy and Brittany)*, 1895, p. 293.

† *cf. Minho, and North Portugal,* by David Wright and Patrick Swift, London 1968, p. 164, 'The shape of the typical boat of the area is said to be definitely Norman in origin.' Yet many words in their dialect are of Arabic derivation.

kingdom. The houses in its winding streets are all gabled, most of them with bay windows and with painted doors; and particularly fine doors for the houses of the presbyter and the apothecary. At back of them are the cottages of the lace-weavers in a curving street, with every door and every set of windows painted a different colour, and a round-topped rose tree growing beside each set of steps. My informants of a few years ago saw them when the roses were in full flower; 'when the tiled roofs glowed like ripe apricots on a south wall and the long pointed shadows lay on the cobblestones'.*

It is places like Tønder, or its satellite Møgeltønder three miles away, with another winding street 'but this one flanked with an avenue of limes', that make one despair of the future. They create a world or cosmogony of their own where, in spite of modern clothes, telephones, motor-cars, bicycles, and so forth, the reality of life in a small painted town in a Fra Angelico picture or a fresco by Benozzo Gozzoli is achieved, and without artiness or affectation. It becomes almost painful to think of, in comparison with the faceless hideosity of Piccadilly Circus, the hub of Empire, or, now, Commonwealth, but it had better go back to being the centre of England which has been as beautiful and wonderful as any country in the world. Yet what chance has it in that welter of ugliness, where even the hidden mid-Victorian interior of the Criterion Theatre down so many flights of stairs speaks as with delegated authority from the theatrical and Italian past. It is a reminder, slight as that is, of what has been and what could well be once more when, if ever, some kind of grammar and discipline were restored to visual life. The past lingered and was left behind, where theatre interiors were concerned, all through the last century, till the surviving fragments of old music-halls have now the solid authority of tradition.

But there is danger in being caught up and delayed by detail. Typical of this is the wild strawberry plant that Ruskin spent so much of his time in copying when he should have been engaged on bigger, more important projects. It is in the foreground of Cima's altar painting in the Madonna dell' Orto, but Ruskin was thoroughly scatterbrained by then, and he was probably as happily and usefully employed there as on any of his other schemes. Impossible not to think of him in the Venetian church he loved so dearly. With the mental blight that was to fall upon him in the not distant future; and not to remember in the same breath Tosca and Cavaradossi in the Roman church of the Madonna della Valle, and *Recondita Armonia* when Cavaradossi looks from his unfinished Madonna and compares it with the miniature of Tosca; which music, yet, is unlike any Roman morning or evening and in its spring-like beauty more suggestive of treading the wild violets on the wooded slopes of Soracte or the Ciminian Forest. It is sung in a church upon the stage, and stays immortally Italian, with all and everything of which the lack and absence turned the brain of Ruskin.

It is perhaps a pathetic sign to see oneself as worked to the death on plans and projects that are of no use to anybody. As to have written as many books as I have written, and all of them really and truly for my own pleasure with no other end in view. As long, though, as some little of it seeps through and simmers

* My informants were John and Fanny Cradock, of *Bon Viveur* fame.

a while, to set someone thinking. For that, and little more than that has been its purpose. Conceived and written in pleasure for pleasure in reading. But of which there are many categories from gay to serious with all the tones and undertones in between. As of voices of the past in contrast to the sirens and hooters and klaxon horns of today. Ancestral voices, not prophesying war but postulating peace, if human beings will but know their limitations, and as well, the marvels that have been and which are still within their grasp. It is indeed world without end in the comprehension and understanding of its wonders, that could last not for one, but for a hundred lifetimes. There need never be a dull moment, though there are times of despairing rage and pity.

II · PROSPECT OF VENICE

This time I have promised to write about what I really like myself, and about the surroundings I would want to live in. Having spent my childhood and youth, for I discount my schooldays, in either of two places. In the big dilapidated old house with the garden my father made, and with a mining village at the park gates; or in the town on the North Sea coast where I was born. But mostly of course at school. For nearly three-quarters of every year from five years old and upwards; and all of it, all of it a waste of time. But where else to be sent, or go? For I could not be kept at home.

Owing much to my father for his intelligence and for his interesting mind, which have been cruelly derided, with no one to speak up for him and protect his memory. And grateful to him for loving me, as did my mother at that age – but above all for taking me to Italy during the Easter holidays so that I remember not only Florence and Venice, but Lucca and Bologna from eight or nine years old. And having a sister and a brother whom I loved and revered, but whom, in the light of later happenings, perhaps I loved more than they loved me.

That was childhood, and then the First World War. And immediately it was over, indeed before that during 1917 and 1918, to meeting with painters and writers. Marrying four or five years later, which lasting happiness of our own may have broken, or snapped, or strained the strings of family attachment. But it gave me my liberty, it made my own life, and let me work in peace. And now, long after, with many illusions formed, and many, but not nearly as many, broken or dispelled – to work upon what was promised in my first sentence.

And to say that there is decidedly such a thing as therapeutic architecture, as I believe all will have experienced who have stood in Brunelleschi's Cappella Pazzi at Florence. And it is the same therapeutic feeling in a fine example of a Palladian villa, the best of which display the frugal magnificence of the Venetians at its greatest. The therapeutics are alive and at work in the architectural proportion. It is this that lifts the heart and mind. All is mathematically ordered and controlled as in the fugal music of the masters, and even the immortal Johann Sebastian Bach did not succeed at every attempt into the ordered universe of sound. He failed; and it moves and rotates in dullness, now and then. The architecture of Palladio, which is much less adventurous, even aims at dullness, and makes a virtue of that in its nature cure. For the proportions have the properties of a diet sheet. You start to get well at sight of it, feel better every day; and depart with appetite restored, and longing for excess again. There is even this feeling after only a few minutes inside San Giorgio Maggiore, coming out onto the limestone quay even in the rain, with all of Venice just opposite across the waves. It is beautiful indeed, but it is not all that we would have it be. Why are there no giant statues in the water? But of that later, after another look around.

The façade of San Giorgio Maggiore, only a few feet at back of where we are standing, is disappointing but, then, it is not by Palladio but from a later hand. Dull, too, for the matter of that, is the façade of the Redentore in its unrivalled opportunity, alone on the island of the Giudecca with nothing to compete with it. And this is by Palladio but, none the less, it fails. It is his villas that are his *forte*, not his façades of churches. His frigid architectural good manners excluded any excess whether of welcome or expectation. He does not come forward to greet you, and even appears indifferent as to whether you push open the door for yourself and step inside. The water sites of both San Giorgio and of the Redentore are unique and inimitable. But the best use has not been made of them; and I suppose (not having been there) that a like opportunity only offered itself, and was perhaps better fulfilled, in the classical buildings along the water front and canal quays of St Petersburg. But the light of the Baltic and the Neva cannot be of the same quality as that of Venice; though it may have been true that 'no city presented a more singular spectacle in winter with its main thoroughfare covered with sledges rapidly and noiselessly drawn over the snow'; for which here substitute the black shadow of a gondola with masked occupants and pair of rowers, one in front and one behind, gliding as on secret orders quietly and swiftly along the Grand Canal; or the lazy slow plash of the oar and corner-cry of 'aoè!' along the *piccoli canali* or side canals of Venice from the lone gondolier.

The conchological triumphs of the dome of the Madonna della Salute, and the marvels of the Molo and of the Piazzetta, are Venice fulfilled. Not least with the pair of granite columns 'from Syria or Constantinople', erected here in 1180, bearing the Winged Lion of St Mark, and, for no such clear reason, St Theodore upon a crocodile. They have the look of the ancient world of Antiquity and of the Orient, against the arcades and Gothic balconies of the Doge's Palace, against the 'howdah' domes of St Mark's, and the statued skyline and colonnaded front of Sansovino's Libreria Vecchia or Old Library. All of which only raises the same query, prompted again by that pair of statue-bearing columns and by the classical imagery of Sansovino's masterpiece. Why are there no statues rising from the water?

Because one may feel that Jacopo Sansovino (1486–1570), to judge from his pair of colossal statues of Mars and Neptune at head of the Scala dei Giganti, or Giant's Stair, leading into the Doge's Palace, would have been more than equal to the opportunity. This must be the grandest entrance into any palace in the world in midst of that unforgettable ensemble of architecture, with those leaden domes of St Mark's in the background telling of that greater Orient upon the Golden Horn, and foreshadowing all of Muscovite history and that pretence of being the Third Rome; and little wonder the Doges of the seventeenth century were crowned on the highest landing of that stair. The statues of Mars and Neptune are worthy of their place at top of the steps, and it is only a pity Sansovino was not entrusted to put statues in the water.

In the glorious Bacino di San Marco, that open stretch of water in front of all this splendour across to San Giorgio and the Giudecca – with the halberd-prow of a gondola showing here and there against the architecture or the green water for insignia of the city as in Canaletto's paintings – and spreading eventually through the lagoon into the open Adriatic. Which reach of water is deep enough to take big vessels, but it must be shallow enough in places just off shore, by the point of the Dogana, and at the mouth of the Grand Canal, which down all its length has an average depth of seventeen or eighteen feet, no more. It would not have been difficult to put down the stone pedestals for statues, and we will take leave of this last chance there will ever be again.*

Such is Venice, the most interesting and fascinating city of the human world but, returning to my theme, I am not enamoured of the interiors of Venetian 'palaces', having spent too much of my youth in midst of crumbling, dusty and decrepit Italian furniture. The water-steps of Venetian houses are ever a delight, but not so the grand staircase and *piano nobile*. It is the water sounds and the view from the windows that are the beauty of Venice, and the paintings. Those apart, and with too much of Tintoretto, even the Venetian *settecento* is a disappointment. I am thinking of the heavy and hideous *stucchi*, and of the ill-painted, flimsy furniture.

But at the time I have in mind the paintings of Magnasco were almost a personal discovery, and one quickly acted upon for with my brother I was founder and instigator of the Magnasco Society in 1922, which held major exhibitions of Italian *seicento* and *settecento* paintings on three successive years at Messrs Agnew's Gallery in Bond Street. Paintings by Canaletto from the Royal Collection and from Castle Howard were on view to the public for the first time and, naturally, Magnasco himself was well represented. His best paintings are probably the interiors of a Synagogue and of a Quaker Meeting House, which pair belonged to the Venetian painter Italico Brass. These two, and the pair of paintings of monks in the refectory and warming themselves at the *calefactorium* from the picture gallery at Belluno. In the course of ages I have come to like his typical landscapes less than his early Gypsy-banditti-charlatan subjects carousing in cellars, which are more than a little reminiscent of the *Harold en Italie* of Berlioz. But it was a delight in those days to have Magnasco as almost a personal possession, as, too, the portraits by Vittore Ghislandi, or 'Fra Galgario', of Bergamo.

The life and vitality of decaying Italy, with little exception, was in Piedmont and in Apulia. In and around Turin, where great architects Guarini and Juvarra and Vittone were at work; and down in the heel of Italy at Lecce, and in a dozen or a score of little towns near by. But, as well, in the megalopolis of Italy, the only

* Recalling in a footnote the account of someone who escaped from Spain during the Civil War through Barcelona, and in the light of dawn saw the giant statues of Karl Marx and Lenin set up in its squares.

town to come down from Antiquity with a large population – Naples, the Parthenopaean city upon the Siren Bay – where there were good painters and fair architects, and which was the capital of music in its day.

Of the same period in Bavaria, and thereabouts, it would be a stony heart that did not warm to the glissandi, the virtuoso handcrossings, the flourishes and fanfares, to apply musical terms to them, of their stuccomeisters, Johann Baptist Zimmermann foremost, but there must be a dozen or a score of others little inferior to him – or that does not find welcome awaiting him in the gaiety and fresh colours, whether in the rose-pink ceiling of the Court Chapel at Bayreuth;* the abbatial guest rooms in their enchanting colour changes at Wilhering upon the Danube; or in so many more places we may leave happily to the imagination where there may be tiled stoves and pretty ceilings in the bedrooms and espaliered apricot trees in the garden. Not to have seen such things is to have missed experiences just as beautiful in their way as uncomfortable old Italian villas, or the inhospitable châteaux of the Loire. Perhaps the only counterpart to the delights just touched on being Danish houses of the eighteenth century such as Wedellsborg or Waldemar Slot; or the palace of Queluz in Portugal, all colour-washed pale pink outside, with a room of *azulejo* wall panels of palm trees and Negroes and Chinamen, in blue on a yellow ground, and a garden canal floored with blue-and-white tile panels of ships in full sail.

Having no desire, myself, for huge oil paintings of whatever school, and genuinely preferring to see them in churches or picture galleries. Disliking the medium of oil-paint in the first place, and fresco being impracticable in this age and day. Were paintings positively forced upon me I would only take or accept oddities, such as small pictures by Otto Marcellis van Schrieck, called Snuffalaer, a Dutchman born at Amsterdam in 1613, who in the rhythmical prose of Fuseli in his *Dictionary of Painters* 'acquired considerable celebrity by his excellence in a very singular branch of art. He painted reptiles, insects, and curious plants, which he designed with surprising fidelity, and finished with extraordinary care.' Drawings or small paintings by Fuseli himself I would much like to possess. And particularly pictures by him in his sinister vein, like the small painting shown at an exhibition in London some years ago of a little supernatural being, female inhabitant or visitant from Elfhame, standing in a room in strange hallucinatory fashion, leaning or slanting slightly forward with no clue whatever to the title or subject. One felt one must watch her and wait for her next move. It can only have been the recapture of one of Fuseli's induced dreams, but it almost made one turn, on leaving, and look back over one's shoulder. Paintings of ancestors in wigs which are not good paintings are acceptable; and they make one regret the ancestral portraits in country homes in Poland, where the men had shaved heads and huge moustachios the ends of which, according to Mickiewicz in his *Pan*

* The one-aisled chapel at Bayreuth has a ceiling painted rose-pink with white figures. It is by Pedrozzi, probably a stuccoist from the Ticino, and it provokes a gasp of pleasure. He, also, worked in the castle of Rudolfstadt, whither, 'in the handsome suite of Rococo rooms' – but it is in East Prussia – he should be worth following, and in Potsdam. This is to pursue the career of one itinerant stuccoist, a minor art now entirely lost and gone.

Tadeusʒ, they twirled with the fingers of one hand when dancing or rather pro-
cessing in stately fashion in the mazurka, while the other hand rested on the hilt of
a curved scimitar, which, also, often appears in their portraits.

It could be in the main the grossly exaggerated prices of paintings that makes
the possession of them less a pleasure than a pain. I have seen more than enough
of the French Impressionists to last a lifetime; though pictures by Manet – about
the only painter not to have been put on view in a huge exhibition, but one who
could fill the big rooms at Burlington House as did Goya a few years back – and
paintings or pastels by Degas are an unfailing revelation. Having been the
former owner of four marvellous, half-length pencil portraits by Ingres, drawn in
1815 during his Roman period, I can understand the remark of Degas to an
English lady who brought a miraculous pencil portrait by Ingres of a mother and
daughter, relations of hers, to Degas' studio to show to him: 'Je deviens comme
un tigre; mais je respecte les traditions de famille.'*

Were they not so insanely valuable, and therefore impossible to insure, one
would like to own portrait drawings by Ingres, preferably those with Roman
details in the background, these are the most precious of all; sepias by Giambattista
Tiepolo of turban'd Orientals and of groups of Pulcinellos; drawings of the
'classical period' of Picasso which must exist in dozens: with designs for theatrical
scenery by the Bibienas; drawings by Richard Dadd, and Spanish or Egyptian
drawings by J. F. Lewis; and the originals, if such still exist, for music hall song
covers by Alfred Concanen.

And then there is the problem of the actual scene. Where is it to be? Because
in spite of a collector's more than a gardener's love of florists' flowers – having
some working knowledge of the illustrations, at least, in old flower books – I
am notably lacking in the gift of 'green fingers'. But, as well, my enthusiasm
coupled with ignorance has been extended to include semi-tropical and tropical
flowers and flowering trees. And in the result the English flowers as they grow in
Anne Hathaway's cottage at Shottery are no longer enough for me. Nor, though
I have not seen them, the camellias and rhododendrons of Cornwall and the West
of Scotland; and although the rhododendrons may grow there better and to greater
perfection than in their native Burma or Western China. I would sooner the tulips
of the 'Tulip Reign'; and would wish to have seen the auricula theatres of the
monks of Tournai. But such in the past have been my stock-in-trade; or, at least,
a part of it, and one lacks the courage and the energy to set it all down again.

Where it is a question of wild flowers one would like to be in Jordan, or in the
Lebanon or in Iran, when the paradoxa and oncocyclus irises are in flower, not
encamped or on safari, but if it could be managed that, like peasants in their
'Sunday best', all the irises could show up in full costume on fixed and pre-
arranged days. In this manner it might be possible to see the true Biblical 'lilies-
of-the-field' in their splendour. The misty and wild mountain gorges of the Shan
States as described by Kingdon Ward have no appeal for me. But wild tulips,
narcissi, peonies, are another matter, as on the morning in Rhodes when we went
up into the forest of Monte Sant'Elia, as it was called by the Italians but it will

* This drawing by Ingres is now in the Fogg Library at Boston, USA.

have got back its Greek name long ago, where many stags were wandering and the wood was full of huge white peonies. And they grew, too, near to a forest of cedar trees in Morocco, which leads on to the subject of the *villes blanches* of the Moors – the white, white houses of Barbary and Salee, alleys paling as we walk in them, and Cordovan courts and patios of the Barrio de la Judería, which it is not altogether incorrect to term white alleys of the Sephardim. Doubtless, in its ramifications from the Aegean to the Atlantic this is an architectural style not to be mistaken or misunderstood; and pertaining to the felicitous range of dwellings that do not require, that even repel the hanging of pictures upon their walls. The scale is completely and entirely suited to modern living where what are to be desired, food and drink apart, are a lot of books to read and a good gramophone – and damn the golf links and the tennis courts! It is those that have spoiled the islands of the Caribbean.

III   RED RAKU TEA BOWL

But the time has come to say where I would sooner be. At the moment. And it is not where the oncocyclus and paradoxa iris grow. Nor yet the wild narcissi.

It is farther afield.

Opening on the sea, that is the first impression, with the sea but a few feet away. Some fishing boats not far out, perhaps half-a-mile away, their bare masts showing silent and busy above the shoals. And where they are just right to give the distance, two more ships, each with a huge sail, of which you almost feel the pull and hear the noise. An island far off in one corner, and the full moon over it with a reef of cloud across the moonface. Nothing else out there except the surf, the sand edge and some boughs of a bamboo.

And suddenly, it must be round seven o'clock in the evening, the moonlight 'turns on' and the moon itself is lifting, climbing, and in a very few moments it will alter. The lamps will be lit. It will be an ordinary evening, but at the moment in the moonlight it is transcendental.

This is not exactly a room for it has no walls, but it has a wooden ceiling of good carpenter's work, at that, with the tie-beams in nice perspective. The wooden floor space set out in rectangles which are units of measurement, and in fact for straw mats to cover, but this is summer. Only four wooden posts of neat carpenter's work to support the ceiling. No walls, as said before, and all open to the evening.

A room easy to escape from in the event of fire or earthquake.

An open stage, and in the wings to one side the open room of the next-door house, but quite far away, with two or three persons leaning on the wooden rail, the roof of a shed below, and some indeterminate boughs intervening. And in the wing opposite a far-off promontory noticed now for the first time, and still more distant sails on the horizon; the paper panes of a house with a woman's shadow behind them, and more neat carpenters' work on which they must set much pride, on joists and ceiling.

Nothing at all in the way of furniture, if you except three or four standing lamps of plain design, and a large dwarfed cedar or cryptomeria in a huge bowl planted with other flowers, chrysanthemums, I am afraid! on a wooden stand. Nothing at all by way of furniture, and for the moment neither radio nor gramophone.

The scene is in fact *Moonlight Revelry at the Dozo Sagami,** presumably one of the 'green mansions', a painting at the Freer Gallery of Art at Washington, DC, attributed to Utamaro. I have often thought this to be an ideal civilization for the poet or artist, so long as one can bear an age that moved at the pace of a bullock-cart at two miles an hour. It is an alien world, but free of the clutter and rubbish that surround ourselves.

We have to go back into another currency of time in order to understand this. In my home, which is a not large seventeenth-century manor house in a village still, mercifully, three miles from anywhere, there are lacquer cabinets belonging to a Suffolk family called Barnardiston, that came here by inheritance in 1773. I have often thought of the journey these and other objects must have had all the way from Brightwell in Suffolk where that family lived, and carried here surely in a farm-waggon at that same two miles an hour. It will have taken a week, at least, or longer in bad weather; and here am I bored and disappointed, when some longed-for book or gramophone record takes a long time in arriving. There must be exquisite sensations of peace and harmony that we are missing, and of a relenting, languishing of time as of that summer afternoon in *Madame Bovary* when nothing at all happens and only a bumble-bee bumps against the window-pane.

The *Moonlight Revelry* in the painting, if it be by Utamaro, which one might guess is doubtful, is of decorous kind. There are ladies in marvellously patterned kimono, and servitors carrying in what look to be cups of *saké*. I have thought this to be an ideal culture for the poet or artist to live in for purely personal reasons, because, impossible as would be the physical transformation which is as unlikely as that I should find myself an active member of a colony of flamingos, none the less if there must be aesthetes, and I have never sought their company, this would seem to me to be the nearest to the ideal. It had been certainly for some eight centuries, as readers of *The Tale of Genji* will appreciate, the most aesthetic civilization there has ever been. Had one been born to it I do not think one would have got it upon one's nerves.

But, if spectacle there must be and there is none in the neighbourhood of Piccadilly Circus, one cannot get out of one's mind what must have been even at the end and decadence of their aestheticism a Flower Festival among the 'green mansions'.† This dazzling procession of inconceivable patternings of kimono under fruit trees in full blossom is something so different in idea and principle

---

* Reproduced in *The Traditional Arts of Japan*, by H. Batterson Boger, London 1964, colour plate 8.

† A so called 'gouache painting' of *The Flower Festival at the Yoshiwara* was on exhibition in a gallery in Paris and is reproduced in colour as endpapers for *The World in Colour: Japan*, edited by Doré Ogrizek, London 1957. Again, the attribution to Utamaro may be uncertain, but the patterns of kimono are marvellous in their profusion.

from the beautiful blonde models sitting on the bonnets of cars, or aboard small yachts and motor-boats in the *Daily Express* sponsored exhibition at Earls Court, that they personify two civilizations as far removed from contact with each other as they could possibly be. The birds of paradise are not more distantly related to the sparrows of Trafalgar Square, or humming-birds to the 'broilers' of the chicken farms. Nothing, nothing whatever is to be transmuted from the one, except perhaps a film contract, irrespective of acting talent and taking regard only of physical appearance, while in the other there are the last shoots or suckers of a whole and entire civilization. The Flower Festival is the lowest ebb of the one, while the height of the other is 'Miss Europe', or whatever, in a beauty competition. 'Hot pants', or the like, are not really 'in the running' where it is a question of aesthetics. Thus, while not wholly disapproving of the one, for present purposes I prefer the other.

There are enough persons now who take trouble to write a good hand for there to be a growing appreciation of calligraphy, though it could never possibly reach the proportions it attained in the Orient. But it can be the start and beginning of aesthetic feeling. And it would be perfectly feasible to be interested in that as an art form, and in nothing else. Into the minutiae of this kind of thing the Japanese entered with an energy that has no parallel elsewhere. What other race, not content with their 'lobster scale' armour would make even their arrow heads into minor works of art? These were produced generally by swordsmiths; but a swordsmith to the tyrant Hideyoshi (d. 1578) was nearly as famous for his arrowheads as for his sword blades. They have pierced and saw-cut patterns of herons and reeds, or, even, unbelievably, of sages in a landscape playing the game of *go*. There were even 'whistling' or 'sounding' arrows which served as signals and frightened the horses of the enemy.

It is no surprise therefore to find that one of their most renowned artists Hon-ami Koetsu (1558-1637) was the adopted son of a priest of the sixth generation of a family of famous swordsmiths, who came of a noted line of priest abbots who had been in charge of the swords of the Ashikaga Shoguns . . . 'They were hereditary sword sharpeners; and the families' profession was the judgment on, sharpening of, preservation and wiping of, swords of which they had accumulated hereditary experience and secret knowledge.'* Against this background it is not astonishing that Koetsu was a famous calligrapher, renowned, also, for his paintings, for his lacquer, and for his pottery; but principally for his calligraphy and for his Raku tea bowls. His fame is in respect of these, and for his friendship and association with the great painter Sotatsu: paintings by whom often bear inscriptions in Koetsu's hand. The great pair of six-fold screens in gold and colours from the *Genji Monogatari* by Sotatsu establish him as the greatest of the decorative painters of Japan.† And the pair of screens of the rocks and waves of Matsushima, in the Freer Gallery of Art, confirm this judgment.

It is in the contrast between the six-fold golden screens – though, again, they are but gold on paper – and the rustic and philosophic simplicity preached by the

* Quoted from *Japanese Pottery*, by Soame Jenyns, London 1971, p. 279.
† In the Seikado Collection in Tokyo.

tea-masters that lies the fascination of their strange, strange aesthetic,* some points of which are almost impossible for a Western mind to appreciate or understand. And it is as though a complicated ceremonial and ritual with its appropriate style in tent and pavilion building, arms and armour – above all, poetry, behaviour at meals, style of dancing, and most things imaginable, had grown up around the tournaments and jousting of our Middle Ages. And of everything in aesthetics which it is difficult to assimilate, probably the most abstruse of all is the adoration of the aesthetes in Japan for their Raku tea bowls. Many of these may seem, to us Occidentals, merely shapeless and ugly; or, as an Italian Jesuit who witnessed the tea-ceremony in 1575 said of their tea bowls: 'We would not know what to do with them in Europe except to put them in a song bird's cage as a drinking vessel.'

Had, then, the highest ideals ever in aesthetics, as present in the person of Hon-ami Koetsu, degenerated into nonsense? He was by now (1615) living on land at Takagamine, outside Kyoto, given him by Ieyasu the tyrant-successor to Hideyoshi – 'where the river is not large but enough for a boatride to Kyoto ... and whence the little hills in the city itself are like those of a miniature garden'† – an artists' colony with fifty-seven houses in it, 'devoted to paper-making', an aesthetic luxury in itself, and the manufacture of paint brushes and lacquers. Of all the products of which, as is to be expected of an artists' colony, practically nothing at all is left, and one might guess that idle talking was the main occupation. Has there ever been an artist's colony of which it was otherwise? The American settlers at San Miguel de Allende in Mexico – and this is typical of so many other similar places – are artists of some sort or other to a man or woman, but it all amounts to very little in the end. More comes out of one household where there is not too much conversation. That there was incessant chatter at Takagamine we may be certain, combined with sand pictures, 'an unusual means of decorative expression which is said to have originated with Koetsu', making use of five different grades or colours of sand which were sieved and combed and pushed about on lacquer trays, with pebbles or stones added, to make landscapes and other scenes.‡ A lot of time will have been spent upon study of *chanoyu* (the tea ceremony), and Koetsu is said to have made cast iron tea kettles and, as well, *No* masks, *netsuke*, *inro*, incense boxes and bamboo vases. But he was supreme as calligrapher and potter, and as friend and catalyst, one might think, to the great Sotatsu.

* Senno Rikyu (1521–1591) and Kobori Enshu (1579–1647) were two of the most famous of the tea-masters. Both men were, also, garden architects within the tenets of their creed. The sentence, *passim*, from the Italian Jesuit, Alessandro Vagliano, is quoted from *They came to Japan*, by Michael Cooper, S. J., London 1965, p. 261.

† Quoted from *Kenzan and his tradition*, by Bernard Leach, 1966, p. 48.

‡ To which I would add a footnote in order to recall the 'sand artists' of my childhood who 'drew' pictures upon the Scarborough sands, portraits of Lord Roberts, Queen Victoria, and even local celebrities; and with a foot as well as a hand in use, or even a pair of feet. It had possibilities for caricature, as well; and all was erased by the next tide. One may guess that Hokusai, certainly, if not Koetsu, would have taken up the challenge to 'draw upon the sands'.

In Koetsu, therefore, we have an artist of the keenest and highest suscepti-
bilities, and to whom there is no parallel one can think of in the Occidental
world. He had lived, also, in his contacts with the court of Hideyoshi and of his
successor Ieyasu, in surroundings of the greatest sartorial and sumptuary
splendour that Japan has ever aspired to, but which indeed many of their scholars
look upon as vulgar and ostentatious. It had however reached to refinements in
glory to which again it is difficult to find an Occidental parallel; and as a spectacle
it must have been beautiful beyond the imagining. Mr Bernard Leach says of
Koetsu, 'He was almost as varied in gifts and skills as Leonardo da Vinci, with
whom it would have been more appropriate to compare him than with Benvenuto
Cellini as has been done.' But, in truth, neither comparison is very apt and the
background of neither artist is in the least comparable to that of Koetsu, in whom
the extreme niceties of largely inherited or transmitted skills come to their climax.
The swordsmith side of his descent, alone, resembles the annals of racehorse
breeding. There are specimens enough of his calligraphy, and two or three pieces
of his lacquer are extant, but his main fame is from his tea bowls.

It must now be explained that there have been no fewer than ten generations of
the Raku family of potters, the last of whom Raku xiv is living today in Kyoto,
though several of these may have been pupils who were adopted members of the
family. It was Chojiro Raku I (1516–92) who worked under the tea-master Senno
Rikyu to the extent that it is supposed every piece made by him was examined
individually by Rikyu, and named by him during his lifetime. After the death of
Chojiro, the tyrant Hideyoshi gave his son a gold seal with the character Raku
on it, meaning enjoyment of freedom; hence the family name. It is the tea bowls
of Chojiro I which the Japanese value and admire inordinately; but perhaps
because Koetsu was other things besides merely a most skilled potter, it is easier
for Occidentals to try to appreciate the bowls of Koetsu.

His bowls, too, are in the Raku style which, as I have said elsewhere in this
book 'are mainly black, while others are rufous, or turkey-wattle red; with black
treacle lip; or splashed with white as from an eagle's droppings'. And I added that
'when properly understood they become works of art'. But it is, in fact, exceed-
ingly difficult for Occidentals not brought up to it, to do this. Koetsu had been a
pupil of Donyu Raku III: of whom admirers wrote that 'his glazing had the
brightness of fireflies' and that his reds, for which he was famous, 'were like red
clouds'.* This was but mild praise compared to the ecstasies accorded to Chojiro
Raku I. In these it would perhaps be too difficult to participate sincerely, but with
the bowls by Koetsu it is different; and one may feel certain in one's mind that Mr
Soame Jenyns is only speaking the truth when he writes that 'once seen they are
not likely to be forgotten', and that 'consciously or unconsciously, in their
incurving lips and irregular profiles they have the shape of some full-blown tulip
or wilting poppy bloom'. But, unhappily, it is the 'once seen' that is the difficulty,
for they are, indeed, generally speaking, inaccessible. That is to say, they are in

---

* And his black, 'smooth and bright like the wing of a black beetle'. *Japanese Pottery*, by
Soame Jenyns, London 1971, p. 255. This is the only and indispensable work upon its
subject, and a mine of erudition.

private collections, are no more than fifteen or eighteen in number, and of inestimable value, if ever considerations of money came even near to them, being rated and considered as national treasures.

It has been difficult indeed to form any considered opinion of these esoteric objects, if only because of the lack of good illustration. And that in the practical impossibility of seeing such objects with one's own eyes. But this has been to some extent remedied with the fine coloured plate of a red Raku tea bowl by Koetsu in Mr Soame Jenyns' book, though he has this to say of the *Fujisan*, Koetsu's most famous tea bowl. 'It is very rarely exhibited in public and it would be a very great honour to have it shown to you privately by Count Sakai' (its owner). And he continues: 'On the occasion of the exhibition in Tokyo *Japanese Pottery and Porcelain through the Ages* in 1958, it was illustrated in the Catalogue but much to my disappointment failed to make an appearance, although I had been assured it would be on show on the day on which the Japanese Emperor and Empress visited the exhibition. So I have never seen it.'

It is the *Otogozen* (moon-faced woman) by Hon-ami Koetsu which forms the subject of colour plate 2 in Mr Soame Jenyns' book, and it features as only number thirteen in the eighteen in all tea bowls by Koetsu which are in existence. And this Mr Jenyns was 'able to handle' at the aforesaid exhibition in 1958. It has, it is true, the shape of a moon face with the wide curve of outline admired in the past in Japan centuries before the plebeian Ukiyo-ye, and which would go with shaved eyebrows, and, to Occidentals, the oddly blackened teeth. Yes! One can see that it has a resemblance to a moon-shaped face. And this affinity with the 'full blown tulip or wilting poppy'. But, indeed, the more you look at it, the more it grows upon one because of its perfectly unique colour and substance. And texture, could one but touch it with one's fingers; more still as it is a tea bowl, lift it to one's lips. Feel the weight of it, too, for that is no less important.

It is entirely ageless in appearance, and at moments, only probably of human origin and the work of human hands. Anybody who has seen puff-balls (mushrooms) blowing about in a field, and one of them coming, tumbling and spinning over the grass, puzzling and unrecognizable for the first moment will see the likeness. And it rolls to your feet, and you put a foot on it and it disintegrates in a little puff of dust. And this could be the bowl and rim of it, and how easily it could topple over on its back! And you could take another look at it and kick it away!

For it does not balance properly. It would topple over and upset very easily. And then the rim, which it seems has been 'repaired with lacquer', is very uneven; almost as if it had been licked or nibbled by a cow mistaking it for rock salt. Very popular with cows and has been left out in the field for nights on end. And found where it has rolled down into a corner near the brook. But the colour, the texture and the fragility are what are extraordinary. A colour of red not found on any other human artifact and that has not the remotest connection with red lacquer. But neither is it as sharp as red cinnamon which is more of a brownish-red. And it would now seem not unlikely that it is of volcanic origin, baked at some inconceivably high temperature, and then spewed out or regurgitated upon earth. At which event it should not be unique, but there must be hundreds of them. And why not at once look for more of them all over the field? No. Because they are too fragile and all the rest will have perished. This is the only one of its kind. But can its colour have been arrived at by accident for we know Koetsu was an amateur, and not a professional potter? Did it just happen, or did he contrive it? Perhaps like the puff-ball it was but one out of many hundreds! But there are Koetsu's inherited and trained skills to consider, and it could happen to him and not to other potters. And he would be the first to take advantage of it.

It changes as you look at it and now becomes an atomic poppy cloud. Lifting, and yet caught and held there. Emerging out of a temperature of how many thousands of degrees which is almost that of the sun! And in fact an extra-terrestrial object plunged down like a meteorite, and coming from outer space. Cloud-like, and could expand and tower up into red cumulus, or blow away. In any case unlikely to keep its shape for long, which is what makes it so entirely and utterly unique. With that rounded moon-face outline which would be admired on a young girl, and that soon goes. But not in this hue and colour. There was never 'Red Indian' of the tepees of the plains, or of the Cliff Palace, the ledge or crevice town of the Mesa Verde in Colorado, of this colour. This is something quite unknown there. Or anywhere else.

The tea bowl, now that we can come back to it as a tea bowl, appears to have a vitreous glaze on it which would scratch or flake with the fingernails. And that would be to take some hundreds or even thousands of pounds off its value? Or even enhance its value for that is possible, too? It has certain decided cracks, three, or perhaps four in number, from top to bottom, but none the less it is an object of beauty and immense value of which there are only a dozen or so others, all by the same hand and by one intent upon rare and unobtrusive skills. He has put all his personality into it without stating anything whatever beyond the plain truth, which is at the same time simple and as abstruse as it could possibly be.

And now the tea bowl is becoming not a gold cup or a silver cup but a blood cup; a sacred object transformed from the butcher's or the knacker's yard, of congealed substance and corresponding colour, and yet of cirrhus-like insubstantiality. In their land of origin such objects were esteemed for their softness of touch to drink from, as well as for qualities which it is near to impossible for an Occidental to understand. Comfortable, too, to hold in the hand in spite of the astronomical sum imperilled in the chance of dropping it. Now looking to be of ripe persimmon colour, this being a fruit as common to them as our pear or apple. With a worn or nibbled rim; and except that it is bigger, no more interesting than an old conker picked up from underneath the chestnut tree. So that, as with their ideals in personal bravery, and with their extreme creative inventions in religious philosophy and in aesthetics, it is all or nothing. Which is to equate the tea bowls of Kenzan and Koetsu with the conundrum arguments of Zen, and with Ryuan-ji, the Kyoto 'dry landscape' garden of fifteen stones and raked sand. And looking at it once more it alters under our eyes from an old conker into a persimmon skin or rind, blossoms into an atomic radiance and could even seem to be in prophecy of the discoveries and disasters of our time.

The Garnering of the Cornstooks

It is time now for the garnering of the cornstooks in hope of having escaped the heavy rains. A latish harvest in mid-August when the first blackberries are in the hedges, and if you listen you can hear the combine-harvester at work not far away. Impossible not to think of it mowing down the poppies in that far corner many miles or even leagues away along the cornfield. And as this is written, it may have passed them and they lie dead or dying.

Ah! if only August were the fourth or fifth, and not the eighth month, which is irrevocable, and before long will be beyond recall. But there is a dual scale or measurement for everything. Alike with the sand in the hourglass, and with the Swiss clock that needs no winding but takes its motion from the variations of temperature within the room. So that it, too, is subject to something and not its own master. In the same way it was a lifetime walking along the margin of the cornfield, and yet no longer in time than it took to pick the stalk of wheat or barley you were holding in your hand. One stalk perhaps out of a million, and all of them identical yet individual, and just alike. 'You', incidentally, being not 'you', but 'me'; though we are all as alike, but different, as those myriads of wheatears. And 'we', that is 'I' give 'you' back yourself again.

We began with death – with the deathbed of a housefly – and, would end with the living. How else? There is too much that is interesting to be depressed and sad. What does it matter if the sand is running out? Only in the individual hourglass, of content, all things considered, of a grain of sand. There are plenty more and it could be the same again; which is mathematically possible for there are recurring numbers – of unknown significance; but it is unlikely. That is the beauty of it. So look again in the looking glass, it is our only chance.

It has been a 'toss-up' whether your skin was yellow like silk, or black like anthracite. And little to do with your parents: it is something more remote than that. Not a mere shaking of the grains or particles. There must surely have been a scheme of some sort? Can it be the same deity you pray to who helped you win the football pool? He must have his hands full. And of course if there is good luck there is bad luck, too. In which event who distributes the disasters? Perhaps the business has been disposed of and is in other hands? That part of it, at least. Or the receiver has taken it over. In any event, if there is the one there is the other, which makes two. Once there is one, it has begun. If there are no numbers there is no existence.

The secret could well be in the flow of numbers. They have order; and unlike the computer, once started they admit of no mistake. Human beings are not infallible; but in abstract mathematics, free from human or mechanical interference, a mistake is physically impossible. But enough of numbers, of which there is – or was – a beginning and no end. It is no use to number the wheatears, so we will think of other things.*

Of the cornstooks and the harvest for those are conceivable in human terms. Which could amount to a few poems, or rather more than that of prose. And it would be enough, more than enough, were that so. But in only one language, and there are many hundreds. Painters, architects, musicians, all arts and craftsmen have that advantage. Except writers, and then only the best and the very worst, in translation. The writer or poet owing to language difficulties is lodged, as it were, in a separate wing with no dining-room – it entails crossing the road for meals – and even unsatisfactory washing arrangements and inadequate 'toilet facilities'. So that, indeed, one might prefer . . . But there is no choice in the matter. What has to be, has to be. Che sara, sara!

Neither is the company so agreeable as all that. One would prefer almost any category of artist, but musicians most of all for they have been polite and kind. Fellow writers, no! But there is no escaping them. And they have brought their pens with them; or whatever is the equivalent now that pens, pen-nibs, blotting-paper, even ink is extinct and no longer on the market. What emblem, then, for the portrait or statue of a writer or poet? His typewriter, or telephone; or his Muse, female or deviationist, it is all the same. Where does the Dark Lady of the Sonnets lie buried? How beautiful it is that no one knows! Or has dared prise open the tomb at Stratford-on-Avon that may have his pen in the dust beside his bones!

A welcoming word – if the juxtaposition to our last sentence be forgiven, and who is there to grant that? – from Ronald Firbank of butterfly talent and moth-like flutter, or a greetings card from Percy Wyndham Lewis? I think not. Nor yet a message from Eliot, on whom more books have been written than on any poet who has ever lived. But Eliot's poetry is quarried for other minerals than poetry by other persons than poets, and has become a scrabble-board. Still less, a word from the 'father-figure' Ezra Pound, most sillily so called. But they were

---

* The composer Anton Bruckner (1824–96), according to one of his pupils, suffered at a period in his life from deep depression, 'fixed ideas', and a 'counting mania'. He tells how, whilst out walking, Bruckner would stop to count the leaves on a tree. Subsequently, he seems to have benefited from a 'cold water cure' at Bad Kreutzen. Bruckner had also 'an obsessional urge' to count windows, weathercocks, church crosses, dots, buttons, and so forth; and an 'unhealthy interest' in corpses. With regard to the former, in a letter to his biographer: 'Excuse me, one more request: I'd so very much like to know the material from which the two pointed finials above the cupola of the municipal towers . . . are made. Next to the cupola is (a) the pommel then (b) the weathercock with ornament, isn't it? Many thanks in advance. Please write it all down.' And with regard to the latter mania: 'I'd give anything in the world to see the body of Maximilian,' who was his 'pet'. 'Even during my illness this was the only thing that was dear to my heart: it was Mexico, Maximilian . . . Please inform me kindly by telegram, so that I may not come too late.' And when attending the exhumation of the mortal remains of Beethoven, Bruckner lost a glass out of his pince-nez in his morbid curiosity. Details garnered from the article on *Bruckner* by Ralph W. Wood in *The Music Masters*, A Pelican Book, 1958, and from *Bruckner and Mahler* by A. F. Redlich in the *Master Musicians Series*, London 1955, pp. 30–31.

not the only poets. There were Wilfred Owen and Dylan Thomas. Why not indulge one's fantasy as none of it can happen? And enlarge the circle?

Why is there no dictionary of poets, as there are dictionaries of painters and musicians? It is because the poetry, or much the larger part of it, is untranslatable. The poems of Mallarmé just do not transfer from the language in which they were written into another, and at the hands of Roger Fry are in their own patois of near-gibberish, though Mallarmé's *Un Coup de Dés* could defy the top precision worker. All who have attempted Baudelaire have made fools of themselves, and it is decidedly not fair to judge of Pushkin in translation. He reads, one might think, like a poor translation of Lord Byron into Russian.

There are poets of whom it is not possible to get the taste or form an opinion unless one knows the language. Luis de Góngora among them, whom one would love dearly to be able to appreciate and understand. Perhaps he is as 'difficult', and as dead to other aesthetics than his own, as the Red Raku tea bowl of a few pages ago. But it is agreeable to think he came from Córdoba, and was a friend of El Greco, by whom there is his portrait. Góngora is mellifluous and high flown, it is evident; and one wants more of poetry than that it should be a dry, hard-shelled acrostic.

There are those, too, one would want to read about without reading them; Torquato Tasso (1544–95) perhaps first among them all because of his plangently romantic and strange career. He was born at Sorrento on the Bay of Naples, and his poems had been the sensation of civilized Europe when he was little more than twenty years old, and living at the court of the d'Estes at Ferrara. But, when only about twenty-five, the strain of his nerves from overwork and probably an unhappy love affair brought on a nervous and mental collapse. The legend is that Tasso was in love with Duke Alfonso's sister, the Princess Lucrezia, which prince and princess with another sister, Leonora, were grandchildren to Lucrezia, sister to Cesare Borgia. It is unnecessary to add that this 'attachment' of Tasso seems to have had a poetical foundation only. But so have many other 'attachments'. Certainly their letters to each other breathe of something more than mere friendship.

But, at least, Tasso was not imprisoned by Duke Alfonso because of it, and probably his detention at the castle of Belriguardo was an act of kindness. The occasion of it was when he was reciting his sorrows one day to Lucrezia, and imagining that a servant was listening rushed upon him, knife in hand. After which he was removed under armed guard and taken, later, to a Capuchin convent. When, after some years, he eventually left Ferrara, it was as a wanderer from court to court over Italy, being received everywhere with the respect due to his genius – whatever that may mean! – but aggravated in his mental condition by being treated by his hosts with a sort of 'amused kindness'. He came, at last, to his sister Cornelia Tasso's house at Sorrento, his birthplace, disguised as a shepherd, and died a year or two later at Rome. At the end of which recital it is interesting to recall that the late Edward J. Dent, the Mozart scholar and friend of Ferruccio Busoni, had the repute perhaps romantically magnified in his honour, of being the only living Englishman who had read through Tasso's *Gerusalemme Liberata*.

Further than that, if the first strophes of Tasso's poem are no longer on the lips of the Venetian gondoliers*

Canto l'armi pietose e'l Capitano
Che'l gran Sepolcro liberò di Cristo

as Liszt heard them and made note of them, the poem is at least in the repertory of the marionette or puppet theatre of Palermo and appears, if now spasmodically, upon the painted carts that rattle about the town.

Tasso is in the category of those poets who will remain more of a legend than a reality. And who will become more so still as time goes on. He is in the same kindly limbo of oblivion as the madrigalist Orlando di Lasso (1532–94) to whom the similarity in name will condone the mention. But Camoens, by contrast to Torquato Tasso, is easier of access or approach. It is possible to spell out lines from his *Lusiad*, word by word, with pleasure; and his poetry read out aloud in the Portuguese is a wonder and delight to listen to. Spanish or Portuguese poetry is to be preferred in all ignorance to the more liquid Italian which is made for music and better suited for singing than mere speaking. But, opposed to social realism in all its forms and wherever it lifts its hydra head, and – were that possible! – absolved from its bonds or shackles by the hard work put into all the unnecessary books I have written, I would like to have been a poet of the *Pléiade* in the time of the Valois kings of France. This, if only because of a youthful affection for the poems of Ronsard and du Bellay, and in modesty, as the phrase goes, not 'aiming at the stars'. This although – poetry apart, and the sculptures of Jean Goujon, the bookbindings and typography of the day given their due – it was an ugly age. It is evident in old houses in the Marais, in towns like Bourges and in the French châteaux. It was an ugly age from the time of François Premier to the reign of Henri Quatre, in all, from 1515 to 1610. But it was a *printemps*, a *primavera* of poets, like the later Elizabethan years, or, unromantically, the reign of James the First. And there is not a hope in hell of there ever being that again It is too late now, and the accent is on other things. It is an awful thought that poetry could end with Eliot and Pound. And it is not to be believed for a moment, any more than it is true that Joyce's *Ulysses* was the novel to end all novels.

What could have been the horn of Herne the Hunter was the siren on Walls Ice Cream van! This, on a foggy late autumn afternoon in 1943 or 1944 when one thought the War would go on for ever. The second World War in a lifetime, and then in its fifth or sixth year. One was ready to think or believe in almost anything, such was the hopelessness and the atrophy of ideas. Walking in the shrubbery or 'wilderness' which has been the launching theme or motif of other pages in this present book – with the dead raindrops still on the yew boughs, fog in their high branches and the path all sodden with beechmast and dead, wet leaves.

---

* Professor Dent could also understand the Venetian dialect and had read the, on occasion, blackmailing letters about their daughters addressed to Lord Byron by the Venetian gondoliers. As postscript to which footnote, on a recent visit to Palermo, where formerly dozens, if not scores of painted carts were to be seen, no more than two, in sorry state, were met with (March 1972).

The first part of the 'wilderness' traversed, and walking by the stream which was in spate and running with a lively noise of waters. More and more dead leaves and twigs upon the wet ground, and the ashes of a dead bonfire.

Here the wood has another character; elms and horse-chestnuts, haunts of the woodpecker where it taps and hammers, or flies across with mocking laughter. But not a sound now, this winter day. All is sodden and noiseless below the leafless trees. There are splendid oak trees at the far end of the field. One of them, which must be hundreds of years old, standing in a world of its own above a cattle pond. And I was thinking of summer in the country here, of the mornings and of the August, the slumbrous Augustan afternoons; but, now it was the dark, stark winter day when, suddenly, there was that horn, and another – or the same one? – not far off. It was entirely magical for the moment, and one only wondered what would happen now. Windsor Great Park, sacred to Falstaff and to Mistress Quickly, and the hanging woods of Marlow are in the next county, not a long day's ride even on a winter's day through the meadows and the beech-woods of Buckinghamshire, and I have to admit that for a moment I wondered and wondered! But in a second or two, like all transitory visions it had vanished. This was no

appel de chasseurs perdus dans les grands bois

it was, just simply, the siren voice on Walls Ice Cream van. This story should be a warning to all sensitive persons who feel they are on the verge of a great discovery; and it applies to nations or races as much as it does to persons. The student on the opposite side of the world who thinks he sees the future in concrete music, or in non-paintings, is not more mistaken and deluded than I was when I thought I heard the horn of Herne the Hunter.

In extenuating circumstances, that is true, for it was a mad time to be alive in. No madder than it is now, but more violent, if in fact less dangerous potentially. For now, to put it crudely, the whole place could go up with a bang. We are told that this is why, quite certainly, it will not happen. And as an argument that is not at all convincing. But, yet, it could be so, though it seems unlikely. But what a moment it has been, from time to time! And what a moment it still could very well be! But will it? It is a question, to so large a degree of mathematics. Not merely of mere numerals, as though it is a matter of number of beds or of seating accommodation; but, also, it is a question of human and natural proportion.

It may be, or is the modern Babylon, but it is this that has gone wrong with midtown, New York. The anthill is too tall for the ants who work in it, and if they possibly can they live outside it. And at the same time more of them keep pouring in. But, also, in our cities the point has been reached when large sections of the population, whether they like it or not, are sent down to live in the country, in inevitably ugly new towns. But, at least, the new towns have not the sheer vertical horror of New York which we have done our best to ape in London, where there is no reason or excuse for it. The towers of flats that shake against the sunset as you come into London, and that are grouped, haphazard, here and there on the horizon, spill out their inhabitants into the country, where they will be unhappier still for they are unused to it. So that all in the big towns is confusion and discontent, muddle and pollution. There are nightmares in which they become the scene of urban guerrilla warfare street by street; and doubtless not a few persons are already at work upon the text books, which will not lack for readers. In desperation, it cannot be a difficult art to learn. And it is easier to dislike and hate your neighbour than to hate the Vietcong or Vietnamese.

It seems hopeless to say how quiet and beautiful are the white-painted wooden houses and the portico'd churches with their wooden spires. For all that is in the past. And it is like being shown a photograph of your grandmother as a young girl when you are in love, yourself. It is no help at all and only an appeal to sentiment. But such is the past of little towns in New England; of Henry James's *The Europeans*. Or even, with pollution just beginning, of the characters in *Madison Square* and *The Bostonians*. Now those towns are congeries of glass towers that empty themselves at evening and are empty at night. The liftmen and dustmen, the motor mechanics and electric power workers, and the airport personnel, have a stranglehold upon them. The grand objective being to bring things to a standstill, with a 'stop-go' attitude about continuing with it at all. For who wants it? Everyone is sick and tired of it. Of course the polyglot population has some connection with this. The inhabitants of the modern Babylon are not Babylonians for nothing. And it is no use wishing yourself back in a village of 'magpie' houses with windowboxes in the Black Forest, in a cubical white house above the wine-blue sea, or where ever has taken your fancy, because it is not the truth of things. That is no longer the world as it is today. Oh! to be the voice from the Command Module and be listened to with attention. In default of which one must live for each morning which is a recurring miracle and wonder, and go on writing for one's own pleasure in the hope that it may please others.

The most important of all projects in aesthetics is to restore the 'media' and this does not mean the newspapers. The invention of the camera a hundred and more years ago made the painting of visual truth an unnecessary trouble and labour, though it took painters some half-century to realize this. And the discovery, needless to say, was almost coincidental with the ultra-realism of our minor pre-Raphaelites. Illusory realism has perhaps never been carried further than in John Brett's *The Stonebreaker*, or in his *Vale of Aosta*, which latter picture was painted, quite literally, with Ruskin standing over and bullying him. So much so that Brett never worked again in this minute manner, and would not undertake the painting of some old Alpine village in a Swiss valley, or in the Tyrol, that Ruskin had suggested.

In his *Academy Notes* for 1859 Ruskin has this to say of *The Stonebreakers*, a picture which has Box Hill in the background: 'In some points of precision it goes beyond anything that the pre-Raphaelites have done yet. I know no such thistle-down, no such chalk and elm trees, no such natural pieces of far away cloud, in any of their work.' Then, for the nonce, more critically; 'the tone of the whole is a little too much as if some of the chalk of the flints had been mixed with all the colours.' . . . 'For all that, it is a marvellous picture, and may be examined inch by inch with delight; though nearly the last stone I should have thought of anyone's sitting down to paint would have been a chalk flint. If he can still make so much of that, what will Mr Brett not make of mica, slate, and gneiss! If he can paint so lovely a distance from the Surrey Downs and railway-traversed dales what would he not make of the chestnut groves of the Val d'Aosta! I heartily wish him good-speed and long exile!' But John Brett, as we have seen, thought otherwise. He painted the Val d'Aosta; but would have no more of it, and declined to let Ruskin make him into a geological, or even a mineralogical painter. And indeed in its way *The Stonebreaker* too, is a beautiful and strange painting with its heap of flint stones, so miraculously rendered. Having said which, it could be left to Andy Warhol to 'manage' the identical mini-skulls in a gas-mantle!

Other painters seemed to have a presentiment that the camera was coming to defeat them. In the 'townscapes' for instance of the 'brick painter' Jan van der Heyden (1637–1712), 'who painted walls and masonry with minute skill', indeed, brick by brick, his renderings of street scenes in Amsterdam or Haarlem being so microscopic in detail that in the result they are not the visual truth at all. The best pair of eyes could not assimilate that number of bricks from any viewpoint in the picture. Could it have been the effect of a ghostly or spiritual Ruskin at his side urging him on to ever closer detail, that in the end deflected van der Heyden from painting bricks 'so that they could be counted', and made him devote his energies to designing fire-engines and street lighting, from which dual theme he made a book of engravings and died a rich man.

The labour-in-vain of the painter becomes more painful the nearer that time approaches to the invention of photography. It is apparent in Ingres, though not foreshadowed in his early and miraculous pencil portraits nor in paintings like his *Madame Rivière*, of 1805 (in the Louvre). But when it comes to marvels such as his Madame d'Haussonville (of the Frick Collection), of the pale blue dress standing with her back to the mirror; to the *Baronne James de Rothschild* (1844–8); to Princess de Broglie (1853); and to his masterpiece Madame de Moitessier (in the National Gallery, London), posed, finger to head, in the attitude of a classical god,* on which Ingres was at work, intermittently, for twelve years (1844–56), there can be no more question about it. Ingres was aware of the coloured daguerreotype; and all of these portraits with their marvellous and meaningful accessories of tassels, cushions, fringed table covers, opera-glasses, pieces of Sèvres, visiting cards, bracelets, bangles, objects worn in the hair, are subservient to their fate. Which is, that after so many months of altering the pose, painting out one accessory and painting in another, changing the whole conception and then changing it back again, and so forth – were the subject for the portrait posed for a few minutes before the camera in the painter's final and last conception, the daguerreotype would be the portrait, finished and complete. Twelve years' work in those few minutes! But not a work of art. Or a gramo-phone record would be no different from a live performance, to which it is at the

---

* Her pose is that of *Hercules finding his son Telephos in Arcadia*, a wall painting from Herculaneum in the museum at Naples. This was a favourite antique of Ingres's *cf.* *Ingres: Peintre de la vie Moderne*, by Sir Kenneth Clark, in *Apollo* for May 1971.

same time a close facsimile. But it is only one sort of truth that the camera under-takes, and there are so many others. The camera is immediately responsive. But it cannot think and it cannot imagine.

Yet an instantaneous colour photograph of great beauty could have been taken from life of *Madame Moitessier*, whereas it would not be possible to simu-late in photography Titian's painting of *Diana and Actaeon*. That is to say, you could photograph the picture itself, but not the arranged theme or subject. No *tableau vivant* could reproduce the effect of the painted figures against the painted landscape, which is where genius defeats the machine. But at the same time it has to be said that the early photograph of Balzac is a masterpiece. Of art, or of *verismo*? Nadar's camera portraits of Baudelaire, of Berlioz, and others besides, are masterpieces – but of photography. And the not long-discovered daguerreo-type of Chopin, taken in the last months of his life and showing the ravages of his disease and his depression, could not have been surpassed by many months or even years of studio painting. It is both astonishing and touching as a human document.

But in the general acceleration during the last two or three decades, all, and indeed everything in the arts, has been by-passed and overtaken. Colour films by their excellence now deprive the painter of most of his abilities except his skill in drawing, which the camera cannot emulate. It is a large part of his labour gone. So why regret it? This is not a reduction, but an extended repertory for the painter. And it is for the writer or poet to inspire and stimulate him.

In so many of the arts it is the want of theme that is the shortcoming. In opera it is the need for finding a good libretto. What torments must Rossini and Donizetti have endured who were bound by contract to produce perhaps three or four operas a year! And what a difference when a good subject has been found and a librettist is at work who knows his business! The music, then, to some large extent depended on the plot, and on the situations and the characters. In default of which the composer was in the place of a doctor longing to set to work but without patients. And therefore in a sense paralysed. When properly supplied with what he needed by da Ponte, the characters project themselves and live within the music and there is no mistaking an air or an ensemble from *Figaro* for one from *Don Giovanni*. How exhausting were the lives of those composers, but, at least, they had an immediacy of success and their failures or half-failures were soon forgotten! Yet just the Köchel index of Mozart's works* or the list of Rossini's operas appals a little. Compared to which the solitary life of a writer

---

* From the January of 1785, when was his twenty-ninth birthday, to the April of the following year, when he completed *The Marriage of Figaro*, Mozart wrote, as well, the one-act opera *The Impresario*, four operatic scenas, two to be inserted in Francesco Bianchi's comic opera *La Villanella rapita* and two for an amateur performance of *Idomeneo*; the cantata *Davidde penitente;* four masonic pieces, including another cantata and the Funeral Music, K477; no fewer than five piano concertos, K466, 467, 482, 488, 491; two of the 'Haydn' string quartets, K464, 465, and the G-minor piano quartet, K478; the C-minor piano fantasy, K475, the D-major rondo for piano, K485, and the E-flat violin sonata, K481, as well as several songs, including his beautiful setting of Goethe's poem, *Das Veilchen.*

may seem idyllic, and I would not have it different for all the world, though long stretches of it have been so quiet that you could hear a pin drop. And drop it has! If only once a year, and there are sixty seconds in a minute. Only a few more seconds, no more than a handful, and it will be nearing the number of years that I have been at work. Which is the reason for saying that it is time now for the garnering of the cornstooks, and in fact the noises of harvesting blow in through the window while I am writing. How much longer it must have been when the reapers were at work with their scythes from the dawn of the summer day, as attempted in the opening pages of *The Green Children*! And in Pieter Bruegel's beautiful and inspiring painting of *The Corn Harvest*. But it has been my endeavour to give it the East Anglian air, within sound, were that possible, of the bells of St Edmund's, and whether I have succeeded in this it is not for me to say.

Here it is different, where have been years of devoted happiness. And the harvest, within the limits of the home or even of a room, is of another order. Which has not prevented the sounds of the outer world from coming in, though limited today to the noises of the combine-harvester and of an aeroplane or two passing overhead. A 'middling' harvest, not much more than that, considering what might have been; and of course neither writer nor farmer is ever satisfied. What is it they want? But this is too obvious to need discussion. We will leave it at that. Like most other individuals, they want more and better. A longer time to live; and in the case of the writer more and more to fill the mind. Of which, never, never can there be too much. Or, indeed, enough. And one could be dying and still wanting more.

Having had a determination to get the knowledge, even if it be useless, and not continue in ignorance. My motto having been pleasure and not improvement, and the aim aesthetic enjoyment and not religious or philosophic instruction. And the purpose, to do my best to give pleasure and inspiration. What I would appreciate above all would be to know I had interested painters and musicians. To which end a very extensive field has been surveyed and explored, much of it superficially or even in hypothesis. But always with the same object, which is no less and little different from that of gathering honey from the flowers. The garnering of the cornstooks, the *vendemmia* or grape harvest, the storing of the hive – they are all alike. It is the gathered richness, and it has its uses. In all three instances it is not the product, itself, in the first stage but what is made of it; the bread, the wine, the honey. It is these that give the sustenance, and do not support life but make life worth living. So that they appear to be the luxuries but are, none the less, necessities. And in the civilized world, if it continues and is not extinguished, they will be the pleasure and the recreation. But with the deeper meaning that it is the human spirit or ethos reborn or made over again, knowing it is god-like of possibilities and that if it keeps its wisdom there is little that it cannot do. From exploring the stars to limiting its own increase, with diseases conquered, and much else besides; but not the unconquerable which are old age and death.

CODA
'I return you now to the studio'

More often it is 'I' who return 'you' to the studio. But, at times, in mock modesty, it is 'we' who return 'you'. Yet who am 'I'? And who are 'we'? And who are 'you'?

'One' is asking this question before the words are out of that mouth, thereby adding a fourth dimension to the mystery. For 'you' – I mean 'one' – is 'oneself' from first consciousness for as long as 'one' can be certain of anything.

Already the persons, first, second, third and fourth are taking over, or changing their identities. Really it is 'you' who are returning 'us' to the studio, and not 'we' 'you'. Who, then, are the 'we' who have become 'you'? And what is intended by the studio?

It was a voice of authority to judge from its sound and tone. No note of indecision in it. And now what happens? What is the next move?

By 'return you now' 'he' seems to mean moving 'you' or 'us' without 'our' permission, even against 'our' will. It is sterner, more peremptory than the 'pass along there, please' of the policeman to the crowd. It intends 'you' are coming along to the studio, willy-nilly, whether 'you' want to, or not.

And if 'you' don't like it, then, in schoolboy language, 'you can just switch it off'. Or worse. It is preposterous.

By 'you' he means 'us', the whole lot of 'us', perhaps twenty or twenty-five millions of 'us', all waiting to hear the nine o'clock news. 'He' is taking too much to 'himself'. We have only to turn a knob. 'We' need not go, nor listen, but can keep on with 'our' own lives.

If 'we' leave it on we have to go with 'him'. But only so long as 'we' don't touch or interfere with 'it' in any way. And go where? Into the earth? Or back again into 'our' mother's womb? 'My' mother died in 1937. 'I' want to keep 'my' identity, and certainly do not want to go back into 'anyone' else's mother's womb. Or does 'it' merge somewhere, somehow, and run back into the human race? With never a separate individuality again. Or never 'our' own, in any case? Whichever way 'one' looks at 'it' the prospect is uninviting. Unless 'one' can learn to regard 'it' as some kind of absurd and ridiculous ball game.

And it seems to 'me' that 'his' or 'their' views are somewhat slanted. Why should it be assumed that 'we' all share the same opinions? I am beginning to regard it impersonally as though it doesn't really matter to me, and I don't care. If I took it all *au pied de la lettre*, I would have been shut up and looked after long ago. For it is as bad as that, or even worse. It is hammering, or, rather, shouting away at one all day long and far into the night. Reminding us of one of those clocks that have a second, as well as a minute hand, so that life is slipping away visibly each time you look up at it, or listen. And no one in his or her senses is going to have an electric clock of that sort in the bedroom, ticking and ticking away the whole time.

What is going on ? Which channel are we on ? Perhaps there will be music, or a joke or two for early risers an hour or more before the sun rises. Are the astronauts, O'Leary, Sweeney, Mitrovitz, still in their sleep period ? But we can confuse their names so easily at this time of the morning with those of the footballers with numbers on their backs. 'Over to Riley'. Or just a stentorian roll call as they move forward: 'Bullen'. Or 'Now, Castro'! And then a wild burst of cheering, and cat-calls, rattles and tin whistles, for we are back in 'Blighty'. How easy it would be if only the affairs of the world could be settled in this way! And why not ? Would it be so different in the end ?

But this is more exciting. It is so much faster. It is ice-hockey. And like a game played in another element, they move so quickly. And the curious, crouching, shaman-goalkeeper. Masked, visored, bent nearly double, hands on knees, as though guarding the flap into the tent or tepee. Huge, and small at the same time, as if with painted war face, but minus the bear's claws or eagle's quills. And a big attack is coming from every way at once, and he crouches lower still. Threatening, and hitting out with his harlequin-bat, in full war paint. And it is a wonder, not killed. And it surges back and slides on again.

There are advertisements all round the ice-rink as though it, too, is padded or wearing armour. In reminder of the magic word Cinzano, already mentioned, on the tin-hoarding at Posilippo to mark the site of Virgil's tomb. Gin and 'it' for the 'eye-ties', as though they have been celebrating ever since for twenty centuries! Do I not remember the bicycle race all over Italy, day and night, to celebrate the six-hundredth anniversary of the death of Dante in 1921, and how difficult it was to get a wink of sleep? This was in Parma, but I was more interested at that moment in Paganini and in the painter Cima da Conegliano.*

How beautiful and quiet are his altarpieces in San Giovanni in Bragora and in the Madonna del Orto in Venice! And this is written never yet having seen the painting in the cathedral at his native town which he so often painted in the background on its little hill. How pleasing to read that 'several of the houses have painted façades', and that 'Conegliano is noted for its wine'! At about the time of the bicycle race it is given as having 4,600 inhabitants, but the latest figure quoted is 29,582, as though to include the last-born pair of twins! On this evidence it is easy to prophesy there will never be such peace and quiet again. It is probable, too, that this is in accord with the wish of the overwhelming majority of the population, which has quintupled in size, as is the case in nearly every town in

---

* Two beautiful little paintings by Cima of 'pagan' subjects, one of *Endymion* and the other of *Midas deciding between Apollo and Pan*, are in the gallery at Parma.

Italy. Twentieth-century Italians are out to get all the noise they can, and if disappointed of it they will just 'up' and move on somewhere else. That is the point of big towns like Naples and Milan. How they love the noise in the latter city – built just at the time that in England we were building seaside piers – but not even Milan airport can compete with Milan railway station for real distraction from sheer noise. And what a nightmare the crowded trains! With those coming from long distance, starting from Hamburg or Bremen, so full that it is impossible to get along the corridors, and with the lavatories 'occupied' in permanence by persons who have stood all night long and want just to be able to sit down and rest, without regard to the possible consequences for other passengers in a train that seems to stop at every station between Milan and Venice. But, then, it is old fashioned indeed to go by train at all. You either fly or hitchhike; or whirl along the autostrada in between those two extremes.

How antediluvian it seems now to have moved stage by stage, from Milan to Bergamo, then Brescia, Verona, Vicenza, Padua, staying a night or two in all five towns to see the churches and palaces and look at the paintings, and so onto Venice! And to have done this, not once or twice, but perhaps half-a-dozen times, or more.

And to have spent a whole night in an uncomfortable railway compartment between Florence and Venice, over and over again through all the tunnels in the Apennines; and the same between Rome and Naples with no breakfast but early morning view of the palace of Caserta from the window. And how the train dawdled on the way, for it was a journey of not more than a hundred and twenty miles at most! And now Venice to Florence, or Rome to Naples, is three or four hours along the motor-road.

But all the cities named are swarming. Towns like Brescia, or Verona, even Vicenza, the town of Palladio, have about quintupled their population. So there are four or five times more Italians, whose soil was once the most fertile in genius for the arts; but is so no longer. Neither has the talent spread conspicuously elsewhere, but it could be said the fields lie fallow everywhere. The talent has gone in other directions, that is all – into science, or medicine, or engineering – and if it is wanted enough it will come back surely. And will likely return without being noticed in the same way that recovery from illness can be a sudden recognition that the symptoms have disappeared. There is all the evidence that it was thought nothing remarkable in its time, was even taken for granted and as expected that the arts should flourish, which is proof of a healthy economy, at least from the writer's hedonistic point of view, who is not interested in a Socialist Britain, or anywhere else for that matter, but only in the arts of human beings and in the wonders of which the human brain and human hands are capable.

It is not therefore the average which is the interest, but the exceptional, which is indeed the point and reason for these pages. If only the human millions all over the world were paper millions as with the votes cast at the Labour Party Conference, now to be called, simply, 'Conference', like 'Congress', or 'British Rail', or 'Transport House': from which it becomes somewhat of an intoxication to turn to the past and the future, leaving out the present which at the moment could be pronounced 'showery', without the 'bright intervals' or 'bright spells' of the weather forecaster. A single word or a name can suffice and be enough for recovery. How lucky, at least, the Italians have been in their personal names, as for instance in their respective kinds of painting. Raffaelle, or Michelangelo, or Leonardo, or Palladio for his particular kind of architecture, or for a great soldier and iconoclast, Napoleone, in all of which examples the name suggests the character. Or is this merely fanciful? But it does seem to have weighted their personalities in a particular direction, and they had these names long before they became famous. In which context, but with no further connotation, one can but quote the names Marco-Antonio, Aspreno, Ascanio of the Roman family of Colonna, and conjecture what a help to them these names should, or may have been during the Middle Ages. If this is not so, then a good title for a book or play means nothing, and the fact that the family in question produced no outstanding genius is no argument at least against making full use of the name. On the other hand, Keats being called John Keats, no more, no less, is as significant, and there need be no more than that upon his passport in this world or into the next.

At the mere mention of the names of certain human beings it is as though the skies clear and the world changes. There was an emptiness before them, and they leave a void behind them. In the same breath it may be no happiness to think of them in their own lives, but only in their lifework. This may seem but a frail raft to ride the stormy waters, but what else is there to hold to? We have no saints to intercede for us. They have lost their efficacy if they ever had any, and the work is being done for us as their legends are dismantled one by one. The common-sense point of view has come late and can only too easily dispel any magic there is left.

There are other shades more substantial to pin our hopes upon. Statesmen and politicians have failed us, that is the universal feeling. There must be a new litany with other names to pray to, and a creed in which saintliness has no part to play. Of what use has been holiness? Human beings have wonderful and incredible achievements to their credit, to the extent and degree that no other god is needed. He is already here in the human race, if of fleeting appearance and transient of form.

There have been more than mere sparks or flashes of the divine being. The whole of creation indeed is too extraordinary for us to understand. Above all, how could it be possible in a single lifetime which is all the time we have? It is as though the truth is concealed on purpose in a determination it should not be found. On whose part, and on whose orders? That is the mystery. The wonders of the morning and the evening are more than just the turning on and turning off of a lamp. And always punctually, if not at the same hour, but in obedience to an ascertainable law and timetable, and never so much as the fraction of a second late. So that it is mathematical truth or certainty, which could be called the only and abiding truth that nothing can gainsay, and which is another thing altogether from poetical truth.

The beauties and terrors of nature, of the natural world, are the mathematical truth which must be predictable from its own premises, a premise being rather more than 'a proposition from which an inference is drawn'. Or it could not have developed and have happened; while the arts of mankind are the poetical truth which is unpredictable, illogical, does not act in obedience to any laws but is entirely arbitrary, and to a degree irresponsible. The one works to strict formulas, however far-fetched and improbable its fantasies, while the other follows no genetic laws, or, at least, none that are understood so far – which is probably a blessing – but is haphazard and for the most part unexpected, both of occurrence and in the forms it takes.

Birth and death apart, and illness, we are hardly any more a part of nature. The Papuan native who has thrown away his crown or tiara of bird-of-paradise feathers and wears instead a Coca-Cola bottle, or a pair of Coca-Cola bottles in his frizzy hair is, by that alone, no nearer nature than a railway ticket-inspector, or than a dog in a dog-collar. Or it could be said that the only touch of nature in a block of offices is the office cold, until it comes to procreation and its preliminaries and aftermaths, when we are no different from the London sparrows, or from the toad that has made a nest for its family in a bed of lilies-of-the-valley. Or, in fact, we are allowed out on a long lead and then drawn back again.

Nothing will ever be done to alter that, but only to delay it for a little. The laws are irremediable and irrevocable. It has to happen, and only because of that there is a continuity. Otherwise it would never alter but always be the same, and permanence is a contradiction of all the natural laws. Even the sun and stars grow older while we look at them. Not appreciably, of course, any more than they, themselves, have the slightest idea or intimation of our existence. If we benefit from them in any way it is accidental; or is that a part of some large design? If this be so, it is a plan that gets thwarted in the sense that the 'benevolent' view of nature has its awkward questions to answer, as for example, the many races in nature that prey upon another. Human beings included, for what else are we but carnivores? Lambs and calves are born in milky innocence, unaware that something akin to the 'final solution' awaits them in the slaughter-house. They know no more of the fate in store for them than the flies of summer are warned of the returning swallows who will take them on the wing. In nature all seems prepared and made ready for the wicked with no precautions whatever taken on behalf of the innocent and harmless. But, also, individual human beings have been, and are, evil and reprehensible, and quite obviously there is no controlling power with the slightest authority over our propensities. The 'flower children' will never inherit the earth. They will always be shaken off and killed. Innocence is synonymous with danger to the innocent, and only by energy can the asperities of the world be softened. It is the catalysts of good and evil who produce this energy and share it out with others or usurp it for themselves.

My object has been to celebrate the glories of being animate and living. It happens once, and only once, and never again. Just as it can only happen to one once to be young and considered a young person of talent. This happened to me when I was nineteen or twenty, and the younger brother of my sister and brother. I have never forgotten that, and have always tried to prove myself, and to remember the birds sing not in fear, but in pleasure and wonder; and, also, perhaps, in awe. For there is much that is inexplicable and is accountable to no form of reason. Why the tiger, the mosquito, the hyena? Except for the tiger's beauty. Or the shark, the crocodile, the stinging-ray? There have been horrors to be written of; it is not all like the Wieskirche, the Rococo church in Bavaria that has been called 'a sacred dancing floor'; there are, as well, the owl and vulture and how many species of bats with leathern, membrane wings! Is the ugly of its own intent an excrescence upon what was calm and beautiful? So that we are to believe there is evil which is active and alive, more so indeed than its opposite which is merely passive and well meaning. Which of the two is combative? But there can be no doubt of that. The spider scuttles along its web to attack the fly which is trussed up and carried away to be sucked dry; and rats, spiders, sharks, too, know no mercy. It is not born in them. Unless we think of an indifferent vital or creative force which is upon too big a scale to bother, and has therefore allowed for such things to happen. It looks as though there is just the gift, or accident of life and all the rest is left to chance. 'The day thou gavest, Lord, is ended', and it is ours till nightfall, or after. But in the end we know no more than when we started.

It would seem that the only answer is to believe in the corporate instinct of the human race. In the same way that the more intelligent creatures, dolphins, whales, bees, and so many others we do not credit with intelligence, could we question them, might answer that they had an allegiance to themselves to do with the preservation of their species, and with the long evolution of rules and customs governing their lives. It could be said of some creatures, storks, swallows and other migratory birds, that there must be some central authority giving orders and governing them. It must be in reality their adaptable, but mass instinct, functioning through all its members. It has been found that storks while migrating sleep upon the wing, keeping just enough of consciousness to be in rhythm with the rest of the flight, and lulled by the waving and swishing of their pinions. Fifteen to twenty minutes' sleep is enough for them, meanwhile flight guidance will have passed from the leader to the next in line. It would be of interest to know what changes, if any, have taken place in the migratory flights of birds since Daedalus, 'the most ingenious artist of his age', made trial of his wings of wax and feathers to escape with his son from the labyrinth of Minos, but Icarus flew too near the sun and perished. And his father, 'by a proper management of his wings, alighted at Cumae', near the Phlegraean Fields, where he built a temple to Apollo; one set of legends where such subjects are concerned being at least as appropriate as another, and finding nothing in Christian mythology on a par with this beyond the dubious feats of the 'flying saint' of Copertino.

The mere gift of life has so many potentialities that it is ungrateful to hope or look for more. There is no shame in being of human flesh and blood, and therefore mortal. But for every man and woman of whom this is true there are and have been so many millions and millions who would not agree and for whom this is not enough. Yet their very insistence in believing and hoping for another life is proof enough that its possibilities have dawned upon them. It is a very limited immortality to hope for; of museum, theatre, concert hall, or lending library capacity. But it is all there is. Yet monarchs survive as patrons. It is impossible to ignore the château or gardens of Versailles, or forget Louis XIV, who was the whole seventeenth century alike in his periwig and in his person. Frederick the Great is remembered for Sanssouci more than for his battles won, and his patronage of Voltaire counts for more than the roll-call of his dead grenadiers. And so forth. Who thinks now of Edison, or Marconi, who effected so much difference in our lives? Who remembers the inventors of salvorsan, insulin or penicillin? News does not travel beyond the human labyrinth or ant-hill, and even there gets lost in its long corridors or tunnels.

What a miracle it is to have been sentient and alive! Something in itself beyond the power of imagining or of expression. But which is self-contradictory, because without the fact of birth there is no such thing as thought. In a sense, and to some little degree, it can continue after death and be carried further of its own volition. Though this is really no more than the wounded hare running on for a little before it jerks its limbs and rolls over, dead. Because we are now unindented slaves to the machine at every hour of our lives and in danger, we are told, of being slowly poisoned or stifled by pollution, we must not pretend to ourselves that we would prefer to have lived at other times than this present. Just because of their wonderful 'hand' in many of the arts there would be no advantage in living in many another age one can think of. Sufficient unto our times the evils but, also, the advantages.

One of which is the greater knowledge that is attainable and the ever widening audience or public. Not, it has to be admitted, if one were born with a different coloured skin and a member, thereby, of the vast numerical majority. But there have been, always, lions, alike, and ant-lions, or dogs and dog-roses that have not had their day, meaning that human beings so alike in outward shape but different in every other respect cannot by the mere law of numbers all attain to their inheritance at one and the same time. Which is quite simply not good enough, and could invalidate the whole of human history, until one knows that this is based on greed and injustice, and not upon its opposites of love and kindness.

One supposes that the Nirvana of the Buddhists is to be forgotten completely as though one had never existed, or ever had the gift of life put into one's hand. In the outermost limbo of oblivion which is, at least, forgiving, if only by forgetting. But it is human vanity to want to be remembered for however little, the merest pittance, or the unpaid inadequate wages of too much writing. How little and small one's own life has been! Going back to its candle-lit beginnings in a night nursery, with memories of persons long dead now and in the pitiful darkness; most, with no one even to remember them. But if the project is for all the unhappiness there has ever been to collect its forces merely in order to overwhelm by weight of numbers, it is soon abandoned. What conceivable good could be done by it? Or by recounting once more the horrors of the Nazi gas-chambers and incinerators. One blind beggar, man, woman, or child is enough. There is no need for more. An extension of the dramatis personae is uncalled for and unnecessary. One is enough for the play and for the player.

Except for one key-figure, which is the skeleton – but it is hardly even a skeleton – of the crucified Jew found a year or two ago in an underground burial chamber in Jerusalem, and of which a full medical examination has been published. His name was scratched in the rock above his remains so that he was a person of some little consequence, whose body must have been reclaimed by his relations. A man, thirty or thirty-five years old, who had been nailed to the cross, almost in a sitting or crouching position with his knees splayed out, and the terrible iron nails hammered in through his wrists and through his ankle bones. He had been given a little wooden slat or shelf to sit on in order to prolong his agony by lessening the strain upon his hands and arms. Having first, of course, undergone the ritual heavy beating that preceded crucifixion. After some hours of day or night his executioners must have come back, wrenched and torn out the nails in order to free his hands from the cross, and broken his legs and ankle-bones with a hammer or iron bar which was the usual end to the drama, by which time it is to be hoped he was no longer alive. And probably his relations took his remains away late in the evening. Nothing is known of what crime he had committed, but it was probably a political offence.

It is by some curious fluke that the posture of this calcareous-looking corpse – it looks as if it had had lime-impregnated water dripping on it through the centuries and had, itself, turned to limestone – has been preserved in order to alter the suppositions concerning another and far more important crucifixion. What is certain is that one cannot even look at the photograph and not be strongly affected by it. There is something so pitifully abject in the attitude, as though the Romans were crucifying their victims by the dozen and either could hardly be bothered to do it properly, or were introducing new and careful refinements into the torment. It has been proved that this poor creature was almost contemporaneous with Christ, and that he suffered at the time when it was said there was hardly enough wood in Jerusalem to make the crosses. He appears, indeed, like a miraculously preserved proxy for that other and parallel death that so much altered history, and probably, we may think, to the astonishment of the victim, had he but known of it.

The other and strange witness or testimony being the Santissimo Sudario, or winding sheet, preserved in the chapel next to the Royal Palace in Turin, and only shown to the public once in a hundred years. But it has been examined and photographed, and is an inexplicably beautiful and sacred object, with certainly the negative impression upon it of a bearded man who has been crucified – there are the marks of the nails on his hands and feet – and who had a beautiful Leonardesque head of terrible intensity of expression, and of Hebraic type and physiognomy. Even if, as has been suggested and is probable, the impression, if it can be called that, on the winding sheet is that of a crucified man of much later date, perhaps of the eleventh or twelfth century – whatever its history, if there be such a thing as a holy or sacred object, it is the Santissimo Sudario* or Santissima

* This holy relic was brought from Cyprus in 1452, and is said to be part of the linen cloth in which the body of Christ was wrapped. It is certainly therefore of Oriental origin, whatever its true story. The beautiful, even terrifying countenance visible thereupon, resembles the twelfth-century mosaic of Christ Pantocrator in the church at Daphni, outside Athens.

Sindone of Turin. And the calcareous corpse found in the burial vault at Jerusalem comes not far behind it.

One cannot look at either of these objects – the one, strange and beautiful beyond imagining and the other pitiful beyond words – and not be strongly moved by them. This, perhaps, all the more to someone who is Christian neither by instinct nor inclination, and who cannot believe in either divine birth or in the resurrection. How much better for us all that Christ should be of human birth, like all other human beings! His teaching, and that he suffered of intention for and on behalf of others, makes him sacred, and leads one to think there could be a spiritual force or accumulation entrusted with the impalpable souls of those who have suffered, and some strength of truth thereby in a martyrology, though the saints and martyrs are not of usual and accustomed kind. It is almost as though there are only two things of importance in the world of human beings – their achievements and their sufferings, and little or nothing in between. There have been monsters and there have been god-like beings, and perhaps it is not necessary to have any religious convictions beyond that and a belief in the powers of good and evil. We are all of the same flesh and blood, and all of us have been born and have to die. The only immortality is of the spirit, and the strongest emotive force should be that of pity, to the extent that spiritual love is compound of care and pity. It is even impossible to love someone without having pity for them.

In which respect it is as the opening of the soup kitchen, as I dimly remember it before two World Wars, and it is a hateful memory. Something which has not been seen for a long time in this kingdom. Not, indeed, that it is comparable to other and worse things. We had no deaths from starvation or malnutrition, but children and old people were going hungry; and one remembers from then, and later, the listless, hopeless 'hanging about' of the unemployed. There was no Ministry of Social Security and no welfare officers in those days. No forms were required, or signatures to be filled in. It was private charity, and charity, now, understandably, has a bad name. A colliery town where the male inhabitants from long habit sit on their heels outside the houses, and if there is the sound of music it is the Salvation Army band. So that it is not indeed at all comparable, but one could say, all the same, that stretching for mile after mile behind them are the starving Biafrans and the starving from East Bengal. Or, at the very least, pitiful and appalling photographs of them. And, unphotographed, the starving Kulaks and the million dead and dying from the siege of Leningrad. The phantom armies of the blind assemble and begin their march; phantoms, if only because they cannot see each other and are as spectres in their own eyes. But, as said already, one blind beggar is enough. The millions more are redundant. Maxim Gorky, in his poverty-stricken *Childhood*, tells how his mother used to say it was the blind beggars who sang best; and who indeed could it have been who wrote the sort of songs they sang, some of which, we may be sure, were touched with genius? On the same principle, linnets and other small birds from Epping Forest, and elsewhere, were blinded to make them sing the better; and in a ruffianly book on cock-fighting in the 'deep South' at about the time of the American Civil War, the 'Old Jacksons' are mentioned, 'a breed of great celebrity in years gone by', having the reputation of fighting better after losing their eyesight from the savagery of their opponent.

* * *

All that is necessary is to turn a knob. And after a moment or two we will be in the thick of it again. And here it comes.

In the meantime where have we been? Or where have we not been, rather? It is *Sportsnight with Coleman,* and a voice saying, 'Lloyd, No. 9'; then 'Regan', with a huge great kick by Regan landing him face down in the mud, and furious. And after a pause, 'Muller in the way', 'over to you, now, Hackenschmidt', then, in melancholy tone, touched with despair, 'Go on, Trautenbeck'. After that, silence. A fade out. Nothing but dazzle, and a notice flashing, *'Do not adjust your sets'.*

* * *

It is over as quick as that. And lasting no longer than rolling up your shirt sleeve in order to be given an injection. An interlude of disconcerting sort making one wonder which is the real, and which the false. Like waking up, and not knowing or remembering for a moment where it is. You know who you are, all right, but not what is going on, or how or why you are here.

Which indeed is the supreme mystery. And even if one knew the answer, it would take a great deal of explaining. Why 'you', in particular, in the first place. Which is to say, oneself. So that it comes down to the simple inquiry, 'Why me?' And there is no answer. Except that it must be something more than that one act of your parents.

After all it is the same for all other animals, except that they do not bother. It does not worry them. Though even an ant gets out of the way if there is danger coming. Except for fighter ants and wasps that take up 'an aggressive posture'. So that there is an animal instinct about death. They do not want to die.

But the importance is in the living, not the dead. The unborn will look after themselves. We can renew and refresh ourselves, and recharge our batteries from the past, mindful of their mistakes and miseries, and lost in wonder at what they achieved, collectively or individually. However did they do it? Or can the answer be that it is not so difficult? That could be the truth. There must be a right and a wrong way to set about such things. It can never be easy, but it is not so difficult. That much of it was accomplished under the worst conditions should be no surprise. Difficulties are the incentive. But with only a little overcrowding and turmoil it may become hopeless. It is not easy, but it is still possible to live away from all this. Which is a scholarly life entailing much solitude and loneliness, and to be half-forgotten before one is even old. But the accumulation of dry knowledge is no true harvest, and to let the stooks or shocks of corn lie rotting. They must be garnered or stored up and put to their proper uses. Not left lying on the bare earth. Nor, in the other sense of it, left to litter the worktable and the bookshelves. There can be poetry long stored that becomes stronger and more potent from long keeping. And in a long life it can be in bulk and quantity, perhaps, the better for that and the more reassuring. Or the enclosed years have been spoiled and wasted. In the course of them I claim in all humility to have discovered or refound some lost secrets, and to have set up an easy flow or fluency. And this according to the principles of poetry, which are the same in practice as those of architecture and of music, the secret in chief being the now despised rules of beauty, which can and do mean many other things beside mere prettiness, including, as they do, the schools of fear and terror and all forms of sensual and visual excitement.

All of which are to be found when needed in Johann Sebastian Bach's *Church Cantatas*; the treading of the grapes in exultation; the longing even for the death knell; the mystical meaning and import – for Christians – of the doctrine of the Trinity (this, in the chorus of *Et in Unum* of the *Mass in B minor*), and doubtless every conceivable expression of spiritual love and pity, together with eternal and extra-mundane mysteries, for which he could find the expression if he did not comprehend the meaning. Or wish to? But just put them down on paper, rather as though they were dictated to him. There are the same effects and sensations in his *Organ Toccatas* and in the *Organ Preludes and Fugues*; a gigantic and rolling rhythm as of a young giant playfully setting things to right; long pleadings for more than forgiveness in the *Passacaglia*; domestic preludes and fugues even suggestive of such household chores as feeding the cat; catechismal secrets; and others that are the solving of musical riddles; and now and again thunder and lightning and the terrors of the storm. There are, also, hair-raising moments of terror and excitement in the *Grande Messe des Morts* of Berlioz; and of Virgilian poetry, but to the rules of his *Grand Traité d'Instrumentation*, in *Les Troyens*.

It has been necessary as well to try to understand and interpret the mystical demonology of Hieronymus Bosch and to try to write in his pictorial idiom. This can come to have an obsessive influence; as can the distortions and mediumistic invocations of El Greco, the latter having been tried experimentally in a part at least of this present book. The attempt has been made to add to the repertory in many directions at the same time, as of not being content only with the ordinary paraphernalia of aesthetics but wishing to add to and extend the areas of experience and appreciation. Here is a picture of the workings of a mind taking pleasure from the contemporary world, but in the same breath puzzled and disturbed by it, and knowing the only solution to it all is in human hands. There is no outside power or influence to help us. There never has been and there is not now. Our fate is in our own hands.

That there was this supreme power has been the grand delusion of human beings over all the ages. That there is good and evil is certain, and that both are all too human. If there is belief only so far as this, then there is a religion and a faith, but not of the old kind. It is free of superstition and of supernatural trappings. There is more than enough to marvel and be astonished at in many a cathedral of the Middle Ages without having to follow its prayers up into the skies. The artificers were no more and no less human than we are ourselves.

What is true is that it was the confidence in their beliefs and prayers that inspired them and gave them strength. But do you have to believe in another life in order to be able to do this? If it is all, and only, of this world, is it not enough? And were it proved beyond doubt that this is all there is for us, would we lie down and die? This world is ours and no one else's, how or why we know not. If we have landed men on the moon, several times now, and brought them back alive, surely there is little we cannot perform and do if we put our minds to it. If in the mood, in the matter of the mediaeval cathedrals, we could do the same or better. That is the trouble, that the mood has changed. We have all of the ability, but not the inspiration. The material world is in triumph over the metaphysical, and the balance is never likely now to be reversed. The other powers are latent, if not sleeping; and how can they be awakened?

Of course such things were possible when there was belief and faith, from which it is easy to argue that the grand deception was worth while. Surely from all the evidence to date we are in a unique position in the universe, with the only and probably inspired handicap against us which is the fact of death. And the whole fabric of the religions has been in order to excuse that or make compensation for it, which in every case has put the holders of the keys to immortality in an enviable situation though subject to the same rule themselves. Political creeds of violent nature are no substitute for religion and only lead to tyranny and persecution. The only solution to all the doubts and misgivings is to realize our unique and scarcely credible birthright and make the most of that.

As the whole of black Africa relapses into sempiternal darkness, and India, where religion was born, pullulates and grows hungrier, there may be little time left. Or all the time in the world, and everything still to learn. Of which we are, as surely, but at the beginning, and of the pains and pleasures of appreciation. For there should not, and cannot be the one without the others. A life lived is to have had this experience. And in time it should take over from religion. For it rests on disappointment and on achievement, not on irredeemable promises. It both mourns and celebrates, for there are the opportunities lost, as well as the miracles achieved. And it is the dual world; of this earth which is the mystery of mysteries, and of the no lesser mystery and potentiality within ourselves. If we are really alone in the universe without other living creatures of whatever form this side of eternity, then it is indeed more extraordinary than can be expressed in words, and would be suggestive of some special purpose or dispensation. And should there be other planets innumerable, with some form of life, but all safely out of reach, then it is no less extraordinary.

The supreme mystery of all would be to receive signals from them, and perhaps lose contact over centuries and get no further with it. Whoever, or whatever they are, could be subject to another time currency altogether. It would be no more than a prisoner knocking on the wall of his cell, and there would be no interchange of information. Just to get the signal, and not be able to answer, would be as mysterious as birth or death. Or is the latter state no more than to be a break on numbers? Against proliferation; and there could be other forms of life, made free of this gift, that are deathless. That have all of time on their hands, and are free in virtue of that from the curse of numbers because if they are death-less they have no increase. In set numbers like the constellation of Cassiopeia which is of thirteen stars, and likely to have been so, and to remain so for the ascertainable rest of time.

The parallel growth to that of ourselves has been that of the natural world we live in, a gift which is only comparable to finding a paradise furnished and equipped with everything needed, and divinely, majestically beautiful, as well, down to perhaps the most extraordinary thing of all, the curative powers of certain plants and herbs, which is equivalent to finding the place furnished down to a medicine chest. This may be naïvely put, but is truly extraordinary when we come to think of it. And every small item of scientific or chemical research only makes the resources of the world the stranger and more inexplicable, and the reason for them more mysterious still. And only here and nowhere else? It would seem so, at least up till the present. And whether this isolation is the more inexplicable, or to have the possibility, or even the certainty that we are not alone in universal time, cannot be answered. For there appears to be no answer. It is left unexplained.

But it is a waste of time to conjecture about what we do not, and probably never will know. That, and futile announcements about the life to come, have been the greatest time-wasters in human history. It is more to the point to narrate and compare deeds of good and evil, thus bring the past alive and into the present, and try to prognosticate the future. Who ever heard of an ivory tower which was inhabited, and genuine? How lucky, though, have been some of the artists in all the arts who become 'old fashioned' in their lifetimes. For instance, Johann Sebastian Bach, or Botticelli, or Piero della Francesca, or Giambattista Tiepolo, and of course there have been many dozens, even many hundreds of others. They, at least, have not tried to be contemporary, or to wind too often and put forward the clock like the pair of nonagenarians, Stravinsky and Picasso. To have been allowed to work in peace, not subject to fluctuations of taste, and able to follow out their own trajectory without premature landing and coming to earth, must be best of all. But, of a certainty, not to have been young and famous. We must admire Domenico Scarlatti, probably the greatest virtuoso till the coming of Liszt, who never gave a public concert and had only thirty of his five hundred and fifty keyboard sonatas published in his lifetime; or Robert Herrick who had his first book of poems printed when he was fifty-seven. Theirs were careers much to be envied compared to that of Rimbaud, or of poor Beardsley. Or, to turn to smaller things, a fluent production such as that of J. J. Kändler, the modeller of Meissen porcelain, with his hundreds of birds and animals, figures from the Italian Comedy, Orientals, the 'crinoline' groups, the celebrated 'Swan service' and so much else, in fact a prodigious programme of dramatis personae – or the work of many scores or hundreds of minor, even anonymous craftsmen – in com-parison to the tortured, difficult birth attendant on some more famous works of art. All, or any of which fertility of production would seem to be nearly impossible given the conditions of our times.

And yet it is to be doubted how far it has ever been different. Human beings do not change so much. It is only the exceptional face that we think typical of no defined period in the past. The rest would be as we see them every day, for better or worse. Crimean faces will have been no different from those in the trenches in the First World War; which, again, is why so many 'hippies' go back with their beards to the days of Beowulf. Perhaps it is true that the same persons given like opportunities will achieve similar results; and the important thing therefore is to make the opportunity and produce the chance, which should not be so difficult as all that. Unfortunately, though it is not the sort of opening likely to be brought about by the standing committee of the Arts Council, or by any municipal or civic body. And the more patronage is taken out of private hands by taxation, and other means, the less likely it is to take root and flourish.

But first of all the leading spirits must come to their senses and make up their minds what it is that they really want; and that is to be lasting. How many times has it been said before that we are nearing the end of the twentieth century in full extremity of sophistication, and that while absorbing all evidences of the past it is of no use to pretend to ourselves that we are in that state of happy and primitive childhood, as regards the arts, of far alien cultures, or of our own Dark Ages! The Victorian architects in their churches and town halls could delude themselves that they were continuing from where it had been left off after the Black Death five centuries before, and with their tenacity of purpose they achieved a measure of success from the mere anachronism fulfilled and finished. It is an anachronism after all to be animal beings, as we are, and no longer living in caves or sleeping under trees. And superior animals, all things considered, we will never cease to be.

But it is time to call in the shadows, which happens before sunrise even at first cockcrow:

Comme un sanglot coupé par un sang écumeux
Le chant du coq au loin déchirait l'air brumeux

and if one reads Baudelaire's couplet twice over the authentic chill of dawn seeps into one's bones.

It is time, too, when the ghosts pack up and go, leaving the stage empty for the moment. But not for long.

It may happen at any moment now. Or in the next few years, at most. When the astronomers, who can watch and listen more millions of years into the past almost with every month that passes, may light upon the secret of the origins of life. When, indeed, the mists and vapours are dispelled and all religions, whatever, should blow up with a bang. Which evidence, on the first hearing, may sound no more interesting than if we owed everything in the universe to the Thames Gas Board.

An elemental beginning, to the comprehension of scientists and mathematicians, but not of theologians. There have been moral teachers; but of this world, not the next. For there is none.

So it all started. It had a beginning out of nothing, like the founding of a fortune.

And just for the sake of argument, can an abstract science like mathematics have had existence by itself; or, even, if infinity be finite, both before itself and after? It must always have had a theoretical existence, and, it could be said, have been waiting in the wings. Once there is one, all the other permutations of numbers are in impalpable but simultaneous being.

A molecular or even gaseous start to things, and a secret wrapped in numbers. A creation which is its own creator, leaving the mystery open. Which is like discovering the course of action, but not the reason.

But will it make all that difference? One was present at one's own birth, if unknowingly; and it is only birth that makes death credible.

Humanity has had its godlike beings, however faulted, and their rights may be restored when history is rewritten. When, if ever, the pandects are balanced and impartial.

The shades foregather, with the death of a common housefly not forgotten, and Blake's *Ghost of a Flea* remembered. Napoleon lies on his camp-bed on St Helena; and the suicide under Cannon Street crossroads with a stake through his heart, in order to keep him earthbound and not let him get away.

There is little pity among the crowd watching. But all is pitiable, and human love must be in part compound of pity.

Does the ghost of Matterig walk in the chalk-white moonlight 'under the East Cliff at Ramsgate, near the Dumpton Stairs'? We will never know what was his trouble. Or, for another throw of fate, the corpse of Johann Sebastian Bach 'mislaid' during a road-widening scheme to lay down a new tramline; and Mozart, given a third-class burial during a snowstorm in a pauper's grave.

In a sense what does it matter to any of them? They are all dead. But there are those who would want to be remembered, and others who only ask to be forgotten. And thus they help the run of numbers.

* * *

The splendours and miseries are all here, in sample. You may choose what you like and help yourselves. I have tried to make it compendious and not overwhelming, and my aim has been entertainment more than instruction.

Above all, no criticism is meant unkindly, for I know how criticism can hurt and injure. Neither would I willingly offend anyone's religious susceptibilities. But it is a sick world which needs a new diet – of old dishes, and a rejuvenation. And so there is a news flash on the screen that says, 'I return you now to the studio'.

But the announcement is not so portentous as it sounds. It means but one thing more, the end of the performance.

Index